Basic
English
Dictionary

Edited by
Shirley Burridge

Oxford University Press

Oxford University Press
Walton Street, Oxford OX2 6DP

Oxford New York
Athens Auckland Bangkok Bombay
Calcutta Cape Town Dar es Salaam Delhi
Florence Hong Kong Istanbul Karachi
Kuala Lumpur Madras Madrid Melbourne
Mexico City Nairobi Paris Singapore
Taipei Tokyo Toronto

and associated companies in
Berlin Ibadan

OXFORD and OXFORD ENGLISH are
trade marks of Oxford University Press

ISBN 0 19 431261 5

© Oxford University Press 1981
First published 1981
Eighteenth impression 1995

Illustrated by
Brian and Constance Dear
Patricia Capon
Bill le Fever
Peter Joyce
Kent Stott
Jim Robins

Set in Univers and Times by
Clays Ltd, St Ives plc.

Printed in Hong Kong

Introduction

We have written this dictionary to help you in your first years of learning English. It is simple and clear and represents the experiences and interests of modern students.

The information for each headword is called an **entry**. The following notes explain the arrangement of entries, so that you can easily find the information you need.

advise /əd'vaɪz/ v. tell someone helpfully what to do or how to do it: *The doctor advised him to stop smoking.*

Headword. This is the first word in the entry and is in heavy, black type (called **bold** type). The headwords in this dictionary include all the important words that you need in your daily life and studies.

double-decker /ˌdʌbl 'dekə(r)/ n. big bus with seats upstairs and downstairs.

In this dictionary most compound words appear as headwords with their own entries. (If a compound word is very close in meaning and spelling to a headword, then you will find it at the end of the entry for that headword.)

flew /flu:/ *past tense* of v. fly.
hooves /hu:vz/ (*pl.*) of n. hoof.

Irregular spellings of verbs and irregular plurals of nouns appear as headwords.

but[1] /bʌt/ conj. however: *She is American but she lives in England.*
but[2] prep. except: *Charles eats nothing but fruit.*

If several headwords have the same spelling, they are in the alphabetical order of their parts of speech and each one has a small number.

absolute /'æbsəlu:t/ adj. total: *I have absolute trust in my doctor.* **absolutely** adv.: *He's absolutely right.*

Derivative. A derivative is a word that comes from another word. For example, **singer** is a derivative of the word **sing**. Derivatives are in **bold** type like the headwords, but smaller.

glimmer /'glɪmə(r)/ n. small, weak light: *the glimmer of a candle.* **glimmer** v. send out a weak light.

Pronunciation and stress. After every headword we give the phonetic spelling and stress marks to show you how to say the word. (If there is no phonetic spelling, the word sounds exactly like the headword before.) Inside the back cover there is a key showing you the sound that each symbol represents.

obstruct /əb'strʌkt/ v. stand in the way of something: *A bus broke down and obstructed the traffic.* **obstruction** /əb'strʌkʃn/ n. something that obstructs.

When a derivative has very different pronunciation or stress from the main headword, we give its phonetic spelling. When the derivative is simply the headword with a common suffix (for example, **quick** + **-ly** = **quickly**), then we do not give the phonetic spelling. Inside the back cover there is a key to the pronunciation of all common suffixes.

foot /fʊt/ n. (pl. feet) **1** part of the leg that you stand on: *I wear sandals on my feet.* **on foot**, walking: *Shall we go by car or on foot?* **2** lowest part; bottom: *the foot of the mountain.* **3** measure of length = 30·5 centimetres: *This fish is one foot long.*

Part of speech. We give the part of speech, in a short form, after every headword and derivative. It is in light, slanting type (called *italic*).

abbrev.	abbreviation
adj.	adjective
adv.	adverb
conj.	conjunction
def. art.	definite article
exclam.	exclamation
indef. art.	indefinite article
n.	noun
past part.	past participle (as a headword)
prefix	
pres. part.	present participle (as a headword)
pron.	pronoun
v.	verb

Plural (*pl.*). To form the plural of most nouns, you simply add -s (for example, bird birds). Whenever a plural form does not follow this rule, we give you full information about it. For example:

child /tʃaɪld/ n. (pl. children) young boy or girl.

Some nouns have completely different plural forms.

aircraft /'eəkrɑ:ft/ n. (pl. aircraft) machine that flies; aeroplane.

Some nouns are the same in the singular and the plural.

froth /frɒθ/ n. (no pl.) white mass of tiny bubbles: *the froth on a glass of beer.*

Sometimes a noun has no plural form.

braces /'breɪsɪz/ n. (pl.) straps that a man wears over his shoulders to keep his trousers up.

Some nouns are always plural.

city /'sɪtɪ/ *n.* (*pl.* cities) big, important town.

Some nouns ending in -y change to -ies in the plural form.

ice[1] /aɪs/ *n.* **1** (no *pl.*) water that has become hard because it is very cold: *In winter there is ice on the pond.* **2** (*pl.* ices) an ice-cream.

Sometimes the different meanings of a word have different plural forms. When this happens, we give the plural after the number of each meaning.

fly[2] *v.* (*past part.* flown /fləʊn/, *past tense* flew /fluː/) **1** move through the air: *In the autumn some birds fly to warmer lands.* **2** travel in an aeroplane: *I'm flying to Brussels tomorrow.* **3** move quickly: *Amanda flew to the telephone.*

Irregular verb. To form the past tense and past participle of most verbs, you add -ed or -d (for example, help help**ed**, fade fade**d**). Whenever a past tense and past participle does not follow this rule, we give you full information about it.

dab /dæb/ *v.* (*pres. part.* dabbing, *past part. & past tense* dabbed /dæbd/) touch something quickly and gently: *She dabbed her eyes with a handkerchief.*

big /bɪg/ *adj.* (bigger, biggest) **1** large: *Manchester is a big city.* **2** important: *I have some big news!*

Doubled consonant. We show you when you must repeat the last consonant of a verb to form the past tense, past participle, and present participle. We also show when you must repeat the last consonant of an adjective in its comparative and superlative forms.

abandon /ə'bændən/ *v.* **1** leave someone or something: *The driver abandoned his car in the snow.* **2** stop doing something: *When the rain started, we abandoned our game.*

Definition. A definition is the explanation of the meaning of the word. We give all the common meanings of a word, and each one has a number.

abolish /ə'bɒlɪʃ/ *v.* stop or end something; say that something must never happen again: *The Americans abolished slavery in 1863.* **abolition** /ˌæbə'lɪʃn/ *n.*

It is important to know whether a verb is 'transitive' or 'intransitive' – that is, whether or not it takes an object. We show this by putting 'someone' or 'something' in the definitions of transitive verbs. For instance, you can see that **abolish** is transitive and takes an object, but **arise** is intransitive and does not take an object.

arise /ə'raɪz/ *v.* (*past part.* arisen /ə'rɪzn/, *past tense* arose /ə'rəʊz/) **1** get up; stand up: *We arose at 5 a.m.* **2** happen; start: *A strong wind arose in the night.*

gleam /gli:m/ v. shine softly: *The cat's eyes were gleaming in the dark.* **gleam** n.

barrier /'bærɪə(r)/ n. something that stops you from passing; fence: *You must show your ticket at the barrier before you can get on to the train.*

about[1] /ə'baʊt/ adv. **1** a little more or less than: *We waited for about twenty minutes.* **2** almost exactly: *Peter is about as tall as John* **3** here and there; in different ways or places: *The children were running about in the rain.* **4** somewhere near; not far away: *Is Judy about?*

Example sentence. In most entries the headwords (and often the derivatives and idioms) are shown in sentences or phrases. These examples are an important part of the dictionary: they help to explain meanings; they show how to use the words; they show when to use the words. Examples are in *italic* type.

hard[1] /hɑ:d/ adj. **1** not soft; firm: *Rock is hard.* **2** difficult; not easy to do or understand: *hard work.* **3** giving trouble, pain, etc.: *He's had a hard life.* **4** not kind; strict: *a hard father.* **be hard on,** be strict with someone. **hard up,** poor; not having much money.

Idiom. Idioms are in heavy, slanting type (called ***bold italic*** type). An idiom (or an idiomatic phrase) is a group of words that have a special meaning. We give full explanations of all the common and important English idioms that you will need and we often give example sentences too.

feel like, **(a)** seem to be another person or thing: *I'm so happy I feel like a king!* **(b)** want something: *I'm so hot I feel like a swim.*

If an idiom has more than one meaning, we mark the meanings **(a)**, **(b)**, etc.

pig /pɪg/ n. **1** fat farm animal. **2** greedy or unkind person. **make a pig of yourself,** eat too much.

talk[2] v. say words; speak to someone: *She is talking to her boyfriend on the telephone.* **talk something over,** talk about something.

high[2] adv. far up: *The plane flew high above the clouds.* **high and low,** everywhere: *Bill looked high and low for his lost shoe.*

Where to find idioms in this dictionary. If the idiom contains a noun, you will find it in the entry for that noun. If it does not have a noun but has a verb, it will be in the entry for that verb. If it has neither a noun nor a verb, decide what the first important word in the idiom is: you will find it in the entry for that word.

Aa

a /ə/ *indef. art.* **1** one: *I want to buy a lemon, please.* **2** each; every: *twice a day.* **3** for each; for every: *Milk costs 30p a litre.*

abandon /ə'bændən/ *v.* **1** leave someone or something: *The driver abandoned his car in the snow.* **2** stop doing something: *When the rain started, we abandoned our game.*

abbey /'æbɪ/ *n.* **1** building where men or women live to serve the Christian God. **2** church that is or was part of an abbey.

abbreviate /ə'bri:vɪeɪt/ *v.* make a word, title, etc. shorter: *The word 'verb' is abbreviated to 'v.' in this dictionary.* **abbreviation** /ə,bri:vɪ'eɪʃn/ *n.* short form of a word or title: *'Jan.' is the abbreviation of 'January'.*

A.B.C. /,eɪ bi: 'si:/ *n.* alphabet; the letters of the English language from A to Z.

ability /ə'bɪlətɪ/ *n.* **1** (no *pl.*) power to do something; cleverness: *Bruce has the ability to score a goal, but will he do it?* **2** (*pl.* abilities) what you can do: *a man of many abilities.*

ablaze /ə'bleɪz/ *adj.* on fire; bright like fire: *Bring some water—the curtains are ablaze!*

able /'eɪbl/ *adj.* **be able to do something**, can do something: *Paul isn't able to come to the party because he's ill.*

aboard /ə'bɔ:d/ *prep.* on, on to, in, or into a ship, aeroplane, train, etc.: *The passengers are all aboard the ship.* **aboard** *adv.*: *The captain went aboard.*

abolish /ə'bɒlɪʃ/ *v.* stop or end something; say that something must never happen again: *The Americans abolished slavery in 1863.* **abolition** /,æbə'lɪʃn/ *n.*

about¹ /ə'baʊt/ *adv.* **1** a little more or less than: *We waited for about twenty minutes.* **2** almost exactly: *Peter is about as tall as John.* **3** here and there; in different ways or places: *The children were running about in the rain.* **4** somewhere near; not far away: *Is Judy about?*

about² *prep.* **1** here and there in a place: *We walked about the town.* **2** to or in many places: *Jean's clothes were lying about the room.* **3** near: *Their house is about here on the map.* **4** of: *a book about American history.* **5** a little before or after a time: *Come about 6 p.m.* **about to**, just going to do something: *It started to rain as I was about to leave the house.*

above¹ /ə'bʌv/ *adv.* at or to a higher place: *I live in the flat above.*

above² *prep.* **1** higher than: *The aeroplane flew above the clouds.* **2** bigger in number, price, etc. than: *I hope the price of the dress will not be above £20.* **above all**, more than anything else: *A clock must above all be exact.*

abroad /ə'brɔ:d/ *adv.* to or in another country or other countries: *Guy came back to Scotland after studying abroad.*

abrupt /ə'brʌpt/ *adj.* sudden: *The train came to an abrupt stop when the driver put on the brake.* **abruptly** *adv.*

absence /'æbsəns/ *n.* (no *pl.*) being away: *In the absence of their parents, the girls stayed with their aunt.*

absent /'æbsənt/ *adj.* not there; away: *Why is Diana absent from school today?*

absolute /'æbsəlu:t/ *adj.* total: *I have absolute trust in my doctor.* **absolutely** *adv.*: *He's absolutely right.*

absurd /əb'sɜ:d/ *adj.* foolish; so silly that it makes you laugh: *The big man looked absurd on the little bicycle.* **absurdly** *adv.*

abuse /ə'bju:z/ *v.* shout at, or talk to, someone angrily and rudely: *She abused the driver who splashed her with mud.* **abuse** /ə'bju:s/ *n.*

academic /,ækə'demɪk/ *adj.* of schools, colleges, universities, learning, or teaching: *A student does academic work.*

accent /'æksənt/ *n.* way of saying words in a language: *I know he is not English because he speaks with a French accent.*

accept /ək'sept/ *v.* **1** take what someone wants to give you: *to accept a* *gift.* **2** say 'yes' to a plan, etc.: *I am pleased to accept your kind invitation.*

accident /'æksɪdənt/ *n.* something, often bad, that happens by chance: *Bad driving causes bad accidents.* **by accident**, by chance: *I found the key by accident when I was cleaning the room.* **accidental** /ˌæksɪ'dentl/ *adj.* not planned: *an accidental meeting.* **accidentally** *adv.*

accommodate /ə'kɒmədeɪt/ *v.* have place for people to live: *The hotel accommodates 100 guests.*

accommodation /ə,kɒmə'deɪʃn/ *n.* (no *pl.*) somewhere to live; rooms in a house or hotel: *Stay with us until you find your own accommodation.*

accompany /ə'kʌmpənɪ/ *v.* **1** go with someone: *I accompanied my aunt to church.* **2** happen at the same time as something else: *Strong winds accompanied the rain.* **3** make music to help a singer or another music player: *Derek accompanies Ann on the guitar.*

accomplish /ə'kʌmplɪʃ/ *v.* do or finish something: *He is so lazy that he will never accomplish anything.*

accord /ə'kɔːd/ *n.* (no *pl.*) **of your own accord**, without being asked: *Alice helps her mother of her own accord.*

according to /ə'kɔːdɪŋ tə/ *prep.* as someone or something says: *According to the radio, it will rain tomorrow.*

accordion /ə'kɔːdɪən/ *n.* sort of musical instrument.

account /ə'kaʊnt/ *n.* **1** piece of paper showing how much money must be paid. **accounts** *n.* writing that shows what money has been paid and received: *A shopkeeper must keep accounts.* **2** way of keeping your money in a bank, post office, etc.: *He has an account with the bank in the High Street.* **3** saying or writing about what happened: *He gave us a long account of Scott's travels.* **on account of**, because of something: *We're late on account of the bad traffic.* **on no account**, never; it is not good to: *On no account must you put your hand in the tiger's cage.* **take something into account**, keep something in your mind when thinking about other things: *I am sorry Eric was rude, but you must take his headache into account.*

accountant /ə'kaʊntənt/ *n.* someone whose job is to keep the money records of a business.

accurate /'ækjʊrət/ *adj.* correct; with no mistakes; right: *If your watch is accurate, you know the exact time.* **accurately** *adv.*

accuse /ə'kjuːz/ *v.* say that someone has done wrong: *The policeman accused the boy of stealing the bicycle.* **accusation** /ˌækjuː'zeɪʃn/ *n.*

accustomed /ə'kʌstmd/ *adj.* **be accustomed to**, know something well because you have done, seen, heard, tasted it, etc. a lot: *English people are accustomed to driving on the left.*

ache /eɪk/ *v.* have a pain: *My legs ached after the long walk.* **ache** *n.*: *tooth-ache; headache.* **aching** *adj.*

achieve /ə'tʃiːv/ *v.* do or finish something well after trying hard: *Maurice has achieved his hope of becoming a doctor.* **achievement** *n.*: *Climbing Mount Everest is a great achievement.*

acid /'æsɪd/ *adj.* with a sharp, bitter taste: *Lemons are acid fruit.*

acknowledge /ək'nɒlɪdʒ/ *v.* say or write that you have received something: *Harry acknowledged my letter.* **acknowledgement** *n.*

acorn /'eɪkɔːn/ *n.* seed of an oak tree.

acquaint /ə'kweɪnt/ *v.* **be acquainted with**, know someone or something: *Are you acquainted with the rules of chess?*

acquaintance /ə'kweɪntəns/ *n.* **1** (*pl.* acquaintances) someone you know a little. **2** (no *pl.*) knowing someone or something: *I am pleased to make your acquaintance.*

acquire /ə'kwaɪə(r)/ *v.* buy, receive, or get something: *Walter has just acquired a car.*

acre /'eɪkə(r)/ *n.* measure of land = 4,074 square metres: *a field of 20 acres.*

acrobat /'ækrəbæt/ *n.* someone who does clever movements with his body. **acrobatic** /ˌækrə'bætɪk/ *adj.* of or like an acrobat.

across¹ /ə'krɒs/ *adv.* from one side to the other: *If the road is busy, don't walk across.*

across² *prep.* **1** over from one side to the other side of something: *Walk across the field.* **2** on the other side of: *Our house is across the river.*

act¹ /ækt/ n. **1** something that you do: *an act of kindness.* **in the act of,** while doing something: *He was caught in the act of stealing the sweets.* **2** law that parliament has made. **3** part of a play: *'Macbeth' has five acts.* **4** piece of entertainment: *the clown's amusing act.*

act² v. **1** do something: *We've talked enough; it's time to act!* **2** be in a play, film, etc. **act as,** work or help in place of the usual person or thing: *Helen sometimes acts as her father's secretary.*

acting /'æktɪŋ/ n. (no pl.) the work of an actor or actress; being in a play, film, etc.

action /'ækʃn/ n. **1** (no pl.) doing things: *A man of action gets things done more quickly than a man who only talks.* **2** (pl. actions) something that you do. **3** (no pl.) working. **in action,** working: *We watched the machine in action.* **out of action,** not working: *I can't go because my car is out of action.*

active /'æktɪv/ adj. **1** able to do things; moving quickly; working; doing a lot of things: *The old man is not as active as he was.* **2** form of a verb: *In 'A dog bit Chris' the verb is active, but in 'Chris was bitten by a dog' the verb is passive.*

activity /æk'tɪvətɪ/ n. **1** (no pl.) doing things; moving quickly: *On the day of the festival there was much activity in the streets.* **2** (pl. activities) what you do: *His main activity after work is playing the drums in a band.*

actor /'æktə(r)/ n. man or boy who acts in plays or films.

actress /'æktrɪs/ n. (pl. actresses) woman or girl who acts in plays or films.

actual /'æktʃʊəl/ adj. real; true. **actually** adv. really: *He said he was going to work but actually he went to the cinema.*

ad /æd/ abbrev. advertisement.

add /æd/ v. **1** find the total of two or more numbers: *If you add two and five, you have seven.* **2** put one thing with another: *Please add Angela's name to the list.* **3** say something more: *'And don't come back again', he added.*

adder /'ædə(r)/ n. small, poisonous snake.

addition /ə'dɪʃn/ n. **1** (no pl.) putting things or numbers together. **2** (pl. additions) something added to another thing:

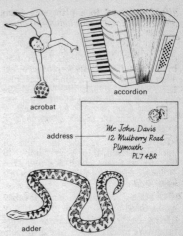

accordion

acrobat

address —

Mr. John Davis
12 Mulberry Road
Plymouth
PL7 4BR

adder

A new baby is an addition to the family. **in addition,** also: *When Diane fell, she hurt her arm and, in addition, broke her glasses.*

address /ə'dres/ n. (pl. addresses) name of the place where someone lives or where a business has its offices: *Write your address clearly at the top of your letter.* **address** v. write the name and address of the person when you send a letter or parcel: *I addressed the envelope to Mr. Jones.*

adequate /'ædɪkwət/ adj. as much as you need; enough: *They were cold because they were not wearing adequate clothing.*

adjective /'ædʒɪktɪv/ n. word that describes something or someone: *The words 'small' and 'bad' are adjectives.*

administration /ədˌmɪnɪ'streɪʃn/ n. (no pl.) controlling or managing a business, office, etc.; people in control.

admiral /'ædmərəl/ n. commander-in-chief of a country's warships; senior officer in the navy.

admire /əd'maɪə(r)/ v. **1** look at something or someone with pleasure, etc.: *The tourists admired the view from the tower.* **2** think well of someone: *I admire you for helping your sister so much.* **admiration** /ˌædmə'reɪʃn/ n.: *When Charles won the prize, his friends were filled with admiration.*

admission /əd'mɪʃn/ n. (no pl.) **1** letting people into a place: *Admission to the cinema was for adults only.* **2** money that you pay to go into a place: *Admission to the zoo is 50p.*

admit /əd'mɪt/ v. (pres. part. admitting, past part. & past tense admitted /əd'mɪtɪd/) **1** say something that you did not want to say: *I admit that I was rude and I am sorry.* **2** let someone or something in: *We do not admit children to this film.*

adopt /ə'dɒpt/ v. take the child of another person into your family to become your own child: *Mr. and Mrs. Williams adopted a child whose parents were dead.*

adorable /ə'dɔːrəbl/ adj. lovable: *an adorable baby.*

adore /ə'dɔː(r)/ v. **1** love someone or something very much: *I adore you!* **2** worship God, etc. **adoration** /ˌædə'reɪʃn/ n.

adult /'ædʌlt/ n. person or animal that is full size, not a child. **adult** adj.: *an adult ticket.*

advance /əd'vɑːns/ v. come or go forward: *The soldiers advanced towards the enemy.* **advance** n. **in advance**, before others; ahead of others: *Neil went in advance to say that we were coming.*

advanced /əd'vɑːnst/ adj. **1** better than others in what you know or can do: *Tim is very young, but his reading is very advanced.* **2** difficult; of or for a high class: *an advanced dictionary.*

advantage /əd'vɑːntɪdʒ/ n. something useful or helpful: *Quick thinking is an advantage for a London taxi-driver.* **take advantage of**, (*a*) use someone or something to help yourself: *Peter took advantage of his visit to Paris to improve his French.* (*b*) be unfair to someone so that you can please yourself: *He takes advantage of her kindness and borrows her bike too much.*

adventure /əd'ventʃə(r)/ n. doing something exciting, dangerous, etc.: *Sherlock Holmes had many adventures.*

adventurous /əd'ventʃərəs/ adj. **1** liking to do exciting, dangerous things. **2** full of danger, excitement, etc.: *an adventurous holiday on a boat.*

adverb /'ædvɜːb/ n. word that answers questions beginning 'How?' 'When?' 'Where?': *The words 'quickly', 'tomorrow', and 'here' are adverbs.*

advertise /'ædvətaɪz/ v. tell people about something by printing a notice in a newspaper, etc. or by talking on radio or television: *When Mr. Hilton wanted to sell his house he advertised it in the newspaper.* **advertisement** /əd'vɜːtɪsmənt/ n. notice telling people about jobs, things to sell, etc.

advice /əd'vaɪs/ n. (no pl.) what you say to help people: *I took my father's advice and went to the station early.*

advise /əd'vaɪz/ v. tell someone helpfully what to do or how to do it: *The doctor advised him to stop smoking.*

aerial /'eərɪəl/ n. part of a radio or television set that sends and gets radio signals.

aerodrome /'eərədrəʊm/ n. place where aircraft can land and take off.

aeroplane /'eərəpleɪn/ n. machine that has wings and can fly.

affair /ə'feə(r)/ n. **1** something that happens; event: *Ruth's birthday party was a happy affair.* **2** business; something to talk about or do: *Go away— this is my affair.*

affect /ə'fekt/ v. make something different: *The noise from the street affected our work.*

affection /ə'fekʃn/ n. (no pl.) love. **affectionate** adj.: *an affectionate smile.* **affectionately** adv. with love. **Yours affectionately**, way of ending a letter to a friend or relative.

afford /ə'fɔːd/ v. have enough money for something: *I can't afford a holiday this year.*

afloat /ə'fləʊt/ adv. on top of water or other liquid; moving on water or air: *The boat was on the sand but when the tide came in, it was afloat.*

afraid /ə'freɪd/ adj. **1** having fear: *Are you afraid of snakes?* **2** worried or sorry about something: *I'm afraid that I have broken your window.*

after[1] /'ɑːftə(r)/ adv. later: *You go first and I'll come after.*

after[2] conj. at a later time than: *Sandra arrived after the film had started.*

after[3] prep. **1** later than: *I'll meet you after dinner.* **2** next to; behind: *Ten comes after nine.* **3** trying to catch: *The cat ran after the* *mouse.* **after all**, when you thought something else would happen: *He was worried about the exam, but he passed it after all.* **after that**, then; next: *What will you do after that?* **be after someone or something**, hunt or want someone or something: *That child is after a sweet!*

afternoon /ˌɑːftəˈnuːn/ *n.* time between midday and evening.

afterwards /ˈɑːftəwədz/ *adv.* later; after a happening: *I did not remember the correct answer until afterwards.*

again /əˈgen/ *adv.* **1** once more; another time: *If you fail the first time, try again!* **2** any more: *Never do that again!* **now and again**, sometimes, but not often. **again and again**, many times. **3** as before: *You'll soon be well again.*

against /əˈgenst/ *prep.* **1** word that shows that you do not like an idea: *I am against your plan.* **2** opposite; on the other side in a sport or fight: *We played against a cricket team from the next village.* **3** to stop something: *an injection against smallpox.* **4** on something: *He banged his head against the wall.*

age /eɪdʒ/ *n.* **1** (*pl.* ages) number of years someone or something has lived: *What age is your son?* **2** (no *pl.*) being old: *His back was bent with age.* **old age**, the time when you are very old. **3** (*pl.* ages) certain time in history: *the Stone Age.* **4** (*pl.* ages) a very long time: *We've been waiting for ages!*

aged /eɪdʒd/ *adj.* at the age of: *I met her son aged 10.*

agency /ˈeɪdʒənsɪ/ *n.* (*pl.* agencies) work or office of someone who does business for others: *A travel agency plans holidays for people.*

agent /ˈeɪdʒənt/ *n.* someone who does business for another person: *The travel agent will get me a ticket for my flight to New York.*

aggressive /əˈgresɪv/ *adj.* wanting or ready to fight: *an aggressive dog.* **aggressively** *adv.*

ago /əˈgəʊ/ *adv.* before now; in the past: *I learned to swim five years ago.* **long ago**, in the distant past.

agony /ˈægənɪ/ *n.* (*pl.* agonies) great pain or suffering of mind or body: *I was in agony with tooth-ache.* **agonizing** /ˈægənaɪzɪŋ/ *adj.* giving you agony.

agree /əˈgriː/ *v.* **1** say 'yes' when

aeroplane

advertisement

aerials

DAVIDSON'S

GARDEN SHEDS
DELIVERED & ERECTED FREE

T. Davidson Ltd

someone has asked you to do something: *Tom agreed to lend me the money that I wanted.* **2** decide together on an idea; have the same ideas: *They all agreed on the plan.* **3** say that something is true: *'It's hot.' 'I agree!'*

agreement /əˈgriːmənt/ *n.* **1** (no *pl.*) having the same answer or idea: *We're all in agreement.* **2** (*pl.* agreements) written promise between people, countries, etc.: *a trade agreement.*

agriculture /ˈægrɪkʌltʃə(r)/ *n.* (no *pl.*) farming; growing crops and keeping animals. **agricultural** /ˌægrɪˈkʌltʃərəl/ *adj.*: *agricultural land.*

aground /əˈgraʊnd/ *adv.* touching the bottom in water: *The ship is aground on the rocks near Plymouth.*

ahead /əˈhed/ *adv.* in front: *Frank ran faster than the others and was soon ahead.* **ahead of**, (*a*) in front of. (*b*) better than another in work, etc.: *Peter's work is ahead of Jack's.* **go ahead**, start, or go on with, something: *If you really need help then go ahead and ask.*

aid /eɪd/ *n.* help; something that gives help: *The old woman walks with the aid of a stick.* **in aid of**, to be used for something or someone: *I am collecting money in aid of deaf people.* **come to someone's aid**, help someone. **first aid**, help that you give to a sick or hurt person before a doctor comes. **aid** *v.* help someone.

aim /eɪm/ v. **1** point a gun, etc. at something or someone: *Pete aimed the gun at the bird, but did not fire.* **2** send or throw something towards another thing: *He aimed the ball into the net, but missed.* **3** plan to do something: *He aims to go to university next year.* **aim** n.: *Pete took aim and fired. Catherine's aim is to be a doctor.*

air[1] /eə(r)/ n. **1** (no *pl.*) what you take in through your nose and mouth when you breathe. **2** *by air*, in an aeroplane: *I travelled to Holland by air.* **air force** n. the military aircraft of a country and the people who fly them and look after them. **3** (no *pl.*) radio. *on the air*, on the radio: *The news will be on the air at 6 p.m.* **4** (*pl.* airs) way someone behaves or looks: *His uniform gives him an air of importance.*

air[2] v. let air come into a place, or on to something, to make it fresh: *Let's open the windows and air this smoky room.*

aircraft /'eəkrɑːft/ n. (*pl.* aircraft) machine that flies; aeroplane; helicopter. **aircraft-carrier** /'eəkrɑːft kærɪə(r)/ n. ship with a flat deck where aeroplanes can take off or land.

airfield /'eəfiːld/ n. place where aircraft take off or land.

air-hostess /'eə həʊstɪs/ n. (*pl.* air-hostesses) woman who looks after passengers on an aeroplane.

airline /'eəlaɪn/ n. business with aeroplanes that carry people or goods: *Lufthansa is a German airline.* **airliner** /'eəlaɪnə(r)/ n. big aeroplane.

airmail /'eəmeɪl/ n. (no *pl.*) letters and parcels that go by aeroplane: *I sent the letter by airmail.*

airport /'eəpɔːt/ n. place where aeroplanes can land to pick up or put down people and goods.

airways /'eəweɪz/ n. (*pl.*) business with aeroplanes that carry people or goods.

aisle /'aɪl/ n. path or way between rows of seats in a church, cinema, or theatre: *The bride walked up the aisle.*

ajar /ə'dʒɑː(r)/ adv. open a little: *The door was ajar and I could hear the people talking in the room.*

alarm[1] /ə'lɑːm/ n. **1** (*pl.* alarms) sound or sign of danger: *The fire alarm rang and everyone ran out of the building.* **2** (no *pl.*) sudden fear: *She cried with alarm when the thunder started.*

alarm[2] v. make someone feel that there is danger: *The noise alarmed the bird and it flew away.* **alarmed** /ə'lɑːmd/ adj. having a feeling of danger.

alarm-clock /ə'lɑːm klɒk/ n. clock with a bell that rings to wake a sleeping person.

alas /ə'læs/ exclam. word that shows sadness or worry: *Alas! The window is broken!*

album /'ælbəm/ n. **1** book with empty pages for photographs, stamps, etc. **2** set of long-playing records: *Have you heard the singer's latest album?*

alcohol /'ælkəhɒl/ n. (no *pl.*) liquid in drinks such as beer, whisky, wine, etc., that can make people drunk. **alcoholic** /ˌælkə'hɒlɪk/ adj.: *an alcoholic drink.*

ale /eɪl/ n. (no *pl.*) beer with a light colour.

alert[1] /ə'lɜːt/ adj. awake; ready to do things.

alert[2] n. signal that warns of danger. *on the alert*, watching for something to happen: *Fireman stay on the alert for fires all day and night.* **alert** v. warn someone.

algebra /'ældʒɪbrə/ n. (no *pl.*) sort of mathematics.

alibi /'ælɪbaɪ/ n. showing that you were not there when a crime happened: *He was at a party with friends when the robbery happened so he has an alibi.*

alien /'eɪlɪən/ n. someone from another country.

alight[1] /ə'laɪt/ adj. on fire; burning: *A fire started in the roof and soon all the house was alight.*

alight[2] v. **1** get down from a bus, horse, etc.: *Don't alight before the bus stops.* **2** come down from the air on to something: *The bird alighted on the fence.*

alike[1] /ə'laɪk/ adj. almost the same; not very different: *The twin sisters are very alike.*

alike[2] adv. in the same way: *Andrew and his father walk alike.*

alive /ə'laɪv/ adj. living: *Only ten people were found alive after the crash.*

all[1] /ɔːl/ adj. **1** every one of: *All my friends like his latest record.* **2** every part of; the whole of: *He spent all his life in India.*

all² *adv.* totally: *They were dressed all in white.* **all along**, for the whole time: *They said he was dead but I knew all along he would come back.* **all out**, doing the best you can: *Nick went all out to win the race.* **all over**, (*a*) in every part of a place: *all over the world.* (*b*) ended: *The party was all over by 10 p.m.* **all over again**, again: *I lost my essay, so I had to write it all over again.*

all³ *pron.* everything; everyone: *I asked twenty people to my party but not all of them came.* **all together**, everyone or everything at the same time. **above all**, more than anything else: *Carol likes fruit and, above all, oranges.* **at all**, in any way: *Can you swim at all?* **not at all**, (*a*) words that make the word 'not' stronger: *He's not at all clever.* (*b*) words that you say to someone who has just said 'thank you', etc.: *'Thanks for helping me, Jill.' 'Not at all, Jack.'*

alley /'ælɪ/ *n.* narrow street between high walls.

alliance /ə'laɪəns/ *n.* agreement between countries or people to work together or fight on the same side.

allied /'ælaɪd/ *past part.* of *v.* ally: *The two countries were allied in the war.*

alligator /'ælɪgeɪtə(r)/ *n.* long, dangerous reptile that lives in hot countries.

allow /ə'laʊ/ *v.* say that someone can have or do something: *Do they allow smoking in the cinema?*

all right¹ /ˌɔːl 'raɪt/ *adj.* good; well: *Is she all right after the accident?*

all right² *exclam.* yes: *All right, I'll help you.*

ally /'ælaɪ/ *n.* (*pl.* allies) person or country that has an agreement with another or gives help. **ally** *v.*

almost /'ɔːlməʊst/ *adv.* nearly: *Don't go away because dinner is almost ready.*

alone /ə'ləʊn/ *adv.* 1 by yourself; with no other people: *When his wife died, he lived alone.* 2 only: *You alone can help me.*

along¹ /ə'lɒŋ/ *adv.* 1 forwards; onwards: *Move along the bus, please!* 2 with you: *Bring your friend along, too.*

along² *prep.* 1 from one end towards the other: *We walked along the road.* 2 at the side of something long: *There are trees along the river bank.*

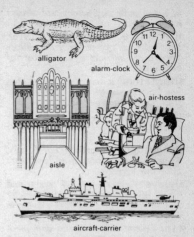

alligator

alarm-clock

air-hostess

aisle

aircraft-carrier

alongside /əˌlɒŋ'saɪd/ *prep.* next to: beside: *He parked his car alongside a bus.*

aloud /ə'laʊd/ *adv.* 1 speaking so that people can hear: *Please read the story aloud.* 2 in a loud voice: *He shouted aloud for help.*

alphabet /'ælfəbet/ *n.* the letters of the English language from A to Z. **alphabetical** /ˌælfə'betɪkl/ *adj.* in the order of the alphabet. **alphabetically** *adv.*: *The teacher calls out the children's names alphabetically: Angela is first and Zoë is last.*

already /ɔːl'redɪ/ *adv.* 1 before that time: *We ran to the station but the train had already left.* 2 before now: *I've been there already so I don't want to go again.*

also /'ɔːlsəʊ/ *adv.* too; as well: *Emma speaks English and also French.*

altar /'ɔːltə(r)/ *n.* 1 table or flat stone where people offer things to a god. 2 Communion table in a Christian church: *The priest kneels in front of the altar.*

alter /'ɔːltə(r)/ *v.* 1 become different; change. 2 make something different; change something: *These trousers are too big so I'll alter them.* **alteration** /ˌɔːltə'reɪʃn/ *n.* change.

alternate /ɔːl'tɜːnət/ *adj.* first one and then the other, in turn: *We have sport and music on alternate days—sport on*

Monday, music on Tuesday, etc. **alternately** *adv.*

alternative[1] /ɔːlˈtɜːnətɪv/ *adj.* different; another: *I can't come tomorrow—please suggest an alternative day.* **alternatively** *adv.*

alternative[2] *n.* one of the things that you can choose: *We have three alternatives for the journey—bus, train, or car.*

although /ɔːlˈðəʊ/ *conj.* though: *Although I am tired, I must go on working.*

altogether /ˌɔːltəˈgeðə(r)/ *adv.* totally: *Some of what you say is true, but I don't altogether agree.*

always /ˈɔːlweɪz/ *adv.* **1** again and again: *Why do you always get up so late?* **2** at all times: *There is always a doctor in a hospital.*

a.m. /ˌeɪˈem/ *abbrev.* (Latin *ante meridiem*) between midnight and midday: *9 a.m. is nine o'clock in the morning.*

am /æm/ part of *v.* be, used with 'I': *I am tall.*

amateur /ˈæmətə(r)/ *adj.* who plays sport, music etc. but does not get money for it: *an amateur cricket player.*

amaze /əˈmeɪz/ *v.* fill someone with great surprise or wonder. **amazing** *adj.*: *What an amazing sight!* **amazingly** *adv.* **amazement** *n.* great surprise or wonder.

ambassador /æmˈbæsədə(r)/ *n.* important person whose job is to speak and act for his government in another country: *the French Ambassador in London.*

amber /ˈæmbə(r)/ *adj.* with an orange colour. **amber** *n.*

ambition /æmˈbɪʃn/ *n.* **1** (no *pl.*) strong wish to do well: *Claire is full of ambition.* **2** (*pl.* ambitions) what you want to do: *Samuel's ambition is to be a doctor.* **ambitious** /æmˈbɪʃəs/ *adj.* wanting to do well.

ambulance /ˈæmbjʊləns/ *n.* special van that carries people who are ill or hurt: *When Bob broke his leg, an ambulance took him to hospital.*

ambush /ˈæmbʊʃ/ *n.* (*pl.* ambushes) sudden attack by people who have hidden and waited. **ambush** *v.*: *The robbers ambushed the travellers.*

ammunition /ˌæmjʊˈnɪʃn/ *n.* (*pl.*) military stores; bullets and bombs.

among /əˈmʌŋ/, **amongst** /əˈmʌŋst/ *prep.* **1** in the middle of: *The house stands among trees.* **2** one of: *The Amazon is among the most famous rivers in the world.* **3** for or by more than two things or people: *He divided the sweets among the children.*

amount /əˈmaʊnt/ *n.* **1** the total sum of money: *He owed me £50, but could only pay half that amount.* **2** quantity: *He likes a large amount of sugar in his coffee.*

ample /ˈæmpl/ *adj.* big; as much as you need: *There's ample room for five people in this car.*

amplifier /ˈæmplɪfaɪə(r)/ *n.* electric machine that makes sounds louder.

amuse /əˈmjuːz/ *v.* make someone smile or laugh: *Richard's jokes amused them.* **amuse yourself**, keep yourself busy and happy: *We amused ourselves with the cat while we waited*

amusement /əˈmjuːzmənt/ *n.* **1** (*pl.* amusements) something that gives people fun or pleasure: *There are many amusements in Liverpool, such as discos and football matches.* **2** (no *pl.*) smiling and laughing.

amusing /əˈmjuːzɪŋ/ *adj.* funny; making you smile and laugh: *an amusing story.*

an /ən/ *indef. art.* **1** a; one: *I ate an egg.* **2** each; every: *three times an hour.* **3** for each; for every: *Parking is 20p an hour.*

anaesthetic /ˌænɪsˈθetɪk/ *n.* something that a doctor gives you so that you will not feel pain: *The dentist gave Audrey an anaesthetic before he pulled out her bad tooth.*

ancestor /ˈænsestə(r)/ *n.* someone who was in your family long ago; grandparents, great-grandparents, etc.: *Paul's ancestors came from Holland in 1700.*

anchor /ˈæŋkə(r)/ *n.* heavy piece of iron dropped from a ship or boat to the bottom of the sea or river to keep the ship in one place: *The sailor dropped anchor when he arrived at the port.* **anchor** *v.*: *The ship anchored at Plymouth.*

ancient /ˈeɪnʃənt/ *adj.* of times long past; very old: *There are ancient walls around the old city of York.*

and /ənd/, /ænd/ *conj.* joining word:

Look at that horse and cart. We danced and sang.

angel /'eɪndʒl/ *n.* messenger, with wings, who comes from God.

anger /'æŋgə(r)/ *n.* (no *pl.*) strong feeling when you are not pleased: *I was filled with anger when I saw him kicking the dog.* **anger** *v.*: *His loud radio angered me.*

angle /'æŋgl/ *n.* space in a corner, where two lines join.

angry /'æŋgrɪ/ *adj.* feeling or showing anger: *Claire was angry when she tore her new dress.* **angrily** /'æŋgrɪlɪ/ *adv.*: *'Stop walking over my corn!' shouted the farmer angrily.*

animal /'ænɪml/ *n.* **1** any living thing that is not a plant: *Men, dogs, birds, and insects are all animals.* **2** creature with four feet, such as a horse, goat, etc.

ankle /'æŋkl/ *n.* part where the foot and leg join.

anniversary /ˌænɪ'vɜːsərɪ/ *n.* (*pl.* anniversaries) same date when something happened in a past year: *We have been married for one year, so today is our first wedding anniversary.*

announce /ə'naʊns/ *v.* tell people some important news: *Jonathan announced that he had found a new job.* **announcement** *n.*: *The children were excited by the announcement that they could have an extra holiday.*

announcer /ə'naʊnsə(r)/ *n.* someone whose job is to tell us about programmes on radio and television.

annoy /ə'nɔɪ/ *v.* make someone rather angry: *Loud music annoys Howard when he is studying.* **annoying** *adj.*: *This rain is annoying.* **annoyed** *adj.* rather angry. **annoyance** *n.* **to your annoyance,** making you rather angry: *To my annoyance, the telephone rang when I was in bed.*

annual /'ænjʊəl/ *adj.* **1** done or happening every year: *Easter is an annual event.* **2** of one year: *Britain's annual exports.*

another[1] /ə'nʌðə(r)/ *adj.* **1** one more: *May I have another potato?* **2** different: *The shop is closed today so we'll come another day.*

another[2] *pron.* (*pl.* others) one more; one of the same kind: *If you finish the book I can give you another.* **one another:** *The three children enjoy playing with one another.*

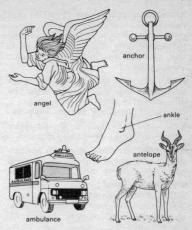

angel

anchor

ankle

antelope

ambulance

answer /'ɑːnsə(r)/ *v.* **1** say or write something when a question has been asked: *What a difficult question—I can't answer it.* **2** write to someone who has written to you: *Mr. Carter answered Mr. Brown's letter.* **answer the door,** go to open the door when someone knocks or rings. **answer the telephone,** pick up the telephone when it rings and speak to the person who is calling. **answer** *n.*: *Have you had an answer to your letter?*

ant /ænt/ *n.* very small insect.

antelope /'æntɪləʊp/ *n.* wild animal that has horns and long, thin legs and that can run fast.

anthem /'ænθəm/ *n.* song: *When the Queen arrived, the band played the National Anthem.*

anti- /'æntɪ/ *prefix* **1** against: *an anti-aircraft gun.* **2** not liking: *He is very anti-British.*

anticipate /æn'tɪsɪpeɪt/ *v.* think that something will happen: *I took my umbrella to work because I anticipated rain.*

antique /æn'tiːk/ *adj.* made long ago: *an antique chair.* **antique** *n.* an old, valuable thing.

anxiety /æŋ'zaɪətɪ/ *n.* **1** (no *pl.*) worry and fear: *We waited with anxiety for our examination results.* **2** (*pl.* anxieties) something that makes you worried and afraid.

anxious /'æŋkʃəs/ adj. **1** afraid and worried: I am anxious about the parcel because it hasn't arrived. **2** wanting something very much: I'm anxious to see what the new neighbours are like. **anxiously** adv.

any[1] /'enɪ/ adj. **1** some; word that you use with questions, 'if', and 'not': Have you any money? I don't have any money. **2** no special one: Come any day this week.

any[2] adv. at all; a little: Is your father any better? If it's any good, I'll buy it.

anybody /'enɪbɒdɪ/ pron. (no pl.) any person; no special person: Anybody will tell you the way to the station.

anyhow /'enɪhaʊ/ adv. **1** with no order; without trying: The chairs were left anyhow and the room looked untidy. **2** no matter what happens: Anyhow, I'll see you tonight.

anyone /'enɪwʌn/ pron. (no pl.) any person; no special person: Did anyone see the accident?

anything /'enɪθɪŋ/ pron. (no pl.) **1** a thing; something: Did anything come in the post today? **2** no matter what thing: I want some food—anything will do.

anyway /'enɪweɪ/ adv. **1** in any way; carelessly. **2** whatever happens: It will probably rain, but we'll go anyway.

anywhere /'enɪweə(r)/ adv. at, in, or to any place: Is there anywhere I can put my books?

apart /ə'pɑːt/ adv. **1** free from each other: The pages are stuck together and I can't pull them apart. **2** away from each other: The two houses are 500 metres apart. **apart from**, as well as; if you do not count: There are ten people in the queue, apart from me.

apartment /ə'pɑːtmənt/ n. flat; group of rooms in a building, where you can live.

ape /eɪp/ n. sort of monkey: Gorillas are apes.

apologetic /ə,pɒlə'dʒetɪk/ adj. showing that you are sorry for doing wrong. **apologetically** adv.: 'I'm sorry, Neville,' said George apologetically.

apologize /ə'pɒlədʒaɪz/ v. say that you are sorry for doing wrong: I apologized to the man for stepping on his foot. **apology** /ə'pɒlədʒɪ/ n.

apostrophe /ə'pɒstrəfɪ/ n. punctuation mark (') **1** to show that you have left a letter out of a word, e.g. I'm = I am. **2** to show who owns something: Peter's piano.

apparent /ə'pærənt/ adj. clear; easy to see; easy to understand: It was apparent that she didn't hear what I said. **apparently** adv. so it seems: She wrote me a nice letter so apparently she is not angry with me.

appeal /ə'piːl/ v. **1** ask for something that you want very much: The police appealed to people to drive slowly in the fog. **2** ask the referee of a football game to change his mind. **appeal to**, please someone: Bright colours appeal to children. **appeal** n. **appealing** adj. pleasing: an appealing picture.

appear /ə'pɪə(r)/ v. **1** be seen; come into view: After the storm, a rainbow appeared in the sky. **2** look as if; seem: She appears older than she really is.

appearance /ə'pɪərəns/ n. **1** what someone or something looks like: She's ill—you can tell from her appearance. **2** being seen; coming: The appearance of clouds often means that rain will fall.

appetite /'æpɪtaɪt/ n. strong wish to have something, usually food: Playing football gave Tony an appetite for dinner.

applaud /ə'plɔːd/ v. clap your hands, etc. to show that you are pleased: We applauded the dancers. **applause** /ə'plɔːz/ n.: There was loud applause when our team scored a goal.

apple /'æpl/ n. round fruit.

applicant /'æplɪkənt/ n. someone who asks for a job, etc.: There were six applicants for the job.

application /,æplɪ'keɪʃn/ n. writing to ask for a job, etc. or to join a club, etc.: Barbara made an application for a job as a nurse.

apply /ə'plaɪ/ v. **apply for**, write to ask for something: Henry applied for a place at the university. **apply to**, have to do with someone or something: This notice applies to all children under 11.

appoint /ə'pɔɪnt/ v. choose someone for a position, job, etc.: The bank appointed Mr. Ford as the new manager.

appointment /ə'pɔɪntmənt/ n. **1** a time that you have fixed to meet someone: an appointment with the dentist. **2** position; job: an appointment as headmaster.

appreciate /ə'priːʃɪeɪt/ v. **1** understand and enjoy something: *You will appreciate that book about England after you have been there yourself.* **2** be thankful for something: *I appreciate your help.* **appreciation** /ə,priːʃɪ'eɪʃn/ n.: *Give Susan some flowers to show your appreciation of her help.*

apprentice /ə'prentɪs/ n. young worker who is learning his job or trade.

approach¹ /ə'prəʊtʃ/ n. (no pl.) going near or nearer to a place: *We heard the approach of the train.*

approach² v. come near or nearer to someone or something: *You must approach the bird very quietly or it will fly away.*

appropriate /ə'prəʊprɪət/ adj. right for that time, place, etc.: *Thin clothes are appropriate for hot weather.* **appropriately** adv.

approve /ə'pruːv/ v. think or say that something or someone is good and right: *Do you approve of Jill's new hairstyle?* **approval** n.: *Yes, it has my full approval.*

approximate /ə'prɒksɪmət/ adj. not exact; very nearly: *Fifteen minutes is the approximate time for boiling potatoes.* **approximately** adv.

apricot /'eɪprɪkɒt/ n. small, soft, yellow fruit.

April /'eɪprəl/ n. fourth month of the year.

apron /'eɪprən/ n. cloth that you tie over the front of your clothes to keep them clean.

arch¹ /ɑːtʃ/ n. (pl. arches) curved part of a bridge or building.

arch² v. make something into a curve: *An angry cat arches its back.* **arched** /ɑːtʃt/ adj. curved: *an arched doorway.*

archaeology /,ɑːkɪ'ɒlədʒɪ/ n. (no pl.) study of very old things like buildings, tombs, etc. **archaeologist** /,ɑːkɪ'ɒlədʒɪst/ n. someone who studies archaeology.

archbishop /,ɑːtʃ'bɪʃəp/ n. chief bishop: *the Archbishop of Canterbury.*

architect /'ɑːkɪtekt/ n. someone whose job is to plan buildings.

architecture /'ɑːkɪtektʃə(r)/ n. (no pl.) **1** planning buildings: *John studied architecture.* **2** shape and plan of build-

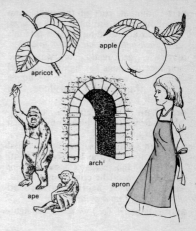

apple

apricot

arch¹

apron

arch

ape

ings: *Coventry Cathedral has very modern architecture.*

are /ɑː(r)/ part of v. be, used with 'you', 'they', 'we': *We are happy.*

area /'eərɪə/ n. **1** part of a country; part of the world: *the desert areas of North Africa.* **2** size of a flat place: *If a room is 3 metres wide by 3 metres long its area is 9 square metres.*

aren't /ɑːnt/ = are not: *Elephants aren't small.*

argue /'ɑːgjuː/ v. **1** say that something is wrong, not true; give a different idea: *Do as I say, and stop arguing!* **2** say why you think something is right or wrong: *Anita argued that she needed a holiday because she had been working hard.*

argument /'ɑːgjʊmənt/ n. quarrel; fight; talk between people with different ideas: *After a long argument, we decided where to go for our holiday.*

arise /ə'raɪz/ v. (past part. arisen /ə'rɪzn/, past tense arose /ə'rəʊz/) **1** get up; stand up: *We arose at 5 a.m.* **2** happen; start: *A strong wind arose in the night.*

aristocrat /'ærɪstəkræt/ n. nobleman or noblewoman. **aristocratic** /,ærɪstə'krætɪk/ adj.: *an aristocratic family.* **aristocracy** /,ærɪ'stɒkrəsɪ/ n. all the nobles.

arithmetic /ə'rɪθmətɪk/ n. (no pl.) working with numbers to find an answer.

arm¹ /ɑ:m/ *n.* part of the body from the shoulder to the hand. **arm in arm**, with your arm holding another person's arm: *Jack and Jill walked arm in arm.*

arm² *v.* get ready for war; give someone weapons for fighting. **armed** /ɑ:md/ *adj.* with a gun, etc.: *an armed robber.* **the armed services**, the army, air force, and navy.

armchair /'ɑ:mtʃeə(r)/ *n.* comfortable chair with high sides where you can rest your arms.

armour /'ɑ:mə(r)/ *n.* (no *pl.*) **1** metal clothing to cover the body when fighting: *Long ago, soldiers wore suits of armour.* **2** metal to cover tanks, ships, cars, etc. when fighting. **armoured** /'ɑ:məd/ *adj.*: *an armoured car.*

arms /ɑ:mz/ *n.* (*pl.*) weapons for fighting.

army /'ɑ:mɪ/ *n.* (*pl.* armies) group of people who fight on land; all the soldiers of a country: *the British Army.*

arose /ə'rəʊz/ past tense of *v.* arise.

around¹ /ə'raʊnd/ *adv.* **1** a little more or less than: *The parcel weighs around three kilos.* **2** here and there; in different ways or places: *In London, there are always tourists looking around.* **3** somewhere near; not far away: *I'll be around if you need me.* **4** in a circle; round: *Turn around!* **5** on every side; everywhere: *From all around we heard music.*

around² *prep.* **1** here and there in a place: *The dogs ran around the garden.* **2** to or in many places: *Jean's clothes were lying around the room.* **3** a little before or after a time: *I'll be there around midday.* **4** in a circle; round: *Ann put a gold chain around her neck.*

arouse /ə'raʊz/ *v.* wake someone up: *A knock on the door aroused us.*

arrange /ə'reɪndʒ/ *v.* **1** put things in a nice, neat way: *The teacher arranged the books on the shelves.* **2** make a plan: *I have arranged to meet Tim at the station.* **arrangement** *n.*: *Have you made arrangements to sell your house?*

arrest /ə'rest/ *v.* make someone a prisoner by law; catch someone who has done a bad thing: *The policeman arrested the thief.* **arrest** *n.* **be under arrest**, be a prisoner of the police or soldiers.

arrival /ə'raɪvl/ *n.* **1** (no *pl.*) getting to a place: *My brother met me on my arrival in Dover.* **2** (*pl.* arrivals) something or someone that has come to a place: *Come and meet the new arrivals!*

arrive /ə'raɪv/ *v.* **1** come to a place: *He was tired when he arrived home.* **2** be born: *Her baby arrived yesterday.* **3** come; happen: *At last, summer has arrived.*

arrow /'ærəʊ/ *n.* **1** thin, pointed stick that you shoot from a bow. **2** sign in the shape of an arrow that points to something or shows the way.

art /ɑ:t/ *n.* studying and making beautiful things. **a work of art**, something beautiful that someone has made: *That painting by Rembrandt is a work of art.*

article /'ɑ:tɪkl/ *n.* **1** thing: *The shop sells many articles of clothing.* **2** piece of writing in a newspaper or magazine: *Did you read the article in 'The Sunday Times'?* **3** sort of word in grammar: *definite article 'the'; indefinite articles 'a', 'an'.*

artificial /ˌɑ:tɪ'fɪʃl/ *adj.* not natural; made by people: *He has an artificial leg.* **artificially** *adv.*

artisan /'ɑ:tɪzæn/ *n.* someone who works with his hands.

artist /'ɑ:tɪst/ *n.* someone who paints pictures, plays music, etc.: *Degas was a famous French artist.*

artistic /ɑ:'tɪstɪk/ *adj.* **1** beautifully and cleverly made: *an artistic flower arrangement.* **2** clever at making beautiful things: *an artistic man.*

as¹ /æz/, /əz/ *conj.* **1** while; when: *I waved as the train left the station.* **2** because: *As he wasn't ready, we left without him.* **3** like; in the same way: *Do as I do.* **as . . . as**, like: *He is as tall as I am.* **as if**, **as though**, in a way that makes you think something: *Fiona is walking slowly as if she were tired.*

as² *prep.* in the job of: *Marion works as a journalist.*

ascend /ə'send/ *v.* come up; go up: *The lift ascended to the top floor.*

ascent /ə'sent/ *n.* way up; going up to the top: *The first ascent of Mount Everest was in 1953.*

ash /æʃ/ *n.* (*pl.* ash or ashes) powder that is left after something has burnt: *cigarette ash.*

ashamed /ə'ʃeɪmd/ *adj.* sorry because you have done something wrong; sad because you are not as good as other people in some way: *Joan was ashamed of her rudeness.*

ashore /ə'ʃɔː(r)/ *adv.* on or on to the land: *The fisherman left his boat and went ashore.*

ash-tray /'æʃ treɪ/ *n.* dish for cigarette ash and cigarette ends.

aside /ə'saɪd/ *adv.* on or to one side; away: *Clive put the book aside while he ate his meal.*

ask /ɑːsk/ *v.* try to get an answer by saying something: *She asked me the way to the market.* **ask for something**, say that you want someone to give you something: *Matthew asked his parents for a bicycle.* **ask someone to something**, invite someone to a place, happening, etc.: *Julian asked me to his house.*

asleep /ə'sliːp/ *adv.* sleeping; not awake: *The cat was asleep in front of the fire.* **fast asleep, sound asleep**, sleeping very well.

aspirin /'æsprɪn/ *n.* medicine to stop pain and fever: *John took an aspirin for his headache.*

ass /æs/ *n.* (*pl.* asses) **1** donkey. **2** someone who is stupid or does something silly.

assassinate /ə'sæsɪneɪt/ *v.* kill a ruler or important person: *John F. Kennedy was assassinated in 1963.* **assassination** /ə,sæsɪ'neɪʃn/ *n.* **assassin** /ə'sæsɪn/ *n.* someone who kills an important person.

assault /ə'sɔːlt/ *v.* attack a place or person.

assemble /ə'sembl/ *v.* **1** meet; come together in a group: *The football team assembled in the dressing-room.* **2** get the parts of something ready so that you can start doing something: *The carpenter assembled his tools.*

assembly /ə'semblɪ/ *n.* (*pl.* assemblies) meeting of a special group of people: *a school assembly.*

assist /ə'sɪst/ *v.* help someone. **assistance** *n.*: *I need your assistance with this heavy load.*

assistant /ə'sɪstənt/ *n.* someone who helps: *a shop assistant.*

associate /ə'səʊʃɪeɪt/ *v.* **1** spend time with someone: *He associates with criminals.* **2** put two ideas together: *We associate smoke with fire.*

association /ə,səʊsɪ'eɪʃn/ *n.* group of

way out ← arrow 1
arrow 2
arm in arm
armour
astronaut
armchair

people with the same interests: *the Automobile Association.*

assorted /ə'sɔːtɪd/ *adj.* of different kinds; mixed: *a bag of assorted sweets.*

assortment /ə'sɔːtmənt/ *n.* group of different things: *Kelly's shop has a large assortment of goods.*

assume /ə'sjuːm/ *v.* think or believe that something is true when you are not totally sure: *Ellen is not here so I assume she is ill.*

assurance /ə'ʃʊərəns/ *n.* **1** (*pl.* assurances) promise: *He gave me his assurance that he would mend my watch by tomorrow.* **2** (no *pl.*) sure feeling that you can do something: *He plays the piano with assurance.*

assure /ə'ʃʊə(r)/ *v.* make someone feel sure about something: *I assure you that the dog isn't dangerous.*

astonish /ə'stɒnɪʃ/ *v.* surprise someone very much: *His rudeness astonishes me.* **astonishing** *adj.* that astonishes you: *astonishing news.* **astonished** /ə'stɒnɪʃt/ *adj.* looking or feeling very surprised. **astonishment** *n.* great surprise.

astound /ə'staʊnd/ *v.* surprise someone very much: *The telegram astounded me.* **astounding** *adj.* that astounds you: *astounding news.* **astounded** /ə'staʊndɪd/ *adj.* looking or feeling very surprised.

astronaut /'æstrənɔːt/ *n.* someone who travels in a spaceship; spaceman.

astronomy /ə'strɒnəmi/ n. (no pl.) study of the sun, moon, planets, and stars. **astronomer** /ə'strɒnəmə(r)/ n. someone who studies astronomy: *Galileo was a famous astronomer.*

at /æt/, /ət/ prep. **1** word that shows where: *Isabel is at home.* **2** word that shows what: *He is good at football.* **3** word that shows when: *We leave at two o'clock.* **4** word that shows how fast, etc.: *We drove at 60 kilometres an hour.* **5** word that shows how much, etc.: *I bought two lemons at 12p each.* **6** towards: *He threw the stone at me.*

ate /et/ *past tense of v.* eat.

athlete /'æθliːt/ n. person trained for sports such as running, jumping, swimming, etc.: *Many athletes took part in the Olympic Games.*

athletic /æθ'letɪk/ adj. good at sports, etc.; having a strong body.

athletics /æθ'letɪks/ n. (pl.) sports like running, jumping, etc.

atlas /'ætləs/ n. (pl. atlases) book of maps.

atmosphere /'ætməsfɪə(r)/ n. **1** (no pl.) all the gases around the earth. **2** (no pl.) air in a place: *The atmosphere in the hall was very hot.* **3** (pl. atmospheres) feeling in a place: *a happy atmosphere.*

atom /'ætəm/ n. smallest part of a chemical: *Water is made of atoms of hydrogen and oxygen.* **atomic** /ə'tɒmɪk/ adj.

attach /ə'tætʃ/ v. join or fix one thing to another thing: *to attach a label to a parcel.* **be attached to,** like someone: *I am very attached to my cousin.*

attack /ə'tæk/ v. **1** start fighting or hurting someone: *The robber attacked the old man.* **2** make someone suddenly ill: *Measles attacks many children.* **attack** n.

attacker /ə'tækə(r)/ n. someone who tries to hurt another person.

attempt /ə'tempt/ v. try to do something: *Don is attempting to swim from England to France.* **attempt** n.: *a brave attempt.*

attend /ə'tend/ v. go to a place where something is happening: *Who attended the meeting?* **attend to,** (**a**) work or listen with care: *Please attend to what you are doing!* (**b**) care for, or serve, someone or something: *A good nurse attends to her patients.*

attendant /ə'tendənt/ n. **1** servant. **2** helper: *a cloakroom attendant.*

attention /ə'tenʃn/ n. (no pl.) interest; thinking carefully about what you are doing. **pay attention,** listen or look with care: *Say that again, please—I wasn't paying attention.* **stand at** or **to attention,** stand straight and still: *The soldiers stood to attention while the governor was passing.*

attic /'ætɪk/ n. room inside the roof of a house.

attitude /'ætɪtjuːd/ n. what you think about something: *What is her attitude to school?*

attract /ə'trækt/ v. **1** make something come nearer: *Magnets attract pins.* **2** make someone want to come nearer, look at it, etc.: *The concert attracted many people.*

attraction /ə'trækʃn/ n. something that makes you want to come nearer, look at it, etc.: *The Tower of London is a great attraction to tourists.*

attractive /ə'træktɪv/ adj. pleasing to see, hear, etc.: *an attractive girl.*

auction /'ɔːkʃn/ n. public sale where each thing is sold to the person who will give the most money for it.

audience /'ɔːdɪəns/ n. group of people listening to a speaker, singer, etc.

August /'ɔːgəst/ n. eighth month of the year.

aunt /ɑːnt/ n. sister of your father or mother; wife of your uncle.

author /'ɔːθə(r)/ n. someone who writes books, stories, etc.: *Dickens was the author of 'Oliver Twist'.*

authority /ɔː'θɒrətɪ/ n. **1** (no pl.) power to tell people what they must do; control: *A manager has authority over his staff.* **2** (pl. authorities) person or people who say what others must do: *the city authorities.*

autobiography /ˌɔːtəbaɪ'ɒgrəfɪ/ n. (pl. autobiographies) book that someone has written about his own life.

autograph /'ɔːtəgrɑːf/ n. person's name written by himself: *Pete collects the autographs of cricketers.*

automatic /ˌɔːtə'mætɪk/ adj. **1** that can work by itself: *an automatic door.* **2** that you do without thinking: *Breathing is automatic.* **automatically** adv.

autumn /'ɔːtəm/ n. time of the year between summer and winter.

available /ə'veɪləbl/ adj. free; ready when you need it: *The hotel is full, so there are no rooms available.*

avenue /'ævənjuː/ n. road with trees on each side; wide street.

average /'ævərɪdʒ/ n. **1** the middle number of a group: *The average of 3, 4, and 5 is 4.* **2** what is ordinary, not special. **average** adj.: *an average student.*

avocado /ˌævə'kɑːdəʊ/ n. avocado pear; fruit with soft, green flesh.

avoid /ə'vɔɪd/ v. keep away or go away from something or someone that you do not like: *We crossed the road to avoid meeting her.*

await /ə'weɪt/ v. be waiting or ready for something or someone: *A big welcome awaits Ben when he comes home.*

awake /ə'weɪk/ adj. not sleeping: *Is the baby awake or asleep?* **awake** v. (*past part.* awoken /ə'wəʊkən/, *past tense* awoke /ə'wəʊk/) stop sleeping.

award /ə'wɔːd/ n. prize, etc. that you give to someone who has done something very well: *Jane saved the child from drowning and they gave her an award for bravery.* **award** v. give someone money, a prize, etc.: *They awarded her first prize when she won the race.*

aware /ə'weə(r)/ adj. **be aware**, know something; know what is happening: *The thief was not aware that I was watching him.*

away /ə'weɪ/ adv. **1** from here; from there: *The sea is two kilometres away.* **2** so that there is less, none: *If you leave the pot on the cooker too long, all the water will boil away.* **3** not here: *Lisa is away today but she will be back tomorrow.*

awe /ɔː/ n. (no pl.) respect and fear.

awful /'ɔːfl/ adj. **1** making you very afraid, very sad, or shocked: *It is awful to read about poverty.* **2** very bad: *awful weather.*

awfully /'ɔːflɪ/ adv. very: *That's awfully kind of you!*

awkward /'ɔːkwəd/ adj. **1** not easy to use: *A narrow road is awkward for big lorries.* **2** not able to move easily: *an awkward dancer.* **awkwardly** adv.: *He walks awkwardly because his leg is hurt.*

awoke /ə'wəʊk/ past tense of v. awake.

axe /æks/ n. tool for cutting wood.

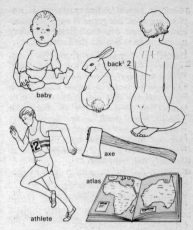

baby

back³ 2

axe

atlas

athlete

Bb

baby /'beɪbɪ/ n. (*pl.* babies) very young child.

babysit /'beɪbɪsɪt/ v. (*pres. part.* babysitting, *past part. & past tense* babysat /'beɪbɪsæt/) look after a child when the parents are away for a short time. **babysitter** /'beɪbɪsɪtə(r)/ n. someone who babysits.

bachelor /'bætʃələ(r)/ n. **1** man who has never had a wife. **2** person who has the first university degree: *a Bachelor of Arts.*

back¹ /bæk/ adj. farthest from the front: *John sits in the back row and cannot see the blackboard very well.*

back² adv. **1** away from the front: *I looked back to see if he was coming.* **2** in or to the place where it was before: *Put the book back when you have read it.* **3** in return; in reply: *Vincent hit me and I hit him back.*

back³ n. **1** part that is behind, farthest from the front: *Your heel is at the back of your foot.* **2** part of the body of a person or animal between the neck and legs: *Neil lay on his back and looked up at the sky.* **go behind someone's back**, do something and not tell someone. **put your back into**, work hard at something. **when someone's**

back is turned, when someone is not looking: *You always stop work when my back is turned.* **3** football player or hockey player who is behind the forwards.

back⁴ *v.* **1** go away from the front; move a vehicle away from the front: *There was no room to turn the car so Mr. Jackson backed it down the road.* **2** help someone; say that you think someone or something is best: *We all back our school team.* **back away**, move away backwards: *Sally backed away from the big dog.* **back out**, give up a plan, promise, etc.: *Paul backed out of the game so we only had ten players.*

backbone /ˈbækbəʊn/ *n.* line of bones down the back of the body.

background /ˈbækɡraʊnd/ *n.* things at the back in a picture: *This is a photo of my house with the mountains in the background.*

backward /ˈbækwəd/ *adj.* **1** towards the back: *a backward step.* **2** not having modern things, ways, etc.: *a backward country.* **3** slow to learn; not as good as others: *a backward pupil.*

backstroke /ˈbækstrəʊk/ *n.* (no *pl.*) way of swimming on your back.

backwards /ˈbækwədz/ *adv.* **1** away from the front; towards the back: *He looked backwards over his shoulder.* **2** with the back or the end first: *Say the alphabet backwards, starting with the letter 'Z'.* **backwards and forwards**, first in one way, then in the other: *The ferry travels backwards and forwards between Dover and Calais.*

bacon /ˈbeɪkən/ *n.* (no *pl.*) salted or smoked meat from a pig.

bad /bæd/ *adj.* (worse, worst) **1** not good; doing wrong: *That bad boy steals money from his friends.* **2** nasty; not pleasant: *There's a bad smell here.* **3** rotten; old and not fresh enough to use. **go bad**, become rotten: *That meat will go bad if you leave it in the sun.* **4** serious: *a bad fire.* **5** poor; not working well: *bad eyesight.* **6** not able to do something well: *a bad driver.*

badge /bædʒ/ *n.* sign that someone wears to show which school, club, army, etc. he belongs to: *a Scout badge.*

badly /ˈbædlɪ/ *adv.* **1** in a bad way; not well: *badly dressed.* **badly off**, poor. **2** very much: *I badly want to go to the festival.*

badminton /ˈbædmɪntən/ *n.* (no *pl.*) game like tennis, where the player hits a small piece of cork with feathers in it.

bad-tempered /ˌbæd ˈtempəd/ *adj.* often cross and angry: *a bad-tempered old man.*

baffle /ˈbæfl/ *v.* be too difficult for you to understand or do: *This sum baffles me.*

bag /bæɡ/ *n.* container made of cloth, leather, paper, etc., with an opening at the top, for holding things: *a shopping bag.*

baggage /ˈbæɡɪdʒ/ *n.* (no *pl.*) luggage; bags, trunks, suitcases, etc. for travelling.

baggy /ˈbæɡɪ/ *adj.* hanging in loose folds: *baggy trousers.*

bagpipes /ˈbæɡpaɪps/ *n.* (*pl.*) musical instrument which Scotsmen often play.

bait /beɪt/ *n.* (no *pl.*) food put on a hook or in a trap, etc. to catch fish or animals.

bake /beɪk/ *v.* **1** cook food in an oven: *My mother bakes bread every day.* **2** make something hard with heat: *The hot sun baked the ground hard.*

baker /ˈbeɪkə(r)/ *n.* someone whose job is to make bread or cakes to sell.

bakery /ˈbeɪkərɪ/ *n.* (*pl.* bakeries) place where bread, cakes, etc. are made or sold.

balance¹ /ˈbæləns/ *n.* **1** (*pl.* balances) instrument for weighing things; scales. **2** (no *pl.*) when two sides are the same; being steady. **keep your balance**, stay steady; not fall: *Derek kept his balance with his arms as he walked on the top of the high wall.* **lose your balance**, become unsteady; fall. **3** (*pl.* balances) the money that is left when you have paid out some of it: *If you earn £100 and spend £60, your balance is £40.*

balance² *v.* make or keep something steady, so it does not fall; stay steady: *That dog can balance a ball on his nose!*

balcony /ˈbælkənɪ/ *n.* (*pl.* balconies) small place on the outside wall of a building above the ground: *They stood on the balcony to watch the festival in the street below.*

bald /bɔːld/ *adj.* with no hair or not much hair.

bale /beɪl/ *n.* big bundle of wool, cotton, etc.: *Farmers keep bales of hay in the barn for cows in winter.*

ball /bɔːl/ n. **1** round thing that you throw or hit in games and sports: *a football; tennis balls.* **2** anything rolled into a round shape: *a ball of wool.* **3** big party where people dance. **ballroom** n. big room for dances.

ballerina /ˌbælə'riːnə/ n. woman who dances in ballet.

ballet /'bæleɪ/ n. sort of dancing.

balloon /bə'luːn/ n. bag that becomes bigger when filled with air or with gas. It can float in the sky.

ballot /'bælət/ n. **1** secret vote on a piece of paper: *We held a ballot to choose a new captain.* **2** piece of paper for secret voting. **ballot box** n. box where people put their voting papers.

ballpoint /'bɔːlpɔɪnt/ n. pen that has a small ball at the end; biro.

ban /bæn/ v. (*pres. part.* banning, *past part. & past tense* banned /bænd/) say that something must stop or must not happen: *The baker bans dogs in his shop.* **ban** n.: *There is a ban on smoking in petrol stations.*

banana /bə'nɑːnə/ n. long, thin, yellow fruit.

band /bænd/ n. **1** flat, thin strip of cloth, etc. to put round something: *Alan put a rubber band round his pencils.* **2** line of colour, etc.: *The French flag has bands of red, white, and blue.* **3** group of people who do something together: *a band of robbers.* **4** group of people who play music together: *a jazz band.*

bandage /'bændɪdʒ/ n. long strip of cloth to put round a part of the body that is hurt. **bandage** v. put a bandage on to someone.

bandit /'bændɪt/ n. robber who attacks travellers.

bang[1] /bæŋ/ n. **1** strong blow: *Arthur fell down and got a bang on the head.* **2** loud, sudden noise: *He shut the door with a bang.*

bang[2] v. **1** hit something hard: *The tall man banged his head as he went through the door.* **2** shut or hit something with a loud noise: *Don't bang the door!*

bangle /'bæŋgl/ n. pretty piece of metal, etc. that you wear round your arm.

banish /'bænɪʃ/ v. send someone away from his own country as a punishment.

banisters /'bænɪstəz/ n. (*pl.*) rail and posts at the side of the stairs.

banjo /'bændʒəʊ/ n. musical instrument with strings.

bank /bæŋk/ n. **1** land along the side of a river: *Jim climbed out of the boat on to the bank.* **2** building or business for keeping money safely, and for lending and exchanging money: *Kevin sold his car and put the money in the bank.*

banker /'bæŋkə(r)/ n. manager or owner of a bank. **bank holiday** n. day when the British have a general public holiday.

banknote /'bæŋknəʊt/ n. piece of paper money.

bankrupt /'bæŋkrʌpt/ adj. not able to pay money that you owe: *John's business had a bad year and he is bankrupt.*

banner /'bænə(r)/ n. flag with words to show what people think.

banquet /'bæŋkwɪt/ n. feast with speeches for a special happening.

baptize /bæp'taɪz/ v. **1** put holy water on someone to show that he or she belongs to the Christian church. **2** give someone a Christian name.

bar[1] /bɑː(r)/ n. **1** long piece of something hard: *a bar of soap; an iron bar.* **2** room where people can buy and have drinks.

bar[2] v. (*pres. part.* barring, *past part. & past tense* barred /bɑːd/) put something across an open place so that people or things cannot pass: *We had to stop the car because sheep were barring the road.*

barbed wire /ˌbɑːbd ˈwaɪə(r)/ *n.* (no *pl.*) wire with short, sharp points, for making fences.

barber /ˈbɑːbə(r)/ *n.* someone whose job is to cut men's hair.

bare /beə(r)/ *adj.* **1** with no clothes, covering, etc.: *The baby is bare.* **2** empty: *Mrs. Jones had no money to buy furniture so her room was bare.*

barefoot /ˈbeəfʊt/ *adv.* with no shoes: *If you go barefoot you will get cold.*

bareheaded /ˌbeəˈhedɪd/ *adj.* with no hat, cap, etc.

barely /ˈbeəlɪ/ *adv.* only just; hardly: *The poor family had barely enough money to buy food.*

bargain¹ /ˈbɑːgɪn/ *n.* **1** agreement to buy, sell, or exchange something; agreement about pay or work, etc.: *Let's make a bargain—if you help me today, I'll help you tomorrow.* **2** something that is very cheap: *I bought this dress because it was a bargain at £2.*

bargain² *v.* talk about making the price of something less: *Perhaps he will sell his house more cheaply if you bargain with him.*

barge /bɑːdʒ/ *n.* boat with flat bottom for carrying goods on rivers.

bark¹ /bɑːk/ *n.* (no *pl.*) outside covering of a tree-trunk and branches.

bark² *n.* cry of a dog or fox. **bark** *v.*: *The dog barked at the stranger.*

barley /ˈbɑːlɪ/ *n.* (no *pl.*) plant that we use for food and to make beer and whisky.

barn /bɑːn/ *n.* building for hay, farm animals, etc.

barometer /bəˈrɒmɪtə(r)/ *n.* instrument that helps to tell what the weather will be.

barracks /ˈbærəks/ *n.* (*pl.*) building where soldiers, etc. live.

barrel /ˈbærəl/ *n.* **1** big container with flat ends and round sides; cask: *a beer barrel.* **2** tube of a gun through which the bullet goes.

barren /ˈbærən/ *adj.* where plants cannot grow: *barren land.*

barricade /ˌbærɪˈkeɪd/ *n.* wall of things that people build quickly to keep others away: *There was a barricade of carts and branches across the road.* **barricade** *v.* block something with a barricade: *He barricaded the door to keep the wolf out.*

barrier /ˈbærɪə(r)/ *n.* something that stops you from passing; fence: *You must show your ticket at the barrier before you can get on to the train.*

barrow /ˈbærəʊ/ *n.* small cart that you push or pull by hand.

base /beɪs/ *n.* **1** bottom; part on which something stands: *This vase falls over a lot because the base is too small.* **2** place to start from and go back to: *That pilot travels all over the world but London is his base.*

baseball /ˈbeɪsbɔːl/ *n.* **1** (no *pl.*) American ball game, with two teams of players. **2** (*pl.* baseballs) ball for this game.

basement /ˈbeɪsmənt/ *n.* part of a building, under the ground: *You can buy garden chairs in the basement of this shop.*

bash /bæʃ/ *v.* hit something very hard.

basin /ˈbeɪsn/ *n.* round, deep dish: *The cook mixed the pudding in a basin.*

bask /bɑːsk/ *v.* enjoy heat and light: *The cat was basking in the sunshine.*

basket /ˈbɑːskɪt/ *n.* container made of thin straw, cane, etc. for carrying things: *a shopping basket.*

basket-ball /ˈbɑːskɪt bɔːl/ *n.* **1** (no *pl.*) game where players try to throw a big ball into a high net. **2** (*pl.* basketballs) ball for this game.

bass /beɪs/ *adj.* with a deep sound: *a bass drum.*

bat /bæt/ *n.* **1** small animal like a mouse with wings, which comes out at night. **2** piece of wood for hitting the ball in a game, etc. **bat** *v.* (*pres. part.* batting, *past part. & past tense* batted /ˈbætɪd/) hit or try to hit a cricket ball: *Tom batted for two hours.*

batch /bætʃ/ *n.* (*pl.* batches) group of things that you make at the same time: *a batch of bread.*

bath¹ /bɑːθ/ *n.* **1** washing the whole body: *I have a bath every evening.* **2** big basin where you sit to wash yourself: *Amelia got into the bath.* **3** (usually *pl.*) public swimming-pool.

bath² *v.* wash the whole body in a big basin: *'I'll bath after Amelia,' said Kim.*

bathe /beɪð/ *v.* **1** wash a part of the body: *The nurse bathed his cut finger.* **2** swim or play in the sea, river, etc.

bather /'beɪðə(r)/ *n.* someone who is bathing in the sea.

bathing-costume /'beɪðɪŋ kɒstjuːm/, **bathing-suit** /'beɪðɪŋ suːt/ *n.* piece of clothing that a woman or girl wears for swimming. **bathing trunks** /'beɪðɪŋ trʌŋks/ *n.* piece of clothing that a man or boy wears for swimming.

bathroom /'bɑːθrʊm/ *n.* room where you can bath and wash.

batsman /'bætsmən/ *n.* (*pl.* batsmen) someone who hits the ball with a bat in a cricket game.

batter /'bætə(r)/ *v.* hit something very hard, again and again, so that it breaks: *The falling rocks battered the roof of the house.*

battery /'bætərɪ/ *n.* (*pl.* batteries) group of cells in a container which give electricity: *I put a new battery into my radio.*

battle /'bætl/ *n.* **1** fight between soldiers, armies, ships, etc.: *The English beat the French at the Battle of Trafalgar.* **2** trying very hard to do something that is not easy: *The doctors had a battle to save Jon's life.* **battle** *v.* try very hard to do something that is not easy: *The doctors battled to save his life.*

bay /beɪ/ *n.* sea with land curving round three sides of it: *the Bay of Biscay.*

bazaar /bə'zɑː(r)/ *n.* **1** sale of goods to make money for a special reason: *a church bazaar.* **2** place in Africa or Asia where there are shops or where goods are sold in the streets.

be /biː/ *v.* (*pres. tense* I am, you are, he is, we are, they are; *past tense* I was, you were, he was, we were, they were; *past perf. tense* I have been, etc.; *pres. part.* being; *past part.* been) **1** word that describes a person or thing: *Kate is a good girl.* **2** become: *Clive hopes to be a farmer.* **3** happen; take place: *Tracey's birthday was in June.* **4** must; have to: *He is to take a tablet every day.* **5** word that you use with another verb to explain when something happens to a person or thing: *The house was built in 1910. Dick has been bitten by a dog.*

beach /biːtʃ/ *n.* (*pl.* beaches) flat strip of sand or stones beside the sea.

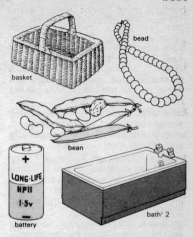

basket

bead

bean

battery

bath¹ 2

bead /biːd/ *n.* small ball of wood, glass, etc. with a hole so that it can go on thread: *My necklace broke and the beads rolled all over the floor.*

beak /biːk/ *n.* hard part of a bird's mouth: *The bird opened its beak and sang.*

beam¹ /biːm/ *n.* **1** long piece of heavy wood, metal, or concrete that holds up a roof, part of a ship, etc. **2** ray of light: *sunbeams.*

beam² *v.* smile in a happy way.

bean /biːn/ *n.* vegetable with seeds in pods.

bear¹ /beə(r)/ *n.* big, wild animal with thick fur.

bear² *v.* (*past part.* borne /bɔːn/, *past tense* bore /bɔː(r)/) **1** carry something: *He bore the crown on a cushion.* **2** keep something up; hold the weight of something: *Is that bridge strong enough to bear a car?* **3** have pain, problems, etc.: *She bore the pain bravely.* **cannot bear**, do not like something: *My mother cannot bear pop music.* **4** produce, or give birth to, a young one or a fruit: *Sarah has borne three children.*

beard /bɪəd/ *n.* hair on a man's chin and cheeks. **bearded** /'bɪədɪd/ *adj.*: *a bearded man.*

beast /biːst/ *n.* **1** animal. **2** bad or cruel person.

beat¹ /biːt/ *n.* sound or stroke that comes again and again: *drumbeats; heartbeats.*

beat[2] *v.* (*past part.* beaten /'bi:tn/, *past tense* beat) **1** hit a person or thing hard, again and again: *He beat the donkey with a stick.* **beat eggs, etc.,** mix eggs well. **2** win a fight or game against others: *Dan always beats me at tennis.* **3** move again and again: *Her heart beat fast as she ran.* **beating** *n.:* *The bad boy had a beating.*

beautiful /'bju:tɪfl/ *adj.* lovely; giving pleasure because it looks or sounds good, etc.: *a beautiful flower.* **beautifully** *adv.: Belinda sings beautifully.*

beauty /'bju:tɪ/ *n.* **1** (no *pl.*) being lovely: *San Francisco is a city of great beauty.* **2** (*pl.* beauties) someone or something that is very lovely or very fine: *Susan is a beauty. These apples are beauties.*

because /bɪ'kɒz/ *conj.* for the reason that: *My sister is in bed because she is ill.* **because of,** as a result of something: *He walked slowly because of his bad leg.*

beckon /'bekən/ *v.* call someone by moving your hand.

become /bɪ'kʌm/ *v.* (*past part.* become, *past tense* became /bɪ'keɪm/) **1** grow to be; develop into: *This little puppy will become a big dog.* **2** change: *We became very brown when we were on holiday.* **become of,** happen to someone or something: *I can't find Joe. What has become of him?*

bed /bed/ *n.* **1** thing that you sleep on: *I was so tired that I went to bed.* **make a bed,** put the coverings neatly on to a bed. **2** bottom of the sea or a river. **3** piece of ground where you grow plants: *flower beds.*

bed-clothes /'bed kləʊðz/ *n.* (*pl.*) sheets, blankets, etc.

bedroom /'bedrʊm/ *n.* room where you sleep.

bee /bi:/ *n.* small, flying insect which makes honey.

beef /bi:f/ *n.* (no *pl.*) meat from an ox, a cow, or a bull.

beehive /'bi:haɪv/ *n.* box where bees live.

been /bi:n/ *past part.* of *v.* be.

beer /bɪə(r)/ *n.* **1** (no *pl.*) sort of alcoholic drink. **2** (*pl.* beers) glass or can of beer: *Three beers, please.*

beetle /'bi:tl/ *n.* insect with hard, shiny wings.

beetroot /'bi:tru:t/ *n.* sweet, round, red vegetable.

before[1] /bɪ'fɔ:(r)/ *adv.* at an earlier time; in the past: *I've never seen him before.*

before[2] *conj.* at an earlier time than: *I said goodbye before I left.*

before[3] *prep.* **1** earlier than: *the day before yesterday.* **2** in front of: *He made a speech before a large audience.*

beforehand /bɪ'fɔ:hænd/ *adv.* earlier; before a happening: *When I travel by ship, I take a tablet beforehand.*

beg /beg/ *v.* (*pres. part.* begging, *past part.* & *past tense* begged /begd/) **1** ask for food, money, etc.: *He was so poor that he had to beg for his meals.* **2** ask for something with strong feeling: *She begged me to wait for her.*

began /bɪ'gæn/ *past tense* of *v.* begin.

beggar /'begə(r)/ *n.* someone who does not work and who asks people for money and food.

begin /bɪgɪn/ *v.* (*pres. part.* beginning, *past part.* begun, *past tense* began) start to do something; start to happen: *School begins again in September.*

beginner /bɪ'gɪnə(r)/ *n.* someone who is starting to do or to learn something.

beginning /bɪ'gɪnɪŋ/ *n.* start.

begun /bɪ'gʌn/ *past part.* of *v.* begin.

behalf /bɪ'hɑ:f/ *n.* **on behalf of, on someone's behalf,** in the place of someone: *Mr. Smith is away, so I am writing to you on his behalf.*

behave /bɪ'heɪv/ *v.* be good or bad; do things well or badly: *Did the children behave well?* **behave yourself,** be good. **behaviour** /bɪ'heɪvɪə/ *n.* how you are: *Robert was pleased with his dog's good behaviour.*

behind[1] /bɪ'haɪnd/ *adv.* coming after; at the back: *The men walked in front and the children followed behind.*

behind[2] *prep.* **1** at the back of: *Oliver hid behind a tree.* **2** slower in work, etc. than: *Barbara is often ill, so she is behind other girls in her school work.*

being[1] /'bi:ɪŋ/ *n.* person: *Men and women are human beings.*

being[2] *pres. part.* of *v.* be.

belief /bɪ'li:f/ *n.* sure feeling that something is true: *belief in God.*

believe /bɪ'li:v/ *v.* think that something is true or right: *Long ago, people believed that the world was flat.*

bell /bel/ n. hollow, metal thing that rings when you hit it: *church bells; a doorbell.*

bellow /'beləʊ/ v. make a loud noise; roar; shout: *A bull bellows when it is angry.*

belly /'belɪ/ n. (*pl.* bellies) part of the body below the waist and above the legs; stomach.

belong /bɪ'lɒŋ/ v. have its right place, etc.: *This book belongs on the top shelf.* **belong to,** (**a**) be owned by someone or something: *That bike belongs to me.* (**b**) be a member of a group, etc.: *She belongs to the tennis club.*

belongings /bɪ'lɒŋɪŋz/ n. (*pl.*) things that you own: *Mr. Day lost all his belongings in the fire.*

below¹ /bɪ'ləʊ/ adv. at or to a lower place: *From the plane, we could see the whole town below.*

below² prep. **1** under; lower than; beneath: *Your mouth is below your nose.* **2** smaller in number, price, etc.: *I hope the cost will be below a pound.*

belt /belt/ n. long piece of cloth, leather, etc. that you wear round your waist.

bench /bentʃ/ n. (*pl.* benches) **1** long seat of wood or stone. **2** work table of a carpenter, shoemaker, etc.

bend¹ /bend/ n. curve; line or shape that is not straight: *I can't see if there is a car coming because there is a bend in the road.*

bend² v. (*past part. & past tense* bent) **1** become curved; make something curved: *It is difficult to bend an iron bar.* **2** make your body curve forward and down: *Enid bent down to put on her sandals.*

beneath /bɪ'niːθ/ prep. under; lower than; below: *The river flows beneath the old bridge.*

benefit /'benɪfɪt/ v. help someone or something; make someone better, happier, etc.: *This sunshine will benefit the farmers.* **benefit from,** be helped by something: *The factory benefited from the new machines.* **benefit** n.

bent /bent/ *past tense* of v. bend.

berry /'berɪ/ n. (*pl.* berries) small, juicy fruit with no stone: *a strawberry; a blackberry.*

berth /bɜːθ/ n. **1** bed on a train or ship. **2** place in harbour or river for a ship or boat.

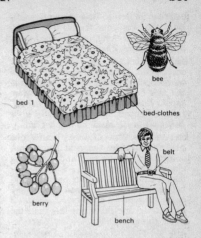

bed 1

bee

bed-clothes

belt

berry

bench

beside /bɪ'saɪd/ prep. at the side of; close to: *Come and sit beside me.*

besides¹ /bɪ'saɪdz/ adv. also: *I don't like this cloth and, besides, it costs too much.*

besides² prep. as well as; if you do not count: *There are many rivers in England besides the Thames.*

besiege /bɪ'siːdʒ/ v. go round a place and attack it from all sides.

best¹ /best/ adj. (good, better) very good; of the most excellent kind: *This is the best ice-cream I have ever eaten!*

best² adv. **1** in a very good way; in the most excellent way: *I work best in the cool weather.* **2** most; more than all others: *Of all games, I like chess best.*

best³ n. (no *pl.*) very good person or thing; most excellent person or thing: *Frank is the best in his class.* **do your best,** do what you can; try hard.

best man /'best mæn/ n. (*pl.* best men) man who helps the bridegroom at his wedding.

bet /bet/ v. (*pres. part.* betting, *past part. & past tense* bet, betted /'betɪd/) **1** say what you think will happen and then get money if you are right: *I bet you £2 that Neil will win.* **2** say you are sure about something: *I bet you can't climb that tree.* **bet** n.: *Mr. Ellis placed a bet on that horse.*

betray /bɪ'treɪ/ v. **1** be untrue to someone who was your friend: *The guards betrayed their king and let the enemy into the castle.* **2** tell a secret, etc.

better /'betə(r)/ adj. (good, best) **1** more good: *I think this looks better than that one, don't you?* **2** less ill: *Jack was ill but he's better now.* **better** adv.: *Alan speaks Italian better than I do.* **better off**, richer, happier, etc.: *I think we'd be better off in the shade on this hot day.*

between /bɪ'twiːn/ prep. **1** after one place and before the next place; with something on one side and something else on the other side: *The letter B is between A and C.* **2** after one time and before the next time: *Please come to my house between 1 o'clock and 2 o'clock.* **3** more than one thing but less than the other thing: *I think the coat costs between £8 and £9.* **4** to and from two places: *This ship sails between Calais and Dover.* **5** for or by two people or things: *You may share the sweets between you.* **6** word for comparing two things or people: *What is the difference between these two dogs?* **between** adv. **in between**, in the middle; in the middle of other things or people: *A sandwich is two pieces of bread with food in between.*

beware /bɪ'weə(r)/ v. **beware of**, be careful of someone or something: *Beware of that dog—it bites!*

bewilder /bɪ'wɪldə(r)/ v. make someone not know what is happening: *The big city bewildered the old woman from the country.*

bewitch /bɪ'wɪtʃ/ v. use magic on someone: *The fairy bewitched the man and turned him into a frog.* **bewitching** adj. very lovely.

beyond[1] /bɪ'jɒnd/ adv. farther on; on the other side: *Pippa climbed the wall and looked into the garden beyond.*

beyond[2] prep. at or on the farther side of; further than: *Penzance is 180 kilometres beyond Exeter.*

bib /bɪb/ n. cloth that a child wears under its chin when it is eating.

bicycle /'baɪsɪkl/ n. machine with two wheels, which you ride.

big /bɪg/ adj. (bigger, biggest) **1** large: *Manchester is a big city.* **2** important: *I have some big news!*

bike /baɪk/ abbrev. bicycle.

bill /bɪl/ n. **1** piece of paper that shows how much money you must pay for something: *After the meal I asked for the bill.* **2** plan for a new law. **3** hard part of a bird's mouth.

bin /bɪn/ n. container, with a lid, for keeping coal, grain, flour, bread, rubbish, etc.

bind /baɪnd/ v. (past part. & past tense bound /baʊnd/) put a piece of string, rope, etc. round something to hold it firm: *They bound the prisoner's legs together so that he could not run away.* **bind up**, put a bandage round someone's arm, leg, etc.: *The doctor bound up Kay's finger.*

binoculars /bɪ'nɒkʊləz/ n. (pl.) special glasses that help you to see things that are far away.

biography /baɪ'ɒgrəfɪ/ n. (pl. biographies) book that tells the story of someone's life.

biology /baɪ'ɒlədʒɪ/ n. (no pl.) study of the life of animals and plants. **biologist** /baɪ'ɒlədʒɪst/ n. someone who studies biology.

bird /bɜːd/ n. animal with feathers and wings: *Swallows and gulls are birds.*

biro /'baɪrəʊ/ n. pen that has a small ball at the end; ballpoint.

birth /bɜːθ/ n. being born; coming into the world: *the birth of a baby.* **give birth to**, have a baby: *My sister gave birth to twins last week.*

birthday /'bɜːθdeɪ/ n. day when you came into the world: *Each year I celebrate my birthday.*

biscuit /'bɪskɪt/ n. kind of thin, dry cake.

bishop /'bɪʃəp/ n. important Christian priest who controls a district of the church.

bit /bɪt/ n. small piece of anything: *He took a bit of paper and a few bits of wood and made a fire.* **a bit**, **(a)** a short time: *They waited a bit before the bus came.* **(b)** a little; rather: *I'm a bit tired.* **a bit of a**, rather a: *That boy's a bit of a clown!* **bit by bit**, slowly: *The old lady was tired but she climbed the hill bit by bit.* **come** or **fall to bits**, break into small pieces: *The chair fell to bits when the fat lady sat on it.*

bite¹ /baɪt/ n. **1** cutting something with teeth: *Susan took a bite from her apple.* **2** sore place on skin made by teeth: *a snake bite.* **3** sting: *a mosquito bite.*

bite² v. (*past part.* bitten /'bɪtn/, *past tense* bit) cut something with the teeth; sting: *The dog has bitten my leg.*

bitter /'bɪtə(r)/ adj. **1** with a sour, sharp taste: *This coffee is too bitter to drink.* **2** making you sad or angry: *a bitter quarrel.* **3** very cold: *a bitter wind.*

black /blæk/ adj. **1** with the colour of night, coal, etc. **2** with a dark skin: *Martin Luther King was a famous black leader.* **black** n.

blackberry /'blækbəri/ n. (*pl.* blackberries) small, soft, red fruit.

blackbird /'blækbɜːd/ n. bird with shiny, black feathers, which you often see in the garden.

blackboard /'blækbɔːd/ n. piece of dark board where the teacher writes with chalk.

blade /bleɪd/ n. **1** cutting part of a knife, sword, razor, etc. **2** long, thin leaf of grass, wheat, etc.

blame /bleɪm/ v. say that it is because of someone or something that wrong happened: *When he arrived late, Mr. Drake blamed the bad traffic.* **blame** n. **take the blame**, say that you are the person who did wrong.

blank /blæŋk/ adj. **1** empty; with no writing on it: *A new exercise book has blank pages.* **2** not showing feelings or understanding: *There was a blank look on his face because he did not know the answer.*

blanket /'blæŋkɪt/ n. thick, woollen cloth to cover someone in bed.

blast¹ /blɑːst/ n. **1** sudden rush of wind. **2** loud sound made by a musical instrument, such as a horn or trumpet.

blast² v. break up or destroy something with a big noise: *The hillside was blasted away so that a road could be built.*

blast-off /'blɑːst ɒf/ n. moment when a rocket or spaceship leaves the ground.

blaze¹ /bleɪz/ n. bright fire, flame, or light: *The fire brigade put out the blaze.*

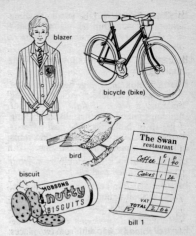

blazer

bicycle (bike)

bird

biscuit

The Swan restaurant

	£	P
Coffee	1	40
Cakes	1	24
VAT		
TOTAL	2	64

bill 1

blaze² v. burn with bright flames; shine brightly and warmly: *The sun blazed in the blue sky.*

blazer /'bleɪzə(r)/ n. light jacket.

bleat /bliːt/ n. cry of a sheep or goat. **bleat** v.

bleed /bliːd/ v. (*past part. & past tense* bled /bled/) lose blood: *He was bleeding to death.*

bless /bles/ v. ask God's help for someone or something: *The priest blessed the crops.*

blessed /'blesɪd/ adj. holy; sacred.

blessing /'blesɪŋ/ n. **1** prayer for good things from God; thanks to God before or after a meal. **2** something that brings happiness: *The rain was a blessing after the long, hot summer.*

blew /bluː/ *past tense* of v. blow.

blind¹ /blaɪnd/ adj. not able to see: *The blind man had a dog to help him.* **blindness** n.

blind² n. roll of cloth or wooden strips that you can pull down to cover a window.

blindfold /'blaɪndfəʊld/ v. cover someone's eyes with a cloth so that he cannot see. **blindfold** n.

blink /blɪŋk/ v. shut and open the eyes quickly: *We blinked when we came out of the dark shop into the bright street.*

blister /'blɪstə(r)/ n. small swelling under the skin, full of water: *Anita's new shoes were too big and made blisters on her heels.*

blizzard /'blɪzəd/ n. snowstorm with a strong wind.

block[1] /blɒk/ n. **1** big, heavy piece of stone, wood, concrete, etc. **2** very big building: *a block of flats.* **3** group of buildings joined together; distance along a group of buildings: *The post office is two blocks away.* **4** something that stops a thing or a person from passing.

block[2] v. stop a thing or person from passing: *A fallen tree blocked the road.*

blockade /blɒ'keɪd/ v. put soldiers, ships, etc. all round a place so that no people or goods can come in or out. **blockade** n.

blond /blɒnd/ adj. with a light or fair colour: *blond hair.* **blonde** /blɒnd/ n. woman with blond hair.

blood /blʌd/ n. (no pl.) red liquid flowing through the body.

bloodshed /'blʌdʃed/ n. (no pl.) killing or wounding of people: *There was no bloodshed when the army entered the town.*

bloodthirsty /'blʌdθɜːstɪ/ adj. cruel; wanting to kill.

bloody /'blʌdɪ/ adj. **1** bleeding; covered with blood: *a bloody nose.* **2** with much killing: *a bloody battle.*

bloom /bluːm/ n. flower. **bloom** v. have flowers; open into flower: *Tulips bloom in the spring.*

blossom /'blɒsəm/ n. (no pl.) all the flowers on a bush or tree. **blossom** v. open into flowers: *The apple trees will blossom soon.*

blot[1] /blɒt/ n. spot of ink.

blot[2] v. (pres. part. blotting, past part. & past tense blotted /'blɒtɪd/) **1** mark something by spilling ink: *He blotted his examination papers when his pen slipped.* **2** dry wet ink with special paper. **blotting-paper** n. paper that dries wet ink.

blouse /blaʊz/ n. piece of clothing that a woman or girl wears on the top part of her body.

blow[1] /bləʊ/ n. **1** hitting something or someone hard; being hit hard: *In the fight, Mick got such a blow that he fell to the floor.* **2** sudden bad luck that makes you shocked and sad: *His father's death was a great blow to him.*

blow[2] v. (past part. blown /bləʊn/, past tense blew /bluː/) **1** move something quickly and strongly in the air; be moved strongly in the air: *The wind blew Rose's hat along the road.* **2** send air out of the mouth: *Uncle blew the dust off his book.* **3** send air from the mouth into a musical instrument, etc. to make a noise: *to blow a whistle.* **blow up, (a)** explode; make something explode: *This bomb will blow up a bridge.* **(b)** fill something with air: *Gerald must blow up his bicycle tyres.*

blue /bluː/ adj. with the colour of a clear sky in the daytime. **blue** n.

bluff /blʌf/ v. trick someone to make him believe something that is not true: *The thief said that he had a gun, but he was really bluffing.* **bluff** n.

blunt /blʌnt/ adj. with an edge or point that is not sharp: *a blunt pencil.*

blush /blʌʃ/ v. become red in the face because of shame, shyness, etc. **blush** n.

boar /bɔː(r)/ n. wild pig; male pig.

board[1] /bɔːd/ n. **1** long, thin, flat piece of wood: *Boards are used to make floors.* **2** flat, square piece of wood fixed on to a wall, etc.: *Please read the list on the notice board.* **3** group of people who control something: *the Examination Board.* **on board,** on a ship, aeroplane, bus, etc.: *How many passengers are on board?*

board[2] v. **1** sleep and eat at a place where you have paid: *Mr. Bond boards in guest houses when he travels for his work.* **2** get on to a ship, plane, train, etc.: *We boarded the plane at Gatwick.*

boarder /'bɔːdə(r)/ n. **1** someone who pays for a room and food in another person's house. **2** child who lives at school.

boast /bəʊst/ v. praise yourself and what you do and have: *He boasted that he had the biggest house in the village.* **boast** n. **boastful** adj. **boastfully** adv.: *'Our team is better than yours!' said Carl boastfully.*

boat /bəʊt/ n. small ship: *a rowing boat; a motor boat.*

bob /bɒb/ v. (*pres. part.* bobbing, *past part. & past tense* bobbed /bɒbd/ move up and down quickly: *The duck bobbed up and down in the water.*

body /'bɒdɪ/ n. (*pl.* bodies) **1** all of a person or animal that you can see and touch: *Arms, legs, hands, and feet are parts of the body.* **2** dead person: *The murderer had put the body under some leaves.*

bodyguard /'bɒdɪgɑːd/ n. man, or group of men, whose job is to keep danger away from an important person.

bog /bɒg/ n. wet, soft ground. **boggy** *adj.*

boil /bɔɪl/ v. **1** heat water or other liquid until it bubbles and steams. **2** become so hot that it bubbles and steams: *Water boils at 100°C. boil over*, bubble over the edge of the pot. **3** cook something in very hot water: *I boiled the rice for fifteen minutes.* **boiled** /bɔɪld/ *adj.* that has been cooked in hot water: *boiled cabbage.*

boiler /'bɔɪlə(r)/ n. big, metal container for heating water, etc.; tank for storing hot water.

bold /bəʊld/ *adj.* **1** with no fear, shame, shyness, etc.: *It was bold of him to make a speech in front of all those people.* **2** clear to see: *the bold shape of a mountain.* **boldly** *adv.* **boldness** n.

bolt /bəʊlt/ n. **1** metal bar used to fasten a door or window. **2** thick, metal pin used with a nut for fastening things together. **bolt** v. lock a door, etc. by putting a metal bar across it: *Bolt the door before you go to bed.*

bomb /bɒm/ n. something filled with an explosive that bursts and hurts people or things. **bomb** v. break something or hurt someone with a bomb: *The city was bombed.*

bomber /'bɒmə(r)/ n. aeroplane for dropping bombs.

bone /bəʊn/ n. one of the hard, white things in the body of a person or animal.

bonfire /'bɒnfaɪə(r)/ n. big fire that you make outside.

bonnet /'bɒnɪt/ n. **1** child's hat tied under the chin, with ribbons, etc. **2** cover of a motor-car engine.

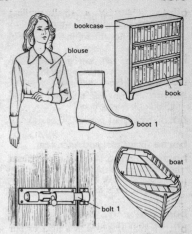

bony /'bəʊnɪ/ *adj.* **1** full of bones: *bony fish.* **2** very thin: *a bony child.*

book¹ /bʊk/ n. **1** sheets of paper fastened together inside a cover, for reading or writing: *a library book; an exercise book.* **2 books** (*pl.*) business accounts, records, etc.: *The clerk looks after the books.*

book² v. ask and pay for a seat for the theatre, a journey, etc.: *He booked a seat on the aeroplane to London.* **booking office** /'bʊkɪŋ ɒfɪs/ n. place where you buy tickets at a station or theatre.

bookcase /'bʊkkeɪs/ n. wooden cupboard, with shelves for books.

book-keeper /'bʊk kiːpə(r)/ n. person in an office who keeps an account of money.

booklet /'bʊklɪt/ n. small book.

boom /buːm/ n. deep, loud sound: *the boom of guns.*

boot /buːt/ n. **1** heavy shoe that covers the ankle and sometimes part of the leg: *football boots.* **2** place for luggage in a car or coach.

border /'bɔːdə(r)/ n. **1** line between two countries: *We stopped at the border and showed our passports.* **2** edge of something: *the border of a cloth.*

bore¹ /bɔː(r)/ n. someone or something that is not interesting.

bore² *past tense* of v. bear.

bore³ *v.* **1** make a narrow, round, deep hole. **2** make someone tired because your talk is not interesting: *His stories bore me.*

bored /bɔ:d/ *adj.* not interested; unhappy because you have nothing interesting to do: *What can I do? I'm bored!*

boring /'bɔ:rɪŋ/ *adj.* dull; not interesting: *What a boring book!*

born /bɔ:n/ *past part.* of *v.* bear; come alive.

borne /bɔ:n/ *past part.* of *v.* bear.

borrow /'bɒrəʊ/ *v.* ask for something that belongs to another person and that you will give back: *May I borrow your bicycle for a day while my car is at the garage?*

boss /bɒs/ *n.* (*pl.* bosses) leader; chief person; important person in a business, office, etc.

bossy /'bɒsɪ/ *adj.* always telling other people what to do, etc.

botany /'bɒtənɪ/ *n.* (no *pl.*) study of plants. **botanist** /'bɒtənɪst/ *n.* someone who studies botany.

both¹ /bəʊθ/ *adj.* the two; not just one but also the other: *Hold this heavy bag in both hands.*

both² *pron.* (*pl.*) the two together: *Both of us want to go.*

bother¹ /'bɒðə(r)/ *exclam.* word that shows you are a little angry.

bother² *v.* **1** trouble someone; make someone cross or worried: *Don't bother me with silly questions!* **2** give yourself extra work, etc.: *Please don't bother to get up.* **bother** *n.* something that gives you worry or trouble: *We had a lot of bother on the journey because the trains were late.* **bothered** /'bɒðəd/ *adj.* worried; unhappy.

bottle /'bɒtl/ *n.* glass or plastic container with a narrow neck, for holding liquids: *a bottle of milk.*

bottom /'bɒtəm/ *n.* **1** lowest part of something: *He fell to the bottom of the stairs.* **2** last part; end: *The cinema is at the bottom of the street.* **3** the part of the body on which you sit. **bottom** *adj.* lowest: *the bottom shelf.*

bough /baʊ/ *n.* big branch of a tree.

bought /bɔ:t/ *past part. & past tense* of *v.* buy.

boulder /'bəʊldə(r)/ *n.* big rock or stone.

bounce /baʊns/ *v.* **1** spring or jump like a ball: *The children bounced on their beds.* **2** make something spring or jump: *Judy bounced her new ball.*

bound¹ /baʊnd/ *adj.* **bound for**, on the way to a place: *This ship is bound for New York.* **bound to**, sure or certain to do something: *I must hide his present or he's bound to see it.*

bound² *n.* **1** jump: *With one bound, the dog was over the fence.* **2** bounds (*pl.*) limit; end. **out of bounds**, in a place where you are not allowed to go: *The river is out of bounds for all pupils.*

bound³ *past part. & past tense* of *v.* bind.

bound⁴ *v.* jump; move or run in small jumps: *The dog bounded along the path.*

boundary /'baʊndrɪ/ *n.* (*pl.* boundaries) line between two countries or other places; edge of a field, etc.

bouquet /bʊ'keɪ/ *n.* bunch of flowers.

bow¹ /bəʊ/ *n.* curved piece of wood with string between the two ends, for shooting arrows.

bow² /bəʊ/ *n.* knot made with loops of ribbon, string, etc.: *My shoelaces are tied in a bow.*

bow³ /baʊ/ *v.* bend the head or body forward to show respect: *They bowed their heads in prayer.* **bow** *n.*

bowl¹ /bəʊl/ *n.* **1** deep, round dish: *a sugar-bowl.* **2** what is in a round dish: *Shirley drank two bowls of soup.*

bowl² *v.* throw the ball towards the wickets in a cricket game.

bowler /'bəʊlə(r)/ *n.* **1** someone who bowls the ball in a cricket game. **2** round, black hat that some businessmen wear in London.

box¹ /bɒks/ *n.* (*pl.* boxes) container made of wood, cardboard, metal, etc.: *a box of matches.*

box² *v.* fight with the fists, in thick gloves, for sport. **boxer** *n.* man who fights with his fists, as a sport. **boxing** *n.* sport of fighting with the fists.

box-office /'bɒks ɒfɪs/ *n.* place where tickets are sold in a theatre, cinema, etc.

boy /bɔɪ/ *n.* male child; young man. **boyfriend** *n.* boy who is the special friend of a girl.

bra /brɑː/ n. brassiere; piece of woman's clothing to cover and support the breasts.

bracelet /'breɪslɪt/ n. pretty piece of metal or chain that you wear on the arm or wrist.

braces /'breɪsɪz/ n. (pl.) straps that a man wears over his shoulders to keep his trousers up.

bracket /'brækɪt/ n. punctuation mark (or).

braid /breɪd/ n. sort of ribbon.

brain /breɪn/ n. the part inside the head of a person or animal, which thinks and feels. *rack your brains*, try hard to think of something: *Steve racked his brains to remember the address.*

brake /breɪk/ n. thing in a motor-car, etc. that you move to make the car stop or go more slowly: *Mr. Edwards put his foot on the brake and we stopped suddenly.* **brake** v. move the brake.

branch /brɑːntʃ/ n. (pl. branches) **1** one of the arms of a tree that grow out from the trunk. **2** part of a business, company, etc.: *The bank has branches all over the country.*

brand /brænd/ n. **1** certain sort of goods; the name of the maker printed on the tin, packet, etc.: *Which brand of tea do you buy?* **2** piece of hot iron to mark something. **brand** v.: *The farmer branded his sheep.*

brand-new /ˌbrænd 'njuː/ adj. totally new.

brandy /'brændɪ/ n. **1** (no pl.) strong alcoholic drink. **2** (pl. brandies) glass of brandy.

brass /brɑːs/ n. (no pl.) bright yellow metal, made by mixing copper and zinc. **brass** adj. made of brass: *a brass letter-box.*

brassiere /'bræsɪə(r)/ n. piece of woman's clothing to cover and support the breasts.

brave /breɪv/ adj. with no fear; not showing fear: *It was brave of him to enter the burning building.* **bravely** adv. **bravery** n.

bread /bred/ n. (no pl.) food made from flour, water, and yeast, and then baked: *a slice of bread.* **breadcrumbs** n. tiny bits of bread.

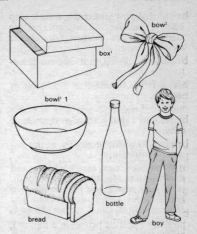

breadth /bretθ/ n. being broad; how wide or broad something is.

break¹ /breɪk/ n. **1** crack; place where something has been broken, etc.: *The sun is shining through a break in the clouds.* **2** short time when you stop doing something: *Let's have a break from T.V.*

break² v. (*past part.* broken /'brəʊkən/, *past tense* broke /brəʊk/) **1** drop, hit, or pull something so that it is in pieces:*He broke a window.* **2** go into smaller pieces by falling, hitting, etc.: *The glass fell and broke.* **3** harm something so that it will not work properly; be harmed: *My watch is broken.* **break down,** (**a**) go wrong and stop working: *We are late because the car broke down.* (**b**) start to cry, etc.: *He broke down when he heard that his horse was dead.* **break in** or **into**, force a way in, to steal, etc.: *Robbers broke into the house.* **break out,** (**a**) start suddenly: *Fighting broke out two days ago.* (**b**) escape; get free: *The prisoners broke out of their cell.* **break up,** (**a**) finish; stop happening: *School breaks up in July.* (**b**) stop something happening: *Jim broke up the fight.* **break the law,** not do what is right: *If you steal money, you are breaking the law.* **break a promise,** not do what you said you would do.

breakable /'breɪkəbl/ adj. not strong; that will easily break.

breakdown /'breɪkdaʊn/ n. total stop when a machine will not work: *There was a breakdown on the railway and all the trains were late.*

breaker /'breɪkə(r)/ n. big wave hitting the shore.

breakfast /'brekfəst/ n. first meal of the day.

breast /brest/ n. **1** part of a woman's or animal's body that gives milk. **2** person's chest.

breaststroke /'brestrəʊk/ n. (no pl.) way of swimming.

breath /breθ/ n. air that you take in and send out through the nose and mouth. **catch your breath**, **hold your breath**, stop breathing for a short time because you are very excited, afraid, etc. **out of breath**, needing to breathe more quickly than usual; panting: *He ran so fast he was soon out of breath.*

breathe /briːð/ v. take air into and send it out from your nose and mouth.

breathless /'breθlɪs/ adj. having little breath because you are tired or excited. **breathlessly** adv.: *They waited breathlessly for the news.*

bred /bred/ past part. & past tense of v. breed.

breed[1] /briːd/ n. sort or group of animals: *A terrier is a breed of dog.*

breed[2] v. (past part. & past tense bred) **1** make young ones: *Birds breed in the spring.* **2** keep animals or birds to make young ones: *Julie breeds rabbits.*

breeze /briːz/ n. light wind. **breezy** adj. windy.

brew /bruː/ v. **1** make drinks such as tea; make beer. **2** start to happen: *A storm is brewing.*

brewery /'brʊərɪ/ n. (pl. breweries) place where beer is made.

bribe /braɪb/ n. money or present that you give to someone to make him do something. **bribe** v.: *The prisoner bribed the guard to let him free.*

brick /brɪk/ n. block of baked clay used for building.

bricklayer /'brɪkleɪə(r)/ n. man whose job is to put bricks together to make walls, buildings, etc.

bridal /'braɪdl/ adj. of a bride or a wedding.

bride /braɪd/ n. woman on her wedding-day.

bridegroom /'braɪdgruːm/ n. man on his wedding-day.

bridesmaid /'braɪdzmeɪd/ n. girl or woman who helps a bride at her wedding.

bridge /brɪdʒ/ n. (pl. bridges) way built for people to cross over a river, railway, or road: *They walked over the bridge to get to the other side of the river.*

bridle /'braɪdl/ n. leather straps that you put over horse's head to control the horse.

brief /briːf/ adj. short: *We had a brief holiday.* **in brief**, in a few words. **briefly** adv.

briefcase /'briːfkeɪs/ n. flat case to carry papers in.

bright /braɪt/ adj. **1** giving out a lot of light; shining: *It is a bright, sunny day.* **2** clear in colour: *bright red.* **3** clever: *a bright child.* **4** cheerful: *a bright smile.* **brightly** adv. **brightness** n.

brighten /'braɪtn/ v. **1** become brighter or lighter; make something brighter or lighter. **2** look happier: *Ken's face brightened when he heard the good news.*

brilliant /'brɪlɪənt/ adj. **1** very bright: *brilliant jewels.* **2** very clever: *a brilliant student.* **brilliantly** adv. **brilliance** /'brɪlɪəns/ n.

brim /brɪm/ n. **1** edge of a cup or bowl. **2** the part of a hat that keeps the sun from the eyes.

bring /brɪŋ/ v. (past part. & past tense brought /brɔːt/) **1** carry or take someone or something to the speaker: *He brought me a cup of tea.* **2** make something happen: *Summer brings warmer weather.* **bring back**, (**a**) return something: *I have brought back the book you lent me.* (**b**) make you remember something: *My photographs of Italy bring back memories of my holiday there.* **bring someone round**, make someone wake up after fainting. **bring up**, (**a**) look after and educate children, etc.: *Mr. Williams brought up his dead brother's children.* (**b**) be sick.

brisk /brɪsk/ adj. active; moving quickly: *Let's go for a brisk walk.*

bristle /'brɪsl/ n. short, stiff hair on an animal or in a brush.

brittle /'brɪtl/ *adj*. that is hard but breaks easily: *Eggshells are brittle*.

broad /brɔːd/ *adj*. wide: *a broad river*.

broadcast /'brɔːdkɑːst/ *v*. (*past part. & past tense* broadcast) send sounds out by radio or television: *The B.B.C. broadcasts news at 9 p.m.* **broadcaster** /'brɔːdkɑːstə(r)/ *n*. someone whose job is to talk on radio or television.

broke /brəʊk/ *past tense* of *v*. break.

broken[1] /'brəʊkən/ *adj*. not whole; in pieces; not working: *A broken clock will not show the right time.*

broken[2] *past part*. of *v*. break.

bronze /brɒnz/ *n*. (no *pl*.) metal made by mixing copper and tin. **bronze** *adj*. made of bronze: *a bronze medal*.

brooch /brəʊtʃ/ *n*. (*pl*. brooches) pretty pin for fastening or wearing on clothes.

brook /brʊk/ *n*. small stream.

broom /bruːm/ *n*. brush on a long handle: *Bill is sweeping up the leaves with a broom.*

brother /'brʌðə(r)/ *n*. boy or man who has the same parents as another: *my younger brother*.

brother-in-law /'brʌðər ɪn lɔː/ *n*. (*pl*. brothers-in-law) brother of your husband or wife; husband of your sister.

brought /brɔːt/ *past part. & past tense* of *v*. bring.

brow /braʊ/ *n*. part of the face above the eyes.

brown /braʊn/ *adj*. with the colour of coffee or cocoa. **brown** *n*.

bruise /bruːz/ *n*. dark mark under the skin that comes after a blow.

brush[1] /brʌʃ/ *n*. (*pl*. brushes) bunch of strong hairs, nylon, wire, etc. fixed in a handle, used for cleaning, painting, making smooth, etc.: *a paint-brush; a hairbrush; a toothbrush.*

brush[2] *v*. do a job with a brush: *He brushed the snow off the path.*

brutal /'bruːtl/ *adj*. very cruel. **brutally** *adv*.: *He beats the donkey brutally.*

brute /bruːt/ *n*. **1** animal. **2** stupid and cruel person.

bubble /'bʌbl/ *v*. send up tiny balls of gas or air: *When water boils it begins to bubble.* **bubble** *n*. tiny ball of gas or air.

brush[1]

bucket

bridge

bud

buckle[1]

briefcase

buck /bʌk/ *n*. male deer, hare, or rabbit.

bucket /'bʌkɪt/ *n*. round container of metal or plastic, with a handle, for holding water, milk, etc.: *The children carried water from the sea in their buckets.*

buckle[1] /'bʌkl/ *n*. fastener for belt or strap.

buckle[2] *v*. **1** clip or fasten a belt, etc. with a buckle. **2** bend; become twisted because of heat or a heavy weight: *The tin roof buckled in the fierce fire.*

bud /bʌd/ *n*. leaf or flower when it starts growing: *There are buds on the trees in the spring.*

budge /bʌdʒ/ *v*. move something a little: *I can't budge this heavy rock.*

budget /'bʌdʒɪt/ *v*. make a plan about how to spend money in the best way: *If you budget carefully you will be able to save enough for a car.* **budget** *n*. plan for money.

budgie /'bʌdʒɪ/ *n*. small blue or green bird, which you keep in a cage.

bug /bʌg/ *n*. **1** small insect. **2** germ; disease: *She has caught some bug and is staying in bed.*

bugle /'bjuːgl/ *n*. sort of musical instrument that you blow.

build /bɪld/ *v*. (*past part. & past tense* built) make something by putting parts together: *Grandpa is building a brick garage at the side of his house.*

builder /'bɪldə(r)/ *n*. someone whose job is to make houses, etc.

building /'bɪldɪŋ/ *n*. place that was made for people to live, work, play, etc. in: *Houses, schools, shops, hotels, and churches are all buildings*.

built /bɪlt/ *past part. & past tense* of *v*. build.

bulb /bʌlb/ *n*. **1** round part from which some plants grow: *a tulip bulb*. **2** round electric thing that makes light.

bulge /bʌldʒ/ *v*. become bigger than usual; curve out: *My bag bulged with the fruit I had bought*. **bulge** *n*.

bulging /'bʌldʒɪŋ/ *adj*. round; curving; swelling: *bulging pockets*.

bull /bʊl/ *n*. **1** big farm animal; male ox. **2** male of some other big animals. **bullock** /'bʊlək/ *n*. young bull that cannot make young animals.

bulldozer /'bʊldəʊzə(r)/ *n*. big machine that moves earth and makes land flat.

bullet /'bʊlɪt/ *n*. piece of lead that shoots out of a rifle or revolver.

bully /'bʊlɪ/ *v*. hurt or frighten a weaker person. **bully** *n*. someone who bullies people.

bump¹ /bʌmp/ *n*. **1** blow or knock when two things hit each other hard: *a bump on the head*. **2** rough point on the road, etc.: *The car hit a bump on the road*. **bumpy** /'bʌmpɪ/ *adj*. with many bumps: *We had a bad journey over the bumpy road*.

bump² *v*. **1** hit or knock something or someone: *The car bumped against the tree*. **2** hurt yourself when you hit against something hard: *I bumped my head*. **bump into someone**, meet someone by chance.

bumper /'bʌmpə(r)/ *n*. bar on the front and back of a car, lorry, etc. It helps to protect the car if it hits something.

bumpy /'bʌmpɪ/ *adj*. rough; that shakes you: *We had a bumpy journey in the old car*.

bun /bʌn/ *n*. small, round cake.

bunch /bʌntʃ/ *n*. (*pl*. bunches) some things of the same kind that you tie together: *a bunch of flowers*.

bundle /'bʌndl/ *n*. number of things that you tie or wrap together: *a bundle of washing*.

bungalow /'bʌŋgələʊ/ *n*. house with only a ground floor.

bunk /bʌŋk/ *n*. narrow bed: *The beds in ships and trains are called bunks*.

buoy /bɔɪ/ *n*. floating thing, put in water to show where there are dangerous rocks, etc.

burden /'bɜːdn/ *n*. something that you carry; a heavy load: *A donkey can carry a heavy burden*.

burglar /'bɜːglə(r)/ *n*. person who breaks into a building to steal. **burglary** *n*. breaking into a building to steal. **burgle** *v*.: *They burgled the museum last Saturday*.

burial /'berɪəl/ *n*. burying or putting a dead body in a grave.

burn¹ /bɜːn/ *n*. mark or scar that fire makes.

burn² *v*. (*past part & past tense* burned /bɜːnd/, burnt /bɜːnt/) **1**. give out flames or light; be on fire: *All the lights are burning. Paper burns easily*. **2** use something to make light or heat: *to burn coal, oil, candles, etc*. **3** hurt someone or something by fire or heat: *She burnt her fingers on the stove*. **burn down**, burn, or make a building burn, until it falls down: *The Smiths have no home because their house has burned down*.

burrow /'bʌrəʊ/ *n*. hole in the ground where rabbits live. **burrow** *v*. make a hole.

burst¹ /bɜːst/ *n*. breaking; sudden hole or crack: *a burst in the water pipe*.

burst² *v*. (*past part. & past tense* burst) **1** break open; make something break open suddenly: *The bag was so full that it burst open*. **2** explode: *The balloon burst*. **3** go, come, or do something suddenly: *Steven burst into the room*. **burst into laughter**, suddenly begin to laugh. **burst into tears**, suddenly begin to cry.

bury /'berɪ/ *v*. put a person or thing in the ground, in a grave, etc.

bus /bʌs/ *n*. (*pl*. buses) big road vehicle for many people to travel in. **bus stop** *n*. place where buses stop to let people get on and off.

bush /bʊʃ/ *n*. **1** (*pl*. bushes) plant like a short tree, with many branches. **2** (no *pl*.) wild country with small trees.

business /'bɪznɪs/ n. **1** (no pl.) buying and selling things: *Business is good at Christmas when people buy presents.* **2** (pl. businesses) shop, factory, etc.: *My uncle has a business in Leeds.* **3** something to talk about or do; what you must do: *It's a mother's business to help her children. it's none of your business,* it has nothing to do with you. *mind your own business,* do your own work and do not be too interested in other people's work.

businessman /'bɪznɪsmæn/ n. (pl. businessmen) man who works in an office and whose job is about buying and selling things.

bust /bʌst/ n. upper front part of the body between the waist and neck; woman's breasts.

busy /'bɪzɪ/ adj. **1** working; with a lot to do: *Can you wait a minute? I'm busy.* **2** with many things happening: *The streets of a big city are always busy.* **busily** adv.

but[1] /bʌt/ conj. however: *She is American but she lives in England.*

but[2] prep. except: *Charles eats nothing but fruit.*

butcher /'bʊtʃə(r)/ n. someone whose job is to cut or sell meat.

butter /'bʌtə(r)/ n. (no pl.) soft, yellow food that comes from milk: *Jane spread butter on her bread.* **butter** v. put butter on to bread, etc.

butterfly /'bʌtəflaɪ/ n. (pl. butterflies) insect with big, pretty wings.

button /'bʌtn/ n. **1** small, round thing that you push through a hole to fasten clothes. **2** small, round thing on a machine, which you push: *When you press this button, the radio will start.* **button** v. fasten a coat, etc. with buttons: *It's cold today so button your coat.* **buttonhole** /'bʌtnhəʊl/ n. hole in clothes for a button.

buy /baɪ/ v. (past part. & past tense bought /bɔːt/) get something for money: *I went to the dairy and bought some milk.*

buzz /bʌz/ v. make a humming sound like bees. **buzz** n.

by[1] /baɪ/ adv. past: *He hurried by without stopping.* *by and by,* later on.

by[2] prep. **1** near; at or to the side of: *Our house is by the river.* **2** past: *He walked*

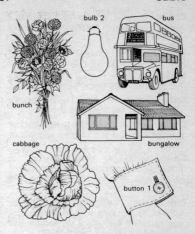

bulb 2   bus

bunch

cabbage   bungalow

button 1

by me without speaking. **3** during: *Do you prefer travelling by day or by night?* **4** not later than: *Be here by 4 o'clock.* **5** through; along; over: *We came through the fields, not by the road.* **6** word that shows the author, painter, etc. of: *a play by Shakespeare.* **7** word that shows how: *This cooker works by electricity.* **8** word that shows what kind of transport, etc.: *to go by train; to send a letter by post.* **9** word that shows which part: *She led the child by the hand.*

bye-bye /ˌbaɪ 'baɪ/ exclam. goodbye.

Cc

cab /kæb/ n. **1** taxi. **2** part of a railway engine, lorry, bus, etc., where the driver sits.

cabbage /'kæbɪdʒ/ n. vegetable with thick, green leaves.

cabin /'kæbɪn/ n. **1** room on a ship or an aeroplane. **2** small, simple house.

cabinet /'kæbɪnɪt/ n. cupboard; piece of furniture with shelves and drawers to keep things. **the Cabinet,** ministers who lead government work.

cable[1] /'keɪbl/ n. **1** thick, strong rope, wire, or chain. **2** telegraph line at the bottom of the sea. **3** message that you send quickly by cable under the sea.

cable[2] v. send a message by cable: *I cabled good wishes to Martin in America yesterday.*

cactus /'kæktəs/ n. (*pl.* cacti) plant that can live in a hot, dry place.

cadet /kə'det/ n. student who is training for the army, air force, navy, or police.

café /'kæfeɪ/ n. place where people can buy and eat food and drink.

cage /keɪdʒ/ n. box or place with bars or a fence round it for keeping animals or birds.

cake /keɪk/ n. sweet mixture of flour, sugar, butter, and eggs, etc. baked in an oven: *We had tea and cakes at 5 o'clock.*

calculate /'kælkjʊleɪt/ v. find an answer by working with numbers: *Can you calculate how much the holiday will cost?* **calculation** /ˌkælkjʊ'leɪʃn/ n.

calculator /'kælkjʊleɪtə(r)/ n. machine that can add, subtract, etc.

calendar /'kælɪndə(r)/ n. list of the days, weeks, months, etc. of one year.

calf /kɑːf/ n. (*pl.* calves) young cow, whale, or elephant.

call[1] /kɔːl/ n. **1** shout; cry: *a call for help.* **2** short visit or stay: *I paid a call on Bob.* **3** using the telephone: *I made a call to Peter.* **4** cry of an animal or bird.

call[2] v. **1** speak loudly and clearly; shout: *Will you come when I call?* **2** send a message to someone; tell someone to come: *Please call the doctor.* **3** give a name to someone or something: *They called the baby Sarah.* **4** visit; arrive: *When does the postman call? call at,* stop at a place: *The train called at every station. call for someone,* go and fetch someone or something: *Please call for me on your way to school. call off,* say that something must stop: *If it rains, we shall call off the picnic. call on, (a)* visit someone for a short time: *Please call on me next time you're in Oxford. (b)* ask someone to do something: *Mr. Woods called on the two boys to help him push the car. call out,* shout. *call someone up,* tell someone to come into the army, air force, or navy: *When the war started, Stuart was called up.*

call-box /'kɔːl bɒks/ n. (*pl.* call-boxes) public telephone box.

caller /'kɔːlə(r)/ n. visitor.

calm /kɑːm/ adj. **1** quiet; not excited; not showing fear, etc.: *Tina was frightened, but she stayed calm.* **2** with no wind: *a calm day.* **3** with no big waves: *a calm sea.* **calm** n. **calm** v. make someone quiet, less afraid, etc.: *The rider calmed the frightened horse. calm down,* become less afraid, excited, etc.

calmly /'kɑːmlɪ/ adv. with no worry or fear.

calves /kɑːvz/ (*pl.*) of n. calf.

came /keɪm/ past tense of v. come.

camel /'kæml/ big animal with one or two humps on its back: *He went across the Sahara on a camel.*

camera /'kæmərə/ n. machine that makes photographs.

camouflage /'kæməflɑːʒ/ v. hide the real shape of something or someone with paint, branches, etc.: *The soldiers camouflaged the gun with leaves.* **camouflage** n.

camp /kæmp/ n. place where people live for a time in tents or huts: *a Scout camp.* **camp** v.: *We walked all day and camped by a river at night.* **camping** n. living in tents or huts, for a holiday, etc.: *Camping isn't fun when it rains!*

campaign /kæm'peɪn/ n. **1** plan for doing something special: *a campaign to stop people drinking when they drive.* **2** plan for fighting part of a war: *a campaign to take the enemy city.*

campus /'kæmpəs/ n. (*pl.* campuses) grounds of a college or university: *The students at Keele live in houses on the campus.*

can[1] /kæn/ n. metal container for keeping foods, etc.; tin: *a can of milk.*

can[2] v. (past tense could /kʊd/) **1** be able to do something: *Pat can write very fast.* **2** be allowed to do something: *Can I go swimming today, please, mum?* **3** be possible; be likely: *It can be very cold in Scotland.*

canal /kə'næl/ n. channel cut through land for boats or ships, or to carry water to places that need it: *the Suez Canal.*

canary /kə'neərɪ/ n. (*pl.* canaries) small, yellow bird, which you keep in a cage.

cancel /'kænsl/ v. (*pres. part.* cancelling, *past part. & past tense* cancelled

/'kænsld/) stop a plan before it happens: *We cancelled the party because I was ill.* **cancellation** /ˌkænsə'leɪʃn/ *n.*

cancer /'kænsə(r)/ *n.* (no *pl.*) dangerous illness; lump that grows in the body.

candidate /'kændɪdət/ *n.* **1** someone who asks for a job, position, etc.: *When the director leaves, there will be many candidates for his job.* **2** someone who is taking an examination.

candle /'kændl/ *n.* stick of wax that gives light when it burns. **candlestick** /'kændlstɪk/ *n.* holder for one candle.

cane¹ /keɪn/ *n.* **1** hollow stem of a sort of plant: *bamboo canes.* **2** stick used to hit people who have done wrong.

cane² *v.* punish someone by hitting him with a stick.

canned /kænd/ *adj.* in a can or tin so that it will stay fresh: *canned meat.*

cannibal /'kænɪbl/ *n.* person who eats other people.

cannon /'kænən/ *n.* big gun.

cannot /'kænət/ = can not; be unable to do something; not know how to do something: *I have hurt my leg and cannot walk.*

canoe /kə'nu:/ *n.* light boat that you move with paddles.

can't /kɑ:nt/ = cannot.

canteen /kæn'ti:n/ *n.* room in a factory, school, etc. where people eat together.

canvas /'kænvəs/ *n.* **1** (no *pl.*) strong cloth for sails, bags, tents, etc. **2** (*pl.* canvasses) piece of strong cloth used by artists for oil-paintings.

cap /kæp/ *n.* **1** sort of soft hat. **2** cover for the top of a tube, bottle, etc.

capable /'keɪpəbl/ *adj.* clever; good at your work: *a capable driver.* **capable of something,** (*a*) able to do something: *John is capable of jumping higher if he tries.* (*b*) likely to do something: *That dog is capable of biting if you go too near!*

capacity /kə'pæsətɪ/ *n.* (no *pl.*) **1** amount that can fit into a container or holder: *What is the capacity of this jug?* **2** number of things or people that can fit into a place: *The seating capacity of this hall is 300.* **3** being able to understand or do something: *Gavin has the capacity to add numbers quickly in his head.*

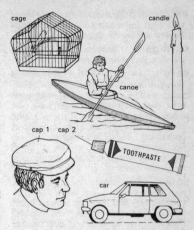

cage

candle

canoe

cap 1   cap 2

TOOTHPASTE

car

cape /keɪp/ *n.* loose piece of clothing, like a coat with no sleeves.

capital /'kæpɪtl/ *n.* **1** (*pl.* capitals) most important city in a country or state: *Paris is the capital of France.* **2** (*pl.* capitals) large letter of the alphabet: *A, B, C, etc. are capitals; a, b, c are not.*

capsize /kæp'saɪz/ *v.* turn over in the water: *The boat hit a rock and capsized.*

captain /'kæptɪn/ *n.* **1** leader of a group of people: *the captain of a football team.* **2** officer in the army or navy; chief person on a ship. **captain** *v.* lead people: *to captain a team.*

captive /'kæptɪv/ *n.* prisoner. **captive** *adj.*: *captive lions in a zoo.*

captivity /kæp'tɪvətɪ/ *n.* (no *pl.*) being a prisoner; being in a place that you cannot leave.

capture /'kæptʃə(r)/ *v.* catch and hold someone or something: *Kate captured a butterfly in her hands.* **capture** *n.*: *the capture of a thief.*

car /kɑ:(r)/ *n.* motor-car; vehicle with four wheels and a small group of people. **car-park** *n.* place where you can put your car for a time.

caravan /'kærəvæn/ *n.* small house on wheels that a car or horse can pull.

card /kɑ:d/ *n.* piece of stiff, thick paper for writing on, etc.: *At Christmas we send Christmas cards to our friends.* **playing cards,** set of cards for playing games.

cardboard /'kɑ:dbɔ:d/ n. (no pl.) thick, stiff card for making boxes, etc. **cardboard** adj.: a cardboard box.

cardigan /'kɑ:dɪgən/ n. knitted woollen jacket with sleeves.

care[1] /keə(r)/ n. **1** (no pl.) serious thought which helps you to do something well: Carry that glass with care. **take care**, be careful: Please take care when you cross the road. **2** (no pl.) help, etc.: **take care of**, look after someone or something: Angela is taking care of her brothers because her mother is ill. **3** (pl. cares) worry; sadness: A poor man has many cares.

care[2] v. feel interest, worry, sadness, etc.: She cares a lot about her cat. **couldn't care less**, have no interest in, or worries about, something: He couldn't care less that his jacket is torn because clothes are not important to him. **care for**, (a) like someone or something: Do you care for him? (b) want to have or do something: Would you care for a cup of coffee, Mrs. Jones? (c) look after a person or animal: Angela is caring for her brothers.

career /kə'rɪə(r)/ n. job for which special training is needed: Carol wants a career in sport.

carefree /'keəfri:/ adj. with no worry or trouble: a carefree holiday.

careful /'keəfl/ adj. having or showing serious thought which helps you to do something well: With careful steps, the old man crossed the road. **carefully** adv.

careless /'keəlɪs/ adj. not having or showing enough thought: Careless drivers have accidents. **carelessly** adv. **carelessness** n.

caretaker /'keəteɪkə(r)/ n. someone whose job is to look after a building.

cargo /'kɑ:gəʊ/ n. (pl. cargoes) things that a ship or aeroplane carries: a cargo of bananas.

carnival /'kɑ:nɪvl/ n. festival; time when many people come together in the streets for dancing, singing, etc.

carol /'kærəl/ n. song; Christmas hymn.

carpenter /'kɑ:pɪntə(r)/ n. man whose job is to make wooden tables, chairs, etc. and the wooden parts of buildings. **carpentry** /'kɑ:pɪntrɪ/ n. job of a carpenter.

carpet /'kɑ:pɪt/ n. big cloth of wool, hair, etc. that covers a floor. **carpet** v. cover the ground or a floor with something: Leaves carpeted the ground.

carriage /'kærɪdʒ/ n. **1** cart pulled by horses, for carrying people. **2** part of a train: The engine was pulling five carriages.

carriageway /'kærɪdʒweɪ/ n. **dual carriageway**, wide road with earth, bushes, etc. down the middle.

carried /'kærɪd/ past part. & past tense of v. carry.

carrier /'kærɪə(r)/ n. box or rack on a bicycle, motor-cycle, etc. for carrying things. **carrier bag** n. shopping bag made of strong paper or plastic.

carrot /'kærət/ n. long, yellow or orange vegetable.

carry /'kærɪ/ v. **1** take someone or something from one place to another: The waiter carried the meal to the table. **2** hold or keep something up; bear the weight of something: The walls of the house carry the roof. **3** contain; be able to have inside it: The car will carry five people. **carry on**, go on doing something: Carry on with your sewing while I read you a story. **carry out**, do or finish what you have planned: When can you carry out the repairs on my car?

cart[1] /kɑ:t/ n. vehicle with two or four wheels, which horses, etc. pull.

cart[2] v. move something or someone: We carted away the rubbish.

carton /'kɑ:tn/ n. thin cardboard box for holding things: a cigarette carton.

cartoon /kɑ:'tu:n/ n. **1** funny drawing, often of well-known people. **2** cinema film made with drawings, not with real people: a Mickey Mouse cartoon.

cartridge /'kɑ:trɪdʒ/ n. small case with gunpowder or a bullet, which goes into a gun.

carve /kɑ:v/ v. **1** cut wood or stone to make a picture or shape: Tony carved his name on a tree with a knife. **2** cut meat into pieces: Father carved the chicken for supper. **carved** /kɑ:vd/ adj.: a carved chair.

case[1] /keɪs/ n. **1** what has really happened. **in case**, because something might happen: *I shall take my umbrella with me in case it rains.* **in any case,** whatever happens: *If it rains we won't have a picnic, but come in any case.* **in that case,** if that happens. **2** example of a bad happening or something special: *There are five cases of food poisoning in the hospital.* **3** question for a law court to decide. **4** problem for the police: *a murder case.*

case² *n.* box; holder: *a suitcase; a bookcase.*

cash¹ /kæʃ/ *n.* (no *pl.*) money in coins or notes. **cash desk** *n.* place in a shop where you pay. **cash register** *n.* machine that holds money and adds up prices.

cash² *v.* give or get coins or notes: *I cashed a cheque at the bank.*

cashier /kæˈʃɪə(r)/ *n.* person working in a bank, shop, etc. who takes in money and pays it out.

cassette /kəˈset/ *n.* small, plastic case holding recording tape.

castle /ˈkɑːsl/ *n.* big, strong building that helped to keep the people inside safe from their enemies long ago: *Windsor Castle.*

casual /ˈkæʒʊəl/ *adj.* **1** not planned: *a casual meeting.* **2** that is not for a special, important time. **casual clothes,** clothes that you wear when you want to be comfortable with family, friends, etc. **casually** *adv.*

casualty /ˈkæʒʊəltɪ/ *n.* (*pl.* casualties) person hurt or killed in an accident or in war: *There were many casualties when the train crashed.*

cat /kæt/ *n.* small, furry animal that often lives with people in a house.

catapult /ˈkætəpʌlt/ *n.* stick like the letter Y, with a piece of elastic, which children use for throwing stones.

catastrophe /kəˈtæstrəfɪ/ *n.* terrible thing that happens suddenly: *The forest fire was a catastrophe.*

catch¹ /kætʃ/ *n.* (*pl.* catches) **1** fish that have been taken out of the water: *The boat brought back a big catch of herring.* **2** something that keeps a door, gate, box, etc. shut.

catch² *v.* (*past part. & past tense* caught) **1** take hold of something to stop it moving; get something in your hands: *Try and catch this ball!* **2** find

carrot

castle

cardigan

cat   cauliflower

and hold someone: *to catch a thief.* **3** find someone suddenly when he is doing a bad thing: *Mr. Bishop caught us taking apples from his tree.* **4** get on to a bus, train, etc. that is going to leave: *I caught a bus to town.* **5** hold something fast: *The nail caught my dress.* **6** get a disease: *Robin caught my cold last week.* **catch alight, catch fire,** start to burn. **catch up with,** reach or go past a person or thing that is going the same way: *Go on and I'll catch up with you in five minutes.*

caterpillar /ˈkætəpɪlə(r)/ *n.* long creature, like a worm with hairs, that changes into a moth or butterfly.

cathedral /kəˈθiːdrəl/ *n.* big, important church with a bishop's chair.

cattle /ˈkætl/ *n.* (*pl.*) cows, bulls, or oxen. **cattle** *adj.*: *Mr. Price has a cattle farm.*

caught /kɔːt/ *past part. & past tense* of *v.* catch.

cauliflower /ˈkɒlɪflaʊə(r)/ *n.* vegetable with a hard, white, round flower.

cause¹ /kɔːz/ *n.* **1** thing or person that makes something happen: *What was the cause of his death?* **have cause,** have a good reason: *Your brakes are working well so you have no cause to worry.* **2** something that people care about and want to help: *We like to give money to a good cause such as a new hospital.*

cause[2] v. make something happen: *A burning cigarette caused the fire.*

caution /'kɔːʃn/ n. (no pl.) taking care to keep away from danger, not make mistakes, etc.: *Handle that gun with caution.*

cautious /'kɔːʃəs/ adj. careful.
cautiously adv.

cave /keɪv/ n. hole in the side of a hill or under the ground: *Many years ago men lived in caves.*

cavern /'kævən/ n. big hole under the ground or in the side of a hill.

cease /siːs/ v. stop: *It is quiet when we all cease talking.*

cease-fire /ˌsiːs 'faɪə(r)/ n. time when soldiers stop fighting.

ceaseless /'siːslɪs/ adj. not stopping.

cedar /'siːdə(r)/ n. sort of tree.

ceiling /'siːlɪŋ/ n. the part of the room over your head: *A light is hanging from the ceiling.*

celebrate /'selɪbreɪt/ v. do something to show that a day or a happening is special: *The church bells ring to celebrate the wedding.*

celebration /ˌselɪ'breɪʃn/ n. party or ceremony for a special reason: *a birthday celebration.*

celery /'seləri/ n. (no pl.) vegetable with long stems which we often eat raw.

cell /sel/ n. 1 small room in a prison or a monastery. 2 small, hollow space: *Bees put honey into the cells of a honeycomb.* 3 very small part of a human, animal, or plant body.

cellar /'selə(r)/ n. room in the ground under a house.

cello /'tʃeləʊ/ n. musical instrument with strings, like a big violin: *Someone who plays a cello is called a cellist.*

cement /sɪ'ment/ n. (no pl.) grey powder that becomes hard like stone when you mix it with water and then leave it to dry. **cement** v. fill holes with cement; stick things together with cement: *The builder cemented bricks together to make a wall.*

cemetery /'semɪtrɪ/ n. (pl. cemeteries) place where dead people lie in the ground.

centimetre /'sentɪmiːtə(r)/ n. measure of length: *There are 100 centimetres in one metre.*

central /'sentrəl/ adj. in the middle of something: *Piccadilly is in central London.*

centre /'sentə(r)/ n. 1 middle part or point: *There is a big stone in the centre of a peach.* 2 place where a lot of people go to do something special: *Shall we buy presents in the shopping centre?*

century /'sentʃʊrɪ/ n. (pl. centuries) 1 a hundred years. 2 one of the periods of one hundred years before or after the birth of Christ: *We live in the twentieth century.*

cereal /'sɪərɪəl/ n. 1 grain such as wheat, maize, rice, etc. used for food. 2 special breakfast food made from grain.

ceremony /'serɪmənɪ/ n. (pl. ceremonies) special programme at an important happening: *a prize-giving ceremony.*

certain[1] /'sɜːtn/ adj. true; sure: *It is certain that the world is round.* **be certain**, feel sure: *I am certain that Clive knows the way because he has been there before.* **make certain**, find out about something so that you are sure: *Please make certain that the river is not deep before you swim there.*

certain[2] adj. some: *Certain plants are good to eat but others are not.*

certainly /'sɜːtnlɪ/ adv. 1 surely; with no doubt: *The glass will certainly break if you drop it.* 2 yes: *'Will you come with me?' 'Certainly.'* **certainly not!** no!

certainty /'sɜːtntɪ/ n. (no pl.) being sure: *I do not know with certainty if Mark will be home tomorrow.*

certificate /sə'tɪfɪkət/ n. piece of paper with writing that tells something about someone: *Your birth certificate says when and where you were born.*

chain /tʃeɪn/ n. row of metal rings joined together: *Mr. Barlow keeps his dog on a chain.* **chain** v. tie someone or something with a chain: *I chained my bicycle to the tree.*

chair /tʃeə(r)/ n. seat with a back.

chairman /'tʃeəmən/ n. (pl. chairmen) man or woman who controls a meeting.

chalk /tʃɔːk/ n. (no pl.) soft, white stuff for writing on a blackboard: *a stick of chalk.*

challenge /'tʃælɪndʒ/ v. **1** tell someone to say what he is doing, who he is, etc. **2** ask someone to fight or run against you because you want to see who will be the winner: *The boys challenged the girls to a race.* **3** ask someone to do something because you want to see if he is brave enough to do it: *Ben challenged Frank to jump into the deep water.*

champion[1] /'tʃæmpɪən/ adj. best in a sport, game, etc.; very good.

champion[2] n. **1** someone who speaks or fights for other people or things. **2** someone who wins a race, game, or sport: *an athletics champion.*

championship /'tʃæmpɪənʃɪp/ n. competition for first place in a sport, game, etc.: *a swimming championship.*

chance /tʃɑːns/ n. **1** (no *pl.*) happening that is not planned: *Harry telephoned by chance and found I was not at home.* **2** (*pl.* chances) hope; opportunity: *Gordon has no chance of winning the race because he has hurt his leg.* **stand a good chance of**, be likely to get or do something: *Arthur stands a good chance of passing the exam.* **take a chance**, do something without knowing if it will end well: *Don took a chance when he picked up the dog, but it didn't bite him.*

change[1] /tʃeɪndʒ/ n. when a difference comes: *a change in the weather.* **for a change**, because you want something new or different: *We normally go to Spain for our holiday but this year we're going to Italy for a change.*

change[2] n. (no *pl.*) money that you give back when someone has paid you too much: *I gave 50p but the jam cost 30p so there was 20p change.*

change[3] v. **1** become different: *In autumn the leaves change from green to yellow.* **2** make something different: *Sheila has changed the colour of her hair.* **3** take or put one thing in place of another: *Tony changed his books at the library.* **4** put on different clothes: *I must change before I go to the party.* **change buses, trains, etc.**, get off one bus, etc., and on to another. **change a pound, etc.**, take one pound and give back 100p, etc.

channel /'tʃænl/ n. **1** narrow way where water can go: *They made a channel to take the water off the camp site.* **2** narrow passage of sea, etc.: *the English Channel.*

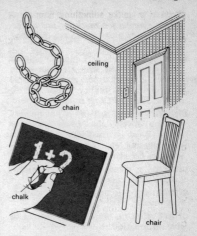

ceiling

chain

chalk

chair

chaos /'keɪɒs/ n. (no *pl.*) when things happen wildly and with no control; when there is no order: *The strong wind left the garden in chaos.* **chaotic** /keɪ'ɒtɪk/ adj.

chap /tʃæp/ n. man; boy.

chapel /'tʃæpl/ n. room or small church where Christians go to pray and worship.

chapter /'tʃæptə(r)/ n. part of a book: *We start a book at chapter 1.*

character /'kærəktə(r)/ n. **1** (no *pl.*) your nature; what sort of person you are: *a gentle character.* **2** (*pl.* characters) someone in a book, play, etc.: *Dr. Watson is a character in the Sherlock Holmes stories.*

charge[1] /tʃɑːdʒ/ n. **1** words that a policeman says when he catches someone who has done wrong. **bring a charge against someone**, say that someone has done wrong: *The police brought a charge against the thief.* **2** sudden attack by soldiers, animals, etc. **3** payment asked for something: *There is a charge of £20 for the use of the hall.* **4** control. **be in charge of, take charge of**, take care of, and have power over, people or things: *The captain is in charge of the ship.*

charge[2] v. **1** say in a law court, etc. that someone has done wrong: *They charged him with murder.* **2** rush forward and attack someone or something: *The angry elephants charged the men.*

3 ask a price for something: *The shop-keeper charged too much for this coffee.* **4** put power into something: *to charge a battery.*

charity /'tʃærətɪ/ *n.* **1** (no *pl.*) help or money for people who are poor or in trouble. **2** (*pl.* charities) group of people who give help, money, food, etc. to others: *The Red Cross is a charity.*

charm¹ /tʃɑːm/ *n.* **1** (no *pl.*) being very pleasing, lovely, etc.: *Linda has great charm.* **2** (*pl.* charms) something that is very pleasing, etc.: *Linda's happy smile is one of her charms.*

charm² *v.* please someone very much: *Linda's smile charmed everyone.*

charming /'tʃɑːmɪŋ/ *adj.* very pleasing; very lovely.

chart /tʃɑːt/ *n.* big drawing or map to give information.

chase /tʃeɪs/ *v.* run after someone: *The police chased the thief.* **chase** *n.: a long chase.*

chat /tʃæt/ *v.* (*pres. part.* chatting, *past part. & past tense* chatted /'tʃætɪd/) talk in a friendly way. **chat** *n.: Let's have a chat.*

chatter /'tʃætə(r)/ *n.* (no *pl.*) sound of people talking quickly. **chatter** *v.* **chatterbox** *n.* someone who talks a lot.

chauffeur /'ʃəʊfə(r)/ *n.* someone whose job is to drive another person's car.

cheap /tʃiːp/ *adj.* low in price; not costing a lot of money: *Food is cheap in the market.*

cheat /tʃiːt/ *n.* someone who is not honest. **cheat** *v.* do something that is not honest: *He cheated in the exam when he copied his friend's work.*

check¹ /tʃek/ *n.* looking to see if something is right, good, etc.: *The police are making a check on all cars to see that their brakes work.* **check** *v.: I must check that your answers are correct.* **check up on**, find out if something is correct, right, or if a person is telling the truth, etc.

check² *n.* pattern made of crossed lines or squares. **checked** /tʃekt/ *adj.: Robert is wearing his checked suit.*

checkout /'tʃekaʊt/ *n.* place in a shop where you pay.

cheek /tʃiːk/ *n.* part of the face below the eye and to the side of the nose.

cheeky /'tʃiːkɪ/ *adj.* too bold; not polite. **cheekily** *adv.*

cheer /tʃɪə(r)/ *v.* **1** shout to show that you are pleased with someone: *The crowd cheered as the Queen drove past.* **2** make someone happy. **cheer up**, become happy; make someone happy: *When I'm feeling sad my mother tells me funny stories to cheer me up.* **cheer** *n.* **three cheers**, the call 'hip, hip, hooray!': *Let's give three cheers for our football team!*

cheerful /'tʃɪəfl/ *adj.* happy; making you happy. **cheerfully** *adv.*

cheese /tʃiːz/ *n.* food made from milk.

chef /ʃef/ *n.* cook; chief cook in a hotel, etc.

chemical /'kemɪkl/ *n.* solid or liquid substance used in chemistry. **chemical** *adj.*

chemist /'kemɪst/ *n.* **1** someone who studies chemistry. **2** someone who makes and sells medicines.

chemistry /'kemɪstrɪ/ *n.* (no *pl.*) study of gases, liquids, and solids to understand how they are made and what they do.

cheque /tʃek/ *n.* special piece of paper that you write on, telling a bank to pay money to someone for you.

cherry /'tʃerɪ/ *n.* (*pl.* cherries) small, round, red fruit.

chess /tʃes/ *n.* (no *pl.*) game that two people play, with little figures on a board.

chest¹ /tʃest/ *n.* front part of the body between the shoulders and above the waist.

chest² *n.* big, strong, wooden box with a lid, for keeping things. **chest of drawers** *n.* big, wooden box with drawers, for keeping things.

chestnut /'tʃesnʌt/ *n.* shiny, brown nut that you can eat.

chew /tʃuː/ *v.* crush and grind food into little bits in your mouth: *Dogs like to chew bones.*

chewing-gum /'tʃuːɪŋ gʌm/ *n.* (no *pl.*) sweet gum that people chew but do not swallow.

chick /tʃɪk/ *n.* baby hen or fowl.

chicken /'tʃɪkɪn/ *n.* young hen; farm bird that lays eggs and that we eat.

chief¹ /tʃiːf/ *adj.* most important: *Glasgow is one of the chief cities of Scotland.*

chief², **chieftain** /'tʃiːftən/ *n.* leader or ruler; head of a group of people.

chiefly /'tʃiːflɪ/ *adv.* mostly; mainly: *Bread is made chiefly of flour.*

child /tʃaɪld/ *n.* (*pl.* children) young boy or girl.

childhood /'tʃaɪldhʊd/ *n.* (no *pl.*) time when you are a child: *I had a happy childhood.*

childish /'tʃaɪldɪʃ/ *adj.* like a young boy or girl; only for young boys and girls: *Now that Charlotte is 15, she thinks dolls are childish.*

chilled /tʃɪld/ *adj.* that has been made cool: *Chilled drinks are nice on a hot day.*

chilly /'tʃɪlɪ/ *adj.* cold.

chime /tʃaɪm/ *v.* make a sound like bells: *On Sundays we can hear the church bells chime.* **chime** *n.*

chimney /'tʃɪmnɪ/ *n.* sort of big pipe that takes smoke from a fireplace out of a building.

chimpanzee /ˌtʃɪmpæn'ziː/ *n.* sort of ape.

chin /tʃɪn/ *n.* part of your face below your mouth.

china /'tʃaɪnə/ *n.* (no *pl.*) **1** special kind of white earth for cups, plates, etc. **2** cups, plates, etc. of china. **china** *adj.*: *china plates.*

chip¹ /tʃɪp/ *n.* small piece of wood, stone, etc., cut from a bigger piece. **chip** *v.* (*pres. part.* chipping, *past part.* & *past tense* chipped /tʃɪpt/) cut or break a small piece off something: *I chipped the plate when I dropped it.*

chip² *n.* small piece of hot, fried potato.

chirp /tʃɜːp/ *n.* short, sharp sound made by birds, insects, etc. **chirp** *v.*

chocolate /'tʃɒklət/ *n.* **1** (no *pl.*) sweet food made from cocoa: *I like chocolate.* **2** (*pl.* chocolates) piece of chocolate: *Have a chocolate.* **chocolate** *adj.*: *a chocolate cake.*

choice /tʃɔɪs/ *n.* **1** (no *pl.*) taking the thing you want; choosing: *There were so many cakes that it was difficult to make a choice.* **2** (no *pl.*) group of things from which you can take something: *a big choice of books.* **3** (*pl.* choices) person or

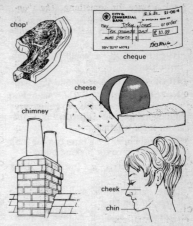

chop¹

cheque

cheese

chimney

cheek

chin

thing that you want or like best: *Amy bought a red bag but my choice was blue.*

choir /'kwaɪə(r)/ *n.* group of people who sing together: *the church choir.*

choke /tʃəʊk/ *v.* stop breathing properly because there is something in your throat: *She choked on a piece of apple.*

choose /tʃuːz/ *v.* (*past part.* chosen, *past tense* chose) take out what you want from several things or people: *Choose one of these kittens.*

chop¹ /tʃɒp/ *n.* thick slice of meat with a bone in it: *a lamb chop.*

chop² *v.* (*pres. part.* chopping, *past part.* & *past tense* chopped /tʃɒpt/) cut something into pieces with an axe, knife, etc.: *I chop up the vegetables before I put them in the stew.*

choppy /'tʃɒpɪ/ *adj.* rough; broken into small waves: *choppy sea.*

chorus /'kɔːrəs/ *n.* (*pl.* choruses) **1** group of singers; group of dancers in the theatre. **2** part of a song that is sung by everyone after each verse.

chose /tʃəʊz/ *past tense* of *v.* choose.

chosen /'tʃəʊzn/ *past part.* of *v.* choose.

christen /'krɪsn/ *v.* **1** put holy water on someone to show that he or she belongs to the Christian Church: *The minister christened the baby.* **2** give a first name to someone: *They christened her Mary.* **christening** *n.*

Christian /ˈkrɪstʃən/ n. someone who believes in Jesus Christ and what He taught. **Christian** adj.: the Christian Church.

chuckle /ˈtʃʌkl/ n. small, soft laugh. **chuckle** v.

chum /tʃʌm/ n. close friend.

church /tʃɜːtʃ/ n. (pl. churches) building where Christians go to pray and worship. **the Church**, all Christian people together.

churn /tʃɜːn/ n. **1** big farm can for fresh milk. **2** machine for making butter.

cider /ˈsaɪdə(r)/ n. (no pl.) drink made from apples.

cigar /sɪˈɡɑː(r)/ n. roll of tobacco leaves for smoking.

cigarette /ˌsɪɡəˈret/ n. tube of paper full of tobacco for smoking.

cinder /ˈsɪndə(r)/ n. dry black or grey stuff that is left after something has burned: The roast meat was burned to cinders.

cine-camera /ˈsɪnɪ kæmərə/ n. machine for taking moving photographs.

cinema /ˈsɪnəmə/ n. place where people go to see films.

circle /ˈsɜːkl/ n. **1** ring; something round. **2** group of people who like the same thing: a circle of friends.

circular /ˈsɜːkjʊlə(r)/ adj. round; making a line that goes round: A wheel is circular.

circulate /ˈsɜːkjʊleɪt/ v. go or pass round something: Blood circulates through our bodies. **circulation** /ˌsɜːkjʊˈleɪʃn/ n.

circumstances /ˈsɜːkəmstənsɪz/ n. (pl.) the facts of a happening; where, when, how, and why something happens. **in** or **under the circumstances**, because things are as they are: There was a snow storm and, under the circumstances, they decided to stay at home. **in** or **under no circumstances**, not at all; never: Under no circumstances must you swim in the deep river!

circus /ˈsɜːkəs/ n. (pl. circuses) show given by clowns, animals, acrobats, etc.

citizen /ˈsɪtɪzn/ n. someone who belongs to a country or town: the citizens of Cardiff.

city /ˈsɪtɪ/ n. (pl. cities) big, important town. **city hall** n. building with offices and meeting rooms for the people who control a city.

civic /ˈsɪvɪk/ adj. of a town: a civic centre.

civil /ˈsɪvl/ adj. belonging to the people of a place. **civil rights** n. things that everyone in a country can have, do, and ask for. **the civil service** n. people who do government work. **civil war** n. war between the people in one country.

civilian /sɪˈvɪlɪən/ n. someone who is not in the army, the navy, the air force, etc.: Civilians and soldiers were killed during the war. **civilian** adj.: civilian dress.

civilization /ˌsɪvəlaɪˈzeɪʃn/ n. people living together at a certain time in a certain way: the Roman civilization.

claim /kleɪm/ v. **1** say that something belongs to you; say that you should have something: Did anyone claim the lost umbrella? **2** say that something is true: Nigel claimed that he had done all the work without help. **claim** n.: a claim for more pay.

clamber /ˈklæmbə(r)/ v. use your hands and feet to climb over something: The children clambered over the rocks.

clan /klæn/ n. large family group of people in Scotland: the Macdonald clan.

clang /klæŋ/ n. loud, ringing noise made by pieces of metal banging together: the clang of a fire bell. **clang** v.

clap[1] /klæp/ n. sound made by hands hitting together. **clap of thunder**, sudden, sharp noise of thunder.

clap[2] v. (pres. part. clapping, past part. & past tense clapped /klæpt/) hit your hands together to show you are pleased, etc.: The boys clapped when their team won the match.

clash /klæʃ/ v. **1** quarrel; fight: The two armies clashed. **2** make a loud, banging noise: The soldiers' swords clashed. **3** happen at the same time: The meeting clashed with my swimming lesson so I could not go. **clash** n.

clasp[1] /klɑːsp/ n. something that holds two things together: the clasp of a necklace.

clasp² *v.* hold someone or something tightly: *She clasped my hand.*

class /klɑːs/ *n.* (*pl.* classes) **1** group of children or students who learn together: *a ballet class.* **2** group of people or things that are the same in some way: *the working class.* **classroom** *n.* room where children have lessons.

classic /ˈklæsɪk/ *n.* book, picture, or piece of music that lasts for always because it is very good: *Shakespeare's plays are classics.*

classical /ˈklæsɪkl/ *adj.* **1** best; that people have thought was the best for many years: *the classical music of Beethoven.* **2** of ancient Greek and Roman times: *The Parthenon is a classical building.*

clatter /ˈklætə(r)/ *n.* (no *pl.*) loud noise of hard things banging together. **clatter** *v.*: *Hailstones clattered down on to the roof.*

clause /klɔːz/ *n.* part of a sentence with its own verb: *I was angry* (= main clause) *because he came late* (= dependent clause).

claw /klɔː/ *n.* **1** one of the pointed nails on the feet of some animals and birds: *Cats have very sharp claws.* **2** hand of a crab, etc.

clay /kleɪ/ *n.* (no *pl.*) heavy earth that is sticky when it is wet and becomes hard when it is dry: *Pots are made from baked clay.*

clean¹ /kliːn/ *adj.* **1** fresh; free from dirt: *clean nails.* **2** new; not yet used: *I have made a mistake so I want a clean sheet of paper.*

clean² *v.* take dirt and marks away from something or someone: *Do you clean your teeth after meals?* **clean** *n.*: *Terry gave the car a good clean.*

clear¹ /klɪə(r)/ *adj.* **1** easy to see: *a clear photograph.* **2** easy to see through: *clear water.* **3** bright; pure: *She has a clear skin.* **4** easy to hear: *Speak so that your words are clear.* **5** easy to understand: *'Do you know the way?' 'Yes, the map is quite clear.'* **6** empty: *The road is clear of traffic so we can cross it safely.*

clear² *v.* take away things that are not wanted: *The waiter cleared the table after the meal.* **clear off**, go away. **clear something out**, make something empty: *to clear out a cupboard.* **clear up**, (a)

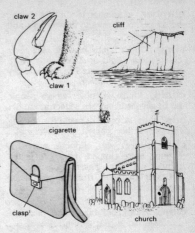

claw 2

claw 1

cliff

cigarette

clasp¹

church

become brighter, less cloudy: *The weather cleared up when the storm was over.* (b) make a place tidy: *We must clear up the classroom before we go home.*

clearly /ˈklɪəlɪ/ *adv.* **1** in a way that is easy to hear, see, etc.: *Try to speak more clearly.* **2** with no doubt; certainly: *He is clearly wrong.*

clergy /ˈklɜːdʒɪ/ *n.* (*pl.*) priests; ministers. **clergyman** *n.* priest.

clerk /klɑːk/ *n.* someone who works in an office, keeping records, writing letters, etc.

clever /ˈklevə(r)/ *adj.* quick to understand and learn. **clever at**, able to do something well: *Stuart is clever at arithmetic.* **cleverly** *adv.*

click /klɪk/ *v.* make a short, sharp sound. **click** *n.*: *the click of knitting-needles.*

client /ˈklaɪənt/ *n.* someone who pays another person, such as a lawyer, builder, etc. to do a job for him.

cliff /klɪf/ *n.* high, steep side of a hill, etc.: *It is dangerous to walk near the edge of a cliff.*

climate /ˈklaɪmɪt/ *n.* sort of weather a place has: *Britain has a colder climate than Italy.*

climb /klaɪm/ *v.* **1** go higher: *The road climbs into the hills.* **2** go up or down with the help of both hands and feet: *We climbed the tree.* **climb** *n.*: *a long climb up the mountain.* **climbing** *adj.* for walking in the mountains: *climbing boots.*

climber /'klaɪmə(r)/ *n.* someone who likes to go up and down rocks and mountains.

cling /klɪŋ/ *v.* (*past part. & past tense* clung /klʌŋ/) hold or stick tightly on to something or someone: *The little monkey is clinging to its mother.*

clinic /'klɪnɪk/ *n.* place where people go to get medicine, see a doctor, etc.

clip[1] /klɪp/ *n.* piece of metal for holding things together: *paper-clip; hair-clip.*

clip[2] *v.* (*pres. part.* clipping, *past part. & past tense* clipped /klɪpt/) **1** fasten things: *to clip papers together.* **2** cut hair or wool from a person or animal: *The barber clipped Murray's hair short.*

cloak /kləʊk/ *n.* big, loose piece of clothing, like a coat with no sleeves.

cloakroom /'kləʊkrʊm/ *n.* **1** place where you can leave coats, hats, and umbrellas. **2** lavatory; toilet.

clock /klɒk/ *n.* instrument that shows the time of day. It stands on a shelf or floor, or hangs on a wall.

close[1] /kləʊs/ *adj.* **1** near: *The shops are close to our home.* **close by**, near: *Alice lives close by.* **close together**, with little space between: *The forest trees are close together.* **2** loving or liking each other: *close friends.* **3** almost happening: *'Did Bob win the race?' 'No, but it was close.'*

close[2] /kləʊz/ *n.* (no *pl.*) end: *We were all tired at the close of the day.*

close[3] /kləʊz/ *v.* **1** shut something: *Please close the door.* **close up**, shut a place: *The caretaker closes up the school at 6 p.m.* **2** stop happening; end: *All the men left when the meeting closed.* **close down**, stop business: *The shop closed down when the owner died.* **closed** /kləʊzd/ *adj.* not open; shut.

cloth /klɒθ/ *n.* **1** (no *pl.*) material; stuff made by weaving threads together: *cotton cloth.* **2** (*pl.* cloths) piece of material that you use for a special job: *face-cloth, table-cloth.*

clothes /kləʊðz/ *n.* (*pl.*) things that you wear to cover your body.

clothing /'kləʊðɪŋ/ *n.* (no *pl.*) coverings for the body: *People wear warm clothing in cold weather.*

cloud /klaʊd/ *n.* mass, made of tiny drops of water, that floats in the air: *Those dark clouds will probably bring rain.* **cloudy** *adj.*: *a cloudy sky.*

clown /klaʊn/ *n.* man in a circus or theatre who makes people laugh.

club[1] /klʌb/ *n.* heavy stick with a thick end.

club[2] *n.* group of people with the same interests: *a tennis club.* **club** *v.* (*pres. part.* clubbing, *past part. & past tense* clubbed /klʌbd/) **club together**, join with other people to buy something: *The children clubbed together to buy a present for their teacher.*

club[3] *n.* the shape ♣ on a playing card.

cluck /klʌk/ *n.* noise made by a hen. **cluck** *v.*

clue /kluː/ *n.* thing, or piece of information, that helps to find the answer to a problem, a crime, etc.: *The police looked for clues.* **have no clue**, understand something: *He hasn't a clue how to dance.*

clump /klʌmp/ *n.* small group of trees or plants.

clumsy /'klʌmzɪ/ *adj.* not able to move easily or carefully: *That clumsy child has just dropped the eggs!* **clumsily** *adv.*

clung /klʌŋ/ *past part. & past tense* of *v.* cling.

cluster /'klʌstə(r)/ *n.* group of things close together: *a cluster of houses.* **cluster** *v.* make a close group around something: *We clustered round the fire.*

clutch /klʌtʃ/ *v.* hold something tightly: *The drowning man clutched the lifebelt.*

co- /kəʊ/ *prefix* together: *A co-educational school has both boys and girls together.*

coach[1] /kəʊtʃ/ *n.* (*pl.* coaches) **1** vehicle, with seats inside, pulled by horses: *The Queen travelled through London in a golden coach.* **2** bus for taking a group of people on long journeys. **3** part of a train where people sit.

coach[2] *n.* (*pl.* coaches) **1** teacher who gives private lessons to people. **2** someone who teaches sport: *The football coach makes his team practise every day.* **coach** *v.* teach someone.

coal /kəʊl/ *n.* **1** (no *pl.*) hard, black stuff from the ground, which gives heat when you burn it. **2** (*pl.* coals) piece of coal.

coarse /kɔːs/ *adj.* not smooth or soft: *coarse cloth.*

coast /kəʊst/ *n.* land by the sea: *Bournemouth is on the coast.* **coastline** /'kəʊstlaɪn/ *n.* edge of the land next to the sea.

coastguard /'kəʊstgɑːd/ *n.* man whose job is to watch the sea and ships carefully and see that all is well.

coat /kəʊt/ *n.* **1** piece of clothing with sleeves and an opening in the front, which you wear outside. **2** animal's covering of hair, fur, etc.: *A tiger has a striped coat.* **3** covering of paint, dust, etc. **coat** *v.* put a thin cover over something: *The wind coated the washing with dust.*

coax /kəʊks/ *v.* persuade someone; make someone or something do something by being kind, careful, etc.: *to coax a child to eat; to coax a fire to burn.*

cobweb /'kɒbweb/ *n.* fine net that a spider makes.

cock /kɒk/ *n.* male bird.

cock-pit /'kɒk pɪt/ *n.* place in an aeroplane where the pilot sits.

cocoa /'kəʊkəʊ/ *n.* (no *pl.*) **1** brown powder from the beans of a tree, made into chocolate. **2** drink that you make with cocoa powder and milk.

coconut /'kəʊkənʌt/ *n.* very big, brown nut that grows on palm trees and has sweet, white milk inside.

cod /kɒd/ *n.* (*pl.* cod) sort of sea-fish that you can eat.

code /kəʊd/ *n.* **1** set of rules for a country or a group of people: *Before Anne learned to drive, she read the Highway Code.* **2** secret writing.

coffee /'kɒfɪ/ *n.* **1** (no *pl.*) drink that you make with hot water and the crushed beans of a plant. **2** (*pl.* coffees) cup of coffee. **coffee bar** *n.* place where you can buy and drink coffee, etc.

coffin /'kɒfɪn/ *n.* box in which a dead person lies.

coil /kɔɪl/ *n.* long piece of rope or wire, twisted round and round. **coil** *v.* twist something into rings; twist round

cloud

clock

collar 1

coat 1

climber

something: *The snake coiled round a branch.*

coin /kɔɪn/ *n.* round piece of metal money.

coincidence /kəʊ'ɪnsɪdəns/ *n.* when things happen at the same time or in the same place by chance: *What a coincidence! I was thinking about Roy when his letter arrived!*

cold¹ /kəʊld/ *adj.* **1** not warm; that feels like snow, ice, etc.: *cold water.* **2** not friendly or cheerful: *a cold smile.* **coldly** *adv.* **coldness** *n.*

cold² *n.* **1** (no *pl.*) being not warm: *The cold makes us shiver.* **2** (*pl.* colds) illness that makes you cough and sneeze. ***catch a cold***, get a cold.

collapse /kə'læps/ *v.* fall down; break into pieces: *The walls of the burning house collapsed.* **collapse** *n.*

collar /'kɒlə(r)/ *n.* **1** the part of your clothes that goes round your neck. **2** band to put round the neck of a dog, horse, etc.

colleague /'kɒliːg/ *n.* person who works with you: *When Robert left his job, his colleagues gave him a present.*

collect /kə'lekt/ *v.* **1** take things from several people or places: *The bus conductor collected money from the passengers.* **2** go and fetch someone or something: *to collect a child from school.* **3** bring together things that are the same in some way, to study or enjoy them: *My niece collects stamps.*

collection /kə'lekʃn/ n. **1** number of things that have been gathered together: *The Tate Gallery has a fine collection of modern pictures.* **2** money that people give at a church service, meeting, etc.

collector /kə'lektə(r)/ n. someone who looks for and keeps things that he likes: *a stamp-collector.*

college /'kɒlɪdʒ/ n. **1** place where people go for more study, after they have left school: *Student teachers study at a training college.* **2** part of a university: *Merton is a college of Oxford University.*

collide /kə'laɪd/ v. hit each other: *The two lorries collided.* **collide with**, hit something hard: *The lorry collided with a tree.* **collision** /kə'lɪʒn/ n.

colon /'kəʊlən/ n. punctuation mark (:) that divides sentences into two or more parts.

colonel /'kɜ:nl/ n. army officer.

colony /'kɒlənɪ/ n. (pl. colonies) **1** country that is ruled by another country: *Hong Kong is a British colony.* **2** group of people from one country who go and live in a new land.

colossal /kə'lɒsl/ adj. very big.

colour /'kʌlə(r)/ n. **1** what we see when light is broken up into parts: *Blue, red, yellow, and green are colours.* **2** paint. **colour** v. put colour on to something: *to colour a drawing.*

coloured /'kʌləd/ adj. **1** with a colour: *Water has no colour, but beer is coloured.* **2** not black or white: *Nick sent a coloured postcard to his parents.* **3** with a dark skin: *Africans and Indians are coloured people.*

colourful /'kʌləfl/ adj. bright: *Gardens are colourful in summer.*

column /'kɒləm/ n. **1** tall pillar of wood, stone, etc. to hold up a building or to make people remember something or someone: *Nelson's Column in Trafalgar Square.* **2** part of a page: *You are now reading the left-hand column of this page.*

comb /kəʊm/ n. the thin piece of metal, plastic, bone, etc. with teeth, for making your hair smooth and tidy. **comb** v. use a comb: *Susan combed her hair.*

combat /'kɒmbæt/ v. fight; fight against something: *The police combat crime.* **combat** n.: *The two armies were in combat.*

come /kʌm/ v. (past part. come, past tense came /keɪm/) **1** move towards or near the person who is speaking: *The dog came when I called him.* **2** arrive: *When is the train coming?* **3** be; happen: *May comes between April and June.* **come about**, happen: *How did the accident come about?* **come across**, find something when you are not looking for it: *I came across my old radio yesterday.* **come apart**, break into pieces: *If you sit on that chair it will come apart!* **come from**, was born or lived in a place: *Joe comes from York.* **come in useful**, be useful. **come on**, follow; hurry: *Oh do come on or we'll be late!* **come to nothing**, not happen: *All my holiday plans came to nothing.* **come true**, be real; happen: *Her dream of visiting Australia came true.* **to come**, in the future: *I think she'll be a famous dancer in years to come.*

comedian /kə'mi:dɪən/ n. actor who plays funny parts; someone who makes people laugh.

comedy /'kɒmədɪ/ n. (pl. comedies) funny or light play in the theatre.

comfort /'kʌmfət/ n. **1** (no pl.) being free from worry, pain, etc.: *We have enough money to live in comfort.* **2** (pl. comforts) someone or something that brings help or kindness: *Your letter was a great comfort to me.* **comfort** v. make someone feel better, happier, etc.: *The mother comforted her crying child.*

comfortable /'kʌmftəbl/ adj. **1** pleasant and easy to sit in, wear, etc.: *a comfortable bed.* **2** with no pain or worry: *The nurse made the sick man comfortable.* **comfortably** adv.

comic¹ /'kɒmɪk/, **comical** /'kɒmɪkl/ adj. funny; making you smile and laugh.

comic² n. children's magazine with picture stories.

comma /'kɒmə/ n. punctuation mark (,) that makes a short stop in a sentence.

command /kə'mɑ:nd/ n. **1** (no pl.) power to tell people what to do: *The general has command over the army.* **2** (pl. commands) order that tells someone what he must do: *The soldiers must obey their general's commands.* **command** v.: *I command you to come here!*

commence /kə'mens/ v. begin: *The meeting will commence at 3 p.m.*

comment /'kɒment/ v. give an opinion. **comment** n.: *Colin made some rude comments about her new hairstyle.*

commentary /'kɒmentrɪ/ n. (pl. commentaries) words spoken about something that is happening: *Let's listen to the radio commentary on the football match.* **commentator** /'kɒmenteɪtə(r)/ n. someone who gives commentaries on radio, television, etc.

commerce /'kɒmɜ:s/ n. (no pl.) buying and selling; trade.

commercial /kə'mɜ:ʃl/ adj. of trade: *commercial news.* **commercial** n. short film that helps to sell something.

commit /kə'mɪt/ v. (pres. part. committing, past part. & past tense committed /kə'mɪtɪd/) do something bad: *to commit murder.*

committee /kə'mɪtɪ/ n. small group of people chosen by others to plan and organize: *the committee of the music club.*

common[1] /'kɒmən/ adj. **1** belonging to, or done by, everyone in a group: *The English and Australians have a common language.* **have something in common**, have some of the same interests as another person; be like another thing in some way: *I have a lot in common with Paul.* **2** happening often; that you often see, hear, etc.: *Double-decker buses are common in London.*

common[2] n. piece of land that anyone can use: *Let's go for a walk on the common.*

commonwealth /'kɒmənwelθ/ n. group of countries that have the same interests and try to help one another.

communicate /kə'mju:nɪkeɪt/ v. **communicate with**, talk, write, or send messages to someone: *A pilot communicates with an airport by radio.*

communication /kə,mju:nɪ'keɪʃn/ n. message; what you tell or write. **in communication with**, sending or getting letters, telephone calls, etc.: *He's in communication with his lawyer about this matter.*

communications /kə,mju:nɪ'keɪʃnz/ n. (pl.) ways of joining places together, such as roads, railways, airways, radio, and telephone.

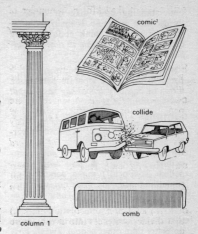

comic[2]

collide

column 1

comb

community /kə'mju:nətɪ/ n. (pl. communities) group of people who live in one place, have the same interests, etc.: *Newquay is a fishing community.*

commute /kə'mju:t/ v. travel a long way from home to work each day. **commuter** n. someone who commutes: *At 5 o'clock the London trains are full of commuters.*

companion /kəm'pæniən/ n. someone who is with another person.

company /'kʌmpənɪ/ n. **1** (no pl.) being with other people: *I am lonely if I have no company.* **be good company**, be a nice or interesting companion. **keep someone company**, be or go with someone: *Please stay and keep me company for a while.* **2** (pl. companies) group of people who work together in a business: *a transport company.*

comparative /kəm'pærətɪv/ adj. form of adjectives and adverbs showing more of something: *'Longer' is the comparative form of 'long'.*

comparatively /kəm'pærətɪvlɪ/ adv. when you see or think about other things: *Standing next to the small children, Alice looks comparatively tall.*

compare /kəm'peə(r)/ v. think about, or look at, two or more things or people so that you can see the differences: *Compare your answers with those at the back of the book to see if they are right.* **comparison** /kəm'pærɪsn/ n. seeing or understanding how alike or different things are. **in** or **by comparison with**, when you see or think about another thing or person: *A train is slow in comparison with a plane.*

compartment /kəm'pɑːtmənt/ *n.* **1** room in a train. **2** separate part inside a box or bag: *My school bag has a small compartment for pens.*

compass /'kʌmpəs/ *n.* (*pl.* compasses) instrument with a needle that always points to the north.

compel /kəm'pel/ *v.* (*pres. part.* compelling, *past part. & past tense* compelled /kəm'peld/) make someone do something when he does not want to: *The rain compelled us to come into the house.*

compete /kəm'piːt/ *v.* try to win; try to do better than other people: *Twenty girls competed in the race.*

competition /ˌkɒmpɪ'tɪʃn/ *n.* **1** (*pl.* competitions) game, sport, or test that people try to win: *a swimming competition.* **2** (no *pl.*) trying hard to be the winner, the best, etc.: *There was keen competition for the job.*

competitor /kəm'petɪtə(r)/ *n.* someone who tries to win in a race or competition.

complain /kəm'pleɪn/ *v.* say angrily that you do not like something; say that you have pain, etc.: *He complained of toothache.* **complaint** /kəm'pleɪnt/ *n.*: *He didn't like the meal so he made a complaint to the manager of the restaurant.*

complete[1] /kəm'pliːt/ *adj.* **1** finished; done: *She stopped when her work was complete.* **2** with no parts missing: *James has arrived so our team is complete.* **3** total: *Gary's visit was a complete surprise!*

complete[2] *v.* finish doing or making something: *The builders will complete the new sports centre next year.*

completely /kəm'pliːtlɪ/ *adv.* totally.

complicated /'kɒmplɪkeɪtɪd/ *adj.* difficult; not easy to do or understand: *a complicated plan.*

compliment /'kɒmplɪmənt/ *v.* say that you think well of something or someone: *May I compliment you on winning the race?* **compliment** *n.* **pay a**

compliment, praise someone: *Simon paid his girlfriend a compliment on her new dress.*

complimentary /ˌkɒmplɪ'mentrɪ/ *adj.* **1** showing that you think well of something or someone: *complimentary remarks.* **2** free: *complimentary tickets for the match.*

compose /kəm'pəʊz/ *v.* make up a poem, song, etc.: *Bizet composed an opera called 'Carmen'.* **be composed of**, be made up of: *The class is composed of twelve boys and eight girls.*

composer /kəm'pəʊzə(r)/ *n.* someone who makes up songs and music: *Mozart was a famous composer.*

composition /ˌkɒmpə'zɪʃn/ *n.* piece of music or writing.

compound /'kɒmpaʊnd/ *adj.* made of two or more parts: *'Fingerprint' is a compound word.*

comprehensive school /ˌkɒmprɪ'hensɪv skuːl/ *n.* secondary school for pupils of all abilities.

compulsory /kəm'pʌlsərɪ/ *adj.* that must be done: *School is compulsory for all children over five.*

computer /kəm'pjuːtə(r)/ *n.* machine that stores information and works out answers.

comrade /'kɒmreɪd/ *n.* friend.

conceal /kən'siːl/ *v.* **1** hide something: *He wears a wig to conceal his bald head.* **2** not tell about something: *He concealed his real name.*

conceited /kən'siːtɪd/ *adj.* thinking too well of yourself and what you can do.

concentrate /'kɒnsntreɪt/ *v.* think hard about, or look hard at, something: *Please concentrate on your typing, Miss Brown, and stop looking out of the window!* **concentration** /ˌkɒnsn'treɪʃn/ *n.*: *Tom paints with great concentration.*

concern[1] /kən'sɜːn/ *n.* **1** (*pl.* concerns) what you are interested in or think is important: *A teacher's biggest concern is his pupils.* **2** (no *pl.*) worry: *He is full of concern about his sick mother.*

concern[2] *v.* **1** interest someone; be about someone: *This report concerns you, John.* **2** be about something: *The next programme concerns the car industry.* **con-**

cern yourself with, be interested in something; do something: *She concerns herself with church work.* **3** worry someone: *The news of the flood concerns us a lot.* **concerned** /kən'sɜːnd/ worried.

concerning /kən'sɜːnɪŋ/ *prep.* about: *I received a letter concerning the meeting.*

concert /'kɒnsət/ *n.* programme of music played or sung for many people.

conclude /kən'kluːd/ *v.* **1** stop happening; end: *The film concluded with a big fight.* **2** come to an idea after thinking: *When he ran away from me, I concluded he was afraid.* **conclusion** /kən'kluːʒn/ *n.*

concrete /'kɒŋkriːt/ *n.* (no *pl.*) hard, grey material for building. **concrete** *adj.* made of concrete: *a concrete path.*

condemn /kən'dem/ *v.* **1** say strongly that someone or something is bad or wrong: *My grandfather condemns all pop music.* **2** punish someone in a law court: *The judge condemned the thief to four years in prison.*

condition /kən'dɪʃn/ *n.* **1** (no *pl.*) how a person, animal, or thing is: *Her teeth are in good condition.* **2 conditions** (*pl.*) how things are around you: *Dad does not like driving in bad traffic conditions.* **3** (*pl.* conditions) what must happen, be done, etc. before another thing can happen. **on condition that**, only if: *You can visit the patient on condition that you only stay five minutes.*

conduct¹ /'kɒndʌkt/ *n.* (no *pl.*) way you behave: *Our teacher praised our good conduct.*

conduct² /kən'dʌkt/ *v.* **1** show someone where to go: *The guide conducted us round Westminster Abbey.* **2** stand in front of an orchestra or singers and control what they do: *to conduct a choir.*

conductor /kən'dʌktə(r)/ *n.* **1** someone whose job is to sell tickets on a bus, etc. **2** someone who leads a group of music players or singers.

cone /kəʊn/ *n.* **1** thing that has one flat, round end and one pointed end: *an ice-cream cone.* **2** dry fruit of a tree with needle leaves: *a fir cone.*

confectionery /kən'fekʃənərɪ/ *n.* (*pl.*) sweets, chocolate, cakes, etc.

conference /'kɒnfərəns/ *n.* meeting of many people to talk about important things: *a press conference.*

confess /kən'fes/ *v.* **1** say that you have done wrong: *She confessed that she had taken the money.* **2** say something that you did not want to say: *I must confess that I'm afraid of spiders.* **confession** /kən'feʃn/ *n.*

confide /kən'faɪd/ *v.* tell a secret, your troubles, etc.: *She always confides in her mother when she has a problem.*

confidence /'kɒnfɪdəns/ *n.* (no *pl.*) **1** sure feeling that you can do something or that something will happen, etc.: *The actress walked on to the stage with great confidence.* **have confidence in someone**, feel sure that someone is right and good: *I have great confidence in my brother.* **2** telling a secret to someone who must not tell it to others: *I am telling you this news in confidence.*

confident /'kɒnfɪdənt/ *adj.* sure about yourself or about something: *Mike is confident that he will arrive in time.*

conflict /'kɒnflɪkt/ *n.* fight; quarrel: *Three soldiers died in the conflict.*

confuse /kən'fjuːz/ *v.* **1** mix your ideas so that you cannot understand: *They asked me so many questions that they confused me.* **2** think one thing is another: *Don't confuse the word 'weather' with 'whether'.* **confusing** *adj.* not clear; difficult to understand: *a confusing answer.*

congratulate /kən'grætʃʊleɪt/ v. tell someone that you are pleased about a good thing he has done or had: *My father congratulated me on passing the exam.*

congratulations /kən,grætʃʊ'leɪʃnz/ n. (pl.) words of joy and praise to someone who has done well, been lucky, etc.: *Congratulations on your new job!*

conjunction /kən'dʒʌŋkʃn/ n. word that joins other words or parts of a sentence: *'And', 'or', and 'but' are conjunctions.*

conjure /'kʌndʒə(r)/ v. do clever tricks that seem to be magic. **conjuror** n. someone who does conjuring tricks: *The conjurer pulled a rabbit out of his hat!*

connect /kə'nekt/ v. join or fix one thing to another thing: *Geoff connected the caravan to the car.*

connection /kə'nekʃn/ n. 1 place or part where things are joined together: *The light goes on and off because there is a loose connection.* 2 when trains, ships, etc. meet so that people can change from one to another quickly: *Ted's train was late so he missed the connection.* **in connection with**, about something: *I went to see the police in connection with the theft of my bicycle.*

conquer /'kɒŋkə(r)/ v. win a fight against others and take their land, etc.: *In 1066 the Normans conquered England.* **conquest** /'kɒŋkwest/ n.

conqueror /'kɒŋkərə(r)/ n. someone who wins.

conscience /'kɒnʃəns/ n. feeling inside your mind what is right and wrong. *have a clear conscience*, feel that you have done nothing wrong. *have a guilty conscience*, feel that you have done wrong.

conscious /'kɒnʃəs/ adj. awake and knowing what is happening: *The police cannot speak to him because he isn't conscious.* **consciousness** n. *lose consciousness*, faint: *He fell on his head and lost consciousness.*

consent /kən'sent/ v. say 'yes' to what someone wants to do, etc.: *I'm pleased because he consented to my idea.* **consent** n.: *The town council gave its consent to the plan for a new swimming pool.*

consequence /'kɒnsɪkwəns/ n. what happens because of something: *Your cough is the consequence of smoking.* *take the consequences*, be ready for the bad things that happen because of what you did: *If you drive so fast, you must take the consequences.*

consequently /'kɒnsɪkwəntlɪ/ adv. therefore; because of that: *John ate too much and consequently was sick.*

consider /kən'sɪdə(r)/ v. 1 think carefully about something or about what to do, etc.: *Matthew is considering my idea.* 2 believe something; think that something is true: *I consider that your bicycle is dangerous.* 3 be thoughtful about the feelings of other people: *A good hotel manager considers his guests.*

considerate /kən'sɪdərət/ adj. kind; thinking and caring about other people. **considerately** adv.: *He considerately gave me his seat.*

consideration /kən,sɪdə'reɪʃn/ n. (no pl.) 1 careful thought about something: *After much consideration, my brother decided to sell his car.* *take into consideration*, remember something important when you are making a plan: *We must take the cost into consideration when we are choosing a hotel.* 2 being thoughtful and careful about people's feelings: *Helen shows great consideration towards younger children.*

consist /kən'sɪst/ v. be made up of something: *The class consists of ten boys and twelve girls.*

console /kən'səʊl/ v. give comfort to someone who is sad, troubled, etc.: *She consoled the crying child.* **consolation** /,kɒnsə'leɪʃn/ n.

consonant /'kɒnsənənt/ n. a letter of the English alphabet that is not one of the vowels a, e, i, o, u.

conspicuous /kən'spɪkjʊəs/ adj. very clear; so big, bright, different, etc. that people look at it: *a conspicuous red hat.* **conspicuously** adv.

conspiracy /kən'spɪrəsɪ/ n. (pl. conspiracies) secret plan to do wrong: *a conspiracy to kill the Prime Minister.* **conspire** /kən'spaɪə(r)/ v.: *Guy Fawkes conspired to blow up the British Parliament.* **conspirator** /kən'spɪrətə(r)/ n. someone who plans secretly with others to do wrong.

constable /'kʌnstəbl/ n. policeman.

constant /'kɒnstənt/ adj. going on and on and not stopping: *the constant noise of traffic.* **constantly** adv.: *She is fat because she eats constantly.*

constituency /kən'stɪtjʊənsɪ/ n. (pl. constituencies) town or area that chooses one member of parliament.

constitution /ˌkɒnstɪ'tjuːʃn/ n. general law of a country.

construct /kən'strʌkt/ v. make or build something: *Brunel constructed railway bridges.*

construction /kən'strʌkʃn/ n. **1** (no pl.) building something: *the construction of the Pyramids.* **2** (pl. constructions) building, bridge, etc.: *St. Paul's Cathedral is a fine construction.*

consul /'kɒnsl/ n. someone whose job is to live in a foreign town and help people from his own country. **consulate** /'kɒnsjʊlət/ n. place where a consul has his office.

consult /kən'sʌlt/ v. ask someone, or read something, to learn what you want to know: *If you are ill, consult a doctor.*

consultation /ˌkɒnsl'teɪʃn/ n. meeting to ask people what should be done, how, etc.

consume /kən'sjuːm/ v. eat, drink, or use up something: *They consumed a lot of food at the party.* **consumption** /kən'sʌmpʃn/ n.: *Our new car has a large petrol consumption.*

contact[1] /'kɒntækt/ n. **1** (pl. contacts) when two things touch each other: *an electric contact.* **2** (no pl.) meeting or writing to people. **come into contact with**, know or meet someone: *A doctor comes into contact with many ill people.* **be in, get into**, or **make contact with**, write to, telephone, or go to see someone: *When I visit York, I shall try to make contact with my friends there.*

contact[2] v. go and see, write to, or telephone someone: *When I saw the broken window, I contacted the police.*

contain /kən'teɪn/ v. hold something; have something inside it: *Does this box contain biscuits?*

container /kən'teɪnə(r)/ n. something that can hold other things inside it: *Baskets, boxes, bottles, and bags are all containers.*

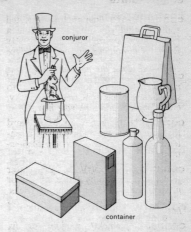

conjuror

container

contempt /kən'tempt/ n. (no pl.) strong feeling that someone or something is no good: *to feel contempt for a liar.*

content /kən'tent/ adj. pleased with what you have; not wanting more. **content to**, willing to do something: *Are you content to eat later?* **contentment** n.: *'What a wonderful meal!' said Arthur with a smile of contentment.* **contented** /kən'tentɪd/ adj. happy; pleased.

contents /'kɒntents/ n. (pl.) **1** what is written or said in a book, etc.: *My mother smiled over the contents of her letter.* **2** what is inside a thing or place: *the contents of a parcel.*

contest /'kɒntest/ n. game, sport, or test, that people try to win: *a boxing contest.* **contest** /kən'test/ v. try to win in a sport, test, etc.: *Many nations contest for medals at the Olympic Games.* **contestant** /kən'testənt/ n. someone who tries to win in a fight, sport, test, etc.: *There were six contestants in the swimming race.*

continent /'kɒntɪnənt/ n. **1** one of the big land masses of the world: *Africa is a continent.* **2** the main part of Europe: *Our friends have gone to the continent for a holiday.* **continental** /ˌkɒntɪ'nentl/ adj.

continual /kən'tɪnjʊəl/ adj. happening often; happening again and again: *The journey was slow because of continual stops.* **continually** adv.

continue /kən'tɪnju:/ v. **1** go on doing something and not stop: *The rain continued all day.* **2** start again after stopping: *We had a meal and then continued our journey at 3 p.m.* **3** go farther: *She continued along the path until she came to the river.* **continuation** /kən,tɪnju'eɪʃn/ n.

continuous /kən'tɪnjʊəs/ adj. going on and on and not stopping: *a continuous line; continuous music.* **continuously** adv.

contract /'kɒntrækt/ n. **1** written agreement between people, countries, etc.: *a marriage contract.* **2** business agreement: *The company won a contract to build the new road.*

contrary /'kɒntrəri/ adj. opposite; not agreeing with: *The rain was heavy but, contrary to our fears, our fields were not flooded.* **contrary** n. **on the contrary**, strong words to show that the opposite is true: *'You look ill, Ben.' 'On the contrary, I feel fine!'*

contrast /kən'trɑ:st/ v. look at, or think about, two or more things so that you can see the differences: *When I contrasted the two bicycles, I saw that one was older.* **contrast** /'kɒntrɑ:st/ n. clear difference between two things: *There is a big contrast between summer and winter weather.*

contribute /kən'trɪbju:t/ v. give a part of something, often help or money: *Everyone contributed food for the picnic.* **contribution** /,kɒntrɪ'bju:ʃn/ n.: *We gave a contribution of clothing to the Red Cross.*

control¹ /kən'trəʊl/ n. (no pl.) power to make people or things do what you want: *A driver must have control of his car.* **get out of control**, behave in a wild way: *The noise frightened the horse and it got out of control.* **lose control**, (a) be unable to make people or things do what you want: *The driver lost control and the bus went into the river.* (b) be unable to keep calm; cry, shout, etc.: *When Ann saw the snake she lost control and screamed.* **under control**, doing what you want it to do: *Don't worry—everything is under control.*

control² v. (pres. part. **controlling**, past part. & past tense **controlled** /kən'trəʊld/) **1** be at the head of

something; make people do what you want: *Who controls the factory?* **2** stop things or people being too wild, fast, free, etc.: *Please control your dog!* **controller** /kən'trəʊlə(r)/ n. someone who controls, organizes, etc.: *an air traffic controller.*

controls /kən'trəʊlz/ n. (pl.) instruments, switches, etc. that make a machine work: *the controls of an aeroplane.*

convenience /kən'vi:nɪəns/ n. **1** (no pl.) being easy to use; making things easy: *She keeps her glasses on a chain round her neck for convenience.* **2** (pl. conveniences) public lavatory.

convenient /kən'vi:nɪənt/ adj. easy or helpful to use; easy to reach; not giving trouble: *Will it be convenient for you to come at 5 p.m.?*

convent /'kɒnvənt/ n. **1** group of religious women, called nuns, who live together to serve the Christian God. **2** building where nuns live and work.

conversation /,kɒnvə'seɪʃn/ n. talking between two or more people: *I had an interesting conversation with my neighbour.*

convey /kən'veɪ/ v. carry someone or something from one place to another: *A taxi conveyed us to the station.*

convict¹ /'kɒnvɪkt/ n. someone who has done wrong and is in prison.

convict² /kən'vɪkt/ v. decide in a law court that someone has done wrong: *The court convicted him of murder.*

conviction /kən'vɪkʃn/ n. **1** deciding in a law court that someone has done wrong: *He has had two convictions for drunken driving.* **2** sure feeling that something is true: *You will not change my father's conviction that all women are bad drivers!*

convince /kən'vɪns/ v. make someone believe something: *Robin's playing convinces me that he is good enough for the team.* **be convinced**, feel certain: *I'm convinced that I'm right.*

cook¹ /kʊk/ n. someone who makes food ready to eat.

cook² v. make food ready to eat by heating it: *My mother cooked the lunch.* **cooking** n.

cooker /'kʊkə(r)/ n. stove; oven; thing in which you can cook food.

cookery /'kʊkərɪ/ n. (no pl.) making things ready to eat; studying how to make food: *a lesson on cookery.*

cool[1] /kuːl/ adj. **1** a little cold: *a cool day.* **2** calm; not excited: *Try to keep cool when you're in danger.*

cool[2] v. make something less hot; become less hot: *A swim in the lake cooled us.* **cool down,** (*a*) become less hot: *At night the air cools down.* (*b*) become calm after you have been excited.

co-operate /kəʊ'ɒpəreɪt/ v. work helpfully together with someone else. **co-operation** /kəʊ,ɒpə'reɪʃn/ n.: *The police thanked Mrs. Brown for her co-operation.*

co-operative /kəʊ'ɒpərətɪv/ adj. willing to work helpfully with other people.

cop /kɒp/ n. policeman.

cope /kəʊp/ v. **cope with,** do a difficult job: *How do you cope with six dogs?*

copper /'kɒpə(r)/ n. (no pl.) red-brown metal. **copper** adj. made of copper.

copy[1] /'kɒpɪ/ n. (pl. copies) **1** something made to look exactly like another thing: *The picture on my wall is a copy of a painting by Turner.* **2** one example of a book or newspaper: *Is this your copy of the dictionary?*

copy[2] v. **1** write or draw something to look like another thing: *Please copy the sentence on the blackboard.* **2** try to be like, or look like, another person: *Tom copied the clothes of the pop star.* **3** cheat by looking at another person's work and writing what that person has written: *You must not copy in an exam.*

cord /kɔːd/ n. thick string; thin rope.

core /kɔː(r)/ n. middle part of some kinds of fruit, where the seeds are: *an apple core.*

cork /kɔːk/ n. **1** (no pl.) light, strong bark of the tree called the cork-oak. **2** (pl. corks) piece of cork used to close a bottle. **cork** v. put a stopper in a bottle: *I corked the bottle carefully so the wine would not run out.*

cork-screw /'kɔːk skruː/ n. instrument for taking corks out of bottles.

corn /kɔːn/ n. (no pl.) seed of grain plants, such as wheat, oats, rye, and maize.

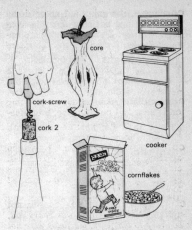

core

cork-screw

cork 2

cooker

cornflakes

corner /'kɔːnə(r)/ n. place where two lines, sides, walls, roads, etc. meet: *He walked round the corner into the next street. The lamp stands in the corner of the room.* **in a tight corner,** in trouble: *My father helped me when I was in a tight corner.*

cornflakes /'kɔːnfleɪks/ n. (pl.) special breakfast food made from small pieces of dried corn.

coronation /,kɒrə'neɪʃn/ n. crowning a king or queen.

corporation /,kɔːpə'reɪʃn/ n. **1** group of people chosen to look after a town. **2** big group of people working together in a business.

corpse /kɔːps/ n. body of a dead person.

correct[1] /kə'rekt/ adj. with no mistakes; right; true: *a correct answer.* **correctly** adv.

correct[2] v. **1** show what is wrong; mark mistakes: *to correct a pupil's homework.* **2** put something right: *The clock was fast so I corrected it.*

correction /kə'rekʃn/ n. right word, answer, etc. put in place of what was wrong.

correspond /,kɒrɪ'spɒnd/ v. **correspond with,** write letters to, and get letters from, someone: *I correspond with many friends in Canada.*

correspondence /ˌkɒrɪˈspɒndəns/ n. (no pl.) writing letters; letters that have been written: *My secretary reads my correspondence.*

correspondent /ˌkɒrɪˈspɒndənt/ n. 1 someone who writes and gets letters. 2 someone whose job is to send news to a newspaper, radio, etc.: *the B.B.C. correspondent in Washington.*

corridor /ˈkɒrɪdɔː(r)/ n. long, narrow passage in a building or train, with doors into rooms or compartments.

cosmetic /kɒzˈmetɪk/ n. something that a woman uses to make her skin or hair more beautiful: *Lipstick and face-powder are cosmetics.*

cost[1] /kɒst/ n. 1 price; money that you must pay for something: *the high cost of oil.* 2 loss; what is given to get another thing: *The fire was put out at the cost of a fireman's life.* **at all costs**, no matter what work, loss, or trouble is needed: *The thief must be caught at all costs.*

cost[2] v. (*past part. & past tense* cost) 1 be the price of something: *How much did the butter cost?* 2 make you lose something: *Bad driving may cost you your life.*

costly /ˈkɒstlɪ/ adj. expensive: *a costly fur coat.*

costume /ˈkɒstjuːm/ n. 1 sort of clothes worn in a country or at a certain time: *national costume.* 2 woman's suit; jacket and skirt.

cosy /ˈkəʊzɪ/ adj. warm; comfortable and friendly: *a cosy room.*

cot /kɒt/ n. baby's bed with high sides to stop it from falling out.

cottage /ˈkɒtɪdʒ/ n. small house in the country.

cotton /ˈkɒtn/ n (no pl.) 1 plant with soft, white stuff round the seeds. 2 thread made from cotton plant. 3 cloth made from cotton plant. **cotton** adj. made from cotton material: *Tracy is wearing a pink cotton dress.*

cotton-wool /ˌkɒtn ˈwʊl/ n. (no pl.) special, soft stuff made from cotton: *The nurse cleaned the cut with cotton-wool.*

couch /kaʊtʃ/ n. (pl. couches) long, soft seat where you can sit or lie.

cough /kɒf/ v. send out air from the mouth and throat in a noisy way:

The smoke made me cough. **cough** n.: *You have a bad cough.*

could /kʊd/ 1 past tense of v. can: *When my father was young he could run fast.* 2 word that shows what will perhaps happen: *It could rain tomorrow.* 3 word that you use when you ask a polite question: *Could I have another cup of tea, please?*

couldn't /ˈkʊdnt/ = could not.

council /ˈkaʊnsl/ n. group of people chosen to work together and make rules: *the town council.* **councillor** /ˈkaʊnsələ(r)/ n. member of a council.

count[1] /kaʊnt/ n. adding up numbers for a special reason: *After an election there is a count of votes.* **lose count of**, stop knowing how many there are: *'I've lost count of the hours I've watched football', said Steve.*

count[2] n. nobleman in some countries.

count[3] v. 1 add up numbers, etc. to see how much there is: *At the end of the day, the shopkeeper counted his money.* 2 say numbers one after the other in the right order: *My little brother can count from 1 to 10.* 3 be important: *A university degree counts if you are looking for a teaching job.* **count on someone**, expect that someone will help you, etc.: *Can we count on Mrs. Benson to bring the food?*

counter /ˈkaʊntə(r)/ n. long table in a shop, bank, or bar, where people buy things: *The baker put the bread on the counter.*

countess /ˈkaʊntɪs/ n. (pl. countesses) 1 wife or widow of a British earl. 2 wife of a count.

countless /ˈkaʊntlɪs/ adj. too many to be counted: *countless stars.*

country /ˈkʌntrɪ/ n. 1 (pl. countries) nation; state: *Italy is a European country.* 2 (no pl.) land not in towns: *My uncle has a farm in the country.*

countryside /ˈkʌntrɪsaɪd/ n. (no pl.) the open land: *In spring, the English countryside is green.*

county /ˈkaʊntɪ/ n. (pl. counties) part of a country: *Kent is an English county.*

couple /ˈkʌpl/ n. 1 two people or things of the same kind that are together: *a couple of friends.* 2 man and his wife; boyfriend and girlfriend: *We invited ten couples to the party.*

coupon /'ku:pɒn/ n. piece of paper that allows you to get something or to do something: *petrol coupons*.

courage /'kʌrɪdʒ/ n. (no *pl.*) bravery; having or showing no fear: *Trevor showed great courage when he saved the child from the burning house*. **courageous** /kə'reɪdʒəs/ adj. brave. **courageously** adv.

course¹ /kɔːs/ n. **1** moving forwards: *during the course of the day*. **2** line in which something moves: *We followed the course of the river*. **change course**, start to go in a different way: *The aeroplane had to change course because of the storm*. **in due course**, later; at the right time: *I wrote to my sister and her reply came in due course*. **of course**, certainly: *Of course I'll help you*.

course² n. ground for sport: *a golf-course; a race-course*.

course³ n. planned programme of study: *Nigel is doing a law course at university*.

course⁴ n. part of a meal: *The first course was soup*.

court /kɔːt/ n. **1** place where judges and lawyers listen to law cases. **2** king or queen and all their followers. **3** place where a king or queen and their followers meet. **4** piece of ground marked for a sport: *a tennis court*.

courteous /'kɜːtɪəs/ adj. polite. **courteously** adv.: *He courteously opened the door for me.* **courtesy** /'kɜːtəsɪ/ n. being polite.

courtyard /'kɔːtjɑːd/ n. open space inside a big building or in front of it.

cousin /'kʌzn/ n. child of your uncle or aunt.

cove /kəʊv/ n. small bay.

cover¹ /'kʌvə(r)/ n. **1** thing that you put over another thing: *The cover of a pot is called a lid*. **2** outside of a book. **3** place that keeps you safe. **take cover**, go into a safe place: *We took cover from the rain under a tree.*

cover² v. **1** put one thing over another thing to hide it, keep it safe, keep it warm, etc.: *Pat covered her head with a scarf*. **2** be all over something: *Flood water covers our fields.* **be covered with**, have something all over yourself or itself: *A bear is covered with fur.* **cover**

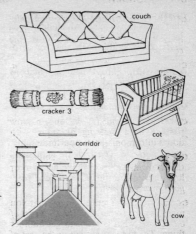

couch

cracker 3

cot

corridor

cow

up, (a) hide your mistakes. **(b)** put one thing over another: *She covered up the baby with a shawl.*

covering /'kʌvərɪŋ/ n. something that you put over another thing or a person.

cow /kaʊ/ n. big farm animal which gives milk.

coward /'kaʊəd/ n. someone who shows fear. **cowardly** adj.

cowboy /'kaʊbɔɪ/ n. man on a horse who looks after cattle in America.

crab /kræb/ n. sea-animal with a hard shell and big claws.

crack¹ /kræk/ n. **1** line or thin hole where something is broken: *cracks in a wall*. **2** sudden, loud noise made by a gun, whip, thunder, etc. **3** hard hit: *a crack on the head*.

crack² v. **1** break something, but not into pieces: *The ball cracked the window*. **2** make a sudden, loud noise: *He cracked his whip*.

cracker /'krækə(r)/ n. **1** kind of thin, dry biscuit. **2** kind of firework. **3** small roll of pretty paper, with a tiny present inside, which makes a noise when two people pull it apart: *Christmas crackers*.

crackle /'krækl/ v. make small, sharp sounds: *The burning wood crackled.*

cradle /'kreɪdl/ n. small bed for a baby.

craft /krɑːft/ n. **1** (pl. crafts) job that needs clever hands which have been trained for a long time: *Weaving is a craft.* **2** (pl. craft) boat, ship, or aeroplane.

craftsman /'krɑːftsmən/ n. someone who has learned to use his hands cleverly.

crafty /'krɑːftɪ/ adj. clever at tricking people. **craftily** adv.

crag /kræg/ n. high, sharp rock.

cram /kræm/ v. (pres. part. cramming, past part. & past tense crammed /kræmd/) **1** make something too full: *The hungry child crammed his mouth with food.* **2** push too much into a small space: *You can't cram eight people into that car!*

crane /kreɪn/ n. machine with a big arm for lifting heavy things: *The crane put the car on to the ship.*

crash[1] /kræʃ/ n. (pl. crashes) **1** an accident; two things coming together hard: *a train crash.* **2** big noise when something falls, breaks, etc.: *I heard a crash as the tree fell.*

crash[2] v. **1** fall or hit something hard and noisily: *A stone crashed through the window.* **2** make something hit another thing hard: *He crashed his car into a wall.*

crash-helmet /'kræʃ helmɪt/ n. hard hat that you wear to keep your head safe: *Motor-cyclists must wear crash-helmets.*

crate /kreɪt/ n. big, wooden box for goods.

crawl[1] /krɔːl/ n. (no pl.) **1** moving slowly: *We drove at a crawl through the busy streets.* **2** way of swimming.

crawl[2] v. **1** move slowly on your hands and knees: *Babies crawl before they walk.* **2** pull the body along the ground: *Worms and snakes crawl.*

crayon /'kreɪən/ n. soft, thick, coloured pencil.

craze /kreɪz/ n. sudden, strong liking for something: *a craze for playing marbles.*

crazy /'kreɪzɪ/ adj. mad; foolish: *You must be crazy to ride a bicycle that has no brakes!* **crazy about**, very interested in something: *Hugh's crazy about football.* **crazily** adv.

creak /kriːk/ n. noise of wood when it bends. **creak** v. **creaky** adj.: *creaky stairs.*

cream[1] /kriːm/ adj. **1** with a yellow-white colour. **2** with the fatty part of milk in it: *a cream cake.*

cream[2] n. (no pl.) **1** yellow-white colour. **2** fatty part of milk that can be made into butter. **3** any thick, soft liquid: *face-cream.*

creamy /'kriːmɪ/ adj. **1** smooth and soft. **2** with cream in it.

crease /kriːs/ v. **1** make paper or cloth full of lines when you fold it, crush it, etc.: *If you push your skirt into the drawer like that you'll crease it.* **2** get too many lines in it: *Does your dress crease?* **crease** n. line made by folding, etc.

create /kriː'eɪt/ v. **1** make something new: *God created the world.* **2** make something happen: *Oh do stop creating such a noise!*

creation /kriː'eɪʃn/ n. **1** (no pl.) making something. **2** (pl. creations) something new that is made: *Mickey Mouse was the creation of Walt Disney.*

creator /kriː'eɪtə(r)/ n. someone who plans or makes new things: *Walt Disney was the creator of Donald Duck.*

creature /'kriːtʃə(r)/ n. living animal or person.

credit /'kredɪt/ n. (no pl.) **1** letting someone take goods now but pay later: *The shop gives me credit.* **2** good name. **be a credit to**, bring a good name to someone: *Alec is a credit to his family.* **credit card** n. card from a bank that lets you borrow money or buy goods and pay for them later.

creep /kriːp/ v. (past part. & past tense crept) move along close to the ground; move slowly, quietly, or secretly: *The cat is creeping towards the bird.*

creeper /'kriːpə(r)/ n. plant that spreads over the ground and climbs over things: *The creeper is growing up the wall.*

crept /krept/ past part. & past tense of v. creep.

crescent /'kresnt/ n. shape like a new moon.

crew /kruː/ n. group of people who work together on a ship or aeroplane.

cricket[1] /'krɪkɪt/ n. brown, jumping insect.

cricket[2] n. (no pl.) ball game with two teams. **cricketer** n. someone who plays cricket.

cried /kraɪd/ past tense of v. cry.

cries /kraɪz/ (pl.) of n. cry. shouts.

crime /kraɪm/ n. something done that is against the law: Murder is a crime.

criminal[1] /'krɪmɪnl/ adj. **1** against the law: a criminal plan. **2** of crime: She's studying criminal law.

criminal[2] n. someone who has broken the law.

crimson /'krɪmzn/ adj. deep red: Blood is crimson. **crimson** n.

cripple[1] /'krɪpl/ n. someone who cannot walk or move well because he is sick or hurt.

cripple[2] v. hurt part of the body so that it cannot work well: The accident crippled my right arm. **crippled** /'krɪpld/ adj. not able to move your arm or leg easily because it is hurt.

crisis /'kraɪsɪs/ n. (pl. crises) very serious time; time of great trouble, danger, etc.: War is a crisis.

crisp[1] /krɪsp/ adj. **1** hard and dry: a crisp biscuit. **2** firm: a crisp lettuce.

crisp[2] n. thin slice of potato, fried in hot oil and then dried: a packet of crisps.

critical /'krɪtɪkl/ adj. **1** very serious: His illness is critical. **2** saying that something is wrong: a critical school report. **critically** adv.

criticize /'krɪtɪsaɪz/ v. **1** say whether things or people are good or bad: Please criticize my painting. **2** say that someone or something is bad or wrong. **criticism** /'krɪtɪsɪzəm/ n.

croak /krəʊk/ n. the noise that a frog makes. **croak** v.

crockery /'krɒkəri/ n. (no pl.) plates, cups, etc.

crocodile /'krɒkədaɪl/ n. long, dangerous reptile that lives in the rivers of Africa.

crook /krʊk/ n. bad person; criminal.

crooked /'krʊkɪd/ adj. **1** not straight; bent; twisting: a crooked path. **2** not honest: a crooked shopkeeper.

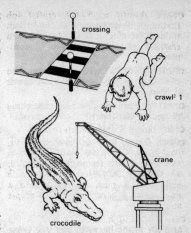

crossing

crawl[2] 1

crane

crocodile

crop /krɒp/ n. all the plants of one kind that the farmer grows in one season: a crop of potatoes.

cross[1] /krɒs/ adj. not pleased; rather angry. **crossly** adv.

cross[2] n. (pl. crosses) mark like (+) or (×).

cross[3] v. go over something from one side to the other: to cross the road.

cross-examine /ˌkrɒs ɪg'zæmɪn/ v. ask someone many important questions in a law court, etc. **cross-examination** /ˌkrɒs ɪgˌzæmɪ'neɪʃn/ n.

crossing /'krɒsɪŋ/ n. (no pl.) special place where you can cross a road.

crossroads /'krɒsrəʊdz/ n. (no pl.) place where two roads meet and go over each other.

crossword, crossword puzzle /'krɒswɜːd pʌzl/ n. game with words on paper.

crouch /kraʊtʃ/ v. bend the body to make it lower: The cat was crouching in the grass, waiting for the bird.

crow[1] /krəʊ/ n. big, black bird with a harsh cry.

crow[2] v. make a cry like a cock when the sun rises.

crowd /kraʊd/ n. many people together: There was a large crowd at the football match. **crowd** v. all come together: They crowded into the hall. **crowded** /'kraʊdɪd/ adj. full of people, etc.

crown /kraʊn/ *n.* special headdress that a king or queen wears at important times. **crown** *v.* put a crown on someone who has become a king or queen.

crucifix /'kru:sɪfɪks/ *n.* (*pl.* crucifixes) small copy of the Cross with the figure of Jesus on it.

crucify /'kru:sɪfaɪ/ *v.* kill someone by nailing him on to a cross. **crucifixion** /ˌkru:sɪ'fɪkʃn/ *n.*

cruel /krʊəl/ *adj.* bringing pain or trouble to others; not kind: *The cruel man was hitting the donkey.* **cruelly** *adv.* **cruelty** /'krʊəltɪ/ *n.*

cruise /kru:z/ *n.* sea-journey for pleasure. **cruise** *v.*

cruiser /'kru:zə(r)/ *n.* sort of boat.

crumb /krʌm/ *n.* very small, broken bit of bread, etc.

crumble /'krʌmbl/ *v.* break or fall into small pieces: *The old castle walls are crumbling.*

crumple /'krʌmpl/ *v.* make paper or cloth full of folds, not smooth. **crumpled** /'krʌmpld/ *adj.: a crumpled shirt.*

crunch /krʌntʃ/ *v.* **1** bite something noisily: *He was crunching nuts.* **2** crush something noisily; be crushed noisily: *The dry leaves crunched under our feet as we walked.*

crush /krʌʃ/ *v.* press something hard and break or harm it: *She stepped on my watch and crushed it.*

crust /krʌst/ *n.* hard, outside part of bread. **crusty** /'krʌstɪ/ *adj.: a crusty loaf.*

crutch /krʌtʃ/ *n.* (*pl.* crutches) long stick to go under the arm and help a hurt person to walk: *After his accident he walked with a pair of crutches.*

cry[1] /kraɪ/ *n.* (*pl.* cries) call that shows pain, fear, sadness, etc.; loud or excited shout: *a cry for help.* **cry-baby** *n.* child who cries often with no real reason.

cry[2] *v.* **1** make a loud noise; shout: *'Help!' cried Beth, when she fell in the river.* **2** weep: *Ann cried when her dog died.*

cub /kʌb/ *n.* young lion, bear, fox, tiger, etc.

cube /kju:b/ *n.* solid shape with six equal, square sides. **cubic** /'kjubɪk/ *adj.*

cuckoo /'kʊku:/ *n.* bird with a call like its name.

cucumber /'kju:kʌmbə(r)/ *n.* long vegetable with a green skin.

cuddle /'kʌdl/ *v.* hold someone close and lovingly in your arms: *She is cuddling her baby.*

cuff /kʌf/ *n.* end of a sleeve by the hand.

culprit /'kʌlprɪt/ *n.* someone who has done wrong: *Are you the culprit who broke this window?*

cultivate /'kʌltɪveɪt/ *v.* **1** make soil ready for growing plants. **2** keep and care for plants: *He works all day cultivating his vegetable garden.* **cultivation** /ˌkʌltɪ'veɪʃn/ *n.*

culture /'kʌltʃə(r)/ *n.* the customs, art, and beliefs of a group of people: *He has studied the cultures of Eastern countries.*

cunning /'kʌnɪŋ/ *adj.* clever at tricking people: *a cunning trick.* **cunning** *n.*

cup /kʌp/ *n.* **1** small bowl with a handle for drinking. **2** drink in a cup: *a cup of coffee.* **3** gold or silver bowl as a prize: *the school swimming cup.*

cupboard /'kʌbəd/ *n.* piece of furniture, with shelves and doors, for keeping things in.

curate /'kjʊərət/ *n.* Christian priest who helps a more senior priest in his church.

curb /kɜ:b/ *n.* edge of the pavement next to the road: *Ted parked his car at the curb.*

cure[1] /kjʊə(r)/ *n.* **1** becoming well from an illness; making someone well: *His cure took six weeks.* **2** something that will end a problem or an illness: *Aspirin is a cure for headaches.*

cure[2] *v.* make a sick person well: *The doctor cured the pain in my back.*

curiosity /ˌkjʊərɪ'ɒsətɪ/ *n.* (no *pl.*) wanting to know about things: *My little brother is full of curiosity.*

curious /'kjʊərɪəs/ *adj.* **1** wanting to know about something: *I am curious to know how that old clock works.* **2** wanting to know too much. **3** strange; unusual: *What is this curious animal?* **curiously** *adv.*

curl¹ /kɜ:l/ *n.* ring or twist of hair. **curly** /ˈkɜ:lɪ/ *adj.: A lamb has a curly coat.*

curl² *v.* twist something into rings: *Jane curled her hair.* **curl up**, make yourself into a ball: *The cat curled up on my knee.*

curler /ˈkɜ:lə(r)/ *n.* small thing that you wind hair round to make the hair curly.

currant /ˈkʌrənt/ *n.* **1** small, sweet, dried fruit. **2** small, juicy fruit.

currency /ˈkʌrənsɪ/ *n.* (*pl.* currencies) kind of money used in a country: *The dollar is American currency.*

current /ˈkʌrənt/ *n.* **1** air or water that is moving along: *We couldn't row against the strong current.* **2** electricity running through a wire.

curry /ˈkʌrɪ/ *n.* (*pl.* curries) dish of food cooked with hot-tasting spices. **curried** /ˈkʌrɪd/ *adj.*

curse /kɜ:s/ *n.* **1** strong wish for something bad to happen to someone: *The witch put a curse on the prince and he became a frog.* **2** rude, angry words: *He gave a curse when he hit his head.* **curse** *v.: He fell off his bicycle and cursed loudly.*

curtain /ˈkɜ:tn/ *n.* piece of cloth that hangs in front of a window. **draw the curtains**, pull the curtains open or closed.

curtsey /ˈkɜ:tsɪ/ *v.* bend your knees to show respect for someone, e.g. a queen.

curve /kɜ:v/ *n.* bend; line or shape that is not straight. **curve** *v.* bend round: *The river curves round the town.* **curved** /kɜ:vd/ *adj.* bent.

cushion /ˈkʊʃn/ *n.* small bag filled with something soft to sit on.

custard /ˈkʌstəd/ *n.* sweet, yellow sauce that you eat with fruit or puddings.

custody /ˈkʌstədɪ/ *n.* (no *pl.*) **1** care; keeping someone or someone safe: *When Jack's parents died, he was put in the custody of his uncle.* **2** being in prison: *The thief was taken into custody.*

custom /ˈkʌstəm/ *n.* what a group of people usually do: *It is a British custom to have a tree in the house at Christmas.*

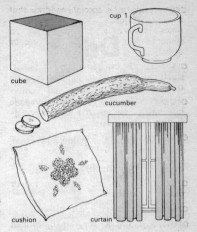

cup 1

cube

cucumber

cushion

curtain

customer /ˈkʌstəmə(r)/ *n.* someone who buys things from a shop.

customs /ˈkʌstəmz/ *n.* (*pl.*) **1** money that you pay when you bring new things into a country from another country: *I had to pay customs on my new camera.* **2** people who collect tax on things that you bring into the country: *We shall have to go through customs at the airport.*

cut /kʌt/ *v.* (*pres. part.* cutting, *past part.* & *past tense* cut) **1** break something with a knife, scissors, etc.: *Please cut this piece of string.* **2** open your skin: *I cut my finger.* **3** make something shorter: *to cut hair.* **4** take one piece from something bigger: *to cut a piece of cake.* **cut down**, chop something so that it falls down: *to cut down a tree.* **cut off**, stop something: *They cut off the electricity today.* **be cut off**, be kept alone, away from others: *The village was cut off by the floods.* **cut** *n.: I have a cut on my finger.* **a short cut**, a way that makes the journey quicker: *Is there a short cut to the station?*

cutlery /ˈkʌtlərɪ/ *n.* (no *pl.*) knives, forks, and spoons.

cycle /ˈsaɪkl/ *n.* bicycle. **cycle** *v.* ride a bicycle. **cycling** *n.* **cyclist** /ˈsaɪklɪst/ *n.* someone who rides a bicycle.

cyclone /ˈsaɪkləʊn/ *n.* dangerous storm with very strong winds.

Dd

dab /dæb/ v. (*pres. part.* dabbing, *past part.* & *past tense* dabbed /dæbd/) touch something quickly and gently: *She dabbed her eyes with a handkerchief.*

dad /dæd/, **daddy** /'dædɪ/ n. (*pl.* daddies) father.

daffodil /'dæfədɪl/ n. yellow flower that comes in spring.

daft /dɑːft/ adj. silly; foolish: *It's daft to play football in the rain!*

dagger /'dægə(r)/ n. short, pointed knife used as a weapon.

daily /'deɪlɪ/ adj. happening every day: *a daily newspaper.* **daily** adv.: *The milkman comes daily to our house.*

dainty /'deɪntɪ/ adj. looking small and pretty: *a dainty little girl.*

dairy /'deərɪ/ n. (*pl.* dairies) **1** place where milk is kept and butter is made. **2** shop that sells milk, eggs, butter, etc.

daisy /'deɪzɪ/ n. (*pl.* daisies) sort of flower.

dam /dæm/ n. wall built across a river, stream, etc. to hold the water.

damage /'dæmɪdʒ/ v. break or hurt something: *The fire has badly damaged the house.* **damage** n.

damp /dæmp/ adj. a little wet: *damp clothes.*

dance¹ /dɑːns/ n. **1** moving to music. **2** party where people dance.

dance² v. move the body, usually to music. **dancer** n. someone who dances.

danger /'deɪndʒə(r)/ n. **1** (no *pl.*) chance that something harmful will happen: *You will be in danger if you walk on a railway line.* **2** (*pl.* dangers) someone or something that may bring harm or trouble: *The busy road is a danger to small children.*

dangerous /'deɪndʒərəs/ adj. that will probably bring harm: *Broken glass is dangerous.* **dangerously** adv.

dare¹ /deə(r)/ n. something bold that you do because another person asks you: *Roy tried to ride on a cow for a dare.*

dare² v. **1** be brave or bold enough to do something: *Dare you swim across the river, John?* **2** ask someone to do something because you want to see if he is brave enough to do it: *'I dare you to climb on to the roof, Larry!' said Bill.* **how dare you**, how can you be so rude and bold: *'How dare you take flowers from my garden!' he shouted angrily.* **I dare say**, I think it is likely: *I dare say it will rain today.*

daring /'deərɪŋ/ adj. brave and bold: *a daring climber.*

dark¹ /dɑːk/ adj. **1** with no light, or not much light: *a dark night.* **2** with a deep colour: *A police uniform is dark blue.* **3** brown or black, not blond: *He has dark hair.*

dark² n. (no *pl.*) where there is no light: *The little boy was afraid of the dark.* **before** or **after dark**, before or after the sun goes down.

darkness /'dɑːknɪs/ n. (no *pl.*) where there is no light. **in darkness**, with no light: *Keith switched the light off and the room was in darkness.*

darling /'dɑːlɪŋ/ n. dear or loved person: *That baby is a little darling.* **darling** adj.

darn /dɑːn/ v. repair a hole in clothes with needle and thread: *My mother is darning Bob's socks.*

dart¹ /dɑːt/ n. small, metal arrow, with feathers, which you throw at a round board in a game called **darts**.

dart² v. move quickly and suddenly: *He darted across the road.*

dash¹ /dæʃ/ n. (*pl.* dashes) sudden, quick run forwards: *We made a dash through the rain to the bus.*

dash² n (*pl.* dashes) punctuation mark (—).

dash³ v. **1** run suddenly: *I must dash or I'll be late for work.* **2** move something strongly and suddenly: *The sea dashed the boat on the rocks.*

date /deɪt/ n. **1** exact day of the month or year: *Tracy's date of birth was 3 June 1966.* **out of date**, too old. **up to date**, modern. **2** meeting that you have planned with someone: *Karen has a date with Paul on Friday.* **3** small, sweet, brown fruit of a tree called the **date-palm**.

daughter /ˈdɔːtə(r)/ *n.* girl child: *Elizabeth is the daughter of Mr. and Mrs. Ellis.*

daughter-in-law /ˈdɔːtər ɪn lɔː/ *n.* (*pl.* daughters-in-law) wife of your son.

dawdle /ˈdɔːdl/ *v.* walk slowly.

dawn[1] /dɔːn/ *n.* the time when day comes: *Do you get up at dawn?*

dawn[2] *v.* begin to be light: *When day dawned, we started our journey.*

day /deɪ/ *n.* **1** (*pl.* days) time of 24 hours: *There are seven days in a week.* **2** (no *pl.*) time between sunrise and sunset: *Most people work in the day and sleep at night.* **3** days (*pl.*) times: *There was no television in the days of Queen Victoria.* **day after day**, every day; all the time: *The rain fell day after day.* **day in, day out**, continuously: *The team trained day in day out for a month.* **I haven't got all day**, I'm in a hurry! **the other day**, a few days ago. **one day, (a)** on a certain day in the past: *One day the temperature was 30°C.* **(b)** at some time in the future: *One day, I'll be grown up.* **some day**, at some time in the future. **in a few days' time**, soon; after a few days: *I am leaving for Sydney in a few days' time.*

day-dream /ˈdeɪdriːm/ *v.* have thoughts of pleasant things. **day-dream** *n.*

daylight /ˈdeɪlaɪt/ *n.* (no *pl.*) time when it is light.

daytime /ˈdeɪtaɪm/ *n.* (no *pl.*) time when it is day and not night.

daze /deɪz/ *v.* make someone not able to think clearly: *The fall dazed him.* **daze** *n.* **in a daze**, not able to think clearly.

dazzle /ˈdæzl/ *v.* shine brightly in someone's eyes so that he cannot see clearly: *The bright lights of the car dazzled me.*

dead[1] /ded/ *adj.* **1** not living; with no life: *Let's throw away those dead flowers and pick some fresh ones.* **2** very quiet: *The streets are dead at night.* **dead to the world**, deeply asleep. **3** total; complete: *a dead stop.*

dead[2] *adv.* quite; totally: *Maurice was dead tired after the race.*

dead[3] *n.* (*pl.*) people who have died: *They buried the dead after the battle.* **at** or **in the dead of night**, late at night when everything is still and quiet.

dance²

daffodil

dart¹

daisy

deadly /ˈdedlɪ/ *adj.* **1** likely to kill people or animals: *a deadly poison.* **2** full of hate: *The two men are deadly enemies.*

deaf /def/ *adj.* not able to hear.

deafen /ˈdefn/ *v.* make so much noise that you cannot hear well: *The noise of the aeroplane deafened us.*

deal[1] /diːl/ *n.* **1** agreement, usually about buying, selling, or working: *The factory has a new deal with a buyer in Canada.* **2** amount. **a good deal**, a lot; much: *We have a good deal of snow in the winter.* **a great deal**, very much: *She's fat because she eats a great deal.*

deal[2] *v.* (*past part. & past tense* dealt /delt/) **deal in**, buy or sell certain goods: *This shop deals in electrical goods.* **deal out**, give a share to each person: *She dealt out the cards for a game.* **deal with, (a)** tell about something: *This book deals with music.* **(b)** look after someone or something: *How can I deal with my work when you play that loud music?*

dealer /ˈdiːlə(r)/ *n.* someone who buys and sells things: *a car dealer.*

dear /dɪə(r)/ *adj.* **1** loved; lovable: *We were sad about the death of our dear grandfather.* **2** way to start a letter: *Dear Sarah.* **3** costing a lot of money: *Bananas are very dear this week.*

dearly /ˈdɪəlɪ/ *adv.* very much: *Kathy dearly loves ice-cream.*

death /deθ/ *n.* dying; end of life: *The child fell to her death from the window.* **put someone to death,** kill someone. **deathly** *adj.* like death: *deathly pale.*

debate /dɪ'beɪt/ *v.* talk about something at a public meeting: *Parliament debates new laws.* **debate** *n.*: *United Nations debates.*

debt /det/ *n.* money that you must pay to someone. **in debt,** owing money: *He's in debt to the bank because he bought that big house.* **out of debt,** not owing money.

decay /dɪ'keɪ/ *v.* go bad: *If you do not clean your teeth they will decay.* **decay** *n.*

deceitful /dɪ'si:tfl/ *adj.* **1** ready to lie, trick, cheat, etc.: *a deceitful child.* **2** that trick and cheat: *deceitful words.*

deceive /dɪ'si:v/ *v.* trick someone to make him believe something that is not true: *Don't try to deceive me—I saw you taking the money!*

December /dɪ'sembə(r)/ *n.* last month of the year.

decent /'di:snt/ *adj.* **1** proper; right: *You must wear decent clothes when you go for a new job.* **2** kind: *It was very decent of you to lend me your bicycle.* **decently** *adv.*

decide /dɪ'saɪd/ *v.* come to an idea or plan after thinking: *I cannot decide which child sings better, Robert or Ian. We have decided to go to France for our holidays.*

decision /dɪ'sɪʒn/ *n.* plan; firm idea: *His decision to leave school was a surprise to his parents.* **come to a decision,** decide.

deck /dek/ *n.* floor of a ship or bus. **deck chair** *n.* folding chair that you can take outside.

declare /dɪ'kleə(r)/ *v.* **1** say something firmly and clearly: *The man declared that he was not the thief.* **2** tell the customs about something: *When you come into England with a lot of wine, you must declare it.* **declaration** /ˌdeklə'reɪʃn/ *n.*

decorate /'dekəreɪt/ *v.* **1** put pretty things on something to make it look nice: *The family decorate the Christmas tree with glass balls and lights.* **2** put paint or paper on to the walls of rooms: *I decorated the room pink.*

decoration /ˌdekə'reɪʃn/ *n.* lights, flowers, pictures, etc. that make a place or a thing prettier and brighter: *At Christmas we put decorations in the house.*

decrease /dɪ'kri:s/ *v.* become smaller, fewer, etc.: *The number of people in the village has decreased from 150 to 100.* **decrease** /'di:kri:s/ *n.*

deed /di:d/ *n.* something you do: *A Scout promises to do one good deed every day.*

deep /di:p/ *adj.* **1** going a long way down: *I cannot stand in the deep end of the swimming pool.* **2** with a darker colour: *deep blue.* **3** with a low sound: *Men usually have deep voices.* **4** total: *Mary was in such a deep sleep that she did not hear her mother call.* **5** with strong feelings: *deep sadness.* **deeply** *adv.*: *deeply worrried; deeply grateful.*

deep-freeze /ˌdi:p 'fri:z/ *n.* box that keeps food very cold and fresh for a long time. **deep-frozen** /ˌdi:p 'frəʊzn/ *adj.*

deer /dɪə(r)/ *n.* (*pl.* deer) wild animal that has horns and long, thin legs.

defeat[1] /dɪ'fi:t/ *n.* losing a game, fight, war, etc.

defeat[2] *v.* win a fight or game against others: *We cheered when our team defeated the other team.*

defence /dɪ'fens/ *n.* **1** (no *pl.*) fighting against people who attack; keeping away dangerous things or people: *Most countries have armies for their defence.* **2** (*pl.* defences) something that keeps away dangerous things or people: *The walls of York were strong defences.*

defend /dɪ'fend/ *v.* **1** guard someone or something; fight to keep away dangerous things or people: *Jack picked up a stick to defend himself against the wild dog.* **2** speak or write to help someone in trouble. **3** say in a court of law that someone has not done wrong. **4** stop the other team from scoring a goal.

defender /dɪ'fendə(r)/ *n.* **1** someone who fights to send away attack. **2** player who must try to stop other players from scoring goals.

defiant /dɪ'faɪənt/ *adj.* bold and not doing what someone tells you to do. **defiantly** *adv.*: *'I won't come!' shouted the child defiantly.*

definite /'defɪnɪt/ *adj.* clear; with no doubts; certain: *I want a definite answer, 'Yes' or 'No'.* **definite article**, the.

definitely /'defɪnɪtlɪ/ *adv.* certainly; surely: *You should definitely stay in bed if the doctor tells you to.*

definition /ˌdefɪ'nɪʃn/ *n.* group of words that tell what another word means.

defy /dɪ'faɪ/ *v.* **1** go boldly against people who have control over you: *to defy the law.* **2** ask someone to do something that you think he cannot and will not do: *The boy ran away and defied his friends to catch him.*

degree /dɪ'griː/ *n.* **1** measure for angles: *There are 90 degrees in a right angle.* **2** measure for temperature: *A person's normal temperature is 37 degrees Centigrade.* **3** title that a university gives to a student who has passed an examination, etc.: *the degree of M.A.*

dejected /dɪ'dʒektɪd/ *adj.* sad: *Harry was dejected when he did not get the job.*

delay¹ /dɪ'leɪ/ *n.* being late; time of being late: *a delay of three hours.* **without delay**, at once.

delay² *v.* **1** make someone or something slow or late: *We arrived late because the bad traffic delayed us.* **2** not do something until a later time: *We shall delay our holiday until the weather is better.*

deliberate /dɪ'lɪbərət/ *adj.* that you want to do or say: *a deliberate lie.* **deliberately** *adv.*: *She broke my bicycle lamp deliberately.*

delicate /'delɪkət/ *adj.* **1** fine and soft: *the delicate skin of a baby.* **2** that will break easily: *delicate glass.* **3** who becomes ill easily: *a delicate child.*

delicious /dɪ'lɪʃəs/ *adj.* very good to eat or to smell: *a delicious stew.*

delight¹ /dɪ'laɪt/ *n.* **1** (no *pl.*) great pleasure or happiness. **take delight in**, enjoy something: *Children take great delight in music and dancing.* **2** (*pl.* delights) something that brings much pleasure: *The lovely garden was a delight.*

delight² *v.* make someone very pleased, happy, etc.: *The new puppy delighted Danny.* **delighted** /dɪ'laɪtɪd/ *adj.* very pleased, happy, etc.

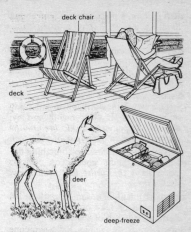

deck chair

deck

deer

deep-freeze

delightful /dɪ'laɪtfl/ *adj.* making you very pleased, happy, etc.: *What a delightful party!* **delightfully** *adv.*

deliver /dɪ'lɪvə(r)/ *v.* take something to the place where it must go: *Every day, the milkman delivers milk to our house.* **delivery** *n.*: *postal deliveries.*

demand /dɪ'mɑːnd/ *v.* **1** say that you must have something: *The workers demanded more money.* **2** need something: *This work demands quick hands.* **demand** *n.* **in demand**, wanted by many people: *Cold drinks are in demand in the summer.*

demolish /dɪ'mɒlɪʃ/ *v.* break something totally, e.g. a building: *They demolished six houses so that they could build a supermarket.*

demonstrate /'demənstreɪt/ *v.* **1** show something clearly: *He demonstrated how to mend a puncture.* **2** walk or stand in public with other people to show that you have strong feelings about something: *The students marched through London to demonstrate against the government.*

demonstration /ˌdemən'streɪʃn/ *n.* **1** showing something: *We watched a cookery demonstration at school.* **2** group of people walking or standing together in public to show that they feel strongly about something: *a workers' demonstration for more money.*

den /den/ n. **1** place where a wild animal lives, e.g. a cave. **2** secret hiding-place: *a den of thieves.*

denim /'denɪm/ n. **1** (no *pl.*) sort of strong, cotton cloth, usually blue. **2** **denims** (*pl.*) trousers or jeans made from denim.

dense /dens/ adj. **1** thick: *Mr. Matthews lost his way in the dense fog.* **2** with many things or people close together: *There was a dense crowd at the match.* **densely** adv.: *a densely crowded street.*

dent /dent/ n. hollow on something flat, which happens when you hit it. **dent** v.: *A taxi drove into my car and dented it.*

dentist /'dentɪst/ n. someone whose job is to mend or take out bad teeth, etc. **dentistry** n. job of a dentist.

deny /dɪ'naɪ/ v. say that something is not true: *He denied that he had stolen the car.*

depart /dɪ'pɑːt/ v. go away: *The train departs from platform 5.* **departure** /dɪ'pɑːtʃə(r)/ n. leaving: *What is the time of departure?*

department /dɪ'pɑːtmənt/ n. part of a big company, university, government, shop, etc.: *Professor Jenkins is the head of the English Department.* **department store** n. big shop that sells different goods in different departments: *Selfridges is a big London department store.*

depend /dɪ'pend/ v. **depend on** or **upon**, (*a*) need someone or something: *Children depend on their parents for food and clothing.* (*b*) trust someone; feel sure that another person or thing will do what you want: *You can depend on him to come if he says he will.* **it depends, that depends**, words to show that something is not certain: *I want to leave early but it depends.*

dependable /dɪ'pendəbl/ adj. that you can trust: *a dependable car; a dependable friend.*

dependent /dɪ'pendənt/ adj. needing someone or something: *A baby is dependent on its mother.*

deposit¹ /dɪ'pɒzɪt/ n. **1** first payment for something: *I paid a deposit on a new bicycle and will pay the rest next week.* **2** money that you put in a bank.

deposit² v. **1** put something down: *He deposited the books on the table.* **2** put something somewhere to keep it safe: *You must deposit the money in a bank.*

depot /'depəʊ/ n. station: *the bus depot.*

depress /dɪ'pres/ v. make someone feel sad and dull: *This grey weather depresses me.* **depressed** /dɪ'prest/ adj.: *You look depressed.*

depth /depθ/ n. being deep; how far it is from the top of something to the bottom: *What is the depth of the well?*

derivative /də'rɪvətɪv/ n. word, etc. that is made from another: *The name 'Cambridge' is a derivative of the name of the River 'Cam'.*

descend /dɪ'send/ v. come down; go down: *Murray descended the steps into the swimming pool.* **be descended from**, come from the family of: *Black Americans are descended from West African people.*

descendant /dɪ'sendənt/ n. someone in a family who comes after you; children, grandchildren, etc.: *Queen Elizabeth II is a descendant of Queen Victoria.*

descent /dɪ'sent/ n. way down; going down: *It's a steep descent from the top of the mountain.*

describe /dɪ'skraɪb/ v. say what something or someone is like: *I have no photograph of my brother but I can describe him to you.* **description** /dɪ'skrɪpʃn/ n.: *We listened to Philip's description of the wedding.*

desert¹ /'dezət/ n. sandy country with little water and few plants: *the Sahara Desert.* **desert island** n. island with no people on it.

desert² /dɪ'zɜːt/ v. go away from a person, the army, etc., when it is wrong to go: *The man deserted his family.*

deserted /dɪ'zɜːtɪd/ adj. empty; with no people: *At night the streets are deserted.*

deserve /dɪ'zɜːv/ v. be worthy of something; have earned something: *Jill deserves a holiday after so much work.*

design¹ /dɪ'zaɪn/ n. **1** drawing or plan that shows how to make something: *a design for a new aeroplane.* **2** pattern: *The wallpaper has a pretty blue design.*

design² v. draw a plan that shows how to make something: *to design dresses*.

desire /dɪ'zaɪə(r)/ n. strong wish. **desire** v. want something very much.

desk /desk/ n. table with drawers where you sit to write, do business, etc.: *In the classroom the pupils sit at desks*.

desolate /'desələt/ adj. **1** empty and unfriendly: *desolate land*. **2** sad and lonely: *The foreigner felt desolate in the strange country*.

despair /dɪ'speə(r)/ n. (no *pl.*) feeling of no hope: *He was in despair when he spent the last of his money*.

despatch, dispatch /dɪ'spætʃ/ v. send someone or something to a place for a special purpose. **despatch, dispatch** n. message or report.

desperate /'despərət/ adj. **1** having no hope and ready to do any wild or dangerous thing: *The desperate man jumped out of the window of the burning house*. **2** very serious: *There is a desperate need for food in poor countries*.

desperation /ˌdespə'reɪʃn/ n. (no *pl.*) feeling of no hope, which makes you do unusual things: *In desperation, the old woman sold her ring to get some money for food*.

despise /dɪ'spaɪz/ v. feel that someone or something is very bad: *I despise people who are cruel to children*.

despite /dɪ'spaɪt/ prep. in spite of; not taking notice of: *I think he is sad, despite his smiles*.

dessert /dɪ'zɜːt/ n. fruit, sweet pudding, etc., that you eat at the end of a meal: *We had ice-cream for dessert*. **dessertspoon** n. big spoon for eating puddings and sweets.

destination /ˌdestɪ'neɪʃn/ n. place where a person or thing is going: *We shall not arrive at our destination before evening*.

destroy /dɪ'strɔɪ/ v. totally break or put an end to something: *Fire destroyed the forest*.

destruction /dɪ'strʌkʃn/ n. (no *pl.*) breaking something totally: *the destruction of a town in an earthquake*.

detach /dɪ'tætʃ/ v. unfasten one thing from another thing: *At Derby they detached two coaches from the train*.

desk

dentist

detergent

detail /'diːteɪl/ n. one of the small parts that make the whole: *I like your plan, now tell me all the details*. **in detail**, with all the facts: *He told us about his plan in detail*.

detective /dɪ'tektɪv/ n. policeman who finds out how a crime happened and then tries to find the person who did it.

detergent /dɪ'tɜːdʒənt/ n. sort of powder or liquid for washing things.

determined /dɪ'tɜːmɪnd/ adj. totally sure; with a firm plan: *Tom is working hard because he is determined to pass the exam*. **determination** /dɪˌtɜːmɪ'neɪʃn/ n. strong will; having a firm plan: *Tom shows great determination*.

detest /dɪ'test/ v. hate someone or something very much: *I detest dirty houses*.

detour /'diːtʊə(r)/ n. way round when you cannot go by the usual road: *There is a detour because the bridge is broken*.

devastate /'devəsteɪt/ v. totally break or destroy something: *Fire devastated the town*.

develop /dɪ'veləp/ v. **1** become bigger, fuller, or more complete: *A boy develops into a man*. **2** make something bigger, etc.: *He developed the little shop into a big store*. **3** treat a photographic film with chemicals so that you can see the picture.

development /dɪ'veləpmənt/ *n.* **1** (no *pl.*) growing: *Parents watch the development of a baby with interest.* **2** (*pl.* developments) new happening: *Tell me the latest developments in the strike.*

devil /'devl/ *n.* **1** wicked spirit; cruel or wicked person. **2 the Devil**, Satan; the enemy of God.

devote /dɪ'vəʊt/ *v.* give a lot of time, money, etc. to something: *Eric devotes all his free time to playing football.*

devoted /dɪ'vəʊtɪd/ *adj.* loving: *a devoted friend.*

devour /dɪ'vaʊə(r)/ *v.* eat all of something quickly: *The hungry dog devoured the dish of meat.*

dew /dju:/ *n.* (no *pl.*) drops of water that form on grass in the night: *In the morning the grass was wet with dew.*

diagram /'daɪəgræm/ *n.* drawing or plan that explains something: *I made a diagram to show how the eye works.*

dial /'daɪəl/ *n.* round, flat face, with numbers and a moving pointer, for showing weight, time, speed, etc.: *the dial of a clock.* **telephone dial**, round part of a telephone, with numbers, which you turn to make a call to someone. **dial** *v.* (*pres. part.* dialling, *past part. & past tense* dialled /'daɪəld/) make a telephone call by turning the dial: *She dialled the number.*

diamond /'daɪəmənd/ *n.* **1** bright, precious stone: *The ring has a diamond in it.* **2** the shape ◆ on a playing card, etc.

diary /'daɪərɪ/ *n.* (*pl.* diaries) book where you write what has happened each day. **keep a diary**, write in a diary every day.

dice /daɪs/ *n.* (*pl.* dice) small piece of wood, plastic, etc., which has dots from 1 to 6 for playing games.

dictate /dɪk'teɪt/ *v.* say words aloud for another person to write down: *The manager dictated a letter to his secretary.* **dictation** /dɪk'teɪʃn/ *n.*

dictator /ˌdɪk'teɪtə(r)/ *n.* person who has total control of a country: *Napoleon was a dictator.*

dictionary /'dɪkʃənrɪ/ *n.* (*pl.* dictionaries) book that gives words from A to Z and explains what each word means.

did /dɪd/ *past tense of v.* do: *What did you say?*

didn't /'dɪdnt/ = did not.

die /daɪ/ *v.* **1** come to the end of life; stop living: *Plants and people die without water.* **die for**, be killed while fighting for something or someone: *Soldiers die for their country.* **die of**, stop living because of something: *He died of smallpox.* **2** want something very much: *'I'm dying for a drink', said Tom when he had finished the race.*

diesel /'di:zl/ *n.* (no *pl.*) engine that uses oil, not petrol. **diesel oil** *n.* heavy sort of oil. **diesel train** *n.* train that runs with diesel oil.

diet /'daɪət/ *n.* **1** usual food: *Cows have a diet of grass.* **2** special programme of food for people who are ill, etc. **go on a diet**, eat only certain food: *You must go on a diet because you are too fat.*

difference /'dɪfrəns/ *n.* **1** being not alike: *There is a difference between winter and summer weather.* **2** how much things are unlike: *The difference between 5 and 7 is 2.* **make a difference**, bring a change: *Your help has made a big difference—I understand the work better now.*

different /'dɪfrənt/ *adj.* **1** not alike: *Boys and girls are different.* **2** many and not alike: *There were six different sorts of ice-cream.*

difficult /'dɪfɪkəlt/ *adj.* **1** not easy to do or understand: *a difficult sum.* **2** that gives trouble: *a difficult child.*

difficulty /'dɪfɪkəltɪ/ *n.* (*pl.* difficulties) problem; something that is not easy to do or understand. **have difficulty**, have trouble: *I'm having difficulty with this work.* **with difficulty**, not easily: *A small child writes with difficulty.*

dig /dɪg/ *v.* (*pres. part.* digging, *past part. & past tense* dug /dʌg/) **1** break earth with a tool, machine, etc.: *You must dig the garden before you can plant the seeds.* **2** make a hole, etc. in the ground: *They are digging a tunnel through the mountain for the new railway.* **dig up**, find something by breaking the ground: *The professor dug up a Roman villa near Bristol.*

dignified /'dɪgnɪfaɪd/ *adj.* calm, quiet, and serious: *a dignified old man.*

dim /dɪm/ adj. **1** not bright: *We can't read because the light is too dim.* **2** not clear: *The old man had only dim memories of the time when he was a boy.* **dimly** adv.

diminish /dɪ'mɪnɪʃ/ v. become less or smaller: *The water in the river diminished during the summer.*

din /dɪn/ n. (no pl.) loud noise: *What a terrible din!*

dine /daɪn/ v. eat an elegant dinner. **dine out**, have a meal away from your home, etc. **dining-room** n. room where people eat.

dinghy /'dɪŋgɪ/ n. (pl. dinghies) small, open boat.

dinner /'dɪnə(r)/ n. main meal of the day.

dinosaur /'daɪnəsɔ:(r)/ n. big, wild animal that lived long ago.

dip /dɪp/ v. (pres. part. dipping, past part. & past tense dipped /dɪpt/) put something into liquid, a container, etc. for a short time and then take it out again: *Jim dipped his spoon into the soup.*

diploma /dɪ'pləʊmə/ n. piece of paper that a student receives when he has passed an examination: *a teaching diploma.*

diplomat /'dɪpləmæt/ n. someone whose job is to speak and act for his government in another country. **diplomatic** /ˌdɪplə'mætɪk/ adj.: *diplomatic talks.*

direct[1] /dɪ'rekt/ adj. **1** as straight as possible; not turning: *If you are in a hurry, take the most direct road.* **2** with nothing or no one between: *The Prime Minister is in direct contact with the President.*

direct[2] adv. not stopping; not going a long way round: *Max had no time in London because he flew direct from Paris to New York.*

direct[3] v. tell or show someone how to do something or to go somewhere: *Can you direct me to the station?*

direction /dɪ'rekʃn/ n. **1** (pl. directions) where someone or something is going or looking: *You must turn back because you are going in the wrong direction.* **2** **directions** (pl.) words telling where to go, what to do, or how to do something: *Before Pam made the cake she read the directions on the packet.*

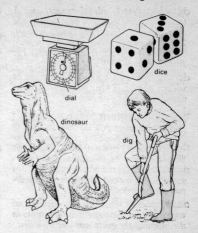

dice

dial

dinosaur

dig

directly /dɪ'rektlɪ/ adv. **1** straight: *The teacher looked directly at Alan.* **2** immediately: *He left directly after the meeting.*

director /dɪ'rektə(r)/ n. one of the chief managers of a business, etc.

directory /dɪ'rektərɪ/ n. (pl. directories) book of people's names, addresses, etc.: *I can find his telephone number in the telephone directory.*

dirt /dɜ:t/ n. (no pl.) mud, dust, or anything not clean: *The farmer came back from the fields with dirt on his boots.*

dirty /'dɜ:tɪ/ adj. not clean; covered with mud, etc.: *Wash those dirty hands!* **dirty** v. make something dirty: *She dirtied her new, white skirt.*

dis- /dɪs/ prefix showing the opposite of something: *'Disbelieve' is the opposite of 'believe'.*

disadvantage /ˌdɪsəd'vɑ:ntɪdʒ/ n. small problem; something that makes things hard to do, etc.: *When you visit France, it is a disadvantage if you cannot speak French.*

disagree /ˌdɪsə'gri:/ v. say that another person's idea is wrong; say that something is not true: *I disagreed with Len—he said the picture was good and I said it was bad.* **disagreement** n.

disagreeable /ˌdɪsə'gri:əbl/ adj. not pleasing; bad-tempered.

disappear /ˌdɪsə'pɪə(r)/ v. go away so that it cannot be seen: *The train disappeared into the tunnel.* **disappearance** n.

disappoint /ˌdɪsə'pɔɪnt/ v. make you sad because the things you hoped for do not happen: *Our football team disappointed us when they lost the match.* **disappointed** /ˌdɪsə'pɔɪntɪd/ adj.: *a disappointed look.*

disappointment /ˌdɪsə'pɔɪntmənt/ n. **1** sadness because you do not do, get, or have what you hope for: *To my great disappointment, I did not get a letter from him.* **2** person or thing that makes you sad because it is not what you hoped: *The holiday was a disappointment because the weather was bad.*

disapprove /ˌdɪsə'pruːv/ v. think or say that someone or something is not good: *Do you disapprove of smoking?*

disaster /dɪ'zɑːstə(r)/ n. very bad happening: *Fires, floods, and earthquakes are disasters.*

disastrous /dɪ'zɑːstrəs/ adj. bringing great danger and trouble: *The heavy rain brought disastrous floods.* **disastrously** adv.

disc, disk /dɪsk/ n. **1** thing that is round and flat. **2** gramophone record.

discipline /'dɪsɪplɪn/ v. train someone; teach someone to do what he is told: *In the army, officers discipline men to make them into good soldiers.* **discipline** n.

disc-jockey /'dɪsk dʒɒkɪ/ n. someone whose job is to talk about and play popular records on the radio, television, or at discos, nightclubs, etc.

discontented /ˌdɪskən'tentɪd/ adj. not happy; not pleased.

disco /'dɪskəʊ/, **discotheque** /'dɪskətek/ n. place where people listen and dance to pop music on records.

discourage /dɪ'skʌrɪdʒ/ v. make someone lose hope: *The difficult work discouraged Alan and he left school.*

discover /dɪ'skʌvə(r)/ v. find out something for the first time: *Fleming discovered penicillin.* **discovery** n.: *the discovery of America.*

discuss /dɪ'skʌs/ v. talk about something: *Shall we discuss where we are going for our holiday?* **discussion** /dɪ'skʌʃn/ n.

disease /dɪ'ziːz/ n. illness: *Malaria is a disease that mosquitoes carry.*

disembark /ˌdɪsɪm'bɑːk/ v. get off a ship or an aeroplane: *When the ship arrived at Southampton, the passengers disembarked.*

disgrace¹ /dɪs'greɪs/ n. (no pl.) person or thing that brings shame because it is so bad: *Your dirty clothes are a disgrace.*

disgrace² v. bring shame to someone: *The girl disgraced her family by stealing.*

disgraceful /dɪs'greɪsfl/ adj. shameful; very bad: *disgraceful behaviour.*

disguise /dɪs'gaɪz/ v. make someone or something look different so that people will not know who or what it is: *We disguised Tom as a clown for the party.* **disguise** n. special clothes, etc. to change how you look: *The guests came to the party in disguise.*

disgust /dɪs'gʌst/ n. (no pl.) strong feeling of dislike: *To his disgust, he saw a dead dog in his garden.* **disgust** v. give someone a strong feeling of dislike: *The dirty plates in the restaurant disgusted us.* **disgusting** adj.

dish /dɪʃ/ n. (pl. dishes) **1** plate or bowl for holding food: *a glass dish.* **2** a particular meal: *Mother cooked a chicken dish for lunch.*

dishonest /dɪs'ɒnɪst/ adj. not honest; ready to lie, cheat, steal, etc.

dishwasher /'dɪʃwɒʃə(r)/ n. machine that washes plates, cups, knives, forks, etc.

disinfectant /ˌdɪsɪn'fektənt/ n. chemical that you use to make a place or a person free from germs.

dislike /dɪs'laɪk/ v. not like someone or something; feel that someone or something is bad: *I don't eat nuts because I dislike them.* **dislike** n.

disloyal /dɪs'lɔɪəl/ adj. not faithful. **disloyalty** n.

dismal /'dɪzməl/ adj. sad; making you feel sad: *dismal weather; dismal news.*

dismay /dɪs'meɪ/ n. (no pl.) feeling of surprise and worry: *He looked at me in dismay when I told him I had crashed the car.* **dismay** v. make someone feel dismay: *The news dismayed him.*

dismiss /dɪs'mɪs/ v. **1** make someone leave his job: *The director dismissed his lazy secretary.* **2** allow people to go away from a place: *The teacher dismisses the class when the bell rings.*

dismount /dɪs'maʊnt/ v. get off a horse, bicycle, etc.

disobey /ˌdɪsə'beɪ/ v. not do what someone has told you to do: *disobedient* /ˌdɪsə'biːdɪənt/ adj.: *a disobedient child.* **disobediently** adv. **disobedience** /ˌdɪsə'biːdɪəns/ n.

disorganize /ˌdɪs'ɔːgənaɪz/ v. stop things working well: *The strike disorganized the train service.*

display /dɪ'spleɪ/ v. show something to people for selling or for interest: *A baker displays his bread in the shop window.* **display** n.: *I watched my sister at the dancing display.*

displease /dɪs'pliːz/ v. make someone rather angry: *The bad food in the restaurant displeased him.* **displeased** /dɪ'spliːzd/ adj. not happy; rather angry: *a displeased look.*

displeasure /dɪs'pleʒə(r)/ n. (no pl.) anger: *a frown of displeasure.*

dispose /dɪ'spəʊz/ v. **dispose of,** throw away or give away something because you do not want it: *Where can I dispose of an old car?*

dispute /dɪ'spjuːt/ n. quarrel; fight: *There is a pay dispute at the factory and the workers are on strike.*

dissatisfied /dɪ'sætɪsfaɪd/ adj. not pleased with what you or others have done: *I must do this work again because I am dissatisfied with it.*

distance /'dɪstəns/ n. space between two things, places, etc.: *The distance from my house to the station is two kilometres.* **in the distance,** far away.

distant /'dɪstənt/ adj. **1** far away in space or time: *If you are very quiet, you can hear distant music from the circus in town.* **2** not close in the family: *distant cousins.* **distantly** adv.

distinct /dɪ'stɪŋkt/ adj. clear; easy to see, hear, or smell: *There is a distinct smell of oranges in this room!*

distinction /dɪ'stɪŋkʃn/ n. **1** (pl. distinctions) small difference; what makes one thing different from another: *What is the distinction between butterflies and*

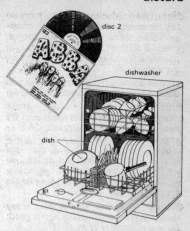

disc 2

dishwasher

dish

moths? **2** (no pl.) being better than many others: *an artist of distinction.* **3** (pl. distinctions) special grade for very good work: *Hugh had a distinction in his music exam.*

distinctly /dɪ'stɪŋktlɪ/ adv. clearly: *Please speak distinctly so that Grandma can hear.*

distress¹ /dɪ'stres/ n. (no pl.) **1** great pain or sadness; suffering because of lack of money, etc.: *The old woman was in distress when her husband died.* **2** trouble: *a ship in distress.*

distress² v. make someone unhappy: *Her son's illness distresses her very much.*

distribute /dɪ'strɪbjuːt/ v. give out or send out things to each person: *The teacher distributed the new books to the pupils.*

district /'dɪstrɪkt/ n. part of a country or town: *They have left this district and gone to live in Bristol.*

distrust /dɪs'trʌst/ v. feel that you cannot trust someone: *I don't lend money to people that I distrust.* **distrust** n. **distrustful** adj.

disturb /dɪ'stɜːb/ v. **1** break the quietness of a place; stop someone thinking or working well: *The music disturbs me when I am working.* **2** move something from its place: *You have disturbed this vase.* **3** make someone worried: *The news of the accident disturbed people.*

disturbance /dɪ'stɜːbəns/ n. 1 breaking the quietness and order: *The drunken man caused a disturbance in the street.* 2 thing or person that breaks the quietness: *Loud music is a disturbance in the countryside.*

disused /dɪs'juːzd/ adj. not used: *A bird has made its nest in that disused tractor.*

ditch /dɪtʃ/ n. (pl. ditches) narrow channel in the fields or at the side of the road to carry away water, etc.

dive /daɪv/ v. 1 jump into water, with your hands and arms first: *Pat dived into the lake.* 2 go under water: *The submarine dived under the water.* **diving-board** n. high board for diving into a swimming-pool.

diver /'daɪvə(r)/ n. person who works under water: *a deep-sea diver.*

divert /daɪ'vɜːt/ v. make something go another way: *When the car crashed, the police diverted the traffic.* **diversion** /daɪ'vɜːʃn/ n.

divide /dɪ'vaɪd/ v. 1 split something into parts; go into parts: *When the path divides you must follow the left way.* 2 share something into parts: *Aunty divided the cake among the children.* 3 find out how often one number will go into a bigger number: *If you divide 20 by 4, the answer is 5.*

divine /dɪ'vaɪn/ adj. of, from, or like God or a god: *a divine plan.*

division /dɪ'vɪʒn/ n. 1 (no pl.) cutting something into parts: *One of the three sons was not pleased with the division of the father's money.* 2 (no pl.) finding out how often a number will go into a bigger number. 3 (pl. divisions) one of the parts of something: *a division of the army.*

divorce /dɪ'vɔːs/ n. end of a marriage by law. **divorce** v.: *She divorced her husband.*

D.I.Y. /ˌdiː aɪ 'waɪ/ abbrev. do it yourself; mending or making something in the house yourself.

dizzy /'dɪzɪ/ adj. feeling that everything is turning round and round and you are going to fall. **dizzily** adv. **dizziness** n.

d.j. /ˌdiː 'dʒeɪ/ abbrev. disc-jockey.

do /duː, də/ v. (pres. part. doing, past part. done /dʌn/, past tense did

/dɪd/) 1 carry out an action: *Do the washing quickly.* 2 finish something; find the answer: *I can't do this difficult sum.* 3 arrange or fix something: *Carol did my hair for the party.* 4 have a job: *'Tell me what he does.' 'He's a doctor.'* 5 study something: *Ken is doing economics at Oxford University.* 6 be all right; be enough: *This soup will do for six people.* 7 word that you put with a main verb when you want to say 'not': *Tom swims well but Dan does not.* 8 word that you put with a main verb to make a question: *He likes ice-cream. Do you like it?* 9 word that you put before another verb to make it stronger: *I am surprised—you do run fast.* **could do with**, wish for or need something: *Those curtains could do with a wash!* **do someone in**, kill someone. **do someone out of something**, take something from someone wrongly: *Ada's uncle did her out of the money her father had left her.* **do up**, (a) clean and fix something: *We bought an old house and are doing it up.* (b) fasten something: *Do up the buttons on your shirt, Richard.* (c) tie up a parcel, etc.: *She did up the package.* **do without**, be all right without something: *Can you do without your car today?* **How do you do?** words you say when you meet a person for the first time: *How do you do, Mr. Smith?*

dock¹ /dɒk/ n. 1 place where ships come to land so that people can load and mend them: *London docks.* 2 place in a law court where the prisoner stands: *The thief stood in the dock.*

dock² v. sail into the place where it can be loaded, etc.: *The ship docked at Liverpool.*

docker /'dɒkə(r)/ n. workman in a port or harbour.

doctor /'dɒktə(r)/ n. 1 someone whose job is to make sick people well again. 2 someone who has the highest university degree.

document /'dɒkjʊmənt/ n. written or printed paper with important information: *a legal document.*

documentary /ˌdɒkjʊ'mentrɪ/ n. film that tells facts about something.

dodge /dɒdʒ/ v. **1** move quickly to get out of the way of something: *Ben threw a stone at me but I dodged it.* **2** not do something that you should do: *He dodged the work by saying he was ill.*

does /dʌz/, /dəz/ part of v. do, used with 'he', 'she', and 'it'.

doesn't /'dʌznt/ = does not.

dog /dɒg/ n. animal that you keep as a pet or on a farm.

doing /'du:ɪŋ/ pres. part. of v. do.

doll /dɒl/ n. toy that looks like a person.

dome /dəʊm/ n. round roof: *the dome of St. Paul's Cathedral.*

domestic /də'mestɪk/ adj. **1** of the home or family: *Cooking and cleaning are domestic jobs.* **2** not wild; that lives with man: *Dogs and cats are domestic animals.*

dominate /'dɒmɪneɪt/ v. control someone; tell someone what to do because you are stronger: *Roy dominates his younger brother.*

done /dʌn/ past part. of v. do.

donkey /'dɒŋkɪ/ n. animal like a small horse, with long ears; ass.

don't /dəʊnt/ = do not.

door /dɔ:(r)/ n. **1** way into a building: *Go through the door on your right and into the office.* **2** piece of wood that closes across the way into a building: *Sheila knocked on the door.* **answer the door**, go to open the door when someone knocks or rings. **from door to door**, (**a**) from one exact place to another: *The journey from college in London to my house in Oxford takes two hours from door to door.* (**b**) to all houses: *The trader goes round the village selling things from door to door.* **next door**, in the next house: *Mr. and Mrs. Jones live next door to us.* **out of doors**, outside in the open air: *It's too cold to sit out of doors in the winter.*

doorbell /'dɔ:bel/ n. bell that a visitor rings to tell you that he is at the door.

doorway /'dɔ:weɪ/ n. opening into a building: *Alison was standing in the doorway when the taxi arrived.*

dormitory /'dɔ:mɪtrɪ/ n. (pl. dormitories) big bedroom for a lot of people: *Boys who live at school sleep in a dormitory.*

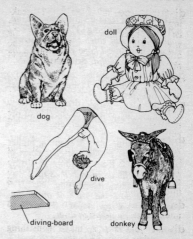

doll

dog

dive

diving-board

donkey

dose /dəʊs/ n. how much medicine you take at one time: *Take three doses every day.* **dose** v.: *She dosed herself with aspirin when she had a headache.*

dot /dɒt/ n. small, round mark: *The letter 'i' has a dot over it.*

double[1] /'dʌbl/ adj. **1** two times as much; twice as much: *You are richer than I am because your pay is double my pay.* **2** with two parts that are the same: *double doors.* **3** for two people or things: *a double bed.* **4** word to show that the same number comes twice: *My telephone number is 49811, four nine eight double one.*

double[2] n. person or thing that looks just like another: *Ann is the double of her twin sister.*

double[3] v. become twice as big; make something twice as big: *The number of children in our school has doubled since 1970.*

double-decker /,dʌbl 'dekə(r)/ n. big bus with seats upstairs and downstairs.

doubt[1] /daʊt/ n. not being sure: *There is some doubt whether the film starts at 7.30 or 8.00.* **in doubt**, not sure: *When I am in doubt about the way, I look at a map.* **no doubt**, certainly: *Walter isn't here but no doubt he will come later.*

doubt[2] *v.* not feel sure about something; not believe something: *You are late so I doubt if you will catch the bus.* **doubtful** *adj.* not sure: *I hope you will like the film but I'm doubtful.* **doubtfully** *adv.*

doubtless /ˈdaʊtlɪs/ *adv.* certainly; probably: *Walter isn't here but doubtless he'll come later.*

dough /dəʊ/ *n.* (no *pl.*) mixture of flour, water, etc. for making bread, biscuits, etc.

down[1] /daʊn/ *adv.* **1** from a higher to a lower place: *The sun goes down in the evening.* **2** from standing to sitting or lying: *to lie down in bed.* **3** in a way that is smaller, less strong, etc.: *I'm pleased because the price of butter has gone down.* **4** on paper: *Write these words down in your notebooks.*

down[2] *prep.* **1** at, in, near, or towards a lower part of something: *The ball is rolling down the hill.* **2** along: *Jim lives further down the road than Duncan.*

downhearted /ˌdaʊnˈhɑːtɪd/ *adj.* sad: *You look downhearted.*

downhill /ˌdaʊnˈhɪl/ *adv.* to a lower place: *A bicycle can go fast downhill.*

downpour /ˈdaʊnpɔː(r)/ *n.* heavy fall of rain.

downstairs /ˌdaʊnˈsteəz/ *adv.* to or on a lower floor of a building: *We went downstairs from the kitchen to the cellar.* **downstairs** /ˈdaʊnsteəz/ *adj.:* *the downstairs rooms.*

downward /ˈdaʊnwəd/ *adj.* moving, going, etc. to a lower place: *a downward path from the top of a hill.* **downwards** /ˈdaʊnwədz/ *adv.:* *The lift went downwards from the sixth to the first floor.*

doze /dəʊz/ *v.* sleep lightly for a short time: *Grandfather often dozes in his chair.* **doze** *n.*

dozen /ˈdʌzn/ *n.* twelve: *Paul gave Andrea a dozen red roses.* **dozens of,** very many: *Sarah is never lonely because she has dozens of friends.*

Dr. /ˈdɒktə(r)/ *abbrev.* Doctor: *If you're ill I'll telephone Dr. Miller.*

drag /dræg/ *v.* (*pres. part.* dragging, *past part. & past tense* dragged /drægd/) **1** pull something slowly along: *He dragged the heavy sack of potatoes into the shop.* **2** seem to go slowly because it is dull: *Time drags when you are waiting for a bus.*

dragon /ˈdrægən/ *n.* big, dangerous animal with fire in its mouth, which lives only in stories.

drain[1] /dreɪn/ *n.* pipe that takes away dirty water, etc.: *He poured the cold tea down the drain.*

drain[2] *v.* **1** make liquid flow away: *Dig a ditch to drain the water away from the garden.* **2** make a place or a thing dry by letting the water run off: *Kate washed the lettuce and drained it.*

draining-board /ˈdreɪnɪŋ bɔːd/ *n.* place beside a sink where you put wet dishes, etc. to dry.

drama /ˈdrɑːmə/ *n.* **1** (*pl.* dramas) story written for people to act; play: *a drama by Shakespeare.* **2** (no *pl.*) study of plays and acting: *a student of drama.* **3** (*pl.* dramas) exciting thing that happens.

dramatic /drəˈmætɪk/ *adj.* **1** of plays: *a dramatic club.* **2** sudden or exciting: *a dramatic jump from a window of a burning house.* **dramatically** *adv.*

dramatist /ˈdræmətɪst/ *n.* writer of plays: *George Bernard Shaw was a famous dramatist.*

drank /dræŋk/ *past tense* of *v.* drink.

draper /ˈdreɪpə(r)/ *n.* shopkeeper who sells cloth, towels, etc.: *Buy me some thread at the draper's shop.*

draught /drɑːft/ *n.* cold air that comes into a room, etc.: *Let's shut the window because I can feel a draught.* **draughty** *adj.:* *a draughty house.*

draughts /drɑːfts/ *n.* (no *pl.*) game for two players with round, flat pieces on a board of black and white squares.

draw[1] /drɔː/ *n.* equal marks, etc. in a game or competition: *The football match ended in a 1–1 draw.*

draw[2] *v.* (*past part.* drawn /drɔːn/, *past tense* drew /druː/) **1** make pictures with a pen, pencil, etc.: *Degas drew wonderful pictures of horses.* **2** pull something to make it move: *Two horses were drawing the cart.* **3** pull or take something out of a place: *I shall draw £50 from the bank.* **4** come: *The end of the holidays is drawing near.* **draw up,** come to a place and stop: *A car drew up at the gate.* **5** end a game or competition with the same marks, etc. for both sides: *Did the school team win or draw yesterday?*

drawer /drɔː(r)/ n. part of a table, cupboard, etc. like a box that you can pull out and push in.

drawing /'drɔːɪŋ/ n. **1** (no pl.) making pictures with a pen, pencil, etc.: *Do you study drawing at college?* **2** (pl. drawings) picture made with a pen, pencil, etc.: *a fine drawing.*

drawing-pin /'drɔːɪŋ pɪn/ n. short pin with a flat top, which fastens papers to a wall, board, etc.

drawn /drɔːn/ past part. of v. draw.

dreadful /'dredfl/ adj. **1** making you very afraid, very sad, or shocked: *a dreadful disaster.* **2** bad: *What dreadful weather!*

dreadfully /'dredfəlɪ/ adv. very: *I'm dreadfully sorry to hear your bad news.*

dream /driːm/ v. (past part. & past tense dreamed /driːmd/, dreamt /dremt/) **1** have a picture or idea in your mind when you are asleep. **2** hope for something nice in the future: *She dreams she will marry a rich man.* **dream** n.

dreary /'drɪərɪ/ adj. **1** not interesting: *a dreary book.* **2** not bright: *dreary weather.*

drench /drentʃ/ v. make someone or something very wet: *The heavy rain drenched us.*

dress¹ /dres/ n. **1** (no pl.) clothing: *The group of dancers wore national dress.* **2** (pl. dresses) piece of clothing for a woman or girl: *Anita wears a dress for school.*

dress² v. **1** put on clothes: *Dress quickly or you'll be late for school.* **2** wear clothes: *The television news readers dress well.* **3** put clothes on to someone. **get dressed,** put clothes on. **dress up, (a)** wear your best clothes: *Let's dress up and go out to the theatre.* (**b**) put on clothes in a game: *The children are dressing up as pirates.*

dressing /'dresɪŋ/ n. bandage that you put on a hurt part of your body: *You must have a dressing on that cut.*

dressing-gown /'dresɪŋ gaʊn/ n. piece of warm clothing that you wear over your night-clothes.

dressing-room /'dresɪŋ rʊm/ n. room where you change your clothes for playing sport, acting in a play, etc.

dressing-table

drawer

dress¹ 2

drink² 1

drawing

dressing-table /'dresɪŋ teɪbl/ n. bedroom table with a mirror.

drew /druː/ past tense of v. draw.

dried /draɪd/ past tense of v. dry.

drier /'draɪə(r)/ n. instrument for drying hair, clothes, etc.

drift¹ /drɪft/ n. (pl. drifts) sand, snow, etc. that the wind has blown into a pile: *The car was stuck in a snow drift.*

drift² v. move slowly and without a plan: *The empty boat drifted on the sea.*

drill¹ /drɪl/ n. tool for making holes: *a dentist's drill.* **drill** v.: *The workmen drilled a big hole in the High Street.*

drill² n. training someone by doing an exercise again and again: *army drill.* **drill** v.: *The teacher drilled the English class until they knew the words well.*

drink¹ /drɪŋk/ n. **1** (pl. drinks) some water, milk, tea, alcohol, etc. that you take in through the mouth: *a drink of water.* **2** (no pl.) alcohol: *Too much drink makes him feel ill.*

drink² v. (past part. drunk /drʌŋk/, past tense drank /dræŋk/) **1** take water, milk, coffee, etc. in through the mouth: *Babies drink milk.* **2** take in alcohol: *He has drunk so much that he cannot stand.* **drink up,** finish all the liquid in a glass, etc. at once: *Drink up and we'll hurry home.*

drip /drɪp/ v. (*pres. part.* dripping, *past part.* & *past tense* dripped /drɪpt/) **1** fall slowly in small drops: *Water dripped from the tap.* **2** have water, etc. falling slowly from it: *The tap was dripping.*

drive[1] /draɪv/ n. **1** journey in a car or bus: *It's a long drive from Glasgow to London.* **2** road from the gate to the house: *Please park your car on the drive.*

drive[2] v. (*past part.* driven /'drɪvn/, *past tense* drove /drəʊv/) **1** control a car, machine, etc.: *Mr. Collins drives a bus.* **2** travel in a car: *We drove to my grandmother's house for lunch.* **drive up**, drive near and stop: *He drove up and got out of his car.* **3** make someone do something: *His hunger drove him to steal food.* **4** hit something hard: *Colin drove a nail into the wall with his hammer.*

driver /'draɪvə(r)/ n. someone who controls a car, bus, train, etc.: *Ralph is a taxi-driver.*

driving /'draɪvɪŋ/ n. controlling a car, etc.: *I enjoy driving.* **driving** adj.: *If you pass your driving test, you will have a driving-licence.*

drizzle /'drɪzl/ v. rain lightly. **drizzle** n.

droop /druːp/ v. bend or hang down because of being tired or weak: *The flowers are drooping because they have no water.*

drop[1] /drɒp/ n. **1** very small spot of liquid, etc.: *a drop of rain.* **2** fall; going down: *a drop in temperature.*

drop[2] v. (*pres. part.* dropping, *past part.* & *past tense* dropped /drɒpt/) **1** fall: *The apple dropped from the tree to the ground.* **2** let something fall: *Gordon dropped the cup and it broke.* **3** become lower or weaker: *The wind dropped.* **4** let someone get out of a car, etc.: *Shall I drop you at your house?* **5** stop doing something: *I have dropped my music lessons.* **drop in**, visit someone who does not know you are coming: *Please drop in to see us if you are in Bradford.* **drop out**, stop doing something with other people: *I dropped out of the play because I had too much work.*

drought /draʊt/ n. long time of dry weather.

drove /drəʊv/ *past tense* of v. drive.

drown /draʊn/ v. **1** die in water because you cannot breathe: *The little girl fell into the lake and drowned.* **2** kill someone or something by putting it in water: *There were too many kittens so the farmer drowned them.* **drowning** adj.: *John pulled the drowning man into the boat.*

drug /drʌg/ n. **1** medicine that makes sick people well or that takes away pain: *The doctor gave my mother a new drug for her headaches.* **2** dangerous stuff that people eat or inject to make them sleep, or do things they usually do not do: *Heroin is a dangerous drug.* **drug addict** n. someone who cannot stop taking drugs. **drug** v. (*pres. part.* drugging, *past part.* & *past tense* drugged /drʌgd/)

drum /drʌm/ n. **1** hollow instrument that you hit to make music. **2** container, with round sides, for holding oil, water, etc.: *an oil drum.*

drummer /'drʌmə(r)/ n. someone who plays a drum.

drunk[1] /drʌŋk/, **drunken** /'drʌŋkən/ adj. with too much alcohol inside you so that you cannot walk or talk well: *He was drunk at the end of the party. There were many drunken men in the streets.*

drunk[2] *past part.* of v. drink.

drunkard /'drʌŋkəd/ n. someone who often drinks too much alcohol.

dry[1] /draɪ/ adj. **1** not wet: *The wood will burn if it is dry.* **2** with no rain: *a dry day.*

dry[2] v. (*past part.* & *past tense* dried /draɪd/) **1** become dry: *The washing is drying in the sun.* **2** make something dry: *Sally dries her hair in front of the fire.* **dry up**, (**a**) have no water: *The river is drying up because there is no rain:* (**b**) dry dishes: *Dad washes the dishes and Anne dries up.*

dry-clean /ˌdraɪ 'kliːn/ v. make something clean without water: *I had my suit dry-cleaned.* **dry-cleaning** n.

dryer /'draɪə(r)/ n. instrument for drying hair, clothes, etc.: *At the hairdresser's there are a lot of hair dryers.*

duchess /'dʌtʃɪs/ n. (*pl.* duchesses) noblewoman; wife of a duke.

duck[1] /dʌk/ n. water-bird that you often see on a farm or in a park.

duck[2] v. **1** move down or to one

side quickly: *The ball did not hit Roger because he ducked.* **2** go under water, or push someone under water, for a short time: *The big boy ducked all the small boys in the river.*

duckling /'dʌklɪŋ/ *n.* young duck.

due /dju:/ *adj.* **1** that you must pay at once: *The rent is due at the beginning of each month.* **2** planned to come: *What time is the train due?* **due to**, because of something: *The accident was due to bad driving.* **due for**, ready for something: *My car is due for a service.*

duel /'dju:əl/ *n.* fight between two people, with swords or guns.

duet /dju:'et/ *n.* music for two people to sing or play on musical instruments: *Bob and Jenny sang a duet.*

dug /dʌg/ *past part.* & *past tense* of *v.* dig.

duke /dju:k/ *n.* nobleman: *The Duke of Edinburgh is the Queen's husband.*

dull /dʌl/ *adj.* **1** not clear or bright: *dull weather.* **2** stupid; not clever: *a dull student.* **3** not interesting: *The book was so dull that I didn't finish it.*

duly /'dju:lɪ/ *adv.* at the right time; in the way that you expect: *The work was duly finished.*

dumb /dʌm/ *adj.* not able to speak.

dump[1] /dʌmp/ *n.* place where you can leave things that you do not want: *a rubbish dump.* **down in the dumps**, sad.

dump[2] *v.* **1** put something down without care: *Can I dump my bags in your room?* **2** throw away things that you do not want.

dune /dju:n/ *n.* low hill of sand: *We walked over the dunes to the beach.*

dungeon /'dʌndʒən/ *n.* dark prison under the ground.

during /'djʊərɪŋ/ *prep.* **1** for all the time of: *The sun gives us light during the day.* **2** at some time in: *He came in during the film.*

dusk /dʌsk/ *n.* (no *pl.*) evening; time when darkness is coming: *Put the car lights on at dusk.*

dust /dʌst/ *n.* (no *pl.*) dry dirt like fine powder. **dust** *v.* brush or wipe dust off something: *I dusted the furniture.* **dusty** *adj.* covered with dust: *a dusty desk.*

dustbin /'dʌstbɪn/ *n.* container for rubbish: *Throw those empty bottles into the dustbin.*

driver

dustbin

drum 1

drummer   duck

duster /'dʌstə(r)/ *n.* cloth for wiping things clean.

dustman /'dʌstmən/ *n.* (*pl.* dustmen) someone whose job is to take away rubbish.

dustpan /'dʌstpæn/ *n.* flat metal or plastic pan where you put dust from the floor, etc.

duty /'dju:tɪ/ *n.* (*pl.* duties) **1** what you do in your job or in everyday life because it is right: *A man has a duty to earn money for his family.* **on duty**, at work: *Some nurses at the hospital are on duty all night.* **off duty**, not at work: *Come and visit us when you're off duty.* **2** money that you pay to the government when you bring things into the country from another country: *import duty.*

duty-free *adj.* that you can bring into the country without paying money in tax to the government: *duty-free cigarettes.*

dwarf /dwɔ:f/ *n.* person, animal, or plant that is smaller than usual.

dye /daɪ/ *n.* something that puts colour into cloth, paper, hair, etc.: *My skirt is wet and the red dye has come out on to my legs.* **dye** *v.* change the colour of something: *She has been dyeing her hair black for years.*

dyed /daɪd/ *past part.* & *past tense* of *v.* dye.

dynamite /'daɪnəmaɪt/ *n.* (no *pl.*) strong explosive: *The terrorists blew up the bridge with dynamite.*

Ee

each /iːtʃ/ *pron.* (*pl.* all) **1** every person or thing in a group: *There are four boys and I have four apples, so I can give an apple to each.* **2** for one: *The peaches cost 10p each.* **each other:** *Anne and Sue write letters to each other.* **each** *adj.: Each child has a chair and a desk.*

eager /ˈiːgə(r)/ *adj.* wanting something, or wanting to do something, very much: *Antony is eager to ride his new bicycle.* **eagerly** *adv.: 'Oh, please let me go in your boat!' said Beth eagerly.*

eagle /ˈiːgl/ *n.* big bird that catches and kills other birds, small animals, etc.

ear /ɪə(r)/ *n.* one of the parts of a person's or an animal's head that hear: *She put her hands over her ears because the music was too loud.*

earl /ɜːl/ *n.* British nobleman.

earlier /ˈɜːlɪə(r)/ *adj.* that comes before another: *The ten o'clock train will be too late so come by the earlier train.* **earlier** *adv.* before: *Adam came earlier than Jack.*

earliest /ˈɜːlɪəst/ *adj.* that comes first. **earliest** *adv.*

early /ˈɜːlɪ/ *adj.* **1** at the beginning: *Spring is the early part of the year.* **2** before the usual time: *An early passenger must wait for the train.* **early** *adv.: The sun sets early in winter.*

earn /ɜːn/ *v.* **1** get money for doing work: *The driver earns £400 a month.* **2** receive something because you have worked well or done something good: *You've earned a holiday!*

earnest /ˈɜːnɪst/ *adj.* serious: *An earnest student works hard.* **earnestly** *adv.*

earnings /ˈɜːnɪŋz/ *n.* (*pl.*) money that you receive for work.

earring /ˈɪərɪŋ/ *n.* pretty ring that you wear on your ear.

earth /ɜːθ/ *n.* (no *pl.*) **1** this world; the planet where we live: *The moon goes round the earth.* **2** land; ground: *Sam shot the bird and it fell to earth.* **3** soil: *Flowers will not grow well in poor earth.*

earthquake /ˈɜːθkweɪk/ *n.* sudden strong shaking of the ground.

earthworm /ˈɜːθwɜːm/ *n.* long, thin worm that lives in the soil.

ease /iːz/ *n.* (no *pl.*) **with ease**, with no trouble: *The cat climbed the tree with ease.*

easel /ˈiːzl/ *n.* thing that holds a blackboard or a picture while the artist is painting it.

easily /ˈiːzəlɪ/ *adv.* with no trouble: *Tom is a good runner and will easily win the race.*

east /iːst/ *n.* (no *pl.*) where the sun comes up in the morning. **east** *adj.: When the wind blows from the east we call it an east wind.* **east** *adv.* towards the east: *The ship sailed east from Plymouth to Southampton.* **easterly** /ˈiːstəlɪ/ *adj.* to or from a place that is east: *an easterly wind.* **eastern** /ˈiːstən/ *adj.* of, from, or in the east part of a town, country, or the world: *Cambridge is in eastern England.* **eastwards** /ˈiːstwədz/ *adv.* towards the east: *From Bristol we drove eastwards to London.*

easy /ˈiːzɪ/ *adj.* **1** simple; that you can do or understand with no trouble: *I did the sum quickly because it was easy.* **2** giving no trouble or pain: *We are not tired because it was an easy journey.* **3** comfortable: *An easy chair has soft arms, back, and seat.* **take things easy, take it easy,** not worry or work too much.

eat /iːt/ *v.* (*past part.* eaten /ˈiːtn/, *past tense* ate /et/) put food in your mouth and swallow it: *She is fat because she eats a lot.* **eat up,** finish what you are eating: *Eat up—we must leave soon!*

echo /ˈekəʊ/ *n.* (*pl.* echoes) sound that a wall sends back so that you can hear it again. **echo** *v.: Our voices echoed when we shouted in the cave.*

economical /ˌiːkəˈnɒmɪkl/ *adj.* using money, goods, etc. well and carefully: *It is more economical to make your clothes than to buy them.* **economically** *adv.*

economics /ˌiːkəˈnɒmɪks/ *n.* (no *pl.*) study of the way countries spend their money, use their goods, workers, etc. **economist** /ɪˈkɒnəmɪst/ *n.* someone who studies economics.

economy /ɪˈkɒnəmɪ/ *n.* (*pl.* economies) **1** way that a country spends its money, uses its goods and workers, etc. **2** using money, goods, etc. well and carefully. **economic** /ˌiːkəˈnɒmɪk/ *adj.*: *The European Economic Community.*

edge /edʒ/ *n.* **1** outside end of something: *If you put that pot on the edge of the table it will fall off.* **2** sharp, cutting part of a knife.

editor /ˈedɪtə(r)/ *n.* someone who prepares or organizes a newspaper, periodical, or book.

educate /ˈedʒʊkeɪt/ *v.* teach someone; show someone how to read, write, and think: *He was educated at a good school.* **education** /ˌedʒʊˈkeɪʃn/ *n.*: *the Minister of Education.*

eel /iːl/ *n.* long fish that looks like a snake.

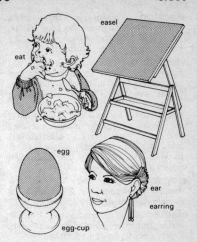

effect /ɪˈfekt/ *n.* what happens because of something: *The brown grass is the effect of the dry weather.* **have an effect on something**, make something change: *Her illness has had a bad effect on her work.*

efficient /ɪˈfɪʃnt/ *adj.* **1** who plans and works well: *an efficient farmer.* **2** that works well: *an efficient machine.* **efficiently** *adv.*

effort /ˈefət/ *n.* trying hard; hard work: *Hugh made a big effort to move the rock.*

e.g. /ˌiːˈdʒiː/ *abbrev.* for example.

egg /eg/ *n.* round thing with a shell, that comes from a bird: *We had eggs and bacon for breakfast.*

egg-cup /ˈeg kʌp/ *n.* small cup to hold a boiled egg when you are eating it.

eiderdown /ˈaɪdədaʊn/ *n.* thick, warm bed-cover.

eight /eɪt/ *n.* number 8. **eight** *adj.*: *I have eight fingers.* **eighth** /eɪtθ/ *adj.* 8th: *I can find seven, but where is the eighth plate?*

eighteen /ˌeɪˈtiːn/ *n.* number 18. **eighteen** *adj.*: *There are eighteen boys in the class.* **eighteenth** /ˌeɪˈtiːnθ/ *adj.* 18th.

eighty /ˈeɪtɪ/ *n.* (*pl.* eighties) number 80. **eighty** *adj.*: *He has eighty cows.* **eightieth** /ˈeɪtɪəθ/ *adj.* 80th.

either¹ /ˈaɪðə(r)/ *adj.* **1** one of two: *Sit on either chair.* **2** each: *There is a path on either side of the road.* **either** *pron.* one of two people or things: *There were two roses on the bush, but I did not pick either.*

either² *adv.* also (after a verb with 'not'): *Amy does not like the blue car and she does not like the red one either.* **either . . . or**, words to show two different things or people that you can choose: *You can either go swimming or play tennis.*

elastic /ɪˈlæstɪk/ *n.* (no *pl.*) material that you can pull or push into another shape. It will go back to its own shape afterwards: *His trousers stay round his waist because they have elastic in the top.* **elastic** *adj.*

elbow /ˈelbəʊ/ *n.* place in the middle of your arm where it bends.

elder /ˈeldə(r)/ *adj.* older of two people: *My younger son is four and my elder son is six.* **elder** *pron.*

elderly /ˈeldəlɪ/ *adj.* rather old: *My parents are elderly and cannot walk very far now.*

eldest /ˈeldɪst/ *adj.* oldest of three or more people: *George is the eldest of our six children.* **eldest** *pron.*

elect /ɪˈlekt/ *v.* choose someone or some people: *to elect a chairman.*

election /ɪ'lekʃn/ n. time when people choose a person to be a leader, etc. **general election**, choosing people for a new government.

electricity /ɪ,lek'trɪsətɪ/ n. (no pl.) power that comes through wires and can make heat and light and move things. **electric** /ɪ'lektrɪk/ adj. making or using electricity: an electric light. **electrical** /ɪ'lektrɪkl/ adj. of electricity: An electrical engineer makes machines that use electricity. **electrician** /ɪ,lek'trɪʃn/ n. someone whose job is to work with electricity: The electrician repaired our television.

elegant /'elɪgənt/ adj. **1** very well dressed: an elegant lady. **2** beautiful: an elegant vase. **elegantly** adv.

elementary /,elɪ'mentrɪ/ adj. **1** of or for beginners: an elementary dictionary. **2** very easy to do or understand.

elephant /'elɪfənt/ n. very big, wild animal, with a long, hanging nose called a trunk.

eleven /ɪ'levn/ n. **1** number 11. **2** cricket or football team. **eleven** adj.: I saw eleven cows. **eleventh** /ɪ'levnθ/ adj. 11th.

else /els/ adv. **1** more; extra: Did anyone else come with James? **2** other; instead: The Grand Hotel was full so we stayed somewhere else. **or else**, if not: You must leave now, or else you'll be late.

elsewhere /'elsweə(r)/ adv. in or to another place: Mr. and Mrs. Houston lived next door but now they live elsewhere.

embark /ɪm'bɑːk/ v. **1** go on to a ship or aeroplane: They embarked at Liverpool. **2** start to do something: When he left school, Frank embarked on a career in industry.

embarrassment /ɪm'bærəsmənt/ n. worry about what other people will think: Jean's big feet are an embarrassment to her. **embarrass** /ɪm'bærəs/ v. make you feel embarrassment: Jean's big feet embarrass her. **embarrassed** /ɪm'bærəst/ adj. feeling or showing embarrassment. **embarrassing** /ɪm'bærəsɪŋ/ adj. making you feel embarrassment.

embassy /'embəsɪ/ n. (pl. embassies) **1** group of people whose job is to speak and act for their own government in

another country. **2** place where embassy people live and work.

embrace /ɪm'breɪs/ v. put your arms around someone to show love. **embrace** n.

embroider /ɪm'brɔɪdə(r)/ v. make beautiful patterns and pictures with thread on cloth. **embroidered** /ɪm'brɔɪdɪd/ adj.: an embroidered blouse. **embroidery** n.: We learn embroidery at school.

emerald /'emərəld/ n. **1** (pl. emeralds) green jewel. **2** (no pl.) green colour. **emerald** adj.

emerge /ɪ'mɜːdʒ/ v. come out from a place: The road was dark and then the moon emerged from behind the clouds.

emergency /ɪ'mɜːdʒənsɪ/ n. (pl. emergencies) sudden, serious happening when people must give quick help. **in an emergency**, when a problem suddenly comes: I can lend you some money in an emergency. **emergency** adj.: When the fire started we left the theatre by the emergency exit.

emigrate /'emɪgreɪt/ v. go away from your country to live in another country: Many Italians emigrated to America. **emigration** /,emɪ'greɪʃn/ n. **emigrant** /'emɪgrənt/ n. someone who emigrates.

emotion /ɪ'məʊʃn/ n. strong feeling: Love, hate, and fear are emotions. **emotional** /ɪ'məʊʃənl/ adj.

emperor /'empərə(r)/ n. king of a big country or a group of countries.

emphasize /'emfəsaɪz/ v. speak firmly to show that what you are saying is important: He emphasized that I must drive slowly.

empire /'empaɪə(r)/ n. country or group of countries that a king or an emperor rules: the Roman Empire.

employ /ɪm'plɔɪ/ v. pay someone to do work for you: My brother employs twelve men. **be employed**, have work: He's employed at the station.

employee /,ɪmplɔɪ'iː/ n. someone who is paid to work.

employer /ɪm'plɔɪə(r)/ n. someone who pays other people to do work for him.

employment /ɪm'plɔɪmənt/ n. (no pl.) job: When he left school he found employment as a lorry driver.

empress /'emprɪs/ n. (pl. empresses) queen of a big country or a group of countries; wife of an emperor: *Queen Victoria was the Empress of India.*

empty[1] /'emptɪ/ adj. **1** with nothing inside: *an empty purse.* **2** with no writing on it: *an empty page.*

empty[2] v. take away everything from inside so that there is nothing left: *Mark drank until he had emptied his cup.*

enable /ɪ'neɪbl/ v. make someone able to do something: *Your help enabled me to finish the job.*

enamel /ɪ'næml/ n. (no pl.) very hard paint for metal. **enamel** adj. covered with enamel: *We have enamel plates when we go camping.*

enchant /ɪn'tʃɑːnt/ v. **1** use magic on someone or something. **2** please someone very much: *Fonteyn's dancing enchanted the audience.* **enchanting** adj. very lovely: *an enchanting face.*

enclose /ɪn'kləʊz/ n. **1** shut a place in on all sides: *A high wall encloses the prison.* **2** put something inside a parcel, letter, etc.: *I enclose my photograph with this letter.*

enclosure /ɪn'kləʊʒə(r)/ n. **1** place that is shut on all sides: *A cage is an enclosure for birds.* **2** something that you have put inside a parcel, letter, etc.

encourage /ɪn'kʌrɪdʒ/ v. give someone hope, courage, support, etc.: *The big crowd encouraged their football team by cheering.* **encouraging** adj.: *We were pleased with Ann's encouraging school report.* **encouragingly** adv.

encouragement /ɪn'kʌrɪdʒmənt/ n. (no pl.) help and support: *My parents give me a lot of encouragement.*

encyclopaedia /ɪn,saɪklə'piːdɪə/ n. book or set of books telling the facts about many things.

end[1] /end/ n. **1** where something stops: *the end of the road.* **2** when something stops: *the end of a story.* **3** small piece that remains: *a cigarette end.* **at an end**, finished: *My holiday is at an end and I must go back to work tomorrow.* **come to an end**, stop: *Jenny turned off the radio when the programme came to an end.* **for days, weeks, months,** or **years on end,** for

embark 1

elephant

embroider

a very long time: *In the winter it rains for days on end.* **in the end**, at last: *We looked everywhere and, in the end, we found the key.* **make ends meet**, earn enough money for living: *When my father died my mother had to get work to make ends meet.* **put an end to something**, stop something happening: *The rain put an end to our netball game.*

end[2] v. **1** stop: *When the concert ended we went home.* **2** finish something: *We ended our holiday with a visit to Stratford.* **end up**, finish: *The bad man ended up in prison.*

ending /'endɪŋ/ n. last part of a word, story, etc.

endless /'endlɪs/ adj. with no end; not stopping: *the endless noise of the sea on the beach.* **endlessly** adv.

endure /ɪn'djʊə(r)/ v. have pain, trouble, problems, etc. but go on bravely: *Captain Scott endured a terrible journey in the Antarctic.* **endurance** n.: *a journey of endurance.*

enemy /'enəmɪ/ n. (pl. enemies) someone who hates or wishes to hurt another person. **make an enemy**, make someone hate you: *The cruel leader made many enemies.* **enemy** adj.: *enemy soldiers.*

energetic /,enə'dʒetɪk/ adj. doing a lot of things because you are strong: *an energetic man.*

energy /'enədʒɪ/ n. (no pl.) 1 power of a person to do many things: *That man has so much energy that he can work as hard as three men!* 2 force or power to make things, machines, etc. move or work: *atomic energy.*

engage /ɪn'geɪdʒ/ v. give work to someone: *The manager of the restaurant engaged a new cook yesterday.*

engaged /ɪn'geɪdʒd/ past part. of v. engage. **be engaged** 1 be busy: *I'm afraid the director can't see you—he's engaged.* 2 be in use: *I couldn't telephone my uncle because his telephone line was engaged.* 3 have promised to marry someone: *Jack and Jill are engaged.*

engagement /ɪn'geɪdʒmənt/ n. 1 promise to marry someone. 2 plan or promise to meet someone: *I can't come at 3 o'clock because I have another engagement then.*

engine /'endʒɪn/ n. 1 machine that gives power or that makes things move: *car engine.* 2 locomotive; part of the train that pulls the rest.

engine-driver /'endʒɪn draɪvə(r)/ n. driver of a railway train.

engineering /ˌendʒɪ'nɪərɪŋ/ n. (no pl.) 1 study of how machines work. 2 job of someone, called an **engineer**, who plans and makes machines.

enjoy /ɪn'dʒɔɪ/ v. like something very much: *Do you enjoy football?* **enjoy yourself**, have a happy time: *I enjoyed myself at the party.*

enjoyable /ɪn'dʒɔɪəbl/ adj. pleasant; nice: *Thank you for a most enjoyable party.* **enjoyably** adv.

enjoyment /ɪn'dʒɔɪmənt/ n. (no pl.) pleasure.

enlarge /ɪn'lɑːdʒ/ v. make something bigger: *Can you enlarge this photograph for me?* **enlargement** n. photograph, etc. that someone has made bigger.

enormous /ɪ'nɔːməs/ adj. 1 very big: *An elephant is an enormous animal.* 2 very great: *The party was enormous fun!*

enormously /ɪ'nɔːməslɪ/ adv. very much: *London has changed enormously since 1900.*

enough /ɪ'nʌf/ adj. as much as you need; as many as you need: *There's enough food for everyone.* **enough** n.: *The poor man doesn't eat enough.* **enough** adv.: *Is Carol old enough to go to school?*

enquire /ɪn'kwaɪə(r)/ v. ask; try to get an answer by saying something: *'How are you feeling?' enquired my uncle.*

enquiry /ɪn'kwaɪərɪ/ n. (pl. enquiries) asking about something: *I want to make an enquiry about train times.*

enter /'entə(r)/ v. 1 come or go into a place: *Please enter the house by the back door.* 2 become a member of a group, etc.: *to enter university.* 3 write down a name or other information: *Please enter your names on this list.* **enter for**, give your name for a competition, examination, etc.: *Lloyd has entered for the big race on Saturday.*

enterprise /'entəpraɪz/ n. (pl. enterprises) plan to do something new that will perhaps be difficult or dangerous: *Building the Panama Canal was a bold enterprise.*

enterprising /'entəpraɪzɪŋ/ adj. being brave enough and ready to do new things.

entertain /ˌentə'teɪn/ v. 1 give food and drink to visitors; have visitors in your home: *Kay is busy cooking because we are entertaining this evening.* 2 make someone laugh or enjoy himself: *Her funny stories entertained us.*

entertaining /ˌentə'teɪnɪŋ/ adj. amusing or interesting: *an entertaining story.*

entertainment /ˌentə'teɪnmənt/ n. show, party, concert, etc. that people enjoy.

enthusiasm /ɪn'θjuːzɪæzəm/ n. (no pl.) great interest and liking: *I don't like golf, but my brother plays it with enthusiasm.* **enthusiastic** /ɪnˌθjuːzɪ'æstɪk/ adj. with enthusiasm: *an enthusiastic footballer.* **enthusiastically** adv.

entire /ɪn'taɪə(r)/ adj. whole; total; with all parts: *The ship sank with the entire crew.*

entirely /ɪn'taɪəlɪ/ adv. totally: *I entirely agree with you.*

entrance /'entrəns/ n. 1 (pl. entrances) way into a place: *The car is waiting at the front entrance.* 2 (no pl.) right to go into a place: *He was refused entrance to the country because he did not have a passport.* 3 (no pl.) becoming a member of a university or a club, etc. **entrance fee** n. money that you pay when you become a member.

entry /'entrɪ/ n. **1** (pl. entries) coming into a place: *Pay on entry into the bus.* **2** (pl. entries) way into a place.

envelope /'envələʊp/ n. paper cover for a letter.

envy /'envɪ/ n. (no pl.) feeling of sadness and anger because you want what another person has: *'You are so lucky to have a brother'*, *said the boy with envy.* **envy** v.: *The poor man envied the rich man.* **envious** /'envɪəs/ adj.: *I am envious of your holiday in Madeira.*

epidemic /ˌepɪ'demɪk/ n. disease that goes quickly from one person to another in the same place: *an epidemic of measles in the village.* **epidemic** adj.

equal¹ /'iːkwəl/ adj. same; as big, as much, or as good as another: *Women ask for equal pay because they work as hard as men.*

equal² v. (pres. part. equalling, past part. & past tense equalled /iːkwəld/) **1** be exactly the same amount as something: *Two plus two equals four.* **2** be as strong, good, etc. as someone: *Simon is younger but he equals his brother in all sports.*

equality /ɪ'kwɒlətɪ/ n. (no pl.) being the same; having the same rights: *In some countries black people do not have equality with white people.*

equally /'iːkwəlɪ/ adv. **1** by the same amount: *If we share the apple equally, we shall each have half.* **2** in the same way: *Chris swims well, but you are equally good.*

equator /ɪ'kweɪtə(r)/ n. (no pl.) line on maps around the middle of the world, from east to west.

equip /ɪ'kwɪp/ v. (pres. part. equipping, past. part. & past tense equipped /iːkwɪpt/) put in a place, or give someone, all the tools, instruments, etc. that are needed: *Alec equipped his boat for the long voyage.*

equipment /ɪ'kwɪpmənt/ n. (no pl.) special things that you need to do a job: *Pens, pencils, and paper are writing equipment.*

erect /ɪ'rekt/ v. build something; put something up: *to erect a tent.* **erection** /ɪ'rekʃn/ n.

errand /'erənd/ n. short journey to fetch something: *My aunt sent me on an errand to get some butter.*

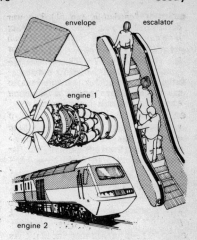

envelope

escalator

engine 1

engine 2

error /'erə(r)/ n. mistake: *He must write the letter again because he has made some errors.*

erupt /ɪ'rʌpt/ v. burst out: *Smoke and flames came out of the volcano as it erupted.* **eruption** /ɪ'rʌpʃn/ n.

escalator /'eskəleɪtə(r)/ n. stairs that move and can carry people up or down.

escape /ɪ'skeɪp/ v. **1** get free from something or someone: *The bird escaped from the cage.* **2** find a way out of a place: *Water is escaping from the broken pipe.* **3** stay, keep, or get away from something that you do not like: *We went to the Bahamas to escape the cold weather in England.* **escape** n. **make your escape**, get free; get away from a place. **have a narrow escape**, be safe from a danger that nearly happened.

escort /'eskɔːt/ n. people, ships, aeroplanes, etc. that go with others to keep them safe: *The king had an escort of soldiers.* **escort** /ɪ'skɔːt/ v. go with someone: *Jim escorted me to the concert.*

especial /ɪ'speʃl/ adj. better, more important, etc. than. **especially** adv. mainly; chiefly: *Kim loves all fruit, especially bananas.*

essay /'eseɪ/ n. short piece of writing on a subject: *Our teacher asked us to write essays on 'My Summer Holidays'.*

essential /ɪ'senʃl/ adj. very important; that you must do or have: *Water is essential for plants.*

estate /ɪ'steɪt/ n. piece of land that one person owns: *The Queen owns the estate of Balmoral.* **housing estate** n. large group of houses that one builder has made. **estate agent** n. someone who buys and sells buildings and land for others.

estimate /'estɪmeɪt/ v. work out how much, big, long, expensive, etc. something is. **estimate** /'estɪmət/ n.: *We made an estimate of the cost of the holiday.*

estuary /'estʃʊərɪ/ n. (pl. estuaries) wide mouth of a river, where it meets the sea.

etc. /ɪt'setərə/ abbrev. (Latin et cetera) and other things; and the rest: *The days of the week are Monday, Tuesday, Wednesday, etc.*

eternal /ɪ'tɜ:nl/ adj. with no beginning or end; lasting for ever: *God is eternal.* **eternally** adv.: *I shall be eternally grateful to you for your help.*

evacuate /ɪ'vækjʊ:eɪt/ v. take people or things away from a place to keep them safe: *When the police heard that there was a bomb in the street, they evacuated everybody from the houses.* **evacuation** /ɪ,vækjʊ:'eɪʃn/ n.

eve /i:v/ n. day or night before a special day: *New Year's Eve is the day before 1 January.*

even[1] /'i:vn/ adj. **1** flat; smooth: *She tripped and fell because the floor was not even.* **2** the same: *Each team had two goals, so they were even.* **3** that you can divide by 2 so that there is nothing left: *4, 6, and 8 are even numbers but 5 and 7 are not even.* **be even, get even**, hurt someone because he has hurt you: *Bill will try to get even because you took his bicycle.*

even[2] adv. word that makes what you say very strong: *This book is so easy that even a child can read it. Ben can run fast but I can run even faster.* **even though**, although: *Even though he was tired, he helped me with my work.*

evening /'i:vnɪŋ/ n. end of the day, between afternoon and night.

event /ɪ'vent/ n. **1** something that happens: *The first day at school is a big event in a child's life.* **2** one of the races,

competitions, etc. in a programme of sport: *The next event will be the high jump.*

eventually /ɪ'ventʃʊəlɪ/ adv. in the end; after some time: *We waited three days for the letter and eventually it came.*

ever /'evə(r)/ adv. at any time: *Have you ever climbed a mountain?* **for ever**, always: *Christians believe that God will live for ever.* **ever since**, from the time when: *I have liked reading ever since I was a child.* **ever so**, very: *Jo is ever so clever!* **ever such a**, a very: *Jo is ever such a clever boy.* **than ever**, than before: *This year records cost more than ever.*

evergreen /'evəgri:n/ adj. with green leaves all the year: *Palm trees are evergreen.*

every /'evrɪ/ adj. each one of: *Julia wears a ring on every finger, but I wear only one.* **every now and then, every so often,** sometimes: *Robert visits us every so often.*

everybody /'evrɪbɒdɪ/ pron. (no pl.) each person; all people: *It will be a big party because everybody in the street is coming.*

everyday /'evrɪdeɪ/ adj. done or happening each day: *School is an everyday event for most children.*

everyone /'evrɪwʌn/ pron. (no pl.) each person; all people: *The office is empty because everyone has gone home.*

everything /'evrɪθɪŋ/ pron. (no pl.) each thing; all things.

everywhere /'evrɪweə(r)/ adv. at, in, or to all places.

evidence /'evɪdəns/ n. (no pl.) proof; something that shows what has happened and why it has happened: *His wet coat was evidence that he had been outside.* **give evidence**, tell what you know about someone or something in a law court: *The woman gave evidence that she had seen the man steal the money.*

evident /'evɪdənt/ adj. clear; easy to see; easy to understand: *It is evident that Jenny is happy, because she is smiling.* **evidently** adv.

evil /'i:vl/ adj. wicked; very bad.

exact /ɪgˈzækt/ adj. with no mistakes; totally correct: *an exact model of an aeroplane.*

exactly[1] /ɪgˈzæklɪ/ adv. **1** correctly: *Please tell me exactly what you saw.* **2** just: *This dress is exactly what I wanted.*

exactly[2] exclam. I quite agree; that is so.

exaggerate /ɪgˈzædʒəreɪt/ v. say that something is bigger, better, worse, etc. than it really is: *The boy exaggerated when he said he was so hungry he could eat an elephant!* **exaggeration** /ɪgˌzædʒəˈreɪʃn/ n.

exam. /ɪgˈzæm/ abbrev. examination.

examination /ɪgˌzæmɪˈneɪʃn/ n. **1** looking at something or someone carefully: *The doctor made an examination of the sick child.* **2** test of what someone knows or can do: *Linda has passed her summer examinations.*

examine /ɪgˈzæmɪn/ v. **1** look at something or someone carefully. **2** ask someone questions to find out what he knows or can do; test someone: *The teacher will examine the class on everything they have learnt this year.* **examiner** /ɪgˈzæmɪnə(r)/ n. someone who tests what people know.

example /ɪgˈzɑːmpl/ n. **1** something that shows how a rule works: *The sentences in this dictionary give examples of how to use words.* **2** one thing that shows what others of the same kind are like: *The Tower of London is a fine example of an English castle.* **for example**, let me give you an example: *Do you have a hobby—for example, painting?*

exasperate /ɪgˈzæspəreɪt/ v. make someone rather angry: *The slow journey exasperated me.* **exasperated** /ɪgˈzæspəreɪtɪd/ adj. rather angry. **exasperation** /ɪgˌzæspəˈreɪʃn/ n.

excavate /ˈekskəveɪt/ v. dig to make or uncover something: *They are excavating a tunnel through the hill.*

exceed /ɪkˈsiːd/ v. be more, greater, etc. than another; go beyond another: *My brother was fined for exceeding the speed limit.*

excellent /ˈeksələnt/ adj. very good: *an excellent film.* **excellently** adv.

except /ɪkˈsept/, **excepting** prep. but

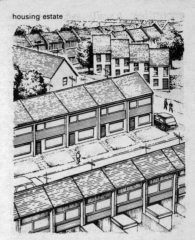

housing estate

not: *He works every day, except Saturday and Sunday.*

exception /ɪkˈsepʃn/ n. something or someone that is not the same as others. **with the exception of**, without; not counting.

exceptional /ɪkˈsepʃənl/ adj. not usual: *Hot weather is exceptional in England.*

exceptionally /ɪkˈsepʃənəlɪ/ adv. unusually; very: *an exceptionally fat man.*

exchange /ɪksˈtʃeɪndʒ/ v. give one thing and get another thing for it: *When I went to France I exchanged my English money for French money.* **exchange** n. **in exchange for**, in the place of something that you have given to someone: *I'll give you three sweets in exchange for an apple.*

excite /ɪkˈsaɪt/ v. make someone full of strong feeling: *The circus tickets will excite the children.* **excitement** n. **excited** /ɪkˈsaɪtɪd/ adj. full of strong feeling: *Paul was excited about his first trip in an aeroplane.* **exciting** adj. making you full of happy interest: *What exciting news!*

exclaim /ɪkˈskleɪm/ v. say something or cry out suddenly and loudly because you feel surprise, anger, pain, etc.: *'Look—there's a fire!' exclaimed Dan.* **exclamation** /ˌekskləˈmeɪʃn/ n. **exclamation mark**, punctuation mark (!) that you put at the end of a sentence to show loud or strong words.

exclude /ɪk'sklu:d/ v. keep out or shut out something or someone: *Little Anita cried because the older children excluded her from their games.*

excluding /ɪk'sklu:dɪŋ/ pres. part. of v. exclude. without; if you do not count: *There are eleven months in the year, excluding January.*

excursion /ɪk'skɜ:ʃn/ n. short journey to see something interesting or to enjoy yourself.

excuse[1] /ɪk'skju:s/ n. what you say or write to explain why you have done something wrong: *He made an excuse for being late.*

excuse[2] /ɪk'skju:z/ v. 1 forgive someone: *Please excuse me for being late.* 2 say that someone need not do something: *The teacher excused me from sport because I had a headache.* **excuse me,** words that you use when you want somebody to listen to you or to say that you are sorry: *Excuse me, is anybody sitting here?*

execute /'eksɪkju:t/ v. kill someone to punish him. **execution** /ˌeksɪ'kju:ʃn/ n.

exercise[1] /'eksəsaɪz/ n. 1 (no pl.) moving your body to keep it strong and well: *I walk to work every day because it is good exercise.* 2 (pl. exercises) special way of training your body to keep it strong and well: *Have you done your exercises today?* 3 (pl. exercises) way of training soldiers, sailors, etc.: *military exercises.* 4 (pl. exercises) way of training the mind; learning something: *We do English exercises to help us learn good English.* **exercise book** n. book of clean pages where a pupil writes.

exercise[2] v. move your body, or make someone move his body, to keep strong and well: *Your dog will get fat if you do not exercise it.*

exhaust /ɪg'zɔ:st/ n. 1 (no pl.) steam, gas, etc. that comes out of an engine. 2 (pl. exhausts) pipe that brings steam, gas, etc. out of an engine.

exhausted /ɪg'zɔ:stɪd/ adj. very tired: *We were exhausted after the long walk.*

exhibit /ɪg'zɪbɪt/ v. show something to people, for selling or for interest: *The gallery is exhibiting French paintings.*

exhibition /ˌeksɪ'bɪʃn/ n. show; group of things for people to see: *an exhibition of paintings.*

exile /'eksaɪl/ n. 1 (no pl.) being sent away from your own country as a punishment, etc. 2 (pl. exiles) someone who must live far away from his own country. **exile** v.

exist /ɪg'zɪst/ v. be; live: *Does life exist on other planets?*

existence /ɪg'zɪstəns/ n. (no pl.) being. **come into existence**, start to be, live, happen, etc.: *We do not know when the world came into existence.*

exit /'eksɪt/ n. 1 way out of a place. 2 going out of a place.

expand /ɪk'spænd/ v. become bigger; make something bigger: *Elastic expands when you pull it.* **expansion** /ɪk'spænʃn/ n.

expect /ɪk'spekt/ v. 1 think that something will happen: *Nick is tired so I expect he will go to bed early.* 2 think that someone or something will come: *I can't go out because I am expecting visitors.* 3 know that you will have a baby: *She is expecting her first child next month.* 4 think that something is true: *I expect the weather is cold in England at the moment.* **I expect so**, I think that is true; I think that will happen. **be expected to**, be supposed to do something; must do something: *I'm expected to arrive at work at 9 a.m.*

expedition /ˌekspɪ'dɪʃn/ n. journey to do something special or find out about something: *Scott's expedition to the South Pole.*

expel /ɪk'spel/ v. (pres. part. expelling, past part. & past tense expelled /ɪk-'speld/) make someone go away from a place: *The headmaster expelled the boy from the school.*

expense /ɪk'spens/ n. (no pl.) cost; how much money, time, etc. you spend on something: *Laurie's holiday was a big expense.* **at someone's expense,** with money from someone: *He was educated at his uncle's expense.*

expensive /ɪk'spensɪv/ adj. costing a lot of money: *expensive clothes.*

experience /ɪk'spɪərɪəns/ n. 1 (no pl.) knowing about things because you have done or seen them: *Has he got any experience of farming?* 2 (pl. experiences) something that happens to you: *The car crash was a bad experience for her.*

experiment /ɪk'sperɪmənt/ n. something that you do to see and study what happens so that you will learn more. **experiment** v.

expert /'ekspɜːt/ n. someone who knows a lot about something: *A gardening expert tells us how to grow plants well.* **expert** adj. clever; knowing a lot about something.

explain /ɪk'spleɪn/ v. **1** show, tell, etc. what something means: *This book explains the meaning of words.* **2** show why something happened: *Can you explain why this window is broken?*

explanation /ˌekspləˈneɪʃn/ n. saying or showing what something means, why something was done, etc.: *'What is the explanation of this water on the floor?' she asked.*

explode /ɪk'spləʊd/ v. burst open dangerously, with a very loud noise: *Bombs explode.*

explore /ɪk'splɔː(r)/ v. go through or into a place to learn about it: *Dr. Livingstone explored Africa.* **exploration** /ˌeksplə'reɪʃn/ n.: *a journey of exploration.* **explorer** /ɪk'splɔːrə(r)/ n. someone who explores.

explosion /ɪk'spləʊʒn/ n. bursting open with a very loud noise.

explosive /ɪk'spləʊsɪv/ adj. that can burst dangerously: *Bombs are explosive.* **explosive** n. thing that can explode: *Dynamite is an explosive.*

export /'ekspɔːt/ n. **1** (pl. exports) something that one country sells to another country: *Tea is an Indian export.* **2** (no pl.) selling things to other countries: *Spain grows oranges for export.* **export** /ɪk'spɔːt/ v. sell goods, etc. to another country: *Brazil exports coffee.*

express¹ /ɪk'spres/ adj. that goes quickly: *express mail.*

express² n. (pl. expresses) fast train.

express³ v. show or say something: *I am writing a letter to express my thanks for a lovely holiday.*

expression /ɪk'spreʃn/ n. **1** look on your face that shows your feeling: *I could tell from his expression that he was angry.* **2** word; group of words; way of saying something: *'Shut up!' is a rude expression.*

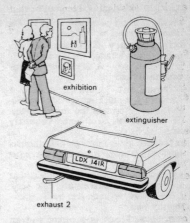

exhibition

extinguisher

exhaust 2

exquisite /'ekskwɪzɪt/ adj. finely made: *an exquisite painting.* **exquisitely** adv.

extend /ɪk'stend/ v. **1** make something longer: *He extended his visit from one week to three weeks.* **2** spread out: *This park extends for a long way.*

extension /ɪk'stenʃn/ n. **1** making something bigger or longer: *I asked my boss for an extension of my holiday.* **2** something that you add on: *We are building an extension on to our house so that my grandmother can live with us.*

extent /ɪk'stent/ n. (no pl.) how big, how long, etc. a place is: *What is the extent of your farm?*

exterior /ek'stɪərɪə(r)/ adj. on, of, in, or from the outside: *Roses grow over the exterior walls of our house.* **exterior** n. part or place outside.

external /ek'stɜːnl/ adj. of, on, or for the outside: *This medicine for insect bites is for external use only, so do not drink it!* **externally** adv.

extinguish /ɪk'stɪŋgwɪʃ/ v. **1** put out a light: *We extinguished the lamp before we went to bed.* **2** put out a fire: *The firemen extinguished the fire with water.*

extinguisher /ɪk'stɪŋgwɪʃə(r)/ n. thing to stop a dangerous fire.

extra /'ekstrə/ adj. more than usual: *I must buy extra bread because friends are coming to tea.* **extra** adv. more than usually: *extra large.*

extract /ık'strækt/ v. take something out of the place where it was: *The dentist extracted my bad tooth.*

extraordinary /ık'strɔ:dnrı/ adj. very unusual; very strange: *An elephant's nose is extraordinary—it is so long!* **extraordinarily** adv.

extravagant /ık'strævəgənt/ adj. **1** spending too much money: *an extravagant man.* **2** costing too much money: *an extravagant meal.* **extravagantly** adv.

extreme /ık'stri:m/ adj. **1** farthest: *I can't see the people at the extreme end of the hall.* **2** very great: *Thank you for your extreme kindness.* **3** with ideas that are too strong. **extremely** adv. very: *I can't work because your radio is extremely loud.*

eye /aı/ n. **1** part of a person's or an animal's head that sees: *Terry has blue eyes.* **catch your eye**, make you look at it: *The pretty girl caught Eric's eye.* **cry your eyes out**, cry very much: *She cried her eyes out when she lost her new sandals.* **in someone's eyes**, as someone thinks: *In his mother's eyes, Richard is the best son in the world.* **keep an eye on**, look after or watch someone or something: *Will you keep an eye on my baby while I go to the shop?* **see eye to eye**, agree with someone: *Mr. Harper doesn't see eye to eye with his neighbour.* **set eyes on**, see or meet someone: *I've never set eyes on that man before.* **turn a blind eye to**, see or know about something that is not right, but not do anything about it. **2** hole like an eye: *You put the thread through the eye of a needle.*

eyebrow /'aıbraʊ/ n. line of short hairs above the eye.

eyelashes /'aılæʃız/ n. (pl.) row of hairs on the eyelid.

eyelid /'aılıd/ n. skin above and below the eye that moves and closes over the eye.

eye-shadow /'aı ʃædəʊ/ n. (no pl.) colour that a girl puts on her eyelids to make her eyes look pretty.

eyesight /'aısaıt/ n. (no pl.) seeing: *I wear glasses because my eyesight is not good.*

eye-witness /'aı wıtnıs/ n. (pl. eye-witnesses) someone who can tell what happened because he saw it: *The police are asking for eye-witnesses to the crime.*

Ff

fable /'feıbl/ n. short story that teaches something: *the fable of the hare and the tortoise.*

face[1] /feıs/ n. front part of the head: *Have you washed your face? **face to face**, looking straight at each other. **keep a straight face**, not laugh at something funny: *I couldn't keep a straight face when he dropped his watch in the soup!* **make a face**, **pull faces**, move parts of your face to show that you do not like something: *She made a face when she saw the pile of work.*

face[2] v. **1** have the face or the front towards something: *The class faces the blackboard. Our house faces the street.* **2** be brave enough to go to someone or something unfriendly or dangerous: *She had to face her angry boss.*

face-cloth /'feıs klɒθ/ n. small cloth for washing the face.

fact /fækt/ n. something that is true or real: *A judge listens to the facts of a crime before he decides how to punish the criminal.* **in fact**, really: *I thought Betty was in the garden, but in fact she was in her room.* **as a matter of fact**, words that you say first to make what you say after more important: *As a matter of fact, we have just bought a new house.*

factory /'fæktərı/ n. (pl. factories) place where people make things, usually with machines: *At the Ford factory, they make cars.*

fade /feıd/ v. lose brightness and colour: *Flowers fade when they come to an end.*

fail /feıl/ v. **1** not be able to do something: *The boys tried to climb the mountain, but they failed because of the bad weather.* **2** not pass an exam, test, etc.: *to fail a driving test.* **3** not do as well as it should; be poor: *The crops failed because of the frost.* **4** not do what is right: *You will be in trouble if you fail to stop at the red light.* **fail** n. **without fail**, for certain: *Bring the money tomorrow without fail.*

failure /'feıljə(r)/ n. someone or something that does not do well: *Our holiday was a failure because we were all ill.*

faint[1] /feɪnt/ *adj.* **1** that you cannot see, smell, or hear clearly: *the faint sound of music from another room.* **2** weak and tired, and feeling that you will fall. **faintly** *adv.*

faint[2] *v.* fall down suddenly because you are weak, ill, or shocked: *She fainted when she heard the terrible news.*

fair[1] /feə(r)/ *adj.* **1** honest; treating people in the right way: *a fair boss.* **2** quite good but not very good: *Your work is good, but Derek's is only fair.* **3** dry and sunny: *fair weather.* **4** with a pale or light colour: *fair hair.*

fair[2] *n.* **1** special market: *We saw new kinds of farm machines at the agricultural fair.* **2** festival in the open air, where you can buy things, play games, hear music, etc.

fairly /'feəlɪ/ *adv.* **1** in a way that is right and honest: *She's a good boss—she treats her workers fairly.* **2** quite; not very: *His work is fairly good.*

fairy /'feərɪ/ *n.* (*pl.* fairies) tiny, magic person with wings.

fairytale /'feərɪteɪl/, **fairy-story** /'feərɪ stɔːrɪ/ (*pl.* fairy-stories) *n.* story about magic, for children: *'Cinderella' is a fairy story.*

faith /feɪθ/ *n.* **1** (no *pl.*) feeling sure that you can trust someone or something: *Do you have faith in Tim?* **2** (*pl.* faiths) religion: *the Christian faith.*

faithful /'feɪθfl/ *adj.* that you can trust; always ready to help: *a faithful friend.*

faithfully /'feɪθfəlɪ/ *adv.* **promise faithfully**, say firmly that you will do something. **Yours faithfully**, way of ending a business letter.

fake[1] /feɪk/ *n.* **1** something copied as a trick: *That's not a Roman vase—it's a fake.* **fake** *adj.*

fall[1] /fɔːl/ *n.* **1** sudden drop from a higher place to a lower place: *a fall from a horse.* **2** getting less, lower, etc.: *There was a fall in the price of apples after the good harvest.* **3** (usually *pl.*) place where a river drops suddenly over a high place: *the Victoria Falls.*

fall[2] *v.* (*past part.* fallen /'fɔːlən/, *past tense* fell /fel/) **1** go down to a lower place; drop: *The rain is falling. Babies often fall when they start to walk.* **2**

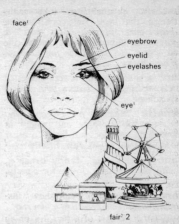

face[1]
eyebrow
eyelid
eyelashes
eye[1]

fair[2] 2

become lower or less: *In winter the temperature falls.* **3** hang down: *Her long hair falls to her waist.* **4** happen: *My birthday falls on a Tuesday this year.* **fall asleep**, start sleeping: *He was so tired that he fell asleep in the car.* **fall behind**, become slower than others: *On the long walk, the small child fell behind her brothers.* **fall behind with**, do something more slowly than others: *He fell behind with his school work because he played too much football.* **fall for**, start to love someone: *Sam fell for the girl he met at the party.* **fall ill**, become ill. **fall out with**, quarrel with someone. **fall over**, fall to the ground.

false /fɔːls/ *adj.* **1** wrong; not true; lying: *The thief gave a false name to the police.* **2** not real; not natural: *false teeth.* **falsely** *adv.*

fame /feɪm/ *n.* (no *pl.*) being well known.

familiar /fə'mɪlɪə(r)/ *adj.* usual; that you often see, hear, etc.: *the familiar faces of your parents.* **be familiar with**, know something well: *I can't drive this tractor because I'm not familiar with the controls.*

family /'fæməlɪ/ *n.* (*pl.* families) **1** mother and father and their children. **2** group of plants, animals, etc.: *A lion belongs to the cat family.*

famous /'feɪməs/ *adj.* well-known: *Oxford is famous for its university.*

fan[1] /fæn/ n. something that moves the air so that you feel cool. **fan** v. (*pres. part.* fanning, *past part.* & *past tense* fanned /fænd/) make the air move: *He fanned the fire to make it burn better.*

fan[2] n. someone who is very interested in something: *The football fans cheered their team.*

fanatic /fə'nætɪk/ n. someone who believes too strongly and wildly in something and does not listen to other ideas. **fanatical** adj. **fanatically** adv.

fancy[1] /'fænsɪ/ adj. **fancy dress** n. funny or interesting clothes for a party, etc.

fancy[2] exclam. word that shows surprise: *Fancy Tom becoming a film star!*

fancy[3] n. (*pl.* fancies) picture that you make in your head: *Did I really hear a voice or was it only my fancy?*

fancy[4] v. **1** think something but not be sure: *I fancy I heard a noise.* **2** think you would like something: *Do you fancy a swim?*

fantastic /fæn'tæstɪk/ adj. **1** very strange; very unusual: *The explorer told fantastic stories of his adventures.* **2** wonderful: *What a fantastic new motorbike!* **fantastically** adv.

far[1] /fɑ:(r)/ adj. **1** a long way off; not near: *a far country.* **2** other: *the far side of the table.*

far[2] adv. **1** how long or short something is: *How far did you walk today?* **2** a long way: *The ship sailed far across the sea.* **far and wide**, everywhere: *People came from far and wide to watch the boat race.* **far apart**, a long way from each other. **far away**, a long way off: *Australia is far away from Europe.* **far behind with**, not doing something as fast or as well as others: *Harry was ill for six weeks and now he is far behind with his work.* **far from**, not at all: *I can't do this work because it is far from easy.* **as far as**, to a place: *We walked as far as the top of the hill.* **so far**, yet; up to now: *He said he would telephone but we haven't heard from him so far.* **3** much: *London is far bigger than Leeds.*

fare /feə(r)/ n. money that you pay to ride on a train, bus, etc.: *How much is the fare from Bristol to Exeter?*

farewell /ˌfeə'wel/ exclam. goodbye. **farewell** adj.: *a farewell party.*

farm /fɑ:m/ n. place where you grow crops and keep animals: *Mr. Stewart has a sheep farm in Australia.* **farm** v. grow crops, keep animals, etc.: *Tony wants to farm in Scotland.* **farmer** n. someone whose job is to grow crops and keep animals, etc. **farm hand** n. worker on a farm. **farm-yard** /'fɑ:m-jɑ:d/ n. open place in the middle of the farm buildings.

farther /'fɑ:ðə(r)/ adv. more far; longer: *Maurice walked two kilometres farther than Basil.* **farthest** /'fɑ:ðɪst/ adv. most far.

fascinate /'fæsɪneɪt/ v. make someone feel so interested that he does not want to go away: *The monkeys in the zoo fascinated John.*

fashion /'fæʃn/ n. **1** way of dressing or doing something that people think best at a certain time: *In 1900 it was the fashion for all small children to wear white.* **2** way of doing, making, or saying something: *My dog has only three legs so he walks in a strange fashion.* **fashionable** /'fæʃnəbl/ adj. in the fashion of the time: *She always wears fashionable clothes.* **fashionably** adv.

fast[1] /fɑ:st/ adj. **1** quick: *a fast car.* **2** showing a time later than it really is: *My watch is fast.* **3** fixed; not easy to move: *Julian made the boat fast to the bank.*

fast[2] adv. **1** quickly: *I can't understand you when you talk so fast.* **2** firmly fixed: *Our car was stuck fast in the mud so we had to walk home.*

fast[3] v. not eat food for a certain time: *Muslims fast during Ramadan.*

fasten /'fɑ:sn/ v. **1** close something so that it will not come open: *to fasten a door; to fasten a coat.* **2** join together: *This dress fastens at the front.* **fasten something to** or **onto**, join one thing to another thing: *He fastened a lamp to his bike.* **fastener** n. thing that joins clothes or paper together: *Your blouse is open because the fastener is broken.* **fastening** n. thing that fixes or closes something: *A bolt is a fastening.*

fat[1] /fæt/ adj. (fatter, fattest) with a lot of flesh: *He's fat because he eats so much.*

fat² *n.* **1** (no *pl.*) oily part of meat or flesh. **2** (*pl.* fats) animal or vegetable oil that you use for cooking: *Butter and margarine are fats.*

fatal /'feɪtl/ *adj.* **1** that brings death: *a fatal fall from a horse.* **2** bad; that brings trouble: *It is fatal to drive when you are very drunk.* **fatally** *adv.*

fate /feɪt/ *n.* (*pl.* fates) what will happen in the future.

father /'fɑːðə(r)/ *n.* male parent.

father-in-law /'fɑːðər ɪn lɔː/ *n.* (*pl.* fathers-in-law) father of your wife or husband.

fault /fɔːlt/ *n.* **1** something wrong or bad in a person: *My secretary's only fault is being late.* **2** something not correct in a thing or in work: *Gail had a lot of faults in her homework because she did it too quickly.* **be someone's fault, be the fault of,** be bad, wrong, etc. because of someone or something: *It is your fault that I am late because you hid my bike.*

faultless /'fɔːltlɪs/ *adj.* perfect; with nothing wrong, bad, etc. **faultlessly** *adv.*

faulty /'fɔːltɪ/ *adj.* wrong; not working well: *Our car will not start because the engine is faulty.*

favour¹ /'feɪvə(r)/ *n.* **1** (no *pl.*) liking or thinking well of someone or something: *A mother must not show favour to one child more than another.* **be in favour of,** like the idea of something: *Alice is in favour of longer holidays!* **be in** or **out of favour with,** be liked or not liked by someone: *Oliver works hard so he is in favour with his boss.* **2** (*pl.* favours) kind thing that you do for someone: *Will you do me a favour and lend me your pencil?*

favour² *v.* give more help, kindness, etc. to one person than to others: *Tilly is unhappy because her mother favours her sister.*

favourable /'feɪvərəbl/ *adj.* **1** good; showing that you like something or someone: *a favourable school report.* **2** good; helpful: *The boat will go fast if the wind is favourable.* **favourably** *adv.*

favourite /'feɪvərɪt/ *adj.* that you like best: *Ice-cream is my favourite food.* **favourite** *n.* person or thing that you like more than others: *I like all flowers but roses are my favourites.*

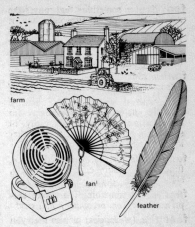

farm

fan¹

feather

fear /fɪə(r)/ *v.* **1** be afraid of something or someone: *Do you fear the dark?* **2** have a feeling that there will be trouble, danger, pain, etc.: *I'll try to hurry but I fear I'll be late.* **fear** *n.* **for fear of,** because you are worried about something: *We talked softly for fear of waking the baby.*

fearful /'fɪəfl/ *adj.* **1** bad: *a fearful car crash.* **2** afraid. **fearfully** *adv.*

fearless /'fɪəlɪs/ *adj.* not afraid. **fearlessly** *adv.*

feast¹ /fiːst/ *n.* very good meal: *What a feast we had when we visited my aunt!*

feast² *v.* eat a lot of good food.

feat /fiːt/ *n.* something you do that is clever, brave, and difficult: *Climbing Mount Everest is a great feat.*

feather /'feðə(r)/ *n.* piece of covering for a bird's body, like a thin stick with fine hairs: *A swan has white feathers.*

feature¹ /'fiːtʃə(r)/ *n.* **1 features** (*pl.*) the face: *Stella has fine features.* **2** important part of something: *A feature of the holiday was a visit to a bull-fight.*

feature² *v.* have an important part for someone: *This film features Charlie Chaplin.*

February /'februərɪ/ *n.* second month of the year.

fed /fed/ *past part & past tense* of *v.* feed. **fed up**, cross because you have had or done too much of something: *I'm fed up with work!*

federal /'fedərəl/ *adj.* joined in a group; united: *the Federal Republic of Germany.*

fee /fiː/ *n.* **1** money that you pay for some special work: *doctor's fees.* **2** (usually *pl.*) money that you pay for classes at a college, university, etc.

feeble /'fiːbl/ *adj.* weak in the body: *a feeble old man.* **feebly** *adv.*

feed /fiːd/ *v.* (*past part. & past tense* fed) give food to a person or animal: *The mother feeds her baby with a spoon.* **feed on**, eat something: *The sheep feed on grass.*

feel /fiːl/ *v.* (*past part. & past tense* felt /felt/) **1** touch something; try to learn by putting your fingers on something: *Feel this soft wool.* **2** be rough, smooth, wet, dry, etc. when you touch it: *My coat feels wet because it is raining outside.* **3** be: *Can we open the window? I feel hot.* **4** think something: *I feel that I should work harder.* **feel as if, feel as though**, seem like: *I'm so hungry that I feel as if I haven't eaten for years!* **feel for something**, put out your hands or feet and try to touch or get something: *I felt in my pocket for some matches.* **feel like**, (a) seem to be another person or thing: *I'm so happy I feel like a king!* (b) want something: *I'm so hot I feel like a swim.*

feeling /'fiːlɪŋ/ *n.* **1** (no *pl.*) power to learn by touching: *My hands were so cold that there was no feeling in them.* **2** (*pl.*feelings) what your body or head tells you about yourself: *a feeling of hunger.* **3** (*pl.* feelings) idea that is not totally certain: *I have a feeling that he is cross with me because he is not speaking to me.* **hurt someone's feelings**, do something that makes someone sad: *Andrew's unkind words hurt her feelings.*

feet /fiːt/ (*pl.*) of *n.* foot. **find your feet**, begin to do things without help: *It takes time to find your feet in another country.* **have** or **get cold feet**, be afraid of doing something: *He made an appointment with the dentist but then he had cold feet and didn't go.* **on your feet**, (a) standing: *I'm tired after being on my feet all day.* (b) well again after being ill. **put your feet**

up, rest: *If your are tired, put your feet up and listen to the radio.* **walk someone off his feet**, make someone walk until he is very tired.

fell /fel/ *past tense* of *v.* fall.

fellow¹ /'feləʊ/ *adj.* of the same kind; like yourself; from the same place, etc.: *The captain of a team organizes his fellow players.*

fellow² *n.* **1** man; boy: *What a nice fellow he is!* **2** (usually *pl.*) people of the same sort; friends: *school-fellows.*

felt /felt/ *past part & past tense* of *v.* feel.

female /'fiːmeɪl/ *n.* woman or girl; animal that can have baby animals; plant that has fruit. **female** *adj.*: *My father does not like female drivers.*

feminine /'femɪnɪn/ *adj.* of or like a woman; right for a woman. **feminine** *n.* word for a female or a woman: *'Princess' is the feminine of 'prince'.*

fence /fens/ *n.* line of wood or metal posts that you build around a place to keep people and animals in or out: *The dog jumped over the fence into the garden.* **fence** *v.* put a fence all round a place: *We fenced our field.*

fern /fɜːn/ *n.* sort of plant.

ferocious /fə'rəʊʃəs/ *adj.* very fierce; savage: *A rhinoceros is a ferocious animal.* **ferociously** *adv.*

ferry /'ferɪ/ *n.* (*pl.* ferries) boat or aeroplane that takes people or goods across a river, channel, etc.: *A channel ferry travels between Dover and Ostend.* **ferry** *v.* move a lot of people or goods from one place to another.

fertile /'fɜːtaɪl/ *adj.* where plants grow well: *fertile land.*

fertilizer /'fɜːtɪlaɪzə(r)/ *n.* food for plants: *The farmer puts fertilizer on his land.*

festival /'festɪvl/ *n.* time when many people come together for singing, dancing, etc.: *the Edinburgh Festival.*

festive /'festɪv/ *adj.*: for special, happy times: *festive music.*

fetch /fetʃ/ *v.***1** go and get someone or something: *I have no margarine. Can you fetch some from the shop?* **2** bring a certain price when you sell it: *This house fetched £20,000.*

fete /feɪt/ *n.* special market to make money for a church, club, etc.

feud /fjuːd/ *n.* quarrel between two people, families, etc. that goes on for many years.

fever /'fiːvə(r)/ *n.* (no *pl.*) **1** high temperature of the body. **2** illness with a high temperature: *scarlet fever.*

feverish /'fiːvərɪʃ/ *adj.* **1** with a high temperature in the body: *If she is feverish, telephone the doctor.* **2** wildly excited or worried. **feverishly** *adv.*: *Dennis was feverishly looking for his lost key.*

few¹ /fjuː/ *adj.* not many: *Few people live to the age of 100.* **a few**, some but not many: *Can I have a few flowers for the table?* **no fewer than**, as many as: *There are no fewer than a thousand people at the festival.*

few² *pron.* (no *pl.*) not many people, things, etc.: *Few were at the seaside because it rained.*

fiancé /fiːˈɒnseɪ/ *n.* man whom you are going to marry. **fiancée** *n.* woman whom you are going to marry.

fib /fɪb/ *n.* small lie; saying something that you know is not true. **fib** *v.* (*pres. part.* fibbing, *past part.* & *past tense* fibbed /fɪbd/) **fibber** *n.* someone who tells small lies.

fiction /'fɪkʃn/ *n.* (no *pl.*) stories that someone has made and that are not true: *The Sherlock Holmes stories are fiction.*

fiddle /'fɪdl/ *n.* musical instrument with strings; violin.

fidget /'fɪdʒɪt/ *v.* be restless.

field /fiːld/ *n.* **1** piece of land with a fence or hedge round it, where crops grow or animals feed: *The sheep are grazing in the field.* **2** piece of land where something special happens: *The aeroplanes landed on the airfield.* **3** place where people find oil, coal, gold, etc.: *an oil-field.*

fierce /fɪəs/ *adj.* **1** savage; ready to hurt; making people afraid, etc.: *a fierce dog.* **2** very strong: *a fierce wind.* **fiercely** *adv.*

fifteen /ˌfɪfˈtiːn/ *n.* **1** number 15. **2** rugby team: *Stephen plays in the first fifteen.* **fifteen** *adj.* **fifteenth** /ˌfɪfˈtiːnθ/ *adj.* 15th: *This is my fifteenth visit to Europe.*

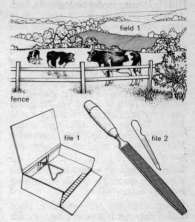

field 1

fence

file 1

file 2

fifth /fɪfθ/ *adj.* 5th: *May is the fifth month.*

fifty /'fɪftɪ/ *n.* (*pl.* fifties) number 50. **fifty** *adj.* **fiftieth** /'fɪftɪəθ/ *adj.* 50th.

fig /fɪg/ *n.* soft, sweet fruit, full of soft seeds.

fight /faɪt/ *v.* (*past part.* & *past tense* fought /fɔːt/) use hands, guns, weapons, etc. against another person: *The English were fighting the French at the Battle of Waterloo.* **fight for**, try very hard to do something: *She is very ill and the doctors are fighting for her life.* **fight** *n.*: *a dog fight.*

fighter /'faɪtə(r)/ *n.* **1** someone who likes to fight others. **2** aeroplane that shoots down other aeroplanes.

figure /'fɪgə(r)/ *n.* **1** sign that shows a number: *2, 4, and 6 are figures.* **2** how much money something costs: *We bought the house for a high figure.* **3** shape of the body: *She has a good figure.* **4** shape of a person or animal in stone, metal, or wood. **5 figures** (*pl.*) sums; arithmetic. **figure of speech** *n.* words that you use in an unusual way to make your meaning stronger: *To say 'he's as brave as a lion' is a figure of speech.*

file¹ /faɪl/ *n.* **1** cardboard cover for keeping papers in. **2** metal instrument with rough sides for making things smooth: *a nail-file.* **3** line of people. **in single file**, one behind the other: *The travellers walked in single file through passport control.*

file² *v.* **1** put papers in a file: *The secretary filed the letters.* **2** make something smooth with a metal file: *I filed my nails.* **3** walk in a long line: *The cows filed into the field.*

fill /fɪl/ *v.* **1** become full: *Her eyes filled with tears.* **2** put things inside something; use all the space inside something: *Clive filled his pockets with apples.* **fill in**, put facts or answers in the spaces that have been left for them: *If you want tickets for the ferry, please fill in this booking form.* **fill up**, make something totally full: *Jim filled up the tank with petrol.*

filling /'fɪlɪŋ/ *n.* something that you put into a space: *The dentist put a filling into my tooth.*

filling station /'fɪlɪŋ steɪʃn/ *n.* place where you can buy petrol, oil, etc. for your car.

film¹ /fɪlm/ *n.* **1** special thin paper that you use for making photographs: *Michael put a new roll of film into his camera.* **2** moving picture that you see at a cinema, etc.

film² *v.* make a moving photograph of news, a story, etc.

film star /'fɪlm stɑː(r)/ *n.* famous film actor or actress.

filthy /'fɪlθɪ/ *adj.* very dirty.

fin /fɪn/ *n.* one of the parts of a fish that move and help it to swim.

final¹ /'faɪnl/ *adj.* last; at the end: *The final word in this dictionary is 'zoom'.*

final² *n.* **1** last match in a competition: *a football final.* **2** (often *pl.*) last examination: *When do you write your finals?*

finally /'faɪnəlɪ/ *adv.* at last; in the end: *After a long time, they finally found the lost child.*

finance¹ /'faɪnæns/ *n.* **1** (no *pl.*) money; planning how to use, get, and save money for a business, country, etc.: *the Minister of Finance.* **2 finances** (*pl.*) money.

finance² /fɪ'næns/ *v.* give money for someone to do something: *Gareth's father financed his visit to Canada.*

financial /faɪ'nænʃl/ *adj.* of or about money: *a financial report.* **financially** *adv.*

find¹ /faɪnd/ *n.* something pleasing that you get by chance or after looking, etc.: *There was an important find of old coins in the farmer's field.*

find² *v.* (*past part. & past tense* found /faʊnd/) **1** discover someone or something after looking: *I hope you will soon find your lost ring.* **2** come to something or someone by chance: *I found that the telephone was ringing when I arrived home.* **3** learn something after much time, work, etc.: *Can you find the answer to this sum?* **4** think; have an idea of something because you have felt, tried, seen it, etc.: *I find this book very interesting.* **find someone guilty** or **innocent**, decide in a law court that someone has or has not done wrong: *They have found the man guilty and he has been sent to prison.* **find someone out**, learn that someone has done wrong, etc. **find something out**, learn something by asking or studying: *Please find out when the train leaves.*

fine¹ /faɪn/ *adj.* **1** bright; not raining: *a fine day.* **2** very pleasant; very good; well made: *a fine painting.* **3** in very tiny bits: *fine sand.* **4** very thin: *fine thread.* **5** very well: *'How are you feeling?' 'Fine, thanks.'*

fine² *n.* money that you must pay because you have done wrong: *a parking fine.* **fine** *v.*: *The police fined me for driving too fast.*

finger /'fɪŋgə(r)/ *n.* one of the parts of the hand: *Beth wears a ring on her little finger.* **have green fingers**, be able to make plants grow well. **keep your fingers crossed**, hope for the best: *I'm keeping my fingers crossed that you'll win.* **lay a finger on**, touch and perhaps hurt someone or something: *If you lay a finger on my brother I'll tell my father.* **not lift a finger**, not do anything to help: *He didn't lift a finger when I was ill.*

fingerprint /'fɪŋgəprɪnt/ *n.* mark that your finger makes when it touches something.

finish¹ /'fɪnɪʃ/ *n.* (no *pl.*) last part; end: *the finish of a race.*

finish² *v.* **1** stop happening: *School finishes at 4 p.m.* **2** stop doing something: *Have you finished your game?* **finish off**, do or eat something until there is no more: *He finished off all the milk and I had to drink black coffee.* **finish up with**, have at the end: *We finished up our* *meal with ice-cream.* **finish with,** not want or need someone or something any more: *Can I read this book when you have finished with it?*

fir /fɜː(r)/ *n.* tree with cones and with leaves like needles.

fire[1] /ˈfaɪə(r)/ *n.* **1** (no *pl.*) burning with flames. **catch fire,** start to burn: *He knocked over the candle and the room caught fire.* **put out a fire,** stop something from burning. **set something on fire, set fire to,** make something begin to burn: *A burning cigarette set the house on fire.* **2** (*pl.* fires) burning wood, coal, etc. for cooking or for making a place warm: *Liz put the pot on the camp-fire.* **3** (no *pl.*) shooting. **cease fire,** stop fighting or shooting: *The captain told his men to cease fire.*

fire[2] *v.* **1** shoot with a gun: *The soldiers fired at the enemy.* **2** make someone leave his job: *The manager fired Mr. Davies because he was always late for work.*

fire-alarm /ˈfaɪər əlɑːm/ *n.* bell that rings to tell people that there is a fire.

fire-brigade /ˈfaɪə brɪɡeɪd/ *n.* group of men whose job is to stop dangerous fires.

fire-engine /ˈfaɪər endʒɪn/ *n.* vehicle that takes men and machines to stop dangerous fires. **fire station** *n.* garage for fire-engines.

fire-escape /ˈfaɪər ɪskeɪp/ *n.* stairs on the outside of a building for people who must get out quickly because there is a fire inside.

fire-extinguisher /ˈfaɪər ɪkstɪŋ-gwɪʃə(r)/ *n.* metal container full of chemicals for stopping a fire.

fireman /ˈfaɪəmən/ *n.* (*pl.* firemen) man whose job is to stop bad fires.

fire-place /ˈfaɪə pleɪs/ *n.* place in a room where you can have a fire for heating or cooking.

fireside /ˈfaɪəsaɪd/ *n.* (no *pl.*) part of the room near the fire: *A cat likes to sit by the fireside.*

firework /ˈfaɪəwɜːk/ *n.* special thing that burns with bright colours or a big noise.

firm[1] /fɜːm/ *adj.* **1** hard; that will not move: *You must hang the picture on a firm nail or it will fall.* **2** showing that

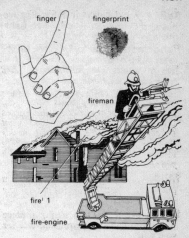

finger   fingerprint

fireman

fire[1] 1

fire-engine

you will make people do what you want: *Nigel was firm with the puppy.*

firm[2] *n.* group of people working together in a business: *My father works for a building firm.*

first[1] /fɜːst/ *adj.* before all others: *January is the first month of the year.*

first[2] *adv.* **1** earliest in place: *He came first in the race.* **2** earliest in time: *Ben first walked when he was 15 months old.* **first of all,** before anything else: *I am going to the market but, first of all, I must find my purse.*

first[3] *n.* (no *pl.*) time that is earliest. **at first,** at the beginning: *At first she was afraid of the water, but she soon learned to swim.*

first[4] *pron.* (no *pl.*) someone or something that comes earliest or before all others: *They were the first to arrive at the party.*

first aid /ˌfɜːst 'eɪd/ *n.* (no *pl.*) quick help that people give to an injured person before the doctor comes.

first-class /ˌfɜːst 'klɑːs/ *adj.* very good; the very best: *What a first-class concert that was!* **first-class** *adv.* **travel first-class,** travel in one of the most expensive seats, etc. in a train, bus, ship, etc.

first-rate /ˌfɜːst 'reɪt/ *adj.* very good.

fish[1] /fɪʃ/ *n.* (*pl.* fish or fishes) animal that lives and breathes in the water and has fins for swimming.

fish² v. try to catch creatures that live in water: *Colin is fishing in the river.* **fishing** n. catching fish.

fisherman /'fɪʃəmən/ n. (pl. fishermen) man who catches creatures that live in water: *The fishermen of Hull catch cod in the North Sea.*

fishmonger /'fɪʃmʌŋgə(r)/ n. someone who sells fish in a shop.

fist /fɪst/ n. hand that is tightly closed: *A boxer hits with his fists.*

fit¹ /fɪt/ adj. (fitter, fittest) **1** good enough: *That dirty dress is not fit to wear.* **2** healthy; well: *Exercise keeps us fit.*

fit² n. **1** sudden illness. **2** doing something suddenly: *He was in fits of laughter.* **3** way clothes look and feel on someone: *My old shoes are a tight fit.* **in fits and starts**, starting and stopping; not happening all the time: *to work in fits and starts.*

fit³ v. (pres. part. fitting, past part. & past tense fitted /'fɪtɪd/) **1** be the right size and shape: *Do your new shoes fit well?* **2** put something into its place: *Mr. Unwin fitted a new lock on the door.* **fit in**, (a) find time to do something: *Can you fit in a visit to me?* (b) find space for something: *Can you fit in another person? Is there room in the car?* **fit in with**, do what someone wants at the right time: *I'll fit in with your plans.*

five /faɪv/ n. number 5. **five** adj.: *Andrew has five sisters.*

fix¹ /fɪks/ n. **in a fix**, in trouble: *I've lost my keys so I'll be in a fix if the door is locked.*

fix² v. **1** put something in place so that it will not move: *to fix a pipe to the wall.* **2** mend something: *Can you fix my broken sandal?* **3** arrange something; make a plan: *Let's fix a time for the party.* **fix someone up with something**, give someone what he needs: *Can you fix me up with a job?*

fixed /fɪkst/ adj. firm; that will not move or change.

fizz /fɪz/ v. make a hissing noise and send out tiny bubbles. **fizzy** adj.: *Coca-cola is a fizzy drink.*

flag /flæg/ n. piece of cloth with a special pattern to show a country, club, etc.: *The British flag is red, white, and blue.* **flagpole** /'flægpəʊl/ n. tall pole where a flag hangs.

flake /fleɪk/ n. small, light piece of something: *a flake of snow; cornflakes.*

flame /fleɪm/ n. a finger of fire: *a candle-flame.* **in flames**, burning: *The house was in flames when the fire-engine arrived.*

flap /flæp/ n. **1** flat piece that hangs down to cover an opening: *He stuck down the flap of the envelope.* **2** moving up and down: *I can hear the flap of wings.* **flap** v. (pres. part. flapping, past part. & past tense flapped /flæpt/): *The bird flapped its wings.*

flare¹ /fleə(r)/ n. flames or bright light.

flare² v. burn brightly. **flare up**, (a) burn suddenly and brightly. (b) become suddenly angry, etc.: *He flared up.*

flash /flæʃ/ v. **1** send out a sudden light: *He flashed his torch into the dark room.* **2** come and go suddenly: *An aeroplane flashed across the sky.* **flash** n.: *a flash of lightning.* **in a flash**, very quickly.

flask /flɑːsk/ n. bottle for holding liquid: *We brought tea in a thermos flask.*

flat¹ /flæt/ adj. smooth; not going up and down: *A table has a flat top.* **a flat tyre**, a tyre with no air inside.

flat² n. group of rooms in a building, where you can live. **block of flats**, big building with many flats, one on top of another.

flatten /'flætn/ v. make something flat.

flatter /'flætə(r)/ v. **1** try to please someone by saying too many nice things about him that are not totally true. **2** make someone look better than he really does: *This photograph flatters me.* **be flattered**, be pleased: *I was flattered by the invitation to speak at the dinner.*

flattery /'flætərɪ/ n. (no pl.) saying too many nice things to someone so as to please him.

flavour /'fleɪvə(r)/ n. the taste of food: *This pudding has a delicious flavour.*

flea /fliː/ n. very small insect that lives on animals and people.

flee /fliː/ v. (past part. & past tense fled /fled/) run away.

fleet /fliːt/ n. big group of ships.

flesh /fleʃ/ n. (no pl.) soft part of a person's or animal's body, under the skin: *The flesh of a cow is called beef.*

flew /flu:/ past tense of v. fly.

flex /fleks/ n. (pl. flexes) piece of covered wire that brings electricity to lamps, etc.

flick /flɪk/ v. touch, move, or hit something quickly and lightly: *She flicked the fly off her sleeve.* **flick** n.

flicker /'flɪkə(r)/ v. shine or burn on and off in a weak way: *The candle flickered and went out.* **flickering** adj.: *a flickering light.* **flicker** n.: *a flicker of lightning.*

flight /flaɪt/ n. 1 (no pl.) flying. 2 (pl. flights) journey in an aeroplane: *a flight from Paris to London.* 3 (pl. flights) group of steps: *a flight of stairs.* 4 (no pl.) running away: *the man's flight from prison.*

fling /flɪŋ/ v. (past part. & past tense flung /flʌŋ/) throw something quickly and strongly: *Did he fling a stone through the window?*

flirt /flɜ:t/ v. be playful with a boyfriend or girlfriend; pretend to love someone: *Stella flirts with all the boys.*

float /fləʊt/ v. 1 stay on top of a liquid: *Cork floats on water.* 2 stay up in the air: *The balloon floated in the sky.*

flock /flɒk/ n. group of birds or animals: *a flock of sheep.*

flog /flɒg/ v. (pres. part. flogging, past part. & past tense flogged /flɒgd/) hit a person or animal very hard and often: *The cruel man flogged his horse.*

flood /flʌd/ n. 1 a lot of water that spreads over land: *After the heavy rain there was a big flood and water came into our house.* **in flood**, with so much water that it spills on to the land: *The river is in flood.* 2 a lot of something: *I had a flood of letters on my birthday.* **flood** v.: *The river flooded the village.*

floor /flɔ:(r)/ n. 1 the part of a room on which you walk: *There were no chairs so we sat on the floor.* 2 all the rooms at the same height in a building: *We went upstairs to the restaurant on the top floor.*

flop /flɒp/ v. (pres. part. flopping, past part. & past tense flopped /flɒpt/) 1 fall

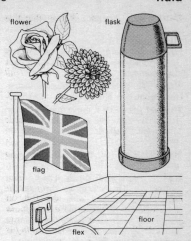

down weakly: *Mother flopped into a chair after her busy day.* 2 fail; not be as good as it should be: *The party flopped because there was no music.* **flop** n. happening that is not a success: *What a sad flop that party was!*

florist /'flɒrɪst/ n. someone who sells flowers.

flour /'flaʊə(r)/ n. (no pl.) soft, white stuff that we use to make bread, cakes, etc.

flourish /'flʌrɪʃ/ v. 1 grow or be well: *The tomato plants flourished in the hot summer.* 2 wave something to show that you are pleased with it, etc.: *Catherine flourished the letter from her mother.*

flow /fləʊ/ n. movement of water, air, etc.: *The doctor stopped the flow of blood from the cut.* **flow** v.: *The river flows to the sea.* **flowing** adj.

flower /'flaʊə(r)/ n. the beautiful part of a plant, which carries the seeds: *A daffodil has yellow flowers.* **flowerbed** n. piece of land where flowers grow.

flown /fləʊn/ past part. of v. fly.

fluent /'flu:ənt/ adj. able to speak easily and smoothly: *Jeremy is fluent in Italian.* **fluently** adv.: *Hans speaks English fluently.*

fluid /'flu:ɪd/ adj. that can flow: *Ice becomes fluid when it melts.* **fluid** n. anything that flows: *Water is a fluid.*

flung /flʌŋ/ *past part. & past tense* of *v.* fling.

flush /flʌʃ/ *v.* **1** become red in the face: *He flushed with anger.* **2** send water through a pipe, etc., to clean it: *to flush the lavatory.*

flute /fluːt/ *n.* sort of musical instrument that you blow.

flutter /'flʌtə(r)/ *v.* move quickly to and fro in the air: *The curtains fluttered in the wind.* **flutter** *n.: the flutter of wings.*

fly[1] /flaɪ/ *n.* (*pl.* flies) sort of flying insect.

fly[2] *v.* (*past part.* flown /fləʊn/, *past tense* flew /fluː/) **1** move through the air: *In the autumn some birds fly to warmer lands.* **2** travel in an aeroplane: *I'm flying to Brussels tomorrow.* **3** move quickly: *Amanda flew to the telephone.* **send something flying**, hit something so that it falls over: *Maurice bumped into the table and sent the cups flying.* **fly off the handle, fly off the deep end, fly into a rage**, suddenly become very angry.

flying /'flaɪɪŋ/ *adj.* moving through the air; able to move through the air: *A flying boat is an aeroplane that can land on water.* **flying saucer** *n.* round flying machine that some people think they see.

flyover /'flaɪəʊvə(r)/ *n.* bridge that carries a road over houses, other roads, etc.

foal /fəʊl/ *n.* young horse or donkey.

foam /fəʊm/ *n.* (no *pl.*) white mass of tiny bubbles that comes when you move liquid quickly.

focus /'fəʊkəs/ *v.* move parts of a camera, microscope, etc. so that you can see things through them sharply: *He focused the camera and took a photo.*

foe /fəʊ/ *n.* enemy.

fog /fɒg/ *n.* thick mist that stops you seeing clearly. **foggy** *adj.: a foggy day.* **fog-horn** *n.* thing that makes a loud noise to warn ships in fog.

fold /fəʊld/ *v.* bend something so that one part is on top of another: *I folded the letter and then put it into the envelope.* **fold** *n.* line made when you bend something. **folding** *adj.: A deck chair is a kind of folding chair.*

folder /'fəʊldə(r)/ *n.* cover of thick, stiff paper, for keeping loose papers, etc.

folk /fəʊk/ *n.* (*pl.*) people: *Some folk like beer and some don't.* **folk-dance** *n.* old dance of the people of a particular place. **folk-song** *n.* old song of the people.

follow /'fɒləʊ/ *v.* **1** come or go after someone or something: *Thursday follows Wednesday. A dog follows its master.* **2** go along a road, etc.: *Follow this path until you reach the village.* **3** understand what someone says: *I couldn't follow that French film.* **4** do what someone says, does, etc.: *I followed your advice.* **as follows**, as you will now hear or read: *The football team will be as follows: Smith, Jenkins, Brown. . . .*

following /'fɒləʊɪŋ/ *adj.* next: *On Saturday we watched football and on the following day we went to church.*

fond /fɒnd/ *adj.* loving; kind: *a fond mother.* **be fond of**, love or like someone or something: *I'm very fond of dancing.*

food /fuːd/ *n.* (no *pl.*) what people and animals eat so that that they live and grow: *Tim is very hungry because he has had no food for ten hours.*

fool[1] /fuːl/ *n.* someone who is stupid or does something silly: *He's a fool because he leaves his door open when he goes out.* **make a fool of**, do something that makes someone look silly: *You made a fool of me when you took away the ladder and left me on the roof.* **play the fool**, do silly things for fun.

fool[2] *v.* **1** do silly things: *Stop fooling and listen to what I am saying.* **2** trick someone and make him think something that is not true: *You can't fool me! I don't believe you.*

foolish /'fuːlɪʃ/ *adj.* stupid; silly. **foolishly** *adv.*

foot /fʊt/ *n.* (*pl.* feet) **1** part of the leg that you stand on: *I wear sandals on my feet.* **on foot**, walking: *Shall we go by car or on foot?* **2** lowest part; bottom: *the foot of the mountain.* **3** measure of length = 30·5 centimetres: *This fish is one foot long.*

football /'fʊtbɔːl/ *n.* **1** (no *pl.*) ball game with two teams of eleven players. **2** (*pl.* footballs) ball for this game. **football pitch** *n.* piece of ground where you play football.

footpath /'fʊtpɑːθ/ *n.* narrow path across fields or at the side of a road.

footprint /'futprɪnt/ *n.* mark that your foot makes when you walk on soft ground.

footstep /'futstep/ *n.* sound of someone walking: *I heard footsteps, then a knock on the door.*

for¹ /fɔː(r)/ *conj.* because: *She went to bed for she was tired.*

for² *prep.* **1** word that shows how far or how long: *We walked for three hours.* **2** word that shows where someone or something is going: *Is this the train for Glasgow?* **3** word that shows who will get or have something: *These flowers are for you.* **4** word that shows whom you are talking about: *It is dangerous for a small child to cross the road alone.* **5** word that shows why you are doing something: *I will bring the letter for you to see.* **6** word that shows how unusual something is: *It is very cold for October.* **7** word that shows that you like an idea: *Some people were for the strike and others were against it.* **8** on the same side in a sport or fight: *Tim plays tennis for his school.* **9** word that shows how much something is: *I bought this bag for £8.* **10** because of: *He got a medal for swimming well.*

forbid /fə'bɪd/ *v.* (*pres. part.* forbidding, *past part.* forbidden /fə'bɪdn/, *past tense* forbade /fə'bæd/) say that someone must not do something: *The guard forbade us to look out of the window when the train was moving.*

force¹ /fɔːs/ *n.* **1** (no *pl.*) power: *He was killed by the force of the blow.* **2** (*pl.* forces) group of men who have power: *the Police Force.* **by force**, with a lot of power, e.g. pushing, pulling, hitting, etc.: *I lost the key so I had to open my door by force.*

force² *v.* **1** make someone do something when he does not want to: *Dennis forced me to lend him my bike.* **2** do something by using a lot of power: *The thief forced the window open.*

forecast /'fɔːkɑːst/ *v.* (*past part. & past tense* forecast) *v.* say what you think will happen: *John forecasts crowded roads at the weekend.* **forecast** *n.*: *The weather forecast says there will be rain.*

foreground /'fɔːɡraʊnd/ *n.* things in the front in a picture: *In this photograph I am in the foreground and our house is behind me.*

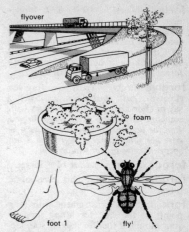

flyover

foam

foot 1   fly¹

forehead /'fɒrɪd/ *n.* part of your face above the eyes.

foreign /'fɒrən/ *adj.* of or from another country or race: *You cannot buy things in England with foreign money.* **foreigner** *n.* someone from another country.

foreman /'fɔːmən/ *n.* (*pl.* foremen) leader of a group of workers.

forest /'fɒrɪst/ *n.* big piece of land with very many trees: *We lost our way in the forest.*

forever /fə'revə(r)/ *adv.* always; at all times: *I can't read because you are forever talking!*

forgave /fə'ɡeɪv/ *past tense* of *v.* forgive.

forge¹ /fɔːdʒ/ *n.* place where a worker heats metal so that he can beat it into another shape.

forge² *v.* shape metal with a hot fire and a hammer: *The blacksmith forged horseshoes.*

forge³ *v.* make a copy of something because you want to trick people: *He forged money.* **forger** /'fɔːdʒə(r)/ *n.* someone who makes very good copies of things that will trick people.

forgery /'fɔːdʒərɪ/ *n.* **1** (no *pl.*) copying something to trick people. **2** (*pl.* forgeries) something copied as a trick: *This picture is not really by Picasso. It is a forgery.*

forget /fə'get/ v. (*pres. part.* forget-ting, *past part.* forgotten, *past tense* forgot) **1** not remember; no longer have something in mind: *I forget the address so I must look in my address book.* **2** stop thinking about something: *Let's forget our quarrel.* **forgetful** *adj.*

forgive /fə'gɪv/ v. (*past part.* forgiven /fə'gɪvn/, *past tense* forgave /fə'geɪv/) say or show that you are not angry with someone any more: *Mrs. Jones forgave Ron for breaking the window because he gave her some flowers.* **forgive me,** I am sorry: *Forgive me for waking you.*

forgot /fə'gɒt/ *past tense* of v. forget.

forgotten /fə'gɒtn/ *past part.* of v. forget.

fork /fɔːk/ n. **1** instrument with long points at the end, for lifting food to your mouth. **2** tool for digging soil, lift-ing plants, etc. **3** place where a road, river, etc. divides into two parts: *At the fork you must take the left road.*

forlorn /fə'lɔːn/ adj. sad and lonely: *the forlorn face of a lost child.*

form[1] /fɔːm/ n. **1** shape of someone or something, not clearly seen: *We could just see the form of a man in the darkness.* **2** sort; kind: *Football and tennis are forms of sport.* **3** printed paper with spaces where you can write your name, etc.: *an application form for a job.* **4** school class: *Joe is in Form 4.*

form[2] v. **1** make something; give a shape to something: *The girls formed a line at the door.* **2** think of something: *The boys formed a plan to visit Strat-ford.* **3** take shape; grow: *The idea began to form in his mind.* **4** start a group, etc.: *Bill wants to form a football team.*

formal /'fɔːml/ adj. that is for a special, important time: *My mother wore a long dress because it was a formal meal.*

former /'fɔːmə(r)/ adj. of an earlier time; that came before: *William went to university and forgot his former friends.* **formerly** *adv.* **former** *pron.*

fort /fɔːt/ n. strong building that helped to keep the people inside safe from their enemies long ago: *The Romans built a fort at York.*

fortieth /'fɔːtɪəθ/ adj. 40th: *my father's fortieth birthday.*

fortification /ˌfɔːtɪfɪ'keɪʃn/ n. strong walls and banks of earth that help to keep a place safe from the enemy.

fortify /'fɔːtɪfaɪ/ v. build walls etc. round a place to make it strong.

fortnight /'fɔːtnaɪt/ n. two weeks: *I'm going on holiday for a fortnight.* **fortnightly** adj. done or happening every two weeks: *a fortnightly visit.* **fortnightly** *adv.*

fortress /'fɔːtrɪs/ n. (*pl.* fortresses) strong building or town that helped to keep the people inside safe from their enemies long ago.

fortunate /'fɔːtʃənət/ adj. lucky. **fortunately** *adv.*: *His car was smashed but fortunately he wasn't killed.*

fortune /'fɔːtʃuːn/ n. **1** what happens to someone or something as life goes on. *tell someone's fortune*, say what will happen to someone in the future: *The old lady looked at my hand and told my fortune.* **2** good luck. **3** a lot of money: *My grandfather made a fortune and was very rich when he died.*

forty /'fɔːtɪ/ n. (*pl.* forties) number 40. **forty** adj.: *There are forty houses in this street.*

forward[1] /'fɔːwəd/ adv. **1** onward; to the front: *Mick went forward to get his prize.* **2** onwards in time. *look for-ward to*, think with pleasure about something that will happen: *I'm looking forward to my holiday next week.*

forward[2] n. front-line player in foot-ball, hockey, etc.

forward[3] v. send letters, etc. to someone's new address: *Please forward my post to me while I'm in Liverpool.*

forwards /'fɔːwədz/ adv. to the front: *When you are driving a car you must look forwards.*

fought /fɔːt/ *past part. & past tense* of v. fight.

foul[1] /faʊl/ adj. **1** dirty; with a bad smell or taste: *a foul stink.* **2** bad: *foul language.* **3** wicked; evil: *Murder is a foul crime.* **4** stormy; rainy: *foul weather.*

foul[2] v. do something against the rules of a game, e.g. football: *He was sent off the field for fouling.* **foul** n.

found[1] /faʊnd/ *past part. & past tense* of v. find.

found² *v.* start a group, school, business, etc.: *Henry VIII founded the Church of England.* **founder** *n.* someone who starts a group, etc.: *Baden-Powell was the founder of the Boy Scout Movement.*

foundation /faʊnˈdeɪʃn/ *n.* **1** (no *pl.*) starting a group, building, etc.: *the foundation of a new school.* **2 foundations** (*pl.*) strong parts of a building which you build first under the ground.

fountain /ˈfaʊntɪn/ *n.* water in a garden or park that springs high in the air and falls down again.

fountain-pen /ˈfaʊntɪn pen/ *n.* pen with a tube of ink inside.

four /fɔː(r)/ *n.* number 4. **on all fours**, on your hands and knees: *Babies crawl on all fours.* **four** *adj.: A chair has four legs.* **fourth** /fɔːθ/ *adj.* 4th.

fourteen /ˌfɔːˈtiːn/ *n.* number 14. **fourteen** *adj.* **fourteenth** /ˌfɔːˈtiːnθ/ *adj.* 14th.

fowl /faʊl/ *n.* bird.

fox /fɒks/ *n.* (*pl.* foxes) wild animal, like a dog, with red fur and a thick tail.

fraction /ˈfrækʃn/ *n.* **1** small part of something: *She only spends a fraction of her time at home.* **2** exact part of a whole number: ½, ¼, and ⅔ are fractions.

fracture /ˈfræktʃə(r)/ *v.* break something: *Ian fell and fractured his arm.* **fracture** *n.*

fragile /ˈfrædʒaɪl/ *adj.* that will break easily: *fragile glass.*

fragment /ˈfrægmənt/ *n.* small piece that has broken off something: *Lorraine dropped the vase but we picked up all the fragments.*

frail /freɪl/ *adj.* weak in the body: *a frail old man.*

frame /freɪm/ *n.* **1** strong bars of wood, metal, etc., that give the main shape to something: *A modern tent has cloth walls over a metal frame.* **2** thin edge of wood, metal, etc. round a picture, door, mirror, or the glass in spectacles.

frantic /ˈfræntɪk/ *adj.* wild with anger, pain, joy, etc.: *We heard frantic cries for help.* **frantically** *adv.*

fraud /frɔːd/ *n.* **1** (no *pl.*) doing things in a way that is not honest: *The bank clerk*

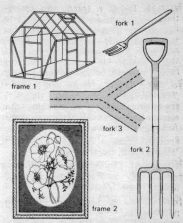

frame 1
fork 1
fork 3
fork 2
frame 2

got money by fraud. **2** (*pl.* frauds) something done that is not honest; something that is not what someone says it is: *This medicine is a fraud—it's only water.* **3** (*pl.* frauds) someone who is not what he seems: *He says he's a policeman but I think he's a fraud.*

frayed /freɪd/ *adj.* worn or ragged: *old, frayed clothes.*

freckle /ˈfrekl/ *n.* tiny, brown mark on the skin: *People with red hair often have freckles on their faces.*

free¹ /friː/ *adj.* **1** able to do what you want and go where you want; not in prison; not in the control of another person. **2** not fixed: *Tie one end of the rope to the tree and leave the other end free.* **3** that costs nothing: *a free ticket.* **4** not busy; not working, etc.: *Will you be free this afternoon?* **free from**, not having something: *'Well done, Robert, your sums are free from mistakes today!'* **free to**, allowed to do something that you want to do: *When the work is finished you are free to go home.* **free with**, ready to give a lot of something: *He is free with his money.* **set free**, let a person or animal go out of a prison, etc.

free² *v.* **1** let a person or animal go out of a place where it was a prisoner: *I wish I could free that bird from its cage.* **2** make someone free from control of another person.

freedom /ˈfriːdəm/ *n.* (no *pl.*) being free: *In 1863 Lincoln gave freedom to all American slaves.*

freeze /fri:z/ v. (past part. frozen /'frəʊzn/, past tense froze /frəʊz/) **1** be so cold that it turns to ice or is hard like ice: *In Russia, the sea sometimes freezes in winter.* **2** feel very cold: *I must put a warm pullover on because I'm freezing.* *freeze to death*, be so cold that you die. **3** stay very still: *The cat froze when it saw the bird.*

freezer /'fri:zə(r)/ n. machine that makes food very cold, like ice, so that it will stay fresh for a long time.

freight /freɪt/ n. (no pl.) goods that a ship or train, etc. transports.

frequent /'fri:kwənt/ adj. happening often: *My girlfriend writes frequent letters to me.* **frequently** adv.

fresh /freʃ/ adj. **1** not old; newly made, grown, etc.: *These are fresh eggs that I bought from the farm today.* **2** not out of a tin: *fresh fruit.* **3** new; not used: *I'll write my letter on a fresh piece of paper.* **4** cool; clean: *fresh air.* **fresh water**, not sea water.

Friday /'fraɪdeɪ/ n. sixth day in the week.

fridge /frɪdʒ/ abbrev. refrigerator; cold cupboard for food.

fried /fraɪd/ adj. cooked in hot oil: *fried fish.*

friend /frend/ n. someone whom you know and like well. *make friends with*, become a friend of someone. **friendship** n. being friends; having someone as your friend.

friendly /'frendlɪ/ adj. kind; helpful; showing that you like someone: *a friendly smile.*

fright /fraɪt/ n. sudden fear.

frighten /'fraɪtn/ v. make someone afraid: *Don't shout or you'll frighten the baby.* **frightened** /'fraɪtnd/ adj.: *She is crying because she is frightened.*

frightening /'fraɪtnɪŋ/ adj. making people afraid: *frightening news from the war.*

frightful /'fraɪtfl/ adj. **1** very bad; terrible: *a frightful crash.* **2** not pleasing; ugly: *What a frightful hat that is!*

fringe /frɪndʒ/ n. **1** edge of loose, hanging threads, etc.: *The table-cloth has a white fringe.* **2** short hair that hangs over the forehead. **3** edge of a place: *Our house is on the fringe of the forest.*

fro /frəʊ/ adv. *to and fro*, backwards and forwards: *The bus travels to and fro between London and Brighton.*

frock /frɒk/ n. dress for a woman or girl.

frog /frɒg/ n. small, jumping animal that lives in water and on land.

from /frɒm/ prep. **1** word that shows where someone or something starts: *We travelled to London from Edinburgh.* **2** word that shows when someone or something starts: *He works from nine o'clock until five o'clock.* **3** word that shows how far away something is: *The house is two miles from the village.* **4** word that shows who gave or sent something: *a letter from Trevor.* **5** word that shows the place where you find something: *water from the tap.* **6** word that shows how something is changing: *The sky changed from blue to grey.* **7** word that shows why: *The child cried from hunger.* **8** word showing the lowest number, price, etc.: *Our handbags cost from £5 to £80.*

front[1] /frʌnt/ adj. furthest from the back; first: *the front row of desks.*

front[2] n. part that looks forwards; part that is ahead of others: *She found a seat at the front of the train.* *in front of,* (a) facing someone or something: *Brian was sitting in front of the television.* (b) when certain other people are there: *Don't cry in front of your friends.*

frontier /'frʌntɪə(r)/ n. border; where one country meets another country: *We must show our passports at the frontier.*

frost /frɒst/ n. (no pl.) thin, white cover of ice on the ground, plants, etc. in very cold weather: *The frost kills flowers.* **frosty** adj.: *frosty air.* **frost-bite** /'frɒst baɪt/ n. where frost damages the body.

froth /frɒθ/ n. (no pl.) white mass of tiny bubbles: *the froth on a glass of beer.* **froth** v. **frothy** adj.: *frothy water.*

frown /fraʊn/ v. move the eyebrows together when angry, worried, thinking, etc.: *Frank frowned when he saw the scratch on his new car.* **frown** n.

froze /frəʊz/ past tense of v. freeze.

frozen /'frəʊzn/ past part. of v. freeze.

fruit /fru:t/ *n.* (*pl.* fruit or fruits) part of a plant that holds the seeds and that you can eat: *Bananas are fruit.*

fry /fraɪ/ *v.* cook something, or be cooked, in very hot oil: *to fry some chips.* **frying** *n.* **frying-pan** *n.* wide, flat, metal dish with a long handle, for frying.

fuel /'fju:əl/ *n.* (no *pl.*) wood, coal, oil, etc. that you burn to make heat or power.

fulfil /fʊl'fɪl/ *v.* (*pres. part* fulfilling, *past part.* & *past tense* fulfilled /fʊl'fɪld/) do what you have planned or promised: *When Stephen grew up, he fulfilled his hopes and became a doctor.*

full /fʊl/ *adj.* **1** holding as much as it can: *We can't go into the theatre because it is full.* **2** complete; with nothing missing: *Please tell me the full story.* **3** as much, great, etc. as possible: *The train was travelling at full speed.* **in full**, saying everything and not leaving out anything: *Please tell me the story in full.* **full up**, with no space for others: *The bus was full up so we waited for the next one.*

full stop /ˌfʊl 'stɒp/ *n.* punctuation mark (.) that shows the end of a sentence.

full-time /'fʊl taɪm/ *adj.* that takes all your working hours: *My brother has a full-time job but I work only in the mornings.*

fully /'fʊlɪ/ *adv.* totally; completely: *I fully agree with you.*

fumble /'fʌmbl/ *v.* move the hands in an unsure way, to do or get something: *In the dark, I fumbled for the key.*

fun /fʌn/ *n.* (no *pl.*) what you like doing, seeing, or hearing: *We had such fun at the festival!* **in fun, for fun**, as a joke: *I didn't want to make Sue cry—I shut her in the cupboard for fun.* **make fun of**, laugh at someone in an unkind way: *They made fun of Robert's big ears.*

function[1] /'fʌŋkʃn/ *n.* **1** special work done by someone or something: *The function of the heart is to send blood round the body.* **2** event; happening: *Our sports day is the most important function of the year.*

function[2] *v.* work: *I couldn't ring you because the phone wasn't functioning.*

fund /fʌnd/ *n.* sum of money for something special: *The money from the school concert will go into the swimming-pool fund.*

fringe 2

fringe 1

frog

funnel

frying-pan

funeral /'fju:nərəl/ *n.* burying or burning a dead person.

funnel /'fʌnl/ *n.* place where smoke comes out of a railway engine, ship, etc.

funny /'fʌnɪ/ *adj.* **1** making you smile and laugh: *a funny story.* **2** strange: *That meat has a funny smell.* **funnily** *adv.* strangely.

fur /fɜ:(r)/ *n.* **1** (no *pl.*) soft, thick hair on animals. **2** (*pl.* furs) animal skin with the fur on it, which you wear. **furry** *adj.*

furious /'fjʊərɪəs/ *adj.* very angry: *Adam was furious with me when I broke his watch.* **furiously** *adv.* wildly.

furnace /'fɜ:nɪs/ *n.* very hot fire in a closed place for making steel, glass, etc.

furnish /'fɜ:nɪʃ/ *v.* put tables, chairs, etc. into rooms. **furnished** /'fɜ:nɪʃt/ *adj.* with furniture: *a furnished flat.*

furniture /'fɜ:nɪtʃə(r)/ *n.* (no *pl.*) tables, chairs, beds, cupboards, etc.: *Mr. and Mrs. Shaw have bought some modern furniture for their living-room.*

further[1] /'fɜ:ðə(r)/ *adj.* more; extra: *Do you need any further help?*

further[2] *adv.* a longer way: *I was too tired to go further so I stopped.*

fury /'fjʊərɪ/ *n.* (no *pl.*) **1** great anger: *To my fury, I saw that the dog had taken our meat.* **2** being strong and wild: *the fury of the storm.*

fuse /fju:z/ *n.* part of an electrical system.

fuss /fʌs/ *n.* (no *pl.*) **1** worry or trouble about small things: *She makes a fuss when I'm five minutes late.* **2** happy excitement. *make a fuss of someone*, give a lot of help, care, etc. to someone: *When Eric came out of hospital his friends made a great fuss of him.* **fuss** *v.*: *Don't fuss over your children too much.* **fussy** *adj.*: *a fussy mother.*

future /'fju:tʃə(r)/ *n.* **1** (no *pl.*) time that is coming. **2** (*pl.* futures) what will happen in coming time: *I wish you a happy future.* *in future*, from now: *In future meetings will start ten minutes earlier.* **future** *adj.* of the time that will be: *Peter's future wife.* **future tense**, form of a verb that shows future time: *In 'David will arrive tomorrow', the verb is in the future tense.*

Gg

gabble /'gæbl/ *v.* talk quickly and not clearly. **gabble** *n.*

gag /gæg/ *n.* something that you put over someone's mouth to stop him speaking. **gag** *v.* (*pres. part.* gagging, *past part.* & *past tense* gagged /gægd/) put a gag on someone: *The thieves gagged the bank manager.*

gaiety /'geiəti/ *n.* (no *pl.*) being or looking happy and full of fun: *Christmas is a time of gaiety.*

gaily /'geili/ *adv.* happily; brightly: *She smiled gaily.*

gain /gein/ *v.* **1** get what you want or need: *Bill gained first prize for swimming.* **2** get more of something: *She was weak after her illness but is now gaining strength.*

gala /'gɑːlə/ *n.* special day for sports, shows, etc.: *a swimming gala.*

gale /geil/ *n.* very strong wind.

gallant /'gælənt/ *adj.* **1** brave. **2** polite and kind to women. **gallantly** *adv.*

gallery /'gæləri/ *n.* (*pl.* galleries) **1** long room in a big house or palace. **2** room or building for showing pictures: *the Tate Gallery.*

gallon /'gælən/ *n.* measure of liquid = 4·5 litres: *This car tank holds 8 gallons of petrol.*

gallop /'gæləp/ *v.* ride or run very fast: *The horses galloped along the road.* **gallop** *n.*

gallows /'gæləʊz/ *n.* (*pl.*) place where criminals were hanged in the past.

gamble /'gæmbl/ *v.* **1** play games of chance for money: *He lost all his money when he gambled at Monte Carlo.* **2** take a chance in business, etc. **gamble** *n.* risk: *This new plan is a gamble.*

gambler /'gæmblə(r)/ *n.* someone who plays games of chance for money.

game[1] /geim/ *n.* **1** playing something with rules: *a game of cards.* **2** secret plan or trick: *I wonder what his game is? give the game away*, tell or show a secret: *I didn't tell her about the accident, but the blood on my jacket gave the game away.*

game[2] *n.* (no *pl.*) animals and birds that people shoot and eat. **big game**, big animals that people shoot for sport.

games /geimz/ *n.* (*pl.*) sports; sports competition: *the Olympic Games.*

gang[1] /gæŋ/ *n.* **1** group of people working together: *a gang of road menders.* **2** group of people who do bad things together: *a gang of robbers.* **3** group of friends.

gang[2] *v.* get together in a group. *gang up on* or *against someone*, get in a group against another person: *Rick was unhappy because the other boys were ganging up on him.*

gangster /'gæŋstə(r)/ *n.* one of a group of bad people who use guns: *Al Capone was a Chicago gangster.*

gangway /'gæŋwei/ *n.* bridge that you put from the side of a ship to the land.

gaol /dʒeil/ *n.* jail; prison. **gaol** *v.* put someone in prison: *The judge gaoled the thief for two years.* **gaoler** *n.* someone whose job is to stop people getting out of prison.

gap /gæp/ *n.* opening, break, or empty place where something usually is: *The sheep got out through a gap in the fence.*

gape /geɪp/ v. look at something with your mouth open because you are surprised: *Colin gaped when he saw the huge aeroplane.* **gaping** *adj.* wide open: *a gaping hole.*

garage /'gærɑːʒ/ n. **1** building where you keep a car. **2** place where you take a car to buy petrol and have repairs, etc.

garden[1] /'gɑːdn/ n. **1** piece of open land by your house where you grow flowers, fruit, and vegetables: *They are playing with a ball in the garden.* **2 gardens** (*pl.*) public park: *Kensington Gardens.*

garden[2] v. grow flowers, etc. **gardening** *n.*: *My mother enjoys gardening.* **gardener** *n.* someone who grows plants.

garlic /'gɑːlɪk/ n. (no *pl.*) plant with a strong taste and smell, that you put in cooking.

garment /'gɑːmənt/ n. piece of clothing: *Socks, blouses, and skirts are all garments.*

gas /gæs/ n. **1** (*pl.* gases) anything like air that you cannot see. **2** (no *pl.*) something like air, that burns to make light and heat: *She cooks with gas.*

gash /gæʃ/ n. (*pl.* gashes) long, deep cut in the body. **gash** *v.*: *He gashed his leg on the broken bottle.*

gasp /gɑːsp/ v. **1** take in a short, quick breath with the mouth open because you are surprised: *The crowd at the circus gasped when the lion jumped on the trainer.* **2** try to get breath: *He was gasping when they pulled him out of the water.* **gasp** *n.*: *a gasp of surprise.*

gate /geɪt/ n. thing that closes over an opening in a wall outside: *Please close the gate so that the cattle cannot get out of the field.*

gateway /'geɪt weɪ/ n. opening that can be closed with a gate.

gather /'gæðə(r)/ v. **1** meet; come together in a group: *Thousands of people gathered for the pop festival.* **2** bring people or things together: *In September the farmers gather the corn.* **3** understand something: *Did you gather what Eric was saying?*

gathering /'gæðərɪŋ/ n. meeting of many people.

garden[1] 1

gag

gate

geese

gangway

gaudy /'gɔːdɪ/ adj. with too many colours; too bright: *gaudy clothes.* **gaudily** adv.

gauge[1] /geɪdʒ/ n. instrument that measures how big, long, fast, etc. something is: *a rain gauge.*

gauge[2] v. measure something exactly.

gave /geɪv/ *past tense* of v. give.

gay /geɪ/ adj. **1** happy; full of fun; making you happy, etc.: *We can hear gay music and laughter from the party.* **2** with a lot of colour: *gay flowers.*

gaze /geɪz/ v. look at someone or something for a long time: *In a train I like to sit and gaze out of the window.*

gear /gɪə(r)/ n. **1** (*pl.* gears) set of wheels, with teeth that work together, in a machine. In a car they connect the road wheels to the engine: *You change gear when you want to go faster or more slowly.* **2** (no *pl.*) special clothes or things that you need for a job or sport: *He can't play cricket because he has left his gear at home.*

geese /giːs/ (*pl.*) of n. goose.

gem /dʒem/ n. jewel; precious stone: *Diamonds and rubies are gems.*

gender /'dʒendə(r)/ n. being masculine, feminine, or neuter in grammar: *'She' is a pronoun of the feminine gender.*

general[1] /'dʒenrəl/ adj. **1** of all, not just of one: *In a general election, we choose all the members of parliament.* **2**

usual; happening everywhere or all the time: *Cold weather is general in Britain in the winter.* **3** not in detail: *a general report.* **in general**, usually.

general² *n.* senior army officer.

generally /'dʒenrəlɪ/ *adv.* usually; mostly: *British children generally have lunch at school.*

generation /,dʒenə'reɪʃn/ *n.* **1** the children, or the parents, or the grandparents, in a family: *Three generations live in our house.* **2** all the people who were born at about the same time: *The older generation doesn't like pop music.*

generosity /,dʒenə'rɒsətɪ/ *n.* (no *pl.*) liking to give things to others.

generous /'dʒenrəs/ *adj.* **1** liking to give things to people: *Aunt Isabel is generous and gives us a lot of presents.* **2** large: *a generous meal.* **generously** *adv.*

genius /'dʒiːnɪəs/ *n.* (*pl.* geniuses) very clever person: *Einstein was a genius.*

gentle /'dʒentl/ *adj.* **1** kind and soft; not rough or wild: *Mothers are gentle with their babies.* **2** that moves softly; that feels soft: *a gentle breeze.* **gently** *adv.* **gentleness** *n.*

gentleman /'dʒentlmən/ *n.* (*pl.* gentlemen) **1** man who is kind, polite, and honest. **2** any man.

genuine /'dʒenjʊɪn/ *adj.* true; real: *Those aren't genuine diamonds—they're pieces of glass!* **genuinely** *adv.*

geography /dʒɪ'ɒɡrəfɪ/ *n.* (no *pl.*) study of the earth, its mountains, rivers, plants, animals, etc.

geology /dʒɪ'ɒlədʒɪ/ *n.* (no *pl.*) study of the history of rocks, soil, etc.

geometry /dʒɪ'ɒmətrɪ/ *n.* (no *pl.*) mathematics of lines, shapes, etc.

germ /dʒɜːm/ *n.* tiny, living thing that may bring illness: *flu germs.*

gesture /'dʒestʃə(r)/ *n.* moving the hand or head to show what you want, feel, think, etc.: *A nod is a gesture.*

get /ɡet/ *v.* (*pres. part.* getting, *past part.* & *past tense* got /ɡɒt/) **1** have something: *Nick's got blue eyes.* **2** buy or take something: *We must get some more butter.* **3** fetch someone or something: *Jenny will get the children from school.* **4** receive something: *I got a lot of presents for my birthday.* **5** catch an

illness: *Sarah got mumps from her brother.* **6** understand something: *I don't get what you are saying.* **7** become: *I'm getting cold—please close the window.* **8** come or go somewhere: *When will the train get to Cambridge?* **9** make someone or something move: *Quick, get the children out of the burning house!* **get about**, go or travel to many places: *The old man doesn't get about much these days.* **get at**, be able to reach or come to a place: *I tried to pick the apple but I couldn't get at it.* **get away**, leave; escape: *Two tigers got away from the zoo last night.* **get away with**, **(a)** do something safely, which usually brings trouble: *He cheated in the exam and got away with it.* **(b)** steal or take something: *The thief got away with £5,000.* **get back**, return: *I got back from my holiday yesterday.* **get in**, come to a place: *The train got in late.* **get someone in**, ask someone to come to the house: *We got the doctor in to see our sick child.* **get into**, put clothes on: *My shoes are too small—I can't get into them.* **get off**, **(a)** leave: *We must get off at once or we'll be late.* **(b)** not be seriously punished, hurt, etc.: *The thief got off with only a month in jail.* **get on**, words that show how work or a job is going: *Philip is getting on well at school.* **get on for**, be nearly: *It's getting on for twelve o'clock.* **get on with someone**, work or live in a friendly way with someone: *Are you getting on with your new neighbours?* **get on with something**, go on doing something: *Stop talking, and get on with your work!* **get out of**, not do something that you do not like: *I'll come swimming with you if I can get out of cleaning my bedroom.* **get your own back on someone**, do something to hurt someone who has harmed you: *She broke my watch and I got my own back on her by hiding her sandals.* **get something ready**, prepare something: *Have you got the dinner ready?* **get through**, **(a)** pass an examination, etc.: *Did you get through your driving test?* **(b)** spend money: *I got through £200 on holiday.* **(c)** be able to speak to someone on the telephone: *I tried to ring Anne but I couldn't get through.* **get to**, come to an idea or feeling: *At first I didn't like my new job, but after a while I got to enjoy it.* **get someone to do something**, make someone do something: *My boss got me to train the new secretary.* **get a thing to do**

something, make a thing do something: *I can't get my car to start.* **get together**, meet; come together in a group: *The whole family got together for Christmas.* **get up**, stand up; get out of bed: *It's time to get up, children!* **get up to**, (*a*) do something, usually bad: *I must go and see what the children are getting up to.* (*b*) come to a place in a book, etc.: *We got up to page 17 in our story today.* **have got to**, must do something: *I have got to leave soon.*

ghastly /'gɑːstlɪ/ *adj.* **1** making you very afraid, very sad, or shocked: *a ghastly crash.* **2** very bad: *a ghastly meal.*

ghost /gəʊst/ *n.* spirit of a dead person that a living person thinks he sees. **ghostly** *adj.* **1** very pale; like a ghost. **2** very strange: *a ghostly noise.*

giant /'dʒaɪənt/ **1** very big, tall man in stories: *the giant Goliath.* **2** any person, animal, or plant that is bigger than usual. **giant** *adj.*

giddy /'gɪdɪ/ *adj.* feeling sick in the head so that everything seems to be turning around you.

gift /gɪft/ *n.* **1** present; something that you give to someone: *birthday gifts.* **2** something that you can do well, without learning it: *Nora has a gift for singing.*

gigantic /dʒaɪˈgæntɪk/ *adj.* very big.

giggle /'gɪgl/ *v.* laugh in a silly way. **giggle** *n.*

ginger¹ /'dʒɪndʒə(r)/ *adj.* with a light brown colour: *a ginger cat.* **ginger** *n.*

ginger² *n.* hot, strong powder that you put in cooking. **gingerbread** *n.* dark brown cake with a hot taste.

gipsy /'dʒɪpsɪ/ *n.* (*pl.* gipsies) someone with dark hair and eyes who lives in a caravan and never stays long in one place.

giraffe /dʒɪˈrɑːf/ *n.* big, wild animal with a very long neck and legs.

girl /gɜːl/ *n.* female child; young woman. **girlfriend** *n.* girl who is the special friend of a boy or man. **Girl Guide** *n.* member of a special club for girls.

give /gɪv/ *v.* (*past part.* given /'gɪvn/, *past tense* gave /geɪv/) **1** hand something to someone: *Mother gave me a glass of milk.* **2** let someone have something: *They gave us a lovely holiday.* **3** pay money for goods: *I gave £60 for my new*

giraffe

Girl Guide   girl

watch. **4** bring a feeling, etc. to someone: *The old car is giving a lot of trouble.* **5** make or bring something: *The sun gives light and heat.* **6** send out a sound, noise, movement, etc.: *Diana gave a cry when she opened the letter.* **7** say that someone may have or do something: *I'll give you ten minutes to change.* **8** use all your time, power, etc. to do something: *Schweitzer gave his life to helping sick people.* **9** pass a sickness to someone else: *Robert gave me his cold.* **10** become weaker and less firm: *The branch of the tree gave, but it did not break.* **give someone away**, (*a*) tell a secret about someone: *I'm going to hide from my brother behind the tree—please don't give me away!* (*b*) hand a bride to her bridegroom at a wedding: *Alice's father will give her away.* **give something away**, (*a*) let someone have and keep something: *St. Francis gave all his money away.* (*b*) share things out to people: *The headmaster gave away the prizes.* (*c*) let people have things free: *They're giving away free glasses at the supermarket.* **give something back**, return something: *Please give me back the book I lent you.* **give in**, stop trying to do something because you are not strong enough, etc.: *Tom always gave in to his big brother.* **give something in**, give work, etc. to someone: *'Please give in your essays now,' said the teacher.* **give out**, (*a*) give things to each person: *Please give out the books.* (*b*) come to an end: *The car* *stopped when the petrol gave out.* **give up**, stop trying to do something or answer a question: *I give up—what's the answer?* **give yourself up**, let someone catch you: *The thief gave himself up to the police.* **give something up**, stop doing, using, or eating something: *The fat girl is giving up sugar.* **give way**, **(a)** agree with someone after not agreeing: *After a long argument, he gave way.* **(b)** break: *The branch gave way and Sheila fell.* **(c)** let another person or thing go first: '*Give way to the left' means that cars coming in from the left side can go first.*

glacier /'glæsɪə(r)/ *n.* river of ice.

glad /glæd/ *adj.* (gladder, gladdest) happy; pleased: *I'm so glad to see you.* **gladly** *adv.* with pleasure: *I'll gladly help you.*

glance /glɑːns/ *v.* look quickly at something: *Beth glanced at her watch.* **glance** *n.*

glare /gleə(r)/ *v.* **1** shine strongly: *The sun glared down from a blue sky.* **2** look angrily: *He glared at the naughty children.* **glare** *n.* **glaring** *adv.*

glass /glɑːs/ *n.* **1** (no *pl.*) hard, clear stuff, that you can see through: *We make windows from glass.* **2** (*pl.* glasses) a glass thing that you drink from: *a glass of milk.* **3** **glasses** /'glɑːsɪz/ (*pl.*) round pieces of glass that you wear over the eyes so that you can see better: *Granny put on her glasses and started to read.*

gleam /gliːm/ *v.* shine softly: *The cat's eyes were gleaming in the dark.* **gleam** *n.*

glide /glaɪd/ *v.* move along smoothly: *The boat glided down the river.*

glider /'glaɪdə(r)/ *n.* aeroplane with no engine, which is pulled up into the air and then moves along on the air. **gliding** *n.:* *Gliding is an exciting sport.*

glimmer /'glɪmə(r)/ *n.* small, weak light: *the glimmer of a candle.* **glimmer** *v.* send out a weak light.

glimpse /glɪmps/ *v.* see someone or something quickly, but not clearly: *I just glimpsed the aeroplane between the clouds.* **glimpse** *n.* **catch a glimpse of**, see someone or something quickly but not clearly.

glisten /'glɪsn/ *v.* shine because the light falls on something wet: *Helen's body glistened when she climbed out of the swimming-pool.*

glitter /'glɪtə(r)/ *v.* shine brightly with small flashes of light: *The broken glass glittered in the sun.* **glitter** *n.* **glittering** *adj.:* *glittering diamonds.*

globe /gləʊb/ *n.* **1** anything round like a ball. **2** round thing with a map of the world on it.

gloomy /'gluːmɪ/ *adj.* sad; with no hope. **gloomily** *adv.:* '*I shan't pass my examination,' he said gloomily.*

glorious /'glɔːrɪəs/ *adj.* **1** with great honour: *a glorious history.* **2** wonderful; very pleasing: *I had a glorious holiday.* **gloriously** *adv.*

glory /'glɔːrɪ/ *n.* **1** (no *pl.*) fame and honour that you win when you do great things. **2** (*pl.* glories) being beautiful; something beautiful: *the glory of a sunset.*

glossy /'glɒsɪ/ *adj.* smooth and shiny: *The horse has a glossy coat.*

glove /glʌv/ *n.* cover of leather, wool, etc. for the hand: *a pair of gloves.*

glow /gləʊ/ *v.* send out soft light and heat with no flame: *The hot metal glowed.* **glow** *n.:* *the glow of a dying fire.*

glue[1] /gluː/ *n.* (no *pl.*) stuff that sticks things together.

glue[2] *v.* stick one thing to another thing: *George glued the pieces of broken vase together.*

glum /glʌm/ *adj.* sad and dull: *Cheer up—don't look so glum!* **glumly** *adv.*

gnarled /nɑːld/ *adj.* rough and twisted: *the gnarled hands of an old man.*

gnaw /nɔː/ *v.* bite at something for a long time with the front teeth: *The dog was gnawing a bone.*

go[1] /gəʊ/ *n.* (*pl.* goes) your turn to do something: *Give the ball to me—it's my go.* **at one go**, with one try: *He blew out all the candles on his birthday cake at one go.* **have a go at**, try to do something: *It's not a difficult game—have a go at it.* **on the go**, very busy; moving around, etc.: *My mother is on the go all day.*

go[2] *v.* (*past part.* gone /gɒn/, *past tense* went /went/) **1** move from one place to another: *I usually go to school at 9 o'clock but yesterday I went early.* **2** travel: *Are you going by train or by bus?* **3** leave: *The train goes at 11.30.* **4** last: *I hope my money will last until next week* *but I'm afraid it will not go so far.* **5** become: *This meat has gone bad.* **6** belong somewhere: *This pot goes on the top shelf.* **7** break: *My roof will go if there's another storm.* **8** work; function: *Gareth dropped my watch and now it doesn't go.* **9** happen; be; do: *How's your work going?* **10** be sent or thrown away: *My car is no good—it must go.* **11** die: *My grandmother is very ill and I think she'll go soon.* **12** have certain words, music, etc.: *How does the new song go?* **13** make a certain sound: *Cats go 'miaow'.* **14** be or live in a certain way: *Poor people often go hungry.* **15** disappear: *Take a tablet and your headache will go.* **16** be sent, kicked, thrown, etc.: *The ball went through the window.* **be going to**, shall or will do something: *He's going to arrive at 10 o'clock tomorrow.* **go about something**, do something: *How do you go about making beer at home?* **go about with**, be often with someone: *Ken goes about with his brother a lot.* **go after**, try to catch or have something: *Alan is going after a new job.* **go against**, say or do things that are not what someone wants: *He went against my wishes.* **go ahead**, **(a)** start to do something; continue to do something: *Here is the book—now go ahead and read it.* **(b)** move in front of someone; leave before someone: *You can go ahead to the station and I'll see you there later.* **go along with someone**, go with someone to a place: *I'll go along to the film with you.* **go and do something**, go to do something: *Please go and shut the door.* **go away**, leave: *My brother went away on holiday yesterday.* **go back**, return to a place: *We're going back to school tomorrow.* **go by**, pass: *Time goes by so slowly when you're waiting for a train.* **go down with**, catch an illness: *Poor Dick has gone down with mumps.* **go down well**, be a success; please someone: *The story went down well with the children.* **go far**, **(a)** buy a lot: *One pound doesn't go far these days.* **(b)** do well; become an important person: *Sandra is very clever and will go far.* **go for someone**, **(a)** be very angry with someone; rush at someone to hurt him: *The dog went for the thief and bit him.* **(b)** go and fetch someone: *Shall I go for a doctor?* **go for something**, **(a)** cost: *The house is going for £30,000.* **(b)** go out to do something: *Let's go for a walk.* **go in for**, give your name for a

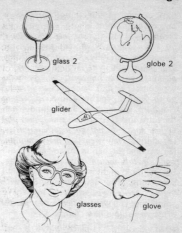

glass 2

globe 2

glider

glasses

glove

competition, examination, etc.: *I'll go in for the swimming race.* **go into**, **(a)** enter a place: *Let's go into the museum.* **(b)** fit inside something: *This small umbrella will go into a handbag.* **(c)** start a job, etc.: *Andrew has gone into the police.* **go off**, **(a)** explode; be fired: *The gun went off with a bang.* **(b)** become bad: *Meat goes off quickly in hot weather.* **go off well, badly, etc.**, happen in a good or bad way: *Did your party go off well?* **go off with someone or something**, go away with someone or something that is not yours: *The thief went off with my earrings.* **go on**, **(a)** happen: *What's going on?* **(b)** behave; do things: *If you go on like that I shall be angry.* **(c)** continue; not stop: *Stop talking and go on with your work.* **go out**, **(a)** leave a building, etc.: *He went out into the street.* **(b)** spend time away from home for amusement: *Are you going out tonight?* **(c)** stop burning or shining: *It's cold because the fire has gone out.* **go out with someone**, have someone as a boyfriend or girlfriend: *Ray is going out with Pauline.* **go over something**, look carefully at something: *The teacher goes over my sums.* **go round**, **(a)** be enough for everyone: *Will the cake go round?* **(b)** travel where you want by another way: *The main road was closed so we went round by the coast road.* **go round to**, go to visit someone or something: *Let's go round to Neville's house this evening.* **go short of**, not have enough of something: *In the snow the animals went short of food.* **go through,** (**a**) suffer: *She went through a lot when she was ill.* (**b**) look inside something carefully; search something: *The policeman went through the thief's pockets.* **go to someone,** be given to someone: *The first prize goes to Martin.* **go to,** lead to; end in: *This road goes to Bradford.* **go together,** look good when they are together: *Those pink shoes and yellow socks do not go together.* **go up,** (**a**) climb: *They went up the mountain.* (**b**) become higher in price: *Eggs have gone up this month.* **go with something,** be or look right when it is next to something: *Pink shoes do not go with yellow socks.* **go without,** not have something you want or need: *Poor people often go without new clothes.*

goal /gəʊl/ *n.* **1** place where a ball must go to win a point in a football match, etc.: *He kicked the ball into goal.* **2** point that a player wins when he sends the ball between the posts: *Liverpool has won by three goals to one.*

goalie /'gəʊlɪ/, **goalkeeper** /'gəʊlkiːpə(r)/ *n.* player in football, etc., who must stop the ball from going between the posts.

goat /gəʊt/ *n.* sort of farm animal.

god /gɒd/ *n.* **1** **God** (no *pl.*) the one great being who made the world and controls all things. **2** (*pl.* gods) any being that people think has power over them and nature: *Mars was the Roman god of war.*

goddess /'gɒdɪs/ *n.* (*pl.* goddesses) female god.

goes /gəʊz/ part of *v.* go.

goggles /'gɒglz/ *n.* (*pl.*) big, round glasses that motor-cyclists and divers etc. wear to keep dust or water from their eyes.

going /'gəʊɪŋ/ *pres. part.* of *v.* go. **be going to,** will happen; will do something: *Come inside—it's going to rain.*

gold /gəʊld/ *n.* (no *pl.*) **1** shiny, yellow metal of great value: *My earrings are made of gold.* **2** with the colour of gold; bright yellow. **gold** *adj.*: *a gold watch.*

golden /'gəʊldən/ *adj.* **1** made of gold. **2** with the colour of gold: *golden hair.*

goldfish /'gəʊldfɪʃ/ *n.* (*pl.* goldfish) small, yellow fish that you keep as a pet.

golf /gɒlf/ *n.* (no *pl.*) sport where the player hits a small ball into a hole with a long stick called a **golf-club. golf-course** *n.* grassy land where you play golf.

gone /gɒn/ *past part.* of *v.* go.

gong /gɒŋ/ *n.* musical instrument that you hit with a stick.

good[1] /gʊd/ *adj.* (better, best) **1** being right; that does what you want: *A good knife cuts well.* **2** pleasing; that you enjoy: *a good party.* **3** kind; doing what is right: *a good mother.* **4** strong; working well: *good eyes.* **5** able to do something well: *a good driver.* **6** total: *He had a good wash after tennis.* **7** hard; strong: *Harry went for a good walk.* **a good,** a whole one and perhaps more: *We waited a good hour.* **as good as,** almost the same as; almost like: *This car is two years old but it looks as good as new.* **good for,** making you well, healthy, happy, etc.: *Fresh fruit is good for you.*

good[2] *exclam.* word that shows that you are pleased.

good[3] *n.* (no *pl.*) something that is right, helpful, valuable, etc. **do good,** do things that are kind, helpful, etc.: *Mrs. Moore does a lot of good in the village.* **do someone good,** (**a**) make someone well, happy, healthy, etc.: *A holiday will do you good.* (**b**) make someone learn: *He's too boastful—losing a race will do him good.* **for good,** for ever; for always: *My uncle went to America for good.* **it's no good,** it's useless: *It's no good telling the rain to stop.*

good afternoon /ˌgʊd ɑːftə'nuːn/ *exclam.* word that you say to someone in the afternoon.

goodbye /ˌgʊd'baɪ/ *exclam.* word that people say when someone goes away: *Goodbye, Ann, see you soon!*

good evening /ˌgʊd 'iːvnɪŋ/ *exclam.* word that you say to someone in the evening.

good-looking /ˌgʊd 'lʊkɪŋ/ *adj.* handsome; beautiful: *What a good-looking boy!*

good morning /ˌgʊd 'mɔːnɪŋ/ *exclam.* word that you say to someone in the morning.

good-natured /ˌgʊd 'neɪtʃəd/ *adj.* kind; friendly.

goodness¹ /'gʊdnɪs/, **goodness me** *exclam.* words that show surprise: *Goodness! What a dirty dress!* **my goodness!** *exclam.* words that show strong feeling: *My goodness, it's hot today!* **goodness knows**, no one knows; I don't know: *Goodness knows what time it is—I haven't a watch.*

goodness² *n.* (no *pl.*) being kind; doing what is right: *I wrote to thank Carol for her goodness to me.*

good night /ˌgʊd 'naɪt/ *exclam.* word that you say when you leave someone at night.

good-tempered /gʊd 'tempəd/ *adj.* not often cross or angry.

goods /gʊdz/ *n.* (*pl.*) **1** things that you sell or buy. **2** things that a train or lorry carries.

goose /guːs/ *n.* (*pl.* geese) big waterbird, with a long neck, that you can eat.

gooseberry /'gʊzbərɪ/ *n.* (*pl.* gooseberries) small, round, green fruit with hairs.

gorgeous /'gɔːdʒəs/ *adj.* **1** with bright colours; beautiful: *a bird with gorgeous feathers.* **2** wonderful; enjoyable: *a gorgeous party.* **gorgeously** *adv.*

gorilla /gə'rɪlə/ *n.* sort of very big ape.

gosh /gɒʃ/ *exclam.* word that shows surprise: *Gosh! Just look at that huge man!*

gossip /'gɒsɪp/ *n.* **1** (no *pl.*) talk, often unkind, about other people. **2** (*pl.* gossips) someone who often talks unkindly about other people. **gossip** *v.*: *The girls were gossiping about Jane's new boyfriend.*

got /gɒt/ *past part. & past tense* of *v.* get.

govern /'gʌvn/ *v.* rule a country, etc.: *Parliament governs Britain.*

governess /'gʌvnɪs/ *n.* (*pl.* governesses) woman who teaches all the children of one family in her home.

government /'gʌvənmənt/ *n.* (*pl.* governments) group of people who rule a country. **local government**, group of people who control a town, state, etc.

goalkeeper

goal 1

goggles

golf-club

golf

goat

governor /'gʌvənə(r)/ *n.* someone who rules a state or province: *Who is the Governor of Hong Kong?*

gown /gaʊn/ *n.* **1** long dress that a woman wears at a special time, etc.: *a wedding-gown.* **2** long, loose clothes for a special job: *a university gown.*

grab /græb/ *v.* (*pres. part.* grabbing, *past part. & past tense* grabbed/græbd/) take something roughly and quickly: *The thief grabbed her purse.* **grab** *n.*: *He made a grab at the purse.*

grace /greɪs/ *n.* **1** (no *pl.*) moving in a pleasing way: *She dances with grace.* **2** (*pl.* graces) thanks that you say before or after a meal.

graceful /'greɪsfl/ *adj.* beautiful; moving or standing easily and in a pleasing way: *a graceful dancer.* **gracefully** *adv.*

gracious /'greɪʃəs/ *adj.* pleasant and kind: *a gracious lady.* **graciously** *adv.*

grade¹ /greɪd/ *n.* rank; sort: *High grade petrol is expensive.*

grade² *v.* sort things into sizes, kinds, etc.: *They grade eggs before they send them to the shops.*

gradual /'grædʒʊəl/ *adj.* happening a little at a time; slow: *A gradual hill is not steep.* **gradually** *adv.*: *We all become gradually older.*

graduate¹ /'grædʒʊət/ *n.* someone who has a university degree: *a graduate of Oxford.*

graduate^2 /'grædʒʊeɪt/ v. get a university degree: *Richard graduated from Leeds University.*

grain /greɪn/ n. **1** seed of a food-plant: *grains of wheat; grains of rice.* **2** tiny, hard bit of something: *grains of sand.*

gram /græm/ n. measure of weight.

grammar /'græmə(r)/ n. (no pl.) study of the right way to put words together when we speak and write. **grammatical** /grə'mætɪkl/ adj. that you have written or said in the right way: *It is not grammatical to say 'They is.'* **grammatically** adv. **grammar-school** n. secondary school for pupils who learn academic subjects.

gramme /græm/ n. measure of weight.

gramophone /'græməfəʊn/ n. machine that plays records.

grand /grænd/ adj. **1** very big, rich, fine, etc.: *a grand palace.* **2** very enjoyable: *Thanks for a grand holiday.* **grandly** adv. in a fine, important way. **grand piano** n. very big piano.

grandchild /'græntʃaɪld/ n. (pl. grandchildren) the child of your child.

granddaughter /'grændɔːtə(r)/ n. the daughter of your child.

grandfather /'grænfɑːðə(r)/, **grandpa** /'grænpɑː/ n. the father of your father or mother.

grandmother /'grænmʌðə(r)/, **grandma** /'grænmɑː/ n. the mother of your father or mother.

grandparents /'grænpeərənts/ n. (pl.) the mother and father of your mother or father.

grandson /'grænsʌn/ n. the son of your child.

grandstand /'grændstænd/ n. rows of seats, with a roof over them, where people sit to watch a sport.

granny, grannie /'grænɪ/ n. child's word for grandmother.

grant^1 /grɑːnt/ n. money that you give for a special reason: *The government gives a grant to every student so that he can buy books.*

grant^2 v. give what someone has asked for: *My boss granted me free time when my mother was ill.*

grape /greɪp/ n. juicy, green or purple fruit, which we can eat or make into wine.

grapefruit /'greɪpfruːt/ n. (pl. grapefruit) fruit like a big, yellow orange.

grasp /grɑːsp/ v. **1** hold something tightly: *Grasp my hand and I will pull you over the wall.* **2** understand: *I can't grasp this maths question.* **grasp** n.: *The ball fell from his grasp.*

grass /grɑːs/ n. **1** (pl. grasses) plant with thin, green leaves that cows eat. **2** (no pl.) place that is covered with grass: *We played cricket on the grass in the park.* **grassy** adj. covered with grass: *a grassy hill.*

grate /greɪt/ v. rub something into small bits: *Mother grated the cheese.*

grateful /'greɪtfl/ adj. thankful; showing thanks: *I am grateful to you for your help.* **gratefully** adv.: *She smiled gratefully when I gave her my seat.*

gratitude /'grætɪtjuːd/ n. (no pl.) feeling or showing thanks: *Tony wrote a letter of gratitude for my help.*

grave^1 /greɪv/ adj. bad; serious: *He made a grave mistake.* **gravely** adv.: *He is gravely ill in hospital.*

grave^2 n. hole that you dig in the ground for a dead person. **gravestone** /'greɪvstəʊn/ n. stone that you put on a grave, with the name of the dead person. **graveyard** /'greɪvjɑːd/ n. place where dead people lie in the ground.

gravel /'grævl/ n. (no pl.) small stones and sand. **gravel** adj.: *a gravel path.*

gravy /'greɪvɪ/ n. (no pl.) **1** juice that comes from meat when it is cooking. **2** thin, meat sauce that you put on food.

gray /greɪ/ adj. grey.

graze^1 /greɪz/ v. **1** go close to something: *The car grazed the wall.* **2** rub along something; rub the skin off part of the body: *He fell and grazed his arm.* **graze** n.

graze^2 v. eat grass: *The sheep are grazing in the field.*

grease^1 /griːs/ n. (no pl.) animal fat; any stuff that is oily, fatty, etc.

grease^2 v. put oil, etc. on to something.

greasy /'griːsɪ/ adj. sticky; slippery; covered with oil, fat, etc.: *My fingers were greasy after the meal.*

great[1] /greɪt/ *adj.* **1** much; a lot of; more than usual: *Take great care when you cross the road.* **2** special; important: *Schweitzer was a great man.* **3** very good: *They are great friends.* **4** wonderful; enjoyable: *It was a great party.* **a great many**, very many: *He made a great many mistakes.*

great-[2] *prefix* showing some parts of a family: *My mother's grandmother is my great-grandmother and I am her great-grandson.*

greatly /'greɪtlɪ/ *adv.* much; very: *I was greatly surprised to see him!*

greedy /'gri:dɪ/ *adj.* wanting too much: *My greedy brother has eaten all the sweets.*

green[1] /gri:n/ *adj.* **1** with the colour of grass: *Laura has green eyes.* **2** not ripe; not ready: *green bananas.*

green[2] *n.* **1** (no *pl.*) colour of grass. **2** (*pl.* greens) piece of open, grassy land in the middle of an English village. **green** *adj.* with the colour of grass.

greenhouse /'gri:nhaʊs/ *n.* building with glass walls and roof, where plants grow.

greet /gri:t/ *v.* say hello: *Amy greeted us with a smile when we arrived.*

greeting /'gri:tɪŋ/ *n.* **1** words that you say when you meet someone: *'Good morning!' is a greeting.* **2** words that you write to someone at a special time: *a birthday greeting.*

grenade /grɪ'neɪd/ *n.* small bomb.

grew /gru:/ *past tense* of *v.* grow.

grey, gray /greɪ/ *adj.* with the colour of ashes, or a winter sky, or an elephant: *The old man's hair is grey.* **grey** *n.*

grief /gri:f/ *n.* (no *pl.*) great sadness: *Her grief was great when her father died.*

grieve /gri:v/ *v.* **1** be very sad: *She grieved over the death of her child.* **2** make someone very sad: *The terrible news grieved us.*

grill /grɪl/ *v.* cook meat, fish, etc. on a frame over or under direct heat: *to grill chops.* **grill** *n.* **1** special frame, or part of a cooker, where you grill meat. **2** meat that you have cooked in a grill: *We had a grill for lunch.*

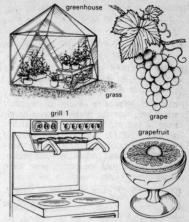

greenhouse

grass

grill 1

grape

grapefruit

grim /grɪm/ *adj.* (grimmer, grimmest) **1** serious; making you feel serious and worried: *grim news.* **2** hard: *a grim fight.*

grin /grɪn/ *n.* big smile. **grin** *v.* (*pres. part.* grinning, *past part.* & *past tense* grinned /grɪnd/).

grind /graɪnd/ *v.* (*past part.* & *past tense* ground /graʊnd/) **1** crush something into very small bits or powder: *Will you grind the coffee for me?* **2** sharpen a knife, tool, etc. on a hard stone, etc.

grip /grɪp/ *v.* (*pres. part.* gripping, *past part.* & *past tense* gripped /grɪpt/) hold something tightly: *She gripped the rail as she climbed the steep stairs.* **grip** *n.* **lose your grip**, stop holding on to something: *He lost his grip on the rocks and fell into the sea.*

gripping /'grɪpɪŋ/ *adj.* very exciting: *a gripping story.*

grit /grɪt/ *n.* (no *pl.*) tiny, hard bits of stone, sand, etc.: *Give me your handkerchief—I have a piece of grit in my eye.*

groan /grəʊn/ *v.* make a deep sound to show that you are hurt, sad, etc. **groan** *n.: He gave a groan of pain.*

grocer /'grəʊsə(r)/ *n.* someone who has a shop that sells tea, coffee, sugar, and all food in tins and packets. **grocery** *n.* grocer's shop.

groceries /'grəʊsərɪz/ *n.* (*pl.*) food in tins, packets, jars, boxes, etc.

groom /gru:m/ *n.* **1** someone whose job is to look after horses. **2** man on his wedding-day.

groove /gru:v/ *n.* long cut: *The needle moves along a groove in the record.*

grope /grəup/ *v.* move the hands in an unsure way, to do or get something: *I groped in the darkness for the door.*

ground¹ /graund *n.* **1** (no *pl.*) earth; soil: *After frost the ground is too hard to dig.* **2** (no *pl.*) top part of the earth: *An apple fell to the ground.* **3** (*pl.* grounds) piece of land for a special use: *a football ground.* **break new** or **fresh ground**, do or find something new: *Dr. Jenner broke new ground in medicine.* **suit someone down to the ground**, please someone in every way: *This house will suit us down to the ground.* **ground** *adj.* **ground floor** *n.* all the rooms in a building at the same height as the street.

ground² *past part.* & *past tense* of *v.* grind.

ground³ *v.* make an aeroplane stay on the ground: *The fog has grounded many planes at Gatwick.*

grounds /graundz/ *n.* (*pl.*) land around a building: *the school grounds.*

group /gru:p/ *n.* **1** number of people or things together: *a group of houses.* **2** club for people who have a special interest: *a drama group.*

grow /grəu/ *v.* (*past part.* grown /grəun/, *past tense* grew/gru:/) **1** become bigger, taller, longer, etc.: *Oranges will not grow well in England.* **2** keep and care for plants: *The farmer grows potatoes in this field.* **3** let something get bigger, longer, etc.: *Annette is growing her hair.* **4** become: *Put the light on—it's growing dark.* **grow out of**, become too big to do or wear something: *She's grown out of her shoes.* **grow up**, become an adult; change from a child to a man or a woman: *I want to be a pilot when I grow up.*

grower /'grəuə(r)/ *n.* farmer; someone who grows things.

growl /graul/ *v.* make a low, angry sound in the throat: *The dog growled at the strange man.* **growl** *n.: The dog gave a growl.*

grown /grəun/ *past part.* of *v.* grow.

grown-up /'grəun ʌp/ *n.* an adult; a man or a woman, not a child. **grown-up** *adj.: She has a grown-up son.*

growth /grəuθ/ *n.* (no *pl.*) getting bigger, etc.: *the growth of a baby.*

grubby /'grʌbɪ/ *adj.* dirty: *Go and wash your grubby hands!*

grudge /grʌdʒ/ *n.* **have** or **bear a grudge**, have a bad feeling, such as envy, hate, etc., against someone: *He bore me a grudge because I got better marks than he did.*

grumble /'grʌmbl/ *v.* say angrily that you do not like something: *You're always grumbling about the weather!* **grumble** *n.: She's always full of grumbles.* **grumbler** *n.* someone who grumbles a lot.

grumpy /'grʌmpɪ/ *adj.* rather angry; not friendly for the moment. **grumpily** *adv.*

grunt /grʌnt/ *v.* make a noise like a pig. **grunt** *n.*

guarantee /ˌgærən'ti:/ *n.* **1** promise: *Arnold has given me a guarantee that he will come back on Sunday.* **2** special promise on paper that a maker will replace or mend goods that go wrong: *This watch has a two-year guarantee.* **guarantee** *v.* make a promise.

guard¹ /gɑ:d/ *n.* **1** (no *pl.*) keeping a place or people safe from harm or attack. **keep** or **stand guard**, stand at a building, etc. to watch for attack. **on guard**, ready for attack. **2** (*pl.* guards) someone who watches a prisoner or keeps a building safe: *a prison guard.* **3** (*pl.* guards) someone whose job is to look after people and goods on a train.

guard² *v.* keep someone or something safe from harm: *Two big dogs guard the farm.* **guard against**, keep away danger: *My grandfather walks with a stick to guard against falling.*

guardian /'gɑ:dɪən/ *n.* someone who looks after a young child with no parents.

guerrilla /gə'rɪlə/ *n.* secret fighter.

guess /ges/ *v.* give an answer without really knowing about it: *Can you guess his age?* **guess** *n.: She made a guess, but was wrong.*

guest /gest/ *n.* someone who stays or eats in another person's house, hotel, etc.: *We had six guests to dinner.*

guidance /'gaɪdəns/ *n.* (no *pl.*) help: *I made a dress with my mother's guidance.*

guide[1] /gaɪd/ *n.* **1** someone who shows people where to go, and tells them about a place, etc.: *The guide took us round Berkeley Castle.* **2** book that tells you how to do something: *a guide to farming.* **3** something that helps you to do things, etc.: *Signposts are a guide to drivers.* **4** member of a special club for girls: *a Girl Guide.* **guide-book** *n.* book that tells people about a town, country, etc.

guide[2] *v.* **1** show someone where to go, etc.: *The dog guided the blind man across the road.* **2** teach or help someone.

guilt /gɪlt/ *n.* (no *pl.*) feeling that you have done wrong; having done wrong: *The court is sure of his guilt.*

guilty /'gɪltɪ/ *adj.* **1** having done wrong: *He was guilty of stealing £200.* **2** feeling or showing that you have done wrong: *He had a guilty look on his face.* **guiltily** *adv.*

guinea-pig /'gɪnɪ pɪg/ *n.* small animal that you keep as a pet.

guitar /gɪ'ta:(r)/ *n.* musical instrument with strings.

gulp /gʌlp/ *v.* swallow food or drink quickly: *He gulped his meal.* **gulp** *n.*

gum /gʌm/ *n.* (no *pl.*) stuff that sticks things together. **gum** *v.* (*pres. part.* gumming, *past part.* & *past tense* gummed /gʌmd/) stick things together with gum or glue. **chewing-gum** *n.* sweet that you chew but do not swallow.

gun /gʌn/ *n.* thing that shoots out bullets to kill people: *A revolver is a sort of gun.* **gunman** *n.* someone who shoots another person.

gunpowder /'gʌnpaʊdə(r)/ *n.* (no *pl.*) powder for guns, bullets, fireworks, etc. that explodes when you put fire to it.

gush /gʌʃ/ *v.* burst or flow out strongly: *Water was gushing from the tap.*

gust /gʌst/ *n.* sudden, strong wind. **gusty** *adj.* stormy; windy: *a gusty day.*

gutter /'gʌtə(r)/ *n.* channel under the edge of a roof or at the side of a road to take away rain-water.

gutter

guitar

gun

guy 2

guinea pig

guy /gaɪ/ *n.* **1** man; fellow: *He's a nice guy!* **2** sort of big doll that English children burn on Guy Fawkes Day.

gym /dʒɪm/ *abbrev.* gymnastics; gymnasium.

gymnasium /dʒɪm'neɪzɪəm/ *n.* room or building where you do physical exercises, sports, etc.

gymnastics /dʒɪm'næstɪks/ *n.* (*pl.*) exercises for the body.

gypsy /'dʒɪpsɪ/ *n.* (*pl.* gypsies) person with dark hair and eyes who lives in a caravan and never stays long in one place.

Hh

habit /'hæbɪt/ *n.* what you usually do: *It's my habit to get up early every morning.*

hack /hæk/ *v.* cut something roughly.

had /hæd/ *past part.* & *past tense* of *v.* have. **you had better**, it is best for you to do something: *We had better go into the house because it is raining.*

haddock /'hædək/ *n.* (*pl.* haddock) sort of sea-fish that you can eat.

ha! ha! /'ha: ha:/ *exclam.* words that show laughing.

hail /heɪl/ n. (no pl.) frozen drops of rain. **hailstone** n. small ball of ice that falls from the sky. **hail** v.: *It was so cold yesterday that it hailed.*

hair /heə(r)/ n. **1** (pl. hairs) fine thread that grows on the skin of animals and people. **2** (no pl.) what grows on the head: *Rose combed her hair.* **make your hair stand on end**, make you very frightened: *That spy film made my hair stand on end!* **not turn a hair**, not show that you are worried or afraid.

haircut /'heəkʌt/ n. **1** cutting the hair: *I need a haircut.* **2** way your hair is cut; hairstyle: *a short haircut.*

hairdresser /'heədresə(r)/ n. someone whose job is to cut and arrange hair.

hairpin /'heəpɪn/ n. pin that holds your hair in place.

hairstyle /'heəstaɪl/ n. way of doing your hair.

hairy /'heərɪ/ adj. covered with hair: *hairy legs.*

half /hɑːf/ n. (pl. halves) one of two equal parts of something: *Half of 6 is 3.* **half** adv. **1** 50 per cent: *This bottle is only half full.* **2** partly: *This work is only half done.* **half past the hour**, 30 minutes after the hour: *It is half past six.*

half-term /ˌhɑːf tɜːm/ n. short school holiday in the middle of term.

half-time /ˌhɑːf 'taɪm/ n. (no pl.) short break in the middle of a game of football, etc.

half-way /ˌhɑːf 'weɪ/ adv. in the middle of a journey or job: *I am half-way through my book.*

hall /hɔːl/ n. **1** big room or building for meetings, concerts, etc.: *the Town Hall.* **2** room in a house, with doors to other rooms.

hallo /hə'ləʊ/ exclam. friendly word that you say when you meet someone or talk on the telephone.

halt /hɔːlt/ v. stop moving; make something stop moving: *He halted the car at the traffic lights.* **halt** n. **come to a halt**, stop.

halve /hɑːv/ v. divide something into two parts that are the same size: *There are two of us, so you must halve the orange.*

halves /hɑːvz/ (pl.) of n. half.

ham /hæm/ n. (no pl.) salted or smoked meat from a pig's leg.

hamburger /'hæmbɜːgə(r)/ n. round sandwich with hot meat in it.

hammer[1] /'hæmə(r)/ n. tool with a handle and a metal head for hitting nails.

hammer[2] v. **1** hit something with a hammer. **2** hit something hard with the hand: *He hammered on the door to wake us.*

hammock /'hæmək/ n. bed of canvas or knotted rope that hangs up between two trees, etc.

hand[1] /hænd/ n. **1** part of the body at the end of the arm. **hands up**, (a) put your hand in the air if you can answer the question. (b) put your hands in the air because I have a gun. **by hand**, without using a machine: *Pam made the dress by hand.* **change hands**, be given or sold by one person to another: *That car has changed hands many times.* **give** or **lend a hand**, help someone: *Please give me a hand with this heavy box.* **have your hands full**, be very busy; have many things to do. **in good hands**, well cared for: *Don't worry—your son is in good hands.* **lay your hands on**, get or find something: *Do you know where I can lay my hands on a pen?* **off your hands**, no longer in your control: *'I'll be glad when this old car is off my hands!' said John.* **get out of hand**, behave in a wild way: *My horse got out of hand when I was away.* **shake hands with**, give your hand to someone when you meet him. **wait on someone hand and foot**, do everything for someone: *Mrs. Law waits on her lazy son hand and foot.* **2** worker in a factory, etc.: *farm hands.* **3** pointer on a clock or watch: *At midday both hands point to twelve.* **4** one side. **on the one hand, on the other hand**, words that show the good and bad sides of an idea: *On the one hand the hotel is near the sea, but on the other hand it costs a lot.*

hand[2] v. put something into someone's hand: *Please hand me that book.* **hand down**, pass a thing, story, etc. on to people who live after you: *This story has been handed down in my family for many years.* **hand in**, give something to someone: *'Hand in your essays now, children,' said the teacher.* **hand over**, give something, which you do not want to give, to someone: *'Hand over that knife!' said the policeman.*

handbag /'hændbæg/ n. woman's bag that holds small things.

handcuffs /'hændkʌfs/ n. (pl.) pair of metal rings with a chain, which you put on a prisoner's arms so that he cannot use his hands well.

handful /'hændful/ n. **1** what you can hold in one hand. **2** small number: *Only a handful of people came to the meeting.*

hand-grenade /'hænd grəneɪd/ n. small bomb that you throw by hand.

handicap /'hændɪkæp/ n. something that stops you doing well: *Bad eyesight is a handicap to a student.* **handicap** v. (*pres. part.* handicapping, *past part. & past tense* handicapped /'hændɪkæpt/) stop you doing well.

handkerchief /'hæŋkətʃɪf/ n. square piece of cloth that you use to wipe your nose.

handle¹ /'hændl/ n. the part of a thing that you hold: *I can't carry the bucket if the handle is broken.*

handle² v. **1** touch something with the hands: *Please wash your hands before you handle the food.* **2** control a person or animal: *A child can't handle that big dog.* **3** look after something: *The clerk handles all letters.*

handlebar /'hændlbɑː(r)/ n. bar that the rider holds at the front of a bicycle or motor-cycle.

hand-made /ˌhænd 'meɪd/ adj. made by a person, not by a machine.

handsome /'hænsəm/ adj. good-looking: *a handsome boyfriend.*

handwriting /'hændraɪtɪŋ/ n. (no pl.) the way you write: *Colin has clear handwriting.*

handy /'hændɪ/ adj. **1** good with the hands: *a handy workman.* **2** useful: *My box of tools is very handy.* **3** near; easy to find: *I always have an extra shirt handy.*

hang /hæŋ/ v. **1** (*past part. & past tense* hung /hʌŋ/) fix something at the top so that the lower part falls freely: *Hilary is hanging her washing on the line.* **2** (*past part. & past tense* hung) be fixed at the top so that it falls freely: *Curtains hang at the windows.* **3** (*past part. & past tense* hanged /hæŋd/) kill someone by holding him above the ground with a rope

hairdresser

hair 2

hammer¹

handkerchief

hand¹ 1

round his neck: *They hanged him for murder.* **hang about**, stand around doing nothing: *Why is he hanging about in the streets?* **hang back**, show that you don't want to do something: *The big boys jumped into the river but little Ned hung back.* **hang on**, wait: *Hang on—don't go yet!* **hang on to**, hold something firmly: *Hang on to my arm in the crowd.*

hangar /'hæŋə(r)/ n. big shed for aeroplanes.

hanger /'hæŋə(r)/ n. bar with a hook for holding clothes: *a coat-hanger.*

hankie, hankey /'hæŋkɪ/ abbrev. handkerchief.

happen /'hæpən/ v. be; take place: *The accident happened at 3 p.m.* **happen to**, do something by chance: *You happened to be out when I came to your house.* **happening** n. something that happens; event.

happy /'hæpɪ/ adj. glad; content: *Mary smiled because she was happy.* **happily** adv. **happiness** n.

harbour /'hɑːbə(r)/ n. place where ships come to land safely.

hard¹ /hɑːd/ adj. **1** not soft; firm: *Rock is hard.* **2** difficult; not easy to do or understand: *hard work.* **3** giving trouble, pain, etc.: *He's had a hard life.* **4** not kind; strict: *a hard father.* **be hard on**, be strict with someone. **hard up**, poor; not having much money.

hard[2] *adv.* **1** strongly: *Geoff hit Mike hard.* **2** a lot: *You must work hard.*

hard-hearted /ˌhɑːd ˈhɑːtɪd/ *adj.* cruel; not kind.

hardly /ˈhɑːdlɪ/ *adv.* only just; not well: *She speaks so quietly I can hardly hear her.*

hardy /ˈhɑːdɪ/ *adj.* strong; able to bear bad conditions: *Sheep must be hardy to live on the hills in winter.*

hare /heə(r)/ *n.* small animal like a rabbit, with long ears.

harm[1] /hɑːm/ *n.* (no *pl.*) hurt; damage. **come to harm**, be hurt.

harm[2] *v.* hurt someone or something: *Hot water will harm the plants.* **harmful** *adj.* dangerous. **harmfully** *adv.* **harmless** *adj.* not dangerous. **harmlessly** *adv.*

harness /ˈhɑːnɪs/ *n.* (*pl.* harnesses) leather straps and metal pieces that a horse wears.

harp /hɑːp/ *n.* big musical instrument with strings, which you play with your fingers.

harsh /hɑːʃ/ *adj.* **1** rough and unpleasant: *a harsh voice.* **2** cruel: *a harsh master.* **harshly** *adv.*

harvest /ˈhɑːvɪst/ *n.* the time when you gather vegetables, corn, or other crops: *The apple harvest comes in September.* **harvest** *v.* gather crops: *When will you harvest your wheat?*

has /hæz/ part of *v.* have: *Edna has an egg.*

hasn't /ˈhæznt/ = has not.

haste /heɪst/ *n.* (no *pl.*) speed; hurry. **in haste**, quickly; in a hurry: *He left in haste because he was late.*

hasten /ˈheɪsn/ *v.* move or do something quickly: *He hastened to catch the train.*

hasty /ˈheɪstɪ/ *adj.* **1** that you do quickly: *We ate a hasty meal.* **2** that you say or do too quickly: *I'm sorry now that my words were so hasty.* **hastily** *adv.*

hat /hæt/ *n.* something that you wear on your head.

hatch /hætʃ/ *v.* come out of an egg; bring young ones out of an egg: *When will the hen's eggs hatch?*

hate[1] /heɪt/, **hatred** /ˈheɪtrɪd/ *n.* (no *pl.*) very great dislike: *He looked at me with hate.*

hate[2] *v.* **1** feel that someone or something is very bad: *Cats hate water.* **2** feel sorry about something: *I hate to trouble you.*

hatred /ˈheɪtrɪd/ *n.* (no *pl.*) very great dislike; hate: *He looked at me with hatred.*

haul /hɔːl/ *v.* pull something heavy: *The elephants were hauling logs.*

haunt /hɔːnt/ *v.* **1** come as a spirit to a place: *A ghost haunts the castle.* **2** visit a place often: *Tony haunts the sports centre.* **3** come to your mind: *Memories of the past haunt her.*

haunted /ˈhɔːntɪd/ *adj.* often visited by spirits: *a haunted house.*

have /hæv/ *v.* (*past part. & past tense* had /hæd/) **1** own or keep something: *Susan has red hair. I have a small car.* **2** word that helps to form perfect tenses of verbs: *I have finished.* **3** eat or drink something: *Do you have tea or coffee in the morning?* **4** feel something: *I have a bad pain in my back.* **5** keep something in your mind: *Have you any idea where he lives?* **will not have**, will not allow something to happen: *I won't have you pulling the cat's tail.* **have to**, must: *I have to go to school on Monday.* **have someone do something**, make someone do something: *I had the mechanic examine the car brakes.* **have something done**, arrange for something to be done: *Pat is having her hair cut by the hairdresser.*

haven't /ˈhævnt/ = have not.

hawk /hɔːk/ *n.* big bird that catches and kills smaller birds.

hay /heɪ/ *n.* (no *pl.*) dried grass that the farmer gathers to feed his animals in the winter. **haystack** /ˈheɪstæk/ *n.* big heap of hay.

hazard /ˈhæzəd/ *n.* risk; danger: *Ice is a hazard for drivers.* **hazardous** *adj.*

haze /heɪz/ *n.* (no *pl.*) thin mist. **hazy** *adj.*: *a hazy day.*

hazel nut /ˈheɪzl nʌt/ *n.* sort of nut that you can eat.

he /hiː/ *pron.* (*pl.* they) word for any male person: *Where is your brother? He is at home.*

head[1] /hed/ *n.* **1** part of the body above the neck: *She tied a scarf round her head.* **a head**, for each person: *This meal will* *cost £10 a head.* **hang your head**, bend your head to show that you know you have done wrong: *Audrey hung her head when I shouted at her.* **2** brain; mind; thinking: *He made the story up in his head.* **go to your head, turn your head**, make you too pleased with yourself: *His prize went to his head.* **keep your head**, stay calm: *You must try to keep your head when you are in danger.* **lose your head**, become too excited to think: *She lost her head and ran in front of a car.* **put heads together**, think about something with other people: *Let's put our heads together and find a plan.* **use your head**, think. **3** front; front part: *the head of the queue.* **4** chief person: *The Pope is the head of the Roman Catholic Church.*

head² *v.* be at the front or top of a group: *Michael's name heads the list.* **head for**, go towards: *Let's head for the river.*

headache /'hedeɪk/ *n.* pain in the head.

heading /'hedɪŋ/ *n.* title; word or words at the top of a piece of writing to show what it is about.

headlamp /'hedlæmp/, **headlight** /'hedlaɪt/ *n.* big, strong lamp at the front of a car, etc.

headline /'hedlaɪn/ *n.* words in big letters at the top of some writing in a newspaper.

headmaster /ˌhed'mɑːstə(r)/ *n.* man in charge of a school.

headmistress /ˌhed'mɪstrɪs/ *n.* (*pl.* headmistresses) woman in charge of a school.

headphones /'hedfəʊnz/ *n.* (*pl.*) things that fit over the head and ears for listening to a radio, etc.

headquarters /ˌhed'kwɔːtəz/ *n.* (*pl.*) main offices where the leaders work.

heal /hiːl/ *v.* become well again: *His burns healed quickly.*

health /helθ/ *n.* (no *pl.*) how the body is; how well you are: *My uncle is in poor health.* **drink someone's health**, have a drink and say you hope someone will stay well.

healthy /'helθɪ/ *adj.* **1** well; not ill: *Those puppies look very healthy.* **2** that will make or keep you well: *The seaside has a healthy climate.*

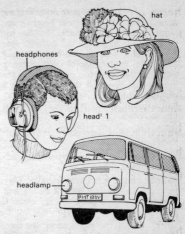

hat

headphones

head¹ 1

headlamp

heap /hiːp/ *n.* pile of things: *a heap of bricks.* **heaps of**, lots of; plenty: *We have heaps of books and toys.* **heap** *v.* put things in a pile: *Mother heaped food on to my plate.*

hear /hɪə(r)/ *v.* (*past part. & past tense* heard /hɜːd/) **1** notice sounds with the ears: *I can hear the neighbour's radio because it is so loud.* **2** receive information: *Have you heard the news?* **hear from**, get a letter, etc. from someone: *Have you heard from your sister?* **hear of**, know about someone or something: *Who is he? I've never heard of him.* **will not hear of**, will not agree to something: *My boss won't hear of my leaving work early.*

hear! hear! *exclam.* words that show you agree.

hearing /'hɪərɪŋ/ *n.* **1** (no *pl.*) noticing sound: *Speak loudly because his hearing is not good.* **2** (no *pl.*) how far you can hear. **out of hearing**, too far away to hear: *I called her but she was out of hearing.*

heart /hɑːt/ *n.* **1** thing inside the chest, that pumps blood round the body: *When I run, my heart beats fast.* **2** your feelings: *Oliver has a kind heart.* **break someone's heart**, make someone very sad. **by heart**, so that you know every word: *I have learned this poem by heart.* **cry your heart out**, cry very much. **have a change of heart**, change your feelings about something: *Let's ask him again—he may have a* *change of heart.* **have your heart in your mouth,** be afraid. **have your heart set on,** want something very much: *Ann has her heart set on going to the festival.* **lose heart,** feel less brave and hopeful. **take heart,** feel more hopeful. **with a heavy heart,** sadly. **3** centre; middle part: *the heart of the forest.* **4** the shape ♥ on a playing card, etc.

heartbroken /'hɑːtbrəʊkən/ *adj.* very sad.

hearth /hɑːθ/ *n.* fireplace: *Cats like to sit by a warm hearth.*

heartless /'hɑːtlɪs/ *adj.* cruel; not kind. **heartlessly** *adv.*

hearty /'hɑːtɪ/ *adj.* **1** very friendly: *They gave me a hearty welcome.* **2** strong and healthy: *a hearty child.* **3** big: *Howard ate a hearty meal.*

heat[1] /hiːt/ **1** (no *pl.*) hotness; the feeling that comes from the sun. **2** (*pl.* heats) one race in a sports competition.

heat[2] *v.* become hot; make something hot: *Pat heated some milk in a saucepan.*

heater /'hiːtə(r)/ *n.* something that gives heat to make a place warm: *an oil-heater.*

heating /'hiːtɪŋ/ *n.* (no *pl.*) **central heating,** system to heat a building.

heather /'heðə(r)/ *n.* (no *pl.*) sort of plant.

heave /hiːv/ *v.* lift or pull something heavy.

heaven /'hevn/ *n.* (no *pl.*) home of God, where many people believe they will go when they die. **heavens** (*pl.*) sky: *The stars shine in the heavens.*

heavy /'hevɪ/ *adj.* **1** with a lot of weight; not easy to lift or move: *I can't carry this bag because it's heavy.* **2** much; a lot of: *heavy rain.* **3** strong: *a heavy blow.* **heavily** *adv.*

hectare /'hektɑː(r)/ *n.* measure of land = 10,000 square metres.

hedge /hedʒ/ *n.* row of bushes that make a wall at the edge of a garden, field, or road.

hedgehog /'hedʒhɒg/ *n.* small animal covered with sharp needles.

heel /hiːl/ *n.* back part of the foot, sock, or shoe. **at** or **on someone's heels,** close behind someone.

height /haɪt/ *n.* **1** being high; how far it is from the bottom of something to the top: *What is the height of the room?* **2** high place: *the mountain heights.* **3** greatest or strongest time: *The storm was at its height.*

heir /eə(r)/ *n.* someone who receives the money, goods, title, etc. when another person dies: *Prince Charles is Queen Elizabeth's heir.* **heiress** /'eərɪs/ *n.* female heir.

held /held/ *past part. & past tense* of *v.* hold.

helicopter /'helɪkɒptə(r)/ *n.* sort of aeroplane with big, turning blades on top.

hell /hel/ *n.* (no *pl.*) place where bad people go after they are dead.

he'll /hiːl/ = he will.

hello /hə'ləʊ/ *exclam.* friendly word that you say when you meet someone or talk on the telephone.

helmet /'helmɪt/ *n.* hard hat that keeps the head safe: *Firemen wear helmets.*

help /help/ *v.* make another person's work easier for him; do something for someone who has problems: *Please help me to lift this heavy box.* **cannot help something,** cannot stop yourself doing something: *Babies can't help wetting their clothes.* **it can't be helped,** there's no way of stopping it. **help someone to something,** give someone food, drink, etc.: *I helped her to a cup of tea.* **help yourself,** take what you want: *She helped herself to a sandwich.* **help** *n.* **1** aid; helping someone: *Thank you for your help.* **2** thing or person that helps: *A walking-stick is a great help to the old lady.* **helper** *n.* someone who helps.

helpful /'helpfl/ *adj.* useful; willing to do what is wanted. **helpfully** *adv.*

helping /'helpɪŋ/ *n.* food on your plate: *Hungry children like big helpings.*

helpless /'helplɪs/ *adj.* not able to take care of yourself: *A baby is totally helpless.* **helplessly** *adv.*

hem /hem/ *n.* neat end of a piece of clothing: *The skirt is too short—let down the hem.*

hen /hen/ *n.* **1** female bird. **2** farm bird that lays eggs and that we eat.

her[1] /hɜ:(r)/ *adj.* of a woman or girl: *That is her book.*

her[2] *pron.* (*pl.* them) word that shows a woman or girl: *Where is Kathy? I can't see her.*

herb /hɜ:b/ *n.* plant, usually with a strong smell and taste, used in medicine or in cooking.

herd /hɜ:d/ *n.* group of animals: *a herd of cattle.*

here /hɪə(r)/ *adv.* in, at, or to this place: *Don't go away—come here. Here is my car.* **here and there,** in different places: *There were boats here and there on the sea.*

hero /'hɪərəʊ/ *n.* (*pl.* heroes) **1** very brave man or boy: *David was a hero when he killed Goliath.* **2** most important man in a story, play, etc.

heroic /hɪ'rəʊɪk/ *adj.* very brave: *heroic deeds.*

heroine /'herəʊɪn/ *n.* **1** very brave woman or girl. **2** most important woman in a story, play, etc.

herring /'herɪŋ/ *n.* sort of sea-fish that you can eat.

hers /hɜːz/ *pron.* (*pl.* theirs) thing that belongs to a woman or girl: *This book is mine and that book is hers.*

herself /hɜː'self/ *pron.* (*pl.* themselves) **1** word that describes the same woman or girl that you have just talked about: *Sarah hurt herself when she fell.* **2** she and no other person: *Sue made a cake herself, without her mother's help.* **by herself,** alone: *Patricia is playing by herself in the garden.*

hesitate /'hezɪteɪt/ *v.* stop for a moment to show that you are not sure about what you are doing: *Andrew hesitated before he took the last cake.* **hesitant** /'hezɪtənt/ *adj.* **hesitantly** *adv.* in an unsure way. **hesitation** /ˌhezɪ'teɪʃn/ *n.*

hey /heɪ/ *exclam.* word to make someone hear you or to show surprise: *Hey! What are you doing?*

hiccup, hiccough /'hɪkʌp/ *n.* sudden loud noise in the throat that comes again and again: *If you eat too fast you'll have hiccups.* **hiccup, hiccough** *v.*

hide /haɪd/ *v.* (*past part.* hidden /'hɪdn/,

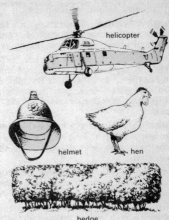

helicopter

helmet　　　hen

hedge

past tense hid /hɪd/) **1** be in a secret place; put something in a secret place: *Peggy hid the broken cup behind her back.* **2** not tell someone about something. **hide-and-seek** *n.* children's game when one child hides and others try to find him.

hideous /'hɪdɪəs/ *adj.* very ugly.

hiding /'haɪdɪŋ/ *n.* (no *pl.*) *be in,* or *go into hiding,* be in, or go into, a place where other people will not see or find you: *The prisoners escaped and went into hiding.*

high[1] /haɪ/ *adj.* **1** how far from top to bottom; tall: *The table is two metres high.* **2** going up a long way: *Mount Everest is very high.* **3** at the top of sound: *high notes.* **4** costing a lot of money: *high prices.* **5** senior: *a high school.*

high[2] *adv.* far up: *The plane flew high above the clouds.* **high and low,** everywhere: *Bill looked high and low for his lost shoe.*

hi-fi /'haɪ faɪ/ *n.* sort of record-player.

highlands /'haɪləndz/ *n.* (*pl.*) part of a country with hills or mountains.

highly /'haɪlɪ/ *adv.* very much; greatly: *The teacher thinks very highly of Frank's work.*

Highness /'haɪnɪs/ *n.* (*pl.* Highnesses) title for a royal person: *Your Highness.*

high school /'haɪ skuːl/ *n.* secondary school.

highway /'haɪweɪ/ n. main road.

highwayman /'haɪweɪmən/ n. (pl. highwaymen) man who stopped travellers and robbed them in old times.

hijack /'haɪdʒæk/ v. **1** stop a car, lorry, etc., on the road and steal from it. **2** make the driver of a car or the pilot of an aeroplane take you somewhere. **hijacker** n. someone who hijacks a vehicle.

hike /haɪk/ v. go for a long walk in the country. **hike** n. long walk. **hiker** n. someone who is walking far in the country.

hill /hɪl/ n. **1** low mountain: the Cotswold Hills. **2** slope on a road, etc.: They pushed their bicycles up the hill.

him /hɪm/ pron. (pl. them) word that shows a man or boy: Where is Jim? I can't see him.

himself /hɪm'self/ pron. (pl. themselves) **1** word that describes the same man or boy that you have just talked about: Bernard hurt himself when he fell over. **2** he, and no other person: Michael made this box himself, without his father's help. **by himself**, alone.

hind /haɪnd/ adj. back: the hind legs of a dog.

hinder /'hɪndə(r)/ v. make another person's work more difficult for him: Don't hinder me when I am trying to work.

hint /hɪnt/ v. say something, but not directly: Una closed her eyes to hint that she was tired. **hint** n.

hip /hɪp/ n. place where the leg joins the side of the body: A cowboy wears his gun on his hip.

hippopotamus /ˌhɪpə'pɒtəməs/ n. (pl. hippopotami or hippopotamuses) big river animal with a thick skin.

hire /'haɪə(r)/ v. pay to use something, or to use someone's help: Can I hire a car for three days? **hire out**, let someone hire something from you: Mr. Jackson hires out bicycles. **hire** n.: Have you any bikes for hire?

his[1] /hɪz/ adj. of a man or boy: That is his book.

his[2] pron. (pl. theirs) thing that belongs to a man or boy: That book is his, not yours.

hiss /hɪs/ v. make a long sound like 's': The snake hissed. **hiss** n.: the hiss of steam.

historic /hɪ'stɒrɪk/ adj. important in past times: 1066 was an historic year for England. **historical** /hɪ'stɒrɪkl/ adj. of past times: an historical film.

history /'hɪstrɪ/ n. **1** (pl. histories) things that happened in the past. **2** (no pl.) study of the past: Our next lesson is history.

hit[1] /hɪt/ n. **1** blow; stroke: The batsman made a good hit. **2** song or film that most people like: That pop group has had many hits. **hit parade** n. list of pop records that sell best.

hit[2] v. (pres. part. hitting, past part. & past tense hit) knock someone or something hard: She cried when he hit her.

hitch-hike /'hɪtʃ haɪk/, **hitch** /hɪtʃ/ v. travel by asking for free rides in cars and lorries. **hitch-hiker** n. someone who hitch-hikes.

hive /haɪv/ n. box where bees live.

hoard[1] /hɔːd/ n. store of money, food, etc.

hoard[2] v. save and keep things secretly: The old man hoarded the gold in a stocking under his bed.

hoarse /hɔːs/ adj. not clear; rough: The preacher talked for such a long time that his voice became hoarse. **hoarsely** adv.

hoax /həʊks/ n. (pl. hoaxes) trick that you play on someone for a joke. **hoax** v.

hobble /'hɒbl/ v. walk painfully and slowly: The old man hobbled along with a stick.

hobby /'hɒbɪ/ n. (pl. hobbies) interest; what you like to do when you are not working: My hobby is collecting stamps.

hockey /'hɒkɪ/ n. (no pl.) game with two teams of players who hit the ball with long, curved sticks.

hoe /həʊ/ n. garden tool that breaks the soil. **hoe** v. work with a hoe.

hoist /hɔɪst/ v. lift or pull something up to a higher place, with ropes, etc.: to hoist a flag.

hold[1] /həʊld/ n. place at the bottom of a ship, where you keep the goods.

hold[2] n. having something in the hands. **get** or **take hold of**, catch something.

lose hold of, let something go: *She lost hold of the rope and fell.*

hold³ *v.* (*past part. & past tense* held /held/) **1** have something in the hand or arms: *The mother is holding her baby.* **2** keep something in place with the hand: *Val is holding her hat on her head because the wind is so strong.* **3** contain; be able to have something inside itself: *How much water will that bucket hold?* **4** have or own something: *Desmond holds a British passport.* **5** make something happen: *to hold a meeting.* **6** control something; keep something in a certain way: *When it started to snow, I couldn't hold the car on the road.* **7** be strong enough to carry something: *That branch won't hold you—it will break!* **hold someone back**, stop someone from moving forward: *The police held back the crowd.* **hold on, hold tight**, grip something and not let it go: *Hold tight when we go round the corner.* **hold up**, stop something for a time: *Rain held up the cricket match.*

hole /həʊl/ *n.* opening, gap, or space in something: *The dentist filled a hole in my tooth.*

holiday /ˈhɒlədeɪ/ *n.* day or time of rest from work: *school holidays.* **on holiday**, not at work, school, etc. **public holiday** *n.* day when everyone in a country has a holiday.

hollow /ˈhɒləʊ/ *adj.* empty; with nothing inside: *A drum is hollow.*

holly /ˈhɒlɪ/ *n.* (*pl.* hollies) tree with prickly, green leaves and red berries.

holy /ˈhəʊlɪ/ *adj.* **1** of God or religion: *the Holy Bible.* **2** religious; very good and pure: *The priest is a holy man.*

home¹ /həʊm/ *adv.* **1** to the place where you live: *Go home quickly!* **2** to your country: *John went home after three years in Holland.*

home² *n.* **1** place where you live: *I leave home at 8 a.m. every day.* **at home**, in your house: *Sandra stayed at home because she was tired.* **feel** or **make yourself at home**, be as easy as you would be in your own house. **2** place where they look after old people, children who have no parents, etc. **home** *adj.* of your home: *What is your home address?*

homeless /ˈhəʊmlɪs/ *adj.* with nowhere to live: *The floods made many people homeless.*

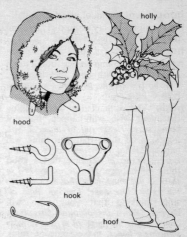

home-made /ˌhəʊm ˈmeɪd/ *adj.* made in your house, not in a shop: *home-made bread, cakes, etc.*

homesick /ˈhəʊmsɪk/ *adj.* sad because you are away from home.

homework /ˈhəʊmwɜːk/ *n.* (no *pl.*) work that a teacher gives a pupil to do at home.

honest /ˈɒnɪst/ *adj.* saying what is true; not stealing or cheating: *An honest man does not tell lies.* **honestly** *adv.* truly: *Tell me honestly if you like my new dress.* **honesty** /ˈɒnɪstɪ/ *n.*

honey /ˈhʌnɪ/ *n.* (no *pl.*) sweet food that bees make.

honeymoon /ˈhʌnɪmuːn/ *n.* holiday that a new husband and wife have just after their marriage.

honour /ˈɒnə(r)/ *n.* (no *pl.*) good name; respect. **in honour of**, to show you think a lot of someone: *There is a party tonight in honour of the new chairman.*

hood /hʊd/ *n.* part of a jacket or coat that goes over the head.

hoof /huːf/ *n.* (*pl.* hoofs or hooves) hard foot of a horse, sheep, cow, etc.

hook /hʊk/ *n.* curved or bent piece of metal **1** for catching something: *a fishhook.* **2** for hanging something: *a picture hook.* **hook** *v.* fasten or hold something with a hook or hooks: *She hooked her dress at the back.*

hoop /hu:p/ n. ring of wood or metal.

hoot /hu:t/ n. **1** cry of an owl. **2** sound that a car-horn makes. **hoot** v.

hooves /hu:vz/ (pl.) of n. hoof.

hop /hɒp/ v. **1** jump on one foot. **2** jump a short way, with both feet together: *The birds were hopping in the garden.* **hop** n. little jump.

hope[1] /həʊp/ n. **1** (no pl.) thinking that your wish will happen, but not being sure: *He is full of hope.* **2** (pl. hopes) good thing that you think will happen: *What are your hopes for the future?* **3** (no pl.) chance that a good thing will happen: *He has not worked so there is not much hope that he will pass the exam.* **lose hope**, **give up hope of**, stop thinking that your wish will happen: *When the postman passed my door, I gave up hope of a letter.* **raise someone's hopes**, make someone think that his wish will happen. **hopeful** adj. with hope. **hopefully** adv.

hope[2] v. wish for something to happen; think that something nice will happen but not be sure: *I hope to see him soon. I hope so*, I think that will happen but I am not sure: *'Will you be at the party?' 'I hope so.'*

hopeless /ˈhəʊplɪs/ adj. **1** with no hope: **2** very bad; useless: *He's hopeless at football.* **hopelessly** adv.

horizon /həˈraɪzn/ n. line where the earth or sea seems to meet the sky: *The sun sank below the horizon.*

horn /hɔ:n/ n. **1** one of a pair of sharp things on an animal's head. **2** musical instrument that you blow. **3** thing in a car that makes warning sounds: *The taxi-driver blew his horn to tell us that he had arrived.*

horrible /ˈhɒrəbl/ adj. **1** making you very afraid, very sad, or shocked: *Murder is a horrible crime.* **2** very bad: *What horrible weather.* **horribly** adv.

horrid /ˈhɒrɪd/ adj. horrible.

horrify /ˈhɒrɪfaɪ/ v. frighten or shock someone: *The pictures of the car crash horrified us.*

horror /ˈhɒrə(r)/ n. (no pl.) great fear or dislike: *She ran away in horror from the snake.*

horse /hɔ:s/ n. big animal that carries people and goods, pulls carts, etc. **on horseback**, riding a horse.

horseshoe /ˈhɔ:sʃu:/ n. metal shoe, like a U, that a horse wears on its foot.

hose /həʊz/, **hosepipe** /ˈhəʊz-paɪp/ n. long, soft tube that brings water to spray on fires, plants, etc.

hospital /ˈhɒspɪtl/ n. place where doctors and nurses look after sick people.

host /həʊst/ n. man who has guests.

hostage /ˈhɒstɪdʒ/ n. prisoner that you keep until people give you what you want. **hold someone hostage**, keep someone as a hostage.

hostel /ˈhɒstl/ n. place where students or travellers can get meals and rooms.

hostess /ˈhəʊstɪs/ n. (pl. hostesses) woman who has guests.

hostile /ˈhɒstaɪl/ adj. like an enemy; not friendly: *a hostile army.*

hot /hɒt/ adj. (hotter, hottest) that feels like the sun; with great heat: *hot weather.*

hotel /həʊˈtel/ n. building where you can buy a meal and hire a bedroom.

hot-water-bottle /ˌhɒt ˈwɔ:tə bɒtl/ n. rubber thing full of hot water, which you put in a bed to warm it.

hour /ˈaʊə(r)/ n. **1** sixty minutes: *a journey of three hours.* **2** time of day: *He came at an early hour.* **hours**, time when you do something, e.g. work: *school hours.*

hourly /ˈaʊəlɪ/ adj. done or happening every hour: *an hourly train.* **hourly** adv.

house /haʊs/ n. **1** building where a person or a family lives: *How many rooms are there in your house?* **2** building for some special purpose: *The House of Commons is part of the British Parliament.*

household /ˈhaʊshəʊld/ n. the people in a house: *There are four in our household.*

housekeeper /ˈhaʊski:pə(r)/ n. woman whose job is to look after a house, do the shopping, etc.

house-wife /ˈhaʊs waɪf/ n. (pl. house-wives) wife or mother who looks after a home.

hover /ˈhɒvə(r)/ v. stay in the air in one place: *A bird hovered over the field, looking for a mouse.*

hovercraft /'hɒvəkrɑːft/ n. special boat that travels across the top of water on a cushion of air.

how[1] /haʊ/ adv. **1** in what way: *She doesn't know how to make tea.* **2** word that you use to ask questions: *How much does that cost? How old is David?* *how are you? how do you feel?* do you feel well? *how do you do*, words that you say when you meet someone for the first time.

how[2] exclam. word that shows surprise or strong feeling: *How big that elephant is!*

however[1] /haʊ'evə(r)/ adv. **1** no matter how: *He won't win however hard he tries.* **2** how? in what way? *However did that happen?*

however[2] conj. but; still: *I want to go to the party—however, I have no transport.*

howl /haʊl/ n. **1** long, loud cry that a wolf or dog makes. **2** sound that strong wind makes. **3** sound that a person makes when he is hurt, angry, or amused. **howl** v.: *The wind howled in the trees.*

huddle /'hʌdl/ v. crowd together.

hug /hʌg/ v. (*pres. part.* hugging, *past part.* & *past tense* hugged /hʌgd/) put your arms round someone: *He hugged his mother.* **hug** n.

huge /hjuːdʒ/ adj. very big.

hullo /hə'ləʊ/ exclam. friendly word that you say you meet someone or talk on the telephone.

hum /hʌm/ v. (*pres. part* humming, *past part.* & *past tense* hummed /hʌmd/) **1** make a sound like bees. **2** sing with closed lips: *She hummed a song.*

human /'hjuːmən/ adj. of man; not animal. **human being** n. a person.

humble /'hʌmbl/ adj. **1** not thinking too well of yourself and what you can do: *He made a humble apology.* **2** simple; poor: *a humble home.* **humbly** adv.

humorous /'hjuːmərəs/ adj. funny; making you smile and laugh. **humorously** adv.

humour /'hjuːmə(r)/ n. (no *pl.*) being funny or amusing: *a story full of humour.* *have a sense of humour*, be able to understand the funny things in life.

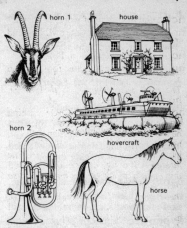

horn 1
house
horn 2
hovercraft
horse

hump /hʌmp/ n. round lump: *a camel's hump.*

hundred /'hʌndrəd/ n. number 100. **hundred** adj.: *two hundred people.* **hundredth** /'hʌndrədθ/ adj.: *a hundredth birthday.*

hung /hʌŋ/ *past part.* & *past tense* of v. hang, used for things, not people: *Father hung the picture on the wall.*

hunger /'hʌŋgə(r)/ n. (no *pl.*) wanting food: *Ted was weak with hunger.*

hungry /'hʌŋgrɪ/ adj. wanting food: *a hungry child.* **hungrily** adv.

hunt /hʌnt/ v. chase wild animals for food or sport. *hunt for*, try to find something: *Don hunted everywhere for his lost cap.* **hunt** n. looking for something. **hunting** n. chasing wild animals.

hunter /'hʌntə(r)/ n. someone who chases wild animals for food or sport.

hurl /hɜːl/ v. throw something strongly.

hurrah /hʊ'rɑː/, **hurray** /hʊ'reɪ/ exclam. word that shows joy, praise, etc.: *Hurrah for the team!*

hurricane /'hʌrɪkən/ n. dangerous storm with very strong winds.

hurry /'hʌrɪ/ v. move or do something quickly. *hurry up*, be quick. **hurry** n. *in a hurry*, wanting to do something quickly: *I can't stop because I'm in a hurry.* **hurried** /'hʌrɪd/ adj. that you do quickly: *We ate a hurried meal.*

hurt /hɜːt/ v. (*past part. & past tense* hurt) **1** break, damage, or give pain to someone or something: *Ben hurt his leg when he fell.* **2** feel pain: *My shoes are so tight that my feet hurt.*

husband /'hʌzbənd/ n. man to whom a woman is married: *Mr. Kent is Mrs. Kent's husband.*

hush /hʌʃ/ exclam. be quiet!

hut /hʌt/ n. small wooden or stone house with one room.

hydrofoil /'haɪdrəfɔɪl/ n. sort of speedboat that moves quickly on top of the water.

hymn /hɪm/ n. song of praise to God.

hyphen /'haɪfn/ n. punctuation mark (-) that joins words, e.g. in 'motor-car'.

hypnotize /'hɪpnətaɪz/ v. put someone into a sort of deep sleep so that he will do what you want.

Ii

I /aɪ/ pron. (*pl.* we) word for myself: *I am happy.*

ice¹ /aɪs/ n. **1** (no pl.) water that has become hard because it is very cold: *In winter there is ice on the pond.* **2** (pl. ices) an ice-cream.

ice² v. **1** make drinks, etc. very cold. **2** put a sweet covering on a cake: *Mother is icing my birthday cake.* **iced** /aɪst/ adj.: *iced water; iced biscuits.*

iceberg /'aɪsbɜːg/ n. very big piece of ice that floats in the sea.

ice-cream /ˌaɪs 'kriːm/ n. kind of sweet, cold food.

icicle /'aɪsɪkl/ n. long piece of ice that hangs from a roof, etc., when it is cold.

icing /'aɪsɪŋ/ n. (no pl.) sweet covering for a cake, etc.: *A wedding cake has white icing.*

icy /'aɪsɪ/ adj. **1** very cold: *an icy wind.* **2** covered with ice: *an icy road.*

I'd /aɪd/ **1** = I had: *I'd planned to go to the market but it rained.* **2** = I should; I would: *I'd like another cup of tea, please.*

idea /aɪ'dɪə/ n. **1** new thought; plan: *It was a good idea to give Dad a pen for his birthday.* **2** what you believe: *My grandmother has very strict ideas about the time when children should go to bed.* **3** picture in your mind: *Rita's letter gave us a good idea of her new job.*

ideal /aɪ'dɪəl/ adj. very best; exactly right: *This place is ideal for a picnic.*

identical /aɪ'dentɪkl/ adj. exactly the same: *The twins are identical.*

identify /aɪ'dentɪfaɪ/ v. say or show who someone is or what something is: *Can you identify your brother in this picture?* **identification** /aɪˌdentɪfɪ'keɪʃn/ n.

identity /aɪ'dentɪtɪ/ n. (pl. identities) who someone is. **identity card** n. piece of paper that shows who you are.

idiom /'ɪdɪəm/ n. group of words with a special meaning: *'To get into hot water' is an English idiom that means 'to be in trouble because of behaving badly'.*

idiomatic /ˌɪdɪə'mætɪk/ adj. in the everyday language of a group of people or a country: *If you live in England, you will soon learn to speak idiomatic English.* **idiomatically** adv.

idiot /'ɪdɪət/ n. someone who is stupid or does something silly. **idiotic** /ˌɪdɪ'ɒtɪk/ adj. foolish: *It is idiotic to go shopping with no money.*

idle /'aɪdl/ adj. **1** not working: *The machines in the factory were idle when the men were on holiday.* **2** lazy: *an idle student.* **idly** /'aɪdlɪ/ adv.

i.e. /ˌaɪ'iː/ abbrev. (of Latin id est) that is to say; this is what I mean: *My best friends, i.e. Robert and Phil, went to the match with me.*

if /ɪf/ conj. **1** on the condition that: *I'll help you today if you help me tomorrow.* **2** supposing that: *If your feet were smaller, you could borrow my shoes. If you visited us, we could show you the photographs.* **3** whenever: *If I am ill, I stay in bed.* **4** whether: *Do you know if Grace is at home?* **as if**, in a way that makes you think something: *Fiona is walking slowly as if she were tired.* **if only**, words that show you want something very much: *If only we could go to the festival today!*

ignorant /'ɪgnərənt/ adj. knowing little; not knowing enough: *That ignorant girl doesn't know where Scotland is.* **ignorantly** adv. **ignorance** /'ɪgnərəns/ n.

ignore /ɪgˈnɔː(r)/ v. know about something but not do anything about it: *Dennis ignored the warning and put his hand into the lion's cage.*

I'll /aɪl/ = I shall; I will: *I'll meet you tomorrow.*

ill[1] /ɪl/ adj. sick; with bad health: *Jill is in bed because she is ill.* **fall ill, be taken ill,** become sick: *Gordon fell ill on holiday.* **illness** n.

ill-[2] prefix bad: *He has ill-health.* **ill-tempered** /ˌɪl ˈtempəd/ adj. often angry.

illegal /ɪˈliːgl/ adj. wrong; not allowed by law: *In Britain, it is illegal to drive when you are drunk.* **illegally** adv.

ill-treat /ˌɪl ˈtriːt/ v. be cruel to a person or animal: *I don't like him because he ill-treats his dog.* **ill-treatment** n.

illuminate /ɪˈluːmɪneɪt/ v. give light to something: *The table was illuminated by candles.*

illustrate /ˈɪləstreɪt/ v. draw a picture to show something more clearly: *The teacher illustrated the history lesson with pictures of castles.* **illustration** /ˌɪləˈstreɪʃn/ n. picture. **illustrated** /ˈɪləstreɪtɪd/ adj. with pictures: *This is an illustrated book.*

I'm /aɪm/ = I am: *I'm twelve years old.*

image /ˈɪmɪdʒ/ n. **1** someone or something that looks exactly like another: *Janet is the image of her mother.* **2** shape of someone or something in stone, metal, or wood.

imaginary /ɪˈmædʒɪnərɪ/ adj. not real; only in the mind: *an imaginary illness.*

imagination /ɪˌmædʒɪˈneɪʃn/ n. **1** (pl. imaginations) making pictures in your mind: *You didn't really see a ghost—it was only your imagination.* **2** (no pl.) thinking of new ideas: *Mark has the imagination to make good new games.* **imaginative** /ɪˈmædʒɪnətɪv/ adj.

imagine /ɪˈmædʒɪn/ v. **1** have a picture of something in your mind: *Can you imagine life on a desert island?* **2** think that something will probably happen: *I imagine that we shall have a holiday in the summer.*

imitate /ˈɪmɪteɪt/ v. copy someone or something; try to do the same as someone or something else.

imitation /ˌɪmɪˈteɪʃn/ n. copy; some-

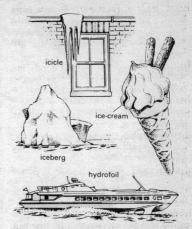

icicle

ice-cream

iceberg

hydrofoil

thing that you make to look like another thing: *The diamond in that ring is only a glass imitation.* **imitation** adj. not real: *imitation leather.*

immediate /ɪˈmiːdɪət/ adj. happening at once: *I can't wait so you must give me an immediate answer.* **immediately** adv.: *Take off your muddy shoes immediately!*

immense /ɪˈmens/ adj. very big: *an immense building.*

immensely /ɪˈmenslɪ/ adv. very much: *We enjoyed the party immensely.*

immigrate /ˈɪmɪgreɪt/ v. come from your own country to live in another country: *Many Pakistani people have immigrated to Britain.* **immigration** /ˌɪmɪˈgreɪʃn/ n. **immigrant** /ˈɪmɪgrənt/ n. someone who immigrates.

imp /ɪmp/ n. little devil; child who plays tricks.

impatient /ɪmˈpeɪʃnt/ adj. not wanting to wait: *The hungry children were impatient for their meal.* **impatiently** adv.: *'Hurry up!' said Richard impatiently.* **impatience** /ɪmˈpeɪʃns/ n.

impertinent /ɪmˈpɜːtɪnənt/ adj. too bold; not polite: *The impertinent boy put his tongue out at me.* **impertinently** adv. **impertinence** /ɪmˈpɜːtɪnəns/ n.

implore /ɪmˈplɔː(r)/ v. ask someone for something with strong feeling: *The mother implored the doctor to save her sick child.*

impolite /ˌɪmpəˈlaɪt/ adj. not polite; talking or acting in a way that makes other people sad, angry, etc.: *It is impolite to sing while I'm talking to you.* **impolitely** adv.

import /ɪmˈpɔːt/ v. bring in goods, etc. from another country: *Britain imports oranges from Spain.* **import** /ˈɪmpɔːt/ n. something that is imported. **importer** n. person or company that imports goods.

importance /ɪmˈpɔːtns/ n. (no pl.) power; great value: *Oil is of great importance to industry.*

important /ɪmˈpɔːtnt/ adj. **1** powerful; special: *The prime minister is an important person.* **2** that you must do or have: *Milk is an important food for babies.*

impossible /ɪmˈpɒsəbl/ adj. that cannot happen: *It is impossible for elephants to fly!* **impossibility** /ɪmˌpɒsəˈbɪlətɪ/ n.

impostor /ɪmˈpɒstə(r)/ n. someone who pretends to be a person he is not: *We knew he was an impostor because he spoke with a foreign accent.*

impress /ɪmˈpres/ v. fix itself firmly in your mind because it is so good, big, fine, etc.: *Diana's singing impressed him so much that he asked her to sing on the radio.* **impressive** /ɪmˈpresɪv/ adj.: *impressive work; an impressive castle.*

impression /ɪmˈpreʃn/ n. thoughts or feelings that you have about something: *What was your first impression of London?* **make an impression**, give someone a certain idea of yourself: *Frank made a good impression so the manager gave him the job.*

imprison /ɪmˈprɪzn/ v. put a person, animal, etc. in a place that he cannot leave: *The bird was imprisoned in a cage.* **imprisonment** n.: *two years' imprisonment.*

improbable /ɪmˈprɒbəbl/ adj. not likely: *When the sky is blue, it is improbable that it will rain.*

improve /ɪmˈpruːv/ v. become better; make someone or something better: *You must improve your cooking before you invite your aunt to dinner.*

improvement /ɪmˈpruːvmənt/ n. **1** (no pl.) becoming better: *The teacher is pleased with the improvement in my* work. **2** (pl. improvements) something that is better: *The new school is a great improvement on the old one.*

impudent /ˈɪmpjʊdənt/ adj. too bold; not polite: *The impudent boys put their tongues out at us.* **impudently** adv. **impudence** /ˈɪmpjʊdəns/ n.

in¹ /ɪn/ adv. **1** word that shows where someone or something is going: *Come in.* **2** word that shows where someone or something is: *Is your brother in or has he gone to the match?* **3** popular; liked by most people: *This year, short skirts are in.* **in for**, likely to have something bad: *I'm afraid we're in for a storm.* **in and out**, coming and going: *The children were in and out all afternoon.* **have it in for**, feel angry with someone and want to hurt him.

in-² prefix **1** showing the way something is coming, etc.: *Incoming flights land on this side of the airport.* **2** not: *The word 'inexpensive' means 'not expensive'.*

in³ prep. **1** word that shows where or what place: *Glasgow is in Scotland.* **2** word that shows where to: *Ray put his hand in the water.* **3** word that shows when: *Margaret started school in 1973.* **4** word that shows how long: *I'll be ready in an hour.* **5** word that shows how someone is: *My mother is in good health. Emma was in tears.* **6** word that shows what sort of clothes: *The policeman is in uniform.* **7** word that tells about what is happening around us: *We walked in the rain. They slept in the shade.* **8** word that shows what way, what language, etc.: *It is written in ink. He spoke in Italian.* **9** word that shows where someone belongs: *He's in the army.* **in all**, altogether: *We were fifteen in all.*

inability /ˌɪnəˈbɪlətɪ/ n. (no pl.) not being able to do something: *She does not learn much because of her inability to listen.*

inaccurate /ɪnˈækjʊrət/ adj. wrong; with mistakes: *She never knows the right time because her watch is inaccurate.* **inaccurately** adv.

inadequate /ɪnˈædɪkwət/ adj. not enough; not as much as you need: *His thin clothes will be inadequate in the winter.* **inadequately** adv.

inaudible /ɪnˈɔːdəbl/ *adj.* that you cannot hear: *Diane speaks so quietly that she is inaudible.* **inaudibly** *adv.*

incapable /ɪnˈkeɪpəbl/ *adj.* **incapable of,** not able to do something: *I'm incapable of walking far today because I've hurt my foot.*

inch /ɪntʃ/ *n.* (*pl.* inches) measure of length = 2·54 centimetres: *She is 26 inches round the waist.*

incident /ˈɪnsɪdənt/ *n.* happening that is not very important: *There was a funny incident when the fat woman couldn't get out of the car!*

incidentally /ˌɪnsɪˈdentlɪ/ *adv.* word that shows you are going to tell a new thing that is not important but perhaps interesting: *Incidentally, did you know that my uncle is visiting us?*

incline /ɪnˈklaɪn/ *v.* **inclined to,** ready and wanting to do something: *I am inclined to leave at once because you are so rude.*

include /ɪnˈkluːd/ *v.* **1** have someone or something as part of the total: *The class of twenty includes seven girls.* **2** think of or count someone or something as part of the total: *Did you include me when you made the list?*

including /ɪnˈkluːdɪŋ/ *pres. part.* of *v.* include. with; counting: *I have seen all his films, including the last.*

income /ˈɪŋkəm/ *n.* money that you receive for your work, etc.: *He is changing his job because he wants a bigger income.* **income tax** *n.* money that the government takes from your income.

incomplete /ˌɪnkəmˈpliːt/ *adj.* **1** not finished: *The artist's picture is incomplete.* **2** with some parts missing: *This set of plates is incomplete.* **incompletely** *adv.*

inconsiderate /ˌɪnkənˈsɪdərət/ *adj.* not thinking or caring about other people: *It is inconsiderate of you to make so much noise when people are asleep.* **inconsiderately** *adv.*

inconvenience /ˌɪnkənˈviːnɪəns/ *n.* **1** (no *pl.*) trouble: *The deep snow made a lot of inconvenience for drivers.* **2** (*pl.* inconveniences) something that gives trouble to someone: *This broken light is an inconvenience.* **inconvenience** *v.*: *Am I inconveniencing you if I park my*

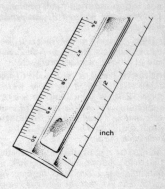

inch

car in front of your house? **inconvenient** /ˌɪnkənˈviːnɪənt/ *adj.*: *He came at an inconvenient time.* **inconveniently** *adv.*

incorrect /ˌɪnkəˈrekt/ *adj.* with mistakes; wrong: *To say 2 + 2 = 5 is incorrect.* **incorrectly** *adv.*

increase /ɪnˈkriːs/ *v.* become bigger or more; make something bigger or more: *People want more money because prices are increasing.* **increase** /ˈɪnkriːs/ *n.*: *There has been a big increase in road accidents.*

incredible /ɪnˈkredəbl/ *adj.* difficult to believe; amazing: *Michael told us an incredible story about his grandmother catching a thief.* **incredibly** *adv.*

indeed[1] /ɪnˈdiːd/ *adv.* **1** very; truly: *I am very glad indeed to hear that you are better.* **2** I agree: *'She's a good rider.' 'Yes, indeed she is!'*

indeed[2] *exclam.* word that shows interest or surprise: *'He told me about your holiday.' 'Oh, indeed!'*

indefinite /ɪnˈdefɪnət/ *adj.* not clear or certain: *indefinite plans.* **indefinite article,** a, an.

indefinitely /ɪnˈdefɪnətlɪ/ *adv.* for a long time, perhaps for ever: *Please write soon because we can't wait indefinitely for your answer.*

independent /ˌɪndɪˈpendənt/ *adj.* **1** free; not controlled by another person, thing, or country: *An independent school*

index /'ɪndeks/ *n.* (*pl.* indexes) list of names, subjects, etc., from A to Z, at the end of a book or in a library, etc.

is not controlled by the state. **2** liking to do things for yourself: *an independent girl.* **independence** /ˌɪndɪ'pendəns/ *n.: In 1948 India received its independence from Britain.*

indicate /'ɪndɪkeɪt/ *v.* **1** point to something: *He indicated the door with his finger.* **2** show something; be a sign of something: *The marks on his face indicate that he's been fighting.* **indication** /ˌɪndɪ'keɪʃn/ *n: The black sky was an indication of rain.*

indicator /'ɪndɪkeɪtə(r)/ *n.* something that tells you what is happening: *The indicator on a car is a flashing light which tells you that the driver is going to turn.*

indignant /ɪn'dɪgnənt/ *adj.* angry about something wrong, unfair, etc.: *She was indignant when I said she was lying.* **indignantly** *adv.* **indignation** /ˌɪndɪg'neɪʃn/ *n.*

indirect /ˌɪndɪ'rekt/ *adj.* not straight; not direct: *We had an indirect journey because the main road was closed.*

individual¹ /ˌɪndɪ'vɪdʒʊəl/ *adj.* for one person or thing only: *She didn't read well so her teacher gave her individual help.* **individually** *adv.* to, by, for, etc. each one: *We packed the cups individually so they would not bang together.*

individual² *n.* each person, by himself, not with others: *We travelled together, but each individual bought his own ticket.*

indoor /'ɪndɔː(r)/ *adj.* that happens inside a building: *Table tennis is an indoor game.*

indoors /ˌɪn'dɔːz/ *adv.* in or into a building: *Catherine stayed indoors because it was raining.*

industrial /ɪn'dʌstrɪəl/ *adj.* **1** with many factories: *Manchester is an industrial city.* **2** of industry: *industrial workers.*

industry /'ɪndəstrɪ/ *n.* (*pl.* industries) making goods in factories, etc.: *the car industry.*

inexpensive /ˌɪnɪk'spensɪv/ *adj.* cheap; not costing a lot of money. **inexpensively** *adv.*

infant /'ɪnfənt/ *n.* baby; very young child.

infect /ɪn'fekt/ *v.* give a disease to someone: *When you have measles, you must stay at home or you will infect the class.* **infected** /ɪn'fektɪd/ *adj.* full of germs: *That cut in your hand will become infected if you don't keep it clean.* **infectious** /ɪn'fekʃəs/ *adj.* that goes from one person to another: *an infectious illness.*

infection /ɪn'fekʃn/ *n.* illness.

inferior /ɪn'fɪərɪə(r)/ *adj.* worse; not as good, clever, important, etc. as another: *Anna's work is so good that the other children feel inferior to her.*

infertile /ɪn'fɜːtaɪl/ *adj.* where plants grow badly: *infertile land.*

infinite /'ɪnfɪnət/ *adj.* with no end; too many to be counted: *There is an infinite number of stars in the sky.*

infinitely /'ɪnfɪnətlɪ/ *adv.* very: *A snail moves infinitely slowly.*

infinitive /ɪn'fɪnətɪv/ *n.* simple form of a verb: *'To go' is an infinitive.*

inflammable /ɪn'flæməbl/ *adj.* that will start to burn easily: *Petrol is very inflammable.*

inflate /ɪn'fleɪt/ *v.* fill something with air: *George mended the tyre and then inflated it.* **inflatable** /ɪn'fleɪtəbl/ *adj.* that you can inflate: *an inflatable rubber boat.*

influence¹ /'ɪnflʊəns/ *n.* **1** (no *pl.*) power to change what someone believes or does: *Television has a strong influence on people.* **2** (*pl.* influences) person or thing that can change someone or something: *Dick is a big influence on his young brother.* **3** (no *pl.*) power that someone has because of his money, job, etc.: *Tony got a job in the factory because his uncle had influence there.*

influence² *v.* change someone or something; make someone do what you want.

influenza /ˌɪnflʊ'enzə/ *n.* (no *pl.*) illness with fever, pain in the muscles, sneezing, etc.

inform /ɪn'fɔːm/ *v.* **inform someone,** tell something to someone: *Have you informed your boss that you will not be at work tomorrow?*

informal /ɪnˈfɔːml/ adj. that is not for a special, important time; casual: *informal clothes*. **informally** adv.

information /ˌɪnfəˈmeɪʃn/ n. (no pl.) what you tell someone; facts; news: *Please give me some information about trains to Edinburgh.*

infrequent /ɪnˈfriːkwənt/ adj. not happening often. **infrequently** adv.: *We go to the theatre infrequently because tickets cost so much.*

ingredient /ɪnˈgriːdɪənt/ n. one of the parts of a mixture: *Eggs are the main ingredients of omelettes.*

inhabit /ɪnˈhæbɪt/ v. live in a place. **be inhabited**, have people or animals living in it: *The South Pole is not inhabited.*

inhabitant /ɪnˈhæbɪtənt/ n. someone who lives in a place: *Our village has five hundred inhabitants.*

inherit /ɪnˈherɪt/ v. receive a house, money, title, etc. from someone who has died: *The children inherited their father's land*. **inheritance** /ɪnˈherɪtəns/ n.: *The inheritance will make him a rich man.*

initial[1] /ɪˈnɪʃl/ adj. first: *'d' is the initial letter of the word 'day'.*

initial[2] n. (usually pl.) first letter or letters of someone's name: *John F. Kennedy's initials were J.F.K.*

inject /ɪnˈdʒekt/ v. put medicine, etc. into the body with a special needle. **injection** /ɪnˈdʒekʃn/ n.

injure /ˈɪndʒə(r)/ v. hurt someone or something: *John fell down from the tree and injured his back*. **injured** /ˈɪndʒəd/ adj. hurt: *After the crash, an ambulance took the injured man to hospital.* **injury** /ˈɪndʒərɪ/ n.: *He fell off the ladder and had serious injuries.*

injustice /ˌɪnˈdʒʌstɪs/ n. **1** (no pl.) being unfair, not right. **2** (pl. injustices) unfair thing.

ink /ɪŋk/ n. coloured liquid for writing and printing: *Write your homework in ink, not in pencil.*

inland /ˈɪnlənd/ adj. not by the sea: *Birmingham is an inland city.* **inland** /ɪnˈlænd/ adv. away from the sea; in or towards the middle of a country: *We left the coast and travelled inland to Cambridge.*

inn /ɪn/ n. house or small hotel where

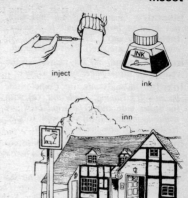

inject

ink

inn

you can buy meals and drinks, and sometimes hire a bedroom. **inn-keeper** /ˈɪnkiːpə(r)/ n. man who controls an inn.

inner /ˈɪnə(r)/ adj. of the inside; in the centre or middle: *Inner London.*

innings /ˈɪnɪŋz/ n. (pl. innings) time when a cricket player or team is batting.

innocent /ˈɪnəsnt/ adj. not having done wrong. **innocently** adv. **innocence** /ˈɪnəsns/ n.: *The friends of the prisoner were sure of his innocence.*

inquire /ɪnˈkwaɪə(r)/ v. ask; try to get an answer by saying something: *At the station my father inquired what time the train left.* **inquire into**, try to learn more about something that has happened: *The police are inquiring into the murder.*

inquiry /ɪnˈkwaɪərɪ/ n. (pl. inquiries) question. **make an inquiry**, ask questions about something: *When I lost my umbrella, I made inquiries about it in all the shops that I had visited.*

inquisitive /ɪnˈkwɪzətɪv/ adj. wanting to know too much; asking too many questions. **inquisitively** adv.: *'What have you got in your handbag?' she asked me inquisitively.*

insane /ɪnˈseɪn/ adj. mad; foolish: *It was insane to take the boat on the sea in that storm.* **insanely** adv.

insect /ˈɪnsekt/ n. small animal with six legs: *Ants, flies, and wasps are insects.*

insecure /ˌɪnsɪ'kjʊə(r)/ adj. not safe; not firm: *A broken ladder is insecure.* **insecurely** adv.: *The picture fell because it was insecurely fixed to the wall.*

inside[1] /'ɪnsaɪd/ adj. on, near, or in the centre: *the inside pages of a newspaper.*

inside[2] /ɪn'saɪd/ adv. in: *Come inside because it's raining.* **inside out,** (a) with the inner side out: *The wind blew my umbrella inside out!* (b) very well; totally: *He knows his homework inside out.*

inside[3] /'ɪnsaɪd/ n. the parts in something: *You must see the inside of a house before you buy it.*

inside[4] /ɪn'saɪd/ prep. in: *Don't let the dog come inside the house.*

insist /ɪn'sɪst/ v. say something again and again, very strongly, although people do not believe you: *Daniel insisted that he had seen a ghost.* **insist on,** say strongly that you must do something; say firmly that something must happen: *I said I'd walk to the station, but he insisted on driving me there.*

insolent /'ɪnsələnt/ adj. too bold; not polite: *An insolent boy stuck his tongue out at us.* **insolently** adv. **insolence** /'ɪnsələns/ n.

inspect /ɪn'spekt/ v. **1** look at something carefully: *Ted inspected the car before he bought it.* **2** visit people or places to see that work is done well: *Someone is coming to inspect the school next week.* **inspection** /ɪn'spekʃn/ n.: *to make an inspection.*

inspector /ɪn'spektə(r)/ n. **1** someone who visits schools, factories, hospitals, etc. to see that all is well. **2** police officer.

inspiration /ˌɪnspə'reɪʃn/ n. **1** (no pl.) thought or idea that helps someone to write a book or music, paint pictures, etc.: *Many artists get their inspiration from nature.* **2** (pl. inspirations) sudden good idea.

inspire /ɪn'spaɪə(r)/ v. **1** put ideas into someone's mind: *The good weather inspired me to work in the garden.* **2** make someone want to write or paint, etc.: *The islands of Scotland inspired Mendelssohn to write some lovely music.*

install /ɪn'stɔːl/ v. put a new thing in its place: *He installed a washing-machine in the kitchen.*

instalment /ɪn'stɔːlmənt/ n. **1** one part of a long story, etc., on the radio or television or in a magazine: *Did you watch the last instalment?* **2** part of the cost of something which you pay over a long time: *He is paying for his new car in twelve monthly instalments.*

instance /'ɪnstəns/ n. example. **for instance,** as an example: *He's a greedy boy—yesterday, for instance, he ate all our biscuits!*

instant[1] /'ɪnstənt/ adj. **1** immediate; happening at once: *He gave an instant answer to my question.* **2** that you can use quickly and easily. **instant coffee** n. coffee that you make with coffee powder and hot water. **instantly** adv. at once.

instant[2] n. very short time; moment: *I'll be with you in an instant.*

instead /ɪn'sted/ adv. in the place of something: *I couldn't find a nice dress so I bought a blouse and skirt instead.*

instead of prep. in place of; rather than: *He has been playing all afternoon instead of studying.*

instinct /'ɪnstɪŋkt/ n. natural feeling, natural thought, etc.: *Birds fly by instinct.* **instinctive** /ɪn'stɪŋktɪv/ adj.: *Animals have an instinctive fear of fire.* **instinctively** adv.

institute /'ɪnstɪtjuːt/ n. **1** group of people who often meet for a special reason, to talk or do something together: *the Women's Institute.* **2** building or office for meetings of a group of people.

instruct /ɪn'strʌkt/ v. **1** teach someone: *My uncle instructs people how to drive cars.* **2** tell someone what he must do: *My boss instructed me to type the letters quickly.*

instruction /ɪn'strʌkʃn/ n. **1** (no pl.) teaching: *Mr. Rivers gives swimming instruction.* **2** (pl. instructions) words that tell how to use or do something: *Read the instructions on the bottle before you take the medicine.*

instructor /ɪn'strʌktə(r)/ n. someone who teaches or trains: *a driving instructor.*

instrument /'ɪnstrəmənt/ n. tool; thing for doing a special job.

insufficient /ˌɪnsə'fɪʃnt/ adj. not enough; not as much or as many as you need: *One sandwich is insufficient for a hungry man.* **insufficiently** *adv.*

insult /ɪn'sʌlt/ *v.* be rude to someone: *You insulted Ralph when you called him a pig.* **insult** /'ɪnsʌlt/ *n.*

insure /ɪn'ʃʊə(r)/ *v.* pay a small sum of money regularly to a company so that it will give you a lot of money if you have an accident, etc.: *Have you insured your house against fire?* **insurance** /ɪn-'ʃʊərəns/ *n.*: *When my car crashed, the insurance paid for the repairs.*

intelligent /ɪn'telɪdʒənt/ *adj.* clever; learning and understanding well: *an intelligent pupil.* **intelligently** *adv.* **intelligence** /ɪn'telɪdʒəns/ *n.*

intend /ɪn'tend/ *v.* plan to do something: *When do you intend to go to London?* **be intended for**, be for: *Small children don't like books that are intended for adults.*

intense /ɪn'tens/ *adj.* very great or strong; that you can feel or hear clearly: *intense heat.* **intensely** *adv.*

intention /ɪn'tenʃn/ *n.* plan; what you are going to do: *He went to Paris with the intention of learning French.*

intentional /ɪn'tenʃənl/ *adj.* that you want to do or say; planned: *I'm sorry I hurt you—it was not intentional.* **intentionally** *adv.*

interest[1] /'ɪntrəst/ *n.* **1** (no *pl.*) wanting to know or learn about something or someone because it is important to you. **take an interest in**, want to know about something: *Farmers always take an interest in the weather.* **2** (*pl.* interests) something you do often because it pleases you: *Football and pop music are Alan's two great interests.*

interest[2] *v.* make someone want to know more about it or him: *I talked to the sailor for a long time because he interested me.* **be interested in**, like something; want to know more about something: *Nigel is interested in aeroplanes.*

interesting /'ɪntrəstɪŋ/ *adj.* making you want to know more about it or him: thing: *He found the film so interesting that he saw it again.* **interestingly** *adv.*

interfere /ˌɪntə'fɪə(r)/ *v.* **1** take part in someone's affairs when he has not asked

inside out

instructor

you to or does not want you to: *Don't interfere! I want to find the answer myself.* **2** do something that makes trouble: *My bicycle chain is stuck. Have you been interfering with it?* **3** stop something from being done well: *Do you let sport interfere with your studies?* **interference** *n.*: *Go away! I don't want any interference while I'm working!*

interior /ɪn'tɪərɪə(r)/ *adj.* on, of, in, or from the inside: *We put paper on the interior walls of our house.* **interior** *n.*

intermediate /ˌɪntə'miːdɪət/ *adj.* coming between; in the middle: *An intermediate class is more difficult than a beginner's class but easier than an advanced one.*

internal /ɪn'tɜːnl/ *adj.* of, on, or for the inside: *He had internal injuries to his stomach.* **internally** *adv.*

international /ˌɪntə'næʃnəl/ *adj.* between countries: *international trade.*

interpret /ɪn'tɜːprɪt/ *v.* say in one language what someone has said in another language: *I couldn't speak Italian so I asked Maria to interpret for me in the shop.* **interpreter** *n.* someone who can interpret: *Maria was my interpreter.*

interrogate /ɪn'terəgeɪt/ *v.* ask someone questions because you want to find out whether he has done wrong, etc.: *The police interrogated the man who had a knife in his pocket.* **interrogation** /ɪnˌterə'geɪʃn/ *n.*

interrupt /ˌɪntəˈrʌpt/ v. **1** stop something for a time: *The floods interrupted railway services.* **2** speak while someone else is speaking or doing something: *She interrupted me to ask a question.* **interruption** /ˌɪntəˈrʌpʃn/ n.: *I can't finish this work because there are so many interruptions.*

interval /ˈɪntəvl/ n. **1** space between two things. **at intervals**, with short spaces or times between: *Lamp-posts stand at intervals in the street.* **2** short time between two parts of a play or concert.

interview /ˈɪntəvjuː/ n. meeting when you can talk to someone to find out more about him or her: *I have an interview for a new job tomorrow.* **interview** v.: *How many people have you interviewed for the job?* **interviewer** n. someone who interviews another person.

into /ˈɪntuː/, /ˈɪntə/ prep. **1** word that shows the way inside something: *Come into the house.* **2** word that shows that something is changing: *When it is very cold, water turns into ice.* **3** word in arithmetic: *If you divide 4 into 12 you will get 3.*

introduce /ˌɪntrəˈdjuːs/ v. bring people together for the first time and tell each of them the name of the other: *He introduced his new girlfriend to his mother.*

introduction /ˌɪntrəˈdʌkʃn/ n. **1** bringing people together to meet each other. **2** piece of writing at the beginning of a book to tell what the book is about.

invade /ɪnˈveɪd/ v. go into a country to attack it: *William the Conqueror invaded England in 1066.* **invasion** /ɪnˈveɪʒn/ n. **invader** n. person or people who invade.

invalid /ˈɪnvəlɪd/ adj. weak because of illness or accident: *She looks after her invalid mother.* **2** for weak and sick people: *an invalid chair.* **invalid** n. weak or sick person.

invent /ɪnˈvent/ v. **1** plan or make something new: *Who invented aeroplanes?* **2** make a story: *When Colin's mother asked him why he was late, he invented a story about football practice.* **invention** /ɪnˈvenʃn/ n.

inventor /ɪnˈventə(r)/ n. person who plans or thinks of something new: *Alexander Graham Bell was the inventor of the telephone.*

inverted commas /ɪnˌvɜːtɪd ˈkɒməz/ n. (pl.) punctuation marks (" ") or (' ') that you put around a word or sentence.

invest /ɪnˈvest/ v. put money into a business so that you will get more money back: *He invested all his money in a boat so that he could catch fish and sell them.* **investment** /ɪnˈvestmənt/ n.

investigate /ɪnˈvestɪɡeɪt/ v. study something with care: *The police are investigating the fire.* **investigation** /ɪnˌvestɪˈɡeɪʃn/ n.: *The police are holding an investigation into the fire.*

invisible /ɪnˈvɪzəbl/ adj. that you cannot see: *Wind is invisible.*

invite /ɪnˈvaɪt/ v. ask someone to come somewhere, or to do something: *Mrs. Roberts invited me to tea.* **invitation** /ˌɪnvɪˈteɪʃn/ n.: *Judith sent me an invitation to her party.*

invoice /ˈɪnvɔɪs/ n. list of goods that have been sold, with the prices that must be paid; bill.

involve /ɪnˈvɒlv/ v. **be involved with** or **in something**, be very busy with something: *Jill does not want to come because she's too involved in her sewing.* **involvement** n.

inward /ˈɪnwəd/, **inwards** /ˈɪnwədz/ adv. towards the inside: *The door opened inwards, so I pushed it.*

iron[1] /ˈaɪən/ n. **1** (no pl.) strong, hard metal. **2** (pl. irons) instrument that you heat for smoothing clothes, etc. **iron** adj. made of iron: *an iron gate.*

iron[2] v. make clothes smooth after washing them, etc.: *Mother is ironing father's shirts.* **ironing** n. things that you must iron: *There's a pile of ironing on the table.* **ironing-board** n. special table where you iron clothes.

irregular /ɪˈreɡjʊlə(r)/ adj. that does not follow the usual rule: *'Mice' is an irregular plural.*

irresponsible /ˌɪrɪˈspɒnsəbl/ adj. whom you cannot trust to be wise, etc. **irresponsibly** adv.

irritable /ˈɪrɪtəbl/ adj. easily becoming angry.

irritate /ˈɪrɪteɪt/ v. **1** make someone

rather angry: *The slow journey irritated me.* **2** make part of the body a little hurt: *The cigarette smoke irritates my eyes.* **irritated** /ˈɪrɪteɪtɪd/ *adj.* rather angry. **irritation** /ˌɪrɪˈteɪʃn/ *n.*

is /ɪz/ part of *v.* be: *Michael is a boy.*

island /ˈaɪlənd/ *n.* **1** piece of land with water all round it: *Malta is an island.* **2** something like an island because it stands on its own: *a traffic island.*

isle /aɪl/ *n.* island: *the British Isles.*

isn't /ˈɪznt/ = is not: *It isn't true!*

isolate /ˈaɪsəleɪt/ *v.* put something away from other things: *Snow has isolated many villages in Scotland.* **isolation** /ˌaɪsəˈleɪʃn/ *n.*: *The old man lives in isolation in the forest.*

issue /ˈɪʃuː/ *v.* **1** come or go out of somewhere: *Smoke was issuing from the chimney.* **2** give something out to someone: *Please issue everyone with a pencil.*

it /ɪt/ *pron.* (*pl.* they, them) **1** word for any thing: *Where's my book? I can't find it.* **2** word that points to an idea that follows: *It is difficult to learn Chinese.* **3** word that shows who someone is or what something is: *Who's at the door? It is your mother. What's that? It is a radio.* **4** word at the beginning of a sentence about the time, weather, distance, etc.: *It is six o'clock. It is hot today. It is 100 kilometres to Bradford.*

itch /ɪtʃ/ *v.* have a feeling on the skin that makes you want to scratch: *These socks make my legs itch.* **itch** *n.* **itchy** /ˈɪtʃɪ/ *adj.* that makes you itch.

item /ˈaɪtəm/ *n.* **1** one in a list of things: *Which items are you bringing for the picnic?* **2** piece of news: *Are there any interesting items in the newspaper today?*

it's /ɪts/ = it is: *It's hot today.*

its *adj.* of it: *The dog wagged its tail.*

itself /ɪtˈself/ *pron.* (*pl.* themselves) **1** word that describes the same thing, animal, or baby that you have just talked about: *The baby hurt itself when it fell out of its cot.* **2** it and no other: *Did you see the explosion itself? by itself,* alone: *The house stands by itself in the forest.*

I've /aɪv/ = I have.

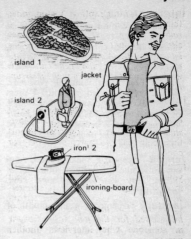

island 1
jacket
island 2
iron¹ 2
ironing-board

ivory /ˈaɪvərɪ/ *n.* **1** (no *pl.*) pale yellow-white colour. **2** (no *pl.*) hard, white bone from the tusks of elephants, which we make into ornaments, etc. **ivory** *adj.*: *an ivory brooch.*

ivy /ˈaɪvɪ/ *n.* (*pl.* ivies) climbing plant with dark, shiny leaves.

Jj

jab /dʒæb/ *v.* (*pres. part.* jabbing, *past part. & past tense* jabbed /dʒæbd/) push something strongly into or at another thing: *John jabbed a knife into the meat.* **jab** *n.*: *He gave me a jab with his finger.*

jacket /ˈdʒækɪt/ *n.* **1** short cooat with sleeves. **2** loose paper cover for a book.

jagged /ˈdʒægɪd/ *adj.* with sharp points and rough edges: *jagged rocks.*

jaguar /ˈdʒægjʊə(r)/ *n.* wild animal like a big cat.

jail /dʒeɪl/ *n.* prison: *The thief went to jail for two years.* **jailer** *n.* someone whose job is to stop people from getting out of prison.

jam¹ /dʒæm/ *n.* (no *pl.*) sweet food made from fruit and sugar: *I'd like some jam on my bread, please.*

jam² *n.* (no *pl.*) crowd of things or people that cannot move because there are too many. **traffic jam** *n.* long line of cars, etc. that cannot go on. *in a jam*, in trouble: *We must help Ernest because he is in a jam.*

jam³ *v.* (*pres. part.* jamming, *past part. & past tense* jammed /dʒæmd/) **1** press something tightly between other things; be pressed tightly: *She jammed the bottle into the basket.* **2** become stuck; not be able to move: *The door jammed and we could not open it.*

jangle /'dʒæŋgl/ *v.* make a loud, ringing noise like big bells or other metal things: *Roy was jangling some keys.* **jangling** *adj.*

January /'dʒænjʊərɪ/ *n.* first month of the year.

jar /dʒɑː(r)/ *n.* pot that holds food: *a jam-jar.*

jaunt /dʒɔːnt/ *n.* short journey to enjoy yourself.

jaw /dʒɔː/ *n.* **1** lower part of the face: *He hit the thief in the jaw.* **2 jaws** (*pl.*) mouth; parts of the head that hold the teeth, etc.: *The dog had a bird in its jaws.*

jazz /dʒæz/ *n.* (no *pl.*) popular music with strong rhythms.

jealous /'dʒeləs/ *adj.* with angry and sad feelings because you are afraid of losing someone's love or because you want what another person has: *Margaret is jealous when Charles talks to other girls.*

jeans /dʒiːnz/ *n.* (*pl.*) trousers of strong blue, cotton cloth.

jeep /dʒiːp/ *n.* small, strong, open car that can go well on bad roads or rough land.

jeer /dʒɪə(r)/ *v.* laugh rudely at someone: *The big boys jeer at Tim because he is so small.* **jeer** *n.* **jeering** *adj.*

jelly /'dʒelɪ/ *n.* (no *pl.*) soft, sweet food made of fruit juice and sugar.

jelly-fish /'dʒelɪfɪʃ/ *n.* (*pl.* jelly-fish or jellyfishes) sea-animal like jelly, that you can see through.

jerk /dʒɜːk/ *v.* move suddenly; make something move suddenly: *The bus jerked along the rough road.* **jerk** *n.*: *The bus stopped with a jerk.* **jerky** *adj.*

jersey /'dʒɜːzɪ/ *n.* piece of woollen clothing that you wear on the top half of your body.

jet /dʒet/ *n.* **1** strong stream of gas, water, etc., which comes very fast out of a small hole: *a jet of water from the fireman's hose; a gas jet.* **2** aeroplane that flies because the engines send out jets of hot gas.

jetty /'dʒetɪ/ *n.* (*pl.* jetties) strong, wide wall built from the land into the sea, so that the harbour is safe.

jewel /'dʒuːəl/ *n.* **1** valuable stone, e.g. a diamond. **2** ring or other ornament with a jewel in it. **jewellery** /'dʒuːəlrɪ/ *n.* necklaces and other ornaments with jewels in them. **jeweller** *n.* someone who sells jewels.

jigsaw puzzle /'dʒɪgsɔː pʌzl/ *n.* picture in many small parts that you must put together.

jingle /'dʒɪŋgl/ *v.* make a soft, ringing sound like small bells or other metal things: *The money jingled in his pocket.* **jingling** *adj.*

job /dʒɒb/ *n.* **1** piece of work: *I have some jobs to do before we go out.* **odd jobs**, bits of work of different kinds. **2** work that you do for money: *Guy has left school and started his first job.* **a good job**, a lucky thing: *It's a good job I was at home when you telephoned.* **make a good job of something**, do something well: *The hairdresser made a good job of my hair.* **be out of a job**, have no paid work.

jockey /'dʒɒkɪ/ *n.* someone whose job is to ride in horse-races.

jog /dʒɒg/ *v.* (*pres. part.* jogging, *past part. & past tense* jogged /dʒɒgd/) **1** shake, or give a small push, to something or someone: *He jogged my elbow and some coffee spilt on to my dress.* **2** move in a shaking way: *We jogged up and down along the bad roads on the old bus.* **3** run slowly, for exercise. **jogger** *n.* someone who jogs.

join /dʒɔɪn/ *v.* **1** fix or stick one thing to another thing: *We joined the caravan to the car.* **2** bring two things together by putting something between them: *A bridge joins the two banks of the river.* **3** come together: *The roads join in two miles.* **4** come and do something with someone: *He joined us for a walk.* **5**

become a member of a group: *Amanda has joined the tennis club.* **join in**, do something with other people: *Kay joined in the game.* **join up**, become a soldier, etc.

joint[1] /dʒɔɪnt/ *adj.* that people do together: *Tina and Jane gave a joint party.*

joint[2] *n.* **1** place where two parts of something come together: *the joints of a chair.* **2** something that holds two parts together: *finger joints.* **3** big piece of meat that you cook: *a joint of beef.*

joke /dʒəʊk/ *n.* something that you say to make people laugh: *He told us a joke about a fat man.* **play a joke on someone**, do something to someone to make people laugh. **practical joke** *n.* trick that you do to make someone look silly. **joke** *v.*: *I didn't really mean what I said—I was only joking.*

jolly[1] /'dʒɒlɪ/ *adj.* full of fun; friendly; happy: *a jolly woman.*

jolly[2] *adv.* very: *Jolly good!*

jolt /dʒəʊlt/ *v.* move something roughly; move quickly and roughly: *The cart jolted along the rough road.* **jolt** *n.* sudden bump.

jostle /'dʒɒsl/ *v.* push roughly against someone: *The crowd jostled us in the market.*

jot /dʒɒt/ *v.* (*pres. part.* jotting, *past part.* & *past tense* jotted /'dʒɒtɪd/) **jot down**, write something quickly: *Before I go shopping, I must jot down a list of things.*

journal /'dʒɜːnl/ *n.* newspaper or magazine.

journalist /'dʒɜːnəlɪst/ *n.* someone whose job is to write for newspapers or magazines.

journey /'dʒɜːnɪ/ *n.* going from one place to another: *Is it a long journey from Glasgow to London?*

joy /dʒɔɪ/ *n.* **1** (no *pl.*) very happy feeling: *Rita is full of joy because she has a new baby sister.* **2** (*pl.* joys) something that makes you happy: *Your letter was a joy when I was in hospital.*

joyful /'dʒɔɪfl/ *adj.* very happy. **joyfully** *adv.*

jubilee /'dʒuːbɪliː/ *n.* special time when you celebrate something important that

jockey

jug

jetty

jaw

happened many years before: *A silver jubilee comes after 25 years.*

judge[1] /dʒʌdʒ/ *n.* **1** person in a law court who decides how someone will be punished: *The judge sent the thief to prison for two years.* **2** someone who decides the winner in a sports contest or competition, etc.

judge[2] *v.* decide if something is right or wrong, good or bad, etc.: *I can't judge which picture is best.*

judgement, judgment /'dʒʌdʒmənt/ *n.* **1** what a judge says: *The prisoner listened to the judgement.* **2** what you think about something: *In my judgement, Arthur will be a good doctor.*

judo /'dʒuːdəʊ/ *n.* (no *pl.*) sort of fighting sport.

jug /dʒʌɡ/ *n.* pot with a handle, for holding and pouring liquid: *a milk jug.*

juggle /'dʒʌɡl/ *v.* do clever tricks by throwing things into the air and catching them. **juggler** *n.* someone who juggles.

juice /dʒuːs/ *n.* liquid part of fruit and vegetables: *a glass of orange juice.* **juicy** *adj.* with a lot of juice: *a juicy orange.*

July /dʒʊ'laɪ/ *n.* seventh month of the year.

jumble /'dʒʌmbl/ *n.* a lot of different, old things. **jumble sale** *n.* market for selling old things to make money for poor people, etc.

jump /dʒʌmp/ v. **1** spring; move quickly off the ground, with both feet in the air: *The cat jumped on to a wall.* **2** move quickly: *He jumped into a car.* **3** move suddenly because you are surprised, frightened, etc.: *When the door banged, he jumped.* **jump at**, say 'yes' to something at once: *Bob jumped at the invitation to watch tennis at Wimbledon.* **jump** n. **long jump**, **high jump**, sports competitions where you jump as far or as high as you can.

jumper /'dʒʌmpə(r)/ n. jersey.

junction /'dʒʌŋkʃn/ n. place where roads, rivers, railway lines, electric cables, etc. meet: *Turn right at the next junction.*

June /dʒuːn/ n. sixth month of the year.

jungle /'dʒʌŋgl/ n. thick forest in hot countries.

junior /'dʒuːnɪə(r)/ adj. **1** younger: *a junior class.* **junior school** n. school for young pupils. **2** less important: *a junior officer.* **junior** n.: *I'm 12 and Jo is 10, so he is my junior by two years.*

jury /'dʒʊərɪ/ n. (pl. juries) group of people who sit in a law court and say whether they think someone has done wrong or not: *The jury decided that the man was guilty of stealing and the judge sent him to prison.*

just¹ /dʒʌst/ adj. fair and right: *a just man.* **justly** adv.

just² adv. **1** exactly; not more or less: *It's just two o'clock.* **2** a very short time before: *The dog is still very wet because he has just come out of the river.* **3** at the moment; now: *We are just going out.* **4** by a little: *They just missed the train by a few minutes.* **5** only: *I came here just to see you.* **6** word that helps to point to what you are saying: *Just look at this funny picture!* **just as**, **(a)** exactly as: *Laura is just as pretty as Jean.* **(b)** at the same time as: *I arrived just as the match started.* **just now**, **(a)** now. **(b)** a very little time ago.

justice /'dʒʌstɪs/ n. (no pl.) **1** being fair and right: *to treat someone with justice.* **2** the law: *British justice.*

Kk

kangaroo /ˌkæŋgə'ruː/ n. Australian wild animal that jumps along on its big, back legs.

keen /kiːn/ adj. **1** sharp: *a knife with a keen edge.* **2** cold: *a keen wind.* **3** that can see well: *keen eyes.* **4** liking something; wanting to do something: *a keen student.* **keen on**, interested in someone or something: *Most girls aren't keen on football.* **keenly** adv.

keep¹ /kiːp/ n. (no pl.) the cost of food, home, clothes, etc.: *That gardener works hard for his keep.* **for keeps**, for ever: *Paul doesn't want this pen so it's mine for keeps.*

keep² v. (past part. & past tense kept /kept/) **1** have something and not give it away: *Please keep these keys while I am on holiday.* **2** stay; remain; not change: *Keep still when I photograph you.* **3** continue; not stop: *Keep knocking until someone opens the door.* **4** take care of someone or an animal; give food, clothes, and a home to someone: *My father keeps a big family.* **5** own or control a shop, business, etc.: *Mr. Smith keeps a fruit shop.* **6** have something to sell: *'Do you sell pens?' 'No, we don't keep them.'* **7** write things often in a book, etc.: *to keep a diary.* **8** stay fresh or good: *Will this meat keep until tomorrow?* **9** take someone's time: *I mustn't keep you when you are so busy.* **keep at**, go on working at something: *He kept at the job until it was finished.* **keep someone at something**, make someone go on working: *His coach kept him at his training.* **keep something back**, not tell about something. **keep someone or something from**, stop someone or something from doing something: *Keep your little brother from playing on the road.* **keep going**, continue; not stop: *Robert was tired but he kept going until the end of the race.* **keep someone in**, make a child stay in school because he has been bad. **keep off**, stay away: *I hope the rain keeps off for sports day.* **keep someone or something off**, make someone or something stay away: *Keep your hands off that wet paint!* **keep on**, **(a)** go farther: *Keep straight on and* *you'll come to the market.* (**b**) continue; not stop: *Laurie was tired but he kept on working.* **keep something to yourself**, not tell others about something: *Ron kept the bad news to himself.* **keep out**, stay outside. **keep someone or something out**, stop someone or something from coming in: *We put a fence round the garden to keep the dogs out.* **keep to**, stay somewhere: *In Britain, cars keep to the left.* **keep up with**, walk or drive as fast as another person or thing so that you are together: *The children can't keep up with you when you walk so quickly.*

keeper /'ki:pə(r)/ *n.* guard; someone who looks after something: *The keeper looks after the animals in the zoo.*

kennel /'kenl/ *n.* small hut where a dog sleeps.

kept /kept/ *past part. & past tense* of *v.* keep.

kerb /kɜ:b/ *n.* edge of a path or pavement: *Don't step off the kerb until the road is clear.*

ketchup /'ketʃəp/ *n.* (no *pl.*) tomato sauce in a bottle.

kettle /'ketl/ *n.* metal pot with a handle on the top, for boiling water.

key /ki:/ *n.* **1** piece of metal that opens a lock: *I turned the key and opened the door.* **keyhole** /'ki:həʊl/ *n.* hole where you put a key. **2** set of answers to tests, etc.: *Check your answers with the key at the back of the book.* **3** part of a piano, a typewriter, etc. that you press with a finger: *A piano has black and white keys.*

khaki /'kɑ:kɪ/ *adj.* with a yellow-brown colour. **khaki** *n.* yellow-brown cloth for soldiers' uniforms.

kick¹ /kɪk/ *n.* **1** moving the foot up suddenly; hitting something or someone with the foot: *Roger gave the ball a kick.* **2** exciting feeling: *Stuart gets a kick out of fast cars.*

kick² *v.* **1** move the foot or feet up suddenly: *The baby was kicking and screaming.* **2** hit something or someone with the foot: *Dick kicked the ball to Jon.* **kick off**, start a game of football. **kick someone out**, make someone go away: *They kicked him out of the party because he was drunk.*

kid /kɪd/ *n.* **1** young goat. **2** child.

key · kettle · kick² 1 · kilt · kangaroo

kidnap /'kɪdnæp/ *v.* (*pres. part.* kidnapping, *past part. & past tense* kidnapped /'kɪdnæpt/) take and hide someone so that his family and friends will pay money to you. **kidnapper** *n.* someone who kidnaps.

kidney /'kɪdnɪ/ *n.* **1** part of a person's or an animal's body. **2** animal's kidney that you can eat.

kill /kɪl/ *v.* make a living person, animal, or plant die: *We kill animals for food.* **killer** *n.* someone who kills.

kilo¹ /'ki:ləʊ/ *abbrev.* kilogram.

kilo-² /'kɪlə/ *prefix* 1,000: *A kilometre is a thousand metres.*

kilogram /'kɪləgræm/ *n.* measure of weight.

kilometre /'kɪləmi:tə(r)/ *n.* measure of length.

kilt /kɪlt/ *n.* short skirt that Scotsmen sometimes wear.

kin /kɪn/ *n.* (*pl.*) family; relatives. **next of kin**, nearest relative or relatives.

kind¹ /kaɪnd/ *adj.* friendly; good to other people: *A kind woman helped the old man to cross the road.* **kind-hearted** *adj.* friendly; showing love for others. **kindness** *n.*

kind² *n.* sort; type: *What kind of dog is that? He's the kind of boy who is always fighting.* **kind of**, words that you use about a thing, idea, etc., when you are not sure: *He looked kind of angry.*

kindle /'kɪndl/ v. start to burn; make something start to burn: *This wood won't kindle because it's wet.*

kindly[1] /'kaɪndlɪ/ adj. friendly and kind: *a kindly smile.*

kindly[2] adv. **1** in a friendly way; gently: *You must treat your new puppy kindly.* **2** please: *Kindly close the window.*

king /kɪŋ/ n. man who rules a country and who belongs to a royal family: *King Arthur.*

kingdom /'kɪŋdəm/ n. country where a king or queen rules: *the United Kingdom.*

kiosk /'kiːɒsk/ n. **1** small, open shop where you can buy newspapers, cigarettes, etc.: *I bought a magazine at the station kiosk.* **2** little building in the street where you can telephone.

kipper /'kɪpə(r)/ n. fish that has been dried or smoked.

kiss /kɪs/ v. touch someone with your lips to show love or to say hello or goodbye: *Rosalind kissed her mother good night.* **kiss** n.: *He gave her a kiss.*

kit /kɪt/ n. (no pl.) **1** special clothes or things that you need for a job or sport: *football kit.* **2** set of tools that a workman has for his job.

kitchen /'kɪtʃɪn/ n. room where you cook food.

kite /kaɪt/ n. toy that children fly in the wind, at the end of a long piece of string.

kitten /'kɪtn/ n. young cat.

knapsack /'næpsæk/ n. bag for food, clothes, etc., that you carry on your back.

knead /niːd/ v. press, pull, and roll something with the hands until it is soft: *She kneaded the dough to make bread.*

knee /niː/ n. **1** place in the middle of your leg where it bends: *She was on her knees planting flowers in the garden.* **2** top part of your leg when you are sitting: *The baby sat on my knee.*

kneel /niːl/ v. (past part. & past tense knelt /nelt/) go down on your knees: *She knelt and looked under the bed.*

knew /njuː/ past tense of v. know.

knickers /'nɪkəz/ n. (pl.) piece of woman's or girl's underclothing; pants.

knife /naɪf/ n. (pl. knives) instrument with a sharp edge and a handle, for cutting or fighting.

knight /naɪt/ n. **1** noble soldier on a horse in old times: *the knights of King Arthur.* **2** man who has the title 'Sir'. **knight** v. make a man a knight: *Queen Elizabeth knighted Francis Chichester after he had sailed alone around the world.*

knit /nɪt/ v. (pres. part knitting, past part. & past tense knitted /'nɪtɪd/, knit) make clothes with wool, etc., on long needles: *My mother knitted me a pullover.* **knitting** n.: *Mother keeps her knitting in a bag.* **knitting-needle** n. long piece of plastic, steel, etc., for knitting.

knives /naɪvz/ (pl.) of n. knife.

knob /nɒb/ n. **1** round handle of a door, drawer, etc. **2** round handle for controlling part of a machine, like a radio or television set.

knock /nɒk/ v. **1** hit something: *The dog knocked the vase off the table.* **2** hit something to make a noise: *Someone is knocking at the door.* **knock someone about**, hit someone often; treat someone roughly: *Alec was badly knocked about in a fight.* **knock something down**, push or pull something so that it falls: *They are knocking down the old school and will build a new one.* **knock someone down**, hit someone so he falls to the ground: *The bus knocked a child down.* **knock off**, stop work: *I knock off at 5 p.m.* **knock someone out**, hit someone so that he falls and lies still. **knock** n.: *Tony got a knock on the head. Did you hear a knock on the door?*

knocker /'nɒkə(r)/ n. piece of metal on a door, for knocking to tell people you are there.

knot[1] /nɒt/ n. **1** place where you have tied two pieces of string, etc. together tightly: *Put the string around the parcel and make a knot.* **2** measurement of how fast ships go: *The ship sailed at 20 knots.*

knot[2] v. (pres. part. knotting, past part. & past tense knotted /'nɒtɪd/) tie or fasten two pieces of string, rope, etc.: *He knotted the tie round his neck.*

know /nəʊ/ v. (past part. known, past tense knew /njuː/) **1** understand; have something in your head because you have learned it: *We all know that two and two make four.* **2** have a picture of someone or something in your head because you have seen it, etc.: *Do you know Canterbury?*

knowledge /'nɒlɪdʒ/ *n.* (no *pl.*) what you have learned: *He has a good knowledge of mathematics.* **general knowledge** *n.* knowing about many different things.

known /nəʊn/ *past part.* of *v.* know: *They sent the letter back because he is not known there.* **well-known** *adj.* famous. *be known as*, have a special name: *Kent is known as 'the garden of England'.*

knuckle /'nʌkl/ *n.* finger-joint: *I hit him with my fist and hurt my knuckles.*

koala /kəʊ'ɑːlə/ *n.* small, wild animal that lives in Australia.

Ll

label /'leɪbl/ *n.* small piece of paper or metal that you fix on something to give information about it: *I don't know what is in this tin because it has no label.* **label** *v.* (*pres. part.* labelling, *past part.* & *past tense* labelled /'leɪbld/) put a label on something: *She labelled the case with her name and address.*

laboratory /lə'bɒrətrɪ/ *n.* (*pl.* laboratories) place where scientists work and study.

labour /'leɪbə(r)/ *n.* (no *pl.*) **1** hard work that you do with your hands. **2** workers in a factory, etc.: *We must have extra labour for the post at Christmas.* **labour** *v.* work hard with your hands.

labourer /'leɪbərə(r)/ *n.* someone who does heavy work with his hands: *farm labourers.*

lace /leɪs/ *n.* **1** (no *pl.*) fine cloth with patterns of tiny holes: *a handkerchief with lace round the edge.* **2** (*pl.* laces) string that fastens a shoe: *She bent down to tie her shoe laces.*

lack /læk/ *v.* **1** not have something important or necessary: *In the hot summer*

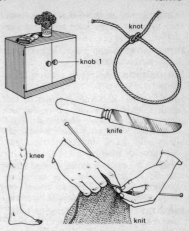

the plants lacked water. **2** not be there; not be enough. **lack** *n.*: *I haven't finished the painting for lack of time.*

lad /læd/ *n.* boy; young man.

ladder /'lædə(r)/ *n.* tall thing made of wooden or metal poles with steps between for climbing: *Jim went up the ladder to mend the roof.*

laden /'leɪdn/ *adj.* *be laden with*, be carrying a lot of something: *The porter at the station was laden with cases.*

ladle /'leɪdl/ *n.* big, deep spoon for taking soup, stew, etc. from a pot. **ladle** *v.* take out soup, etc. with a ladle: *The cook ladled the soup into bowls.*

lady /'leɪdɪ/ *n.* (*pl.* ladies) **1** woman who is kind, polite, and honest. **2** any woman. **3** **Lady**, title for the wife and daughter of some noblemen.

lager /'lɑːgə(r)/ *n.* **1** (no *pl.*) light beer. **2** (*pl.* lagers) glass or can of lager.

laid /leɪd/ *past part.* & *past tense* of *v.* lay.

lain /leɪn/ *past part.* of *v.* lie.

lake /leɪk/ *n.* big area of water, with land all round it: *Lake Windermere.*

lamb /læm/ *n.* **1** (*pl.* lambs) young sheep. **2** (no *pl.*) meat from a lamb: *roast lamb.*

lame /leɪm/ *adj.* not able to walk easily because your leg or foot is hurt: *He walks with a stick because he is lame.* **lamely** *adv.*

lamp /læmp/ *n.* thing that gives light: *She switched on the lamp because it was dark.*

lamp-post /'læmp pəʊst/ *n.* post that holds a street lamp.

lampshade /'læmpʃeɪd/ *n.* cover for a lamp.

land[1] /lænd/ *n.* **1** (no *pl.*) part of the earth that is not water: *After the bad boat journey we were glad to arrive on land.* **2** (no *pl.*) ground; earth: *good land; stony land.* **3** (*pl.* lands) country: *Japan is an eastern land.*

land[2] *v.* **1** come on to the ground from the air or from water: *The aeroplane landed at Gatwick.* **2** put an aircraft on to the ground: *The pilot landed the plane.*

landing /'lændɪŋ/ *n.* **1** coming on to the land; bringing an aircraft on to the land: *The spaceship made a safe landing on the moon.* **2** flat place at the top of stairs in a house or hotel.

landlady /'lændleɪdɪ/ *n.* (*pl.* landladies) **1** woman who has a house and lets people live there, for money. **2** woman who controls a hotel or pub.

landlord /'lændlɔːd/ *n.* **1** man who has a house and lets people live there, for money. **2** man who controls a hotel or pub.

Landrover /'lændrəʊvə(r)/ *n.* strong car that can drive well on bad roads or over the fields.

landscape /'lændskeɪp/ *n.* view of the countryside.

landslide /'lændslaɪd/ *n.* earth, rock, etc. that falls from the side of a hill or mountain.

lane /leɪn/ *n.* **1** narrow road in the country. **2** one part of a wide road: *He was driving in the middle lane of the motorway.*

language /'læŋgwɪdʒ/ *n.* how people talk; speaking: *English is a modern language and Latin is an old language.*

lantern /'læntən/ *n.* light in a glass box, which will stay bright in wind and rain.

lap[1] /læp/ *n.* top part of your legs when you are sitting: *The mother held her baby on her lap.*

lap[2] *n.* going once round a race track: *Peter did not win the race because he fell on the last lap.*

lap[3] *v.* (*pres. part.* lapping, *past part. & past tense* lapped/læpt/) drink liquid like an animal: *The cat lapped up the milk from a bowl.* **lap** *n.*

larder /'lɑːdə(r)/ *n.* small room or cupboard where you keep food.

large /lɑːdʒ/ *adj.* big: *A horse is a large animal.*

lash /læʃ/ *v.* **1** hit something or someone hard: *The rider lashed his horse with a whip.* **2** wave something suddenly and quickly: *The lion lashed its tail angrily.*

lass /læs/ *n.* (*pl.* lasses) girl; young woman.

lasso /læ'suː/ *n.* (*pl.* lassoes or lassos) long rope with a loop at one end, which a cowboy carries for catching horses and cows.

last[1] /lɑːst/ *adj.* **1** at the end, after all others: *December is the last month in the year.* **2** coming just before the present: *It's June now, so last month was May.* **3** only one left: *This is your last chance.* **lastly** *adv.* as the last thing.

last[2] *adv.* **1** after all others: *He came last in the race.* **2** at a time before the present: *When did you last see Penelope?*

last[3] *n.* (no *pl.*) what comes at the end: *These roses are the last of the summer.* **at last,** in the end, after some time: *We had a long journey by train, then at last we reached Aberdeen.*

last[4] *v.* **1** go on: *The film lasted for three hours.* **2** be enough: *Will this loaf of bread last until tomorrow?*

latch /lætʃ/ *n.* (*pl.* latches) thing for closing a door, gate, or window. **latch** *v.*: *If you don't latch the gate, the cows will get out.*

late[1] /leɪt/ *adj.* **1** coming at the end: *In summer the sun goes down in late evening.* **2** coming after the usual time: *There was no food left for the late arrivals.* **at the latest,** not later than that time: *Be here by twelve o'clock at the latest.* **3** no longer alive: *her late husband.*

late[2] *adv.* after the right or usual time: *We always go to bed late on Saturday night.* **later on,** afterwards; at a later time: *I'll see you later on.* **sooner or later,** some time or other.

lately /'leɪtlɪ/ *adv.* recently; not long ago: *Have you seen Mark lately?*

latest /'leɪtɪst/ *adj.* newest: *Irene has all the latest pop records.*

latter /'lætə(r)/ *adj.* last: *October and November come in the latter half of the year.* **latter** *pron.*

laugh /lɑːf/ *v.* show that you are pleased, amused, or happy by opening your mouth and making a noise: *The children laughed when the clown's trousers fell down.* **laugh at someone or something,** laugh to show that you think someone or something is funny or silly: *All the children laugh at Colin's big ears.* **burst out laughing,** suddenly start to laugh loudly. **laugh** *n.: Dennis has a very loud laugh.* **laughter** /'lɑːftə(r)/, **laughing** /'lɑːfɪŋ/ *n.: John and Nina roared with laughter.*

launch¹ /lɔːntʃ/ *n.* (*pl.* launches) fast motor-boat.

launch² *v.* **1** put a ship or boat into the water. **2** start something: *The enemy launched an attack.* **3** send a spacecraft or rocket into the air.

launching-pad /'lɔːntʃɪŋ pæd/ *n.* starting place for a spaceship.

launderette /ˌlɔːndə'ret/ *n.* shop where you can pay to put your clothes in a washing machine.

laundry /'lɔːndrɪ/ *n.* **1** (*pl.* laundries) place where you send clothes, sheets, etc. for washing and ironing. **2** (no *pl.*) clothes that must be washed and ironed.

lavatory /'lævətrɪ/ *n.* (*pl.* lavatories) toilet; W.C.

law /lɔː/ *n.* **1** rule for all the people of a country: *There is a law against murder.* **pass a law,** make a law in parliament. **the law,** all the laws of a country: *If a man murders someone, he is breaking the law.* **law court** *n.* place where judges and lawyers listen to law cases. **2** rule of a game: *the laws of football.*

lawful /'lɔːfl/ *adj.* allowed by the law. **lawfully** *adv.*

lawn /lɔːn/ *n.* area of short grass in a garden or park. **lawn-mower** /'lɔːn məʊə(r)/ *n.* machine that cuts grass on lawns.

lawyer /'lɔːjə(r)/ *n.* someone who has studied law; someone whose job is to help people with the law or talk for them in court.

lay¹ /leɪ/ past tense of *v.* lie.

lay² *v.* (*past part. & past tense* laid /leɪd/) **1** put something on top of another thing: *She laid the papers on my desk.* **2** make an egg: *Birds, fishes, and insects lay eggs.* **lay something out,** put something ready so that you can use it or see it: *Tessa laid out her best dress to wear at the party.*

layer /'leɪə(r)/ *n.* one of several things on top of each other: *I have three layers of blankets on my bed in winter.*

laze /leɪz/ *v.* do nothing: *He lazed on the beach all day.*

lazy /'leɪzɪ/ *adj.* not wanting to work; not working: *My lazy brother never cleans his car.* **lazily** *adv.* **laziness** *n.*

lb *abbrev.* pound, in weight: *1 lb sugar and 2 lbs butter.*

lead¹ /led/ *n.* (no *pl.*) **1** heavy, grey metal for making water-pipes, etc. **2** the black part in the middle of a pencil. **lead** *adj.* made of lead.

lead² /liːd/ *n.* **1** (no *pl.*) going in front; doing something first. **take the lead,** go first; show others what to do: *Godfrey takes the lead because he is oldest.* **2** (no *pl.*) first place. **be in the lead,** be in front: *Harry was in the lead from the beginning of the race.* **3** (no *pl.*) how far someone is in front: *Harry had a lead of two metres.*

lead³ *n.* rope or chain that you tie to an animal so that it walks with you.

lead⁴ v. (*past part. & past tense* led /led/)
1 walk in front of someone to show him the way: *Sidney led us through the wood.* **2** take someone or something by holding the hand, by a rope, etc.: *The dog led the blind man across the road.* **lead someone astray,** make someone do something wrong. **3** be the person who gives orders to others: *The captain leads his team.* **4** be first in something: *Who's leading in the race?* **5** be a way to somewhere: *This path leads to the next village.*

leader /'li:də(r)/ n. **1** someone who goes in front. **2** chief person.

leadership /'li:dəʃɪp/ n. (no pl.) leading or controlling people: *The club is under new leadership.*

leading /'li:dɪŋ/ adj. **1** first: *the leading runner.* **2** important: *a leading writer.*

leaf /li:f/ n. (pl. leaves) one of the green parts of a plant or tree, which grow from the side of a stem or branch: *In autumn the leaves turn brown.* **leafy** adj. covered with leaves.

leaflet /'li:flɪt/ n. printed piece of paper that tells people about something.

league /li:g/ n. **1** group of people or countries that have agreed to work together for something: *the League of Nations.* **2** group of teams that play against one another: *Our team is top of the football league this year.*

leak² /li:k/ v. flow slowly in or out through a small hole: *Oil was leaking from the bottom of the car.* **leak** n.: *There's a leak in the roof.* **leaky** adj. that leaks: *a leaky pipe.*

lean¹ /li:n/ adj. **1** thin: *a lean man.* **2** with no fat: *lean meat.*

lean² v. (*past part. & past tense* leaned /li:nd/, leant /lent/) **1** bend yourself or itself: *Nora leaned out of the window.* **2** put something against another thing: *The window-cleaner leaned the ladder against the wall.*

leap /li:p/ v. (*past part. & past tense* leaped /li:pt/, leapt /lept/) make a big jump: *The cat leapt from the wall to the tree.* **leap** n. a big jump. **by leaps and bounds,** very quickly: *A clever child will learn by leaps and bounds.*

learn /lɜ:n/ v. (*past part. & past tense* learned /lɜ:nd/, learnt /lɜ:nt/) **1** get to know something, or how to do something, by studying or practising: *Anita is learning to swim.* **2** hear about something; find out something: *I learnt from her letter that she was ill.*

learner /'lɜ:nə(r)/ n. someone who is learning: *This dictionary is for learners of English.*

least¹ /li:st/ adj. smallest in amount; less than all others: *Which shirt costs the least money?* **least** adv. less than all others: *That shirt's the least expensive.*

least² n. (no pl.) smallest amount, etc.: *Audrey has a little money, Brenda has less, and Rita has the least.* **at least,** no less than: *That book will cost at least £6.* **not in the least,** not at all: *He's not in the least angry.*

leather /'leðə(r)/ n. (no pl.) animal skin for making shoes, bags, etc. **leather** adj.

leave¹ /li:v/ n. **1** (no pl.) allowing someone to do something: *She gave me leave to borrow her book.* **2** (pl. leaves) holiday from work. **on leave,** having a holiday: *My uncle is on leave for a month.* **take your leave of,** say goodbye to someone.

leave² v. (*past part. & past tense* left /left/) **1** go away from somewhere: *What time will you leave home to go to the station?* **2** go away from someone or something and never come back: *Colin left his job in May.* **3** let someone or something stay in the same place or way: *Did you leave the window open?* **4** cause something to remain: *3 from 7 leaves 4.* **5** give something to someone when you die: *My father left me his farm.* **leave someone alone,** let someone be in peace: *Please leave me alone—I'm busy!* **leave something alone,** not touch or take something: *Leave my sewing alone!* **leave someone or something behind,** not take someone or something: *Mike left his money behind when he went shopping.* **leave for,** start a journey to a place: *We're leaving for the festival soon.* **leave go,** stop holding something: *Don't leave go or you'll fall.* **leave off,** stop: *Has the rain left off yet?* **leave out,** not put someone or something in: *We left Bob out of the team because he is ill.* **leave something to someone,** (a) say that someone will have your money, house, goods, etc. when you die. (b) let someone do a job for you: *Can I leave the arrangements to Wendy?*

leaves /li:vz/ (*pl.*) of *n.* leaf.

lecture /'lektʃə(r)/ *n.* planned talk to teach a group of people something: *The students were at a history lecture today.* **lecture** *v.* **lecturer** *n.* someone who lectures.

led /led/ *past part. & past tense* of *v.* lead.

ledge /ledʒ/ *n.* narrow shelf: *a window-ledge.*

leek /li:k/ *n.* vegetable like a long onion.

left[1] /left/ *adj.* opposite of right: *I always kick the ball with my left foot.* **left** *adv.*: *Turn left when you reach the church.* **left** *n.*: *In England we drive on the left.*

left[2] *past part. & past tense* of *v.* leave.

left-hand /'left hænd/ *adj.* **1** for your left hand: *a left-hand glove.* **2** on the left side: *She was sitting on the left-hand side of the room.* **left-handed** /ˌleft 'hændɪd/ *adj.* using your left hand more easily than the right.

leg /leg/ *n.* **1** one of the long parts of the body for walking and standing: *A man has two legs and a horse has four legs.* *pull someone's leg*, try, for fun, to make someone believe something that is not true: *Colin was pulling your leg when he said that sausages grow on trees.* **2** part of a chair, table, etc. on which it stands.

legacy /'legəsɪ/ *n.* (*pl.* legacies) money that someone leaves to another person when he dies.

legal /'li:gl/ *adj.* **1** of the law: *a legal case.* **2** allowed by the law: *It is not legal to drive without lights at night.* **legally** *adv.*

legend /'ledʒənd/ *n.* old story.

legislate /'ledʒɪsleɪt/ *v.* make laws.

leisure /'leʒə(r)/ *n.* (no *pl.*) time when you are not working and can do what you want.

leisurely /'leʒəlɪ/ *adj.* slow and pleasant: *We had a leisurely lunch.*

lemon /'lemən/ *n.* yellow fruit with a sour taste.

lemonade /ˌlemə'neɪd/ *n.* (no *pl.*) drink made from lemon juice and sugar.

lend /lend/ *v.* (*past part. & past tense* lent) give something to someone for a time: *Please lend me your bicycle for an hour, Andrew.*

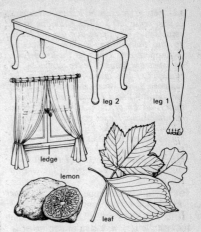

leg 2   leg 1

ledge

lemon

leaf

length /leŋθ/ *n.* **1** being long; how long something is: *What is the length of the car?* **2** piece of cloth, etc.: *a length of silk.*

lengthen /'leŋθən/ *v.* become longer; make something longer: *to lengthen a dress.*

lengthy /'leŋθɪ/ *adj.* very long; too long: *a lengthy telephone call.*

lens /lenz/ *n.* (*pl.* lenses) special piece of glass in a camera, microscope, or pair of spectacles.

lent /lent/ *past part. & past tense* of *v.* lend.

leopard /'lepəd/ *n.* big, wild animal with yellow fur and dark spots.

less[1] /les/ *adj.* not so much; smaller in amount: *A poor man has less money than a rich man.*

less[2] *adv.* word that makes an adjective or adverb weaker: *Jack was careful but Peter was less careful. Harry swims fast but Tom swims less fast.* **less than**, not so much as: *I like bananas less than apples.*

less[3] *n.* (no *pl.*) smaller amount: *There is too much sugar in this tea—please put in less next time.*

lessen /'lesn/ *v.* become smaller, fewer, weaker, etc.; make something smaller, etc.: *A tablet will lessen the pain.*

lesson /'lesn/ *n.* **1** time when you learn something with a teacher: *We have an English lesson every day.* **2** what you learn.

let[1] /let/ v. (*pres. part.* letting, *past part.* & *past tense* let) **1** allow someone to do something: *The fierce dog did not let us go into the garden.* **2** allow something to happen, etc.: *Don't let the fire go out.* **let someone alone**, leave someone in peace: *Let me alone—I'm reading.* **let someone down**, break a promise: *I've let you down—I said I would help you but I didn't.* **let go of**, stop holding someone or something: *He let go of the coat and it fell in the water.* **let off**, fire a gun; light a firework so that it explodes: *We let off rockets on Guy Fawkes Day.* **let someone off**, not punish someone. **let's, let us**, I suggest that we: *Let's go to the cinema this evening.*

let[2] v. allow someone to live in your house or use your land if he pays you: *Have you any rooms to let?*

letter /'letə(r)/ n. **1** sign in writing: *Z is the last letter in the English alphabet.* **2** piece of writing that one person sends to another: *I must post the letter to my boyfriend.*

letter-box /'letə bɒks/ n. (*pl.* letter-boxes) **1** box in the street where you put letters for the post. **2** hole for letters in the door of a house.

lettuce /'letɪs/ n. green plant that you eat in salads.

level[1] /'levl/ adj. **1** flat; smooth: *We need level ground for a tent.* **2** equal: *The two teams are level with 40 points each.*

level[2] n. **1** where something is: *The cellar is below road level.* **2** how high something is: *The river level rose after the rain.*

level crossing /ˌlevl 'krɒsɪŋ/ n. place where a railway line goes over a road.

lever /'li:və(r)/ v. lift something heavy or force something open with a strong bar: *They levered the lid off the box with an iron bar.*

liar /'laɪə(r)/ n. someone who does not tell the truth: *Don't believe him—he's a liar.*

liberal /'lɪbərəl/ adj. **1** giving things freely: *He is liberal with his money and buys a lot of presents.* **2** freely given: *liberal help.* **3** not strict: *liberal parents.* **liberally** adv.

liberate /'lɪbəreɪt/ v. make someone free: *Lincoln liberated American slaves.*

liberty /'lɪbətɪ/ n. (no *pl.*) being free: *Lincoln gave liberty to black slaves.* **at liberty,** (**a**) free to do what you want: *You are at liberty to use my bicycle.* (**b**) not in prison.

library /'laɪbrərɪ/ n. (*pl.* libraries) room or building for books. **librarian** /laɪ-'breərɪən/ n. someone who works in a library.

licence /'laɪsns/ n. piece of paper showing that the law allows you to do or have something: *You must have a driving licence before you can drive a car.* **license** /'laɪsns/ v.: *You must license your dog every year.*

lick /lɪk/ v. pass the tongue over something: *The cat was licking its paws.* **lick** n.: *He gave the envelope a lick and closed it.*

lid /lɪd/ n. **1** cover for a box, pot, etc.: *Where's the lid of the teapot?* **2** skin above and below the eye, which moves and closes over the eye.

lie[1] /laɪ/ v. say something that you know is not true: *Don't believe her because she always lies.* **lie** n.: *He told me a lie.*

lie[2] v. (*pres. part* lying, *past part.* lain /leɪn/, *past tense* lay /leɪ/) **1** put the body flat on something; rest flat: *Kathy lay on the bed and read.* **2** rest flat; be on something: *In the autumn, leaves lie on the ground.*

lieutenant /lef'tenənt/ n. officer in the army or navy.

life /laɪf/ n. **1** (no *pl.*) what animals and plants have but stone, metal, and water do not have: *Is there any life on the moon?* **2** (*pl.* lives) being alive: *Many people lost their lives in the fire.* **lead a life,** live in a certain way: *We lead a quiet life in the country.* **not on your life!** certainly not: *'Shall we walk home?' 'Not on your life—it's too far!'* **run for your life,** run very fast away from something dangerous. **spare someone's life,** not kill someone when you could. **3** (*pl.* lives) time that you have been alive: *Have you lived in Scotland all your life?* **4** (no *pl.*) the way you live: *Do you like life in the country better than town life?* **5** (*pl.* lives) story of someone's life in a book, etc.: *Have you read the life of Albert Schweitzer?* **6** (no *pl.*) energy; being busy and interested: *The children are full of life.*

lifebelt /'laɪfbelt/ n. special ring that you can put round yourself to stop you from drowning.

life-boat /'laɪf bəʊt/ n. boat that helps people or ships in trouble at sea.

life-jacket /'laɪf dʒækɪt/ n. jacket that you wear in a boat to stop you from drowning if you fall into the water.

lifeless /'laɪflɪs/ adj. **1** still. **2** dead.

lifetime /'laɪftaɪm/ n. all the time that you are alive: *There were no aeroplanes in Napoleon's lifetime.*

lift¹ /lɪft/ n. **1** journey in another person's car: *Can you give me a lift to the station?* **2** machine that takes people or goods up and down in a high building: *Shall we go up the stairs or take the lift?*

lift² v. **1** take something or someone up: *He lifted the lid and looked into the box.* **2** go up and away: *The cloud has lifted and we can see the mountains.*

light¹ /laɪt/ adj. **1** bright; not dark: *This room has a lot of windows and is very light.* **2** with a pale colour: *Blue and white make light blue.*

light² adj. **1** with little weight; easy to lift or move: *The little girl is so light I can lift her with one hand.* **2** a little; not much: *light rain.* **3** gentle; not strong: *Your footsteps were so light I didn't hear them.* **lightly** adv. **get off lightly**, be punished less than you expect.

light³ n. **1** (no pl.) where there is no darkness; brightness: *The sun gives us light.* **2** (pl. lights) instrument or thing that makes brightness for us; lamp, etc.: *Turn off the lights when you go out of the room.* **3** (pl. lights) fire from a match, etc.: *Can you give me a light for my cigarette?*

light⁴ v. (past part. & past tense lighted/'laɪtɪd/, lit /lɪt/) **1** make something start to burn or shine: *Please light the fire.* **2** give light to something so that you can see it clearly: *He carried a torch to light the way.*

lighten /'laɪtn/ v. **1** become brighter; make something brighter: *When the sun rises the sky lightens.* **2** become less heavy; make something less heavy: *It will lighten the basket if I take out the potatoes.*

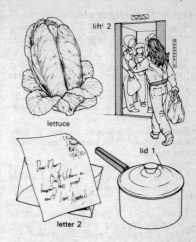

lift¹ 2

lettuce

lid 1

letter 2

lighter /'laɪtə(r)/ n. thing for lighting cigarettes, pipes, etc.: *a cigarette lighter.*

lighthouse /'laɪthaʊs/ n. high tower by or in the sea, with a strong light that shines at night to warn ships that there are rocks.

lightning /'laɪtnɪŋ/ n. (no pl.) sudden flash of bright light in the sky: *Two people were killed by lightning in the storm.*

like¹ /laɪk/ prep. **1** such as; the same as: *She was carrying a bag like mine.* **2** in the same way as: *She sings like a bird.*

like² v. feel that someone or something is good, lovely, interesting, etc.; enjoy something: *Grace drinks a lot of milk because she likes it.*

likeable /'laɪkəbl/ adj. pleasing: *a likeable girl.*

likely /'laɪklɪ/ adj. probable; almost certain: *Tony is the most likely winner of the race. Tony is likely to win.* **likely** adv. **most likely, very likely,** probably.

likeness /'laɪknɪs/ n. (no pl.) being the same: *There's not much likeness between you and your brother.*

liking /'laɪkɪŋ/ n. (no pl.) **have a liking for,** be fond of someone or something. **to your liking,** in a way that pleases you: *Is the coffee to your liking?*

lily /'lɪlɪ/ n. (pl. lilies) sort of flower.

limb /lɪm/ *n.* leg or arm.

lime /laɪm/ *n.* round, green fruit like a lemon. **lime-juice** *n.* drink made from limes.

limit /'lɪmɪt/ *n.* **1** edge: *That fence shows the limit of my garden.* **2** the most that is allowed: *a speed limit.* **limit** *v.* allow only a certain amount, number, sort, etc.: *He must limit the number of cigarettes he smokes.*

limp¹ /lɪmp/ *adj.* soft; not stiff or firm. **limply** *adv.*: *The washing hung limply on the line.*

limp² *v.* walk with one foot that is hurt or stiff: *She hurt her ankle and limped back home.* **limp** *n.*: *He walks with a limp.*

line¹ /laɪn/ *n.* **1** piece of string, rope, or wire: *We hang our washing on a clothes-line.* **2** long, thin mark: *He drew a line with his pencil and ruler.* **3** row of people or things: *Please stand in a straight line.* **4** row of written or printed words: *There are 58 lines on this page.*

line² *v.* stand or be in rows along a street, etc.: *Crowds of people lined the streets to see the Royal Wedding.* **line up**, stand, or make people stand, in a row: *The customers lined up at the counter.*

lined /laɪnd/ *adj.* **1** with another piece of cloth, etc. on the inside: *a lined dress.* **2** with lines across it: *lined paper.*

linen /'lɪnɪn/ *n.* (no *pl.*) **1** sort of cloth. **2** things made from linen cloth: *table linen.*

liner /'laɪnə(r)/ *n.* big ship that carries people.

linger /'lɪŋgə(r)/ *v.* stay near a place: *A hungry dog lingered around the dustbin and looked for food.*

link¹ /lɪŋk/ *n.* **1** one of the rings in a chain. **2** something that holds things or people together: *Letters are a link with friends who live far away.*

link² *v.* **1** join one thing to another thing: *The friends linked hands.* **2** join two things by putting something between them: *A bridge links the two banks of the river.*

lino /'laɪnəʊ/, **linoleum** /lɪ'nəʊlɪəm/ *n.* (no *pl.*) sort of smooth, hard covering for the floor.

lion /'laɪən/ *n.* sort of big, wild animal.

lioness /'laɪənes/ *n.* (*pl.* lionesses) female lion.

lip /lɪp/ *n.* one of the two soft front edges of the mouth: *She had a cigarette between her lips.*

lipstick /'lɪpstɪk/ *n.* pink or red colour that women put on their lips.

liquid /'lɪkwɪd/ *n.* anything that flows, and is not a solid or a gas: *Oil and water are liquids.* **liquid** *adj.*

list /lɪst/ *n.* a lot of names or things that you have written one under another: *a shopping list.* **list** *v.* write things in a list.

listen /'lɪsn/ *v.* **listen to**, hear sounds carefully; try to hear sounds: *Did you listen to the news on the radio this morning?* **listener** *n.* someone who listens: *The announcer tells the listeners what programme comes next.*

lit /lɪt/, **lighted** /'laɪtɪd/ *past part.* & *past tense* of *v.* light.

literature /'lɪtrətʃə(r)/ *n.* (no *pl.*) **1** writing books, plays, poetry, etc. **2** books and writing of a country or a time: *French literature.*

litre /'liːtə(r)/ *n.* measure of liquid.

litter¹ /'lɪtə(r)/ *n.* **1** (no *pl.*) bits of paper, bottles, etc. that people do not want and leave lying on the ground: *Litter covered the cinema floor after the film.* **2** (*pl.* litters) family of new young animals: *a litter of puppies.*

litter² *v.* make a place untidy by leaving things everywhere; lie everywhere in an untidy way: *Books and papers littered his desk.*

little¹ /'lɪtl/ *adj.* **1** small: *a little village.* **2** young: *little children.* **3** not much: *A busy farmer has little free time.* **a little**, some but not much: *I can speak a little French.*

little² *adv.* not much: *I am tired because I slept very little last night.*

little³ *n.* (no *pl.*) not much; only a small amount: *He did very little on his first day at work.* **a little**, (*a*) in a small way: *Try to help your mother a little.* (*b*) slightly; rather: *This dress is a little too short for me.* **for a little**, for a short time or distance. **little by little**, slowly: *Little by little, our English is getting better.*

live¹ /laɪv/ *adj.* **1** having life; not dead: *You won't see live animals in a museum.* **2** happening now; not recorded: *The concert is live from the Royal Festival Hall.* **3** burning: *live coals.* **4** full of electricity: *live wires.*

live² /lɪv/ *v.* **1** be alive, not dead: *Samuel's grandfather lived until he was 90.* **2** have your home: *Where do you live? I live in Norwich.* **3** spend your life in a certain way: *We live very quietly.* **live on**, eat or drink only one thing: *Sheep live on grass and babies live on milk.*

lively /'laɪvlɪ/ *adj.* full of life; moving quickly: *lively kittens.*

liver /'lɪvə(r)/ *n.* **1** part inside a person's or an animal's body. **2** animal's liver that you can eat.

lives /laɪvz/ (*pl.*) of *n.* life.

livestock /'laɪvstɒk/ *n.* (no *pl.*) all the animals on a farm.

living¹ /'lɪvɪŋ/ *adj.* **1** alive: *a living creature.* **2** of or for life; for living in: *poor living conditions.*

living² *n.* **1** (no *pl.*) way of life. *standard of living*, rich or poor way of living. **2** (*pl.* livings) *earn your living, make a living*, work to pay for the things that you need: *Most people in this city earn their living by working in the car factory.*

living-room /'lɪvɪŋ ruːm/ *n.* main room of a house.

load¹ /ləʊd/ *n.* something that you carry: *The lorry had a load of wood.*

load² *v.* **1** put things on to a vehicle or ship: *The two men loaded the furniture on to the van.* **2** put bullets into a gun: *Have you loaded your gun?*

loaf /ləʊf/ *n.* (*pl.* loaves) big piece of bread: *I bought a loaf of bread at the baker's.*

loan /ləʊn/ *v.* lend something: *The public library loans books to people.* **loan** *n.*: *Henry asked his father for a loan of £10.*

loathe /ləʊð/ *v.* hate someone or something: *I loathe rats.* **loathing** *n.*

loaves /ləʊvz/ (*pl.*) of *n.* loaf.

lobster /'lɒbstə(r)/ *n.* big shellfish that you can eat.

local /'ləʊkl/ *adj.* of that place: *We go to the town for clothes but we buy food in local shops.* **locally** *adv.*

lock¹ /lɒk/ *n.* thing that keeps a door, gate, drawer, etc. closed, so that you cannot open it without a key. *under lock and key*, locked up in something.

lock² *v.* **1** close something with a key: *At night we lock the door.* **2** have a lock; become locked: *This suitcase won't lock because it is too full.* *lock something away*, put something away in a locked place. *lock someone out*, lock the door from inside so that someone cannot come in. *lock something up*, lock something in a place so that it will be safe: *We lock up our house when we go out.* *lock someone up*, put someone in a place that he cannot leave.

locked /lɒkt/ *adj.*: *a locked door.*

locker /'lɒkə(r)/ *n.* small cupboard with a lock for one person's things: *At the swimming pool I put my clothes in a locker.*

locomotive /ˌləʊkə'məʊtɪv/ *n.* railway engine.

lodge /lɒdʒ/ *v.* pay to live in rooms in another person's house: *In the summer a foreign student lodged in our house.*

lodger /'lɒdʒə(r)/ *n.* someone who pays to live in another person's house. **lodgings** /'lɒdʒɪŋz/ *n.* room or rooms in a family house where you pay to live: *Does your brother have good lodgings in London?*

loft /lɒft/ *n.* room where you store things at the top of a house, under the roof.

log /lɒg/ n. piece of a tree that has fallen or that you have cut; short, thick piece of wood for a fire.

loiter /'lɔɪtə(r)/ v. walk slowly, often stopping; stand and not do anything: *Why is that boy loitering at the street corner?*

lollipop /'lɒlɪpɒp/, **lolly** /'lɒlɪ/ n. (pl. lollies) big sweet on a stick.

lonely /'ləʊnlɪ/ adj. **1** sad because you are alone, with no friends: *Sarah felt lonely when her best friend left the town.* **2** far away from other places: *a lonely farm.* **loneliness** n.

long[1] /lɒŋ/ adj. **1** from one end to the other: *The snake is a metre long.* **2** from beginning to end: *Our holidays are two weeks long.* **3** far from one end to the other: *long hair.* **4** lasting a lot of time: *a long film.* **no longer**, not now: *He's no longer living in Edinburgh.*

long[2] adv. for a lot of time: *We are in a hurry, so we can't stay long.* **so long as, as long as**, if: *You may borrow this book so long as you keep it clean.* **long before**, at a time much before: *Mark learned to read long before he started school.* **long after**, at a time much after.

long[3] n. (no pl.) **before long**, soon: *I shall see you before long.*

long[4] v. **long for**, want something very much: *We're longing for the holidays.* **long to**, want very much to do or have something: *I'm longing to see you.* **longing** adj.: *a longing look.* **longingly** adv.: *Nora looked longingly at the cakes in the shop window.* **longing** n. strong wish: *After two weeks in London Una had a longing for her family in Scotland.*

look[1] /lʊk/ n. **1** seeing. **have** or **take a look at**, try to see something: *Let me have a look at your new dress.* **2** appearance; how something or someone seems: *I don't like the look of the weather.* **3 looks** (pl.) appearance of the face and body: *good looks*, beauty.

look[2] v. **1** watch; try to see: *You must look both ways before you cross a road.* **look after**, take care of someone or something: *A nurse looks after sick people in a hospital.* **look as if, look as though**, be probable or likely that: *It looks as though he will win the race.* **look at**, watch someone or something: *The children are looking at television in their

room.* **look for**, try to find someone or something: *Grace is looking for a job.* **look forward to**, wait for something with pleasure: *I'm looking forward to our holiday next week.* **look into**, study something carefully: *to look into a problem.* **look on** or **upon**, think of someone or something: *He looks upon me as his best friend.* **look out for**, watch and wait for someone or something. **look out!** be careful! **look something up**, try to find the meaning of something in a book, etc.: *I looked up the word in a dictionary.* **2** appear; seem to be: *You're looking cheerful today.* **look like, (a)** seem to be: *That looks like an interesting film,* **(b)** have the appearance of: *She looks like her mother.*

look-out /'lʊk aʊt/ n. **1** (no pl.) watching. **on the look-out for**, looking for something: *I am on the look-out for a good, cheap bicycle.* **2** (pl. look-outs) place where you can watch for something coming.

loom /luːm/ n. machine for weaving cloth.

loop /luːp/ n. round shape of a piece of string, ribbon, etc. when it crosses itself: *A bow has two loops.*

loose /luːs/ adj. **1** free; not tied, etc. **get loose**, become free: *The dog broke its chain and got loose.* **2** not tight: *Loose clothes are more comfortable than tight ones.* **loosely** adv. **loosen** /'luːsn/ v. become loose; make something loose: *The knot is so tight that I can't loosen it.*

lord /lɔːd/ n. **1** nobleman: *the House of Lords.* **2 the Lord**, God; Christ.

lorry /'lɒrɪ/ n. (pl. lorries) big vehicle that carries heavy loads; truck.

lose /luːz/ v. (past part. & past tense lost /lɒst/) **1** not have something or someone that you had before: *Paul has lost his job because the factory has closed.* **2** not be able to find something: *I can't open the door because I've lost the key.* **3** not win: *Our team is losing the match.*

loser /'luːzə(r)/ n. one who is not the winner.

loss /lɒs/ n. (pl. losses) **1** losing: *He told the police about the loss of his car.* **2** something that is lost; waste: *The wrecked ship was a serious loss.* **at a loss**, for less money than you paid for it: *If you buy a house for £22,000 and sell it* *for £20,000, you are selling at a loss.* **be at a loss**, be uncertain: *I'm at a loss to know what to do.*

lost /lɒst/ *past part. & past tense* of *v.* lose. **be lost**, not know where you are: *I can't find my way home—I'm lost.*

lot[1] /lɒt/ *n.* **a lot**, very much: *It's a lot warmer today.* **a lot of, lots of**, a great number or amount of things or people: *We spent a lot of money in the shop. He bought lots of new clothes.* **the lot**, all; everything: *There were two kilos of onions in the shop and I bought the lot.*

lot[2] *n.* **draw lots, cast lots**, choose people by taking pieces of paper with numbers, etc. from a box: *They drew lots to see who would speak first.*

lotion /ˈləʊʃn/ *n.* soft liquid that you put on the skin: *suntan lotion.*

loud /laʊd/ *adj.* making a lot of noise; that you can hear clearly: *I couldn't hear what he said because the radio was so loud.* **loud** *adv.*: *Speak louder, I can't hear you.* **loudly** *adv.*

loud-speaker /ˌlaʊd ˈspiːkə(r)/ *n.* part of a radio, etc. from which you hear sound.

lounge /laʊndʒ/ *n.* room in a house or hotel, where you can sit comfortably.

lovable /ˈlʌvəbl/ *adj.* that people love very much: *a lovable child.*

love /lʌv/ *v.* **1** have a warm feeling for someone; like someone very much: *I love my parents.* **2** like something very much: *I'd love to come and see you again.* **love** *n.* **be in love with**, love someone. **fall in love with**, begin to love someone. **loving** *adj.* feeling or showing love. **lovingly** *adv.*

lovely /ˈlʌvli/ *adj.* **1** giving pleasure because it looks or sounds good, etc.: *a lovely woman.* **2** that you enjoy very much: *a lovely party.* **loveliness** *n.* beauty.

low[1] /ləʊ/ *adj.* **1** not high: *She jumped over the low wall.* **2** not loud: *I can't hear her because she has a low voice.*

low[2] *adv.* down; in or to a place that is not high: *They bowed low to the Queen.*

lower /ˈləʊə(r)/ *v.* take something or someone down: *to lower a flag.* **lower** *adj.* that is under another; bottom: *my lower lip.*

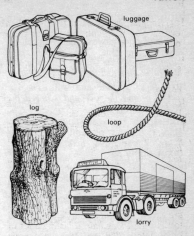

luggage

log

loop

lorry

loyal /ˈlɔɪəl/ *adj.* true and faithful: *He is loyal to his firm.* **loyally** *adv.* **loyalty** /ˈlɔɪəlti/ *n.*: *loyalty to your friends.*

l.p. /ˌel ˈpiː/ *abbrev.* long-playing record.

luck /lʌk/ *n.* (no *pl.*) chance; what happens to someone or something: *Please wish me good luck for my exams!* **be in luck**, have good things happen. **be out of luck**, have bad things happen. **for luck**, so that good things will happen: *Cross your fingers for luck!* **hard luck**, bad luck.

lucky /ˈlʌki/ *adj.* **1** having good luck: *You're lucky to own a car.* **2** bringing good luck: *a lucky number.* **luckily** *adv.*: *I got to the station late, but luckily the train was still there.*

luggage /ˈlʌgɪdʒ/ *n.* (no *pl.*) bags, trunks, suitcases, etc. for travelling.

lull /lʌl/ *n.* short time when it is quiet: *a lull in the storm.*

lullaby /ˈlʌləbaɪ/ *n.* (*pl.* lullabies) song to make a baby go to sleep.

lump /lʌmp/ *n.* **1** hard piece of something: *a lump of sugar.* **2** swelling or hard place in part of your body: *a lump on the head.* **lumpy** *adj.* full of lumps: *lumpy sauce.*

lunatic /ˈluːnətɪk/ *n.* mad person; someone who does very foolish things.

lunch /lʌntʃ/ *n.* (*pl.* lunches) meal that you eat in the middle of the day. **lunch** *v.* eat lunch.

lung /lʌŋ/ *n.* part of the body with which you breathe.

lurch /lɜ:tʃ/ *v.* move suddenly and clumsily to one side: *The drunken man lurched along the street.* **lurch** *n.*: *A big wave came and the ship gave a lurch.*

lurk /lɜ:k/ *v.* hide and wait: *The cat lurked behind the tree and watched the bird.*

luxurious /lʌg'ʒʊərɪəs/ *adj.* **1** comfortable, rich, and pleasant: *a luxurious house.* **2** expensive: *luxurious clothes.* **luxuriously** *adv.*

luxury /'lʌkʃərɪ/ *n.* **1** (no *pl.*) way of living when you have all the rich things that you want: *He lives in luxury.* **2** (*pl.* luxuries) something pleasant that you do not really need: *Wine is a luxury in England.* **luxury** *adj.*: *a luxury hotel.*

lying /'laɪŋ/ *pres. part.* of *v.* lie.

Mm

ma /mɑ:/ *n.* mother.

mac /mæk/ *abbrev.* mackintosh.

machine /mə'ʃi:n/ *n.* instrument with many parts that move together to do work: *a sewing-machine.*

machine-gun /mə'ʃi:n gʌn/ *n.* gun that can fire many bullets, one after the other.

machinery /mə'ʃi:nərɪ/ *n.* (no *pl.*) **1** parts of a machine: *the complicated machinery of a lift.* **2** group of machines: *We need heavy machinery to build the new road.*

mackintosh /'mækɪntɒʃ/ *n.* (*pl.* mackintoshes) raincoat.

mad /mæd/ *adj.* (madder, maddest) **1** with a sick mind. *go mad*, become mad. *like mad*, wildly: *He ran like mad.* **2** very foolish: *You're mad to go out in this thunder-storm!* **3** having very strong feelings: *to be mad with excitement.* **4** very angry: *He was mad with me for losing his watch. drive someone mad*, make someone angry. *mad about*, very fond of something: *Julie is mad about pop music.* **madly** *adv.* very: *madly excited.* **madness** *n.*

madam /'mædəm/ *n.* polite word that you say when you speak to a woman who is a stranger or when you write a business letter to a woman: *Can I help you, madam?*

made /meɪd/ *past part. & past tense* of *v.* make.

magazine /ˌmægə'zi:n/ *n.* book with a paper cover which comes every week, month, etc.: *Have you read the articles in this magazine?*

magic /'mædʒɪk/ *n.* (no *pl.*) **1** strange powers that make wonderful or unusual things happen: *The good fairy made Cinderella's coach come by magic.* **2** clever tricks that a person can do to surprise people. **magic, magical** *adj.* **magically** *adv.*

magician /mə'dʒɪʃn/ *n.* **1** someone who does strange things: *The magician turned the boy into a frog.* **2** someone who does clever tricks to make people laugh, etc.

magistrate /'mædʒɪstreɪt/ *n.* sort of judge in a law court that looks at small crimes: *The magistrate fined him £50 for driving too fast.*

magnet /'mægnɪt/ *n.* piece of iron that can pick up other pieces of metal. **magnetic** /mæg'netɪk/ *adj.*

magnificent /mæg'nɪfɪsnt/ *adj.* very great, fine, or beautiful: *a magnificent palace.* **magnificently** *adv.* **magnificence** /mæg'nɪfɪsns/ *n.*

magnify /'mægnɪfaɪ/ *v.* make something look bigger. **magnifying-glass** *n.* a special glass that can magnify things: *He looked at the little insect through a magnifying-glass.*

magpie /'mægpaɪ/ *n.* black and white bird.

maid /meɪd/ *n.* woman servant.

mail /meɪl/ *n.* (no *pl.*) post; letters and parcels that you send: *The mail was late because the postman was ill.* **mail** *v.* send things in the mail.

main /meɪn/ *adj.* chief; most important: *Piccadilly is one of London's main streets.* **mainly** *adv.* mostly; chiefly: *Babies drink mainly milk.*

maintain /meɪn'teɪn/ *v.* **1** go on with something: *If he can maintain this speed he will win the race.* **2** keep something working well: *You must maintain your bicycle brakes.* **maintenance** /'meɪntənəns/ *n.*

maize /meɪz/ n. (no pl.) plant with big, yellow seeds that we use for food.

majesty /'mædʒəstɪ/ n. (pl. majesties) word that you say when you speak to or about a king or queen: *Her Majesty will arrive at 10 o'clock.* **majestic** /mə-'dʒestɪk/ adj. like a king or queen; looking very rich and important. **majestically** adv.

major¹ /'meɪdʒə(r)/ adj. bigger; most important; very great: *Liverpool is a major British port.*

major² n. army officer.

majority /mə'dʒɒrətɪ/ n. (no pl.) most things or people in a group: *The majority of British people have television.*

make¹ /meɪk/ n. sort; kind: *What make of car do you have?*

make² v. (past part. & past tense made /meɪd/) **1** build something by putting parts together: *I bought some wood and made a house for my rabbit.* **2** cause something to appear or to happen; produce something: *The plane made a loud noise when it landed.* **3** prepare something; put something in order: *He got up and made his bed.* **4** cause someone to feel something: *Do birthdays make you happy?* **5** cause something to be: *The sun made the washing dry.* **6** put someone in a job: *The club made him secretary.* **7** cause someone to do something: *The onions made me cry.* **8** force someone to do something: *The government makes us pay tax.* **make do with**, use something that is not the best for the job: *We had no table, but we made do with boxes.* **make for**, go straight to something: *When the children have money, they make straight for the sweet shop.* **make off**, hurry away. **make off with someone or something**, go away with someone or something that is not yours: *The thief made off with her watch.* **make out**, be able to see or understand something that is not clear: *The night was so dark that he couldn't make out the path.* **make sure, make certain**, find out about something so that you are sure, certain: *Please make sure that the door is locked.* **make up**, (a) think of a story; imagine something that is not

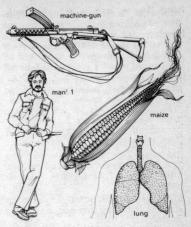

machine-gun

man¹ 1

maize

lung

true: *No one believes that story—he made it up!* (b) end a quarrel: *The brothers quarrelled last year, but now they have made it up.* (c) put something on the skin to make it look more beautiful or different. **maker** /'meɪkə(r)/ n. someone who has made something: *If your watch does not work, send it back to the makers.*

make-up /'meɪk ʌp/ n. (no pl.) something that women and actors put on the skin to make it different or more beautiful: *Lipstick and face-powder are kinds of make-up.*

male /meɪl/ n. man or boy; animal that cannot have baby animals; plant that does not have fruit. **male** adj.: *A cock is a male bird.*

mama, mamma /mə'mɑː/ n. mother.

man¹ /mæn/ n. **1** (pl. men) grown-up male person: *Boys become men when they grow older.* **2** (pl. men) male person who is strong and brave: *Don't cry—be a man!* **3** (pl. men) male worker or soldier: *The builder said his men would start work the next day.* **4** (no pl.) all human beings: *How long has man lived on this earth?* **5** (pl. men) any person: *All men must have water to live.*

man² v. (pres. part. manning, past part. & past tense manned /mænd/) get enough people for a job: *We need twelve people to man the ship.*

manage /'mænɪdʒ/ v. **1** control someone or something: *Only a good rider can manage this horse.* **2** be able to do something that is difficult: *The box was heavy but he managed to carry it.* **3** be able to eat or drink something: *Can you manage another cup of tea?*

management /'mænɪdʒmənt/ n. **1** (no pl.) control of a business, factory, etc.: *The old director has left and the firm is under new management.* **2** (pl. managements) all the people who control a firm, business, etc.

manager /'mænɪdʒə(r)/ n. someone who controls a business, a bank, a hotel, etc. **manageress** /ˌmænɪdʒə'res/ n. female manager.

managing director /ˌmænɪdʒɪŋ daɪ'rektə(r)/ n. the top person in a big business.

mane /meɪn/ n. long hair on the neck of an animal.

maniac /'meɪnɪæk/ n. wild, mad person; someone who does very foolish things: *Be careful! That man is driving like a maniac!*

mankind /ˌmæn'kaɪnd/ n. (no pl.) all human beings; all the people in the world.

manner /'mænə(r)/ n. **1** (no pl.) way something happens; way you do something: *He was walking in a strange manner because he was drunk.* **2** (no pl.) way that you talk to someone: *That boy has an unfriendly manner.* **3 manners** (pl.) general way you behave when other people are there: *It's bad manners to talk with a full mouth.* **ill-mannered** adj. rude. **well-mannered** adj. polite.

mansion /'mænʃn/ n. very big house.

mantelpiece /'mæntlpiːs/ n. shelf above a fireplace in a house.

manual[1] /'mænjʊəl/ adj. that you do with the hands: *manual work.* **manually** adv.

manual[2] n. small book that tells you how to do something.

manufacture /ˌmænjʊ'fæktʃə(r)/ v. make things with machines in a factory: *BL manufactures cars.* **manufacture** n.: *Japan is famous for the manufacture of radios.* **manufacturer** n. person or business that makes things with machines: *Cadburys are famous chocolate manufacturers.*

manuscript /'mænjʊskrɪpt/ n. book, speech, etc.

many[1] /'menɪ/ adj. a lot of: *There are many flats in this block.* **how many,** what number of: *How many cups are there?*

many[2] n. (pl.) lots of things, animals, or people: *All the children play tennis and many play netball too.* **a good many, a great many,** a lot of: *A good many people go on holiday in August.* **many a,** many: *I've had many a good meal in that restaurant.*

map /mæp/ n. flat plan of the world, a country, or a town: *Sue looked at the map to find the way to Sheffield.*

marble[1] /'mɑːbl/ n. (no pl.) hard stone for statues and special buildings. **marble** adj. made of marble.

marble[2] n. small, glass ball for a children's game called **marbles**.

march[1] /mɑːtʃ/ v. **1** walk like a soldier: *The army marched past the general.* **2** make someone walk quickly: *The police marched the thief out of the house.* **march** n. **1** long walk. **2** piece of music for marching people: *The band played a march.*

March[2] /mɑːtʃ/ n. third month of the year.

marg. /mɑːdʒ/ **margarine** /ˌmɑːdʒə'riːn/ n. (no pl.) soft food, like butter, that you put on bread or in cooking.

margin /'mɑːdʒɪn/ n. space with no writing or printing round the edges of a page or sheet of paper.

mark[1] /mɑːk/ n. **1** line, scratch, spot, etc. that spoils something: *What are those dirty marks on your shirt?* **2** spot, shape, etc. on something or someone: *Roger's horse has a white mark on its head.* **3** point that your teacher gives for a piece of work, examination paper, etc., to show how good you are: *Irene got good marks for her essay.*

mark[2] v. **1** put a sign on something by writing on it, etc.: *Can you mark your house on this map?* **2** spoil something with a line, spot, etc.: *Your pen has marked my blouse.* **3** put a number, √, or × on written work to show whether it is right or wrong: *In the test the teacher marked all my answers right.* **4** be a special sign of something: *A Silver Wedding marks 25 years of marriage.*

market /'mɑːkɪt/ n. group of shops or pens in the open air where people go to buy and sell goods: *There is a cattle market in the middle of town every Friday.* **be on the market**, be for sale: *There is a new sort of record-player on the market.*

marmalade /'mɑːməleɪd/ n. (no *pl.*) orange jam that British people eat at breakfast.

marrow /'mærəʊ/ n. sort of vegetable.

marry /'mærɪ/ v. **1** take someone as a husband or wife: *Samuel is going to marry my sister.* **2** join a man and woman as husband and wife: *The priest married Derek and Jane last month.* **get married**, marry: *Sue and Mike got married last month.* **married** adj. /'mærɪd/. **marriage** /'mærɪdʒ/ n. time when a man and a woman are married.

marsh /mɑːʃ/ n. (*pl.* marshes) wet, soft ground.

marvel /'mɑːvl/ n. wonder; wonderful and surprising happening or person: *It's a marvel that you weren't killed in the car crash!* **marvel** v. (*pres. part.* marvelling, *past part. & past tense* marvelled /'mɑːvld/) be very surprised: *We marvelled at his excellent piano playing.*

marvellous /'mɑːvələs/ adj. wonderful; that pleases and surprises very much. **marvellously** adv.

masculine /'mæskjʊlɪn/ adj. of or like a man; right for a man. **masculine** n. word for a male or a man: *'Prince' is the masculine of 'princess'.*

mash /mæʃ/ v. crush or squash food to make it soft.

mask /mɑːsk/ n. **1** cover that you put over the face to hide it: *The thief was wearing a mask.* **2** covering for the face to stop gas, smoke, or germs. **mask** v. cover the face with a mask.

mass /mæs/ n. (*pl.* masses) crowd; many things or people together: *There were masses of dark clouds in the sky.*

massacre /'mæsəkə(r)/ v. kill a big group of people in a cruel way. **massacre** n.

massive /'mæsɪv/ adj. very big and heavy: *We needed six men to lift the massive table.*

mast /mɑːst/ n. **1** tall, straight piece of wood or metal that stands on a boat to

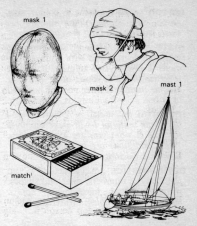

mask 1

mask 2

mast 1

match¹

hold the sails, flag, etc. **2** very tall, steel post to send out radio or television signals.

master¹ /'mɑːstə(r)/ n. **1** chief man; head of the family. **2** male teacher: *Mr. Davies is our maths master.* **3** male owner of a horse, dog, etc. **4** expert; someone who is the best in his sort of work: *Rembrandt was a master of painting.* **5** title for a boy: *Master John Smith is seven years old.*

master² v. learn how to do something: *You will soon master French when you live in Paris.*

masterpiece /'mɑːstəpiːs/ n. very good piece of work; fine piece of writing, music, painting, etc.

mat /mæt/ n. small piece of covering for the floor: *Wipe your feet on the door mat before you go in.*

match¹ /mætʃ/ n. (*pl.* matches) special small stick that makes fire when you rub it on a rough place: *He struck a match to light his cigarette.*

match² n. (*pl.* matches) **1** game between two people or teams: *a boxing match; a football match.* **2** someone who is as strong, clever, etc. as another. **meet your match**, find someone who is as good as, or better than, you in a sport, etc.: *Roy was the best tennis player until he met his match in Barry.* **3** something that is the same shape, colour, size, etc. **be a good match**, be nearly the same colour, etc. as each other: *Ruth's skirt and blouse are a good match.*

match[3] v. be the same in colour, size, shape, etc.: *Ruth's blouse matches her skirt.* **matching** adj.: *matching gloves.*

mate /meɪt/ n. **1** friend; someone who works or learns, etc. with you: *a classmate.* **2** one of two animals that come together to make young ones: *The tiger and his mate had three cubs.* **3** husband or wife.

material /mə'tɪərɪəl/ n. **1** cloth: *If you buy some material I will make the dress for you.* **2** what you are working with: *Wood and stone are building materials. Soap is a cleaning material.*

mathematics /ˌmæθə'mætɪks/ n. (no pl.) study of numbers, sizes, and shapes. **mathematical** /ˌmæθə'mætɪkl/ adj.: *a mathematical problem.* **maths** /mæθs/ abbrev. mathematics.

matinée /'mætɪneɪ/ n. afternoon show at a cinema or theatre.

matron /'meɪtrən/ n. **1** female housekeeper in a school or college. **2** chief nurse in a hospital.

matter[1] /'mætə(r)/ n. **1** (no pl.) what everything is made of. **2** (pl. matters) affair; something to talk about or do: *There is a business matter I must talk to you about.* **as a matter of fact**, words that you say when you are going to tell someone a new, true, and interesting thing: *I'm going home early—as a matter of fact it's my birthday.* **what's the matter?** what is wrong? **3** (no pl.) being important. **no matter**, it's not important. **no matter how**, in any way. **no matter who**, whoever it is: *Don't open the door—no matter who knocks.* **no matter what**, whatever happens. **no matter why**, whatever the reason.

matter[2] v. be important: *It doesn't matter that you came late.*

mattress /'mætrɪs/ n. (pl. mattresses) long, flat bag, full of feathers or soft rubber, which you put on a bed so that you can lie comfortably.

mature /mə'tʃʊə(r)/ adj. fully grown; no longer a child: *a mature man.* **maturely** adv. **mature** v. grow or develop fully; become ready to use, eat, etc.

mauve /məʊv/ adj. with a pale purple colour. **mauve** n.

maximum /'mæksɪməm/ n. most; biggest possible size, amount, number, etc.: *The plane will carry a maximum of 150 people.* **maximum** adj.: *What is the maximum speed of this car?*

May[1] /meɪ/ n. fifth month of the year.

may[2] v. **1** word that shows what will perhaps happen: *It may rain today.* **2** be allowed to do something: *You may have another cake.* **3** I hope that this will happen: *May you have a safe journey.*

maybe /'meɪbi/ adv. perhaps; possibly.

mayor /meə(r)/ n. chief person of a city or town. **mayoress** /ˌmeə'res/ n. female mayor; wife of a mayor.

me /mi:/ pron. (pl. us) word for myself: *I was thirsty so Susan gave me a drink.*

meadow /'medəʊ/ n. field of grass for cows, etc. to eat.

meal /mi:l/ n. food that you eat at a certain time.

mean[1] /mi:n/ adj. **1** wanting to keep everything for yourself: *She is mean and never invites people to meals.* **2** unkind; unfriendly: *It was mean of you to tease the little boy.* **meanness** n.

mean[2] v. (past part. & past tense meant /ment/) **1** say something in different words: *'Tag' in German means 'day' in English.* **mean something to someone**, be important to someone: *My friends mean a lot to me.* **2** want or plan to do something: *I didn't mean to hurt you.* **3** make something likely: *This snow means no sport this afternoon.*

meaning /'mi:nɪŋ/ n. what a word or person is saying: *This dictionary gives the meanings of many words.* **what is the meaning of this?** why have you done this?: *'What is the meaning of this?' asked Trish, when she saw the water on the carpet.*

means /mi:nz/ n. (no pl.) **1** way; how you can do something; how you can go somewhere: *Mrs. Taylor can't go to church because she has no means of transport.* **by means of**, with the help of something: *The thief got into the house by means of a ladder.* **by all means**, certainly. **by no means**, not at all; certainly not. **2** money. **a man of means**, a rich man.

meant /ment/ past part. & past tense of v. mean.

meantime /'mi:ntaɪm/ n. (no pl.) **in the meantime**, meanwhile: *Please find a taxi, and in the meantime I'll pack some food.* **meantime** adv.: *I'll pack the food meantime.*

meanwhile /ˌmi:n'waɪl/ adv. in the time between two happenings; in the time that something else is happening: *Jane was painting the walls and meanwhile Pat was watching T.V.*

measles /'mi:zlz/ n. (no pl.) illness with small, red spots on the skin.

measure[1] /'meʒə(r)/ n. **1** way of saying the size, amount, etc. of something: *A metre is a measure of length.* **2** something that helps you to find out how long, heavy, etc. something is: *Don't guess how tall she is—fetch a tape-measure.*

measure[2] v. **1** find the size, amount, etc. of something or someone: *The tailor measured Harry for a new jacket.* **2** be a certain length, etc.: *This room measures 5 metres across.*

measurement /'meʒəmənt/ n. how long, wide, high, etc. something is: *I will make the dress for you if you give me your measurements.*

meat /mi:t/ n. (no pl.) flesh of animals: *Pork is meat from a pig.*

mechanic /mɪ'kænɪk/ n. someone whose job is to make or work with machines.

mechanical /mɪ'kænɪkl/ adj. of or with a machine: *a mechanical pump.* **mechanically** adv.

mechanics /mɪ'kænɪks/ n. (no pl.) the study of how machines work.

medal /'medl/ n. piece of metal, like a coin, that you give to someone to show that he has done something special: *In the Olympic Games the winner will get a gold medal.*

meddle /'medl/ v. take part in someone's affairs when he has not asked you to or does not want you to: *Who has been meddling with my books?*

medical /'medɪkl/ adj. of medicine, hospitals, or doctors: *a medical student.*

medicine /'medsn/ n. **1** (no pl.) study of health and illness: *Sandra studied medicine for five years before she became a doctor.* **2** (pl. medicines) tablets, pills, special drinks, etc. that help you get

meat

medal

mattress

melon

better when you are ill: *Penicillin is a medicine.*

medium /'mi:dɪəm/ adj. middle; not big and not small: *a man of medium height.* **medium** n.

meet /mi:t/ v. (past part. & past tense met /met/) **1** come to someone: *I met Mr. Butler in the library.* **2** come together at a place: *Shall we all meet at my house?* **3** join at a place: *The river Humber meets the sea at Grimsby.* **4** get to know someone: *I don't think we have met before—what's your name?* **meet with**, have or find something: *We met with a storm on our way here.*

meeting /'mi:tɪŋ/ n. **1** many people who come together at a planned time and place: *There will be a committee meeting at the club this evening.* **2** any coming together: *an unexpected meeting at the bus-stop.*

megaphone /'megəfəʊn/ n. special horn that makes the voice louder so that one man can speak to a big crowd, etc.

melody /'melədɪ/ n. (pl. melodies) sweet piece of music; tune.

melon /'melən/ n. big, round, juicy fruit.

melt /melt/ v. become liquid in heat; make something liquid in heat: *The ice quickly melted in the sunshine.*

member /'membə(r)/ n. someone who is in a group: *Gordon is a member of the football team.* **membership** n. belonging to a group: *You must pay £10 a year for membership of the club.*

memorable /'memərəbl/ *adj.* so special that you will remember it for a long time: *a memorable day.*

memorandum /ˌmeməˈrændəm/ (*pl.* memoranda), **memo** /'meməʊ/ *n.* note that you write to help you remember something.

memorial /mɪˈmɔːrɪəl/ *n.* building or statue to remind people of someone or something: *The theatre at Stratford-on-Avon is a memorial to Shakespeare.*

memorize /'meməraɪz/ *v.* learn every word exactly: *An actor must memorize his part in a play.*

memory /'meməri/ *n.* **1** (*pl.* memories) power to remember things. **have a good memory**, be able to remember things well. **have a bad memory**, forget things easily. **2** (*pl.* memories) what you remember: *happy memories of a lovely holiday.*

men /men/ (*pl.*) of *n.* man.

menace /'menəs/ *n.* danger; someone or something that makes trouble: *Bad drivers are a menace.* **menace** *v.* say or show that you will hurt someone or bring trouble. **menacing** *adj.* full of danger; frightening; bringing trouble. **menacingly** *adv.*

mend /mend/ *v.* repair something; make something good again: *Can you mend this broken chair?*

mending /'mendɪŋ/ *n.* (no *pl.*) **1** sewing clothes to repair them. **2** clothes that you must mend; clothes that you are mending: *a basket full of mending.*

mental /'mentl/ *adj.* of the mind: *mental illness.* **mentally** *adv.*

mention /'menʃn/ *v.* speak or write a little about something: *When my father wrote, he mentioned that my young brother had a new bicycle.* **don't mention it**, words that you say when someone thanks you: *'You are so kind,' said Mrs. Grafton. 'Don't mention it,' said Mrs. Goddard.* **mention** *n.*: *I am surprised that there is no mention of the accident in the newspaper.*

menu /menjuː/ *n.* list of food dishes for a meal in a restaurant, hotel, etc.: *What sort of soup is on the menu today?*

merchant /'mɜːtʃənt/ *n.* trader; someone whose job is to buy and sell goods, especially from other countries: *The Horniman family were famous tea-merchants.*

mercy /'mɜːsɪ/ *n.* (no *pl.*) kindness; not punishing someone when you have the right or power to punish him: *The judge had mercy on the young criminal.* **be at the mercy of**, be in the power of someone or something: *Farmers are at the mercy of the weather.* **merciful** *adj.* with kindness. **mercifully** *adv.* **merciless** *adj.* cruel; with no kind feelings. **mercilessly** *adv.*

mere /mɪə(r)/ *adj.* not more than; only: *The new king was a mere child.*

merely /'mɪəlɪ/ *adv.* only: *I didn't stop to speak to him—I merely smiled.*

merit[1] /'merɪt/ *n.* what is good in someone or something: *Don't buy that painting because it hasn't much merit.*

merit[2] *v.* deserve something; be worthy of something: *This good work merits a prize.*

mermaid /'mɜːmeɪd/ *n.* girl in children's stories, who lives in the sea and has a fish's tail.

merry /'merɪ/ *adj.* happy; cheerful: *a merry laugh.* **merrily** *adv.* **merriment** *n.*

merry-go-round /'merɪ gəʊ raʊnd/ *n.* round machine where children can ride wooden horses, etc. at a fair.

mess[1] /mes/ *n.* (*pl.* messes) many things, all in the wrong place, untidy and dirty: *After the party there was a terrible mess in the room.* **in a mess**, (a) untidy: *The room was in a mess.* (b) in trouble: *Can you help me? I'm in a mess.*

mess[2] *v.* **mess about, mess around**, do something in a silly way; play when you should be working: *You'll never finish this job if you mess about.* **mess something up**, make something go wrong: *The pilots' strike messed up our holiday.*

message /'mesɪdʒ/ *n.* piece of information, order, or question, etc., that one person sends to another: *Please give Julia a message to say that we shall be late.* **messenger** /'mesɪndʒə(r)/ *n.* someone who carries a message from one person to another: *The hotel messenger told me that my friend was waiting in the bar.*

messy /'mesɪ/ *adj.* **1** dirty; untidy: *a messy kitchen.* **2** that makes you dirty: *Cleaning the car is a messy job.*

met /met/ *past part. & past tense* of *v.* meet.

metal /'metl/ *n.:* Tin, iron, silver, and gold are metals. **metal** *adj.* made of metal: *a metal ring.* **metallic** /mə'tælık/ *adj.* like metal: *the metallic sound of bells.*

meter /'mi:tə(r)/ *n.* machine that counts things: *A man comes to read the gas meter to find out how much gas you have used.*

method /'meθəd/ *n.* way of doing something: *What's the best method of cooking beef?*

metre /'mi:tə(r)/ *n.* measure of length = 100 centimetres. **metric** /'metrɪk/ *adj.* that you count in tens: *There are 1,000 grams in a kilogram, which is the metric way of saying how heavy something is.*

mice /maɪs/ *(pl.)* of *n.* mouse.

microphone /'maɪkrəfəʊn/ *n.* electrical instrument that makes sound louder or sends it a long way, as in a radio or a telephone.

microscope /'maɪkrəskəʊp/ *n.* instrument with special glass that makes very small things look much bigger: *Under a microscope a hair looks like a thick stick.*

mid- /mɪd/ *adj.* in the middle of: *mid-June.*

midday /ˌmɪd'deɪ/ *n.* 12 o'clock in the day.

middle /'mɪdl/ *n.* centre: *There is a stone in the middle of a peach.* **in the middle of**, busy doing something: *I can't help you because I am in the middle of cooking dinner.* **middle** *adj.:* There are three houses and ours is the middle house.

middle-aged /ˌmɪdl 'eɪdʒd/ *adj.* not old and not young: *a middle-aged man of 47.*

midnight /'mɪdnaɪt/ *n.* 12 o'clock at night.

midst /mɪdst/ *n.* middle part. **in the midst of**, in the middle of; in the centre of a group: *I couldn't see the pop star because he was in the midst of a crowd of fans.* **in our midst**, among us; with us.

mid-way /ˌmɪd'weɪ/ *adv.* half-way.

might¹ /maɪt/ *n.* (no *pl.*) great power; strength: *He had to work with all his might to move the big rock.* **mighty** *adj.* great; strong; powerful: *The Atlantic is a mighty ocean.*

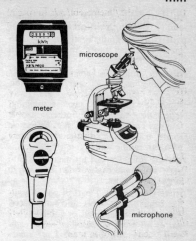

microscope

meter

microphone

might² **1** *past tense* of *v.* may: *I said he might borrow my car.* **2** very polite way of asking for something: *Might I come past, please?* **3** word that shows what will perhaps happen: *Don't run because you might fall.*

mike /maɪk/ *abbrev.* microphone.

mild /maɪld/ *adj.* **1** gentle; moving softly: *a mild breeze.* **2** not hot and not cold: *Spring brings mild weather after the cold winter.*

mile /maɪl/ *n.* measure of length = 1·6 kilometre.

military /'mɪlɪtrɪ/ *adj.* of soldiers: *a military camp.*

milk¹ /mɪlk/ *n.* (no *pl.*) white liquid that a mother makes in her body to give to a baby. People drink the milk that cows make; *Have a glass of milk with your lunch.* **milk** *adj.* made from milk: *milk chocolate.* **milky** *adj.* with a lot of milk in it: *milky coffee.*

milk² *v.* take milk from an animal: *When does the farmer milk the cows?*

milkman /'mɪlkmən/ *n.* (*pl.* milkmen) man whose job is to take milk to people's homes.

mill /mɪl/ *n.* **1** building where a machine makes corn into flour. **2** building or factory where people make things: *a cotton-mill; a steel-mill.* **miller** *n.* someone who makes grain into flour.

million /'mɪlɪən/ *n.* one thousand thousand (1,000,000). **million** *adj.*

millionaire /ˌmɪlɪə'neə(r)/ *n.* very rich man who has more than a million pounds, dollars, etc.

mimic /'mɪmɪk/ *v.* (*pres. part.* mimicking, *past part.* & *past tense* mimicked /'mɪmɪkt/) copy the way someone does or says something, especially to make other people laugh: *Tom mimicked his fat uncle riding a bicycle.* **mimic** *n.* someone who can mimic well.

mince /mɪns/ *v.* cut up meat, etc. into very small pieces. **mince** *n.* meat in very small pieces.

mind[1] /maɪnd/ *n.* **1** part of you in your head that thinks, feels, and remembers. *out of your mind*, mad or foolish: *He's out of his mind to smoke so many cigarettes.* *take someone's mind off something*, make someone stop thinking about something: *The music took her mind off her problem.* **2** opinion; ideas; what you think. *change your mind*, have an idea and then decide to do something different: *I planned a holiday in May but then I changed my mind and went in June.* *give someone a piece of your mind*, tell someone angrily what you think about him. *make up your mind*, decide: *Ken's made up his mind to become a doctor.*

mind[2] *v.* **1** take care of someone or something; look after someone: *I must mind the baby while Mum goes to the shops.* *mind! mind out!* be careful!: *Mind out! There's a car coming.* **2** have a feeling against something: *I don't mind cigarette smoke.* *do you mind, would you mind*, please would you: *It's cold—do you mind closing the window?*

mine[1] /maɪn/ *n.* big hole in the ground that people make when they are looking for coal, metal, diamonds, etc. **mine** *v.* dig for coal, gold, etc. in the ground. **miner** *n.* someone who works in a mine.

mine[2] *n.* sort of bomb that you hide under the ground or sea. **mine** *v.* put bombs and mines in a place; blow up something with a mine: *The ship was mined, and sank in five minutes.*

mine[3] *pron.* (*pl.* ours) thing that belongs to me: *You do your work and I do mine.*

mineral /'mɪnərəl/ *n.* coal, tin, ore, gold, etc. that comes from under the ground. **mineral water** *n.* special sort of water with minerals in it.

mingle /'mɪŋgl/ *v.* mix; go among: *The president mingled with the crowds at the football match.*

mini- /'mɪnɪ/ *prefix* very small or very short: *The club bought a minibus which can carry 14 people.*

miniature /'mɪnɪtʃə(r)/ *adj.* very small: *The doll's house had miniature tables and chairs.*

minimum /'mɪnɪməm/ *n.* least; smallest possible size, amount, number, etc. **minimum** *adj.*

minister /'mɪnɪstə(r)/ *n.* **1** one of the chief people in a government: *the Minister of Education.* **2** Christian priest.

ministry /'mɪnɪstrɪ/ *n.* (*pl.* ministries) government department: *He works in the Ministry of Health.*

minor /'maɪnə(r)/ *adj.* smaller; not very important: *a minor road; a minor accident.*

minority /ˌmaɪ'nɒrɪtɪ/ *n.* (no *pl.*) small part of a group.

mint /mɪnt/ *n.* (no *pl.*) small plant with leaves that you put in cooking and drink. **mint** *adj.*: *mint tea.*

minus /'maɪnəs/ *prep.* less; when you take away: *Nine minus four is five* (9 − 4 = 5).

minute[1] /maɪ'njuːt/ *adj.* very small: *minute grains of sand.*

minute[2] /'mɪnɪt/ *n.* part of an hour: *There are sixty minutes in one hour. It's three minutes past six.* *in a minute*, soon: *I'll be ready in a minute.* *just a minute!* wait!: *Just a minute—there's someone at the door.* *the minute*, at the exact time that: *I'll tell Robert the news the minute he comes home.*

miracle /'mɪrəkl/ *n.* wonderful and surprising happening: *It was a miracle that she did not die when she fell from the window.* **miraculous** /mɪ'rækjʊləs/ *adj.*: *a miraculous escape from the burning aeroplane.* **miraculously** *adv.*

mirror /'mɪrə(r)/ *n.* piece of glass where you can see yourself: *Margaret combed her hair in front of the mirror.*

mis- /mɪs/ *prefix* bad; badly; wrong; wrongly: *misunderstood.*

misbehave /ˌmɪsbɪˈheɪv/ *v.* be naughty; behave badly: *The referee sent the player off the field because he misbehaved.*

mischief /ˈmɪstʃɪf/ *n.* (no *pl.*) trouble. *be up to mischief, get into mischief,* do silly or bad things that make trouble: *I hope that the children are not up to mischief.* **mischievous** /ˈmɪstʃɪvəs/ *adj.*: *a mischievous child.* **mischievously** *adv.*

miser /ˈmaɪzə(r)/ *n.* someone who keeps a lot of money and never spends it. **miserly** *adj.*

miserable /ˈmɪzrəbl/ *adj.* **1** very sad; feeling very sorry for yourself: *He was miserable when he failed his driving test.* **2** making people unhappy: *It's raining again—what miserable weather!* **miserably** *adv.*: *The little boy was crying miserably.*

misery /ˈmɪzəri/ *n.* (no *pl.*) being very unhappy, poor, ill, lonely, etc.

misfortune /ˌmɪsˈfɔːtʃuːn/ *n.* something bad that happens; bad luck: *What a misfortune that you were ill on the day of the party.*

mislay /ˌmɪsˈleɪ/ *v.* (*past part. & past tense* mislaid /ˌmɪsˈleɪd/) forget where you have put something: *I often mislay my umbrella.*

Miss[1] /mɪs/ *n.* (*pl.* Misses) title for a girl or an unmarried woman: *Mrs. Baker and her daughter, Miss Baker.*

miss[2] *v.* **1** feel sad when someone has gone away: *We shall miss Rachel when she goes to live in Canada.* **2** learn that something is lost or is not there: *When did you miss your shopping bag?* **3** not hit, hold, catch, or see what you want: *I threw the ball to Colin but he missed it and it broke the window. Their house is at the end of the road—you can't miss it.* ***miss something out,*** not put something in: *The letter did not arrive because she missed out part of the address.* **missing** *adj.* that you cannot find: *The police are looking for the missing child.*

missile /ˈmɪsaɪl/ *n.* something that you throw or fire from a gun to hurt someone: *The missile that killed Goliath was a stone.*

mission /ˈmɪʃn/ *n.* journey to do a special job.

mitten

mirror

mistletoe   miner

missionary /ˈmɪʃənri/ *n.* (*pl.* missionaries) someone who goes to a foreign country to tell people about his religion. **missionary** *adj.*

mist /mɪst/ *n.* sort of thin cloud near the ground: *We had to drive slowly because of the mist.* **misty** *adj.*: *a misty morning.*

mistake[1] /mɪˈsteɪk/ *n.* something that you do or say wrongly: *If you say that 2 + 2 = 5 you are making a mistake.* ***by mistake,*** done wrongly but not planned: *I took your book by mistake.*

mistake[2] *v.* ***be mistaken,*** have the wrong idea: *I said she was 20 but I was mistaken because she is only 18.*

mistletoe /ˈmɪsltəʊ/ *n.* (no *pl.*) plant with white berries that British people put in the house at Christmas.

mistress /ˈmɪstrɪs/ *n.* (*pl.* mistresses) female teacher: *Mrs. Williams is our history mistress.*

misunderstand /ˌmɪsʌndəˈstænd/ *v.* (*past part. & past tense* misunderstood /ˌmɪsʌndəˈstʊd/) not understand something correctly. **misunderstanding** *n.* **1** thinking wrongly. **2** angry talk between people that comes because one has understood the other wrongly.

mitten /ˈmɪtn/ *n.* cover of leather, wool, etc. for the hand.

mix /mɪks/ *v.* **1** put different things together; bring different people together: *You mix flour, yeast, and water* *to make bread.* **2** stay together: *Oil doesn't mix with water.* **3** spend time together: *Do the boys mix with the girls in your class?* **mix one thing up with another thing,** (*a*) put things together so that you do not know which is which: *You have mixed up all our pencils and I can't find mine.* (*b*) think one thing or person is another; not know which of two things or people it is: *I always mix Susan up with Yvonne because they are both blonde.*

mixed /mɪkst/ *adj.* of many different kinds: *mixed sweets.*

mixer /'mɪksə(r)/ *n.* machine that mixes things: *a food mixer.*

mixture /'mɪkstʃə(r)/ *n.* group or mass of different things: *a cake mixture.*

moan /məʊn/ *v.* **1** make a long, sad sound to show that you are hurt, unhappy, etc.: *After the car hit him, the boy lay on the ground and moaned.* **2** say how sad, unlucky, etc. you are; talk about your troubles; ask for pity: *He is always moaning about his bad luck.* **moan** *n.*: *a loud moan.*

moat /məʊt/ *n.* deep ditch round a castle, etc., filled with water, to keep enemies away.

mob /mɒb/ *n.* big, noisy crowd of people, who have come together to shout, fight, etc.: *The police arrived to control the football mob.*

mobile /'məʊbaɪl/ *adj.* that can move easily from place to place: *A mobile clinic visits this village every week.*

mock /mɒk/ *v.* laugh at someone in an unkind way: *The other boys mocked the fat pupil in the sports lesson.* **mocking** *adj.*: *a mocking laugh.*

model[1] /'mɒdl/ *adj.* copied in a small size: *a model aeroplane.*

model[2] *n.* **1** small copy of something: *On the table we have a model of the Eiffel Tower.* **2** first example from which you make other copies: *Have you seen the latest Volkswagen model?* **3** someone who sits or stands so that an artist can paint a picture of him, etc. **4** someone whose job is to wear clothes at a special show so that people will see them and buy them.

model[3] *v.* (*pres. part.* modelling, *past. part.* & *past tense* modelled /'mɒdld/) **1**

copy something; make a shape of something out of clay, etc.: *The sculptor modelled a horse.* **2** get money by putting on and showing new clothes, etc., for sale: *Kate models dresses for a shop in Paris.*

moderate /'mɒdərət/ *adj.* in the middle; not too big and not too small; not too much and not too little: *moderate heat.* **moderately** *adv.*

modern /'mɒdn/ *adj.* of the present time; of the sort that is usual now: *modern furniture.*

modest /'mɒdɪst/ *adj.* **1** not thinking too well of yourself: *You are modest— you didn't tell me you could swim so well.* **2** not very big or very grand: *He is a rich man, but he lives in a modest little house.* **modestly** *adv.* **modesty** *n.*

moist /mɔɪst/ *adj.* a little wet: *A healthy dog has a moist nose.*

moisture /'mɔɪstʃə(r)/ *n.* (no *pl.*) a little wetness; tiny drops of water in the air or on something.

mole /məʊl/ *n.* small animal that lives under the ground and makes tunnels. **mole-hill** *n.* little pile of earth that a mole has made.

moment /'məʊmənt/ *n.* very short time. **the moment,** at the exact time that; as soon as: *The moment I saw Andrew's smile, I knew he'd won the prize.* **at the moment,** now: *At the moment she's on holiday, but she'll be back tomorrow.* **in a moment,** very soon: *I'll be with you in a moment.*

monarch /'mɒnək/ *n.* king, queen, emperor, or empress. **monarchy** *n.* country that has a king, emperor, etc., at the top.

monastery /'mɒnəstrɪ/ *n.* (*pl.* monasteries) place where a group of men live to serve the Christian God.

Monday /'mʌndeɪ/ *n.* second day of the week.

money /'mʌnɪ/ *n.* (no *pl.*) metal coins and paper banknotes. **make money,** get or earn money. **money-box** *n.* box with a hole in the top where you put money when you want to keep it for a time.

monk /mʌŋk/ *n.* man who lives with a group of other men to serve the Christian God.

monkey /'mʌŋkɪ/ n. sort of animal that is most like man: *A chimpanzee is a sort of monkey.*

monotonous /mə'nɒtənəs/ adj. dull because it does not change; not interesting: *It is monotonous to do the same work each day.*

monster /'mɒnstə(r)/ n. **1** very big person or animal, with a strange shape. **2** very bad, cruel person or animal. **monster** adj. very big: *a monster potato.*

monstrous /'mɒnstrəs/ adj. very cruel, terrible, ugly, etc. **monstrously** adv.

month /mʌnθ/ n. one of the twelve parts of a year: *December is the last month of the year.*

monthly /'mʌnθlɪ/ adj. done or happening every month: *Our club has a monthly meeting.* **monthly** adv.

monument /'mɒnjʊmənt/ n. building, statue, or stone to remind people of someone or something: *There is a tall monument in London at the place where the Great Fire of London started.*

mood /muːd/ n. how you feel: *Is the boss in a good mood today?* **be in the mood for**, want something: *I'm in the mood for music.*

moon /muːn/ n. **the moon**, the big, round thing that shines in the sky at night. **full moon**, time when you can see all the moon. **new moon**, time when you can only see the first thin part of the moon. **moonbeam** /'muːnbiːm/ n. line of light from the moon. **moonlight** /'muːnlaɪt/ n. light from the moon. **moonlit** /'muːnlɪt/ adj. full of moonlight: *the moonlit countryside.*

moor¹ /mʊə(r)/, **moorland** /'mʊələnd/ n. open, rough land on hills where only sheep can feed.

moor² v. tie up a boat, ship, etc., to a post, stone, etc., to keep it in one place: *Have you moored the dinghy safely?*

moorings /'mʊərɪŋz/ n. (pl.) place where you tie up a boat or ship.

mop¹ /mɒp/ n. sort of soft brush for washing floors, etc.

mop² v. (*pres. part.* mopping, *past part.* & *past tense* mopped /mɒpt/) clean or wipe something. **mop up**, take up a lot of liquid, water, etc. with a cloth: *I mopped up the milk that I'd spilled.*

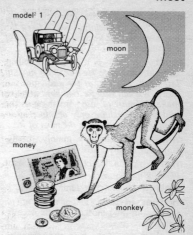

model² 1

moon

money

monkey

moped /'məʊped/ n. vehicle like a bicycle with a small engine.

more¹ /mɔː(r)/ adj. bigger in number, amount, size, etc.: *I'm still hungry—can I have some more pudding?*

more² adv. **1** word that makes an adjective or adverb stronger: *Robert is careful but Henry is more careful. Denise speaks quietly but you speak more quietly. He is more intelligent than his brother.* **2** in a greater way: *I like bananas more than apples.* **once more**, again: *Play that music once more.* **any more**, any longer: *He works in a garage; he doesn't go to school any more.*

more³ n. (no *pl.*) larger number, amount, etc.: *That's not enough—give me more.*

morning /'mɔːnɪŋ/ n. early part of the day; time between sunrise and midday: *I start work at nine in the morning.* **morning** adj.: *morning newspapers.*

mosque /mɒsk/ n. building where Muslims go to worship.

mosquito /mə'skiːtəʊ/ n. (*pl.* mosquitoes) flying insect that bites people and drinks blood.

moss /mɒs/ n. (*pl.* mosses) soft, green plant that grows like a carpet on walls, trees, etc. **mossy** adj. covered with moss.

most¹ /məʊst/ adj. biggest in number, amount, etc.: *Most children like ice-cream but a few don't.*

most² *adv.* **1** more than all others: *That's the most helpful book. I liked the last song most.* **2** very: *It is most kind of you to help me.*

most³ *n.* (no *pl.*) biggest number, amount, part, etc.: *He was ill for most of last week.* **at most, at the most,** but not more: *We can stay for two days at most.* **make the most of,** use something in the best way: *We have only one free afternoon, so we must make the most of it.*

mostly /'məʊstlɪ/ *adv.* mainly; chiefly: *Cows eat mostly grass.*

moth /mɒθ/ *n.* insect that flies at night near lights.

mother /'mʌðə(r)/ *n.* female parent.

mother-in-law /'mʌðər ɪn lɔ:/ *n.* (*pl.* mothers-in-law) mother of wife or husband.

motion /'məʊʃn/ *n.* (no *pl.*) **in motion,** moving: *Don't put your head out of the window while the train is in motion.*

motive /'məʊtɪv/ *n.* reason why you do or say something: *What was the murderer's motive?*

motor /'məʊtə(r)/ *n.* **1** machine or engine that makes something move. **2** motor-car.

motor-bike /'məʊtə baɪk/, **motor-cycle** /'məʊtə saɪkl/ *n.* vehicle like a heavy bicycle with a strong engine. **motor-cyclist** *n.* someone who rides a motor-cycle.

motor-boat /'məʊtə bəʊt/ *n.* small boat with an engine.

motor-car /'məʊtə kɑ:(r)/ *n.* vehicle with four wheels for a small group of people.

motorist /'məʊtərɪst/ *n.* someone who drives a car, etc.

motorway /'məʊtəweɪ/ *n.* wide, modern road where cars and lorries can travel a long way fast: *The M4 is the motorway from London to the West.*

mould¹ /məʊld/ *n.* what grows on food when you leave it too long in the cupboard. **mouldy** *adj.*: *mouldy cheese.*

mould² *v.* give something a shape; make a shape out of something soft: *The children moulded animals out of clay.* **mould** *n.* shape for making things: *They poured the hot metal into the mould.*

mound /maʊnd/ *n.* small hill; pile of earth, etc.

mount¹ /maʊnt/ *n.* mountain; very high hill: *Mount Everest.*

mount² *v.* **1** go up something: *to mount a ladder.* **2** get on to a horse, bicycle, etc.: *Dave mounted his horse and rode away.*

mountain /'maʊntɪn/ *n.* very high hill: *Everest is the highest mountain in the world.* **mountainous** *adj.* **1** with many mountains: *mountainous country.* **2** very big: *mountainous waves.*

mountaineer /ˌmaʊntɪ'nɪə(r)/ *n.* someone who likes to climb mountains. **mountaineering** *n.* sport of climbing mountains.

mourn /mɔ:n/ *v.* feel or show that you are sad because someone is dead, something is lost, etc.: *He mourned his dead dog.* **mourner** *n.* family member or friend who is sad about someone's death.

mourning /'mɔ:nɪŋ/ *n.* (no *pl.*) **1** great sadness because someone has died. **2** black clothes, etc. that you wear to show that you are sad when someone has died: *The family was dressed in mourning for the funeral.*

mouse /maʊs/ *n.* (*pl.* mice) small animal with a long tail, which lives in a hole: *The cat was chasing a mouse.*

moustache /mə'stɑ:ʃ/ *n.* hair on a man's top lip, below his nose.

mouth /maʊθ/ *n.* **1** part of the face that holds the teeth, tongue, etc. **2** end of a river, where it comes to the sea: *the mouth of the Thames.*

mouthful /'maʊθfʊl/ *n.* as much as you can put into your mouth at one time.

mouth-organ /'maʊθ ɔ:gən/ *n.* small musical instrument that you blow.

move¹ /mu:v/ *n.* **1** going from one place to another; change of position: *If you make a move, you will frighten the bird away.* **get a move on,** hurry: *Get a move on, or you'll be late for work!* **2** changing from one house to another: *We must hire a big van for the move.*

move² *v.* **1** go from one place to another: *This is my seat—will you move, please?* **2** put something in another place: *It's cold—move your chair nearer to the fire.* **3** change the position of part of your body: *Please move your head so*

that I can see the screen. **4** change your house: *We're going to move next week.* ***move in***, go into a house, etc., to live there. ***move out***, leave a room, house, etc., where you have been living.
moving /'mu:vɪŋ/ *adj.* not still; that is going: *Don't get off a moving bus.*

movement /'mu:vmənt/ *n.* moving or being moved: *I stopped because I saw a movement in the grass.*

movie /'mu:vɪ/ *n.* film that you see at a cinema.

mow /məʊ/ *v.* (*past part.* mown /məʊn/, *past tense* mowed /məʊd/) cut grass short: *Larry is mowing the lawn.*
mower *n.* machine that cuts grass.

Mr. /'mɪstə(r)/ *abbrev.* Mister; title for a man: *Mr. John Williams.*

Mrs. /'mɪsɪz/ *abbrev.* Mistress; title for a married woman: *Mrs. Dorothy Williams.*

Ms. /mɪz/ title for any woman, instead of 'Miss' or 'Mrs.'

Mt. /maʊnt/ *abbrev.* mount; word before the name of a mountain: *Mt. Kilimanjaro.*

much¹ /mʌtʃ/ *adj.* large in number, size, amount, etc.; a lot of: *There was so much food that we couldn't eat it all.* ***how much***, what amount of: *How much paper do you want?*

much² *adv.* a lot: *After a good sleep I felt much better.*

much³ *n.* (no *pl.*) a lot; plenty. ***this much, that much***, words that you say when you show how much with your hands: *I'd like this much, please.* ***be too much for***, be too difficult, too clever, etc. for someone: *This cold wind is too much for me.* ***as much***, the same amount: *Give me as much as you gave Jane.* ***how much***, (*a*) what amount: *How much do you read?* (*b*) what price; what cost: *How much is that picture?*

mud /mʌd/ *n.* (no *pl.*) soft, wet earth: *After the football match Philip was covered with mud.*

muddle /'mʌdl/ *v.* **1** put everything in the wrong place so that it is difficult to find what you want: *The cat knocked the table over and muddled all my papers.* **2** mix your ideas so that you cannot understand: *The lesson was not clear and it has muddled me.* **muddle** *n.*

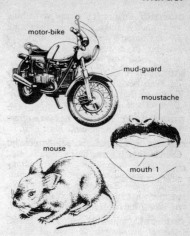

motor-bike

mud-guard

moustache

mouse

mouth 1

muddy /'mʌdɪ/ *adj.* covered with earth and dirt: *muddy shoes.*

mud-guard /'mʌd gɑ:d/ *n.* cover over the top of a bicycle wheel, which keeps mud, etc. off the rider.

mug¹ /mʌg/ *n.* big cup or glass with a handle: *a mug of cocoa.*

mug² *v.* (*pres. part* mugging, *past part.* & *past tense* mugged /mʌgd/) hit or attack someone and take his money.

mule /mju:l/ *n.* animal that is part horse and part donkey.

multi- /'mʌltɪ/ *prefix* with many.
multi-coloured *adj.* with many colours. **multi-storey** *adj.* with many floors: *The new multi-storey car-park holds 200 cars.*

multiply /'mʌltɪplaɪ/ *v.* make something bigger by a certain number of times: *2 multiplied by 3 is 6; 2 × 3 = 6.* **multiplication** /ˌmʌltɪplɪˈkeɪʃn/ *n.*

mum /mʌm/, **mummy** /'mʌmɪ/ (*pl.* mummies) *n.* mother.

mumble /'mʌmbl/ *v.* say something in a voice that is not loud and clear: *I couldn't hear what she said because she was mumbling.*

mumps /mʌmps/ *n.* (no *pl.*) illness that makes the neck fat.

murder /'mɜ:də(r)/ *v.* kill someone on purpose: *Macbeth murdered the king with a knife.* **murder** *n.* **murderer** *n.* man who has murdered someone. **murderess** *n.* woman who has murdered someone.

murmur /'mɜ:mə(r)/ *v.* say something very quietly; make a low, gentle sound: *He murmured a prayer.* **murmur** *n.: the murmur of a stream; the murmer of voices in the next room.*

museum /mju:'zɪəm/ *n.* building where we keep beautiful, old, and interesting things so that people can see them: *the Victoria and Albert Museum.*

mushroom /'mʌʃrʊm/ *n.* plant with no leaves, which we can eat.

music /'mju:zɪk/ *n.* (no *pl.*) **1** pleasant sounds that pianos, harps, drums, etc., or singing voices, etc. make; making these sounds: *Let's listen to some music on the radio.* **2** signs on paper to show people what to sing or play: *I can't play because I have lost my music.*

musical /'mju:zɪkl/ *adj.* **1** of music: *musical instruments.* **2** fond of music; clever at making music, singing, etc.: *a musical child.* **musical** *n.* musical play.

musician /mju:'zɪʃn/ *n.* someone who writes music or plays a musical instrument.

Muslim /'mʊzlɪm/ *n.* someone who believes in Muhammad and what he taught.

must /mʌst/ *v.* word to tell someone what to do; word that tells what is necessary: *You must have a passport before you go abroad.* **must be**, certainly is; probably is: *You must be tired after your long journey.* **must have done something**, words that show what probably happened: *If you were at the party you must have seen Colin.*

mustard /'mʌstəd/ *n.* (no *pl.*) very thick, yellow sauce, with a strong taste, which you make from powder and eat on meat.

mustn't /'mʌsnt/ = must not.

mutiny /'mju:tɪnɪ/ *n.* (*pl.* mutinies) time when soldiers or sailors attack their own leaders and officers. **mutiny** *v.*

mutter /'mʌtə(r)/ *v.* say words in a low voice so that other people will not hear. **mutter** *n.*

mutton /'mʌtn/ *n.* (no *pl.*) meat from a sheep.

my /maɪ/ *adj.* of me: *I brushed my teeth.*

myself /maɪ'self/ *pron.* (*pl.* ourselves) **1** word that you say when you talk about yourself: *I hurt myself.* **2** I and no other person: *I can do it myself.* **by myself**, alone: *I live by myself.*

mysterious /mɪ'stɪərɪəs/ *adj.* strange; that you do not know about or understand: *There were mysterious lights at night in the empty house.* **mysteriously** *adv.: She smiled mysteriously when I asked her about my birthday present.*

mystery /'mɪstərɪ/ *n.* (*pl.* mysteries) strange happening or person that you cannot understand or explain: *Have you heard about the mystery of the ship that disappeared?*

Nn

n. *abbrev.* for noun in this dictionary.

nail[1] /neɪl/ *n.* **1** hard part at the end of the finger or toe: *Norah paints her finger-nails red.* **2** small piece of metal with one pointed end, which you hit into wood to fasten things together.

nail[2] *v.* fasten or fix something with a nail: *David nailed the broken box together again.*

naked /'neɪkɪd/ *adj.* with no clothes: *We were naked when we went swimming.*

name /neɪm/ *n.* **1** word or words that we give to a person or animal when they are born: *His name is Colin Brown.* **call someone names**, say bad, unkind words about someone. **2** being famous. **make a name for yourself**, become well-known: *Henry Ford made a name for himself building cars.* **name** *v.* **1** give a name to someone or something: *They have named their new baby Sophie.* **2** know and say the name or names of someone or something: *Can you name all the flowers in your garden?*

namely /'neɪmlɪ/ *adv.* that is to say: *Only one boy, namely Nicholas, was late.*

nanny /'nænɪ/ *n.* (*pl.* nannies) woman whose job is to look after the small children of a rich family.

nap /næp/ *n.* short sleep.

napkin /'næpkɪn/ *n.* small piece of cloth that each person has at the table to keep his clothes clean, and wipe his fingers on, etc.

nappy /'næpɪ/ n. (pl. nappies) special cloth that you put round a baby's bottom.

narrow /'nærəʊ/ adj. not wide; not far from one side to the other: *The road was so narrow that two cars could not pass.*

narrowly /'nærəʊlɪ/ adv. only just: *The bus narrowly missed me because I jumped to one side.*

nasty /'nɑːstɪ/ adj. not pleasant; bad: *Bad meat smells nasty; a nasty accident.* **nastily** adv. **nastiness** n.

nation /'neɪʃn/ n. big group of people who live in one country, under one government; country: *France is a European nation.*

national /'næʃənl/ adj. of a country: *The British national flag is red, white, and blue.* **national** n. someone who belongs to a certain country: *His passport shows that he is a British national.*

nationality /ˌnæʃə'nælətɪ/ n. (pl. nationalities) belonging to a certain country: *What is your nationality?*

native[1] /'neɪtɪv/ adj. of the place where you were born: *John's native language is English and Karl's native language is German.*

native[2] n. person born in a place, country, etc.: *David Livingstone was a native of Scotland.*

natural /'nætʃrəl/ adj. **1** made by nature, not made or changed by people: *A river is a natural waterway but a canal is not.* **2** normal; usual: *It is natural to laugh when you are happy.*

naturally /'nætʃrəlɪ/ adv. **1** by nature: *Kittens are naturally playful.* **2** in an ordinary way, not trying too hard: *Just smile naturally while I take your photograph.* **3** of course: *Naturally I want to pass the exam!*

nature /'neɪtʃə(r)/ n. **1** (no pl.) the sun, the stars, the sky, etc., and everything in the world that was not made by people; the power that makes all things live, die, and change: *Nature makes most trees lose their leaves in winter.* **2** (pl. natures) how someone or something is: *It is a lion's nature to kill.* **3** (pl. natures) character; what sort of a person you are: *She has a sweet nature.* **good-natured** adj. kind; pleasant. **ill-natured** adj. unkind; unfriendly.

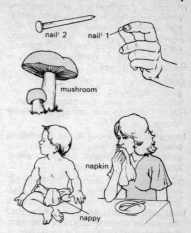

nail[1] 2   nail[1] 1

mushroom

napkin

nappy

naughty /'nɔːtɪ/ adj. behaving badly; making trouble: *naughty children.* **naughtily** adv. **naughtiness** n.

naval /'neɪvl/ adj. of a navy: *Admiral Nelson was a naval officer.*

navigate /'nævɪgeɪt/ v. **1** control the way that a ship or aeroplane must go. **2** sail in a ship. **navigator** /'nævɪgeɪtə(r)/ n.: *Columbus was a famous navigator.*

navy /'neɪvɪ/ n. (pl. navies) all the warships of a country, with officers and men: *The British navy beat the French navy at the Battle of Trafalgar.*

navy-blue /ˌneɪvɪ 'bluː/ adj. dark blue.

near[1] /nɪə(r)/ adj. **1** not far; close: *The station is near so we shall get there soon.* **2** close in family, feelings, etc.: *A brother is a near relation.*

near[2] adv. not far; close: *Do you live near?* **draw near**, come closer: *They became excited as the holidays drew near.*

near[3] prep. close to: *I don't need a car because I live near the city centre.*

near[4] v. come closer; go closer: *It's nearing the end of summer.*

nearby /'nɪəbaɪ/ adj. close: *the nearby village.* **nearby** /nɪə'baɪ/ adv.: *Let's visit Tim—he lives nearby.*

nearly /'nɪəlɪ/ adv. almost: *It's nearly lunchtime so we must go home.* **not nearly**, not at all: *Robin has £20 but that's not nearly enough to buy a new bicycle.*

neat /niːt/ adj. **1** tidy; in good order: neat clothes. **2** doing things carefully; liking to have things in good order: Carol is a neat writer and her letters are carefully written. **neatly** adv.: neatly dressed. **neatness** n.

necessary /'nesəsərɪ/ adj. that you need; important: Food and water are necessary to man. **necessarily** /'nesəserəlɪ/ adv.: Big men are not necessarily strong.

necessity /nɪ'sesətɪ/ n. (pl. necessities) something that you need; what you must have: Food and clothes are necessities of life.

neck /nek/ n. **1** part of the body between the shoulders and head: Elsie wears a gold chain round her neck. **neck and neck**, exactly equal in a race, etc.: The horses were running neck and neck. **2** thin part at the top of a bottle, etc.

necklace /'neklɪs/ n. string of beads, jewels, etc. that you wear round your neck.

need /niːd/ v. want something important and necessary that is not there; must have something: The leaves of this plant are yellow because it needs water. **need to**, must: Colin's very ill—he needs to go to hospital. **need** n. **in need of**, wanting something important: You are tired—you are in need of sleep.

needle /'niːdl/ n. **1** very small, thin piece of steel with a sharp point at one end, for sewing: I'll mend the hole in your blouse if you give me a needle and thread. **2** long, thin piece of wood, plastic, or metal with a pointed end, for knitting: knitting needles. **3** any small, sharp thing like a sewing needle: the needle on a record-player.

needless /'niːdlɪs/ adj. that is not useful, etc.: It is needless to sweep a clean floor. **needlessly** adv.

needn't /'niːdnt/ = need not.

negative /'negətɪv/ n. piece of film in which dark things are light and light things are dark, which we use to make photographs.

neglect /nɪ'glekt/ v. not take enough care of something; not do what you should do for someone: He neglects his dog and it is always dirty and hungry. **neglect** n. **neglected** /nɪ'glektɪd/ adj.: a dirty, neglected house.

negro /'niːɡrəʊ/ n. (pl. negroes) someone with a black skin: American negroes. **negress** /'niːɡrɪs/ n. negro woman or girl.

neigh /neɪ/ n. cry of a horse. **neigh** v.

neighbour /'neɪbə(r)/ n. someone who lives in the next house or near you; thing or country that is near another: Holland is one of Germany's neighbours. **neighbouring** adj. that is near: We went to a cinema in the neighbouring town.

neighbourhood /'neɪbəhʊd/ n. the streets or land around a place: There are not enough doctors in this neighbourhood.

neither[1] /'naɪðə(r)/ adj. not one and not the other of two people, things, etc.: Neither book was very interesting. **neither** pron.: Neither was very interesting.

neither[2] /'naɪðə(r)/ conj. (after a verb with 'not') then not: If you do not go, neither will I. **neither ... nor**, not ... and not: He neither wrote nor telephoned.

nephew /'nevjuː/ n. son of your brother or sister.

nerve /nɜːv/ n. **1** (pl. nerves) thing that carries feelings and messages through the body. **2 nerves** (pl.) feelings. **get on your nerves**, annoy, upset you, etc.: The noisy children got on my nerves. **3** (no pl.) being brave and bold. **lose your nerve**, become afraid.

nervous /'nɜːvəs/ adj. **1** of the nerves: the nervous system of the human body. **2** afraid; worried: Are you nervous when you are alone in the house? **nervously** adv. **nervousness** n.

nest /nest/ n. **1** home of a bird; place where a bird lays its eggs: Alan found a bird's nest in the tree. **2** place where some insects, snakes, etc. lay their eggs and keep their babies: an ants' nest. **nest** v. make and live in a nest: The ducks are nesting by the river.

net /net/ n. **1** (no pl.) cloth of threads that are knotted together with big holes between. **2** (pl. nets) thing made of this cloth, for a special job: a hairnet; a football net; a fishing net. **net** adj.: net curtains.

netball /'netbɔːl/ n. **1** (no pl.) game where players try to throw a big ball into a high net. **2** (pl. netballs) ball for this game.

netting /'netɪŋ/ n. (no pl.) string, rope, wire, etc. that is knotted to make a strong cover or fence with big holes: *We put wire netting round the garden to keep the dog in.*

nettle /'netl/ n. plant with leaves that hurt or sting you.

neuter /'njuːtə(r)/ adj. not masculine or feminine in grammar: *'It' is a neuter pronoun.*

never /'nevə(r)/ adv. not at any time: *Children in Nigeria never see snow.* **never mind**, don't worry about it: *It's too late to go to the film now—never mind, we'll go tomorrow.* **well I never!** I'm very surprised: *'Well I never!' said John's father when he won the prize.*

nevertheless /ˌnevəðə'les/ conj. but; however; still: *Freda knew that she would not win; nevertheless she went on trying.* **nevertheless** adv.

new /njuː/ adj. **1** that has just been made or bought; fresh: *I must buy a new pen because this one is broken.* **2** that you are seeing, hearing, etc. for the first time: *I've started learning a new language—Italian.* **3** starting again: *the new moon.* **new** adv.: *a new-born baby.* **new to**, at a place, or doing something, for the first time: *Will you help Janet—she is new to the school.*

new-comer /'njuː kʌmə(r)/ n. someone who has just come to a place: *On the first day of term the headmaster welcomed all the new-comers.*

newly /'njuːlɪ/ adj. **1** not long ago; just: *Mr. and Mrs. Owen are newly married.* **2** in a different way: *a newly painted room.*

news /njuːz/ n. (no pl.) report or programme that tells about things that have just happened: *We heard about the air crash on the news.* **break the news**, tell someone about something important that has happened: *When will you break the news to your family?*

newsagent /'njuːzeɪdʒənt/ n. shopkeeper who sells newspapers, magazines, etc.

newspaper /'njuːspeɪpə(r)/ n. sheets of printed paper with news and advertisements, which you can buy every day or every week: *The 'Guardian' and 'Daily Telegraph' are newspapers.*

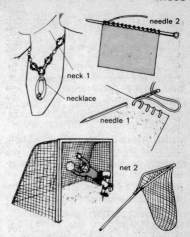

needle 2

neck 1

necklace

needle 1

net 2

next¹ /nekst/ adj. **1** nearest: *Our bus could not stop and bumped into the next bus.* **2** the first that comes after; following: *We missed the 5 o'clock train so we caught the next one.* **next to nothing**, very little: *When she was ill Helen ate next to nothing.*

next² adv. afterwards; then: *I've done this job—what shall I do next?* **next to**, at the side of; beside: *My best friend sits next to me in class.*

next³ n. (no pl.) **1** person or thing that is nearest: *This is the Carters' house and ours is the next.* **2** person or thing coming just after: *Amy was the first to arrive and Mary was the next.*

next door /ˌnekst 'dɔː(r)/ adv. in the nearest house: *Who lives next door?* **next-door** adj.: *the next-door garden.*

nib /nɪb/ n. pointed piece of metal at the end of a pen.

nibble /'nɪbl/ v. take very small bites of something: *The mouse nibbled the bread.* **nibble** n.

nice /naɪs/ adj. pleasant; good: *It's a nice day for a walk.* **nice and . . .**, nice because . . .: *Your bedroom is nice and tidy.* **nicely** adv.

nickname /'nɪkneɪm/ n. name that you give to someone instead of his real name: *They gave John the nickname 'Fatty' because he was so fat.*

niece /niːs/ n. daughter of your brother or sister.

night /naɪt/ n. **1** time when it is dark because there is no light from the sun: *We sleep at night.* **all night**, for the whole of the night. **night and day**, all the time: *Elsie studied night and day before the exams.* **2** evening: *We want to go to a film on Friday night.* **first night**, first time a play or film happens.

nightdress /'naɪtdres/ (*pl.* nightdresses), **nightie** /'naɪtɪ/ n. long, loose dress that a woman or girl wears in bed.

nightingale /'naɪtɪŋɡeɪl/ n. small bird that sings sweetly.

nightly /'naɪtlɪ/ adj. done or happening every night. **nightly** adv.: *We have to feed the baby twice nightly.*

nightmare /'naɪtmeə(r)/ n. bad dream.

night-watchman /ˌnaɪt 'wɒtʃmən/ n. (*pl.* night-watchmen) man whose job is to look after a building, factory, etc. at night.

nil /nɪl/ n. (no *pl.*) nothing: *Our team won the football match three-nil.*

nine /naɪn/ n. number 9. **nine** adj.: *a train with nine coaches.* **ninth** /naɪnθ/ adj. 9th: *the ninth time.*

nineteen /ˌnaɪn'tiːn/ n. number 19. **nineteen** adj.: *Jeff is nineteen years old.* **nineteenth** /ˌnaɪn'tiːnθ/ adj. 19th.

ninety /'naɪntɪ/ n. (*pl.* nineties) number 90. **ninety** adj. **ninetieth** /'naɪntɪəθ/ adj. 90th.

nip /nɪp/ v. (*pres. part.* nipping, *past part.* & *past tense* nipped /nɪpt/) take something tightly between fingers or teeth, etc.: *A crab nipped my toe while I was walking in the sea.* **nip** n.

no[1] /nəʊ/ adj. not a; not one; not any: *There is no money in my purse—it is empty.* **no** adv. in no way; not any: *He could walk no faster because he was tired.*

no[2] exclam. word to show that you do not agree; not yes.

noble /'nəʊbl/ adj. **1** of the family of a king; of high rank: *a man of noble birth.* **2** fine and good: *noble thoughts.* **3** great; fine; beautiful: *a noble building.* **nobly** adv. **the nobility** /nəʊ'bɪlətɪ/ n. all the people of noble families.

nobody /'nəʊbədɪ/ pron. (no *pl.*) no person: *Nobody met me when I arrived so I was alone.*

nod /nɒd/ v. (*pres. part.* nodding, *past part.* & *past tense* nodded /'nɒdɪd/) **1** bend your head forward quickly, to show that you know someone or that you agree with something: *He nodded when I asked if he understood.* **2** let your head fall forward when you are going to sleep in a chair, etc. **nod** n.: *He gave me a nod as we passed each other in the street.*

noise /nɔɪz/ n. **1** sound: *I think there's a mouse in the cellar because I heard a little noise.* **2** loud sound that you do not like: *Don't make so much noise!* **noiseless** adj. silent; with no sound. **noiselessly** adv.: *The cat walked noiselessly through the grass.*

noisy /'nɔɪzɪ/ adj. **1** making a lot of loud sound: *noisy children.* **2** full of loud sound: *a noisy restaurant.* **noisily** adv.

non- /nɒn/ prefix not; that is not, does not, etc.: *We took a non-stop train from London to Oxford.*

none[1] /nʌn/ adv. **none the worse for**, not hurt or damaged by something: *Adrian was none the worse for his car crash and went to work next day.*

none[2] pron. (no *pl.*) not any things or people; not one thing or person: *You can't have an apple because there are none in the house.*

nonsense /'nɒnsns/ n. (no *pl.*) silly ideas: *It's nonsense to say that eggs grow on trees!*

noon /nuːn/ n. 12 o'clock in the day.

no one /'nəʊ wʌn/ pron. (no *pl.*) no person: *No one met me when I arrived so I was alone.*

nor /nɔː(r)/ conj. (after a verb with 'not') then not: *If Jack doesn't go, nor will Jill.* **neither ... nor**, not ... and not: *Neither Tom nor Jerry can swim.*

normal /'nɔːml/ adj. usual; ordinary: *Will you be late for lunch or will you have it at the normal time?* **normally** adv. usually; mostly: *Hilda normally goes to bed at nine o'clock.*

north /nɔːθ/ n. (no *pl.*) one of the points of the compass: *England lies to the north of France.* **north** adj.: *the North Pole.* **north** adv.: *They travelled north from England to Scotland.* **northerly** /'nɔːðəlɪ/ adj. **1** in or to a place that is north: *a northerly direction.* **2** from the north: *a northerly wind.* **northern** /'nɔːðən/ adj.

of the north part of a town, country, the world, etc.: *Leeds is in northern England.*
northwards /ˈnɔːθwədz/ *adv.* towards the north: *From London we drove northwards to Birmingham.*

nose /nəʊz/ *n.* **1** part of the face that breathes and smells. ***blow your nose***, blow air through your nose to empty it, into a piece of cloth called a handkerchief. ***under your nose***, in front of you: *I thought I'd lost my pen, but it was right under my nose!* **2** part like a nose, on the front of something: *the nose of an aeroplane.*

nosy /ˈnəʊzɪ/ *adj.* wanting to know too much; asking too many questions.

not /nɒt/ *adv.* word that gives an opposite meaning to another word or sentence: *He likes bananas but I do not like them.* ***not at all***, **(a)** polite words that you say when someone has thanked you, etc.: *'It was kind of you to help me.' 'Not at all.'* **(b)** no; not a little bit: *'Are you tired?' 'Not at all.'*

note¹ /nəʊt/ *n.* **1** few words that you write down to help you remember something: *Sally made a note of the meeting in her diary.* ***take note of***, listen to or watch something carefully so that you will not forget it. **2** short letter: *a note of thanks.* **3** piece of paper money: *a pound note.* **4** one sound in music; mark that shows a sound in music.

note² *v.* **1** write something so that you remember it: *The policeman noted the driver's name and address.* **2** listen to or watch something carefully: *Drivers must note road signs.*

notebook /ˈnəʊtbʊk/ *n.* small book where you write things that you want to remember.

note-paper /ˈnəʊt peɪpə(r)/ *n.* (no *pl.*) paper for letters.

nothing¹ /ˈnʌθɪŋ/ *adv.* not at all: *He's nothing like his brother.*

nothing² *n.* (no *pl.*) not anything: *There's nothing in this purse—it's empty.* ***come to nothing***, not happen: *Jim's holiday plans came to nothing because he didn't have enough money.* ***for nothing***, **(a)** with no payment; free: *You can have these apples for nothing.* **(b)** without a good result: *He went to the station for nothing because she wasn't on the train.* ***have nothing on***, have no clothes on: *I can't open the door because I have nothing on.* **have**

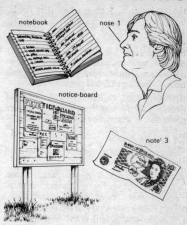

notebook · nose 1 · notice-board · note¹ 3

nothing to do with someone, **(a)** stay away from, and not talk to, someone: *He is a bad man and you must have nothing to do with him.* **(b)** not be the business of someone: *What I do in my free time has nothing to do with the teacher.* ***mean nothing to***, not be important to someone: *Money means nothing to him so he gives most of it away.*

notice¹ /ˈnəʊtɪs/ *n.* **1** (*pl.* notices) piece of writing to tell people something: *There's a notice on that gate saying 'NO PARKING'.* **2** (no *pl.*) warning telling someone that something will happen: *I must have notice when you want me to do the work.* ***at short notice***, with very little time to get ready: *We went on holiday at such short notice that I didn't say goodbye to Eric.* ***hand in***, or ***give in, your notice***, tell your boss that you will be leaving your job. **3** (no *pl.*) looking at, or listening to, something carefully; attention. ***take notice of***, not listen to, or look at, someone or something: *Take no notice of his angry words—he's not well.*

notice² *v.* see something or someone: *Did you notice that Mr. Bennet was driving a new car?*

noticeable /ˈnəʊtɪsəbl/ *adj.* clear; easy to see: *I've had no time to wash my hair—is it noticeable?* **noticeably** *adv.*: *She is noticeably thinner after her illness.*

notice-board /ˈnəʊtɪs bɔːd/ *n.* flat piece of wood fixed on to a wall, etc., where you can put papers to tell people about things.

notorious /nə'tɔːrɪəs/ adj. famous because he or it is so bad: a notorious criminal.

nought /nɔːt/ n. the number 0; zero.

noun /naʊn/ n. word that is the name of a person, thing, idea, etc.: The words 'boy', 'cat', 'pen', and 'lesson' are nouns.

novel /'nɒvl/ n. book that is one long story: 'David Copperfield' is a novel by Charles Dickens. **novelist** n. someone who writes novels: Charles Dickens was a famous novelist.

November /nəʊ'vembə(r)/ n. eleventh month of the year.

now /naʊ/ adv. **1** at the present time: You can't see Trevor because he's at school now. **2** at once; immediately: Don't wait—do it now! **from now on**, after this; in future: This is the last time I go with you—from now on you must go alone. **now and then, now and again**, sometimes: Susan comes to see me now and then but not very often.

nowadays /'naʊədeɪz/ adv. at the present time: There were no televisions when my grandmother was a child but nowadays most people have one.

nowhere /'nəʊweə(r)/ adv. at, in, or to no place; not anywhere: He went to look for Maurice but could find him nowhere.

nudge /nʌdʒ/ v. touch or push someone gently with your elbow: Nudge me if I fall asleep in the film, will you? **nudge** n.: He gave me a nudge.

nuisance /'njuːsns/ n. person or thing that gives you worry or trouble: The rain is a nuisance when we want to have a picnic.

numb /nʌm/ adj. with no feeling: My hands were numb because they were so cold.

number¹ /'nʌmbə(r)/ n. **1** word or figure like '2', 'two', '40', 'forty', etc.: There is a large number of boys in this class. **2** group of more than one person or thing. **a number of**, some; a lot of: I have a number of letters to write.

number² v. put a figure on something; give a figure to someone: Number the pages of your exercise book. **numbered** /'nʌmbəd/ adj. with a number: The seats in a theatre are usually numbered.

number-plate /'nʌmbə pleɪt/ n. flat piece of metal at the front and back of a car, which shows the car's licence number: The number-plate on my car is HYN 765N.

numeral /'njuːmərəl/ n. number; figure: '2', '7', and '140' are numerals.

numerous /'njuːmərəs/ adj. very many: She writes a lot of letters because she has numerous friends.

nun /nʌn/ n. woman who lives with a group of other women to serve the Christian God. **nunnery** /'nʌnərɪ/ n. place where nuns live and work.

nurse¹ /nɜːs/ n. **1** someone whose job is to look after people who are sick or hurt: In hospital the nurses helped me to wash. **2** woman or girl whose job is to look after babies and small children. **nursing** n. **nursing** adj.

nurse² v. look after people who are sick or hurt: Mother nursed Bob until he was well again.

nursery /'nɜːsərɪ/ n. (pl. nurseries) **1** special room for small children. **2** place where a baby or small child can stay while the mother goes out to work. **nursery rhyme** n. poem or song for young children. **nursery school** n. school for very young children.

nut /nʌt/ n. **1** hard fruit of a tree or bush: walnuts; peanuts; hazelnuts. **nutshell** /'nʌtʃel/ n. hard outside case of a nut. **be nuts**, be mad. **2** small piece of metal with a hole that you can put on the end of a screw or bolt to hold it tightly: nuts and bolts.

nylon /'naɪlɒn/ n. (no pl.) strong thread, made by machines, for making cloth, brushes, etc. **nylon** adj. **nylons** /'naɪlɒnz/ n. women's stockings.

Oo

O, oh /əʊ/ exclam. word that shows any strong feeling: Oh what a lovely rose! **Oh dear!** exclam. words to show that you are surprised or not happy: Oh dear! I've broken a cup!

oak /əʊk/ n. **1** (pl. oaks) sort of tree. **2** (no pl.) wood of an oak tree. **oak** adj.: an oak table.

oar /ɔː(r)/ *n.* long piece of wood, with one flat end, for rowing a boat.

oasis /əʊˈeɪsɪs/ *n.* (*pl.* oases) place with water and trees in a desert.

oath /əʊθ/ *n.* serious promise: *He took an oath on the Bible to tell the truth in court.*

oats /əʊts/ *n.* (*pl.*) plant that we use for food: *We make porridge from oats.*

obey /əˈbeɪ/ *v.* do what someone has told you to do: *A good dog obeys his master.* **obedient** /əˈbiːdɪənt/ *adj.: an obedient child.* **obediently** *adv.* **obedience** /əˈbiːdɪəns/ *n.*

object¹ /ˈɒbdʒɪkt/ *n.* **1** thing that you can see or touch: *There are three objects on my desk: a book, a pencil, and a ruler.* **2** what you plan to do: *The object of the journey was to visit Grandma.* **3** In the sentence 'Frank kicked the ball', the word 'ball' is the object of the verb 'kicked'.

object² /əbˈdʒekt/ *v.* say that you are against something; say that you do not like something: *He objects to muddy shoes in the house.* **objection** /əbˈdʒek-ʃn/ *n.* **have an objection to**, be against something: *Have you any objection to my smoking?*

oblige /əˈblaɪdʒ/ *v.* **be obliged to**, have to do something: *I was obliged to walk home because the car would not start.*

oblong /ˈɒblɒŋ/ *n.* shape with four straight sides and four right angles. **oblong** *adj.: Most envelopes are oblong.*

observation /ˌɒbzəˈveɪʃn/ *n.* (no *pl.*) watching carefully; being watched carefully. **be under observation**, be watched: *The sick man is under observation in hospital.* **keep someone under observation**, watch someone carefully: *The detective was keeping the house under observation because he thought the murderer lived there.*

observe /əbˈzɜːv/ *v.* see or watch someone or something carefully: *The trainer observed the players as they trained on the field.*

obstacle /ˈɒbstəkl/ *n.* something that stands in your way so you must get over or round it before you can go on: *He jumped over the obstacle and ran on.*

obstinate /ˈɒbstɪnət/ *adj.* not willing to change your ideas: *The obstinate donkey*

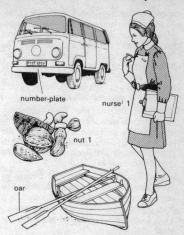

number-plate   nurse¹ 1

nut 1

oar

would not walk any further. **obstinately** *adv.*

obstruct /əbˈstrʌkt/ *v.* stand in the way of something: *A bus broke down and obstructed the traffic.* **obstruction** /əbˈstrʌkʃn/ *n.* something that obstructs: *The train had to stop because of an obstruction on the line.*

obtain /əbˈteɪn/ *v.* get or buy something: *Where can I obtain tickets for the boxing match?*

obvious /ˈɒbvɪəs/ *adj.* very clear; easy to see or understand. **obviously** *adv.* in a way that is easy to see or understand: *She was obviously thirsty because she drank a lot.*

occasion /əˈkeɪʒn/ *n.* **1** a certain time; time when something happens: *I have travelled in an aeroplane on three occasions.* **2** special time: *A wedding is a big family occasion.*

occasional /əˈkeɪʒənl/ *adj.* happening sometimes, but not very often: *an occasional visit.* **occasionally** *adv.* sometimes: *I occasionally play badminton but I don't often have time.*

occupation /ˌɒkjʊˈpeɪʃn/ *n.* **1** (*pl.* occupations) job: *What is your father's occupation?* **2** (*pl.* occupations) anything that keeps you busy: *Swimming and canoeing are my favourite occupations.* **3** (no *pl.*) living in a house, country, etc.: *Their occupation of the flat lasted only for six months.* **4** taking and keeping a country, town, etc. in war.

occupy /'ɒkjʊpaɪ/ v. **1** live in a place: *Grandmother occupies two rooms on the ground floor of our house.* **2** take and keep a country, town, etc., in war: *The Normans occupied England from 1066.* **3** fill time; take someone's time: *The repair occupied him for five hours.* **occupied** /'ɒkjʊpaɪd/ adj. busy: *I can't come for a moment—I'm occupied.*

occur /ə'kɜː(r)/ v. (*pres. part.* occurring, *past part.* & *past tense* occurred /ə'kɜːd/) happen: *The accident occurred when the bus hit a big lorry.* **occur to**, come into your mind: *It occurred to me that she didn't know our new address.*

ocean /'əʊʃn/ n. great sea: *If you go from England to America by ship, you will sail across the Atlantic Ocean.*

o'clock /ə'klɒk/ adv. word that shows what hour of the day it is: *What time is it? It's six o'clock.*

October /ɒk'təʊbə(r)/ n. tenth month of the year.

odd /ɒd/ adj. **1** that you cannot divide exactly by 2: *1, 3, 5, and 7 are odd numbers; 2, 4, 6, and 8 are even numbers.* **2** not with the other of the pair: *Here's an odd sock—do you know where the other is?* **3** strange; not usual: *He's an odd man—he never talks to anyone.* **oddly** adv. strangely: *oddly dressed.*

odds /ɒdz/ n. (*pl.*) chance that something will or will not happen: *Shall we reach the boat in time—what are the odds? The odds are against us in the match because our best player is ill.*

odds and ends /'ɒdz ənd 'endz/ n. (*pl.*) different small things that are not important: *Ruth went out to buy a few odds and ends.*

of /ɒv/ prep. **1** word that shows what you have and own: *a book of mine.* **2** word that shows what you are to another person: *a cousin of ours; a friend of my mother's.* **3** word that shows amount: *a pound of butter.* **4** word that shows what is inside a thing: *a cup of tea.* **5** word that shows what sort: *a piece of wood.* **6** word that shows how something is made: *a ring of gold.* **7** word that describes: *a man of wealth.* **8** word that shows place: *the end of the road.* **9** word that shows how far: *20 miles north of Bradford.* **10** word that shows who has written something: *the plays of Shakespeare.* **of course**, certainly.

off[1] /ɒf/ adv. **1** not on; away from the place where it was: *Carol took her clothes off to have a bath.* **2** not on; out, so that it is not working: *Please put the lights off when you leave the room.* **3** away: *We can walk to the station because it is not far off.* **4** away to another place: *He went off by train at 11 o'clock.* **5** apart; not joined: *The cup's handle broke off.* **6** not at work: *The cook is having a day off today.* **7** not fresh: *This meat is going off.* **badly off**, poor. **on and off, off and on**, from time to time. **well off**, rich.

off[2] prep. **1** from; down from; away from: *He fell off the roof on to the ground.* **2** near: *an island off the coast.* **3** joining: *a track off the main road.* **4** not wanting; not liking: *I'm off my food.* **5** free from: *A policeman does not wear a uniform when he is off duty.*

offence /ə'fens/ n. **1** (*pl.* offences) something that you do against the law or against the rules; crime: *Driving without lights at night is an offence.* **2** (no *pl.*) feeling upset and angry. **take offence**, become angry: *He took offence when I said his car was dirty.*

offend /ə'fend/ v. make someone angry; hurt the feelings of someone: *I offended him when I said he was fat.*

offender /ə'fendə(r)/ n. someone who does something wrong.

offer /'ɒfə(r)/ v. **1** hold out something that you want to give to someone: *Gail offered me a chocolate.* **2** say that you will give, do, or pay something if the other person wants it: *At the end of the interview they offered me a job.* **offer** n.: *Thank you for your offer of help.*

office /'ɒfɪs/ n. **1** room or rooms where you do business: *My sister is a secretary in the office of a big school.* **office block** n. big building with many offices. **2** building for government work: *a post office.* **3** important job in the government, in a society, etc. **take office**, get an important job: *The new prime minister has just taken office.*

officer /'ɒfɪsə(r)/ n. **1** someone who gives orders to others in the army, navy, etc. **2** someone who does important work, especially for the government: *a customs officer; police officers.*

official[1] /ə'fɪʃl/ adj. from a person with authority: *an official report.* **officially**

adv.: We think he has got the job but they will tell him officially on Friday.

official[2] *n.* someone who does important work, especially for the government: *An official at the railway station said the train would arrive late.*

often /'ɒfn/ *adv.* many times: *We often play football after school.* **every so often,** sometimes.

oh, O /əʊ/ *exclam.* word that shows any strong feeling.

oil /ɔɪl/ *n.* **1** fatty liquid that comes from plants or animals: *She cooked the fish in oil in a pan.* **2** thick liquid that comes from under the ground: *I must put some more oil in the car.* **strike oil,** find oil in the ground. **oil** *v.* put oil on to a machine, etc.: *Rachel oiled her bicycle.*

oil-colours /'ɔɪl kʌləz/, etc. **oils** /ɔɪlz/ *n.* (*pl.*) oily sort of paint for painting pictures.

oil-drilling /'ɔɪl drɪlɪŋ/ *n.* (no *pl.*) digging for oil under the ground.

oil-painting /'ɔɪl peɪntɪŋ/ *n.* picture painted with oily paints.

oil-rig /'ɔɪl rɪg/ *n.* special building with machines that dig for oil under the sea or on land.

oil-tanker /'ɔɪl tæŋkə(r)/ *n.* ship or big lorry that carries oil.

oil-well /'ɔɪl wel/ *n.* deep hole in the ground, where petroleum oil comes from.

oily /'ɔɪlɪ/ *adj.* **1** of oil; like oil: *Butter gets oily on a hot day.* **2** covered with oil, fat, etc.: *oily fingers.*

ointment /'ɔɪntmənt/ *n.* cream that you put on the skin, etc. to make it well.

O.K., okay /ˌəʊ'keɪ/ *exclam.* yes; all right: *'Will you come with me?' 'O.K., I will.'* **O.K., okay** *adj.* all right: *Is it O.K. to park my car here?*

old[1] /əʊld/ *adj.* **1** of age; long since birth: *How old are you? I am twelve years old.* **2** not young; having lived a long time: *My great-grandfather is very old.* **3** not new; that was made or bought long ago; not fresh: *She gave away her old coat and bought a new one.* **4** known a long time: *Grace is an old friend; I have known her since we first went to school.*

old[2] *pron.* (*pl.*) **the old,** old people.

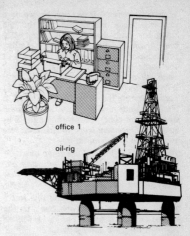

office 1

oil-rig

old-fashioned /ˌəʊld'fæʃnd/ *adj.* not modern; old in style: *Clothes of 20 years ago look very old-fashioned today.*

omelette /'ɒmlɪt/ *n.* eggs that you beat together and cook in butter.

omit /ə'mɪt/ *v.* leave something out: *When we sing the next hymn, we shall omit the second verse.*

on[1] /ɒn/ *adv.* **1** word that shows where: *It's cold, so put a warm coat on.* **2** so that it is working: *It's dark, so put the lights on.* **3** moving forward or ahead: *You can't park here, so drive on.* **4** happening: *We'll go to the cinema if there's a good film on.* **from now on,** after this: *He's left school and will go to work from now on.* **and so on,** and other things of the same kind; et cetera: *Grandma knits pullovers, gloves, scarves, and so on.* **on and on,** without stopping: *It was a very long concert; the music went on and on.*

on[2] *prep.* **1** word that shows where: *The boat is on the river. The number is on the door.* **2** word that shows when: *Shall we meet on Sunday?* **3** about: *a book on cars.* **4** word that shows you are part of a group: *My brother is on the committee.* **5** word that shows what you are doing, how you are, how something is, etc.: *They are on holiday.*

once /wʌns/ *adv.* **1** one time: *I've only been to Brighton once.* **once more,** again: *Tell me the story once more.* **once or twice, once in a while,** a few times: *It has been a* *very dry summer—it has only rained once or twice.* **once and for all,** for the last time; for ever: *He closed his shop once and for all and retired.* **at once, (a)** now; immediately: *Come here at once!* **(b)** at the same time: *I can't do two things at once.* **all at once,** suddenly: *All at once, a bird flew out of the bushes.* **2** at some time in the past: *Once he lived in America but now he lives in England.* **once upon a time,** a long time ago. **3** as soon as: *Once you learn to ride a bicycle you can go to school on it.*

one[1] /wʌn/ *adj.* **1** a: *I am going away for one week.* **2** single: *I can only find one sandal.* **3** the same: *The birds all flew away in one direction.*

one[2] *n.* number 1: *One and one make two (1 + 1 = 2).* **one by one,** one after the other; one at a time: *The cows walked through the gate one by one.*

one[3] *pron.* (no *pl.*) **1** a single thing: *I'll have one of those oranges, please.* **2** a person; any person: *One can fly to America in Concorde in three hours.* **one another,** each other: *The three men never speak because they don't like one another.* **3** word that we have instead of a person or thing: *Two boys were playing and the fat one hit the thin one.*

oneself /wʌn'self/ *pron.* (no *pl.*) a person's own self: *One can see oneself in the mirror.* **by oneself,** alone.

onion /'ʌnɪən/ *n.* round vegetable with a strong smell and taste.

only[1] /'əʊnlɪ/ *adj.* **1** that is the one person, thing, or group of a certain sort: *Jeremy is the only friend who lives near; all my other friends live far away.* **an only child,** a child with no brothers or sisters. **2** best: *The only thing to do on a hot day is to go swimming.*

only[2] *adv.* **1** no one more than; nothing more than; exactly: *Only five children came to the party because the others are all sick.* **2** just: *He only walks to save money—he doesn't really like walking.*

only[3] *conj.* but: *That bag is just what I want, only it costs too much.*

on to /'ɒn tu:/, /'ɒntə/ *prep.* to a place: *I threw a log on to the fire.*

onward /'ɒnwəd/, **onwards** /'ɒnwədz/ *adv.* **1** to the front; forward: *He drove onwards.* **2** after a certain time: *I shall be at home from 8 o'clock onwards.*

ooze /u:z/ *v.* flow out slowly: *Blood oozed out when David cut his hand.*

open[1] /'əʊpən/ *adj.* **1** not closed; so that people or things can go in and out: *Leave the windows open, so that fresh air can come into the room.* **2** not covered: *an open market.* **3** not closed, so that you can look in: *an open box; an open book.* **4** ready for business: *When is the post office open?* **5** not for a special group: *The competition is open to all children.*

open[2] *n.* (no *pl.*) **in the open,** in the open air; outside.

open[3] *v.* **1** unfasten something so that people or things can go in, out, or through it: *He opened the door so that I could come in.* **2** move so that you can see inside, underneath, etc.: *The baby's mouth opened and it began to cry.* **3** unfold something: *Open your hand and let me see what you have in it.* **4** begin; start to happen: *The meeting opens at ten o'clock.* **open fire,** start shooting. **5** say that something can begin or is ready: *The governor opened the new hospital.*

opener /'əʊpnə(r)/ *n.* thing that takes the lid, etc. off something: *a tin-opener.*

opening /'əʊpnɪŋ/ *n.* **1** way in or out: *The cattle got out of the field through an opening in the fence.* **2** beginning: *We were too late to see the opening of the game.*

openly /'əʊpənlɪ/ *adv.* not secretly; freely.

opera /'ɒprə/ *n.* a play where the actors sing but do not speak much. **opera house** *n.* theatre for operas. **operatic** /ɒpə'rætɪk/ *adj.: operatic music.*

operate /'ɒpəreɪt/ *v.* **1** function; work: *How does this machine operate?* **2** make something work: *It is not difficult to operate a lift.* **3** cut into someone's body to mend a part inside: *The doctor will operate on her leg tomorrow.*

operation /ɒpə'reɪʃn/ *n.* **1** (no *pl.*) working; the way something works. **2** (*pl.* operations) doctor's work when he cuts into your body to mend a part inside: *an operation to take out the appendix.*

operator /'ɒpəreɪtə(r)/ *n.* someone who makes something work: *a telephone operator.*

opinion /ə'pɪnɪən/ n. what you believe or think about something: *What is your opinion of her work?*

opponent /ə'pəʊnənt/ n. someone with whom you fight, argue, or play a game: *The boxer beat his opponent.*

opportunity /ˌɒpə'tjuː:nətɪ/ n. (pl. opportunities) chance; what will perhaps happen; time for you to do something: *I was in a hurry this morning so I had no opportunity to read my letters.*

oppose /ə'pəʊz/ v. be against someone or something; fight someone or something: *His father did not oppose his plan to study in America.*

opposite¹ /'ɒpəzɪt/ adj. **1** across from where you are; other: *You must cross the bridge if you want to get to the opposite bank of the river.* **2** totally different: *North is the opposite direction to south.* **opposite** adv.: *They don't live on this side of the road—they live opposite.*

opposite² n. word or thing that is totally different: *Hot is the opposite of cold.*

optimist /'ɒptɪmɪst/ n. someone who believes the best will happen, and is full of hope: *Don't worry about the exams—be an optimist.* **optimistic** /ˌɒptɪ'mɪstɪk/ adj. **optimistically** adv.: *'I'm sure I'll do well', said Susan optimistically.*

option /'ɒpʃn/ n. one of the things that you can do, choose etc.: *If you want to learn a foreign language, French and German are the options.*

optional /'ɒpʃənl/ adj. that you can choose to do or have: *All pupils must learn English but music is an optional subject.*

or /ɔː(r)/ conj. **1** word that shows another person, thing, idea, etc.: *Is the light red or green?* **2** if not, then: *Hurry or you'll be late.* **or else**, if not, then: *Hurry or else you'll be late.* **either . . . or**, words to show two different things or people that you can choose: *You can either walk or come by car.*

oral /'ɔːrəl/ adj. speaking, not writing: *an oral examination.*

orange /'ɒrɪndʒ/ n. **1** (pl. oranges) round, juicy fruit with a thick, yellow-red skin. **2** (no pl.) colour between yellow and red; gold. **orange** adj.

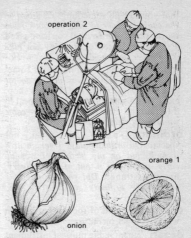

operation 2

orange 1

onion

orbit /'ɔːbɪt/ v. move round another thing in space, etc.: *The spacecraft is orbiting the moon.* **orbit** n.

orchard /'ɔːtʃəd/ n. big group of fruit trees.

orchestra /'ɔːkɪstrə/ n. group of people who play musical instruments together. **orchestral** /ɔː'kestrəl/ adj.: *an orchestral concert.*

ordeal /ɔː'diːl/ n. time of great trouble or pain: *He had a terrible ordeal when he was lost in the mountains for a week with no food.*

order¹ /'ɔːdə(r)/ n. **1** (no pl.) way you arrange or place things or people: *He wrote a list of children in order of age.* **2** (no pl.) when things are placed with care, working well, etc.: *There is always order on a good ship.* **in order, in good order,** (a) neat; tidy. (b) as it should be: *Sam always keeps his bicycle in good order.* **out of order,** not working: *I couldn't ring because the phone was out of order.* **3** (no pl.) when there is peace and calm and everyone is doing what is right: *Our boss likes order in the office.* **keep someone in order,** control someone: *The police kept the crowd in order.* **4** (pl. orders) words that tell someone to do something: *The officer gave the soldiers an order to march.* **5** (pl. orders) asking a shop, etc. to get or send something to you: *He sent an order for groceries.* **in order that,** so that: *I posted the letter today in order that you'd get it tomorrow.* **in order to,** so that you can do something: *He stood on the chair in order to take the book from the top shelf.* **on order**, that you have asked a shop, etc. to get for you: *My new bike is on order and should arrive next week.*

order[2] *v.* **1** tell someone to do something: *When Muriel was ill the doctor ordered her to stay in bed.* **2** ask a shop, etc. to send something; ask for a meal in a restaurant, etc.: *When the waiter came we ordered steak and chips.*

ordinary /'ɔ:dnrɪ/ *adj.* usual; not special: *On ordinary days I get up at 8 o'clock, but on my birthday I was up early.* **ordinary** *n.* **out of the ordinary**, unusual; strange: *Did you see anything out of the ordinary?* **ordinarily** *adv.* usually.

ore /ɔ:(r)/ *n.* kind of rock or earth from which you get metal: *iron ore; tin ore.*

organ /'ɔ:gən/ *n.* big musical instrument with keys like a piano: *There is usually an organ in a church.* **organist** /'ɔ:gənɪst/ *n.* someone who plays an organ.

organization /ˌɔ:gənaɪ'zeɪʃn/ *n.* **1** (no *pl.*) planning something: *She's busy with the organization of her daughter's party.* **2** (*pl.* organizations) group of people, countries, etc., who are working together for some purpose: *United Nations Organization.*

organize /'ɔ:gənaɪz/ *v.* plan something; control things or people: *Our teacher has organized a class trip to Stratford-upon-Avon.*

oriental /ˌɔ:rɪ'entl/ *adj.* eastern: *China is an oriental country.*

origin /'ɒrɪdʒɪn/ *n.* beginning; start of anything: *What was the origin of Man?*

original[1] /ə'rɪdʒənl/ *adj.* **1** first; earliest: *I have the bicycle now but my sister was the original owner.* **2** that is real, not a copy: *original paintings.*

original[2] *n.* thing of which there are copies: *This is a good copy of the painting—the original is in the National Gallery.*

originally /ə'rɪdʒənəlɪ/ *adv.* in the beginning; at first: *This hotel was originally the house of a duke.*

ornament /'ɔ:nəmənt/ *n.* extra thing that you add to make something beautiful: *stone ornaments of animals in a garden.* **ornamental** /ˌɔ:nə'mentl/ *adj.*

orphan /'ɔ:fn/ *n.* child whose parents are dead. **orphanage** /'ɔ:fənɪdʒ/ *n.* home for orphans.

ostrich /'ɒstrɪtʃ/ *n.* (*pl.* ostriches) very big bird from Africa that runs fast but cannot fly.

other[1] /'ʌðə(r)/ *adj.* not the same; opposite: *He walked across the road to the other side.* **the other day**, not many days ago: *I saw your brother the other day.* **some . . . or other**, words that show you are not sure: *I'll come and see you some time or other when I am free.*

other[2] *pron.* (no *pl.*) someone or something that is not the same: *This book is mine and the other is Adrian's.*

otherwise /'ʌðəwaɪz/ *adv.* **1** differently: *My father wanted me to become a farmer, but I decided otherwise.* **2** apart from that; if you forget that: *The house is small, but otherwise it is comfortable.* **otherwise** *conj.* if not: *Walk slowly on the ice, otherwise you'll fall.*

ought /ɔ:t/ *v.* **ought to,** (**a**) words that tell someone what is the right thing to do: *It's late so I ought to go home.* (**b**) words that show what you think will happen: *Bruce is the fastest runner, so he ought to win the race.*

ounce /aʊns/ *n.* measure of weight = 28·3 grams.

our /ɑ:(r)/, /'aʊə(r)/ *adj.* of us: *Come and see us at our house.* **ours** *pron.* thing that belongs to us: *This house is ours.*

ourselves /ɑ:'selvz/, /aʊə'selvz/ *pron.* (*pl.*) **1** word that describes us when we have just been talked about: *We hurt ourselves when we fell over.* **2** we and no other people: *We made this ourselves.* **by ourselves**, alone.

out /aʊt/ *adv.* **1** away from a place; from inside: *When you go out, please close the door.* **2** not at home, in the office, etc.: *Mr. Johnson is out and will be back in two hours.* **3** open; that you can see clearly: *It was hot when the sun came out.* **4** not shining or burning: *It was dark because the light had gone out.* **5** loudly; clearly: *He cried out in pain.* **6** forwards; towards someone or something: *Hold your hands out.* **all out, flat out**, doing the best you can: *He can run 100 metres in fifteen seconds when he's going all out.* **out and out**, total: *He's an out and out thief!*

outbreak /'aʊtbreɪk/ n. sudden beginning: *There was an outbreak of typhoid in the city.*

outdoor /aʊt'dɔː(r)/ adj. in the open air; that happens outside a building: *Football and cricket are outdoor games.*
outdoors adv. in the open air; outside: *We had our lunch outdoors.*

outer /'aʊtə(r)/ adj. of or for the outside; farther from the centre: *the outer parts of the city.*

outfit /'aʊtfɪt/ n. set of clothes that you wear together, for sport or a special happening.

outgrow /aʊt'grəʊ/ v. (*past part.* outgrown /aʊt'grəʊn/, *past tense* outgrew /aʊt'gruː/) **1** grow too big for your clothes: *The baby has outgrown her shoes.* **2** grow too old for something: *She doesn't play with dolls now—she's outgrown them.*

outing /'aʊtɪŋ/ n. short journey to enjoy yourself: *We went for an outing to the sea on Sunday.*

outlaw /'aʊtlɔː/ n. someone who lives in a secret place away from other people because he has broken the law: *Robin Hood was a famous outlaw.*

outline /'aʊtlaɪn/ n. line that shows the shape of something: *We could see the outline of the castle through the fog.*

outnumber /aʊt'nʌmbə(r)/ v. be more in number than others: *Male doctors outnumber female doctors.*

out of /'aʊt əv/ prep. **1** words that show where: *Fish cannot live out of water.* **2** words that show where from: *It's time you got out of bed.* **3** words that show why: *Audrey helped us out of kindness.* **4** words that show part of a group; from among: *Twenty out of a class of thirty children were ill.* **5** with; from: *He made a table out of an old box.* **6** without; not having: *We were out of breath after running up the hill.*

out-of-date /ˌaʊt əv 'deɪt/ adj. **1** not modern: *out-of-date clothes.* **2** with old information: *an out-of-date list.*

output /'aʊtpʊt/ n. (no *pl.*) amount of things that you have made: *What is the output of the factory?*

outside¹ /ˌaʊt'saɪd/ adj. on, near, or in the part away from the centre: *an outside toilet.*

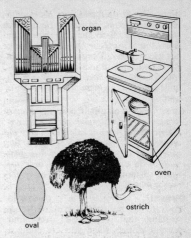

organ

oven

ostrich

oval

outside² adv. out; from a place: *He went outside to look at the garden.*

outside³ n. outer part of something: *The outside of the car is blue.*

outside⁴ prep. on or at the outer part of: *He parked his car outside the theatre.*

outskirts /'aʊtskɜːts/ n. (*pl.*) outer parts of a town or city: *Heathrow airport is on the outskirts of London.*

outstanding /ˌaʊt'stændɪŋ/ adj. very good; much better than others: *Jeff is an outstanding boxer and will probably become a champion.*

outward /'aʊtwəd/, **outwards** /'aʊtwədz/ adv. towards the outside: *Does that window open inwards or outwards?*

oval /'əʊvl/ n. shape like an egg. **oval** adj.

oven /'ʌvn/ n. inside part of a cooker; thing in which you can cook food.

over¹ /'əʊvə(r)/ adv. **1** across: *Let's row over to the other side of the river.* **2** from one place to another: *Come over and see us on Saturday.* **3** in all parts. **all over**, everywhere: *The dog went in the water and now it's wet all over.* **4** through; from beginning to end: *I'll read the question over once more.* **all over again**, **over again**, another time: *The audience liked the song so much that she sang it all over again.* **over and over again**, many

times: *Say it over and over again until
you remember it.* **5** down: *He tripped
and fell over.* **6** so that the other
side is on top: *Turn your books over.* **7** left;
not used: *If there's any soup over, we can
eat it tomorrow.* **8** more: *The race is for
children of ten and over.* **9** ended;
finished: *We'll go home when the class is
over.*

over² *prep.* **1** on top of; covering: *I put a
blanket over the sleeping child.* **2** above;
higher than: *When it rains you carry an
umbrella over your head.* **3** across; to the
other side of: *Can you jump over that
wall?* **4** in every part of: *all over the
world.* **5** more than: *He was away for
over a month.*

overall /'əʊvərɔːl/ *n.*, **overalls**
/'əʊvərɔːlz/ *n.* (*pl.*) piece of loose
clothing that you wear over your
normal clothes when you are doing a
dirty job.

overboard /'əʊvəbɔːd/ *adv.* over the
side of a boat and into the water: *They
jumped overboard when the ship caught
fire.*

overcoat /'əʊvəkəʊt/ *n.* long coat that
you wear over other clothes in cold
weather.

overcome /,əʊvə'kʌm/ *v.* (*past part.*
overcome, *past tense* overcame /,əʊvə-
'keɪm/) **1** beat someone because you
are too strong for him: *The army overcame
the enemy.* **2** find an answer to a difficult thing in your life: *We overcame the
problem.*

overcrowded /,əʊvə'kraʊdɪd/ *adj.* too
full of people: *an overcrowded train.*

overdue /,əʊvə'djuː/ *adj.* **1** late: *The
train is two hours overdue.* **2** not yet
paid: *The landlady is angry because the
rent is overdue.*

overflow /,əʊvə'fləʊ/ *v.* flow over the
edge of something: *The river overflowed
its banks.*

overgrown /,əʊvə'grəʊn/ *adj.* covered
with plants that have grown everywhere: *The garden of the empty house is
overgrown with weeds.*

overhaul /,əʊvə'hɔːl/ *v.* check something and mend it if necessary: *The
garage will overhaul the car for you.*
overhaul /'əʊvəhɔːl/ *n.*

overhead /,əʊvə'hed/ *adv.* above your
head: *The sun is hottest when it is over-*

head. **overhead** *adj.* high above the
ground: *an overhead railway.*

overhear /,əʊvə'hɪə(r)/ *v.* (*past part. &
past tense* overheard /,əʊvə'hɜːd/) hear
something by chance when the speaker
does not know that you are listening.

overjoyed /,əʊvə'dʒɔɪd/ *adj.* very
happy.

overlook /,əʊvə'lʊk/ *v.* **1** look down at
something from above: *My room over-
looks the sea.* **2** forget; not see something important: *I overlooked this mistake in your paper the first time I read it.*
3 not be angry about a bad thing: *I will
overlook your late arrival because it is
the first time.*

overnight /,əʊvə'naɪt/ *adv.* for the
night: *They stayed at our house overnight.* **overnight** *adj.*: *an overnight
journey.*

overpower /,əʊvə'paʊə(r)/ *v.* beat
someone because you are too strong for
him: *Three policemen overpowered the
robber.*

overseas /,əʊvə'siːz/ *adj.* in, to, or from
places across the sea; foreign: *overseas
news.* **overseas** *adv.* abroad: *He is
living overseas.*

oversleep /,əʊvə'sliːp/ *v.* (*past part. &
past tense* overslept /,əʊvə'slept/) sleep
too long; not wake at the right time.

overtake /,əʊvə'teɪk/ *v.* (*past part.* over-
taken /,əʊvə'teɪkn/, *past tense* overtook
/,əʊvə'tʊk/) go past someone or something that is going more slowly: *I was
riding my bicycle along the road when a
car overtook me.*

overthrow /,əʊvə'θrəʊ/ *v.* (*past part.*
overthrown /,əʊvə'θrəʊn/, *past tense*
overthrew /,əʊvə'θruː/) conquer a ruler,
country, etc. *Oliver Cromwell overthrew
King Charles I.*

overtime /'əʊvətaɪm/ *n.* (no *pl.*) extra
time at work. **overtime** *adv.*: *They will
be home late because they are working
overtime.*

overtook /,əʊvə'tʊk/ *past tense* of *v.*
overtake.

overturn /,əʊvə'tɜːn/ *v.* turn over; turn
something over: *A big wave overturned
the boat.*

overweight /,əʊvə'weɪt/ *adj.* too heavy:
*He had to pay more at the airport be-
cause his case was overweight. He eats
too much and is very overweight.*

owe /əʊ/ v. **1** have to give back money that you have borrowed from someone; have to give someone money that you have not yet paid for something: *I owe my brother £2 that he lent me last week.* **2** feel that someone has done a lot for you: *She owes her life to that man who pulled her out of the river.*

owing to /'əʊɪŋ tʊ/ prep. because of: *They call him 'Carrots' owing to his red hair.*

owl /aʊl/ n. bird that flies at night.

own[1] /əʊn/ adj. word that shows that something belongs to a person or thing or is a special part of something: *This is my own camera, which I bought with my own money.* **own** pron.: *Those books belong to the library but this is my own.* **get your own back on**, harm someone who has harmed you: *I'll get my own back on that boy who broke my watch!* **of your own**, belonging to you and to no one else: *a home of my own.* **on your own**, alone: *He lives on his own.*

own[2] v. have something that is yours: *We don't rent our house; we own it.* **own up to**, say that you have done something wrong: *No one owned up to the broken window.*

owner /'əʊnə(r)/ n. someone who has something: *Who is the owner of that red car?*

ox /ɒks/ n. (pl. oxen) bull used for farm work.

oxygen /'ɒksɪdʒən/ n. (no pl.) gas in the air that we must breathe to go on living.

oz. abbrev. ounce.

Pp

p /piː/ abbrev. pence: *This lemon cost 10p.*

pa /pɑː/ father.

pace /peɪs/ n. **1** step: *Take two paces forward!* **2** speed of walking or running. **keep pace with**, go as fast as someone: *The little boy can't keep pace with his big brothers.*

pack[1] /pæk/ n. **1** bag or bundle of

packet
pad 1
pad 2
overall
owl

things that you have tied together so that they are easy to carry: *The hikers had packs on their backs.* **2** group of animals that run and hunt together: *a pack of wolves.* **3** group of people or things: *a pack of thieves.* **a pack of cards**, a set of cards for playing games.

pack[2] v. **1** put things into a box, bag, etc. until it is full. **2** put clothes into a case ready for a journey: *I must pack quickly for my trip to London.* **3** put something firmly into a tight place: *Frank packed earth round the fence-post.* **pack up**, stop doing something: *At 2 o'clock we'll pack up and go home.*

package /'pækɪdʒ/ n. parcel; bundle.

packed /pækt/ adj. **1** full: *The train was packed.* **2** in a small parcel: *a packed lunch.*

packet /'pækɪt/ n. small parcel or box: *a packet of cigarettes.*

packing /'pækɪŋ/ n. (no pl.) **1** putting things into boxes, bags, etc.: *Finish your packing and let's go.* **2** paper, straw, etc. that you put round something to stop it from breaking, etc.: *Put plenty of packing round this vase before you post it.*

pact /pækt/ n. agreement to do something.

pad /pæd/ n. **1** thick piece of soft stuff that you put on a wound or part of your body to keep it safe: *an eye-pad; cricket pads.* **2** a lot of new pieces of paper, fixed at one end: *a writing pad.*

paddle[1] /'pædl/ n. long piece of wood with a flat end, for making a canoe, etc. move through the water.

paddle[2] v. **1** make a canoe, etc. move through the water with a paddle: *They paddled their boat up the river.* **2** play and walk in shallow water with bare feet: *The children were paddling in the sea.*

paddock /'pædək/ n. small field for horses.

padlock /'pædlɒk/ n. sort of lock: *Dawn fastened her bike to the fence with a padlock and chain.*

page[1] /peɪdʒ/ n. **1** piece of paper in a book, magazine, etc. **2** one side of a piece of paper in a book, etc.: *You are reading page 178 of this book.*

page[2] n. boy servant to a king, queen, etc. long ago.

paid /peɪd/ past part. & past tense of v. pay.

pail /peɪl/ n. bucket: *a pail of water.*

pain /peɪn/ n. hurt in the body or mind: *His broken leg gave him a lot of pain.*

painful /'peɪnfl/ adj. giving pain: *a painful bee sting.* **painfully** adv.

painless /'peɪnlɪs/ adj. not giving pain. **painlessly** adv.

pains /peɪnz/ n. (pl.) **take pains with** or **over**, spend a lot of time and care on someone or something: *Ann takes great pains over her hair.*

paint[1] /peɪnt/ n. coloured liquid that you put on something with a brush to change the colour or make a picture: *Wet paint—do not touch!*

paint[2] v. **1** cover something with a coloured liquid: *We painted the door blue.* **2** make a picture with paints: *Picasso painted that picture.*

painter /'peɪntə(r)/ n. **1** someone who paints pictures; artist: *Picasso was a painter.* **2** someone whose job is to paint houses, ships, etc.

painting /'peɪntɪŋ/ n. **1** (no pl.) using paint; making pictures by using different colours: *The painting was a long job because the room was very big.* **2** (pl. paintings) pictures made with paint.

pair /peə(r)/ n. **1** two things of the same kind that are together: *a pair of socks.* **2** thing with two parts that are joined together: *a pair of trousers; a pair of scissors.* **3** two people: *a happy pair.*

pal /pæl/ n. friend.

palace /'pælɪs/ n. house of a king or other ruler; very big, beautiful house.

pale /peɪl/ adj. **1** with little colour in the face. **2** not bright; with a light or weak colour: *The sky is pale blue.*

palm[1] /pɑːm/ n. inside, flat part of the hand: *I put the coins into his palm.*

palm[2] n. sort of tree: *a coconut palm.*

pan /pæn/ n. flat dish for cooking: *a frying-pan.*

pancake /'pænkeɪk/ n. very thin, round cake that you make with milk, eggs, and flour and cook in a frying pan.

pane /peɪn/ n. piece of glass in a window.

panel /'pænl/ n. **1** flat piece of wood, glass, metal, etc., often part of a door or wall. **2** board or shelf on a machine, in a car, etc., with dials, switches, etc.: *an instrument panel.*

panic /'pænɪk/ n. strong fear that spreads quickly and makes people do wild things: *There was panic in the shop when a fire started.* **panic** v. (pres. part. panicking, past part. & past tense panicked /'pænɪkt/): *The children panicked.* **panic-stricken** /'pænɪk strɪkn/ adj. full of panic.

pant /pænt/ v. breathe quickly through the mouth: *The dog was panting after chasing the cat.*

pantihose /'pæntɪhəʊz/ n. (pl.) stockings and pants all in one piece of clothing, which a woman or girl wears.

pantomine /'pæntəmaɪm/ n. sort of play, with music, dancing, singing, and jokes.

pantry /'pæntrɪ/ n. (pl. pantries) small room next to a kitchen, where you keep food.

pants /pænts/ n. (pl.) **1** trousers. **2** piece of clothing that you wear on your bottom, under a skirt or trousers.

papa /pə'pɑː/ n. father.

paper[1] /'peɪpə(r)/ n. **1** (no pl.) thin sheets of stuff for writing, printing, packing, etc.: *This book is made of paper.* **2** (pl. papers) newspaper: *Have you read* *today's paper?* **3 papers** (*pl.*) special pieces of paper that show who you are, what you do, etc.: *The police asked to see his papers.* **4** (*pl.* papers) set of examination questions: *The history paper was easy.*

paper² *v.* stick paper on to a wall to make it pretty.

paperback /'peɪpəbæk/ *n.* book with paper covers.

paper-clip /'peɪpə klɪp/ *n.* small piece of wire that holds pieces of paper together.

parachute /'pærəʃuːt/ *n.* thing like a big umbrella that you wear when you jump out of an aeroplane so that you will come down to earth safely. **parachute** *v.* jump, or drop things, from an aeroplane with a parachute: *They parachuted slowly down on to the island.*

parade /pə'reɪd/ *v.* walk or march together on an important occasion: *The scouts paraded in front of the Queen.* **parade** *n.*: *Let's go and watch the Easter parade.*

paradise /'pærədaɪs/ *n.* (no *pl.*) **1** heaven. **2** place where you are totally happy.

paraffin /'pærəfɪn/ *n.* (no *pl.*) oil from petrol, coal, etc., for lighting and heating.

paragraph /'pærəgrɑːf/ *n.* group of lines of writing.

paralyse /'pærəlaɪz/ *v.* make someone or something lose the feeling or power to move: *The accident has paralysed his legs.* **paralysed** /'pærəlaɪzd/ *adj.*

parcel /'pɑːsl/ *n.* thing or things that you wrap and tie up so that you can send it by post or carry it easily.

pardon /'pɑːdn/ *v.* say that you forgive someone for the wrong he has done: *Please pardon me for waking you.* **pardon** *n.* **1** forgiving someone. **2** being forgiven. *beg someone's pardon*, say to someone that you are sorry for the bad or rude thing you have done: *I begged Jon's pardon for arriving late.*

parent /'peərənt/ *n.* father or mother. **parents** *n.* father and mother.

parish /'pærɪʃ/ *n.* (*pl.* parishes) one church and the area that it controls: *The vicar visits all the old people in his parish.*

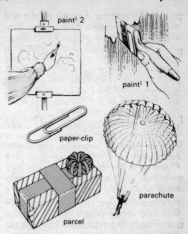

paint² 2

paint² 1

paper-clip

parcel

parachute

park¹ /pɑːk/ *n.* public garden or place in a town where you can walk, sit, and play games: *Hyde Park.*

park² *v.* put or leave a car, lorry, etc. somewhere for a time: *Where can we park the car?* **parking** *n.* leaving cars, etc. for a time: *You can't leave a car where it says 'No Parking'.* **parking-meter** *n.* machine that takes your money and shows the time that you can leave the car in the **parking place.**

parliament /'pɑːləmənt/ *n.* people who discuss and make the laws in a country. **member of parliament** *n.* someone that people have chosen to be in their parliament. **parliamentary** /ˌpɑːlə'mentrɪ/ *adj.*

parrot /'pærət/ *n.* bird that can copy what people say.

parsley /'pɑːslɪ/ *n.* (no *pl.*) small plant with curly leaves that you put in cooking.

parson /'pɑːsn/ *n.* Christian priest.

part¹ /pɑːt/ *n.* **1** some, but not all, of a thing or things: *We spend part of the day at school.* **2** one of several equal bits: *A minute is the sixtieth part of an hour.* **3** someone's share in doing something: *What's your part in the plan?* *take part in something*, work or play with other people in a particular happening: *Please may I take part in your game?* *take someone's part*, help one side in a quarrel, etc.: *When the other boys teased me,* *my brother took my part.* **4** a person in a play, etc. *play a part*, be in a play, film, etc.: *Jane played the part of Cinderella in the school pantomime.* **5** one piece of a machine, watch, bicycle, etc.: *The chain is an important part of a bicycle.* **spare part**, piece of a machine that you keep to use when an old part breaks or wears out. **6 parts** (*pl.*) area; place: *It never gets very cold in these parts.*

part² *v.* go away from each other; make people leave each other: *He waved goodbye when we parted.* **part with**, give something away: *He hates to part with his money so he never buys any gifts.* **part your hair**, make a line or lines by combing the hair in different directions.

participate /pɑːˈtɪsɪpeɪt/ *v.* work or play with other people in a particular happening: *Terry can't participate in the match because he has hurt his foot.* **participation** /pɑːˌtɪsɪˈpeɪʃn/ *n.*

participle /ˈpɑːtɪsɪpl/ *n.* form of a verb: *The present participle of 'hurry' is 'hurrying' and the past participle is 'hurried'.*

particular /pəˈtɪkjʊlə(r)/ *adj.* **1** one only, and not any other: *Are you interested in a particular radio or shall I show you several?* **2** special: *Walk on the icy path with particular care.* **3** careful; wanting something to be exactly right: *Grandad is very particular about his food.*

particularly /pəˈtɪkjʊləlɪ/ *adv.* especially: *I particularly want to see that new film.*

parting /ˈpɑːtɪŋ/ *n.* **1** line where the hair is combed in different directions. **2** leaving: *a sad parting.*

partly /ˈpɑːtlɪ/ *adv.* in some way but not totally: *It was partly my fault, and partly yours.*

partner /ˈpɑːtnə(r)/ *n.* **1** other person, whom you play or dance with; husband or wife. **2** someone who shares a business with another. **partnership** /ˈpɑːtnəʃɪp/ *n.*: *The two brothers are going into partnership in a shop.*

part-time /ˈpɑːt taɪm/ *adj.* that takes some, but not all, of your usual working hours: *a part-time job.*

party /ˈpɑːtɪ/ *n.* (*pl.* parties) **1** meeting of friends to eat, drink, play games, dance, etc.: *a birthday party.* **2** group of

people who have the same political ideas: *the Conservative Party.* **3** group of people travelling or working together: *a party of American tourists.*

pass¹ /pɑːs/ *n.* (*pl.* passes) **1** narrow road or path through high hills or mountains: *the St. Bernard Pass.* **2** doing well enough in an examination, test, etc.: *How many passes did you have in your exams?* **3** special piece of paper that says that you can go into a place, etc.: *Roger has a pass to get into the hospital after visiting hours.* **4** kicking, throwing, or hitting the ball to someone in the same team in football, netball, hockey, etc.

pass² *v.* **1** go by someone or something: *Hugo waved as he passed Hilary in his car.* **2** spend time: *We played cards to pass the evening until the train came.* **3** go by: *A week passed before his letter arrived.* **4** give something to someone: *Please pass me the salt.* **5** do well enough in an examination, etc.: *Arthur passed his driving test.* **pass on**, tell something to another person: *Will you pass on a message to George for me?* **pass out**, faint: *It was so hot that two girls passed out.* **pass through**, go through a place: *The train passes through Reading on its way to Bristol.*

passage /ˈpæsɪdʒ/ *n.* **1** narrow way in a building that leads to other rooms; corridor: *Go along this passage to the library.* **2** part of a book, story, speech, etc.: *an interesting passage.*

passenger /ˈpæsɪndʒə(r)/ *n.* someone who is travelling on a bus, train, ship, aeroplane, etc. **passenger** *adj.*: *a passenger train.*

passer-by /ˌpɑːsə ˈbaɪ/ *n.* (*pl.* passers-by) someone who passes you in the street: *When I fell down, a passer-by helped me to get up.*

passion /ˈpæʃn/ *n.* (no *pl.*) strong feeling of love, hate, or anger.

passive /ˈpæsɪv/ *adj.* form of a verb: *In 'A dog bit Chris' the verb is active, but in 'Chris was bitten by a dog' the verb is passive.*

passport /ˈpɑːspɔːt/ *n.* important little book with your name, photograph, etc. that shows which country you come from.

password /ˈpɑːswɜːd/ *n.* secret word

pause

that you say to show that you are a friend, not an enemy.

past¹ /pɑːst/ *adj.* **1** of the time that has gone: *Henry VIII was a past king of England.* **2** last: *He has been ill for the past two weeks.* **past tense**, form of a verb that shows past time: *In 'James sang in the choir yesterday,' the verb is in the past tense.*

past² *adv.* by: *We couldn't get on the bus because it drove past.*

past³ *n.* **1** (no *pl.*) the time before now; times long ago: *In the past, people had candles to light their homes.* **2** (*pl.* pasts) your life before now: *Tell me about his past.*

past⁴ *prep.* **1** later than; after: *It's seven minutes past three. It's past dinner-time and I'm hungry.* **2** by: *Marie took an apple as she walked past the tree.*

paste /peɪst/ *n.* (no *pl.*) stuff that sticks things together. **paste** *v.* stick something on to another thing with paste: *We pasted the paper on to the wall.*

pastime /'pɑːstaɪm/ *n.* what you like to do when you are not working: *Dancing is Mary's favourite pastime.*

past part. *abbrev.* for past participle in this dictionary.

pastry /'peɪstrɪ/ *n.* **1** (no *pl.*) crust made of flour, fat, and water. **2** (*pl.* pastries) cake or biscuit.

pat /pæt/ *v.* (*pres. part.* patting, *past part.* & *past tense* patted /'pætɪd/) touch something or someone gently with your hand several times: *The little boy patted the dog.* **pat** *n.: a pat on the shoulder.*

patch¹ /pætʃ/ *n.* (*pl.* patches) **1** piece of cloth that you put over a hole in clothing, sheets, etc.: *I sewed a patch over the hole in my jeans.* **2** small part of something that is a different colour: *a dog with a white patch on its back.* **3** place; small piece of ground: *our vegetable patch.*

patch² *v.* put a piece of cloth over a hole or torn place; repair something: *I am patching the elbows of his old pullover.* **patch something up**, mend something roughly. **patch things up, patch up a quarrel**, become friends again after a quarrel.

path /pɑːθ/ *n.* narrow way for people to walk on.

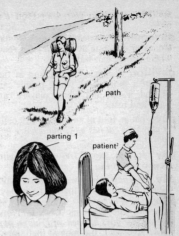

path

parting 1

patient²

patience /'peɪʃns/ *n.* (no *pl.*) being calm when you are waiting or when you have trouble, problems, etc.: *We must have patience until the exam results come out. The job needs a lot of patience.* **lose patience with, be out of patience with,** become angry with someone who is slow or stupid: *He walked so slowly that his brother lost patience with him.*

patient¹ /'peɪʃnt/ *adj.* having or showing patience. **patiently** *adv.: Mr. Scott stood patiently at the bus-stop.*

patient² *n.* sick person whom a doctor is looking after: *Dr. Dyson goes out to visit his patients at 11 o'clock.*

patrol /pə'trəʊl/ *n.* **1** (no *pl.*) **on patrol**, going round a town, camp, etc. to see that all is well: *Why are police on patrol at the airport?* **2** (*pl.* patrols) group of men, ships, aircraft, etc., that go around to look after a place: *an army patrol.* **patrol** *v.* (*pres. part.* patrolling, *past part.* & *past tense* patrolled /pə'trəʊld/): *A guard patrols the gate at night.*

patter /'pætə(r)/ *v.* make quick, light sounds: *Rain was pattering on the windows.* **patter** *n.*

pattern /'pætn/ *n.* **1** plan that you can copy when you want to make something: *Stephanie bought a pattern and made a new dress.* **2** shapes and colours on something; design: *My new curtains have a pretty blue and red pattern.*

pause /pɔːz/ *n.* short stop or wait.

pause v.: *Pause before you cross the road.*

pavement /'peɪvmənt/ n. path of flat stones or concrete at the side of a road where people can walk.

pavilion /pə'vɪlɪən/ n. building at the side of a sports field, where people can sit and watch and where players can wash and rest.

paw /pɔ:/ n. foot of an animal with nails or claws: *A cat has paws but a horse has hooves.*

pay[1] /peɪ/ n. (no pl.) money that you receive for work.

pay[2] v. (past part. & past tense paid /peɪd/) **1** give money for what you buy: *I paid £50 for this dress.* **2** give money to someone who has done work for you: *The builder pays his men on Fridays.* **pay back**, give back the money that someone has lent you. **pay someone back**, harm someone who has harmed you: *One day I'll pay back that boy who broke my bike!* **pay for**, (a) give money for what you buy. (b) be hurt or punished for doing wrong: *He paid for his laziness by not passing his exam.*

payment /'peɪmənt/ n. **1** (no pl.) paying: *This money is in payment for the work you have done.* **2** (pl. payments) sum of money that you pay: *I am buying my bicycle with monthly payments of £4.*

pea /pi:/ n. vegetable like a very small, green ball.

peace /pi:s/ n. (no pl.) **1** time when there is no fighting, war, or trouble between countries. **make peace**, end a war or a fight: *The two countries made peace.* **2** quiet; rest: *There is peace in the countryside at night.* **in peace**, quiet; calm and happy: *Leave me in peace to read my book.*

peaceful /'pi:sfl/ adj. **1** quiet: *a peaceful evening.* **2** with no fighting: *a peaceful discussion.* **peacefully** adv.

peach /pi:tʃ/ n. (pl. peaches) round, juicy fruit with a yellow-red skin.

peacock /'pi:kɒk/ n. big, male bird with beautiful, long tail feathers.

peak /pi:k/ n. **1** pointed top of a hill or mountain. **2** hard front part of a cap.

peal /pi:l/ v. ring loudly: *The bells were pealing.* **peal** n.: *peals of laughter; a peal of thunder.*

peanut /'pi:nʌt/ n. sort of nut that you can eat.

pear /peə(r)/ n. juicy green or yellow fruit.

pearl /pɜ:l/ n. precious stone like a small, white ball, which comes from an oyster. **pearl** adj. with a pearl in it: *a pearl ring.*

peasant /'peznt/ n. poor person who lives in the country and works on his own small piece of land.

pebble /'pebl/ n. small, round stone on a beach or in a river.

peck /pek/ v. eat or bite something with the beak: *The hens pecked corn from the ground.* **peck** n.

peculiar /pɪ'kju:lɪə(r)/ adj. strange; not usual: *a peculiar noise.*

pedal /'pedl/ n. part of a bicycle, or other machine, that you move with your feet. **pedal** v. (pres. part. pedalling, past part. & past tense pedalled /'pedld/) move pedals with your feet: *You must pedal hard when you ride a bicycle up a hill.*

pedestrian /pɪ'destrɪən/ n. someone who is walking in a street, etc. **pedestrian** adj.: *A pedestrian crossing is a place where cars must stop so that people can walk over the road.*

peel[1] /pi:l/ n. (no pl.) skin of some fruit or vegetables: *orange peel.*

peel[2] v. **1** take the skin off fruit, etc.: *I peeled the potatoes before boiling them.* **2** come off in thin pieces: *Your skin will peel if you lie in the sun too much.*

peep /pi:p/ v. **1** look at something quickly: *She peeped through the keyhole.* **2** come out for a short time; be partly seen: *The moon peeped out from behind the clouds.* **peep** n.: *Can we have a peep at your holiday photographs?*

peer /pɪə(r)/ v. look at something closely because you cannot see well: *He had to peer at his book because the room was dark.*

peg[1] /peg/ n. **1** piece of wood, metal, or plastic on a wall or door, where you can hang clothes, etc.: *He put his hat on the peg.* **2** wood or metal thing that you put into the ground to hold a rope: *a tent-*

peg. **3** wooden or plastic clip that holds wet clothes on a line when they are drying.

peg² *v.* (*pres. part.* pegging, *past part.* & *past tense* pegged /pegd/) fix something with pegs: *I pegged the washing on the line.*

pen¹ /pen/ *n.* instrument for writing with ink.

pen² *n.* small place where you can keep sheep, cattle, etc. safe.

penalty /'penəltɪ/ *n.* punishment: *What is the penalty for speeding?*

pence /pens/ *n.* (*pl.*) pennies.

pencil /'pensl/ *n.* instrument for writing and drawing, made of a thin piece of wood with lead, etc. inside it.

penetrate /'penɪtreɪt/ *v.* go into or through something: *A nail penetrated the car tyre.*

pen-friend /'pen frend/ *n.* someone in another country whom you write to but probably have never seen.

penguin /'peŋgwɪn/ *n.* bird that lives in very cold places and can swim but not fly.

peninsula /pə'nɪnsjʊlə/ *n.* long, narrow piece of land with water on three sides: *Italy is a peninsula.*

pen-knife /'pen naɪf/ *n.* (*pl.* pen-knives) small knife that folds, so that you can put it in your pocket.

penny /'penɪ/ *n.* (*pl.* pence or pennies) piece of British money.

pension /'penʃn/ *n.* money that you receive from a company or a government when you are old and do not work any longer. **pensioner** *n.* someone who has a pension.

people /'pi:pl/ *n.* (*pl.*) persons; men, women, and children: *The streets were crowded with people.*

pepper /'pepə(r)/ *n.* (no *pl.*) powder with a hot taste, which we put on food. **pepper** *v.* put pepper on food. **peppery** *adj.*: *a peppery dish.*

peppermint /'pepəmɪnt/ *n.* **1** (no *pl.*) sort of plant that gives an oil with a nice taste. **2** (*pl.* peppermints) sort of sweet.

per /pɜː(r)/ *prep.* for each; in each: *My car can do 140 kilometres per hour.* **per cent** %, for each hundred: *If her*

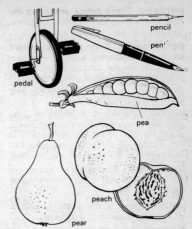

pencil

pen¹

pedal

pea

peach

pear

answers are all correct, she'll get a mark of one hundred per cent.

perch¹ /pɜːtʃ/ *n.* (*pl.* perches) place where a bird sits.

perch² *v.* **1** fly down and rest on something: *The birds perched on the big tree.* **2** sit or be on something high: *Sandra perched on a tall stool in the coffee bar.*

perfect /'pɜːfɪkt/ *adj.* completely correct and good; with nothing wrong: *a perfect diamond.* **perfect tense**, form of a verb that shows past time: *In the sentence 'He has seen the film', the verb is in the perfect tense.*

perfectly /'pɜːfɪktlɪ/ *adv.* **1** totally: *He is perfectly happy in his new job.* **2** extremely well: *Janet sings perfectly.*

perform /pə'fɔːm/ *v.* **1** do work, etc.; function: *Is the new car performing well?* **2** be in a play, film, concert, etc.: *The clown performed tricks in the circus ring.* **performer** *n.* someone who acts or sings.

performance /pə'fɔːməns/ *n.* **1** doing work; something that you do: *Val's poor performance at school.* **2** being in a play, concert, etc.: *The pianist gave a fine performance.* **3** time when you can go to a play, etc.: *Shall we go to the afternoon or the evening performance of the ballet?*

perfume /'pɜːfjuːm/ *n.* **1** scent; liquid with a sweet smell, which you put on your body. **2** any sweet smell: *the perfume of roses.*

perhaps /pə'hæps/ *adv.* maybe; possibly: *Perhaps I'll see him tomorrow, but I'm not sure.*

peril /'perɪl/ *n.* **1** (no *pl.*) great danger: *He was in great peril when the wind sent his boat on the rocks.* **2** (*pl.* perils) something that brings great danger: *Ice is a peril on the road.* **perilous** *adj.* dangerous. **perilously** *adv.*

period /'pɪərɪəd/ *n.* **1** length of time: *One day is a period of twenty-four hours.* **2** certain time in the life of a person, in the history of a country, etc.: *the Victorian period.* **3** lesson: *the maths period.*

periodical /,pɪərɪ'ɒdɪkl/ *n.* newspaper or magazine that comes every week, month, etc.

perish /'perɪʃ/ *v.* die; come to an end: *Many people perished in the fire.*

permanent /'pɜːmənənt/ *adj.* for always; for a long time; not changing: *a permanent job.* **permanently** *adv.* always.

permission /pə'mɪʃn/ *n.* (no *pl.*) allowing someone to do something: *May I have permission to leave early?*

permit[1] /'pɜːmɪt/ *n.* letter or paper that says you can do something, go somewhere, etc.: *You must get a permit if you want to keep a gun.*

permit[2] /pə'mɪt/ *v. pres. part.* permitting, *past part. & past tense* permitted /pə'mɪtɪd/) allow someone to do something: *They do not permit smoking in the theatre.*

persecute /'pɜːsɪkjuːt/ *v.* be very cruel to someone because of what he believes: *The Romans persecuted the first Christians.* **persecution** /,pɜːsɪ'kjuːʃn/ *n.*

persist /pə'sɪst/ *v.* go on doing something: *The rain persisted all day.* **persistent** *adj.* **persistently** *adv.*

person /'pɜːsn/ *n.* man, woman, or child: *We have room for another person in the car.* **in person**, yourself: *I was there in person, so I saw what happened.*

personal /'pɜːsnl/ *adj.* private; of or for one person: *This letter is personal, and I don't want anyone else to read it.*

personality /,pɜːsə'nælətɪ/ *n.* (*pl.* personalities) **1** character; what sort of person you are: *Ray has a happy personality.* **2** well-known person: *Mohammed Ali is a boxing personality.*

personally /'pɜːsənəlɪ/ *adv.* speaking for yourself: *Personally, I like him, but many people do not.*

perspire /pə'spaɪə(r)/ *v.* sweat. **perspiration** /,pɜːspə'reɪʃn/ *n.*

persuade /pə'sweɪd/ *v.* make someone believe or do something by talking to him: *I persuaded Robert that the journey was too dangerous and he didn't go.* **persuasion** /pə'sweɪʒn/ *n.*

pessimist /'pesɪmɪst/ *n.* someone who believes the worst will happen. **pessimistic** /,pesɪ'mɪstɪk/ *adj.*: *That pessimistic boy thinks that he will fail his exams.* **pessimistically** *adv.*

pest /pest/ *n.* **1** insect or animal that eats crops or damages them. **2** person or thing that gives you worry or trouble: *My little brother is a pest when he spoils my games.*

pester /'pestə(r)/ *v.* trouble someone; go to someone again and again and make him rather angry: *Don't pester me with questions when I'm busy!*

pet /pet/ *n.* **1** animal, etc. that you like very much and keep in the garden or house: *Sammy has two pets—a goldfish and a cat.* **2** child that a parent or teacher likes best of all.

petition /pɪ'tɪʃn/ *n.* special letter from a group of people that asks for something: *Many people signed the petition for a pedestrian crossing.*

petrol /'petrəl/ *n.* (no *pl.*) sort of oil that makes car-engines go. **petrol station** *n.* place where you can buy petrol. **petrol tanker** *n.* big lorry that carries petrol. **petrol** *adj.*: *a petrol tank.*

petticoat /'petɪkəʊt/ *n.* piece of clothing that a woman or girl wears under her dress, etc.

phantom /'fæntəm/ *n.* ghost.

philosophy /fɪ'lɒsəfɪ/ *n.* **1** (no *pl.*) study of life; thinking about life and man. **2** (*pl.* philosophies) what one person thinks about life. **philosopher** /fɪ'lɒsəfə(r)/ *n.* someone who studies philosophy.

phone /fəʊn/ *abbrev.* telephone: *I phoned my sister last night. She speaks quietly on the phone.* **phone box, phone booth** *n.* small building with a public telephone.

phonetics /fə'netɪks/ n. (no pl.) study of the sounds of a language; the signs that you use to write the sounds of a language. **phonetic** adj.: *Each new word in this dictionary has phonetic symbols after it to show you how to say the word.*

phoney /'fəʊnɪ/ adj. that seems to be real or true but is not: *a phoney story.*

photo /'fəʊtəʊ/, **photograph** /'fəʊtə-grɑ:f/ n. picture that you make with a camera. **photograph** v.: *They photographed the winning team.* **photographer** /fə'tɒɡrəfə(r)/ n. someone who takes pictures with a camera. **photography** /fə'tɒɡrəfɪ/ n. **photographic** /fəʊtə'ɡræfɪk/ adj.

phrase /freɪz/ n. group of words in a sentence: *The words 'a quiet little village' make a phrase.*

physical /'fɪzɪkl/ adj. **1** of things that you can see, touch, etc.: *the physical world.* **2** of the body: *physical pain.* **physically** adv.

physician /fɪ'zɪʃn/ n. doctor of medicine.

physics /'fɪzɪks/ n. (no pl.) study of heat, light, sound, etc. **physicist** /'fɪzɪsɪst/ n. someone who studies physics.

piano /pɪ'ænəʊ/ n. big musical instrument with black and white keys that you press to make music. **pianist** /'pɪənɪst/ n. someone who plays a piano.

pick[1] /pɪk/ n. heavy instrument for breaking roads, stones, etc.

pick[2] n. (no pl.) choosing; what you choose. **take your pick**, choose what you like: *The greengrocer told me to take my pick of the apples, so I chose the big, ripe ones.*

pick[3] v. **1** take something up with the fingers; gather things: *Pat picked some flowers to put in a vase.* **2** choose someone or something: *The sports-master picked the best boys for the team.* **pick someone or something out**, be able to see someone or something in a lot of others: *There's such a big crowd that I can't pick Samuel out.* **pick up, (a)** lift someone or something from the ground: *He picked up his crying child.* **(b)** learn something without studying it especially: *If you go to England, you'll soon pick up English.*

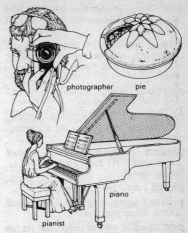

photographer   pie

piano

pianist

picket /'pɪkɪt/ v. stand outside a factory, office, etc., trying to stop other people from going inside to work, when there is a strike. **picket** n. someone who pickets: *Are there pickets outside the docks?*

pickpocket /'pɪkpɒkɪt/ n. someone who steals things from people's pockets.

picnic /'pɪknɪk/ v. (pres. part. picnicking, past part. & past tense picnicked /'pɪknɪkt/) eat a meal outside, away from home: *We picnicked on the beach yesterday.* **picnic** n.: *We had a picnic by the river.* **picnic** adj.: *a picnic basket.*

picture /'pɪktʃə(r)/ n. **1** drawing, painting, or photograph of someone or something: *Annette painted a picture of a flower.* **take a picture**, make a photograph. **2** film that you can see at a cinema. **the pictures**, the cinema.

pie /paɪ/ n. dish of meat or fruit covered with pastry and cooked.

piece /pi:s/ n. **1** bit or part of something: *Will you have a piece of cake?* **give someone a piece of your mind**, tell someone angrily what you think about him. **in pieces**, broken: *She has dropped the cup and it is now in pieces.* **take something to pieces**, divide something into its parts: *He's taking his bicycle to pieces to see how it works.* **2** one single thing: *a piece of furniture.* **3** coin: *a 50p piece.* **4** one of a set or group: *A three-piece suite has two chairs and a sofa.*

pier /pɪə(r)/ n. wall from the land into the sea, where people can get on and off boats.

pierce /pɪəs/ v. go into or through something; make a hole in something: *The pin pierced his finger and it began to bleed.*

piercing /'pɪəsɪŋ/ adj. sharp; very clear and loud: *a piercing cry.*

pig /pɪg/ n. **1** fat farm animal. **2** greedy or unkind person. *make a pig of yourself,* eat too much.

pigeon /'pɪdʒɪn/ n. bird that you often see in towns: *We fed the pigeons in Trafalgar Square.*

piglet /'pɪglɪt/ n. young pig.

pigsty /'pɪgstaɪ/ n. (pl. pigsties) place on a farm where pigs live.

pile¹ /paɪl/ n. a lot of things, one on top of the other; heap: *a pile of books.*

pile² /paɪl/ v. put a lot of things on top of one another: *He piled food on to his plate.* *pile up,* become bigger, more, etc.: *His work at the office piled up when he was in hospital.*

pilgrim /'pɪlgrɪm/ n. someone who travels a long way to a place because it is holy. **pilgrimage** /'pɪlgrɪmɪdʒ/ n. journey of a pilgrim.

pill /pɪl/ n. small, round hard piece of medicine, which you swallow.

pillar /'pɪlə(r)/ n. tall, strong piece of wood, stone, etc., to hold up a building.

pillar-box /'pɪlə bɒks/ n. (pl. pillar-boxes) tall letter-box in the street.

pillow /'pɪləʊ/ n. soft thing where you put your head when you are in bed. **pillow-case, pillow-slip** n. cover for a pillow.

pilot /'paɪlət/ n. **1** someone who flies an aeroplane. **2** someone who guides a ship the safe way up a river into harbour, etc. **pilot** v. fly an aeroplane; guide a boat.

pimple /'pɪmpl/ n. small, sore place on skin. **pimply** adj.

pin¹ /pɪn/ n. very small, thin piece of metal with a flat head at one end and a sharp point at the other, which holds together pieces of cloth, paper, etc. *pins and needles,* funny feeling in part of your body: *She had pins and needles in her hand after she had been lying on it.* **drawing-pin** n. short pin with a flat top, which fastens papers to a wall, board, etc. **safety-pin** n. pin with a cover over its point.

pin² v. (pres. part. pinning, past part. & past tense pinned /pɪnd/) **1** fasten things together with a pin or pins: *Judy pinned the pieces of cloth together before she sewed them.* **2** hold someone or something so that he or it cannot move away: *The car turned over and pinned the driver underneath it.*

pinafore /'pɪnəfɔː(r)/ n. apron; piece of clothing that a woman or girl wears over other clothes to keep them clean.

pinch¹ /pɪntʃ/ n. (pl. pinches) **1** holding or pressing something between your thumb and first finger: *He gave my arm a pinch.* **2** how much you can hold with your thumb and first finger: *a pinch of salt.*

pinch² v. **1** take something tightly between your thumb and first finger: *Don't pinch me, it hurts!* **2** catch or trap something in a tight place: *Ow! I've pinched my fingers in the car door!* **3** hurt someone because it is too tight: *These shoes pinch.* **4** steal something; take something without asking: *Who has pinched my pencil?*

pine /paɪn/ n. tree that has leaves like long needles.

pineapple /'paɪnæpl/ n. big, juicy fruit.

ping-pong /'pɪŋpɒŋ/ n. (no pl.) table-tennis; game where players hit a small white ball over a net on a big table. **ping-pong** adj.: *a ping-pong ball.*

pink /pɪŋk/ adj. with a pale red colour. **pink** n.

pint /paɪnt/ n. measure of liquid = 0.57 litre.

pioneer /ˌpaɪə'nɪə(r)/ n. someone who goes to a new country to live or work: *The Pilgrim Fathers were pioneers.*

pip /pɪp/ n. seed in a lemon, orange, apple, grapefruit, etc.

pipe /paɪp/ n. **1** tube that takes water, oil, gas, etc. from one place to another. **2** thing for smoking tobacco, etc. **3** sort of musical instrument.

piper /'paɪpə(r)/ n. someone who makes music with a pipe or bagpipes.

pirate /'paɪrət/ *n.* someone who sails on the sea and robs other ships.

pistol /'pɪstl/ *n.* small gun.

pit /pɪt/ *n.* **1** deep hole in the earth. **2** coal-mine: *Gareth works down the pit.*

pitch[1] /pɪtʃ/ *n.* **1** (*pl.* pitches) piece of ground where you play cricket. **2** (*pl.* pitches) how high or low a voice or other sound is.

pitch[2] *v.* **pitch a tent**, put up a tent.

pitiful /'pɪtɪfl/ *adj.* making you feel pity: *The hungry dog was a pitiful sight.* **pitifully** *adv.*

pity[1] /'pɪtɪ/ *n.* (no *pl.*) sadness for the troubles, pain, etc. of another person: *I felt pity for the blind child.* **take** or **have pity on**, feel sorry for someone and help him: *She took pity on the beggar, and gave him some food.* **it's a pity, what a pity**, it is sad: *What a pity you can't come to the party.*

pity[2] *v.* feel sorry for someone: *I pity people who cannot sleep at night.*

pl. *abbrev.* for plural in this dictionary.

placard /'plækɑːd/ *n.* big piece of card or paper with something written on it, which you put up or carry so that people can see it.

place[1] /pleɪs/ *n.* **1** where something or someone is: *That table is the best place for the flowers.* **2** town, village, etc.: *What's the name of this place?* **3** building or piece of land for something special: *An office is a place of work.* **4** seat: *Another boy was sitting in my place.* **5** page that you are reading in a book: *I dropped the book and lost my place.* **6** where you finish in a race: *Percy was first, and Jim was in second place.* **in place**, where you want them; tidy: *Are all the chairs in place?* **in place of**, instead of: *Sebastian became captain in place of Miles who had broken his leg.* **take place**, happen; occur: *When did the accident take place?* **take the place of**, do the job of someone: *When his secretary went on holiday, Miss Tyson took her place for a week.*

place[2] *v.* **1** put something somewhere: *The waiter placed the meal in front of me.* **2** give someone a certain job to do: *They placed Giles in charge of the group.* **3** give an order to a shop, etc.: *I've placed an order for a new car with a firm in Nottingham.*

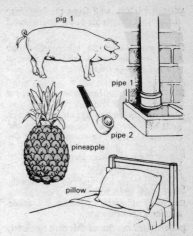

pig 1

pipe 1

pipe 2

pineapple

pillow

plain[1] /pleɪn/ *adj.* **1** easy to hear, see, or understand; clear: *It's plain that she doesn't like the job because she's trying to find another.* **2** ordinary; simple: *plain food.* **3** not pretty: *a plain girl.* **4** with no pattern: *plain blue material.* **plain-clothes** *adj.* not in uniform: *a plain-clothes policeman.*

plain[2] *n.* piece of flat country.

plainly /'pleɪnlɪ/ *adv.* clearly.

plait /plæt/ *v.* take three or more pieces of hair, string, straw, etc. and weave or twist them together: *Will you plait my hair for me?* **plait** *n.*: *I wear my hair in plaits.*

plan[1] /plæn/ *v.* (*pres. part.* planning, *past part & past tense* planned /plænd/) think or say what you will do, how you will do it, etc.: *We're planning a tour of Italy this summer.*

plan[2] *n.* **1** idea or arrangement for the future: *What are your holiday plans?* **2** drawing for a new building, machine, etc. **3** map: *a plan of the town.*

plane /pleɪn/ *abbrev.* aeroplane.

planet /'plænɪt/ *n.* thing in the sky that moves round the sun: *Mars and Venus are planets of the sun.*

plank /plæŋk/ *n.* long, flat piece of wood; board.

plant[1] /plɑːnt/ *n.* any thing that grows from the ground.

plant² *v.* put seeds, flowers, vegetables, etc. in the ground to grow: *We planted some roses.*

plantation /plɑ:n'teɪʃn/ *n.* piece of land where trees or bushes grow as crops: *a plantation of fir trees.*

plaster /'plɑ:stə(r)/ *n.* **1** (no *pl.*) stuff that you put over bricks, etc. to make a smooth wall. **2** (no *pl.*) stuff that you put round a broken leg, etc. It becomes hard and keeps the leg safe: *After the accident Dorothy's arm was in plaster for three weeks.* **3** (*pl.* plasters) piece of sticky cloth that you put over a cut to keep it clean and safe.

plastic /'plæstɪk/ *n.* (no *pl.*) light, strong stuff made in factories: *Our picnic plates are made of plastic.* **plastic** *adj.* made of plastic: *plastic cups.*

plate /pleɪt/ *n.* round, flat dish for food.

platform /'plætfɔ:m/ *n.* **1** part of a railway station where you get on and off trains: *Which is the platform for the London train?* **2** place higher than the floor or the ground where a speaker, etc. stands: *Each pupil came up to the platform for his prize.*

play¹ /pleɪ/ *n.* (no *pl.*) **1** games; what children do for fun: *Is it time for play?* **2** way of doing a game, sport, etc.: *There was a lot of rough play in the football match.*

play² *n.* story that you act on the stage, radio, etc.: *'Hamlet' is a play by Shakespeare.*

play³ *v.* **1** have fun; do things to enjoy yourself: *The children are playing with their toys.* **2** take part in a game: *Do you play tennis?* **play fair**, (*a*) keep the rules. (*b*) be fair to people. **3** make music with a musical instrument: *Do you play the piano?* **4** act a part in a play: *Quentin will play Hamlet.*

player /'pleɪə(r)/ *n.* **1** someone who plays a game: *football players.* **2** someone who makes music on an instrument: *the best player in the orchestra.*

playful /'pleɪfl/ *adj.* wanting to play; not serious: *a playful puppy.* **playfully** *adv.*

playground /'pleɪɡraʊnd/ *n.* piece of ground where children play in a school, park, etc.

playing-field /'pleɪɪŋ fi:ld/ *n.* field for games of cricket, football, etc.

playmate /'pleɪmeɪt/ *n.* child who plays with another child.

plea /pli:/ *n.* asking for something with strong feeling: *a plea for help.*

plead /pli:d/ *v.* **1** beg; ask strongly. **plead with**, ask someone for something, with strong feeling. **2** speak for your own case in a court of law. **plead guilty**, say that you did the crime. **plead not guilty**, say that you did not do the crime.

pleasant /'pleznt/ *adj.* nice; that you enjoy: *We had a pleasant evening at Alan's house.* **pleasantly** *adv.*: *It is pleasantly warm in May.*

please /pli:z/ *v.* **1** word that you say when you ask for something politely: *Will you give me an apple, please?* **2** make someone happy; satisfy someone: *That picture pleases me.* **as you please**, as you wish: *Stay as long as you please.*

pleased /pli:zd/ *adj.* glad; happy: *I'm pleased to see you, Adam.*

pleasing /'pli:zɪŋ/ *adj.* nice; that you like or enjoy: *pleasing music.*

pleasure /'pleʒə(r)/ *n.* **1** (no *pl.*) feeling of being happy; enjoyment: *I go sailing for pleasure.* **take pleasure in**, enjoy something: *I take pleasure in gardening.* **with pleasure**, gladly: *I'll help you with pleasure.* **2** (*pl.* pleasures) thing that gives happiness: *His work leaves him no time for pleasures.*

pleated /'pli:tɪd/ *adj.* with regular folds: *a pleated skirt.*

plenty /'plentɪ/ *n.* (no *pl.*) a large number; as much as you need: *I didn't hurry because I had plenty of time.* **plentiful** /'plentɪfl/ *adj.*: *Tomatoes are plentiful in the summer.* **plentifully** *adv.*

pliers /'plaɪəz/ *n.* (*pl.*) instrument for holding things tightly, pulling nails out of wood, etc.

plod /plɒd/ *v.* (*pres. part.* plodding, *past part.* & *past tense* plodded /'plɒdɪd/) walk slowly, in a heavy, tired way.

plot¹ /plɒt/ *n.* **1** secret plan, usually to do wrong: *a plot to rob the bank.* **2** small piece of land: *a vegetable plot.* **3** what happens in a story or play: *an exciting plot.*

plot² *v.* (*pres. part.* plotting, *past part.* &

past tense plotted /'plɒtɪd/) make a secret plan for doing wrong: *Guy Fawkes plotted to blow up parliament.*

plough /plaʊ/ *v.* cut and turn over the soil: *The farmer ploughed the field before he planted the corn.* **plough** *n.* thing that a tractor pulls to plough soil.

pluck /plʌk/ *n.* (no *pl.*) courage; bravery. **plucky** *adj.*

plug /plʌg/ *n.* **1** round thing that you put in the hole in a wash-basin or bath: *Take the plug out of the sink and let the water out.* **2** thing that joins a lamp, machine, etc. to the point in the wall where there is electricity. **plug** *v.* (*pres. part.* plugging, *past part.* & *past tense* plugged /plʌgd/) **1** fill a hole in something with a plug. **2** *plug in*, put the electric plug of a machine, etc. into the electric point in the wall: *The lamp will not work until you plug it in.*

plum /plʌm/ *n.* round, juicy fruit.

plumber /'plʌmə(r)/ *n.* someone whose job is to put in and mend water-pipes, wash-basins, etc.

plump /plʌmp/ *adj.* round and fat: *plump cheeks.*

plunge /plʌndʒ/ *v.* jump down suddenly; fall fast: *Rebecca plunged into the pool.* **plunge** *n.*

plural /'plʊərəl/ *n.* form of a word that shows that there is more than one: *The plural of 'dog' is 'dogs'.* **plural** *adj.*: *'Dogs' is a plural noun.*

plus /plʌs/ *prep.* and; added to: *Four plus five is nine.*

p.m. /ˌpi: 'em/ *abbrev.* (Latin *post meridiem*) between midday and midnight: *Our friends came at 5 p.m.*

pneumonia /njuː'məʊnɪə/ *n.* (no *pl.*) serious illness of the lungs.

poach[1] /pəʊtʃ/ *v.* cook food gently in water or other liquid. **poached** /pəʊtʃt/ *adj.*: *a poached egg.*

poach[2] *v.* kill and steal animals, fish, or birds from another person's land. **poacher** *n.* someone who poaches.

P.O. Box /ˌpi: əʊ bɒks/ *abbrev.* Post Office Box; box in a post office to take the letters of one person or office.

pocket /'pɒkɪt/ *n.* small bag in your clothes for carrying things: *I have a handkerchief in my pocket.* **pick**

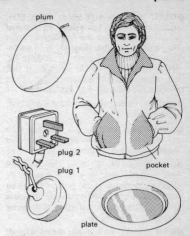

plum

plug 2

plug 1

pocket

plate

someone's pocket, steal from someone's pocket.

pocket-money /'pɒkɪt mʌnɪ/ *n.* (no *pl.*) money that parents give to a child each week to buy small things.

pod /pɒd/ *n.* long, narrow part of a plant, that holds peas, beans, and other seeds.

poem /'pəʊɪm/ *n.* piece of writing in verse.

poet /'pəʊɪt/ *n.* writer of poems: *Keats is a famous poet.*

poetry /'pəʊɪtrɪ/ *n.* (no *pl.*) poems: *Wordsworth wrote beautiful poetry.*

point[1] /pɔɪnt/ *n.* **1** thin, sharp end: *the point of a pin.* **2** dot (·) **decimal point** *n.* dot that shows part of a whole number: *2·5 (two point five).* **3** certain place or time: *It started to rain and, at that point, we went home.* **4** most important idea; purpose: *The point of going to school is to learn.* **5** mark that you win in a game or sport: *Our team scored five points.* **points of the compass**, 32 marks on a compass that show direction. *point of view*, way of thinking about something: *I understand your point of view. miss the point*, not understand what someone is trying to say. *on the point of*, just going to do something: *I was on the point of going out when the phone rang. there's no point in*, there's no good reason for doing something: *There's no point in hanging out washing when it is raining.*

point² *v.* show with your finger, arm, stick, etc. where something is: *I asked where the bank was and he pointed across the road.* **point something at**, hold something towards someone or something: *He pointed a gun at the deer.* **point out**, tell about or show something: *Evan pointed out that my bag was open.*

pointed /'pɔɪntɪd/ *adj.* with a sharp end: *a pointed stick.*

pointless /'pɔɪntlɪs/ *adj.* wasted; with no purpose: *It is pointless to hang out washing when it is raining.*

poison /'pɔɪzn/ *n.* thing that will kill you or make you very ill if you eat or drink it. **poison** *v.* use poison to kill or hurt someone. **poisonous** *adj.* that will bring illness or death if you eat it: *Some berries are poisonous.*

poke /pəʊk/ *v.* **1** push something or someone with your finger, a stick, etc. **2** move something to a place: *Poke your head through the door and see who is there.* **poke** *n.*: *She gave the potatoes a poke to see if they were soft.*

poker /'pəʊkə(r)/ *n.* **1** (*pl.* pokers) long stick of metal for moving wood, coal, etc. in a fire. **2** (no *pl.*) sort of card game.

polar /'pəʊlə(r)/ *adj.* of the North or South Pole: *a polar expedition.*

pole¹ /pəʊl/ *n.* tall piece of wood or metal that stands in the ground to hold something up: *a flag pole; telegraph poles.*

pole² *n.* **North Pole, South Pole**, the north and south points of the earth.

police /pə'li:s/ *n.* (*pl.*) group of men and women whose job is to keep order and see that people do not break the law of the country. **policeman** /pə'li:smən/, **policewoman** /pə'li:swʊmən/ *n.* member of the police. **police-station** *n.* office of the police.

policy /'pɒləsɪ/ *n.* (*pl.* policies) general plan of a government, business, company, etc.: *What is the government's policy on education?*

polish /'pɒlɪʃ/ *v.* rub something so that it shines: *She polished her dirty shoes.* **polish** *n.* **1** polishing something: *I gave the window a polish.* **2** oily stuff that you use to polish something: *a tin of shoe-polish.*

polite /pə'laɪt/ *adj.* not rude; talking and acting in a way that does not make other people sad, angry, etc.: *It is polite to say 'Please' when you ask for something.* **politely** *adv.* **politeness** *n.*

political /pə'lɪtɪkl/ *adj.* of government: *A political party is a group of people who have the same ideas about the government of their country.* **politically** *adv.* **politician** /ˌpɒlɪ'tɪʃn/ *n.* someone who works in politics: *Members of Parliament are politicians.*

politics /'pɒlɪtɪks/ *n.* (no *pl.*) **1** work of government. **2** study of government.

polytechnic /ˌpɒlɪ'teknɪk/ *n.* place where people go to study technical subjects.

pond /pɒnd/ *n.* small lake.

pony /'pəʊnɪ/ *n.* (*pl.* ponies) small horse.

pool¹ /pu:l/ *n.* **1** hollow in the ground, where water lies: *There were pools of water on the road after the storm.* **2** place for swimming: *Perry dived into the pool.*

pool² *v.* put money, etc. together for something that all can use: *The three brothers pooled their money to buy a car.*

poor¹ /pʊə(r)/ *adj.* **1** with very little money: *She is too poor to buy a warm coat.* **2** that makes you feel sad: *That poor man has no friends.* **3** not good: *Vegetables don't grow well in poor soil.*

poor² *n.* (*pl.*) **the poor**, people who have very little money, etc.

poorly /'pʊəlɪ/ *adv.* badly: *The streets were poorly lit.* **poorly off**, having very little money: *She was very poorly off when her husband died.*

pop¹ /pɒp/ *abbrev.* popular music. **pop stars, pop groups**, singers and players that make pop music.

pop² *n.* short, sharp sound: *The cork came out of the bottle with a pop.*

pop³ *v.* (*pres. part.* popping, *past part.* & *past tense* popped /pɒpt/) **1** burst with a short, sharp sound: *The balloon will pop if you put a pin in it.* **2** go quickly: *I'll pop over the road and buy an ice-cream.* **3** do something quickly: *Kay popped a sweet in her mouth.*

popular /'pɒpjʊlə(r)/ *adj.* that many

people like: *Football is a popular sport.*
popularity /ˌpɒpjuˈlærətɪ/ *n.*

population /ˌpɒpjuˈleɪʃn/ *n.* the number
of people who live in a place, country,
etc.: *What is the population of London?*

porcelain /ˈpɔːsəlɪn/ *n.* (no *pl.*) sort of
white china. **porcelain** *adj.* made of
porcelain.

porch /pɔːtʃ/ *n.* (*pl.* porches) roof and
walls round the outside of a doorway: *We
sheltered from the rain in the church
porch.*

pork /pɔːk/ *n.* (no *pl.*) meat from a pig.

porridge /ˈpɒrɪdʒ/ *n.* (no *pl.*) soft food
made from oats and water, which
British people eat for breakfast.

port /pɔːt/ *n.* town or city with a harbour: *Liverpool is a big port.*

portable /ˈpɔːtəbl/ *adj.* that you can
carry about; not fixed: *a portable radio.*

porter /ˈpɔːtə(r)/ *n.* man in a hotel, station, or airport, who carries your baggage.

porthole /ˈpɔːthəʊl/ *n.* small, round
window in the side of a ship or aeroplane.

portion /ˈpɔːʃn/ *n.* share; how much
one person gets.

portrait /ˈpɔːtrɪt/ *n.* painting or picture
of someone: *There is a portrait of the
mayor in the city hall.*

position /pəˈzɪʃn/ *n.* **1** place where
someone or something is: *Can you show
me the position of your village on the
map?* **in position**, in the right place. **out of
position**, not in the right place. **2** way in
which someone or something is placed:
Are you sitting in a comfortable position?
3 how things are: *He's in a difficult position because he hasn't enough money to
finish his studies.* **4** job: *My brother has
a position in a bank.*

positive /ˈpɒzɪtɪv/ *adj.* sure; certain: *Are
you positive that you put the key in your
pocket?* **positively** *adv.* definitely; certainly.

possess /pəˈzes/ *v.* have or own something: *He lost all that he possessed when
his house burned down.*

possession /pəˈzeʃn/ *n.* **1** (no *pl.*)
having or owning something. **for possession of**, to get or take something: *The
players fought for possession of the ball.*

policeman

porch

pool² 2

2 (*pl.* possessions) something that you
have or own: *We lost all our possessions
in the floods.*

possibility /ˌpɒsəˈbɪlətɪ/ *n.* (*pl.* possi-
bilities) something that can happen:
*Take your umbrella because there's a
possibility it will rain.*

possible /ˈpɒsəbl/ *adj.* that can
happen: *Is it possible to walk there in
an hour?*

possibly /ˈpɒsəblɪ/ *adv.* **1** in a way that
can be done: *I'll come as soon as I possibly can.* **2** perhaps: *Will it be ready
tomorrow? Possibly.*

post¹ /pəʊst/ *n.* tall piece of wood or
metal that stands in the ground to hold
something up or to mark something: *a
signpost.*

post² *n.* (no *pl.*) letters and parcels that
you send: *I sent her birthday present by
post.* **postal** /ˈpəʊstl/ *adj.* of the post:
postal charges.

post³ *n.* **1** place where a soldier is on
duty. **2** job: *a teaching post.*

post⁴ *v.* **1** send letters, parcels, etc. by
mail. **2** send someone to a place to do a
certain job: *Sandra's firm has posted her
abroad for two years.*

postage /ˈpəʊstɪdʒ/ *n.* (no *pl.*) money
that you must pay when you send a
letter, etc.: *What is the postage for a
letter to Australia?* **postage stamp** *n.*
small piece of paper that you stick on a

letter, etc., to show how much you have paid to send it.

post-box /'pəʊst bɒks/ n. (pl. post-boxes) box in the street where you put letters for the post.

postcard /'pəʊstkɑːd/ n. card that you write a message on and send by post.

poster /'pəʊstə(r)/ n. big piece of paper that you put where people can see it, to tell them about something: a poster about the pop festival.

postman /'pəʊstmən/ n. (pl. postmen) man whose job is to take letters, etc. to people's houses, offices, etc.

postmaster /'pəʊstmɑːstə(r)/, **postmistress** /'pəʊstmɪstrɪs/ (pl. postmistresses) n. someone who controls a post office.

post office /'pəʊst ɒfɪs/ n. building where you can send letters and telegrams, buy stamps, etc.

postpone /pə'spəʊn/ v. not do something until a later time: Because it was raining, we postponed the match until tomorrow.

pot /pɒt/ n. **1** deep, round dish for cooking: I put the potatoes in a pot and boiled them. **2** jar that holds food: a pot of honey.

potato /pə'teɪtəʊ/ n. (pl. potatoes) round, white vegetable that grows under the ground.

pottery /'pɒtərɪ/ n. **1** (no pl.) making dishes, jars, plates, etc. from clay: We are learning pottery at school. **2** (no pl.) clay dishes, etc.: I bought my sister some pottery. **3** (pl. potteries) place where clay dishes, etc. are made.

poultry /'pəʊltrɪ/ n. (pl.) farm birds that lay eggs and that you can eat.

pounce /paʊns/ v. **pounce on** or **at**, jump on to someone or something: The cat pounced on the mouse. **pounce** n.

pound /paʊnd/ n. **1** measure of weight = 0·4 kg. **2** unit of British money = £1.

pour /pɔː(r)/ v. **1** empty liquid from something; tip a jug, etc. so that liquid comes out: She poured wine into my glass. **2** stream; flow fast: The rain poured down for hours.

poverty /'pɒvətɪ/ n. (no pl.) being poor. **live in poverty**, live in a very poor way. **poverty-stricken** adj. very poor.

powder /'paʊdə(r)/ n. any fine stuff like dust: baking powder; soap-powder. **powder** v. put powder on someone or something. **powdered** /'paʊdəd/ adj. made into powder: powdered milk.

power /'paʊə(r)/ n. **1** (no pl.) being strong; being able to do something. **do everything in your power**, try very hard: He did everything in his power to help me. **2** (no pl.) energy; force that makes things work: electric power. **power point** n. set of holes in a wall, where you can put an electric plug. **power station** n. place where electricity, etc. is made. **3** (pl. powers) having the right to do something: A policeman has the power to arrest a criminal. **4** (pl. powers) strong person or country: America and Russia are great powers.

powerful /'paʊəfl/ adj. **1** with a strong body; able to move heavy things easily: a powerful car. **2** that you can smell or hear clearly, or feel strongly: a powerful smell. **3** with the right to do important things; able to make other people do what you want: a powerful president. **powerfully** adv.

powerless /'paʊəlɪs/ adj. weak; not able to do something: A bird with a broken wing is powerless to fly.

practical /'præktɪkl/ adj. **1** of doing: a practical lesson. **2** able to do useful things: a practical leader. **3** sensible and possible: Rowing across the Atlantic is not a practical idea.

practically /'præktɪkəlɪ/ adv. almost; nearly: Lunch is practically ready so come to the table.

practice /'præktɪs/ n. **1** (no pl.) doing something; training; doing something often, so that you will do it well: It takes a lot of practice to play the piano well. **in practice**, good at something because you have trained well. **out of practice**, not good at something, because you have not trained much. **2** (pl. practices) work of a doctor or lawyer: Dr. Price has a large practice.

practise /'præktɪs/ v. do something often so that you will be good at it: The team is practising for the match on Saturday.

praise /preɪz/ v. say that something or someone is good: The teacher praised Mike's work. **praise** n.

pram /præm/ *n.* small cart that holds a baby.

pray /preɪ/ *v.* speak to God or a god: *He was kneeling down and praying.* **prayer** /'preə(r)/ *n.*

preach /priːtʃ/ *v.* talk about God to a group of people. **preacher** *n.*

precaution /prɪ'kɔːʃn/ *n.* taking care so that something will not happen: *You should put lotion on yourself as a precaution against sunburn.*

precious /'preʃəs/ *adj.* **1** very valuable: *Diamonds are precious stones.* **2** loved very much: *His children are very precious to him.*

precipice /'presɪpɪs/ *n.* high cliff or steep side of a mountain.

precise /prɪ'saɪs/ *adj.* exact; not more or less: *precise orders.* **precisely** *adv.* exactly: *at twelve o'clock precisely.*

predict /prɪ'dɪkt/ *v.* say what you think will happen: *He looked at the clouds and predicted rain.* **prediction** /prɪ'dɪkʃn/ *n.*

prefect /'priːfekt/ *n.* one of a group of senior pupils in a school, who must keep the younger children in order.

prefer /prɪ'fɜː(r)/ *v.* (*pres. part.* preferring, *past part. & past tense* preferred /prɪ'fɜːd/) like someone or something better: *Do you prefer tea or coffee?* **preference** /'prefrəns/ *n.* what you like: *There is tea and coffee—have you a preference?* **preferable** /'prefrəbl/ *adj.* better; that you like more: *I think riding a bicycle is preferable to walking.* **preferably** *adv.*

prefix /'priːfɪks/ *n.* (*pl.* prefixes) group of letters that you add to the front of one word to make another word: *'Semi-' is a prefix that means 'half', so a semi-circle is half a circle.*

pregnant /'pregnənt/ *adj.* having a baby in your body, before it is born.

prejudice /'predʒədɪs/ *n.* having a feeling against something before you know much about it: *Old people often have a prejudice against new ideas.* **prejudiced** /'predʒədɪst/ *adj.* with strong and unfair ideas.

preparation /ˌprepə'reɪʃn/ *n.* **1** (no *pl.*) getting ready for something. **in preparation for**, ready for something: *He packed his bags in preparation for the journey.* **2**

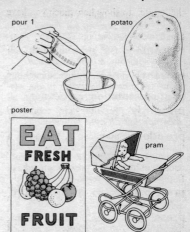

pour 1

potato

poster

EAT FRESH FRUIT

pram

preparations (*pl.*) what you do to get ready for something: *What preparations have you made for the party?*

preparatory school /prɪ'pærətrɪ skuːl/, **prep school** /'prep skuːl/ *n.* private school for young pupils.

prepare /prɪ'peə(r)/ *v.* make something ready: *She is in the kitchen preparing the dinner.* **prepared for**, ready to face something: *Sit down and be prepared for a shock.* **prepared to**, ready and willing to do something: *If the bus doesn't come, we must be prepared to walk.*

preposition /ˌprepə'zɪʃn/ *n.* word that you put in front of a noun or pronoun to show where, how, etc.: *The words 'in', 'from', 'out', and 'of' are prepositions.*

prescribe /prɪ'skraɪb/ *v.* say that someone must take a medicine: *The doctor prescribed some tablets for her.*

prescription /prɪ'skrɪpʃn/ *n.* note from a doctor to a chemist to give some medicine to someone.

presence /'prezns/ *n.* (no *pl.*) being in a place. **in the presence of**, with another person or other people there: *Anna and Neville got married in the presence of their family and friends.*

present¹ /'preznt/ *adj.* **1** being here; being there: *Is all the class present?* **2** being or happening now: *my present job.* **at the present time**, now. **present** *n.* the time now. **at present**, now. **for the present**, for now; until later: *I've got enough money for the present, but I must go to the bank tomorrow.*

present[2] *n.* gift; something that you give to someone: *a birthday present.*

present[3] /prɪˈzent/ *v.* give something: *Who will present the prizes to the winners?* **presentation** /ˌprezn̩ˈteɪʃn̩/ *n.*

presently /ˈprezntlɪ/ *adv.* soon: *I'm busy now but I'll come presently.*

president /ˈprezɪdənt/ *n.* **1** head of a government, especially in a country that has no king or queen. **2** head of a club, etc. **presidential** /ˌprezɪˈdenʃl̩/ *adj.* of a president or his work.

pres. part. *abbrev.* for present participle in this dictionary.

press[1] /pres/ *n.* (*pl.* presses) **1** pushing something: *Give the doorbell a press.* **2** ironing clothes, etc. to make them smooth: *Your trousers need a press.* **3** machine for printing newspapers, books, etc. **4 the press**, newspapers and magazines, and the people who write them: *We read news in the daily press.*

press[2] *v.* **1** push something: *You must press this button to start the radio.* **2** iron clothes, etc.: *to press trousers.* **3** try to make someone do something: *She pressed me to stay to lunch.* **press on**, go on doing something: *I must press on with my work because it is late.*

pressure /ˈpreʃə(r)/ *n.* force: *the air pressure in a tyre.*

pretend /prɪˈtend/ *v.* make it seem that something is true when it is not: *She didn't want to talk so she pretended she was asleep.* **pretence** /prɪˈtens/ *n.*

pretty[1] /ˈprɪtɪ/ *adj.* lovely: **prettily** *adv.*

pretty[2] *adv.* quite; fairly: *Your work is pretty good, but it could be better!*

prevent /prɪˈvent/ *v.* **1** stop someone from doing something: *She closed the gate to prevent the dog from going out of the garden.* **2** stop something happening: *Bill stopped the car quickly and prevented a crash.* **prevention** /prɪˈvenʃn̩/ *n.: the prevention of crime.*

previous /ˈpriːvɪəs/ *adj.* of an earlier time; that came before: *I had already visited Italy on a previous holiday.* **previously** *adv.* before.

prey /preɪ/ *n.* (no *pl.*) animal or bird that another one kills for food: *The lion was eating its prey.*

price /praɪs/ *n.* money that you must pay for something; cost: *What was the price of your new car?*

prick /prɪk/ *v.* make a little hole in something, or hurt someone, with a sharp point: *She pricked her finger with a needle.* **prick** *n.*

prickle /ˈprɪkl̩/ *n.* sharp point that grows on a plant or an animal: *Holly leaves have prickles.* **prickly** *adj.* covered with sharp points: *The holly is a prickly plant.*

pride /praɪd/ *n.* (no *pl.*) **1** feeling pleased about something that you or others have done, own, etc.: *The parents took pride in their children's good work.* **2** thinking too much that you are good, clever, etc.

priest /priːst/ *n.* religious man who looks after a church and its people.

primary /ˈpraɪmərɪ/ *adj.* first; earliest. **primary school** *n.* school for young pupils.

prime minister /ˌpraɪm ˈmɪnɪstə(r)/ *n.* leader of the government in some countries.

prince /prɪns/ *n.* **1** son of a king or queen. **2** ruler.

princess /prɪnˈses/ *n.* (*pl.* princesses) daughter of a king or queen; wife of a prince.

principal[1] /ˈprɪnsɪpl̩/ *adj.* most important.

principal[2] *n.* head of a school or college.

principally /ˈprɪnsɪplɪ/ *adv.* mainly; chiefly.

principle /ˈprɪnsɪpl̩/ *n.* rule for living: *He has strong principles.*

print[1] /prɪnt/ *n.* **1** (no *pl.*) letters, etc., that a machine makes on paper: *The words in this book are in black print.* **2** (*pl.* prints) mark where something has pressed: *footprints.* **3** (*pl.* prints) sort of picture.

print[2] *v.* **1** make marks on paper, etc., by pressing it with a machine; make books, pictures, etc., in this way: *They print the newspaper daily.* **2** write words with separate letters, not with joined letters: *Please print your name and address clearly.* **printer** *n.* person or firm whose job is to print books, etc.

prison /'prɪzn/ *n.* place where they lock up criminals: *The thief went to prison for six years.*

prisoner /'prɪznə(r)/ *n.* **1** someone who is in a locked place. **2** enemy that soldiers catch in a war. *take someone prisoner*, catch someone.

private /'praɪvɪt/ *adj.* **1** of or for one person or a small group of people; secret: *a private swimming pool.* **2** not of your job: *In his private life, the president likes to play golf.* *in private*, alone; away from other people: *The boss wants to see me in private.*

privilege /'prɪvəlɪdʒ/ *n.* special right; nice thing that only one or a few people can do: *The eldest boy has the privilege of going to bed later than his brothers.* **privileged** /'prɪvəlɪdʒd/ *adj.*

prize /praɪz/ *n.* what you give to someone who has won a contest, competition, etc. **prize-giving** /'praɪz gɪvɪŋ/ *n.* time when a school gives prizes to pupils.

probable /'prɒbəbl/ *adj.* likely; almost certain: *Rain seems probable so take your umbrella.* **probably** *adv.*: *She is very ill and will probably die.*

problem /'prɒbləm/ *n.* **1** question that is hard to answer or understand: *a mathematical problem.* **2** something that is difficult: *Driving is a problem in deep snow.*

proceed /prə'siːd/ *v.* go on doing something: *We stopped for lunch and then proceeded on our journey.*

process /'prəʊses/ *n.* (*pl.* processes) how you do or make something; piece of work, step by step: *He explained the process of building a boat.*

procession /prə'seʃn/ *n.* line of people, cars, etc. following one another: *We watched the Royal procession on Jubilee Day.*

prod /prɒd/ *v.* (*pres. part.* prodding, *past part. & past tense* prodded /'prɒdɪd/) push someone or something with your finger, a stick, etc.: *Tracy prodded the potatoes with a fork to see if they were ready.*

procession

produce¹ /'prɒdjuːs/ *n.* (no *pl.*) what you grow on a farm, etc.: *My cousin sells her garden produce in the market.*

produce² /prə'djuːs/ *v.* **1** bring something out to show it: *The taxi driver produced his licence for the policeman.* **2** make something: *David produced a fine meal.* **3** give fruit, crops, etc.: *What does this farm produce?* **4** have young ones: *The cat produced six kittens.* **5** make something happen: *Eric's hard work produced good results.* **6** organize a play, etc.

producer /prə'djuːsə(r)/ *n.* someone who organizes a play, film, etc.: *a TV producer.*

product /'prɒdʌkt/ *n.* something that you have made or grown: *Coffee is Brazil's main product.*

production /prə'dʌkʃn/ *n.* **1** (no *pl.*) making things: *the production of cars.* **2** (*pl.* productions) showing a play, drama, etc.: *the school production of 'Macbeth'.*

profession /prə'feʃn/ *n.* job that needs special training and a lot of thinking: *He is a doctor by profession.*

professional /prə'feʃənl/ *adj.* **1** who belongs to a profession: *A doctor is a professional man.* **2** who plays sport, music, etc. for money: *a professional footballer.* **professionally** *adv.*

professor /prə'fesə(r)/ *n.* senior teacher at a university.

profit /'prɒfɪt/ n. money that you make when you sell something for more than you paid for it: *If you buy a bike for £20 and sell it for £30, you make a profit of £10.*

profitable /'prɒfɪtəbl/ adj. that brings money: *profitable business.*

programme /'prəʊɡræm/ n. **1** list of things in a concert, etc.: *Look at the programme and see who is singing.* **2** plan or list of times when something will happen, be done, etc.: *What is our programme for tomorrow?* **3** one piece on radio or television: *Did you see that programme on animals?*

progress /'prəʊɡres/ n. (no pl.) **1** moving forward: *The old lady made slow progress up the hill.* **2** how you are learning or working: *my progress at school.* **in progress**, happening: *When we arrived, the match was in progress.* **make progress**, do quite well: *Austin is making progress at school.*

prohibit /prə'hɪbɪt/ v. say that something must not happen: *Smoking is prohibited in the theatre.*

project /'prɒdʒekt/ n. big plan: *a building project.*

projector /prə'dʒektə(r)/ n. machine that shows films or slides on a wall, screen, etc.

promenade /ˌprɒmə'nɑːd/ n. road that runs along by the sea in a seaside town.

prominent /'prɒmɪnənt/ adj. **1** easy to see because it is bigger than normal: *prominent teeth.* **2** important and well-known: *a prominent writer.*

promise /'prɒmɪs/ v. say that you will definitely do something: *Philip has promised to take me to the cinema tomorrow.* **promise** n. **break a promise**, not do what you promised. **keep a promise**, do what you promised. **make a promise**, say that you will definitely do something, etc.

promote /prə'məʊt/ v. give someone a higher job, etc. **promotion** /prə-'məʊʃn/ n.

prompt /prɒmpt/ adj. quick: *a prompt answer.* **promptly** adv. on time, not late: *David arrived promptly at 2 o'clock.*

pron. abbrev. for pronoun in this dictionary.

pronoun /'prəʊnaʊn/ n. word in place of a noun: *'I', 'you', 'he', 'she', 'it', 'we', and 'they' are pronouns.*

pronounce /prə'naʊns/ v. make the sound of a letter or word: *The phonetic signs in this dictionary tell you how to pronounce words.* **pronunciation** /prəˌnʌnsɪ'eɪʃn/ n. how you say a word or words.

proof /pruːf/ n. thing that shows what is true: *His passport is proof that he comes from Canada.*

propeller /prə'pelə(r)/ n. thing that is joined to the engine on a boat or aeroplane. It goes round fast to make the boat or plane go forward.

proper /'prɒpə(r)/ adj. right; correct: *You work better if you have the proper tools.* **properly** adv.: *The wind blew the door open because you hadn't closed it properly.*

property /'prɒpətɪ/ n. **1** (no pl.) what belongs to you: *Those books are my property.* **2** (pl. properties) piece of land; piece of land and buildings: *The family lives on a large property in Scotland.*

prophet /'prɒfɪt/ n. someone from God who tells what will happen in the future.

proportion /prə'pɔːʃn/ n. size; measurement; how big something is: *a building of huge proportions.*

proposal /prə'pəʊzl/ n. **1** plan: *a peace proposal.* **2** saying that you want to marry someone: *How many proposals has she had?*

propose /prə'pəʊz/ v. **1** say what you will do or what you think should be done, etc.: *I propose we should have another meeting.* **2** ask someone to marry you: *Mark proposed to Valerie.*

proprietor /prə'praɪətə(r)/ n. someone who owns a shop, hotel, school, etc.

prosperous /'prɒspərəs/ adj. rich.

protect /prə'tekt/ v. keep something or someone safe: *The sheepdog protects the sheep from danger.* **protection** /prə-'tekʃn/ n.: *An umbrella is a protection against the rain.*

protest /prə'test/ v. complain; say firmly that you do not like something: *The workers protested about their pay.*

protest /'prəʊtest/ *n.*: *They made a protest.*

proud /praʊd/ *adj*. **1** feeling pleased about something you have or did: *Susan is proud of her new baby brother.* **2** thinking too well of yourself: *The famous man was too proud to go back to his parents' poor home.* **proudly** *adv.*: *He walked proudly to receive his prize.*

prove /pru:v/ *v.* (*past part.* proved /pru:vd/, proven /'pru:vn/) show that something is true: *These footprints prove that someone came to the door.*

proverb /'prɒvɜ:b/ *n.* wise saying: *'The early bird catches the worm' is an English proverb.*

provide /prə'vaɪd/ *v.* give things that someone needs: *I'll provide food for the picnic.* **provision** /prə'vɪʒn/ *n.* **provisions** *n.* food for a journey, etc.

provided /prə'vaɪdɪd/, **providing** /prə'vaɪdɪŋ/ *conj.* if: *I'll go, providing Pete can come with me.*

province /'prɒvɪns/ *n.* part of a country; state. **provincial** /prə'vɪnʃl/ *adj*.

provoke /prə'vəʊk/ *v.* make someone angry: *If you provoke that cat it will scratch you!*

prowl /praʊl/ *v.* walk slowly and quietly like an animal that wants to kill: *The cat prowled round the bird's cage.* **prowl** *n.*: *A fox is on the prowl!*

prune /pru:n/ *n.* dried plum.

pry /praɪ/ *v.* ask too many questions; try to find out too much about other people.

psalm /sɑ:m/ *n.* religious song or hymn.

P.T.O. /ˌpi: ti: 'əʊ/ *abbrev.* please turn over; words that tell you to turn the page.

pub /pʌb/, **public house** /ˌpʌblɪk 'haʊs/ *n.* building where you go to drink beer, etc. and to talk to friends.

public[1] /'pʌblɪk/ *adj*. of everyone; for all people: *public transport; a public library.* **public school** *n.* private school for pupils of 13–18. **publicly** *adv*.

public[2] *n.* (no *pl.*) **the public**, people in general. **in public**, where other people are; openly: *She is too shy to sing in public.*

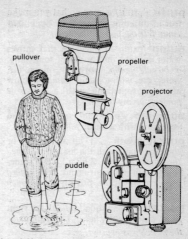

publish /'pʌblɪʃ/ *v.* prepare a book, magazine, newspaper, etc. for selling: *Oxford University Press published this dictionary.* **publisher** *n.* person or business that publishes books, magazines, etc.

pudding /'pʊdɪŋ/ *n.* sweet food that you eat at the end of a meal.

puddle /'pʌdl/ *n.* small pool of dirty water, on the ground.

puff[1] /pʌf/ *n.* short, quick burst of air, wind, smoke, etc.: *A sudden puff of wind blew off his hat.*

puff[2] *v.* **1** breathe quickly: *He ran so fast that he was puffing.* **2** send out a short burst of air, smoke, etc.: *The wind puffed my hat over the wall.* **puff out a candle, etc.**, blow on to a candle flame so that it goes out.

pull /pʊl/ *v.* move something strongly towards yourself: *She pulled the drawer open.* **pull something down**, take down a building: *They pulled down the old school.* **pull in**, drive the car to the side of the road and stop: *Keith pulled in for a minute to look at the map.* **pull up**, stop the car: *The bus pulled up because the lights were red.* **pull** *n.*: *He gave my hair a pull.*

pullover /'pʊləʊvə(r)/ *n.* jersey; sweater.

pulpit /'pʊlpɪt/ *n.* place where the priest stands when he preaches in church.

pulse /pʌls/ n. beat of the heart that you feel in different parts of the body: *The nurse felt the pulse in his wrist.*

pump /pʌmp/ n. machine that moves water, air, etc. into or out of something: *a bicycle pump.* **pump** v. move air, water, etc. with a pump. *pump up,* blow air into something with a pump: *I pumped up my bicycle tyre.*

pumpkin /'pʌmpkɪn/ n. big, round vegetable with a hard, yellow skin.

punch /pʌntʃ/ v. **1** hit something or someone hard with the fist: *He punched the boy in the face.* **2** hit a hole in something with an instrument: *The guard punched my ticket.* **punch** n.: *a punch on the chin.*

punctual /'pʌŋktjuəl/ adj. at the right time; **punctually** adv.: *The train came punctually.*

punctuate /'pʌŋktjʊeɪt/ v. put marks such as (.) (,) (;) (:) (?) into a piece of writing. **punctuation** /ˌpʌŋktjʊ'eɪʃn/ n.

puncture /'pʌŋktʃə(r)/ n. small hole in something, which lets the air out: *He mended a puncture in his bicycle tyre.* **puncture** v. make a puncture in something: *A piece of glass punctured our tyre.*

punish /'pʌnɪʃ/ v. make someone suffer because he has done wrong. **punishment** n.: *The thief was sent to prison as a punishment.*

pupil /'pju:pl/ n. someone who is learning in school or from a private teacher: *There are twenty pupils in the class.*

puppet /'pʌpɪt/ n. doll or toy animal, etc. that will move if you pull strings, or put your hand inside it.

puppy /'pʌpɪ/ n. (pl. puppies) young dog.

purchase /'pɜ:tʃəs/ v. buy something. **purchase** n. something that you have bought. *make a purchase,* buy something.

pure /pjʊə(r)/ adj. **1** totally clean; not mixed with any other thing: *pure water from a spring.* **2** good; with no evil: *a pure mind.* **3** total; complete: *What you are saying is pure nonsense.* **purely** adv. totally; only.

purple /'pɜ:pl/ adj. with a blue-red colour: *purple grapes.* **purple** n.

purpose /'pɜ:pəs/ n. plan; intention; what you are going to do: *He went to the library with the purpose of finding a book about guns.* **purposely** adv., *on purpose,* because you want to; with a particular idea: *I came here purposely to see you. Was it a mistake or did you kick him on purpose? for the purpose of,* for this reason; to do a particular job: *Scissors are for the purpose of cutting.*

purr /pɜ:(r)/ v. make the sound of a happy cat: *The cat purred when I gave it some milk.* **purr** n.

purse /pɜ:s/ n. small bag where you keep money.

pursue /pə'sju:/ v. chase or follow someone because you want to catch him: *They pursued the thief down the road.* **pursuit** /pə'sju:t/ n.: *The policeman was in pursuit of the thief.*

push /pʊʃ/ v. move something strongly away from yourself: *She pushed the drawer shut.* **push** n.: *I fell because he gave me a push.* **push chair** n. seat on wheels for a small child.

puss /pʊs/ (pl. pusses), **pussy** /'pʊsɪ/ (pl. pussies) n. cat.

put /pʊt/ v. (pres. part. putting, past part. & past tense put) move something to another place: *He put his hat on his head. put something away,* store something in its usual place: *I put my jacket away in the wardrobe. put something off,* not do something until a later time: *I'm not well today, so I'll put off my visit until tomorrow. put someone off, (a)* ask someone to do something later than he planned: *I'm busy today, so I shall have to put Jack off until tomorrow. (b)* make you feel angry, sick, etc. so that you do not do something: *I didn't eat the fish because the smell put me off. put something on,* put on some clothes: *She put something on and answered the door. put on,* press a switch to start something: *It's very dark—I'll put the lights on. put out a fire* or *light,* make a fire or light stop burning or shining: *I put out the fire with a bucket of water. put something right,* mend something; change something so that it is correct: *My car won't start—can you put it right? put up,* stay at a place: *They put up at a hotel. put someone up,* let someone sleep in your home: *When I was in Cardiff, my cousin put me up.* **put up with**, bear something or someone: *We can't change the bad weather, so we must put up with it.*

puzzle[1] /'pʌzl/ *n.* **1** problem; something that is difficult to understand: *His wife has disappeared—it's a puzzle.* **2** game where you must find an answer. **3** jigsaw puzzle; picture in many small parts that you must put together.

puzzle[2] *v.* make you think a lot because you do not understand it: *This mystery puzzles me.* **puzzle over**, think hard about something. **puzzled** /'pʌzəld/ *adj.* not understanding something: *She had a puzzled frown.* **puzzling** /'pʌzlɪŋ/ *adj.* that you do not understand: *a puzzling letter.*

pyjamas /pə'dʒɑ:məz/ *n.* (*pl.*) loose jacket and trousers that you wear in bed.

pyramid /'pɪrəmɪd/ *n.* thing with a flat bottom and three or four sides that come to a point at the top: *the pyramids of Egypt.*

Qq

quack /kwæk/ *v.* make the sound of a duck. **quack** *n.*

quake /kweɪk/ *v.* shake; tremble: *Gordon quaked with fear when he heard the lion roar.*

qualification /ˌkwɒlɪfɪ'keɪʃn/ *n.* what you must know in order to do special work.

qualified /'kwɒlɪfaɪd/ *adj.* with the right knowledge and training: *a qualified doctor.*

quality /'kwɒlətɪ/ *n.* (no *pl.*) how good or bad something is: *I want meat of the best quality.*

quantity /'kwɒntətɪ/ *n.* (*pl.* quantities) how much, how many, etc. of something; amount: *I can only eat a small quantity of rice.*

quarrel /'kwɒrəl/ *v.* (*pres. part.* quarrelling, *past part.* & *past tense* quarrelled /'kwɒrəld/) argue; talk angrily because

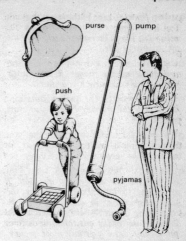

you cannot agree: *We were quarrelling because we both wanted to use the car.* **quarrel** *n.* fight; argument: *The two boys had a quarrel over a bicycle.* **pick a quarrel with someone**, find some reason to argue or fight with someone. **quarrelsome** /'kwɒrəlsəm/ *adj.* often fighting or arguing.

quarry /'kwɒrɪ/ *n.* (*pl.* quarries) place where you take stone from the ground for making buildings, roads, etc.

quart /kwɔ:t/ *n.* measure of liquid = 1·14 litre.

quarter /'kwɔ:tə(r)/ *n.* **1** one of four equal parts of something. *a quarter past the hour*, 15 minutes after the hour: *It's a quarter past two. a quarter to the hour*, 15 minutes before the hour. **2** special part of a town: *the poor quarter of Glasgow.* **3** quarters (*pl.*) place where you live or sleep: *The captain sent the soldiers back to their quarters.*

quarterly /'kwɔ:təlɪ/ *adj.* done or happening every three months: *a quarterly telephone bill.* **quarterly** *adv.*

quay /ki:/ *n.* place in a harbour where you tie a boat or ship so that you can go on and off.

queen /kwi:n/ *n.* **1** woman who rules a country and who belongs to a royal family: *Elizabeth II is Queen of England.* **2** wife of a king.

queer /kwɪə(r)/ *adj*. **1** strange; not usual: *You have some very queer ideas.* **2** not well; sick: *If you feel queer I will stop the car.* **queerly** *adv*.

quench /kwentʃ/ *v*. **1** stop fire: *The firemen quenched the flames.* **2** end thirst: *Have a drink to quench your thirst.*

query[1] /'kwɪərɪ/ *n*. (*pl*. queries) question: *Have you any queries before you start your work?*

query[2] *v*. ask about something that you do not think is correct: *He queried the bill from the shop.*

question[1] /'kwestʃən/ *n*. **1** what you ask: *He did not answer my question.* **2** something to talk about; problem: *the housing question*. **in question**, that we are talking about: *Where is the house in question? out of the question*, impossible: *No, I won't give you any more money. It's out of the question!*

question[2] *v*. ask someone about something: *The police questioned him about the stolen car.*

question-mark /'kwestʃən mɑːk/ *n*. punctuation mark (?) that comes at the end of a sentence, to show that it is a question.

queue /kjuː/ *n*. line of people who are waiting to do something: *a queue at the bus-stop*. **queue** *v*., *queue up*, stand in a queue: *We queued up for half an hour to get into the cinema.*

quick /kwɪk/ *adj*. fast; that takes little time: *a quick worker*. **quick, quickly** *adv*.: *She finished before I did because she writes quickly*. **quickness** *n*.

quiet /kwaɪət/ *adj*. **1** not loud; with a gentle sound; with no sound: *Be quiet— the baby is asleep.* **2** peaceful; with no trouble: *a quiet life*. **3** secret. **keep something quiet**, not tell other people about something. **quietly** *adv*.: *I didn't hear Jane because she came in so quietly*. **quiet, quietness** *n*.: *I need quiet when I do my homework.*

quilt /kwɪlt/ *n*. thick, warm bed-cover.

quite /kwaɪt/ *adv*. **1** totally: *You're quite right.* **2** rather; fairly; not very: *It's quite warm today.*

quiver /'kwɪvə(r)/ *v*. shake; tremble.

quiz /kwɪz/ *n*. (*pl*. quizzes) game where you try to answer questions.

Rr

rabbit /'ræbɪt/ *n*. small animal, with long ears, which lives in holes under the ground.

race[1] /reɪs/ *n*. group of people of the same sort with the same colour of skin, etc. **the human race**, all people. **racial** /'reɪʃl/ *adj*. of race: *racial problems.*

race[2] *n*. competition or contest to see who can run, drive, ride, etc. fastest: *Who will win the 200 metres race?* **the races**, horse-races: *He lost a lot of money at the races*. **race-course** *n*. place where you go to see horse-races.

race[3] *v*. **1** run, drive, etc. in a competition: *Top drivers race at Brands Hatch.* **2** run fast: *We raced to put out the fire.* **3** do something fast: *Kim raced through his homework.*

racing /'reɪsɪŋ/ *n*. (no *pl*.) sport where horses, cars, etc. race against each other.

rack /ræk/ *n*. sort of shelf or frame on the wall for holding things: *Put your case on the luggage rack.*

racket, racquet /'rækɪt/ *n*. instrument for hitting the ball in tennis, etc.

radar /'reɪdɑː(r)/ *n*. (no *pl*.) instrument in a ship or aeroplane that tells you where things are when you cannot see them.

radiator /'reɪdɪeɪtə(r)/ *n*. **1** instrument that has hot water flowing through to heat the room. **2** part of a car that holds water to cool the engine.

radio /'reɪdɪəʊ/ *n*. **1** (no *pl*.) sending people's voices, music, and other sounds a long way through the air by special waves. **2** (*pl*. radios) instrument that receives sounds from the air and lets people hear them: *We were listening to some music on the radio*. **radio** *v*. send a message by radio: *The pilot radioed the airport for help.*

raft /rɑːft/ *n*. sort of flat boat with no sides and no engine.

rag /ræg/ *n*. **1** any small piece of cloth:

Can I have a rag to clean my bicycle? **2 rags** (*pl.*) clothes that are old and torn: *The beggar was dressed in rags.*

rage /reɪdʒ/ *n.* great anger; fury: *Dad was in a rage when he found that thieves had taken his car.* ***fly into a rage***, become very angry.

ragged /'rægɪd/ *adj.* **1** badly torn: *a ragged coat.* **2** wearing clothes that are old or torn: *a ragged old man.* **3** with rough edges: *ragged clouds.*

raid /reɪd/ *v.* make a sudden attack on a place: *The fox raided the hen house.* **raid** *n.: a bank raid.* **raider** *n.* person, ship, aeroplane, etc. that raids.

rail /reɪl/ *n.* **1** long piece of wood or metal, fixed to a wall: *She hung her towel on the towel rail.* **2** long pieces of steel that are joined together to make a track where a train or tram can run. **3** train transport. ***by rail***, in a train: *I went from London to Leeds by rail.*

railing /'reɪlɪŋ/ *n.* fence made with thin rails.

railway /'reɪlweɪ/ *n.* **1** rails where a train runs: *a bridge over the railway.* **2** train service that carries people and goods: *a railway timetable.* **railway station** *n.* place where a train stops so that people can get on and off.

rain /reɪn/ *n.* (no *pl.*) drops of water that fall from the sky: *Her coat is wet because she was out in the rain.* **rainy** *adj.* with a lot of rain: *It's a rainy day, so we can't play outside.* **rain** *v.* fall from the sky as water: *I wear a mac when it rains.*

rainbow /'reɪnbəʊ/ *n.* half circle of bright colours that you see in the sky when rain and sun come together.

raincoat /'reɪnkəʊt/ *n.* coat that you wear when it rains.

raise /reɪz/ *v.* **1** lift something or someone up: *He raised the lid and looked into the box.* **2** make prices, wages, etc. higher: *The shopkeeper raised the price of sugar from 30p to 35p.* **3** grow plants: *We raised a good crop of tomatoes this year.* **4** keep animals to make young animals: *The farmer raises cattle.* **5** have and bring up children: *My grandmother raised a family of ten.* **6** fetch something; bring something together: *He ran to raise help.*

raisin /'reɪzn/ *n.* dried grape.

queue

rabbit

radiator 1

radio 2

rake /reɪk/ *n.* garden instrument with a long handle, for making soil flat, etc. **rake** *v.: Rake the dead leaves off the grass.*

rally /'rælɪ/ *n.* (*pl.* rallies) **1** big meeting of people who are asking for something: *a peace rally.* **2** big meeting of people who are all playing a sport: *a car-rally.* **rally** *v.* gather; come together.

ram /ræm/ *v.* (*pres. part.* ramming, *past part.* & *past tense* rammed /ræmd/) push or hit something very hard: *He rammed the cork into the bottle.*

ramble /'ræmbl/ *v.* walk for pleasure in the country. **ramble** *n.*

rampart /'ræmpɑ:t/ *n.* wall or big bank of earth round a town, castle, etc., to hold back enemies.

ran /ræn/ *past tense* of *v.* run.

ranch /rɑ:ntʃ/ *n.* (*pl.* ranches) big cattle farm.

rang /ræŋ/ *past tense* of *v.* ring.

range¹ /reɪndʒ/ *n.* **1** line or row of things: *a mountain range.* **2** a lot of different sorts: *This shop sells a wide range of bicycles.* **3** how far you can see, call, drive, shoot, etc.: *What is the range of these binoculars?*

range² *v.* be at different points between two ends: *The prices ranged from £2 to £10.*

rank /ræŋk/ *n.* **1** line of soldiers who are

standing side by side. **2** grade in the armed forces: *the rank of captain.* **3** social class: *people of high rank.*

ransom /'rænsəm/ *n.* money that you pay so that a criminal will free a person that he has taken: *The hijackers demanded a ransom of a million pounds before they would free the passengers.*

rap /ræp/ *v.* (*pres. part.* rapping, *past part.* & *past tense* rapped /ræpt/) hit something quickly and lightly: *He rapped on the door and waited.* **rap** *n.*

rapid /'ræpɪd/ *adj.* quick; fast: *a rapid journey.* **rapidly** *adv.*

rare /reə(r)/ *adj.* not happening often; that you do not often see, hear, etc.: *It is rare to see snow in summer.* **rarely** *adv.*: *My grandmother cannot walk far and rarely leaves her house.*

rascal /'rɑːskl/ *n.* **1** bad person whom you cannot trust. **2** child or other person who likes to play tricks: *That young rascal has hidden his mother's purse!*

rash[1] /ræʃ/ *adj.* that you say or do too quickly, without thinking: *It was rash of you to leave your job before you have found a new one.* **rashly** *adv.*

rash[2] *n.* (*pl.* rashes) group of small, red spots on the skin.

raspberry /'rɑːzbrɪ/ *n.* (*pl.* raspberries) small, soft, pink fruit.

rat /ræt/ *n.* animal like a big mouse.

rate /reɪt/ *n.* **1** speed: *When he is excited he talks at a great rate.* **2** way of measuring how much something costs, how much you receive, etc.: *£100 a week is a higher rate of pay than £90 a week.* **rate of exchange**, how much money of one country you can buy with the money of another country. **at this rate**, if this is true; if this goes on: *We're working so slowly that, at this rate, we'll never finish the job.* **at any rate**, whatever happens: *I hope to be back by 10 p.m.—at any rate I'll be back before midnight.*

rather /'rɑːðə(r)/ *adv.* fairly; quite; not very: *We were rather tired after our long walk.* **would rather**, would prefer to do something: *I can come today but I would rather come tomorrow.* **rather than**, which is better than; instead of: *Shall we go for a walk rather than watch television?*

ration /'ræʃn/ *v.* give out only a certain amount of something: *After the very dry summer they rationed water.* **ration**, **rations** *n.*: *food rations.*

rattle[1] /'rætl/ *n.* baby's toy that makes a noise when you shake it.

rattle[2] *v.* **1** make a lot of short, sharp sounds because it is shaking: *The bus rattled as we drove along the bumpy road.* **2** shake something, or move, so that it makes short, sharp sounds: *The strong wind rattled the windows.*

ravenous /'rævənəs/ *adj.* very hungry. **ravenously** *adv.*

raw /rɔː/ *adj.* **1** not cooked: *Animals eat raw meat.* **2** natural; just as it comes from the soil, from plants, etc.: *raw cotton.*

ray /reɪ/ *n.* line or beam of light, heat, etc.: *the rays of the sun.* **a ray of hope**, some hope.

razor /'reɪzə(r)/ *n.* sharp instrument for taking hair off the body: *My father shaves his face with a razor every morning.* **razor blade** *n.* piece of metal with a sharp edge that you put in a razor.

re- /riː/ *prefix* again: *The work was wrong, so I'll re-do it.*

reach[1] /riːtʃ/ *n.* (no *pl.*) how far you can put your hand. **beyond reach, out of reach**, too far away: *We keep tablets out of the reach of young children.* **within reach**, near enough to touch or go to: *The station is within easy reach of my house.*

reach[2] *v.* **1** put your hand out and touch something; be able to touch something: *I'm too short to reach the apples on the tree.* **2** get to a place; arrive somewhere: *Telephone me when you reach London.*

read /riːd/ *v.* (*past part.* & *past tense* read /red/) **1** look at words and understand them: *She was reading a book in her room.* **2** say aloud words that you can see: *Will you read this letter to me?* **read through**, study a book or piece of writing from the beginning to the end: *Please read through Chapter 1 for your homework.* **read out**, read something aloud: *The headmaster read out the list of names.*

reader /'riːdə(r)/ *n.* **1** someone who is reading; someone who reads books a lot. **2** story book for pupils.

readily /'redɪlɪ/ adv. **1** gladly: *I'll readily help you.* **2** easily and quickly: *She answered the question readily.*

ready /'redɪ/ adj. **1** prepared; waiting because you have done all that is necessary: *I'll be ready to leave in five minutes.* **get ready**, prepare for something: *I must get ready for the party.* **2** willing; happy to do something: *The teacher was always ready to help the children in their work.*

real /'rɪəl/ adj. true; natural; not just in the mind: *This is real gold, not cheap yellow metal.*

realize /'rɪəlaɪz/ v. understand or know something: *When Stephen heard the car, he realized his father had come home.* **realization** /ˌrɪəlaɪˈzeɪʃn/ n. understanding.

really[1] /'rɪəlɪ/ adv. truly: *What do you really want to do?*

really[2] exclam. word that shows surprise, interest, etc.: *'I'm going to China next year.' 'Really!'*

reap /riːp/ v. cut and gather grain: *The farmer reaped the corn in September.*

rear[1] /rɪə(r)/ adj. at the back: *the rear lights of a car.*

rear[2] n. back part: *The kitchen is at the rear of the house.*

rear[3] v. **1** keep animals to make young animals. **2** have and bring up children: *She reared a big family.* **3** lift animal up: *The snake reared its head.* **4** rise up on the back legs: *The horse reared up when the car frightened it.*

reason /'riːzn/ n. **1** (pl. reasons) cause; why you do or say something: *What is the reason for your hurry?* **2** (no pl.) clear thinking; being able to put ideas together sensibly: *Man is different from the other animals because he has reason.*

reasonable /'riːznəbl/ adj. **1** willing to listen to what someone says; willing to think carefully about something: *You must be reasonable, I can't meet you at the station while I am at work.* **2** fair; right: *That seems a reasonable price.* **reasonably** adv.

reassure /ˌriːəˈʃʊə(r)/ v. say something to make someone feel happier, safer, etc.: *The doctor reassured her that she was not very ill.* **reassuring** adj. **reassuringly** adv.: *The doctor spoke reassuringly.* **reassurance** n.

raspberry

read 1

receiver

rat

rebel[1] /'rebl/ n. **1** someone who fights against the government of his country. **2** someone who does not do what you tell him to do.

rebel[2] /rɪ'bel/ v. (pres. part. rebelling, past part. & past tense rebelled /rɪ'beld/) **1** fight against the government of your country. **2** not do what someone has told you to do: *The dog rebelled against his master.* **rebellion** /rɪ'belɪən/ n. **rebellious** /rɪ'belɪəs/ adj. **rebelliously** adv.

recall /rɪ'kɔːl/ v. remember something: *What was the name of the hotel? I can't recall it.*

receipt /rɪ'siːt/ n. piece of paper that shows you have received money for goods, etc.: *When Maurice paid for his bicycle, he got a receipt for his money.*

receive /rɪ'siːv/ v. **1** be given something; get something: *Did you receive many presents on your birthday?* **2** welcome someone: *He received his visitors with a smile.*

receiver /rɪ'siːvə(r)/ n. part of a telephone that you pick up and hold next to your mouth and ear.

recent /'riːsnt/ adj. that happened, etc. a short time ago: *a recent letter.* **recently** adv.: *She's very brown because she's been on holiday recently.*

reception /rɪ'sepʃn/ n. **1** (pl. receptions) official party: *There was a reception* *after the wedding.* **2** (no *pl.*) office in a big business, hotel, etc. where people go when they arrive: *He went to reception for his room key.*

receptionist /rɪ'sepʃənɪst/ *n.* someone who helps people when they arrive at a hotel, doctor's surgery, hairdresser's, etc.

recipe /'resəpɪ/ *n.* piece of writing that tells you how to make food: *a cake recipe.*

reckless /'reklɪs/ *adj.* not thinking about danger. **recklessly** *adv.: He drove recklessly along the narrow road.*

reckon /'rekən/ *v.* **1** calculate an amount; work with numbers to find out how much, how many, etc.: *He reckoned the cost of the holiday.* **2** think, consider, or believe something: *I reckon I'll be too tired to go out tonight.*

recognize /'rekəgnaɪz/ *v.* **1** know someone when you see him again; know something because you have seen it, heard it, etc. before: *You've grown so tall that I did not recognize you!* **2** understand or guess what someone or something is: *You can recognize a tiger by its stripes.* **recognition** /,rekəg'nɪʃn/ *n.*

recommend /,rekə'mend/ *v.* **1** tell someone helpfully what to do or how to do it: *What can you recommend for taking this mark off my shirt?* **2** say that you think that a certain thing or person is good: *Can you recommend a hotel in this town?* **recommendation** /,rekəmen'deɪʃn/ *n.* **at** or **on someone's recommendation**, because someone recommends it: *I bought this book on Jo's recommendation.*

record[1] /'rekɔːd/ *adj.* best, most, highest, lowest, fastest, etc. that has ever been done: *He ran the race in record time.*

record[2] *n.* **1** exact notes about things that have happened: *A doctor keeps a record of his patients' illnesses.* **2** round thing that you play on a gramophone when you want music, etc. **3** the biggest, fastest, highest, lowest, etc. of its sort; the greatest that has ever been done: *Who holds the record for swimming 500 metres?* **beat** or **break the record**, do better in a sport than anyone has done before.

record[3] /rɪ'kɔːd/ *v.* **1** write notes about things that happen: *In his diary he re-*

corded everything that he did. **2** put sound on a disc, tape, etc. so that you can hear it again: *I recorded the concert so that I can hear it tomorrow.* **3** take a photograph of something: *Film cameras recorded the president's arrival.* **recording** *n.: My sister in America sent a recording of her family.*

recorder /rɪ'kɔːdə(r)/ *n.* musical instrument that you blow.

record-player /'rekɔːd pleɪə(r)/ *n.* machine that plays records; gramophone.

recover /rɪ'kʌvə(r)/ *v.* **1** find or get back something that you have lost: *Someone stole my car, but the police have recovered it.* **2** become well, happy, etc. again: *He is slowly recovering from his illness.* **recovery** *n.: I am glad to hear of his recovery.*

recreation /,rekrɪ'eɪʃn/ *n.* playing games; what you like to do when you are not working: *Playing the organ is his favourite recreation.* **recreation ground**, piece of land where you can play football, etc.

recruit /rɪ'kruːt/ *n.* new soldier; new member of a group, etc. **recruit** *v.* find someone to join the army, a group, etc.: *They are recruiting young men for the police force.*

rectangle /'rektæŋgl/ *n.* shape with four straight sides and four right angles. **rectangular** /rek'tæŋgjʊlə(r)/ *adj.: This is a rectangular page.*

red /red/ *adj.* with the colour of blood. **red-hot**, extremely hot. **catch someone red-handed**, catch someone when he is doing something wrong: *The police caught the thief red-handed.* **see red**, become very angry. **red** *n.*

reduce /rɪ'djuːs/ *v.* make something less or smaller: *She's too fat—she must reduce her weight.* **reduction** /rɪ'dʌkʃn/ *n.: a big reduction in prices.*

reed /riːd/ *n.* sort of tall grass that grows in or near water.

reel /riːl/ *n.* thing with round sides that holds thread, film, etc.: *a reel of cotton.*

refer /rɪ'fɜː(r)/ *v.* (*pres. part.* referring, *past part. & past tense* referred /rɪ'fɜːd/) **refer to,** (*a*) go to a book or person for information: *You can't refer to your book when you are in the exam.* (*b*) speak about something: *When I said that some people are stupid, I wasn't referring to you!*

referee /ˌrefəˈriː/ *n.* someone who controls a sports match and sees that the players obey the rules.

refill /ˌriːˈfɪl/ *v.* fill a container again: *Your glass is empty—let me refill it.*

reflect /rɪˈflekt/ *v.* **1** give back light, pictures, etc.: *The glass reflected her face.* **2** think carefully and deeply: *He reflected on what he had read.*

reflection /rɪˈflekʃn/ *n.* **1** (no *pl.*) giving back light, pictures, etc.: *the reflection of light from a white wall.* **2** (*pl.* reflections) picture that a mirror, glass, or water gives back: *Tessa looked into the pool and saw a reflection of herself.* **3** (no *pl.*) thinking carefully and deeply: *After much reflection I decided to stay at home.*

refresh /rɪˈfreʃ/ *v.* make someone feel brighter, less tired, cooler, etc.: *A holiday refreshes us after a lot of work.* **refreshing** *adj.*: *a refreshing drink.* **refreshingly** *adv.*: *a refreshingly cool breeze.*

refreshments /rɪˈfreʃmənts/ *n.* snack; food or drink that you can buy in a public place: *We had refreshments in the interval.*

refrigerator /rɪˈfrɪdʒəreɪtə(r)/ *n.* cold cupboard for food.

refuge /ˈrefjuːdʒ/ *n.* place where you are safe from danger, trouble, etc. **take refuge from something**, go to a safe place to get away from something: *The bird took refuge from the cat in the tree.*

refugee /ˌrefjʊˈdʒiː/ *n.* someone who is running away from danger and trying to find a new, safe home.

refuse /rɪˈfjuːz/ *v.* say 'no' to what someone wants to do, etc.: *I asked Donald to play with me, but he refused.* **refusal** /rɪˈfjuːzl/ *n.*: *I was sad at Donald's refusal.*

regard¹ /rɪˈɡɑːd/ *n.* **1** (no *pl.*) care; thought: *He drove with no regard for safety.* **2** (no *pl.*) what you think about someone or something: *I have a high regard for my uncle because he is a brave man.* **3 regards** (*pl.*) kind thoughts and wishes: *Please give my regards to your mother.*

record² 2   record-player

recorder

refrigerator

regard² *v.* **1** believe something: *Many people regard Martin Luther King as a hero.* **as regards, regarding** *prep.* concerning; about: *I telephoned him regarding his invitation.* **2** look at someone or something: *He regarded me with a smile.*

regiment /ˈredʒɪmənt/ *n.* part of an army.

region /ˈriːdʒən/ *n.* part of a country; part of the world: *Monkeys live in hot regions.*

register¹ /ˈredʒɪstə(r)/ *n.* list of names, etc.: *a register of voters.*

register² *v.* **1** put a name, etc. on a list: *New guests must register in the hotel book.* **2** point to a number: *It was so hot that the thermometer registered 40°C.* **3** send a letter or parcel by special post so that you will get money back if it is lost. **registration** /ˌredʒɪˈstreɪʃn/ *n.*

regret /rɪˈɡret/ *v.* (*pres. part.* regretting, *past part. & past tense* regretted /rɪˈɡretɪd/) **1** feel sorry: *He regrets that he was rude to her.* **2** say 'no' politely: *I regret that we cannot give you the job.* **regret** *n.*

regular /ˈreɡjʊlə(r)/ *adj.* **1** happening again and again at the same time, or at fixed times, etc.; not changing or stopping: *regular heart-beats.* **2** usual: *I have never seen him before—he's not one of my regular customers.* **3** that follows the usual rule: *regular verbs.* **regularly** *adv.*: *The milkman comes regularly every day.*

regulation /ˌregjʊˈleɪʃn/ n. rule; order: *traffic regulations.*

rehearse /rɪˈhɜːs/ v. practise music, a play, etc. before doing it for other people: *Anita rehearsed her song until it was perfect.* **rehearsal** /rɪˈhɜːsl/ n.

reign[1] /reɪn/ n. time when someone is a king or queen: *The reign of Queen Elizabeth II began in 1953.*

reign[2] v. be king or queen of a country: *Queen Victoria reigned for a long time.*

rein /reɪn/ n. long, thin strap that a horse wears on its head so that a rider can control it.

reindeer /ˈreɪndɪə(r)/ n. (pl. reindeer) animal that lives in cold, northern countries.

reject /rɪˈdʒekt/ v. say 'no' to something; not take something: *She rejected my offer of help.*

rejoice /rɪˈdʒɔɪs/ v. feel or show that you are very happy: *They rejoiced at the good news.* **rejoicing** n. happiness; joy.

relate /rɪˈleɪt/ v. **be related**, be in the same family: *Are those two boys related?*

relation /rɪˈleɪʃn/ n. **1** someone in your family: *An uncle is a relation.* **2** what one person, group, country, etc. is to another: *America and Britain have friendly relations.*

relationship /rɪˈleɪʃnʃɪp/ n. how people, things, or ideas are to each other: *We have a good relationship with our neighbours.*

relative /ˈrelətɪv/ n. someone in your family: *Aunts, uncles, and cousins are all relatives.*

relax /rɪˈlæks/ v. **1** become less tight; make something less tight: *She relaxed her grip and let me go.* **2** rest from work, etc.: *Let's relax for an hour and go for a swim.* **relaxation** /ˌriːlækˈseɪʃn/ n.

release /rɪˈliːs/ v. let someone or something go free: *We released the bird from the cage and it flew away.* **release** n.

reliable /rɪˈlaɪəbl/ adj. that you can trust: *a reliable car; a reliable person.* **reliably** adv.

relied /rɪˈlaɪd/ past part. & past tense of v. rely.

relief /rɪˈliːf/ n. (no pl.) **1** taking away pain, worry, etc.: *These tablets give relief from headaches.* **2** something that takes away pain, worry, etc.: *The rain was a great relief after many weeks of hot, dry weather.* **3** food, money, or other help: *Many countries sent relief for the people who lost their homes in the floods.*

relieve /rɪˈliːv/ v. take away pain or worry: *Take this pill to relieve your headache.*

relieved /rɪˈliːvd/ adj. glad that a problem has gone away: *I am relieved that Gwen is better.*

religion /rɪˈlɪdʒən/ n. **1** (no pl.) believing in a god. **2** (pl. religions) one of the different ways of believing in a god: *Christianity and Islam are two of the great religions of the world.* **religious** /rɪˈlɪdʒəs/ adj.

reluctant /rɪˈlʌktənt/ adj. not wanting to do something: *Gillian enjoyed the party so much that she was reluctant to leave.* **reluctantly** adv. **reluctance** /rɪˈlʌktəns/ n.

rely /rɪˈlaɪ/ v. **rely on**, trust someone; be sure that someone will do what he says: *You can rely on him because he always keeps his promises.*

remain /rɪˈmeɪn/ v. **1** stay after a part has gone: *We ate and ate until nothing remained on the plates.* **2** stay or continue in the same place: *We remain at home on Sundays.* **3** stay or continue in the same way; not change: *I asked her a question but she remained silent.*

remains /rɪˈmeɪnz/ n. (pl.) what is there when most has gone: *She couldn't finish her lunch so I threw the remains away.*

remark /rɪˈmɑːk/ v. say something: *Peter remarked that the pudding was too sweet.* **remark** n.: *They all made nice remarks about the good food.*

remarkable /rɪˈmɑːkəbl/ adj. unusual and surprising: *a remarkable discovery.* **remarkably** adv. very: *a remarkably clever boy.*

remedy /ˈremədɪ/ n. (pl. remedies) something that will end a problem or an illness: *A long drink of water is a good remedy for hiccups.*

remember /rɪˈmembə(r)/ v. keep something in your mind; not forget something: *Did you remember to post the letter? Do you remember what we* *learned in class yesterday?* **remember one person to another person**, take greetings from one person to another: *Please remember me to your brother when you see him.*

remind /rɪ'maɪnd/ v. **1** make you think of someone or something: *These photographs remind me of our holiday.* **2** tell someone to remember something: *Please remind me to buy a loaf of bread.* **reminder** n.

remote /rɪ'məʊt/ adj. far from other places: *a remote farm.*

remove /rɪ'muːv/ v. take something or someone away: *She washed her hands to remove the dirt.* **removal** /rɪ'muːvl/ n. **removal** adj.: *The removal van took our furniture to the new house.*

rent /rent/ v. **1** pay to use something; pay to live or work in another person's house, office, etc.: *He rents a room near the office where he works.* **2** let someone use your rooms, land, etc. if he pays you for it: *We rent a flat to him for £100 a month.* **rent** n.: *How much rent do you pay for your house?*

repaid /rɪ'peɪd/ past part. & past tense of v. repay.

repair /rɪ'peə(r)/ v. mend something: *There is a hole in my shoe—can you repair it?* **repair** n. **under repair**, being mended: *The road is closed because it is under repair.*

repay /rɪ'peɪ/ v. (past part. & past tense repaid /rɪ'peɪd/) **1** pay back money: *If you lend me 50p, I'll repay you next week.* **2** do something to show your thanks to someone: *What can I do to repay you for your help?* **repayment** n.: *the repayment of a loan.*

repeat /rɪ'piːt/ v. **1** say or do something again: *I repeated my words because he had not heard.* **2** tell other people what someone has told you: *If I tell you a secret, you must promise not to repeat it.* **repeat** n. doing something again.

repeatedly /rɪ'piːtɪdlɪ/ adv. again and again: *He knocked repeatedly but no one came to the door.*

repetition /ˌrepɪ'tɪʃn/ n. (no pl.) saying or doing something again.

replace /rɪ'pleɪs/ v. **1** put something back in its place again: *When you have finished the book, please replace it on the*

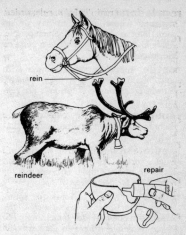

rein

reindeer   repair

shelf. **2** put one thing in place of another thing: *The gate was broken, so we replaced it with a new one.*

replacement /rɪ'pleɪsmənt/ n. **1** (no pl.) putting something or someone in place of another: *The replacement of the tyre was a dirty job.* **2** (pl. replacements) person or thing that you put in the place of another: *This battery is finished and I need a replacement.*

reply /rɪ'plaɪ/ v. answer: 'Yes, sir,' he replied. **reply** n. answer: *I asked if she was enjoying the music but I couldn't hear her reply.* **in reply**, as an answer: *What did you say in reply to his question?*

report[1] /rɪ'pɔːt/ n. piece of news; telling about something that has happened, etc.: *Did you read the newspaper report of the match?*

report[2] v. **1** tell or write about something that has happened: *He reported that there had been a plane crash near Exeter.* **2** go and see someone: *When you start your new job, you must report to the manager.*

reporter /rɪ'pɔːtə(r)/ n. someone who works for a newspaper, radio, etc. and tells about things that have happened.

represent /ˌreprɪ'zent/ v. **1** be a sign for something: *On the map dots represent towns.* **2** speak or do something in the name of other people: *Chris represented his school in the swimming match.*

representative /ˌreprɪˈzentətɪv/ *n.* someone whose job is to say or do something in the name of other people: *There is a representative of each class on the school committee.*

reptile /ˈreptaɪl/ *n.* sort of animal with cold blood, which lays eggs: *Snakes, lizards, crocodiles, and tortoises are reptiles.*

republic /rɪˈpʌblɪk/ *n.* country where there is a president and parliament that people choose.

reputation /ˌrepjʊˈteɪʃn/ *n.* (no *pl.*) what people think or say about someone or something: *Graham has the reputation for being greedy.*

request /rɪˈkwest/ *v.* **1** ask for something: *The prisoner requested a cigarette.* **2** ask someone to do something: *The police requested drivers to take care on the icy road.* **request** *n.*

require /rɪˈkwaɪə(r)/ *v.* need something: *This job requires a clear head.* **requirement** *n.* something that you need.

rescue /ˈreskjuː/ *v.* save someone or something from danger: *Arthur jumped into the river and rescued the child from drowning.* **rescue** *n.* **come** or **go to someone's rescue**, help someone: *I was trapped in the burning house but the fireman came to my rescue.*

research /rɪˈsɜːtʃ/ *n.* (*pl.* researches) studying to find out more about things, life, etc.: *medical research.*

resemble /rɪˈzembl/ *v.* look like someone or something: *Lisa resembles her mother.* **resemblance** /rɪˈzembləns/ *n.*

resent /rɪˈzent/ *v.* feel angry with someone or about something: *I resent your reading my letters.* **resentful** *adj.* feeling or showing anger. **resentfully** *adv.*

reserve[1] /rɪˈzɜːv/ *n.* **1** something that you keep to use later. **in reserve**, for later: *We must keep some money in reserve because you never know what will happen.* **2** piece of land for a special reason: *nature reserve.*

reserve[2] *v.* **1** keep something for a later time. **2** arrange to have something; ask and pay for a seat for the theatre, a journey, etc.: *He reserved two seats on the train to Dover.* **reservation** /ˌrezəˈveɪʃn/ *n.* booking; arrangement to keep a seat in a train, a room in a hotel, etc. for someone: *We have reservations on the midday plane to Washington.*

reservoir /ˈrezəvwɑː(r)/ *n.* lake where a town stores water.

residence /ˈrezɪdəns/ *n.* **1** (no *pl.*) living in a place: *They took up residence in their new house.* **2** (*pl.* residences) house: *a residence in town.*

resident /ˈrezɪdənt/ *n.* someone who lives in a place: *I'm a visitor, not a resident.*

resign /rɪˈzaɪn/ *v.* leave your job: *The director has resigned and a new one will take his place.* **resign yourself to**, accept something you do not like: *There were a lot of people at the doctor's so she resigned herself to a long wait.* **resignation** /ˌrezɪgˈneɪʃn/ *n.* **hand in** or **send in your resignation**, write a letter to say that you are leaving your job.

resist /rɪˈzɪst/ *v.* **1** be against someone; try to stop someone who is attacking you: *They tried to push Ken into the pool but he resisted.* **2** be strong and say no to something: *Chocolates make me fat but I can't resist them.* **resistance** *n.*

resolution /ˌrezəˈluːʃn/ *n.* plan; something that you decide to do: *At New Year my father made a resolution to stop smoking.*

resolve /rɪˈzɒlv/ *v.* decide; make a firm plan: *Mary resolved to work harder.*

resort /rɪˈzɔːt/ *n.* **1** (no *pl.*) using something to help you; someone or something that you use to help you. **the last resort**, the only thing or person left to help you: *No one else will lend me any money, so you are my last resort.* **2** (*pl.* resorts) place that many people visit for holidays: *Brighton is a seaside resort.*

respect[1] /rɪˈspekt/ *n.* **1** (no *pl.*) good opinion; thinking well of someone: *I have no respect for a man who drinks too much.* **2** **respects** (*pl.*) polite greetings: *Please give your father my respects.*

respect[2] *v.* think well of someone: *Everyone respects a brave man.*

respectable /rɪˈspektəbl/ *adj.* proper; wearing the right kind of clothes and doing things in the right way. **respectably** *adv.*: *respectably dressed.*

respond /rɪˈspɒnd/ *v.* do or say something in answer to someone: *When I said* *hello he responded by smiling.* **response** /rɪ'spɒns/ *n.*

responsibility /rɪˌspɒnsə'bɪlətɪ/ *n.* (*pl.* responsibilities) **1** having a duty to care for someone or something: *It is the responsibility of parents to look after their children.* **2** what you must look after: *The dog is my sister's responsibility.*

responsible /rɪ'spɒnsəbl/ *adj.* **1** with a duty to look after someone or something: *The driver is responsible for the lives of the people on the train.* **2** whom you can trust to be good and wise: *Leave the keys with Anne—she's very responsible.* **be responsible for something**, cause something; make something happen: *Who's responsible for this broken window?* **responsibly** *adv.*

rest[1] /rest/ *n.* sleep; being still and quiet: *After walking for an hour, we stopped for a rest.*

rest[2] *n.* (no *pl.*) **the rest, (a)** what is there when most has gone; the other things: *Eat what you want, and throw the rest away.* **(b)** the other people: *Sarah and I are going swimming—what are the rest of you going to do?*

rest[3] *v.* **1** be still or quiet: *We rested for an hour in the afternoon.* **2** let someone or something be still or quiet: *He stopped for an hour to rest his horse.* **3** lie: *Her arms were resting on the table.* **4** put something somewhere: *She rested her head on his shoulder.*

restaurant /'restrɒnt/ *n.* place where you go to buy a meal and eat it.

restful /'restfl/ *adj.* quiet; giving rest: *We had a restful day and didn't do any work.* **restfully** *adv.*

restless /'restlɪs/ *adj.* never still or quiet; unable to sleep or be still: *The animals were restless because of the storm.* **restlessly** *adv.* **restlessness** *n.*

restore /rɪ'stɔ:(r)/ *v.* give or put something back: *The police restored the lost child to its parents.*

restrain /rɪ'streɪn/ *v.* hold someone or something back; stop someone or something from doing something: *Joe could not restrain his anger.*

restrict /rɪ'strɪkt/ *v.* allow only a certain amount, number, sort, etc.: *You must restrict your speed when you drive in a town.*

restriction /rɪ'strɪkʃn/ *n.* rule to stop or control something: *The coast is dangerous so there are restrictions on swimming.*

result /rɪ'zʌlt/ *n.* **1** what happens because of something; what follows from something: *The accident was the result of bad driving.* **2** what you have after hard work, study, an exam, etc.: *Michael worked well and got good results.* **3** score: *football results.* **4** answer to a sum in mathematics, etc.: *If you add 2 and 3, the result is 5.*

resume /rɪ'zju:m/ *v.* begin doing something again after a break: *We resumed work after lunch.*

retire /rɪ'taɪə(r)/ *v.* **1** go back; go away: *The player was hurt and retired from the match.* **2** leave your work when you become old: *My father retired when he was 65.* **retirement** *n.* **1** time when an old person leaves work for ever. **2** rest of an old person's life after he has stopped work. **retired** /rɪ'taɪəd/ *adj.*: *a retired judge.*

retreat /rɪ'tri:t/ *v.* move back; go away from a fight that you have lost: *We won and the enemy retreated.* **retreat** *n.*

return[1] /rɪ'tɜ:n/ *adj.* **1** for a journey to a place and back again: *a return ticket.* **2** coming back: *my return journey.* **return match** *n.* another game against a team who have just played against you.

return[2] *n.* **1** (no *pl.*) coming, going, taking, sending, or putting back: *a return to work.* **by return**, by the next post: *Please answer my letter by return.* **in return**, in exchange: *Lend me your bicycle, and you can borrow my radio in return.* **many happy returns**, words that you say to someone on his birthday. **on your return**, when you get back: *I'll meet you at the airport on your return.* **2** (*pl.* returns) ticket for a journey to a place and back again.

return[3] *v.* **1** come back; go back: *When does he return from work?* **2** give, put, take, or pay something back: *We must return these books to the library.*

reunion /ˌriːˈjuːnɪən/ *n.* meeting of old friends, etc. after a long time: *a family reunion at a wedding.*

Rev., Revd. /ˈrevərənd/ *abbrev.* Reverend: *the Revd. Mark Brown.*

reveal /rɪˈviːl/ *v.* **1** show something that was hidden before: *The clouds lifted and revealed the mountains.* **2** tell something that was a secret: *Please don't reveal the secret.*

revenge /rɪˈvendʒ/ *v.* **revenge yourself on**, harm someone who has harmed you or your friends: *He revenged himself on his wife's killers.* **revenge** *n.* **take, have,** or **get your revenge on someone**, harm someone who has harmed you or your friends: *If you spoil his picture, he'll get his revenge on you.*

Reverend /ˈrevərənd/ *n.* title of a Christian priest: *the Reverend Mark Brown.*

reverse /rɪˈvɜːs/ *v.* **1** turn something the other way round. **2** go backwards in a vehicle; make something go backwards or in the other way: *You can't drive forwards—you must reverse.* **reverse** *n.* **in reverse**, the other way round.

revise /rɪˈvaɪz/ *v.* **1** change or correct a plan, piece of writing, etc. **2** read school books or notes, etc. again, before you do an exam. **revision** /rɪˈvɪʒn/ *n.*: *You must do some revision before your exam, Bill.*

revive /rɪˈvaɪv/ *v.* become better or stronger; make someone or something stronger: *When Edna fainted, the cold water revived her.*

revolt[1] /rɪˈvəʊlt/ *n.* (no *pl.*) fighting against the government of your country:

The people were in revolt against their ruler.

revolt[2] *v.* **1** fight against the government of your country. **2** shock someone; be so bad that it makes you feel sick: *The restaurant food revolted me.*

revolting /rɪˈvəʊltɪŋ/ *adj.* horrible; shocking: *a revolting crime.*

revolution /ˌrevəˈluːʃn/ *n.* **1** total change in the way of doing things: *the Industrial Revolution.* **2** total change in the way of governing a country: *the French Revolution.*

revolutionary[1] /ˌrevəˈluːʃənərɪ/ *adj.* bringing or wanting total change: *revolutionary ideas.*

revolutionary[2] *n.* (*pl.* revolutionaries) someone who wants to change things totally.

revolver /rɪˈvɒlvə(r)/ *n.* small gun.

reward /rɪˈwɔːd/ *n.* present or money that you give to thank someone for something: *There will be a reward for the person who finds my dog.* **reward** *v.*: *I shall reward the person who finds my dog.*

rhinoceros /raɪˈnɒsərəs/ *n.* (*pl.* rhinoceroses) big, wild animal with a horn on its nose.

rhyme[1] /raɪm/ *n.* **1** (no *pl.*) when two words have the same sound at the end, like 'bell' and 'well'. **2** short poem where lines end in the same sounds: *Young children often learn nursery rhymes.*

rhyme[2] *v.* **rhyme with**, have the same sound at the end as another word: *'Drip' rhymes with 'trip'.*

rhythm /ˈrɪðəm/ *n.* regular beat in music: *I like the slow rhythm of that song.*

rib /rɪb/ *n.* one of a set of bones round your chest: *He fell off his bicycle and broke his ribs.*

ribbon /ˈrɪbən/ *n.* narrow band of cloth for tying things: *Anne tied her hair back with a ribbon.*

rice /raɪs/ *n.* (no *pl.*) plant that we use for food: *We eat curry with rice.*

rich /rɪtʃ/ *adj.* **1** with a lot of money, land, etc.: *a rich man.* **2** valuable; fine: *a crown full of rich jewels.* **3** with a lot of

fat, oil, sugar, etc. in it: *rich food.*
richly *adv.* beautifully; expensively:
richly dressed. **richness** *n.*

riches /'rɪtʃɪz/ *n.* (*pl.*) much money,
land, etc.; wealth.

rid /rɪd/ *v.* (*pres. part.* ridding, *past part.*
& *past tense* rid) **get rid of,** (*a*) throw
something away: *Get rid of that old coat!*
(*b*) free yourself from someone or
something: *That dog is always following
me around, and I can't get rid of him.*

ridden /'rɪdn/ *past part.* of *v.* ride.

riddle /'rɪdl/ *n.* game with words; trick
question: *Here's a riddle: What has four
legs but can't walk? The answer is 'a
chair'.*

ride /raɪd/ *v.* (*past part.* ridden /'rɪdn/,
past tense rode /rəʊd/) **1** go on a horse
or a bicycle: *Victor jumped on his bicycle
and rode away.* **2** travel in a bus, car,
etc.: *We rode in the back of the car.* **ride**
n. journey on a horse, bicycle, etc., or in
a bus, car, etc. **rider** *n.* someone who
rides. **riding** /'raɪdɪŋ/ *n.* (no *pl.*) sport
of riding horses.

ridge /rɪdʒ/ *n.* **1** long, narrow top of
something: *the ridge of a roof.* **2** long
top of a hill or line of hills: *a mountain
ridge.*

ridiculous /rɪ'dɪkjʊləs/ *adj.* foolish; so
silly that it makes you laugh: *It is ridiculous to play tennis with a football!* **ridi-
culously** *adv.*

rifle /'raɪfl/ *n.* sort of gun that you hold
against your shoulder when you fire it.

right[1] /raɪt/ *adj.* opposite of left: *Most
people write with their right hands.* **right**
adv.: *Turn right at the end of the street.*
right *n.*: *Our house is the first one on
the right.*

right[2] *adj.* **1** good; what the law allows:
It's not right to steal. **2** true; correct: *the
right answer. I was right and he was
wrong.* **3** best; most suitable: *the right
man for the job.* **all right,** (*a*) good; well:
Are you all right? (*b*) yes, I agree: *All
right, I'll come.*

right[3] *adv.* **1** straight; directly: *The wind
blew right in our faces.* **2** exactly: *Our
house is right in the middle of the town.* **3**
all the way: *Go right to the end of the
road.* **4** correctly: *Did you guess right or
wrong?* **rightly** *adv.* correctly: *You
rightly decided to leave early.*

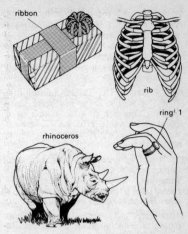

ribbon

rib

ring[1] 1

rhinoceros

right[4] *n.* **1** (no *pl.*) what is good, true,
etc.: *Our parents teach us about right and
wrong.* **2** (*pl.* right) being able to do
something by law: *All citizens have the
right to a passport.*

right-hand /'raɪt hænd/ *adj.* **1** for your
right hand: *a right-hand glove.* **2** on the
right side: *a right-hand bend.* **right-
handed** /ˌraɪt 'hændɪd/ *adj.* working
with your right hand more easily than
the left.

rim /rɪm/ *n.* **1** edge of something round:
the rim of a pot. **2** frame round the glass
of spectacles.

rind /raɪnd/ *n.* hard skin of some fruit,
and of bacon, cheeses, etc.

ring[1] /rɪŋ/ *n.* **1** round band of metal that
you wear on your finger: *a wedding-ring.*
2 round band of any sort: *a key-ring.* **3**
circle: *Please stand in a ring.* **4** place for a
boxing-match, circus, etc.: *The clowns
ran into the ring.*

ring[2] *n.* **1** (*pl.* rings) sound of a bell or a
piece of metal when you hit it: *a ring at
the door.* **2** (no *pl.*) telephone call: *I'll
give you a ring later.*

ring[3] *v.* (*past part.* rung /rʌŋ/, *past tense*
rang /ræŋ/) **1** make a sound like a bell:
The telephone is ringing. **2** pull or move
a bell so that it makes a sound: *She went
to the door and rang the bell.* **3** telephone
someone: *I'll ring you tomorrow.* **ring off,**
finish telephoning. **ring someone up**, telephone someone: *When can I ring you up?*

rink /rɪŋk/ n. place for skating.

rinse /rɪns/ v. **1** wash something away with water: *Rinse the tea-leaves out of the teapot.* **2** wash something with clean water after washing it with soap. **rinse** n.: *Give your hair a good rinse to wash the soap out.*

riot /'raɪət/ n. **1** (pl. riots) fighting in a crowd of people. **2** (no pl.) being noisy and wild. **run riot**, go wild; make a lot of noise and trouble. **riot** v.: *The crowds were rioting all night.* **rioter** n. someone who riots.

rip /rɪp/ v. (pres. part. ripping, past part. & past tense ripped /rɪpt/) **1** pull or tear something quickly and roughly: *He ripped the letter open with a knife.* **2** tear: *Her skirt ripped on a nail.*

ripe /raɪp/ adj. ready for picking and eating: *A green banana is not ripe enough to eat.*

rise[1] /raɪz/ n. **1** becoming higher, more, etc.: *a rise in the price of sugar.* **2** small hill: *a rise in the ground.*

rise[2] v. (past part. risen /rɪzn/, past tense rose /rəʊz/) **1** become higher or more: *After the heavy rain the river will rise.* **2** stand up: *He rose from his chair.* **3** get out of bed: *When do you rise in the morning?*

risk /rɪsk/ n. danger; chance of being hurt or losing something: *The water is not deep, so there is no risk of your drowning.* **take a risk**, do something although there is a chance of danger, loss, etc. **risk** v. put someone or something in danger: *Norman risked his own life when he saved the girl from the burning house.*

risky /'rɪskɪ/ adj. dangerous. **riskily** adv.

rival /'raɪvl/ n. someone who wants to do as well as you; someone who is trying to take what you want: *business rivals.* **rival** adj.

river /'rɪvə(r)/ n. big stream of water that flows to the sea or to a big lake: *the River Thames.*

road /rəʊd/ n. way from one place to another, where cars, buses, etc. can drive; street: *Is this the road to York?* **main road**, big, important road between two towns. **by road**, in a car, bus, etc.: *Shall we go by road or by rail?* **on the road**, travelling: *We were on the road for two days.*

roam /rəʊm/ v. wander; walk or travel about with no special plan: *Wolves roam in the forest.*

roar /rɔː(r)/ n. loud, deep sound: *the roar of a tiger.* **roar** v.: *They roared with laughter.*

roast /rəʊst/ v. cook meat or vegetables in a hot oven or over a fire: *Shall we roast the potatoes?* **roast** adj.: *roast beef.* **roast** n. piece of meat that you have cooked in an oven, or over a fire.

rob /rɒb/ v. (pres. part. robbing, past part. & past tense robbed /rɒbd/) take something that is not yours: *The thief knocked him down and robbed him of his watch.* **robber** n. thief. **robbery** n. stealing.

robe /rəʊb/ n. long, loose piece of clothing.

robin /'rɒbɪn/ n. small, brown bird with a red front, which you often see in the garden.

rock[1] /rɒk/ n. **1** (no pl.) stone; very hard part of the ground. **2** (pl. rocks) big piece of rock: *The ship went on the rocks and sank.*

rock[2] v. go, or move something, gently backwards and forwards, or from side to side: *She rocked her baby to sleep.*

rocket /'rɒkɪt/ n. **1** firework that goes up into the air very fast and then bursts into fire with a loud noise. **2** engine that pushes a spacecraft up into space.

rocky /'rɒkɪ/ adj. covered with stones and rocks: *a rocky coast.*

rod /rɒd/ n. thin, straight piece of wood or metal: *a fishing-rod.*

rode /rəʊd/ past tense of v. ride.

rogue /rəʊg/ n. bad person whom you cannot trust.

role /rəʊl/ n. one person's part in a play: *the role of Hamlet.*

roll[1] /rəʊl/ n. **1** (no pl.) moving from side to side; turning over: *the roll of a ship.* **2** (pl. rolls) something that you have folded over and over: *a roll of cloth.* **3** (pl. rolls) list of names. **call the roll**, read a list of names to see who is there and who is not. **4** (pl. rolls) small piece of bread baked in a ball.

roll[2] v. **1** move along by turning over and over; make something go over and over: *The coin rolled under the table.* **2**

move on wheels: *The cart rolled along the road.* **3** move from side to side: *The ship rolled in the big waves.* **4** make something into the shape of a ball: *He rolled the clay into a ball.* **5** push a round instrument over something to make it flat: *Mother rolled the pastry on the table.* **6** make long, deep sounds: *The drums rolled.* **roll up**, turn something over and over into the shape of a tube: *The campers rolled up their sleeping-bags.*

roller-skate /'rəʊlə skeɪt/ *n.* sort of shoe with small wheels, which children wear for fun and play.

rolling-pin /'rəʊlɪŋ pɪn/ *n.* wooden instrument that you roll over pastry to make it flat.

romance /rəʊ'mæns/ *n.* **1** story about love. **2** being in love. **romantic** /rəʊ'mæntɪk/ *adj.: a romantic story.*

roof /ruːf/ *n.* top of a building, car, etc.

room /ruːm/ *n.* **1** (*pl.* rooms) part of a house or other building: *We sleep in the bedroom and wash in the bathroom.* **rooms**, lodgings; rooms that you rent: *My brother has rooms near the university.* **2** (no *pl.*) space; enough space: *This big table takes up too much room.*

root /ruːt/ *n.* the part of a plant, tree, etc. that is under the ground.

rope /rəʊp/ *n.* very thick, strong string: *They tied the ship to the quay with ropes.* **rope** *v.* tie something with rope: *Father roped the cases on to the roof of the car.*

rose¹ /rəʊz/ *n.* **1** (*pl.* roses) sort of flower. **2** (no *pl.*) pink or red colour. **rose** *adj.*

rose² past tense of *v.* rise.

rosy /'rəʊzɪ/ *adj.* pink or red: *rosy cheeks.*

rot /rɒt/ *v.* (*pres. part.* rotting, *past part.* & *past tense* rotted /'rɒtɪd/) make something go bad; become bad, as things do when they die: *No one picked the apples so they rotted on the tree.*

rota /'rəʊtə/ *n.* list of people who do things in turn: *There is a rota of pupils to clean the blackboard.*

rotten /'rɒtn/ *adj.* **1** old and not fresh enough to use: *Rotten eggs smell horrible.* **2** not pleasant; not good: *What rotten weather!* **3** not well: *I shall go to the doctor because I feel rotten.*

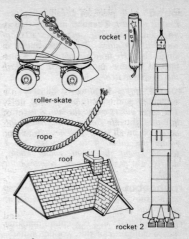

rocket 1

roller-skate

rope

roof

rocket 2

rough /rʌf/ *adj.* **1** not smooth; not flat: *The bus bumped up and down on the rough road.* **2** not behaving gently: *a rough boy.* **3** not moving gently: *rough sea.* **4** not pleasant to hear: *a rough voice.* **5** that shakes and bumps you: *a rough ride.* **roughness** *n.*

roughly /'rʌflɪ/ *adv.* **1** not gently; in a violent way: *If you play with the baby so roughly, you'll hurt him!* **2** not finely: *a roughly made table.* **3** about: *The holiday will cost roughly £200.*

round¹ /raʊnd/ *adj.* with the shape of a circle or a ball: *a round plate.*

round² *adv.* **1** in a half-circle; in the opposite direction: *She turned round and went back again. Turn your chair round.* **2** in a full circle: *In one hour the minute-hand of a clock goes right round.* **round and round**, round many times: *The dog chased the cat round and round the room.* **3** making a ring or circle: *The garden has a high wall all round.* **4** from one place or person to another: *Pass these pictures round so you can all look at them.* **5** by a longer road, etc.: *If you can't get across the river, you'll have to go round by the bridge.* **6** to a place where someone is: *When can you come round and fetch the eggs?* **7** better, after being ill. **come round,** (*a*) wake up, after fainting. (*b*) visit me; come to see me: *Come round at 2 o'clock.* **go round,** (*a*) be enough for everyone: *Is there enough coffee to go round?* (*b*) visit someone; go somewhere.

round³ *n.* **1** piece of bread, etc.: *two rounds of toast.* **2** regular journey that is your daily job: *The postman starts his round at 8 o'clock.* **3** a single bullet; a single shot: *He fired his last round.* **4** one part of a game, etc.: *the sixth round of the boxing match.*

round⁴ *prep.* **1** going to all sides of something and coming back to the start: *The earth moves round the sun.* **2** turning left or right: *He followed me round the corner.* **3** on all sides of: *They are sitting round the table.* **4** to all parts of: *I looked round the room.* **round about**, nearly; not exactly: *It costs round about £100.*

roundabout¹ /'raʊndəbaʊt/ *adj.* longer than usual: *The bridge had fallen down, so we had to go a roundabout way.*

roundabout² *n.* **1** big, round machine where children can ride wooden horses, etc. at a fair. **2** crossroads where cars cannot drive straight forward but must drive round a circle in the middle.

rouse /raʊz/ *v.* wake someone up: *A knock at the door roused me.*

route /ru:t/ *n.* way from one place to another: *Which is the quickest route from London to Paris?*

row¹ /rəʊ/ *n.* line of people or things: *We sat in the front row of seats at the theatre.*

row² /raʊ/ *n.* **1** (no *pl.*) loud noise: *What's that row in the street?* **2** (*pl.* rows) noisy quarrel.

row³ /rəʊ/ *v.* move oars to make a boat go; take something or someone in a boat with oars: *Please row me across the river.* **row** *n.*: *Let's go for a row.* **rowing** *adj.*: *a rowing boat.*

rowdy /'raʊdɪ/ *adj.* noisy and rough: *a rowdy party.* **rowdily** *adv.*

royal /'rɔɪəl/ *adj.* of a king or queen: *the Royal Family.* **royally** *adv.*

royalty /'rɔɪəltɪ/ *n.* (no *pl.*) kings, queens, and their families.

rub /rʌb/ *v.* (*pres. part.* rubbing, *past part.* & *past tense* rubbed /rʌbd/) move something backwards and forwards on another thing: *Rub oil on your skin before you sit in the sun.* **rub something out**, take marks, writing, etc. off something: *Rub out the word you spelled wrongly and write it again.* **rub** *n.*

rubber /'rʌbə(r)/ *n.* **1** (no *pl.*) stuff from a special tree that we use for tyres, balls, etc. **2** (*pl.* rubbers) small piece of rubber that takes away pencil marks, etc. **rubber** *adj.* made of rubber: *a rubber band.*

rubbish /'rʌbɪʃ/ *n.* (no *pl.*) **1** things that you throw away because they are not useful: *Burn this rubbish on the fire.* **2** nonsense; silly ideas: *He's talking a lot of rubbish.*

rucksack /'rʌksæk/ *n.* bag for food, clothes, etc. that you carry on your back.

rudder /'rʌdə(r)/ *n.* flat piece of wood at the back of a boat or ship that you move to make the boat go left or right.

rude /ru:d/ *adj.* not polite; talking or acting in a way that makes other people sad, angry, etc.: *It's rude to turn your back when someone is talking to you.* **rudely** *adv.* **rudeness** *n.*

rug /rʌg/ *n.* **1** small carpet; small piece of covering for the floor. **2** thick covering to keep you warm.

rugby /'rʌgbɪ/, **rugger** /'rʌgə(r)/ *n.* (no *pl.*) ball game with two teams of fifteen players.

rugged /'rʌgɪd/ *adj.* rough and rocky: *a rugged coast.*

ruin¹ /'ru:ɪn/ *n.* **1** (no *pl.*) bad damage; disaster: *The war brought ruin to the country.* **2** (*pl.* ruins) building, etc. that has been broken, etc. **in ruins**, broken; destroyed; finished: *The house was in ruins after the fire.*

ruin² *v.* spoil or damage something so that it is no longer good; break something totally: *The storm ruined our picnic.*

rule¹ /ru:l/ *n.* **1** (*pl.* rules) what you must, or must not, do in a game, at school, at work etc.: *It's a rule of chess that a player can move only one piece at a time.* **2** (no *pl.*) what you usually do; what usually happens. **as a rule**, usually: *As a rule, I get up at six, but today I woke up late.* **3** (no *pl.*) government; control: *India was once under British rule.*

rule² *v.* **1** be king, queen, etc.; be in control: *Queen Victoria ruled for many years.* **2** say what is right; decide: *The referee ruled that the player must leave* *the field.* **3** draw a straight line on paper, etc. with an instrument.

ruler /ˈruːlə(r)/ *n.* **1** someone who governs: *A king is a ruler.* **2** long piece of wood, plastic, etc. that helps you to draw straight lines or to measure things.

rum /rʌm/ *n.* (no *pl.*) sort of alcoholic drink.

rumble /ˈrʌmbl/ *v.* make a long, deep noise: *Thunder rumbled in the sky.* **rumble** *n.*

rumour /ˈruːmə(r)/ *n.* story that goes from person to person but that is perhaps not true: *There is a rumour that our teacher is leaving.*

run[1] /rʌn/ *n.* **1** moving fast on your feet: *Let's go for a run across the fields.* **2** journey in a car, train, etc.: *It's a long run from London to Edinburgh.* **3** place where you keep birds, animals, etc.: *a chicken run.* **4** single point in cricket.

run[2] *v.* (*pres. part.* running, *past part.* run, *past tense* ran /ræn/) **1** go with very fast steps: *I was late for the bus so I ran to the bus-stop.* **2** go; make a journey: *The bus was not running because of the snow.* **3** work; function: *Don't leave the engine of your car running too long.* **4** flow; let something flow: *Rivers run into the sea.* **run dry**, become dry. **5** control or organize a business, club, etc.: *Who runs the business?* **6** stand; be placed: *The fence runs all the way round the garden.* **run across, run into**, meet, by chance, someone whom you did not expect to meet. **run after**, try to catch a person or animal: *I ran after the dog that had taken my hat.* **run away**, go quickly away, and stay away, from a place: *He has run away from home.* **run away with someone or something**, go away with someone or something that is not yours: *Who's run away with my pen?* **run someone down**, knock someone over: *A lorry ran the cyclist down.* **run out of**, have no more of something: *We've run out of sugar, so I must buy some more.* **run over**, drive over someone or something: *A bus ran over the cow and killed it.* **run wild**, be excited or uncontrolled: *The children ran wild while their mother was away.*

runaway /ˈrʌnəweɪ/ *n.* person or animal that has left home, escaped, etc. **runaway** *adj.*: *a runaway horse.*

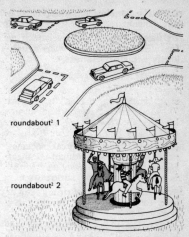

roundabout[2] 1

roundabout[2] 2

rung[1] /rʌŋ/ *n.* one of the steps of a ladder.

rung[2] *past part.* of *v.* ring.

runner /ˈrʌnə(r)/ *n.* person or horse that runs: *How many runners are there in the race?*

runner-up /ˌrʌnər ˈʌp/ *n.* (*pl.* runners-up) person or team that comes second in a race, etc.

running /ˈrʌnɪŋ/ *adj.* **1** happening one after the other: *We won three times running.* **2** for sport, etc.: *running shorts.*

runway /ˈrʌnweɪ/ *n.* wide road where a plane takes off and lands.

rush /rʌʃ/ *v.* **1** move, or do something, quickly; hurry: *The children rushed out of the classroom at the end of their lesson.* **2** make someone do something quickly: *This is a difficult job—don't rush me.* **3** take someone or something quickly: *They rushed him to hospital.* **rush** *n.*: *There was a rush to get the best seats.* **the rush hour**, time when everyone is travelling to work, or back home again.

rust /rʌst/ *n.* (no *pl.*) hard red-brown covering that forms on metals when they get wet. **rust** *v.*: *A bicycle will rust if you leave it in the rain.* **rusty** /ˈrʌstɪ/ *adj.* covered with rust: *a rusty nail.*

rustle /ˈrʌsl/ *v.* make a gentle, light sound: *The leaves rustled in the wind.* **rustle** *n.*

rut /rʌt/ n. deep line that wheels make in soft ground.

ruthless /'ru:θlɪs/ adj. cruel; with no kind feelings: a ruthless killer. **ruthlessly** adv. **ruthlessness** n.

Ss

sabotage /'sæbəta:ʒ/ v. break machines, etc. so that the enemy cannot use them: They sabotaged the railway lines so that the trains could not run. **sabotage** n.

sack[1] /sæk/ n. big bag of strong cloth or paper for carrying heavy things: a sack of potatoes.

sack[2] v. make someone leave his job: The manager sacked him because he stole some money. **sack** n. **get the sack**, lose your job. **give someone the sack**, make someone leave his job.

sacred /'seɪkrɪd/ adj. of god or religion; holy: A church is a sacred building.

sacrifice /'sækrɪfaɪs/ v. **1** kill an animal, etc. as a present to a god: They sacrificed a lamb. **2** give up something important so that you can help someone: He sacrificed his life to save the child. **sacrifice** n.: Harry made big sacrifices to send his brother to America.

sad /sæd/ adj. (sadder, saddest) **1** unhappy: The children are sad because their dog has died. **2** that makes you feel unhappy: sad news. **sadly** adv. **sadness** n.

saddle /'sædl/ n. seat for a rider on a horse, donkey, bicycle, etc. **saddle** v. put a saddle on to a horse or other animal: Will you saddle the black horse for me?

safari /sə'fa:rɪ/ n. journey to see or hunt wild animals.

safe[1] /seɪf/ adj. **1** not hurt; not in danger: Will the baby be safe alone? **2** not dangerous: A knife is not a safe toy. **safe and sound**, not hurt or harmed: They found the lost climber safe and sound in a cave. **safely** adv.: The children can play safely in the garden. **safety** /'seɪftɪ/ n. being safe.

safe[2] n. metal box with a strong lock, where you can keep money, jewels, etc.

safety-belt /'seɪftɪ belt/ n. belt that a traveller wears in a car or aeroplane to keep him safe in an accident.

safety-pin /'seɪftɪ pɪn/ n. pin with a cover over the point.

sag /sæg/ v. (pres. part. sagging, past part. & past tense sagged /sægd/) bend in the middle; hang down: The washing line sagged when I hung the wet clothes on it.

said /sed/ past part. & past tense of v. say.

sail[1] /seɪl/ n. **1** big piece of cloth on the mast of a boat. The wind blows it and moves the boat along. **set sail**, begin a voyage: When do you set sail for America? **2** journey in a boat: Let's go for a sail this afternoon.

sail[2] v. **1** travel on the sea: The QE2 sails between New York and Southampton. **2** control a boat that sails: Where did you learn to sail? **3** begin a voyage: The ship sails at 11 o'clock. **sailing** adj.: a sailing boat. **sailing** n.: Sailing is a wonderful sport.

sailor /'seɪlə(r)/ n. someone who helps to control a boat or ship.

saint /seɪnt/ n. very good, holy person: Saint Peter.

sake /seɪk/ n. **for the sake of, for someone's sake**, because of someone; to help someone: Try to get home early for your mother's sake.

salad /'sæləd/ n. dish of cold, raw vegetables.

salary /'sælərɪ/ n. (pl. salaries) money that you receive every month for work.

sale /seɪl/ n. **1** (no pl.) selling something. **for sale**, to be sold: The Browns are leaving town, so their house is for sale. **2** (pl. sales) time when people come together in one room to buy things. Each thing goes to the person who will pay the most money for it. **3** (pl. sales) time when a shop sells things at lower prices than normal: Harrods is holding its summer sale this month.

salesman /'seɪlzmən/ (pl. salesmen), **saleswoman** /'seɪlzwʊmən/ (pl. saleswomen) n. someone whose job is to sell goods.

salmon /'sæmən/ n. (pl. salmon) big fish that lives in the sea and in rivers.

salt /sɔːlt/ n. (no pl.) stuff like white sand, which we put on food to give it taste. **salty** adj. with the taste of salt: Sea-water is salty.

salute /sə'luːt/ v. lift your hand to your head in a military sign: The soldier saluted his officer. **salute** n.

same¹ /seɪm/ adj. not different; that and no other: I have no time to change so I shall wear the same clothes.

same² pron. **the same**, not in a different way. **all the same**, still; however: He's not very clever, but I like him all the same. **be all the same to**, not matter to someone: You can do it now or later—it's all the same to me.

sample /'sɑːmpl/ n. small piece that shows what the rest is like; one example of a group of things: a sample of curtain material.

sand /sænd/ n. **1** (no pl.) fine white, yellow, or grey powder, really crushed stone, that you find in the desert, by the sea, or by a river: We swam in the sea and then lay on the sand. **2 sands** (pl.) beach, where there is sand: The children were playing on the sands. **sandy** adj. of sand; covered with sand: a sandy beach.

sandal /'sændl/ n. light, open shoe.

sandwich /'sændwɪdʒ/ n. (pl. sandwiches) two pieces of bread with other food between: a ham sandwich.

sane /seɪn/ adj. not mad; healthy in the mind.

sang /sæŋ/ past tense of v. sing.

sank /sæŋk/ past tense of v. sink.

sarcastic /sɑː'kæstɪk/ adj. with unkind words. **sarcastically** adv.

sardine /sɑː'diːn/ n. small fish that we usually buy in tins.

sat /sæt/ past part. & past tense of v. sit.

satchel /'sætʃl/ n. bag for carrying school-books, etc.

satellite /'sætəlaɪt/ n. **1** thing that goes around a planet: The moon is a satellite of the earth. **2** spacecraft that goes around the earth and sends back radio and television signals, etc. to earth.

satin /'sætɪn/ n. (no pl.) very shiny, smooth cloth.

satisfaction /ˌsætɪs'fækʃn/ n. (no pl.)

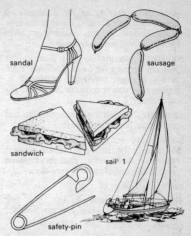

sandal / sausage / sandwich / sail¹ / safety-pin

being pleased with what you or others have done: My garden gives me great satisfaction.

satisfactory /ˌsætɪs'fæktərɪ/ adj. good enough: Is your new car satisfactory? **satisfactorily** adv.

satisfy /'sætɪsfaɪ/ v. give someone what he wants or needs; be good enough to please someone: I hope this painting will satisfy my art teacher. **satisfied** /'sætɪsfaɪd/ adj. pleased with what you or others have done: She looked at the cake with a satisfied smile. **satisfying** /'sætɪsfaɪŋ/ adj. that pleases you because it is what you want: a satisfying meal.

Saturday /'sætədeɪ/ n. seventh day of the week.

sauce /sɔːs/ n. thick liquid that you eat with other food: We eat pork with apple sauce.

saucepan /'sɔːspən/ n. deep, round dish for cooking.

saucer /'sɔːsə(r)/ n. small, round plate under a cup.

sausage /'sɒsɪdʒ/ n. long roll of minced meat in a thin skin.

savage /'sævɪdʒ/ adj. wild; very fierce: The savage dog bit many people. **savagely** adv.

save /seɪv/ v. **1** take someone or something out of danger: Help! Save the little boy! **2** keep money, etc. for a later time. **save up for**, keep money to buy something later: *Jill is saving up for a bicycle.* **3** help you to find time, money, etc. for other things: *If you make your own clothes, it will save you money.*

savings /'seɪvɪnz/ n. (pl.) money that you are keeping for later: *Dick has £100 in his savings.* **savings account** n. money that you keep in the bank, etc. for some time.

saviour /'seɪvɪə(r)/ n. someone who has saved you from sin or harm.

saw[1] /sɔː/ n. metal instrument with sharp teeth for cutting wood, etc. **saw** v. (*past part.* sawn /sɔːn/, *past tense* sawed /sɔːd/): *He sawed the tree into logs.*

saw[2] *past tense* of v. see.

sawdust /'sɔːdʌst/ n. (no pl.) fine powder that falls when you saw wood.

sawn /sɔːn/ *past part.* of v. saw.

saxophone /'sæksəfəʊn/ n. sort of musical instrument that you blow.

say /seɪ/ v. (*past part. & past tense* said /sed/) **1** speak a word or words: *Say 'please' when you ask for something.* **2** give information to someone: *She said that she was cold.* **I say!** *exclam.* words that show surprise or call someone: *I say! you look wonderful!* **that is to say**, what I mean is …: *I'll see you in a week's time—that is to say, next Monday.* **say** n. **have your say, have a say**, give your opinion: *Before you make any plans, I want to have my say!*

saying /'seɪɪŋ/ n. wise thing that people often say: *'Many hands make light work' is an English saying.*

scab /skæb/ n. hard kind of skin that grows over a cut or sore on the body.

scaffolding /'skæfəldɪŋ/ n. (no pl.) frame of ladders, planks, and metal bars, where workmen can stand while they are working on high parts of a building.

scald /skɔːld/ v. burn someone with hot liquid or steam: *Ada scalded her hand with boiling water.* **scald** n.

scale /skeɪl/ n. **1** set of marks on an instrument for measuring: *The ruler has a scale marked in centimetres.* **2** **scale, scales** /skeɪlz/ instrument for weighing things.

scamper /'skæmpə(r)/ v. run quickly with small steps.

scandal /'skændl/ v. **1** (no pl.) unkind talk about a person, which gives you bad ideas about him: *Don't listen to scandal!* **2** (pl. scandals) bad thing that makes people angry: *The dirty trains are a scandal.*

scar /skɑː(r)/ n. mark on the skin, which an old wound has left. **scar** v. (*pres. part.* scarring, *past part. & past tense* scarred) make a scar: *The cut will scar his face.* **scarred** /skɑːd/ adj.: *a scarred face.*

scarce /skeəs/ adj. rare; difficult to find; not enough: *Flowers are scarce in winter.*

scarcely /'skeəslɪ/ adv. only just: *He was so frightened that he could scarcely speak.*

scare /skeə(r)/ v. frighten someone; make someone afraid: *The thunder scared the children.* **scare** n. **scared** /skeəd/ adj. frightened.

scarecrow /'skeəkrəʊ/ n. figure of sticks and old clothes, that a farmer puts in a field to frighten birds away from crops.

scarf /skɑːf/ n. (pl. scarves) piece of cloth that you wear round your neck, over your shoulders, or over your head.

scarlet /'skɑːlət/ adj. bright red. **scarlet** n.

scatter /'skætə(r)/ v. **1** go in different directions; send people in many directions: *The crowd scattered when the storm broke.* **2** throw things here and there: *We scattered crumbs for the birds.*

scene /siːn/ n. **1** place where something is happening or has happened: *The police arrived at the scene of the crime.* **2** view; something that you can look at: *a beautiful scene.* **3** part of a play: *'Hamlet', Act I, Scene 2.* **4** background on the stage of a theatre: *The scene of the play is a kitchen.*

scenery /'siːnərɪ/ n. (no pl.) **1** countryside; the look of the land: *the mountain scenery of Scotland.* **2** things on the stage of a theatre that make it look like a real place.

scent[1] /sent/ n. **1** (no pl.) sweet smell: *the scent of roses.* **2** (no pl.) liquid with a sweet smell, which you put on your body: *a bottle of scent.* **3** (pl. scents) smell of an animal or person, which another animal can follow: *The hounds were on the scent of a fox.*

scent² v. **1** smell something: *The dog scented a rat.* **2** give out a sweet smell: *The rose scented the air.*

schedule /ˈʃedjuːl/ n. programme; plan or list of times when something will happen, be done, etc. **behind schedule**, late. **on schedule**, at the right time: *The train arrived on schedule.*

scheme¹ /skiːm/ n. plan: *'Meals-on-Wheels' is a scheme to bring hot food to old people.*

scheme² v. make secret plans to do something, usually wrong: *They were scheming to steal money from the bank.*

scholar /ˈskɒlə(r)/ n. **1** someone who is learning in school; student. **2** someone who has learned a lot about something: *a famous Latin scholar.*

scholarship /ˈskɒləʃɪp/ n. special sum of money to help a clever student go on studying: *Fergus won a scholarship to Cambridge.*

school /skuːl/ n. **1** (pl. schools) place where people learn things: *primary and secondary schools.* **2** (no pl.) lessons: *There will be no school tomorrow because it's a holiday.* **schoolboy** /ˈskuːlbɔɪ/, **schoolgirl** /ˈskuːlɡɜːl/ n. boy or girl at school. **schoolfellow** /ˈskuːlfeləʊ/, **schoolmate** /ˈskuːlmeɪt/ n. boy or girl in the same school as you. **schooldays** /ˈskuːldeɪz/ n. time when you are at school.

schoolmaster /ˈskuːlmɑːstə(r)/ n. man teacher. **schoolmistress** /ˈskuːlmɪstrɪs/ n. (pl. schoolmistresses) woman teacher.

science /ˈsaɪəns/ n. study of natural things: *Biology, Chemistry, and Physics are sciences.* **science fiction** n. stories about what will perhaps happen in the future or may perhaps be happening in other parts of the universe. **scientific** /ˌsaɪənˈtɪfɪk/ adj. of science: *scientific instruments.* **scientifically** adv. **scientist** /ˈsaɪəntɪst/ n. someone who studies science or works with science.

scissors /ˈsɪzəz/ n. (pl.) instrument with two blades, for cutting.

scold /skəʊld/ v. speak angrily to a child because he has done something wrong: *Don't scold her—she's too young to understand.* **scolding** n.: *You'll get a scolding if you're late!*

saw¹

scarf

scales

scissors   scooter 1

scoop /skuːp/ v. **1** take something out or up with a spoon, etc.: *Miranda scooped the ice-cream out of the bowl.* **2** make a round hole in something: *The baby scooped a hole in the sand.*

scooter /ˈskuːtə(r)/ n. **1** light motorcycle with small wheels. **2** toy on wheels, which a child can ride.

scorch /skɔːtʃ/ v. **1** burn something lightly: *The hot iron scorched the shirt.* **2** make plants, etc. dry and brown: *The hot sun scorched the grass.*

score /skɔː(r)/ n. number of points, goals, runs, etc. that you win in a sport: *What was the score at half-time?* **keep the score**, write down the points; remember the points. **score** v. **1** win a point: *Who scored the goal?* **2** write down or remember the points: *Will you score for this match, Ralph?*

scorn /skɔːn/ v. feel that someone or something is bad, weak, poor, etc.: *I scorn people who cheat.* **scorn** n. **scornful** adj. with no respect. **scornfully** adv.: *He looked at my old bicycle scornfully.*

scoundrel /ˈskaʊndrəl/ n. bad person.

scout /skaʊt/ n. **1 Scout**, member of a special club for boys. **2** soldier, etc. who goes to find where the enemy is.

scowl /skaʊl/ v. look angry. **scowl** n.

scramble /ˈskræmbl/ v. walk or climb with difficulty over rough land: *They scrambled up the side of the mountain.*

scrambled eggs /ˌskræmbld 'egz/ n. (no pl.) eggs that you beat with milk and cook in butter.

scrap /skræp/ n. small piece of something: *a scrap of paper*.

scrape /skreɪp/ v. **1** rub or scratch something with a hard instrument, etc. so that you take something off it: *Scrape the mud off your shoes!* **2** go too close to something: *The car scraped along the wall*. **scrape through**, only just pass an exam, etc. **scrape** n.: *She fell and got a scrape on the knee*.

scratch[1] /skrætʃ/ n. **1** (pl. scratches) cut or mark that something sharp or rough has made: *Hilda's hands were covered with scratches from the rose bush.* **2** (no pl.) rubbing the skin with nails, claws, etc., when it itches: *The dog was having a scratch*. **start from scratch**, start again from the beginning. **up to scratch**, good enough: *Is Jo's work up to scratch?*

scratch[2] v. **1** cut or mark something with a rough or sharp thing: *The cat scratched me with its claws.* **2** rub the skin with nails, claws, etc. because it itches: *Stop scratching those spots!*

scream /skri:m/ v. cry out loudly: *She screamed when she saw a snake*. **scream** n. loud cry or noise.

screech /skri:tʃ/ v. make a loud, hard noise: *The brakes screeched when the car stopped suddenly*. **screech** n.

screen[1] /skri:n/ n. **1** piece of cloth, wood, etc. that you put in front of a place to keep away wind, light, etc. or to stop people from watching: *The nurse put a screen around his bed*. **2** part of the television or cinema where the pictures appear.

screen[2] v. hide something from wind, bright light, or watchers: *She put up her hand to screen her eyes from the sun*.

screw /skru:/ v. **1** twist something to open or close it: *He screwed the lid on the jar.* **2** fasten something with a special sort of nail that you twist into the wood, etc.: *He screwed the box together*. **screw** n. sort of nail that you twist into wood, etc. **screw-driver** /'skru:draɪvə(r)/ n. instrument for turning screws.

scribble /'skrɪbl/ v. write something quickly and carelessly: *I'll scribble a note*.

scripture /'skrɪptʃə(r)/ n. the Bible; a holy book.

scrub[1] /skrʌb/ n. (no pl.) rough land with poor trees and bushes.

scrub[2] v. (pres. part. scrubbing, past part. & past tense scrubbed /skrʌbd/) rub something hard with a brush and soap and water to clean it: *He scrubbed the floor.* **scrub** n.: *This floor needs a good scrub*. **scrubbing-brush** n. hard brush for cleaning floors, etc.

sculptor /'skʌlptə(r)/ n. someone who makes statues or other shapes from metal, wood, stone, etc.

sculpture /'skʌlptʃə(r)/ n. **1** (no pl.) making statues or other shapes from metal, clay, wood, stone, etc. **2** (pl. sculptures) shape in metal, clay, etc.

scurry /'skʌrɪ/ v. run quickly with small steps: *The mouse scurried across the floor*.

sea /si:/ n. **1** (no pl.) the salty water that covers most of the earth wherever there is no land: *Fish swim in the sea.* **2** (pl. seas) big area of sea: *the Mediterranean Sea*. **at sea**, while you are on the sea: *We had a storm at sea.* **by sea**, in a ship: *Did you fly to New York or did you go by sea?* **go to sea**, become a sailor.

seagull /'si:gʌl/ n. sort of sea-bird.

seal[1] /si:l/ n. furry animal that lives in the sea and on the land.

seal[2] v. stick something down so that it is tightly closed: *She licked the envelope and sealed it*.

seam /si:m/ n. line of stitches where you have sewn two pieces of cloth together.

seaman /'si:mən/ n. (pl. seamen) sailor.

search /sɜ:tʃ/ v. look carefully at a person or thing because you want to find something: *The customs officer searched my bags for drugs.* **search for**, try to find someone or something: *I searched everywhere for my pen.* **search** n.: *the search for the lost children.* **in search of**, looking for something: *We drove round the town in search of a good hotel*.

seashell /'si:ʃel/ n. hard covering of some sea-animals.

seashore /'si:ʃɔ:(r)/ n. ground next to

the sea; beach: *We pulled the boat out of the water on to the seashore.*

seasick /'si:sɪk/ *adj.* feeling sick because the boat moves up and down. **seasickness** *n.*

seaside /'si:saɪd/ *n.* (no *pl.*) land by the sea: *We always go to the seaside for our holidays.* **seaside** *adj.*: *Brighton is a seaside town.*

season /'si:zn/ *n.* **1** one of the four parts of the year: *Winter is the coldest season in Britain.* **2** special time of the year for something: *the holiday season.*

seat¹ /si:t/ *n.* **1** chair; place where you sit: *We had good seats at the front of the theatre.* **take a seat**, sit down: *Please take a seat—the manager will soon be here.* **2** part of a chair where you sit: *Who has spilled water on the seat of this chair?*

seat² *v.* have places where people can sit: *The hall seats 200 people.* **be seated**, sit down: *'Please be seated', said the chairman.* **seat yourself**, sit down: *He seated himself in the corner.*

seat-belt /'si:t belt/ *n.* belt that a traveller wears in a car or aeroplane to keep him safe in an accident.

seaweed /'si:wi:d/ *n.* sort of plant in the sea and on rocks by the sea.

second¹ /'sekənd/ *adj.* **1** next after the first: *February is the second month of the year.* **2** extra; another: *Your shoes may get wet, so bring a second pair.*

second² *n.* person or thing that comes after the first: *Today is the first of May, so tomorrow will be the second.*

second³ *n.* sixtieth part of a minute: *The winner's time was one minute and ten seconds.* **in a second**, soon: *I'll be ready in a second.*

secondary school /'sekəndrɪ sku:l/ *n.* school for pupils of 11–18.

second-best /,sekənd 'best/ *adj.* not the best: *my second-best coat.*

second-class /,sekənd 'klɑ:s/ *adj.* not the best. **second-class** *adv.* **travel second-class**, travel in one of the usual seats, not in one of the most expensive.

second-hand /,sekənd 'hænd/ *adj.* not new; that another person has used before: *second-hand books.*

second-rate /,sekənd 'reɪt/ *adj.* not very good; poor: *a second-rate restaurant.*

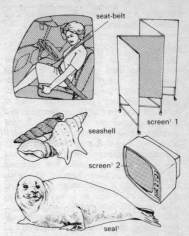

seat-belt

screen¹ 1

seashell

screen¹ 2

seal¹

secret¹ /'si:krɪt/ *adj.* that other people do not know: *a secret hiding-place.* **secretly** *adv.* not telling other people; so that other people do not know about it: *Spies do their work secretly.* **secrecy** /'si:krəsɪ/ *n.* **in secrecy**, secretly.

secret² *n.* something that you do not tell other people. **in secret**, so that others do not see it, hear it, etc.: *They made their plans in secret.* **keep a secret**, not tell other people about something. **let someone into a secret**, tell someone about something that not many others know about.

secretarial /,sekrə'teərɪəl/ *adj.* of the work of a typist or secretary: *a secretarial college.*

secretary /'sekrətrɪ/ *n.* (*pl.* secretaries) **1** someone whose job is to type letters, look after papers, answer the telephone, etc. **2** government minister: *the Secretary of State for Education.*

secretive /'si:krətɪv/ *adj.* not wanting to tell other people about yourself, your plans, etc.: *Why is he so secretive about his new job?* **secretively** *adv.*

section /'sekʃn/ *n.* part of something: *You will find that book in the historical section of the library.*

secure¹ /sɪ'kjʊə(r)/ *adj.* safe; firm; that will not easily move or fall: *Don't climb that ladder—it's not secure.* **securely** *adv.*: *Is the window securely closed?* **security** /sɪ'kjʊərətɪ/ *n.*

secure[2] *v.* make something safe; lock or fasten something: *We must secure the doors and windows before we go out.*

see /si:/ *v.* (*past part.* seen, *past tense* saw /sɔ:/) **1** use your eyes: *If you shut your eyes, you can't see.* **2** notice someone or something with your eyes: *Did you see that aeroplane?* **3** understand something: *Do you see what I mean?* **4** find out about something: *Go and see whether the shop is open.* **5** visit someone: *I went to see the doctor today about my cough.* **6** make certain about something; arrange something: *I'll see that everything is ready.* **see someone off**, go to a station, airport, etc. with someone who is going away: *I saw Vera off at 6 o'clock this morning.* **see to**, do what is necessary; mend something: *I have to see to a puncture in my bicycle tyre.* **seeing that**, since; because: *Stay in bed longer today, seeing that you were late last night.*

seed /si:d/ *n.* little thing that grows into a new plant or tree.

seek /si:k/ *v.* (*past part. & past tense* sought /sɔ:t/) **1** try to find something. **2** ask for something: *He sought help from a lawyer.*

seem /si:m/ *v.* make you think that something is so: *That apple is bad but this one seems all right.* **seem as if, seem as though**, be likely that: *It seems as though Ken will win the race.*

seen /si:n/ *past part.* of *v.* see.

seep /si:p/ *v.* flow out slowly: *Water was seeping through the roof of the shed.*

seesaw /'si:sɔ:/ *n.* special piece of wood that can move up and down when a child sits on each end. **seesaw** *v.*

seize /si:z/ *v.* take something roughly and quickly: *The thief seized my bag and ran away.*

seldom /'seldəm/ *adv.* not often: *The old lady seldom leaves her house because she can't walk far.*

select /sɪ'lekt/ *v.* choose someone or something: *Hilary always selects the best fruit in the market.*

selection /sɪ'lekʃn/ *n.* **1** (no *pl.*) choosing. **2** (*pl.* selections) group of things from which you can choose; group of things that you have chosen: *Ricky has a good selection of records.*

self /self/ *prefix* by yourself; for yourself: *He is self-taught and never went to school.*

selfish /'selfɪʃ/ *adj.* thinking too much about yourself and what you want; not thinking about other people: *That selfish boy won't let other children play with his toys.* **selfishly** *adv.* **selfishness** *n.*

self-service /,self 'sɜ:vɪs/ *adj.* where you can serve yourself: *There are no waiters in a self-service restaurant.*

sell /sel/ *v.* (*past part. & past tense* sold /səuld/) **1** give something to someone who pays you money for it: *Ann sold me her old piano.* **2** have things that you give people for money: *That shop sells bread.* **sell out**, sell all that you have of something: *We have those shoes in small sizes only —we've sold out all the bigger ones.* **seller** *n.* someone who sells things: *a bookseller.*

semi- /'semɪ/ *prefix* half: *A semi-circle is a half circle.*

semi-colon /,semɪ 'kəulən/ *n.* punctuation mark (;).

semi-final /,semɪ 'faɪnl/ *n.* match that comes before the final match in a competition.

senate /'senɪt/ *n.* one of the parts of parliament in some countries. **senator** /'senətə(r)/ *n.* member of a senate.

send /send/ *v.* (*past part. & past tense* sent /sent/) **1** make someone go somewhere: *Peter's boss has sent him to New York.* **2** make something go somewhere: *Have you sent a letter to John?* **3** make someone feel something: *The noise is sending me mad!* **send for**, ask for someone or something: *The manager sent for his secretary.* **send off**, post something: *Have you sent off Lesley's birthday present?* **send out**, give out something: *The sun sends out light and warmth.*

senior /'si:nɪə(r)/ *adj.* **1** older: *a senior class.* **2** more important: *a senior officer.*

sensation /sen'seɪʃn/ *n.* **1** feeling: *a sensation of fear.* **2** great excitement and interest; something that makes people excited: *The news of the fire in the factory caused a sensation.*

sensational /sen'seɪʃənl/ *adj.* making people interested and excited: *sensational news.* **sensationally** *adv.*

sense /sens/ n. **1** (pl. senses) one of the powers of the body: *Sight, smell, hearing, taste, and touch are the main senses.* **2** (no pl.) right and wise ideas. **common sense**, natural good thinking. **3** (pl. senses) meaning: *The word 'bear' has several senses.* **make sense**, have a meaning that you can understand: *I can't follow these instructions—they don't make sense.*

senseless /'senslıs/ adj. **1** foolish; stupid: *It is senseless to leave your house open at night.* **2** unconscious: *He was hit on the head and fell senseless to the ground.* **senselessly** adv.

sensible /'sensəbl/ adj. **1** wise; knowing what is right and good: *Let John decide—he's very sensible.* **2** right and good; useful: *Wear sensible shoes for a walk in the country.* **sensibly** adv.: *She was sensibly dressed.*

sensitive /'sensətıv/ adj. feeling things quickly and deeply; that you can easily hurt: *Don't shout at her—she's very sensitive.* **sensitively** adv.

sent /sent/ past part. & past tense of v. **send**.

sentence[1] /'sentəns/ n. group of words that you put together to tell an idea or ask a question.

sentence[2] v. give a punishment to someone in a law court: *The judge sentenced the thief to five years.* **sentence** n.: *a sentence of five years in prison.*

sentry /'sentrı/ n. (pl. sentries) soldier who is guarding a building, camp, etc.

separate[1] /'seprət/ adj. **1** divided; not joined: *Will you cut the little boy's meat into separate pieces?* **2** different; not the same: *My brothers sleep together but my sister and I have separate rooms.* **separately** adv.

separate[2] /'sepəreıt/ v. **1** divide something; keep things apart: *The Mediterranean Sea separates Europe and Africa.* **2** go in different ways: *We went to the bank together, then said goodbye and separated.* **separation** /ˌsepə'reıʃn/ n.

September /sep'tembə(r)/ n. ninth month of the year.

sergeant /'sɑːdʒənt/ n. junior officer in the police or army.

serial /'sıərıəl/ n. story, play, etc. that

seesaw

sentry

comes in weekly parts on the radio or television or in a magazine.

series /'sıəriːz/ n. (pl. series) number of things that come one after the other: *There was a series of bangs as the box fell down the stairs.*

serious /'sıərıəs/ adj. **1** thinking a lot; not playing or joking: *a serious boy.* **2** not funny: *a serious film.* **3** very bad: *a serious accident.* **4** important: *a serious discussion.* **seriously** adv.: *seriously ill.* **seriousness** n.

sermon /'sɜːmən/ n. talk that a priest gives in church.

servant /'sɜːvənt/ n. someone who works in another person's house, cooking, cleaning, etc.

serve /sɜːv/ v. **1** work for an employer: *He served in the army for three years.* **2** sell things to someone in a shop: *Can I serve you, madam?* **3** put a meal on the table: *I shall serve lunch at 1 o'clock.* **serve as**, be useful for something: *This box will serve as a table.* **it serves him** or **her right**, it is right that this bad thing has happened to him: *It serves her right that she feels sick—she ate too much.*

service /'sɜːvıs/ n. **1** (pl. services) help. **at your service**, ready to help you; ready for you: *I am at your service if you need me.* **2** (pl. services) work of someone who helps other people: *Do you need the services of a doctor?* **3** (no pl.) the staff and their work in a hotel or restaurant:

The food was good but the service was poor. **4** (*pl.* services) transport for the public: *This town has a good bus service.* **5** (*pl.* services) meeting in a church for prayers, singing, etc.: *Shall we go to the evening service?* **6** (*pl.* services) time when a car goes into a garage so that a mechanic can check it and oil it: *The car must have a service before we go on holiday.* **7** (*pl.* services) set of plates, bowls, cups, etc. for the table: *a tea service of 22 pieces.* **8** (usually *pl.*) **the services, the armed services**, the army, air force, and navy.

serviette /ˌsɜːvɪˈet/ *n.* small piece of cloth or paper that each person has at the table to keep his clothes clean, wipe his fingers on, etc.

set¹ /set/ *n.* **1** group of things of the same sort; group of things that you use together: *a set of tools.* **2** radio or television instrument: *We bought a new television set.*

set² *v.* (*pres. part.* setting, *past part.* & *past tense* set) **1** put something somewhere: *He set the suitcase on the floor.* **2** fix something firmly in a tight place: *The jeweller set a diamond in the ring.* **3** put something together in a certain way; make something ready: *The farmer set a trap for rats.* **set a bone**, put a broken bone together so that it will mend: *The doctor set my arm.* **4** go down from the sky: *The sun sets and night comes.* **5** make something happen; start something: *The book set me thinking.* **set fire to something, set something on fire**, make something burn: *The cigarette set the house on fire.* **set someone free**, let someone go out of prison, etc. **6** give work to someone to do: *Our teacher is setting us an exam.* **set about**, begin to do something: *How do I set about this job?* **set off, set out**, start a journey, race, etc.: *Mr. Carter set out for London at 11 o'clock.* **set sail**, start a voyage: *The liner set sail for New York at 8.30.*

settee /seˈtiː/ *n.* long, soft seat.

settle /ˈsetl/ *v.* **1** stop and rest somewhere: *The bird settled on a branch of the tree.* **2** be happy in a new job, position, etc.: *Has Dick settled in his new job?* **3** make your home in a new place: *Roy left England and went to settle in Australia.* **4** end a discussion, argument, etc.; decide something after

discussing it: *to settle an argument.* **5** pay money that you owe: *to settle a bill.*

settlement /ˈsetlmənt/ *n.* **1** agreeing about something after discussing it: *After long talks about pay, the managers and workers reached a settlement.* **2** group of homes in a place where no people have lived before: *The Pilgrim Fathers made a settlement in America.*

seven /ˈsevən/ *n.* number 7. **seven** *adj.*: *There are seven days in a week.* **seventh** /ˈsevənθ/ *adj.* 7th: *Saturday is the seventh day in the week.*

seventeen /ˌsevənˈtiːn/ *n.* number 17. **seventeen** *adj.*: *Tracy is seventeen.* **seventeenth** /ˌsevənˈtiːnθ/ *adj.* 17th.

seventy /ˈsevəntɪ/ *n.* (*pl.* seventies) number 70. **seventy** *adj.*: *seventy years old.* **seventieth** /ˈsevəntɪəθ/ *adj.* 70th.

several /ˈsevrəl/ *adj.* some, but not many: *I've read this book several times.* **several** *pron.*: *Several of us went to the theatre yesterday.*

severe /səˈvɪə(r)/ *adj.* **1** hard; strict: *a severe boss.* **2** that you feel strongly: *a severe pain.* **severely** *adv.*

sew /səʊ/ *v.* (*past part.* sewn /səʊn/, sewed /səʊd/, *past tense* sewed) make stitches with a needle and cotton to put pieces of cloth together; make clothes: *to sew a dress.* **sewing** *n.* **sewing-machine** *n.* machine that sews.

sex /seks/ *n.* (*pl.* sexes) being a male or a female: *What sex is the new baby?*

shabby /ˈʃæbɪ/ *adj.* **1** old and worn because you have used it a lot: *a shabby coat.* **2** with poor clothes: *a shabby man.* **shabbily** *adv.*: *She was shabbily dressed.*

shack /ʃæk/ *n.* hut; small, rough house.

shade¹ /ʃeɪd/ *n.* **1** (no *pl.*) where it is dark because the sun does not shine directly there: *Let's sit in the shade of the tree.* **2** (*pl.* shades) thing that keeps strong light from your eyes: *a sun-shade.* **3** (*pl.* shades) colour: *a dress in several different shades of blue.*

shade² *v.* stop light from shining straight on to something: *He shaded his eyes with his hand.*

shadow¹ /ˈʃædəʊ/ *n.* **1** (no *pl.*) darkness: *The north side of the mountain was in shadow.* **2** (*pl.* shadows) area of shade where the sunlight cannot fall because someone or something is standing in the way: *Our shadows get shorter as the sun goes higher*. **shadowy** *adj*. **1** with shadows: *a shadowy forest*. **2** not clear; like a shadow: *a shadowy figure in the darkness*.

shadow[2] *v*. follow and watch someone secretly: *The spy was shadowed by a policeman wearing plain clothes*.

shady /ˈʃeɪdɪ/ *adj*. not in bright sunshine; rather dark: *the shady side of the street*.

shake /ʃeɪk/ *v*. (*past part*. shaken /ˈʃeɪkən/, *past tense* shook /ʃʊk/) **1** move quickly, from side to side, up and down, etc.; tremble: *The house shook in the gale. She was shaking with fear*. **2** make something or someone tremble or move quickly from side to side, up and down, etc.: *An earthquake shook the city. The cat shook the rat*.

shaky /ˈʃeɪkɪ/ *adj*. **1** shaking or trembling: *shaky hands*. **2** not firm; not strong: *a shaky bridge*. **shakily** *adv*.

shall /ʃl̩/, /ʃæl/ *v*. **1** word that forms the future with other verbs; word that shows something is going to happen: *I shall come tomorrow*. **2** word that you say when you are asking for advice: *'Shall I help him?' asked Rob*.

shallow /ˈʃæləʊ/ *adj*. not deep; with not much water: *The river is shallow here—we can walk across*.

shame /ʃeɪm/ *n*. (no *pl*.) unhappy feeling because you have done something wrong or foolish: *She felt shame after she told the lie*. **it's a shame, what a shame**, it's sad: *It's a shame to work on a nice day!*

shameful /ˈʃeɪmfl̩/ *adj*. very bad: *a shameful lie*. **shamefully** *adv*.

shampoo /ʃæmˈpuː/ *n*. special sort of soap for washing hair. **shampoo** *v*. wash hair: *Will you shampoo my hair for me?*

shan't /ʃɑːnt/ = shall not.

shape[1] /ʃeɪp/ *n*. form: *What is the shape of the table—round or square?* **in good shape**, well. **in bad shape**, in bad condition; not well: *Roger is in bad shape after the accident*.

shape[2] *v*. make something; give a form to something: *She shaped the dough into*

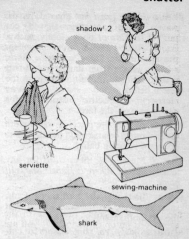

shadow[1] 2

serviette

sewing-machine

shark

biscuits. **shaped like**, with the form of something: *a brooch shaped like a flower*.

share[1] /ʃeə(r)/ *n*. how much one person gets or has: *Here is your share of the cake. I did my share of the work*.

share[2] *v*. **1** divide something and give parts to different people: *Share this bag of sweets with your friends*. **2** have or use something with another person: *I share a bedroom with my sister*.

shark /ʃɑːk/ *n*. big, fierce fish.

sharp[1] /ʃɑːp/ *adj*. **1** with an edge that cuts easily: *a sharp knife*. **2** with a fine point; that makes holes easily: *a sharp needle*. **3** clear; that you can see or smell clearly: *the sharp outline of mountains against the sky*. **4** that you hear loudly and suddenly: *a sharp cry*. **5** that can see, hear, etc. well: *sharp eyes; sharp ears*. **6** angry; severe: *sharp words*. **sharply** *adv*. **sharpness** *n*. **sharpen** /ˈʃɑːpən/ *v*. become sharp; make something sharp or sharper: *to sharpen a knife*. **sharpener** *n*. thing for making something sharp: *a pencil-sharpener*.

sharp[2] *adv*. **1** not later; exactly: *Come at six o'clock sharp*. **2** with a big change of direction: *Turn sharp right*.

shatter /ˈʃætə(r)/ *v*. break completely into small bits; break something into small bits: *The stone hit the window and shattered the glass*.

shave /ʃeɪv/ v. (*past part.* shaved /ʃeɪvd/, shaven /'ʃeɪvn/, *past tense* shaved) cut hair off the face or body closely, with a razor: *Father shaves every morning.* **shave** n. *a close shave, a narrow shave,* a lucky escape from danger. **shaving brush** n. brush for putting soap on the face before you shave. **shaver** /'ʃeɪvə(r)/ n. electric instrument for taking hair off the face.

shawl /ʃɔːl/ n. big piece of warm cloth that a woman wears round her shoulders or wraps round a baby.

she /ʃiː/ pron. (*pl.* they) word for any female person: *Where is Isabel? She is at home.*

shear /ʃɪə(r)/ v. (*past part.* shorn /ʃɔːn/, sheared /ʃɪəd/, *past tense* sheared) cut the wool off sheep.

shears /ʃɪəz/ n. (*pl.*) big scissors for cutting cloth, grass, sheep's wool, etc.

shed[1] /ʃed/ n. building for animals, tools, etc.: *a cow-shed.*

shed[2] v. (*pres. part.* shedding, *past part.* & *past tense* shed) take something off; let something fall: *Some trees shed their leaves in autumn.*

sheep /ʃiːp/ n. (*pl.* sheep) farm animal that gives us wool and meat.

sheer /ʃɪə(r)/ adj. **1** going straight up or down: *a sheer cliff.* **2** total: *a sheer waste of time.*

sheet /ʃiːt/ n. **1** big piece of thin cloth for a bed. **2** big, flat piece of something thin: *sheets of paper.*

shelf /ʃelf/ n. (*pl.* shelves) flat piece of wood, etc. on a wall or in a cupboard, where things can stand: *Please put the book back on the shelf when you have read it.*

she'll /ʃiːl/ = she will.

shell /ʃel/ n. hard, outside covering of birds' eggs, nuts, peas, etc., and of crabs, lobsters, and some other animals.

shellfish /'ʃelfɪʃ/ n. (*pl.* shellfish) crabs, shrimps, and other water-animals that have a hard, outside covering.

shelter[1] /'ʃeltə(r)/ n. **1** (no *pl.*) being safe from bad weather, danger, etc.: *We took shelter from the rain under a tree.* **2** (*pl.* shelters) place where you can be safe from bad weather, danger, etc.: *a shelter at a bus-stop.*

shelter[2] v. **1** make someone or something safe from bad weather, danger, etc.: *The wall sheltered him from the wind.* **2** go where you can be safe from bad weather, danger, etc.: *Let's shelter under this tree until the rain stops.*

shepherd /'ʃepəd/ n. man who looks after sheep. **shepherdess** /,ʃepə'des/ n. woman who looks after sheep.

shield[1] /ʃiːld/ n. piece of metal, wood, etc. that a soldier carried in wars long ago to keep himself safe from arrows, swords, etc.

shield[2] v. keep something or someone safe from danger, hurt, etc.: *He shielded his eyes from the bright sun.*

shift[1] /ʃɪft/ n. **1** group of workers who begin work when another group finishes: *Each shift in the factory works for eight hours.* **2** time when one group of workers are working: *the night shift.*

shift[2] v. move to another place; move something to another place: *Let's shift the beds so that we can sweep the floor.*

shine /ʃaɪn/ v. (*past part.* & past tense shone /ʃɒn/) **1** give out light; be bright: *The moon shines at night. The sun shines in the day.* **2** rub something to make it bright: *Go and shine your shoes.* **shine** n. brightness. **shiny** adj. bright: *a shiny, new bike.*

ship /ʃɪp/ n. big boat that sails on the sea. **ship** v. (*pres. part.* shipping, past part. & past tense shipped /ʃɪpt/) send something in a ship: *Australia ships meat to Britain.*

shipwreck /'ʃɪprek/ n. accident when a ship breaks up in a storm or on the rocks. **shipwreck** v.: *Many boats have been shipwrecked on the dangerous coast of Cornwall.*

shipyard /'ʃɪpjɑːd/ n. place where people build ships.

shirt /ʃɜːt/ n. piece of thin clothing that a man wears on the upper part of his body, under a jacket.

shiver /'ʃɪvə(r)/ v. shake because of cold, fever, or fear: *He shivered in the cold wind.*

shock[1] /ʃɒk/ n. **1** strong blow or shaking: *earthquake shocks.* **2** sudden pain when electricity passes through the body: *an electric shock.* **3** nasty surprise: *The news was a terrible shock.*

shock[2] *v.* **1** upset someone; give someone a nasty surprise: *His murder shocked everyone.* **2** give someone a sudden pain by electricity.

shocking /'ʃɒkɪŋ/ *adj.* surprising in a very bad way: *a shocking crime.*

shoe /ʃuː/ *n.* covering of leather, rubber, etc. that you wear on your foot: *a pair of shoes.*

shoe-lace /'ʃuː leɪs/ *n.* string that fastens a shoe.

shone /ʃɒn/ *past part.* & *past tense* of *v.* shine.

shook /ʃʊk/ *past tense* of *v.* shake.

shoot[1] /ʃuːt/ *n.* bud; new, green point of a plant.

shoot[2] *v.* (*past part.* & *past tense* shot /ʃɒt/) **1** send a bullet from a gun or an arrow from a bow; hurt or kill a person or animal with a bullet or arrow: *He shot the dying horse.* **2** move suddenly or quickly: *The cat shot out of the house with the dog behind her.* **3** make a film: *They are shooting the last scene now.*

shop[1] /ʃɒp/ *n.* building or part of a building where you buy things. **shop assistant** *n.* someone who works in a shop and sells things to people.

shop[2] *v.* (*pres. part.* shopping, *past part.* & *past tense* shopped /ʃɒpt/) buy things: *I always shop on Fridays.* **go shopping**, go out to buy things: *Will you buy some butter for me when you go shopping?* **shopping** *n.*: *She does her shopping after work.* **shopper** *n.* someone who is buying things.

shopkeeper /'ʃɒpkiːpə(r)/ *n.* someone who owns a shop.

shore /ʃɔː/ *n.* ground next to the sea or a big lake. **on shore,** (*a*) on the land: *Sailors enjoy their holidays on shore.* (*b*) on to the land from a boat or ship: *We tied up our boat and went on shore.*

shorn /ʃɔːn/ *past part.* of *v.* shear.

short[1] /ʃɔːt/ *adj.* **1** not long; very little from one end to the other: *It's only a short way, so you can walk there in a few minutes.* **2** very little from bottom to top; not tall: *She's too short to reach the top shelf.* **3** less than usual. **be** or **go short of,** not have enough: *Hilary went to the bank because she was short of money.*

sheep
shirt
shorts
shield[1]
shoe
shelf

short[2] *adv.* suddenly: *We stopped short because there was a big hole in the road.*

shortage /'ʃɔːtɪdʒ/ *n.* not enough of something: *After the hot summer, there was a shortage of water.*

shorten /'ʃɔːtn/ *v.* become shorter; make something shorter: *My dress is too long—I must shorten it.*

shorthand /'ʃɔːthænd/ *n.* (no *pl.*) way of writing quickly, with special signs: *A secretary must learn shorthand and typing.* **shorthand-typist** *n.* someone who does shorthand and typing in an office.

shortly /'ʃɔːtlɪ/ *adv.* soon: *We'll follow you shortly.* **shortly after,** soon after: *He left shortly after six.* **shortly before,** not long before: *We arrived shortly before the film started.*

shorts /ʃɔːts/ *n.* (*pl.*) short trousers. *Football players wear shorts.*

shot[1] /ʃɒt/ *n.* **1** firing a gun; noise made when a gun is fired: *We heard two shots.* **have a shot at,** try to do something: *It's a difficult job but I'll have a shot at it.* **2** photograph: *This is a good shot of the boat.*

shot[2] *past part.* & *past tense* of *v.* shoot.

should /ʃʊd/ *v.* **1** *past tense* of *v.* shall: *I said I should go to town.* **2** word that shows what you think will happen: *He should arrive soon.* **3** word to tell someone what is the right thing to do:

It's cold so you should wear a coat. **4** word that you say when you are asking for advice: *Should I wear a coat?*

shoulder /'ʃəʊldə(r)/ *n.* part where the arm joins the main part of the body: *Her bag hangs over her shoulder.*

shouldn't /'ʃʊdnt/ = should not.

shout /ʃaʊt/ *v.* cry words out loudly and strongly: *I have to shout at granny because she's deaf.* **shout for,** shout that you want something: *He shouted for help.* **shout** *n.*

shove /ʃʌv/ *v.* push someone or something. **shove** *n.*

shovel /'ʃʌvl/ *n.* spade; instrument for digging. **shovel** *v.* (*pres. part.* shovelling, *past part.* & *past tense* shovelled /'ʃʌvld/) move something with a shovel: *Dad shovelled snow off the path.*

show¹ /ʃəʊ/ *n.* **1** group of things for people to see: *the Boat Show.* **on show,** for people to see: *There's a new car on show at the garage.* **2** play, music and singing, etc. in a theatre, on radio or television, etc.: *a film show.* **give the show away,** tell people about a secret plan.

show² *v.* (*past part.* shown /ʃəʊn/, showed /ʃəʊd/, *past tense* showed) **1** let someone see something: *You must show your train ticket when the collector asks for it.* **2** appear; be seen: *Light was showing under the door.* **show someone round,** let someone see in a building, etc.: *David showed me round his old school.* **show that,** be a sign of something: *His cough shows that he smokes too much.* **show someone to a place,** take someone to a place: *He showed us to our room.* **show off,** talk loudly, etc. because you want people to think you are important. **show something off,** let people see something new, beautiful, etc.: *Sue wanted to show off her new dress.*

shower /'ʃaʊə(r)/ *n.* **1** brief fall of rain. **2** place where you can wash under water that falls from above: *There is a shower in our bathroom.* **3** washing yourself in a shower: *Bob took a shower after the game of football.*

shown /ʃəʊn/ *past part.* of *v.* show.

shrank /ʃræŋk/ *past tense* of *v.* shrink.

shred /ʃred/ *n.* small piece that you tear off something. **tear something to shreds,** tear something totally: *He angrily tore the letter to shreds.*

shriek /ʃriːk/ *v.* cry out loudly; scream. **shriek** *n.*

shrill /ʃrɪl/ *adj.* with a high, sharp sound: *a shrill whistle.*

shrine /ʃraɪn/ *n.* holy place: *the shrine at Lourdes.*

shrink /ʃrɪŋk/ *v.* (*past part.* shrunk /ʃrʌŋk/, shrunken /'ʃrʌŋkən/, *past tense* shrank /ʃræŋk/, shrunk) become smaller; make something smaller: *Woollen clothes shrink in hot water.*

shrivel /'ʃrɪvl/ *v.* (*pres. part.* shrivelling, *past part.* & *past tense* shrivelled /'ʃrɪvld/) dry up and die; make something dry up and die: *The corn shrivelled in the hot wind.*

shrub /ʃrʌb/ *n.* low bush.

shrug /ʃrʌg/ *v.* (*pres. part.* shrugging, *past part.* & *past tense* shrugged /ʃrʌgd/) move your shoulders to show that you do not know or do not care about something. **shrug** *n.: He answered my question with a shrug of the shoulders.*

shrunk /ʃrʌŋk/, **shrunken** /'ʃrʌŋkən/ *past part.* of *v.* shrink.

shudder /'ʃʌdə(r)/ *v.* **1** shake because you are afraid or do not like something: *He shuddered when he drank the horrible medicine.* **2** shake: *The building shuddered when the bomb exploded.* **shudder** *n.*

shuffle /'ʃʌfl/ *v.* drag your feet along the ground when you walk: *The old man was shuffling along the road.*

shut /ʃʌt/ *v.* (*pres. part.* shutting, *past part.* & *past tense* shut) **1** close something: *Please shut the door so that the dog cannot come out.* **2** close: *When does the supermarket shut?* **shut someone in** or **up,** keep a person or animal in a place: *He shuts his dog in the flat when he goes to work.* **shut someone out,** keep someone out of a place: *Shut the dog out of the room while we're eating.* **shut up,** stop talking; make someone stop talking: *Shut up, children—I can't hear the radio!* **shut something up,** close a box, place, etc. completely: *He shut up his shop at Christmas.*

shutter /'ʃʌtə(r)/ *n.* wooden or metal cover for a window.

shy /ʃaɪ/ *adj.* not sure about yourself; not finding it easy to talk to new people:

The shy boy blushed when I spoke to him.
shyly *adv.*

sick /sɪk/ *adj.* ill: *Sick people go to see a doctor.* **be sick,** throw up food from the stomach. **be sick of,** be tired of something: *I'm sick of all this rain.* **sickness** *n.* illness; disease.

side¹ /saɪd/ *n.* **1** one of the outer parts of something that is not the top or bottom: *A box has a top, a bottom, and four sides. The front door was closed so we went in by a door at the side of the house.* **2** the back or the front of a piece of paper, cloth, etc.: *There is printing on both sides of this paper.* **3** inner or outer part of something: *You've put your socks on with the wrong side out!* **4** right or left part: *He carries a gun at his side.* **by the side of,** next to: *They built a house by the side of the river.* **side¹ by side,** close together: *They walked side by side.* **5** part of a thing, place, etc. that is away from the middle; edge: *They rowed the boat to the side of the lake and got out.* **on every side,** everywhere: *In spring there are wild flowers on every side.* **put something on one side,** keep something until later: *Martha is too busy to finish her new dress this week, so she has put it on one side.* **6** team of players in sport: *Our school has a good football side.* **7** one of two groups of people who are quarrelling or fighting: *America and Japan were on different sides in the Second World War.* **on the side of,** with the same ideas as another person; helping another person in a quarrel: *Mel said I was wrong, but Andy was on my side.* **take the side of someone,** help someone in a quarrel, fight, etc.

side² *v.* **side with,** help someone, or agree with someone, in a fight, quarrel, etc.: *Mel said I was wrong, but Andy sided with me.*

sideboard /'saɪdbɔːd/ *n.* long, low cupboard in a dining-room, where you keep cups, plates, glasses, etc.

sideways /'saɪdweɪz/ *adv.* **1** to one side: *She looked sideways at the girl in the next seat.* **2** with a side or edge first: *We can drive a car forwards or backwards, but not sideways.*

siege /siːdʒ/ *n.* long attack on a town or camp so that people inside cannot get out or fetch help.

shower · shoulder · sideboard · shovel · sign¹ 1

sigh /saɪ/ *v.* take a long, deep breath when you are tired, sad, glad, etc.: *She sighed when she saw the hole in her blouse.* **sigh** *n.:* *'I wish I had a friend,' she said with a sigh.*

sight /saɪt/ *n.* **1** (*no pl.*) seeing: *She wears glasses because she has bad sight.* **catch sight of,** see someone or something suddenly: *I caught sight of Tim's face in the crowd.* **come into sight,** come near so that you can see it: *We ran to the bus-stop when the bus came into sight.* **out of sight,** where you cannot see it: *We waved until the car was out of sight.* **2** (*pl.* sights) something that you see: *After the fire, the house was a terrible sight.*

sightseer /'saɪtsiːə(r)/ *n.* someone who comes to look at an interesting building or happening: *The castle was full of sightseers.* **sightseeing** *n.:* *a day's sightseeing in Stratford-on-Avon.*

sign¹ /saɪn/ *n.* **1** mark, word, picture, or movement to show something: *+ and − are signs for 'plus' and 'minus' in arithmetic. The policeman made a sign for us to stop.* **2** something that tells you about another thing: *Dark clouds are a sign of rain.*

sign² *v.* write your name in your own way on something: *His secretary typed the letter and he signed it.*

signal /'sɪɡnəl/ *v.* (*pres. part.* signalling, *past part.* & *past tense* signalled /'sɪɡnəld/) tell people something by moving your hand, a flag, etc. or by putting on a light: *The policeman signalled the children to cross the road.* **signal** *n.*: *A red light is usually a signal of danger.*

signature /'sɪgnətʃə(r)/ *n.* your name that you have written in your own way.

significant /sɪg'nɪfɪkənt/ *adj.* with a meaning; important: *Do you think that her silence is significant?* **significantly** *adv.*

signpost /'saɪnpəʊst/ *n.* sign by the road that shows the way to a place, how far the place is, etc.

silence[1] /'saɪləns/ *n.* **1** (no *pl.*) total quiet: *I must have silence for my work.* **2** (*pl.* silences) time of quiet, no talking, etc.: *There was a long silence before she answered the question.*

silence[2] *v.* make someone or something quiet: *The chairman silenced the meeting.*

silent /'saɪlənt/ *adj.* **1** with no sound; quiet: *The house was silent because everyone was asleep.* **2** saying nothing; giving no answer. *keep silent,* (*a*) say nothing. (*b*) keep a secret. **silently** *adv.*

silk /sɪlk/ *n.* (no *pl.*) fine, soft thread from an insect called a **silkworm**, which people make into cloth; cloth made of silk. **silk** *adj.* made of silk: *a silk scarf.*

sill /sɪl/ *n.* flat shelf at the bottom of a window: *The cat sat on the sill and looked out of the window.*

silly /'sɪlɪ/ *adj.* foolish; stupid.

silver /'sɪlvə(r)/ *n.* (no *pl.*) **1** shiny, white metal of great value. **2** things made of silver. **silver** *adj.* **1** made of silver: *a silver teapot.* **2** with the colour of silver: *silver shoes.* **silvery** *adj.* like silver.

similar /'sɪmɪlə(r)/ *adj.* alike; almost the same: *Rats and mice are similar animals.* **similarly** *adv.*

simple /'sɪmpl/ *adj.* **1** easy to do or understand: *I did the work quickly because it was so simple.* **2** plain; ordinary: *a simple meal.* **3** foolish; stupid: *She's so simple that she thinks babies grow on bushes!*

simplify /'sɪmplɪfaɪ/ *v.* make something easy to understand or do: *This dictionary tries to simplify the meanings of words.* **simplification** /ˌsɪmplɪfɪ'keɪʃn/ *n.*

simply /'sɪmplɪ/ *adv.* **1** in a plain, ordinary way: *simply dressed.* **2** really; quite: *Your French accent is simply terrible!*

sin /sɪn/ *n.* breaking of God's laws; doing something wicked. **sin** *v.* (*pres. part.* sinning, *past part.* & *past tense* sinned /sɪnd/) **sinful** *adj.* **sinner** *n.* someone who has sinned.

since[1] /sɪns/ *adv.* from then until now: *Alan went away two years ago and we have not seen him since.* *ever since,* in all the time from then until now: *Jack went to Canada in 1974 and has lived there ever since.*

since[2] *conj.* **1** from the time when: *What have you done since I saw you last?* **2** because; as: *Since I have no money, I can't buy any food.*

since[3] *prep.* in all the time after: *She has been ill since last Sunday.*

sincere /sɪn'sɪə(r)/ *adj.* honest; meaning what you say: *Are you sincere when you say you will work harder?* **sincerely** *adv.* *Yours sincerely,* way of ending a letter to someone you know.

sing /sɪŋ/ *v.* (*past part.* sung /sʌŋ/, *past tense* sang /sæŋ/) make music with your voice: *Robert sings in a church choir.* **singer** *n.* someone who sings.

single[1] /'sɪŋgl/ *adj.* **1** one: *I haven't a single enemy.* **2** not married: *a single man.* **3** for or by one person: *a single bed.* **4** for a journey to a place but not back again: *a single ticket.*

single[2] *n.* **1** ticket for a journey to a place but not back again: *A single to London, please.* **2** record with one song on each side.

single-handed /ˌsɪŋgl 'hændɪd/ *adj.* by one person alone. **single-handed** *adv.*: *He caught the thief single-handed.*

singular /'sɪŋgjʊlə(r)/ *n.* form of a word for one person or thing: *'Chair' is singular; 'chairs' is plural.* **singular** *adj.*: *a singular noun.*

sink[1] /sɪŋk/ *n.* place in a kitchen where you wash dishes, etc.

sink[2] *v.* (*past part.* sunk /sʌŋk/, *past tense* sank /sæŋk/) **1** go under water; make a ship, etc. go under water: *He dropped a stone into the river and it sank to the bottom.* **2** go down; go lower: *The sun was sinking in the west.*

sip /sɪp/ v. (*pres. part.* sipping, *past part.* & *past tense* sipped /sɪpt/) drink a little at a time: *She sipped the hot tea.* **sip** *n.*: *Have a sip of my wine to see if you like it.*

sir /sɜː(r)/ n. **1** polite word that you say when you speak to a man who is older, more important, or a stranger, or when you write a business letter to a man. **2** **Sir**, word before the name of a knight: *Sir Winston Churchill.*

siren /'saɪərən/ n. thing that makes a long, loud noise to warn people: *a fire siren.*

sister /'sɪstə(r)/ n. **1** girl or woman who has the same parents as you. **2** nurse in a hospital. **3** nun. **sisterly** *adj.* of or like a sister.

sister-in-law /'sɪstər ɪn lɔː/ n. (*pl.* sisters-in-law) sister of your wife or husband; wife of your brother.

sit /sɪt/ v. (*pres. part.* sitting, *past part.* & *past tense* sat /sæt/) put yourself down on your bottom; rest on your bottom: *John sat on the most comfortable chair.* **sit down**, sit when you have been standing: *He came in and sat down.* **sit up**, sit when you have been lying: *She sat up in bed and looked at the clock.* **sitting-room** /'sɪtɪŋ rʊm/ n. room in a house where you can sit comfortably.

site /saɪt/ n. place where something is, was, or will be: *London is on the site of a Roman fort. We put up our tent in the camp site.*

situated /'sɪtʃʊeɪtɪd/ adj. **be situated**, be in a place: *The house is situated near the station.*

situation /ˌsɪtʃʊ'eɪʃn/ n. **1** place where a town, building, etc. is: *The castle has a lovely situation on a hill.* **2** the way things are at a certain time: *The family was in a difficult situation when mother was in hospital.*

six /sɪks/ n. (*pl.* sixes) number 6: *Alex was six today.* **six** *adj.* **sixth** /sɪksθ/ *adj.* 6th: *Alexander's sixth birthday.*

sixteen /sɪk'stiːn/ n. number 16. **sixteen** *adj.* **sixteenth** /sɪk'stiːnθ/ *adj.* 16th.

sixty /'sɪkstɪ/ n. (*pl.* sixties) number 60. **sixty** *adj.* **sixtieth** /'sɪkstɪəθ/ *adj.* 60th.

size /saɪz/ n. **1** (no *pl.*) how big or small

skate

signpost

skeleton

skateboard

something is: *You can wear my dress because we are the same size.* **2** (*pl.* sizes) exact measurement: *Her shoes are size 5.*

skate /skeɪt/ n. piece of metal with a sharp edge that is fixed under a boot for moving on ice: *a pair of skates.* **skate** v. move on skates: *The children skated over the frozen river.* **skating-rink** n. special place where you can skate.

skateboard /'skeɪtbɔːd/ n. long piece of wood or plastic on wheels. You stand on it while it runs quickly over the ground.

skeleton /'skelɪtn/ n. bone frame in the body of an animal or person.

sketch /sketʃ/ v. draw something quickly. **sketch** n. quick drawing.

ski /skiː/ n. one of two long pieces of wood that you fix under your boot for moving quickly and smoothly over snow: *a pair of skis.* **ski** v. move over snow on skis: *We skied down the hill.* **skiing** n. sport of moving over snow on skis. **skier** n. person who skis. **ski-slope** /'skiː sləʊp/ n. hill or mountain where you can ski.

skid /skɪd/ v. (*pres. part.* skidding, *past part.* & *past tense* skidded /'skɪdɪd/) move or slip dangerously to the side: *The car skidded on the wet road.* **skid** n.: *The car went into a skid.*

skies /skaɪz/ (*pl.*) of n. sky.

skill /skɪl/ n. **1** (no *pl.*) being able to do something well and in the right way: *She* *plays the piano with great skill.* **2** (*pl.* skills) something you can do well. **skilful** *adj.: a skilful athlete.* **skilfully** *adv.*

skilled /skɪld/ *adj.* trained; good because you have learned for a long time: *a skilled workman.*

skin /skɪn/ *n.* **1** (no *pl.*) thin stuff that covers the body of a person or animal: *Most Africans have darker skins than Europeans.* **by the skin of your teeth**, only just: *I passed the test by the skin of my teeth!* **2** (*pl.* skins) total outside covering of an animal: *bear skins.* **3** (*pl.* skins) outside covering of some vegetables and fruit: *banana skins.*

skinny /'skɪnɪ/ *adj.* thin: *a skinny child.*

skip /skɪp/ *v.* (*pres. part.* skipping, *past part.* & *past tense* skipped /skɪpt/) **1** run, jumping lightly with each foot: *The little girl skipped down the road.* **2** jump again and again over a rope that you are swinging. **skipping-rope** *n.* piece of rope for skipping. **skip** *n.* little jump.

skipper /'skɪpə(r)/ *n.* **1** captain of a boat or small ship. **2** captain of a football or cricket team.

skirt /skɜːt/ *n.* piece of clothing for a woman or girl, which hangs from the waist.

skull /skʌl/ *n.* bones of the head.

sky /skaɪ/ *n.* (*pl.* skies) space above the earth with the sun, moon, and stars: *a blue sky.*

skyline /'skaɪlaɪn/ *n.* the shape of the land or a town against the sky.

skyscraper /'skaɪskreɪpə(r)/ *n.* very high building.

slab /slæb/ *n.* big, flat piece of something: *a slab of concrete.*

slack /slæk/ *adj.* **1** lazy; not working hard: *a slack student.* **2** with little work or business to do: *February is a slack time for hotels by the sea.* **3** loose; not tight: *a slack rope.* **slackly** *adv.* **slackness** *n.*

slam /slæm/ *v.* (*pres. part.* slamming, *past part.* & *past tense* slammed /slæmd/) close something loudly and strongly; throw something down with a loud noise: *He slammed the door angrily.* **slam** *n.: He closed the door with a slam.*

slang /slæŋ/ *n.* (no *pl.*) words for ordinary talk, but not for writing or fine talk: *The word 'copper' is slang for policeman.*

slant /slɑːnt/ *v.* lean to one side. **slanting** *adj.* with one side higher than the other: *slanting eyes.* **slant** *n.*

slap /slæp/ *v.* (*pres. part.* slapping, *past part.* & *past tense* slapped /slæpt/) **1** hit someone with your open hand: *Why did you slap my cheek?* **2** put something down hard: *He slapped the money on the counter.* **slap** *n.*

slash /slæʃ/ *v.* make a long cut in something. **slash** *n.*

slaughter /'slɔːtə(r)/ *v.* **1** kill an animal for food: *to slaughter a lamb.* **2** kill a big group of people. **slaughter** *n.*

slave /sleɪv/ *n.* servant who belongs to a master and receives no money. **slavery** *n.* **1** being a slave: *They lived in slavery.* **2** having slaves: *William Wilberforce worked hard to end slavery.*

sledge /sledʒ/ *n.* sort of cart that moves on long pieces of metal or wood over the snow.

sleep /sliːp/ *v.* (*past part.* & *past tense* slept /slept/) rest yourself totally, with your eyes closed, as in bed at night. **sleep** *n.* **go to sleep**, start to sleep: *She will go to sleep quickly because she's very tired.* **sleeping bag** *n.* big, warm bag that you sleep inside when you are camping, etc. **sleepless** /'sliːpləs/ *adj.* not able to sleep.

sleepy /'sliːpɪ/ *adj.* **1** tired; wanting to sleep: *I'm sleepy after my long walk.* **2** quiet; with not many things happening: *a sleepy village.* **sleepily** *adv.: Richard yawned sleepily.*

sleet /sliːt/ *n.* (no *pl.*) falling snow with rain.

sleeve /sliːv/ *n.* part of a dress, shirt, coat, etc. that covers your arm.

sleigh /sleɪ/ *n.* sort of cart that moves on long pieces of metal or wood over the snow.

slender /'slendə(r)/ *adj.* nicely thin: *a slender girl.*

slept /slept/ *past part.* & *past tense* of *v.* sleep.

slice /slaɪs/ *n.* thin piece that you cut off bread, meat, or other food: *a slice of cake.* **slice** *v.* cut something into slices: *Heather sliced the ham for sandwiches.*

slide¹ /slaɪd/ *n.* **1** moving smoothly over or down something: *The children were having a slide down the icy path.* **2** special thing for children where they can climb up steps and slide down the other side: *There are swings and slides in the children's playground.* **3** piece of film that you put in a projector which shows the picture on a screen: *Have you seen the slides of our holiday?*

slide² *v.* (*past part. & past tense* slid /slɪd/) move smoothly; make something move smoothly: *The drawers of my desk slide in and out easily.*

slight /slaɪt/ *adj.* small; not important or bad: *a slight mistake.*

slightly /'slaɪtlɪ/ *adv.* a little: *I'm feeling slightly better today.*

slim¹ /slɪm/ *adj.* (slimmer, slimmest) nicely thin: *slim legs.*

slim² *v.* (*pres. part.* slimming, *past part. & past tense* slimmed /slɪmd/) try to get thinner by eating less food, etc.

sling¹ /slɪŋ/ *n.* piece of cloth that holds up a broken or hurt arm.

sling² *v.* (*past part. & past tense* slung /slʌŋ/) **1** throw something: *The boys were slinging stones into the river.* **2** hang something in a place: *Molly slung her bag over her shoulder.*

slink /slɪŋk/ *v.* (*past part. & past tense* slunk /slʌŋk/) walk quietly, with your head down, because you are in trouble: *The dog slunk under the chair when the boy kicked him.*

slip¹ /slɪp/ *n.* **1** sliding and falling, or almost falling: *He had a nasty slip on the icy path.* **2** small mistake that you make when you are not careful: *There are too many slips in your work.* **3** small piece of paper: *Paul gave me a slip with his telephone number.*

slip² *v.* (*pres. part.* slipping, *past part. & past tense* slipped /slɪpt/) **1** fall or almost fall: *She broke her leg when she slipped on the ice.* **2** go quickly and quietly so that no one notices: *She slipped out of the room.* **3** take something, or put something somewhere, quickly and quietly: *He slipped the money into his pocket.* **slip something on** or **off**, put something on or off quickly and easily: *He slipped his coat on.* **slip up**, make a mistake.

slipper /'slɪpə(r)/ *n.* light, soft shoe that you wear in the house: *a pair of slippers.*

slippery /'slɪpərɪ/ *adj.* so smooth, wet,

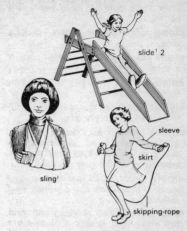

etc. that you cannot hold it or stand on it easily: *The slippery fish dropped from his hands.*

slit /slɪt/ *n.* long, narrow hole: *Post the letter through the slit in the letter-box.*
slit *v.* (*pres. part.* slitting, *past part. & past tense* slit) make a slit: *to slit an envelope open.*

slither /'slɪðə(r)/ *v.* slide; slip.

slope /sləʊp/ *n.* **1** line that has one end higher than the other: *the slope of a roof.* **2** piece of ground that goes up or down: *He skied fast down the mountain slope.* **slope** *v.*: *The field slopes down to the river.* **sloping** *adj.*: *sloping roofs.*

slot /slɒt/ *n.* narrow hole where you can push something through.

slot-machine /'slɒt məʃi:n/ *n.* machine that pushes out a packet of cigarettes, sweets, etc. when you put a coin through a hole.

slow¹ /sləʊ/ *adj.* **1** not quick; that takes a long time: *A slow runner will not win many races.* **2** showing a time earlier than it really is: *My watch is five minutes slow.* **slow** *adv.* word that you usually put with an adjective: *a slow-moving train.* **slowly** *adv.*: *The old lady walked slowly up the hill.* **slowness** *n.*

slow² *v.* **slow down, slow up**, go slower; make something go slower: *The train slowed down as it came to the station.*

slum /slʌm/ *n.* poor building; part of a

town where there are many poor, dirty houses.

slung /slʌŋ/ *past part. & past tense* of *v.* sling.

slunk /slʌŋk/ *past part. & past tense* of *v.* slink.

slush /slʌʃ/ *n.* (no *pl.*) soft, melting snow; soft mud.

sly /slaɪ/ *adj.* doing things secretly; ready to lie, trick, etc. **slyly** *adv.*

smack /smæk/ *v.* hit a person or animal with your open hand: *She smacked the dog because it was on her chair.* **smack, smacking** *n.*: *She gave it a smack.*

small /smɔːl/ *adj.* **1** not big; little: *A mouse is a small animal.* **2** young: *small children.*

smart /smɑːt/ *adj.* **1** clean and neat; new and bright; elegant: *a smart suit; a smart new car.* **2** clever; with a quick mind: *a smart pupil.* **smartly** *adv.*

smash¹ /smæʃ/ *n.* (*pl.* smashes) **1** accident; two things coming together hard: *a car smash.* **2** big noise when something falls, breaks, etc.: *The vase fell with a smash.*

smash² *v.* **1** drop or hit something and break it: *The ball smashed a window.* **2** break into pieces: *Did the glass smash when it fell?*

smashing /'smæʃɪŋ/ *adj.* very good; wonderful: *a smashing film.*

smear /smɪə(r)/ *v.* **1** spread soft stuff on something: *She smeared suntan oil on her legs.* **2** make dirty marks on something: *You smeared your face when you rubbed it.* **smear** *n.*

smell /smel/ *v.* (*past part. & past tense* smelt, smelled /smelt/) **1** notice something with your nose: *Can you smell smoke?* **2** give out something that you notice with your nose: *That fish smells bad. These roses smell lovely.* **3** give out something that seems bad to the nose: *Those dirty socks smell!* **smell** *n.* what you smell: *a smell of cooking from the kitchen.*

smelly /'smelɪ/ *adj.* with a bad smell: *dirty, smelly clothes.*

smile /smaɪl/ *v.* have a happy look on your face: *Lisa smiled because she was pleased to see us.* **smile** *n.*: *She answered with a smile.*

smoke¹ /sməʊk/ *n.* **1** (no *pl.*) grey or black stuff that goes up into the air from fire, etc.: *cigarette smoke.* **2** (*pl.* smokes) having a cigarette, pipe, etc.: *They stopped work for a smoke.*

smoke² *v.* **1** give out smoke: *The chimney was smoking.* **2** have a lighted cigarette, pipe, etc. in the mouth: *He smoked a cigar after lunch.* **smoking** *n.*: *No smoking in the theatre.*

smoked /sməʊkt/ *adj.* dried over a wood fire so that it will keep for a long time: *smoked ham.*

smoker /'sməʊkə(r)/ *n.* someone who smokes cigarettes or tobacco.

smoky /'sməʊkɪ/ *adj.* **1** full of smoke: *a smoky room.* **2** giving out a lot of smoke: *a smoky fire.*

smooth /smuːð/ *adj.* **1** not rough; flat: *A baby has a smooth skin.* **2** that does not shake or bump you; gentle: *a smooth ride.* **3** not difficult; with no problems: *a smooth meeting.* **smoothly** *adv.*

smother /'smʌðə(r)/ *v.* **1** kill someone by stopping him breathing. **2** put out a fire by covering it with sand, etc. **3** cover something totally or thickly: *The wind smothered the houses with dust.*

smoulder /'sməʊldə(r)/ *v.* burn slowly with no flames: *The fire was still smouldering the next morning.*

smuggle /'smʌgl/ *v.* **1** take things secretly into a country and not pay tax: *He hid a hundred gold watches in his car and smuggled them into the country.* **2** take something secretly into a place: *She smuggled a gun to the man in prison.* **smuggler** *n.* someone who smuggles.

snack /snæk/ *n.* small, quick meal. **snack-bar** *n.* place where you can buy and eat snacks.

snag /snæg/ *n.* small problem that you did not expect: *The house will be ready next week if there are no snags.*

snail /sneɪl/ *n.* small, soft animal with a shell on its back.

snake /sneɪk/ *n.* long reptile with no legs.

snap¹ /snæp/ *v.* (*pres. part.* snapping, *past part. & past tense* snapped /snæpt/) **1** try to bite: *The dog snapped at my leg.* **2** break with a sharp sound: *Sam pulled* *the rubber band until it snapped.* **3** say something quickly and angrily: *'Go away—I'm busy!' he snapped.* **snap** *n.*

snap², **snapshot** /'snæpʃɒt/ *n.* photograph.

snarl /snɑːl/ *v.* show the teeth and make a low, angry sound: *The dog snarled at the stranger.* **snarl** *n.*

snatch /snætʃ/ *v.* take something roughly and quickly: *The thief snatched her handbag and ran off.*

sneer /snɪə(r)/ *v.* talk or smile in a nasty way to show that you think someone is poor, weak, stupid, etc.: *The boys sneered at him because his family was poor.* **sneer** *n.*

sneeze /sniːz/ *v.* suddenly send out air from your nose and mouth: *Ann had a cold and was sneezing and coughing.* **sneeze** *n.*

sniff /snɪf/ *v.* **1** take air noisily through your nose because you do not have a handkerchief. **2** smell something: *The dog sniffed the meat.* **sniff** *n.*

snip /snɪp/ *v.* (*pres. part.* snipping, *past part.* & *past tense* snipped /snɪpt/) cut something with scissors: *to snip off the end of a thread.* **snip** *n.*

snooze /snuːz/ *v.* sleep for a short time. **snooze** *n.*

snore /snɔː(r)/ *v.* breathe roughly and noisily while you are asleep. **snore** *n.*

snow /snəʊ/ *n.* (no *pl.*) soft, white stuff that falls from the sky when it is very cold: *The road was blocked with snow.* **snowflake** /'snəʊfleɪk/ *n.* one piece of falling snow. **snow** *v.*: *It often snows in Scotland in the winter.* **snowed up**, unable to leave a place because there is so much snow on the ground.

snowy /'snəʊɪ/ *adj.* **1** with a lot of snow: *snowy weather.* **2** white, like snow: *a snowy beard.*

snug /snʌg/ *adj.* (snugger, snuggest) warm and comfortable.

so¹ /səʊ/ *adv.* **1** word that you say when you tell how much, how big, etc. something or someone is: *The bag is so heavy that I can't carry it.* **so . . . as**, words that you use with 'not' to show how different two things or people are: *He is not so tall as his brother.* **2** very: *Why are you so late?* **3** in this way; in that way: *Don't*

shout so! **4** also: *Carol is very pretty; so is her sister.* **5** word to show that you agree: *'Tomorrow is a holiday.' 'So it is.'* **so as to**, in order to: *I'll get up early, so as to be ready when you come.* **so far**, up to now, etc.: *So far, I have understood the lesson.* **so that**, in order that: *Speak loudly, so that I can hear what you say.*

so² *conj.* for this reason; for that reason: *The shop is closed, so I can't buy the bread.*

so³ *exclam.* word that shows you are a little surprised: *So you've come back again!*

soak /səʊk/ *v.* **1** be in liquid; put something in liquid: *The dirty clothes were soaking in soapy water.* **2** make something or someone wet: *The rain soaked us.* **soaked** /səʊkt/, **soaking** *adj.* very wet. **soak up**, take in liquid: *Dry ground quickly soaks up water.*

soap /səʊp/ *n.* (no *pl.*) stuff that you put with water for washing and cleaning. **soap-powder** *n.* soap in the form of powder for washing clothes, etc. **soapy** *adj.* full of soap: *soapy water.*

soar /sɔː(r)/ *v.* fly; go up into the air: *The bird soared in the sky.*

sob /sɒb/ *v.* (*pres. part.* sobbing, *past part.* & *past tense* sobbed /sɒbd/) cry: *The child started to sob when he couldn't find his mother.* **sob** *n.*

sober /'səʊbə(r)/ *adj.* not drunk: *A driver must stay sober.*

soccer /'sɒkə(r)/ *n.* (no *pl.*) football.

social /'səʊʃl/ *adj.* of people together; of being with other people: *Rosemary has a busy social life.*

society /sə'saɪətɪ/ *n.* **1** (no *pl.*) people living together: *A murderer is a danger to society.* **2** (*pl.* societies) club; group of people with the same interests: *the Music Society.*

sock /sɒk/ *n.* piece of clothing that you wear on your foot, inside a shoe.

socket /'sɒkɪt/ *n.* hole where something goes: *She pushed the plug into the electric socket on the wall.*

soda-water /'səʊdə wɔːtə(r)/ *n.* (no *pl.*) water with gas-bubbles in it, which you drink.

sofa /'səʊfə/ *n.* long, soft seat.

soft /sɒft/ *adj.* **1** not hard; not firm: *Feet leave prints in soft ground.* **2** not rough; smooth: *soft hands.* **3** not strong in colour: *soft blue.* **4** that you cannot see or hear clearly; not bright; not loud: *a soft light.* **5** too kind or gentle: *a soft person.* **6** that does not move strongly: *a soft wind.* **7** with no alcohol: *Lemonade is a soft drink.* **softly** *adv.* gently; quietly: *Speak softly—the baby's asleep.*

soft-hearted /ˌsɒft 'hɑːtɪd/ *adj.* kind; gentle: *a soft-hearted mother.*

soggy /'sɒgɪ/ *adj.* very wet: *soggy ground.*

soil¹ /sɔɪl/ *n.* ground; earth: *Plants grow well in good soil.*

soil² *v.* make something dirty.

sold /səʊld/ *past part.* & *past tense* of *v.* sell. *sold out*, with no more to sell: *I'm sorry—the bananas are sold out.*

soldier /'səʊldʒə(r)/ *n.* person in an army.

sole¹ /səʊl/ *adj.* only; single: *Her aunt is her sole relative—all the rest of the family are dead.*

sole² *n.* the under part of a foot, or of a sock, shoe, etc.

sole³ *n.* flat sea-fish that you can eat.

solemn /'sɒləm/ *adj.* serious: *a solemn face.* **2** slow and sad: *solemn music.* **solemnly** *adv.*

solid /'sɒlɪd/ *adj.* **1** hard; not liquid or gas: *Ice is solid water.* **2** with no hollow inside; the same all through: *a plate of solid gold.* **3** strong: *I want a good, solid box that won't break easily.*

solitary /'sɒlɪtrɪ/ *adj.* alone; with no other people: *He went for a solitary walk.*

solo /'səʊləʊ/ *n.* music for one person to sing or play: *a piano solo.* **solo** *adv.* alone: *Has Mark flown solo yet?*

soloist /'səʊləʊɪst/ *n.* someone who sings or plays a musical instrument alone.

solve /sɒlv/ *v.* find the answer to a question or a problem: *Will you help me to solve this puzzle?* **solution** /sə'luːʃn/ *n.*: *The solutions to the questions are at the back of the book.*

some¹ /sʌm/ *adj.* **1** a number of; an amount of: *Go to the supermarket and buy some tomatoes and some meat.* **2** part of a number or amount: *Some of these children can swim, but the others can't.* **3** word to show that you do not know who or what: *There's some man at the door—go and see what he wants.* *some more*, a little more; a few more. *some time*, quite a long time: *We waited for some time, but Fay didn't come.*

some² *pron.* (no *pl.*) an amount; a number: *Those apples look lovely—can I have some?*

somebody /'sʌmbədɪ/ *pron.* (no *pl.*) a person; a person whom you do not know: *Somebody knocked at the door.*

someone /'sʌmwʌn/ *pron.* (no *pl.*) a person; a person whom you do not know: *Can someone answer the question?*

somersault /'sʌməsɔːlt/ *n.* jumping and turning over completely and land on your feet again. **somersault** *v.*

something /'sʌmθɪŋ/ *pron.* (no *pl.*) a thing; a thing that you cannot name: *There's something on the floor—what is it?*

sometime /'sʌmtaɪm/ *adv.* at a time that you do not know exactly: *I saw him sometime last year.*

sometimes /'sʌmtaɪmz/ *adv.* not very often: *We sometimes visit our grandmother.*

somewhere /'sʌmweə(r)/ *adv.* at, in, or to a place that you do not know exactly: *I left my book somewhere near here.*

son /sʌn/ *n.* boy child: *The man was walking with his son.*

song /sɒŋ/ *n.* **1** (no *pl.*) singing; music of

voices: *bird-song.* **2** (*pl.* songs) piece of music that you sing: *'Greensleeves' is an old English song.*

son-in-law /ˈsʌn ɪn lɔː/ *n.* (*pl.* sons-in-law) husband of your daughter.

soon /suːn/ *adv.* in a short time from now: *Will Neville come home soon?* **as soon as,** when; at the exact time that: *I'll leave as soon as I'm ready.* **soon after,** not long after a time: *We arrived soon after three o'clock.* **sooner or later,** some time or other: *I expect I'll see him again sooner or later.* **sooner than, (a)** earlier than: *Neville arrived sooner than we expected.* (**b**) rather than; which is better than: *He'll change his job sooner than work for that boss.* **too soon,** too early: *We got to the station twenty minutes too soon for the train.*

soot /sʊt/ *n.* (no *pl.*) black powder that comes from smoke in chimneys.

soothe /suːð/ *v.* make someone quiet or calm: *The rider soothed the frightened horse.* **soothing** *adj.: a soothing voice.* **soothingly** *adv.*

sore /sɔː(r)/ *adj.* giving pain: *My feet are sore after the long walk.*

sorrow /ˈsɒrəʊ/ *n.* sadness. **sorrowful** *adj.* **sorrowfully** *adv.*

sorry¹ /ˈsɒrɪ/ *adj.* sad: *I am sorry that your father has died.*

sorry² *exclam.* word to say 'no' politely: *Sorry—I can't help you.*

sort¹ /sɔːt/ *n.* kind; group of people or things that are the same: *What sort of music do you like best—pop or classical?* **sort of,** words that you use about a thing, idea, etc. when you are not sure: *He looks sort of ill.*

sort² *v.* put things in groups: *I sorted the shoes into pairs.*

S.O.S. /ˌes əʊ ˈes/ *n.* call for help from a ship, aeroplane, etc. that is in danger.

sought /sɔːt/ *past part.* & *past tense* of *v.* seek.

soul /səʊl/ *n.* **1** your spirit; the part of you that does not die with your body. **2** one person: *Everyone had gone out and there was not a soul in the house.*

sound¹ /saʊnd/ *adj.* **1** healthy; strong: *He has sound teeth with no holes in them.* **2** sensible: *a sound idea.* **3** total; complete: *He's in such a sound sleep*

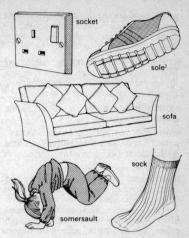

socket

sole²

sofa

sock

somersault

that he won't hear anything. **soundness** *n.*

sound², **soundly** *adv.* totally: *to be sound asleep.*

sound³ *n.* **1** (*pl.* sounds) noise; what you can hear: *I heard the sound of church bells.* **2** (no *pl.*) thought or idea that you have when you hear about or read something: *They say that food prices will soon go up—I don't like the sound of that.*

sound⁴ *v.* **1** make something give out a noise; make a noise: *The doorbell sounded.* **2** seem: *He told me about the book—it sounds interesting.*

soup /suːp/ *n.* liquid food that you eat with a spoon.

sour /ˈsaʊə(r)/ *adj.* **1** with a sharp, bitter taste: *A lemon is sour.* **2** bad, not fresh: *sour milk.*

source /sɔːs/ *n.* **1** place where a river starts: *Where is the source of the Thames?* **2** place where something comes from: *a source of information.*

south /saʊθ/ *n.* (no *pl.*) one of the points of the compass. **south** *adj.: a south wind.* **south** *adv.: England is south of Scotland.* **southerly** /ˈsʌðəlɪ/ *adj.* in or from a place that is south: *We drove in a southerly direction from Manchester to London.* **southern** /ˈsʌðən/ *adj.* of, from, or in the south part of a town, country, the world, etc.: *Brighton* *is in southern England.* **southwards** /'saʊθwədz/ *adv.* towards the south: *We drove southwards from Manchester to London.*

souvenir /ˌsuːvə'nɪə(r)/ *n.* something that you buy or give because it will bring memories: *He brought back a cowboy hat as a souvenir of America.*

sovereign /'sɒvrɪn/ *n.* ruler; king, queen, or emperor.

sow /saʊ/ *v.* (*past part.* sown /saʊn/, sowed /saʊd/, *past tense* sowed) put seed in the earth: *The farmer sows the corn in the spring.*

space /speɪs/ *n.* **1** (no *pl.*) the sky and all that is beyond, where all the stars are: *The men who landed on the moon travelled through space.* **spacecraft, spaceship** *n.* machine for travelling through space. **spaceman** *n.* man who travels in a spaceship. **spacesuit** *n.* special clothing for a traveller in space. **2** (no *pl.*) enough room for someone or something: *Is there space for another bed in the room?* **3** (*pl.* spaces) place: *parking space.* **4** (*pl.* spaces) empty part between two or more things: *Leave a space after each word when you write.*

spacious /'speɪʃəs/ *adj.* big; with a lot of room: *a spacious hall.*

spade /speɪd/ *n.* **1** instrument for digging. **2** the shape ♠ on a playing card.

spank /spæŋk/ *v.* hit a child on the bottom with your open hand.

spanner /'spænə(r)/ *n.* instrument for holding and turning nuts and bolts.

spare[1] /speə(r)/ *adj.* **1** free: *spare time.* **2** extra: *We always have a spare wheel in our car.*

spare[2] *n.* extra tyre or wheel for a car; extra part that you can put in a machine when a part breaks: *Do you keep spares?*

spare[3] *v.* **1** not hurt or kill someone when you could: *He spared his prisoner.* **2** find enough money, time, etc. to give someone: *Can you spare a few minutes— I can't carry this box on my own.*

spark /spɑːk/ *n.* tiny bit of fire.

sparkle /'spɑːkl/ *v.* give flashes of light: *Diamonds sparkle in the light.* **sparkle** *n.* **sparkling** *adj.*: *sparkling eyes.*

sparrow /'spærəʊ/ *n.* small bird that you often see in towns.

spat /spæt/ *past part. & past tense* of *v.* spit.

speak /spiːk/ *v.* (*past part.* spoken /'spəʊkən/, *past tense* spoke /spəʊk/) **1** say words; talk to someone: *She speaks very fast.. Did you speak to the doctor about your back?* **2** know and use a language: *Martin speaks English, German, and French.* **3** make a speech: *The chairman spoke for half an hour at the meeting.* **speak up**, talk clearly and loudly: *Speak up—I can't hear you!*

speaker /'spiːkə(r)/ *n.* **1** someone who talks to a big group of people. **2** part of a radio, etc. from which you hear the sound.

spear /spɪə(r)/ *n.* long stick with a metal point on the end, for hunting and killing.

special /'speʃl/ *adj.* **1** for a particular person or thing: *You must have special boots for skiing.* **2** better, more important, etc. than others: *Johnny is my special friend.* **specially** *adv.* mainly; chiefly: *I came here specially to see you.*

specialist /'speʃəlɪst/ *n.* **1** expert; someone who knows a lot about something: *a specialist in racing bikes.* **2** doctor who knows a lot about one part of the body or one sort of disease: *an eye-specialist.*

specialize /'speʃəlaɪz/ *v.* **specialize in**, know or learn a lot about one thing so that you can do it well: *In the sixth form, Andrew specialized in Maths and Physics.*

specimen /'spesɪmən/ *n.* small piece that shows what the rest is like; one example of a group of things: *a specimen of rock.*

speck /spek/ *n.* tiny bit or spot of something: *specks of dust.*

speckled /'spekld/ *adj.* with small, coloured marks on the skin, shell, feathers, etc.: *a speckled hen.*

spectacle /'spektəkl/ *n.* something that a lot of people watch: *The coronation was a wonderful spectacle.*

spectacles /'spektəkəlz/ *n.* (*pl.*) glasses; round pieces of glass that you wear over your eyes so that you can see better: *He put on his spectacles and started to read.*

spectacular /spek'tækjʊlə(r)/ *adj.* wonderful to watch: *a spectacular jump.* **spectacularly** *adv.*

spectator /spek'teɪtə(r)/ *n.* someone who watches a happening: *There were 2,000 spectators at the match.*

sped /sped/ *past part. & past tense of v.* speed.

speech /spi:tʃ/ *n.* **1** (no *pl.*) speaking: *A dog has no speech—he cannot tell you what he thinks.* **2** (*pl.* speeches) talk that you give to a lot of people: *The president made a speech today.*

speechless /'spi:tʃlɪs/ *adj.* so surprised or angry that you cannot speak.

speed[1] /spi:d/ *n.* **1** (*pl.* speeds) how quickly something goes: *We drove at a speed of 50 kilometres an hour.* **2** (no *pl.*) going fast: *Please slow down—I don't like speed.* **at full speed**, as fast as you can. **at high speed**, very fast. **speed limit** *n.* the fastest that you may go: *The speed limit in this town is 40 miles per hour.*

speed[2] *v.* (*past part. & past tense* sped /sped/, speeded /'spi:dɪd/) **1** go quickly: *The cars were speeding along the road.* **2** go too quickly: *The policeman stopped him because he was speeding.* **speed up**, make something go more quickly: *The driver speeded up the train.*

speedy /'spi:dɪ/ *adj.* quick; fast: *a speedy journey.* **speedily** *adv.*

spell[1] /spel/ *n.* magic words. **put a spell on, cast a spell over**, say magic words to someone, which make him do what you want.

spell[2] *n.* time: *a long spell of wet weather.*

spell[3] *v.* (*past part. & past tense* spelt /spelt/, spelled /speld/) give the letters of a word, one by one: *How do you spell your name?* **spelling** *n.* way of writing a word correctly.

spend /spend/ *v.* (*past part. & past tense* spent /spent/) **1** pay money for something: *Maisie spends a lot of money on records.* **2** give time, energy, etc. to something: *George spends a lot of time listening to music.*

spice /spaɪs/ *n.* things like ginger, pepper, cinnamon, cloves, etc. that we put into food.

spider /'spaɪdə(r)/ *n.* small animal with eight legs, which makes webs to catch insects for food.

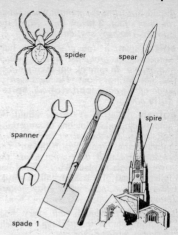

spider   spear   spire   spanner   spade 1

spied /spaɪd/ *past part. & past tense of v.* spy.

spike /spaɪk/ *n.* pointed piece of metal, etc.: *running-shoes with spikes on them.*

spill /spɪl/ *v.* (*past part. & past tense* spilt /spɪlt/, spilled /spɪld/) shake liquid out of something by mistake: *He knocked his cup over and spilt tea on the carpet.*

spin /spɪn/ *v.* (*pres. part.* spinning, *past part. & past tense* spun /spʌn/) **1** make thread by twisting cotton, silk, wool, etc.: *to spin wool.* **2** make something with threads: *The spider was spinning a web.* **3** go round fast; make something go round fast: *The skater spun round and round on the ice.*

spine /spaɪn/ *n.* backbone.

spinster /'spɪnstə(r)/ *n.* woman who has never had a husband.

spiral /'spaɪərəl/ *adj.* that goes round as it goes up: *a spiral staircase.*

spire /'spaɪə(r)/ *n.* tall, pointed roof of a church.

spirit /'spɪrɪt/ *n.* **1** (*pl.* spirits) your soul; the part of you that does not die with your body. **2 spirits** (*pl.*) how you feel. **in high spirits**, very happy. **in low spirits**, sad. **3 spirits** (*pl.*) strong, alcoholic drink: *Whisky and brandy are spirits.* **4** (no *pl.*) alcohol for burning: *We put spirit in the lamp.*

spit /spɪt/ *v.* (*pres. part.* spitting, *past part. & past tense* spat /spæt/) **1** send liquid out from the mouth: *She spat in the man's face.* **2** throw food out of the mouth: *The baby spat out the egg.*

spite /spaɪt/ *n.* (no *pl.*) wish to hurt someone: *She broke her brother's watch out of spite.* **in spite of,** not taking notice of, not caring about: *He slept well in spite of the noise.* **spiteful** *adj.* **spitefully** *adv.*

splash /splæʃ/ *v.* **1** throw liquid on something; make someone or something wet: *He splashed his sister with water.* **2** move so that liquid flies in the air: *The children splashed their way across the river.* **splash** *n.* place where liquid has fallen; sound of a sudden fall of water: *There was a splash when May jumped into the river.*

splendid /'splendɪd/ *adj.* very fine, beautiful, etc.: *a splendid sunset; splendid robes.* **splendidly** *adv.*

splinter /'splɪntə(r)/ *n.* thin, sharp piece of wood, glass, etc. that has broken off a bigger piece: *I pulled a splinter out of my finger.*

split /splɪt/ *v.* (*pres. part.* splitting, *past part. & past tense* split) **1** break something into two parts: *He split the wood with an axe.* **2** break open: *Your dress has split at the side.* **3** share something into parts: *They split the cost of the party between them.* **split** *n.* breaking; place where something has broken or torn: *a split in your trousers.*

spoil /spɔɪl/ *v.* (*past part. & past tense* spoilt /spɔɪlt/, spoiled /spɔɪld/) **1** damage or hurt something so it is no longer good: *The baby tore my book and spoilt it.* **2** give someone everything he wants so that he becomes greedy or difficult: *Jenny spoils her little sister.* **spoilt** *adj.:* a *spoilt child.*

spoilsport /'spɔɪlspɔːt/ *n.* someone who does something to stop the fun of other people.

spoke[1] /spəʊk/ *n.* one of the thin bars from the middle to the edge of a wheel.

spoke[2] *past tense* of *v.* speak.

spoken /'spəʊkən/ *past part.* of *v.* speak.

sponge /spʌndʒ/ *n.* soft thing that we use for washing and cleaning: *He was washing his car with a sponge.* **sponge** *v.* wash or clean something with a sponge.

spool /spuːl/ *n.* thing with round sides that holds thread, film, etc.

spoon /spuːn/ *n.* instrument with a round end, for putting food in your mouth, etc.: *We put sugar in our coffee with a spoon.*

sport /spɔːt/ *n.* **1** (no *pl.*) what you do for exercise and enjoyment; physical games: *Do you like playing sport?* **2** (*pl.* sports) game: *Football and swimming are popular sports in this country.* **3 sports** (*pl.*) meeting for running and jumping competitions, etc.: *the school sports.* **sportsman** /'spɔːtsmən/ man who plays sport. **sportswoman** /'spɔːtswʊmən/ *n.* woman who plays sport.

spot[1] /spɒt/ *n.* **1** small, round mark: *A tiger has stripes and a leopard has spots.* **2** dirty mark: *What are those spots on your clean shirt?* **3** small, sore place on the skin. **4** place: *a shady spot under a tree.* **spotted** /'spɒtɪd/ *adj.* with small, round marks: *a spotted tie.* **spotty** *adj.* with small, sore places on the skin: *a spotty face.*

spot[2] *v.* (*pres. part.* spotting, *past part. & past tense* spotted /'spɒtɪd/) **1** make a mark on something: *The ink has spotted my clean shirt.* **2** see someone or something: *He spotted his friend in the crowd.*

spotless /'spɒtlɪs/ *adj.* very clean. **spotlessly** *adv.*

spout /spaʊt/ *n.* short pipe on a teapot, watering-can, etc. where the liquid comes out.

sprain /spreɪn/ *v.* pull or twist your arm or leg so that it is hurt: *Scott fell over and sprained his ankle.* **sprain** *n.*

sprang /spræŋ/ *past tense* of *v.* spring.

spray /spreɪ/ *n.* **1** (no *pl.*) liquid going through the air in tiny drops: *Clouds of spray rose from the sea as it crashed on the rocks.* **2** (*pl.* sprays) can with liquid that shoots out in fine drops when you press a button: *a hair spray.* **spray** *v.* shoot out in spray; make liquid shoot out: *He sprayed the plants to kill the insects.*

spread /spred/ *v.* (*past part. & past tense* spread) **1** become wider; open something to make it wider: *The bird spread its wings and flew away.* **2** open something and lay it down: *We spread a rug on the grass for the picnic.* **3** smear or rub soft stuff all over something: *He spread butter on a piece of bread.* **4** go to other places; take something to other places: *The boy's measles soon spread to other children in the class.* **spread** *n.*: *Doctors try to stop the spread of disease.*

spring¹ /sprɪŋ/ *n.* **1** sudden, strong jump. **2** place where water comes out of the ground. **3** thin piece of metal or wire that is twisted round and round so that it will jump back into place if you pull or push it.

spring² *n.* time of the year after the winter, when the plants begin to grow.

spring³ *v.* (*past part.* sprung /sprʌŋ/, *past tense* sprang /spræŋ/) jump suddenly and strongly: *The cat sprang on the mouse.*

sprinkle /'sprɪŋkl/ *v.* throw little bits or drops on to something: *Mother sprinkled salt on the potatoes.*

sprint /sprɪnt/ *v.* run.

sprout¹ /spraʊt/, **Brussels sprout** /ˌbrʌslz 'spraʊt/ *n.* round, green vegetable like a small cabbage.

sprout² *v.* begin to grow: *New leaves are sprouting on the trees.*

sprung /sprʌŋ/ *past part.* of *v.* spring.

spun /spʌn/ *past part. & past tense* of *v.* spin.

spurt /spɜːt/ *v.* burst or flow out strongly and suddenly: *Blood spurted out of the cut in his leg.*

spy /spaɪ/ *v.* try to learn secrets about another country. **spy on**, watch something or someone secretly. **spy** *n.* someone who spies.

squabble /'skwɒbl/ *v.* quarrel about something that is not important. **squabble over**, fight for something small: *The children squabbled over the last sweet.* **squabble** *n.*

squad /skwɒd/ *n.* small group of soldiers, policemen, etc. who are working together.

square¹ /skweə(r)/ *adj.* with four sides of the same length and four right angles: *a square table.*

square² *n.* **1** shape like □, with four straight sides of the same length and four right angles. **2** open space in a town with buildings round it: *Trafalgar Square.*

spot¹ 1

sponge

spoon

spout

sprout¹

squash¹ /skwɒʃ/ *n.* (no *pl.*) game where two players hit a ball hard against a wall.

squash² *n.* (no *pl.*) too many people or things in a small space: *It's a squash in this car with five people.*

squash³ *n.* (*pl.* squashes) fruit drink.

squash⁴ *v.* **1** press something hard and break it or harm it: *Don't sit on my hat or you'll squash it!* **2** push too much into a small space: *He squashed three suits into the suitcase.*

squashy /'skwɒʃɪ/ *adj.* soft and wet: *squashy tomatoes.*

squat /skwɒt/ *v.* (*pres. part.* squatting, *past part. & past tense* squatted /'skwɒtɪd/) sit on your heels: *Betty squatted down to light the fire.*

squeak /skwiːk/ *v.* make a short, high sound: *Mark put some oil on the door because it was squeaking.* **squeak** *n.*: *the squeak of a mouse.* **a narrow squeak**, a lucky escape from danger. **squeaky** *adj.*

squeal /skwiːl/ *v.* make a loud, high sound: *Pigs squeal.* **squeal** *n.*: *There was a squeal of brakes as the car suddenly stopped.*

squeeze /skwiːz/ *v.* **1** press something hard: *The child squeezed his mother's hand.* **2** press something hard to get liquid out of it: *to squeeze a lemon.* **3** get into a small space; push too much into a small space: *We squeezed into the crowded room.* **squeeze** *n.*: *He gave my arm a squeeze.* **a tight squeeze**, too many people or things in a small space: *It's a tight squeeze with six people in this little car.*

squirrel /'skwɪrəl/ *n.* small grey or brown animal with a big, furry tail, which lives in trees.

squirt /skwɜ:t/ *v.* **1** burst or flow out suddenly: *Water was squirting out from a hole in the pipe.* **2** make liquid, etc. shoot out. **squirt** *n.*

St. *abbrev.* **1** /sɪnt/ saint: *St. Paul.* **2** /stri:t/ street: *Oxford St.*

stab /stæb/ *v.* (*pres. part.* stabbing, *past part. & past tense* stabbed /stæbd/) push a knife or other sharp weapon into a person or thing. **stab** *n.*

stable[1] /'steɪbl/ *adj.* firm; that will not move: *Don't sit on that chair—it's not stable.*

stable[2] *n.* building where you keep horses.

stack /stæk/ *n.* big pile or heap of something: *a stack of wood; a haystack.* **stack** *v.* put things into a pile: *I stacked the books on my desk.*

stadium /'steɪdɪəm/ *n.* place for games and sports, with seats around the sides: *Wembley Stadium.*

staff /stɑ:f/ *n.* (*pl.*) group of people who work together under a leader: *The headmaster has a staff of twenty teachers.*

staff-room /'stɑ:f rʊm/ *n.* room in a school where teachers can sit, talk, work, etc.

stag /stæg/ *n.* male deer.

stage[1] /steɪdʒ/ *n.* part of the theatre where actors, dancers, etc. stand and move. **go on the stage**, become an actor, etc.

stage[2] *n.* **1** certain point or time while things are happening or changing: *The baby has reached the stage where he can stand up.* **at this stage**, now. **at a later stage**, later. **2** part of a journey: *We travelled the first stage by train; then we went by ship.*

stagger /'stægə(r)/ *v.* walk in an unsteady way: *The drunken man staggered across the room and fell.*

stain /steɪn/ *v.* make coloured or dirty

marks on something: *The pen stained the cloth with ink.* **stain** *n.*: *blood stains.*

stair /steə(r)/ *n.* one of a group of steps that go from one floor to the next: *She ran up the stairs to the bathroom.* **flight of stairs**, set of stairs. **the foot of the stairs**, the bottom of a set of stairs. **staircase, stairway** *n.* group of steps.

stake /steɪk/ *n.* strong post of wood or metal that stands in the ground: *The farmer tied the bull to a stake in the field.*

stale /steɪl/ *adj.* not fresh: *stale bread; stale air.*

stalk /stɔ:k/ *n.* tall part of a plant that has leaves, flowers, fruit, etc. on it.

stall /stɔ:l/ *n.* small, open shop in a street, railway station, etc.; table in a market: *a flower stall.*

stammer /'stæmə(r)/ *v.* say the same sounds several times when you are trying to say a word: *'G-g-go b-b-back,'* he stammered. **stammer** *n.*

stamp[1] /stæmp/ *n.* **1** putting your foot down hard. **2** small, hard instrument that you press on paper to make a mark or word: *a rubber stamp.* **3** small piece of paper that you stick on to a letter, etc. to show how much you have paid to send it.

stamp[2] *v.* **1** put your foot down hard: *Samuel stamped on the spider and killed it.* **2** press a small, hard instrument on a piece of paper, etc. to make a mark or word: *The potter stamped his sign on the bottom of the pot.* **3** put a small piece of paper on a letter, parcel, etc. to show how much money you have paid to send it: *You must stamp your letters before you post them.*

stand[1] /stænd/ *n.* **1** upright piece of furniture that holds something: *a hat-stand.* **2** place where people can sit or stand to watch races, sports, etc.

stand[2] *v.* (*past part. & past tense* stood /stʊd/) **1** get up on to your feet: *At the end of the concert, the audience stood and clapped the singer.* **2** be on the feet or legs: *All the seats in the bus were full so we had to stand.* **3** move; go: *He stood back so that I could pass.* **4** be in a certain place: *The house stands on the hill.* **5** put something upright: *Stand the ladder against the wall.* **6** bear something that you do not like: *I can't stand*

a lot of noise when I'm trying to read.
stand by, (a) watch but not do anything:
*How can you stand by when those boys
are kicking the cat?* (**b**) be ready to do
something: *Stand by until I call you!*
stand by someone, help someone. **stand
for**, be the sign or short word for
something: *B.B.C. stands for British
Broadcasting Corporation:* **stand out**, be
easy to see because bigger, better, etc.:
Ruth stands out because she is so lovely.
stand still, not move: *Stand still while I
photograph you.* **stand up**, get up on to
your feet. **stand up for**, say that someone
is right; support someone: *Stuart always
stands up for his brother.* **stand up
to**, show that you are not afraid of
someone: *My little brother always stands
up to the bigger boys.*

standard[1] /'stændəd/ *adj.* usual: *A standard bottle of milk holds one pint.*

standard[2] *n.* **1** how good something or
someone is: *Her work is of a high standard.* **standard of living**, rich or poor
way of living. **2** special flag: *the Royal
Standard.* **standard lamp** *n.* lamp on
a tall pole in a house.

standstill /'stændstɪl/ *n.* total stop: *The
traffic is at a standstill because of an
accident.*

stank /stæŋk/ *past tense* of *v.* stink.

star[1] /stɑ:(r)/ *n.* **1** one of the bright
things that shine in the sky at night. **2**
shape with points, like a star.

star[2] *n.* famous actor, singer, sportsman, etc.: *pop stars; football stars.* **star**
adj.: *She has the star part in the film.*
star *v.* (*pres. part.* starring, *past part.* &
past tense starred /stɑ:d/) be the star:
She starred in the play.

stare /steə(r)/ *v.* **1** look at someone or
something for a long time: *She was star-
ing out of the window.* **2** look at
someone or something with wide open
eyes: *She stared at me with surprise.*
stare *n.*: *a rude stare.*

starry /'stɑ:rɪ/ *adj.* full of stars: *a starry
sky.*

start[1] /stɑ:t/ *n.* **1** (*pl.* starts) beginning
of a happening, journey, etc.: *She came
late after the start of the meeting.* **make
a start**, begin to do something or go
somewhere: *We have a long way to go,
so we'll make an early start.* **2** (no *pl.*)

stamp[1] 3

squirrel

stairs

stall

extra help in a race, etc. **give someone a
start**, let someone begin ahead of you:
*Dennis is the smallest boy in the race, so
we'll give him a start of 10 metres.* **3** (*pl.*
starts) moving suddenly because you are
surprised, frightened, etc.: *Steve sat up
with a start when I called him.*

start[2] *v.* **1** begin to do something: *She
put up her umbrella when it started to
rain.* **2** begin to happen: *Does the match
start at 3 p.m.?* **3** make something begin
to work: *I can't start the car.* **4** leave on
a journey: *When do you start for Scotland?* **5** move suddenly because you are
surprised, frightened, etc.: *Eric started
when I banged the door.*

startle /'stɑ:tl/ *v.* surprise or shock
someone: *You startled me when you
knocked on the window!*

starve /stɑ:v/ *v.* not have enough to eat;
not give someone enough food. **starving** *adj.*: *a starving cat.* **starvation**
/stɑ:'veɪʃn/ *n.*: *The dog died of starvation.*

state[1] /steɪt/ *n.* **1** (no *pl.*) how someone
or something is, looks, etc.: *The room
was in an untidy state.* **2** (*pl.* states)
country: *France is a European state.* **3**
(*pl.* states) part of a country: *the state of
Texas.* **state** *adj.*

state[2] *v.* say or write something. **statement** /'steɪtmənt/ *n.*: *Robert made a
statement to the police about the robbery that he saw.*

statesman /'steɪtsmən/ n. (pl. states-men) important person in the government.

station /'steɪʃn/ n. **1** place where trains or buses stop for people to get on and off: a railway station. **2** building for a particular sort of work: a fire station; a police station.

stationary /'steɪʃənrɪ/ adj. standing in one place; not moving: He crashed into a stationary bus.

stationery /'steɪʃənrɪ/ n. (no pl.) paper, pens, and other things for writing, etc. **stationer** n. someone who sells stationery.

statue /'stætju:/ n. stone, metal, or wooden figure of a person or animal: There is a statue of Nelson in Trafalgar Square.

stay[1] /steɪ/ n. visit; time in a place: Ed is back from a short stay with his uncle.

stay[2] v. **1** remain or continue in the same place: On Sundays we stay at home. **2** remain or continue in the same way; not change: My sister stayed single and didn't marry. **3** be a guest for a time: I stayed with my aunt when I was in London. **stay behind**, not go with others: My sisters have gone out but I am staying behind to do some work. **stay up**, not go to bed: We stayed up until after midnight.

steady /'stedɪ/ adj. **1** not moving; firm: Hold the ladder steady while I stand on it. **2** regular; not changing or stopping: a steady wind; a steady worker. **steadily** adv.: He walked steadily up the hill.

steak /steɪk/ n. thick piece of meat or fish for cooking.

steal /sti:l/ v. (past part. stolen /'stəʊlən/, past tense stole /stəʊl/) **1** secretly take something that is not yours: Someone has stolen my money. **2** move quietly, so that people do not hear you: I was late for work so I stole past my boss's office.

steam[1] /sti:m/ n. (no pl.) cloud of gas that rises from very hot water: the steam from a boiling kettle. **steaming** adj. very hot, with steam rising from it: a steaming cup of coffee. **steamy** adj. with steam on or in it: steamy windows.

steam[2] v. **1** give out steam: The kettle was steaming on the stove. **2** move with steam: The train steamed into the sta-

tion. **3** cook something in steam: Shall we steam or fry the fish?

steam-engine /'sti:m endʒɪn/ n. engine that works with steam.

steamer /'sti:mə(r)/, **steamship** /'sti:mʃɪp/ n. ship with engines that work with steam.

steel /sti:l/ n. (no pl.) strong, hard metal for making knives, tools, machines, etc.

steep /sti:p/ adj. with a sharp slope: Sandy walked slowly up the steep hill. **steeply** adv.

steeple /'sti:pl/ n. tall, pointed roof of a church.

steer v. turn a wheel or handle to guide a boat, car, bike, etc. **steering-wheel** n. wheel that turns a boat, car, etc. left or right.

stem /stem/ n. stalk; tall part of a plant that has leaves, flowers, fruit, etc. on it: A rose has thorns on its stem.

step[1] /step/ n. **1** one movement forwards or backwards when you walk, dance, etc.; sound of walking, etc.: The dog barked when he heard steps in the garden. **watch your step**, (a) be careful not to fall. (b) be careful of trouble: Watch your step today—the boss is in a bad mood. **2** stair; place to put your foot when you go up or down stairs: Walk carefully in the dark, because there are three steps down into the kitchen. **3** one in a list of things that you must do: What is the first step in planning a holiday? **step by step**, slowly; doing one thing at a time.

step[2] v. (pres. part. stepping, past part. & past tense stepped /stept/) move your foot to go forwards or backwards; walk: Can you step across the stream, or is it too wide? **step aside**, move to one side: She stepped aside to let me pass.

step-[3] prefix showing that a member of the family has come with a second marriage: A step-mother is the woman who married your father when your own mother was dead or divorced.

step-ladder /'step lædə(r)/ n. short ladder.

sterling /'stɜ:lɪŋ/ n. (no pl.) British money.

stern /stɜ:n/ adj. hard; strict: a stern father.

stew /stju:/ v. cook something slowly in water or juice. **stewed** /stju:d/ adj.: stewed beef; stewed pears. **stew** n. dish of cooked meat, vegetables, etc.

steward /'stju:əd/ n. man who looks after passengers on a ship or aeroplane. **stewardess** /ˌstju:ə'des/ n. woman who looks after passengers on a ship or aeroplane.

stick¹ /stɪk/ n. **1** thin piece of wood: Let's find some sticks to make a fire. **2** piece of wood that helps you to walk: The old man walks with a stick. **3** thin piece of something: a stick of chalk.

stick² v. (past part. & past tense stuck /stʌk/) **1** go into something; push a pointed thing into something: Don't stick that needle into your finger! **2** fix or fasten one thing to another thing with glue, paste, etc.: She stuck a stamp on to the envelope. **3** become fixed or fastened; not be able to move: The car stuck in the mud. **stick at**, keep on doing something: If you stick at that job, you'll soon finish it. **stick something out**, push or hold something out: It's rude to stick out your tongue! **stick to something**, go on doing something: Stick to your work, Joe! **stick together**, stay together: Let's stick together in the crowd. **stick up for**, say that someone is right; support someone: The other children laughed at Godfrey, but Oliver stuck up for him.

sticky /'stɪkɪ/ adj. **1** that stays on your finger, etc. when you touch it: Jam is sticky. **2** covered with stuff that you have touched: sticky fingers.

stiff /stɪf/ adj. not bending easily: a stiff brush. **stiffly** adv.

stile /staɪl/ n. step or steps for climbing over a fence.

still¹ /stɪl/ adj. not moving or making any sound: The air is so still that the smoke is rising straight up from the fire. **stillness** n.

still² adv. without moving or making any sound; quietly: Please sit still while I cut your hair.

still³ adv. **1** up to now; even now: I can't go because I'm still busy. **2** up to then and at that time: When I left the fire was still burning. **3** even; more: Grace is tall, but Catherine is still taller.

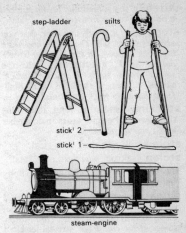

step-ladder · stilts · stick¹ 2 · stick¹ 1 · steam-engine

still⁴ conj. but; however: I don't want to get up—still, it's time for work.

stilts /stɪlts/ n. (pl.) long sticks for walking high above the ground.

sting¹ /stɪŋ/ n. **1** sharp part of an insect that pricks and hurts: The sting of a wasp is in its tail. **2** small hairs on the leaves of some plants that hurt you when you touch them. **3** pain or sore place that an insect or a plant makes: Her face was covered with bee stings.

sting² v. (past part. & past tense stung /stʌŋ/) **1** prick or hurt someone: A wasp stung him. **2** feel sharp pain: His face was stinging where Harry hit him.

stink /stɪŋk/ n. bad smell. **stink** v. (past part. stunk /stʌŋk/, past tense stank /stæŋk/): This bad fish stinks!

stir¹ /stɜː(r)/ n. (no pl.) **1** moving or being moved: He gave his coffee a stir with the spoon. **2** excitement and interest: The pop star's visit made a big stir in the village.

stir² v. (pres. part. stirring, past part. & past tense stirred /stɜːd/) **1** move a little; make something move a little: The wind stirred the leaves. **2** move a spoon, etc. round and round to mix something: Have you stirred your tea?

stitch¹ /stɪtʃ/ n. (pl. stitches) one movement in and out with a needle when you are sewing or knitting.

stitch² v. sew something: *Sheila stitched a patch on to her trousers.*

stock /stɒk/ n. goods in a shop that you are keeping to sell: *That shoe-shop has a big stock of boots.* **in stock**, ready to sell. **out of stock**, not there to sell: *I'm sorry—brown sugar is out of stock.* **stock** v. keep a stock of something: *Does that shop stock raincoats?*

stocking /'stɒkɪŋ/ n. long, thin thing that a woman or girl wears to cover her leg: *a pair of stockings.*

stole /stəʊl/ *past tense* of v. steal.

stolen /'stəʊlən/ *past part.* of v. steal.

stomach /'stʌmək/ n. place in the body where food goes when you eat it.

stone /stəʊn/ n. **1** (no *pl.*) very hard part of the ground; rock: *a wall of stone.* **2** (*pl.* stones) piece of stone: *Don't throw stones at the cat.* **3** (*pl.* stones) jewel: *A diamond is a precious stone.* **4** (*pl.* stones) measure of weight = 6·3 kilograms. **5** (*pl.* stones) hard part in the middle of some fruit.

stony /'stəʊnɪ/ adj. covered with stones: *a stony road.*

stood /stʊd/ *past part. & past tense* of v. stand.

stool /stuːl/ n. small seat with no back.

stoop /stuːp/ v. bend forward and down: *She stooped to pick up her bag from the ground.* **stoop** n. bending of the body: *The old woman walks with a stoop.*

stop¹ /stɒp/ n. **1** the moment when someone or something no longer moves: *The train came to a sudden stop.* **put a stop to**, make something end: *We must put a stop to parking in this narrow street.* **2** place where buses, trains, etc. stop moving to let people on and off: *Please can I get off the bus at the next stop?* **3** punctuation mark (.) that shows the end of a sentence.

stop² /stɒp/ v. (*pres. part.* stopping, *past part. & past tense* stopped /stɒpt/) **1** end what someone or something is doing: *He stopped his car at the traffic lights.* **stop someone from doing something**, not allow someone to do something: *He stopped the child from playing near the river.* **2** finish moving; become still: *The train stopped at the station.* **3** not do something, or not work, any more: *We stopped talking.*

stopper /'stɒpə(r)/ n. round thing that you push into the top of a bottle to close it.

store¹ /stɔː(r)/ n. **1** big shop: *Selfridges is a London store.* **2** place for keeping a lot of things: *a furniture store.* **3** what you put away and keep for a later time: *a store of food.* **4 stores** (*pl.*) goods of a certain kind: *military stores.*

store² v. keep something for a later time: *The farmer stores hay for his cows to eat in winter.*

storey /'stɔːrɪ/ n. floor in a building: *A skyscraper has many storeys.*

storm¹ /stɔːm/ n. time of bad weather, strong wind, heavy rain, thunder, lightning, etc.

storm² v. **1** show that you are very angry; shout angrily: *He stormed out of the room.* **2** attack a place violently and take it: *The soldiers stormed the castle.*

stormy /'stɔːmɪ/ adj. **1** with strong wind, rain, etc.: *a stormy day.* **2** angry: *a stormy meeting.* **stormily** adv.

story /'stɔːrɪ/ n. (*pl.* stories) telling about happenings that are true or untrue: *Hans Christian Anderson wrote stories for children. Granny tells us stories about her childhood.*

stove /stəʊv/ n. cooker or heater: *She warmed a pan of soup on the stove.*

stowaway /'stəʊəweɪ/ n. someone who hides in a ship or aeroplane so that he can travel without paying.

straight¹ /streɪt/ adj. **1** not bent; with no curve or curl: *straight hair.* **2** tidy. **put something straight**, make something tidy: *I put my desk straight before I went on holiday.*

straight² adv. **1** not in a curve; not bending: *The smoke rose straight up because there was no wind.* **2** directly; by the shortest way, not stopping: *Come straight home.* **straight away**, now: *I'll do it straight away.* **straight on**, ahead; in the same direction: *Don't turn left— walk straight on.*

straighten /'streɪtn/ v. become straight; make something straight.

straightforward /ˌstreɪt'fɔːwəd/ adj. easy to understand or do: *a straightforward task.*

strain /streɪn/ v. **1** pull something as

hard as you can: *The dog was straining at his lead.* **2** try very hard: *I strained to hear her quiet voice on the telephone.* **3** damage part of your body because you have pulled or twisted it, or made it work too hard: *You'll strain your eyes if you read in bad light.* **4** pass liquid, food, etc. through cloth or netting. **strain** *n.*

strainer /'streɪnə(r)/ *n.* piece of metal or plastic net that you pour liquid or food through: *We pour tea through a strainer.*

strand[1] /strænd/ *n.* long piece of thread, hair, etc.

strand[2] *v.* **be stranded,** be left with no help: *The car broke down and we were stranded on a lonely road.*

strange /streɪndʒ/ *adj.* that you do not know; surprising because it does not often happen: *What is that strange noise?* **strangely** *adv.*: *She usually talks a lot, but today she was strangely quiet.*

stranger /'streɪndʒə(r)/ *n.* **1** someone whom you do not know: *There's a stranger at the door—who is he?* **2** someone in a place that he does not know: *I'm a stranger in this town.*

strangle /'stræŋgl/ *v.* hold someone's throat so tightly that you kill him.

strap /stræp/ *n.* narrow piece of leather, etc. that holds things together or keeps something in its place: *A watch-strap holds a watch on your wrist.* **strap** *v.* (*pres. part.* strapping, *past part.* & *past tense* strapped /stræpt/) tie something with a strap: *Bill strapped his bag on to his bicycle.*

straw /strɔː/ *n.* **1** (no *pl.*) dry, cut stalks of wheat, etc.: *My rabbit sleeps on a bed of straw.* **2** (*pl.* straws) one dry stalk of a wheat plant, etc. **the last straw**, a bad thing which happens after so many other bad things that you lose hope. **3** (*pl.* straws) thin tube of paper or plastic for drinking a cold drink: *He sucked Coke through a straw.*

strawberry /'strɔːbrɪ/ *n.* (*pl.* strawberries) small, soft, red fruit.

stray[1] /streɪ/ *adj.* that has lost its way; that has left its correct place: *a stray sheep.* **stray** *n.* person or animal that has lost its way or has no home.

stray[2] *v.* leave the right place or road;

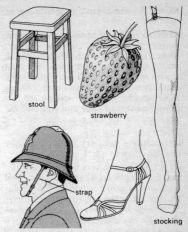

stool

strawberry

strap

stocking

lose your way: *Don't let the dog stray from the garden.*

streak /striːk/ *n.* long, thin line: *There are streaks of grey in Dad's hair.* **streak** *v.* mark something with streaks.

stream[1] /striːm/ *n.* **1** small river. **2** a lot of moving liquid or moving things: *Streams of cars were driving into the city.*

stream[2] *v.* move like water; flow: *Tears were streaming down her cheeks.*

street /striːt/ *n.* road in a town or village with buildings along the side: *Regent Street.*

strength /streŋθ/ *n.* (no *pl.*) being strong: *The little boy hasn't the strength to lift that heavy box.*

stress[1] /stres/ *n.* (*pl.* stresses) saying one word or part of a word more strongly than another: *The stress is on the first part of the word 'paper'.*

stress[2] *v.* **1** say one word or part of a word more strongly than another: *You must stress the first part of the word 'London'.* **2** speak firmly to show that what you are saying is important: *Mum stressed that Jacky should be home by ten o'clock.*

stretch[1] /stretʃ/ *n.* (*pl.* stretches) **1** pushing your arms and legs out as far as you can: *He got up with a stretch and a yawn.* **2** time. **at a stretch**, without stopping: *He can work for eight hours at a* *stretch.* **3** piece of land: *long stretches of moorland.*

stretch² *v.* **1** pull something to make it longer, wider, etc.; become longer, wider, etc.: *Rubber bands stretch.* **2** reach; be long enough: *Will this rope stretch round the box?* **3** push your arms and legs out as far as you can: *The cat woke up and stretched.* **stretch out**, lie down and spread arms and legs out: *He stretched out on the grass and went to sleep.*

stretcher /'stretʃə(r)/ *n.* sort of light bed for carrying a sick person.

strict /strɪkt/ *adj.* very firm with people; making people do what you want: *Our boss is very strict so we have to arrive on time.* **strictly** *adv.* firmly; definitely: *Swimming in the river is strictly forbidden—it's very dangerous.*

stride /straɪd/ *v.* (*past part.* stridden /'strɪdn/, *past tense* strode /strəʊd/) walk with long steps: *The farmer strode across his fields.* **stride** *n.*

strike¹ /straɪk/ *n.* time when workers will not work because they want more money or are angry about something. **on strike**, refusing to work: *There are no trains because the train-drivers are on strike.*

strike² *v.* (*past part.* struck /strʌk/, stricken /'strɪkən/, *past tense* struck) **1** hit someone or something: *He struck me with a stick.* **2** hit a bell to tell the hour: *At midday the clock strikes twelve.* **3** stop working because you want more money or are angry about something: *The workers at the factory are striking for more pay.* **4** make someone think something. **it strikes me**, I think: *It strikes me that he is worried about something.*

striker /'straɪkə(r)/ *n.* worker who will not work because he wants more money or is angry about something.

striking /'straɪkɪŋ/ *adj.* very unusual and interesting: *a striking dress.* **strikingly** *adv.*

string /strɪŋ/ *n.* **1** (no *pl.*) piece of cord for tying things: *Jon tied up the parcel with string.* **2** (*pl.* strings) line of things on a piece of cord: *a string of beads.* **3** (*pl.* strings) piece of cord, wire, etc. on a musical instrument: *the strings of a violin.*

strip¹ /strɪp/ *n.* long, narrow piece of something: *a strip of paper; a strip of land.*

strip² *v.* (*pres. part.* stripping, *past part. & past tense* stripped /strɪpt/) **1 strip** take away the outside part of something: *He stripped the paper off the parcel.* **2 strip, strip off**, take off your clothes: *He stripped off and got into the bath.*

stripe /straɪp/ *n.* long, narrow band of colour: *The American flag has stars and stripes.* **striped** /straɪpt/ *adj.* with stripes: *a striped shirt.*

strode /strəʊd/ *past tense* of *v.* stride.

stroke¹ /strəʊk/ *n.* **1** hitting; blow: *He cut off the dragon's head with one stroke of his sword.* **2** way of moving arms or body in swimming, etc.: *breaststroke.* **3** sound of the bell in a clock: *We have dinner on the stroke of twelve.* **4** sudden illness, when the brain stops working.

stroke² *v.* move your hand gently across something, again and again, to show love: *He stroked the horse's neck.*

stroll /strəʊl/ *v.* walk slowly. **stroll** *n.*: *We had a stroll by the river before dawn.*

strong /strɒŋ/ *adj.* **1** with a powerful body; able to move heavy things easily: *He lifted the heavy box in his strong arms.* **2** that will not break easily: *Don't sit on that chair—it's not very strong.* **3** that you can see, smell, taste, or feel very clearly: *a strong smell of oranges.* **4** able to make other people do what you want: *a strong government.* **strongly** *adv.*: *He swims strongly.*

struck /strʌk/ *past part. & past tense* of *v.* strike.

structure /'strʌktʃə(r)/ *n.* building; what you have put together: *The Severn Bridge is a huge structure.*

struggle /'strʌgl/ *v.* **1** fight: *He struggled with the burglar.* **2** try very hard to do something that is not easy: *She struggled to lift the heavy basket.* **struggle** *n.*: *In 1862 the American slaves won their struggle for freedom.*

stub /stʌb/ *n.* short end of a pencil, cigarette, etc.

stubborn /'stʌbən/ *adj.* not willing to change; determined: *A donkey is a stubborn animal.* **stubbornly** *adv.*

stuck /stʌk/ *past part. & past tense* of *v.* stick.

student /'stju:dnt/ *n.* someone who is learning at college or university: *Medical students are training to be doctors.*

studio /'stju:dɪəʊ/ *n.* **1** room with a lot of light where a painter works. **2** room where people make films and radio or television programmes.

study[1] /'stʌdɪ/ *n.* (*pl.* studies) **1** learning: *When are you beginning your studies at college?* **2** private room where you study, read, and write.

study[2] *v.* **1** read about, think about, and learn something: *Miles is studying medicine because he wants to be a doctor.* **2** look at something carefully: *We must study the map before we start our journey.*

stuff[1] /stʌf/ *n.* (no *pl.*) sort of thing; material: *What is this sticky stuff on the carpet?*

stuff[2] *v.* **1** push a lot into a small space: *She stuffed the apples into her pockets.* **2** put special filling into a chicken, etc. before cooking it.

stuffing /'stʌfɪŋ/ *n.* (no *pl.*) **1** what you put inside a cushion, pillow, etc. **2** special filling that you put into a chicken, etc. before you cook it.

stuffy /'stʌfɪ/ *adj.* with no fresh air: *a stuffy room.*

stumble /'stʌmbl/ *v.* **1** hit your foot against something and almost fall: *He stumbled over the doorstep.* **stumble upon**, find something that you did not expect: *He was digging in the garden and stumbled upon a gold coin.* **2** walk like an ill or drunk person: *The old woman stumbled along the road.*

stump /stʌmp/ *n.* what remains when the main part has gone: *We sat on a tree stump.*

stun /stʌn/ *v.* (*pres. part.* stunning, *past part. & past tense* stunned /stʌnd/) **1** hit a person or animal on the head so hard that he cannot see, think, or talk for a while: *The blow stunned him.* **2** shock or surprise someone: *His father's death stunned him.*

stung /stʌŋ/ *past part. & past tense* of *v.* sting.

stunk /stʌŋk/ *past part.* of *v.* stink.

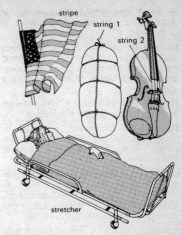

stripe

string 1

string 2

stretcher

stunning /'stʌnɪŋ/ *adj.* wonderful.

stunt /stʌnt/ *n.* something that you do to make people look or watch: *The aeroplanes were flying upside down and doing other stunts.*

stupid /'stju:pɪd/ *adj.* foolish; with very slow thinking. **stupidly** *adv.* **stupidity** /stju:'pɪdətɪ/ *n.*

stutter /'stʌtə(r)/ *v.* say the same sounds several times when you are trying to say a word: *'I c-c-can't talk prop-p-perly', she stuttered.* **stutter** *n.*

sty /staɪ/ *n.* (*pl.* sties) building where you keep pigs.

style /staɪl/ *n.* **1** way of doing, making, or saying something: *He writes in an amusing style.* **2** fashion: *the latest style.*

subject /'sʌbdʒɪkt/ *n.* **1** someone who belongs to a certain country: *Nigel is a British subject.* **2** something to talk or write about: *What is the subject of that book?* **3** what you learn at school, college, etc.: *Maths and Geography are my favourite subjects.* **4** part of a sentence that goes with the verb: *In the sentence 'Barry likes chocolate', 'Barry' is the subject.*

submarine /ˌsʌbmə'ri:n/ *n.* ship that can travel under the sea.

subscribe /səb'skraɪb/ *v.* join with other people to buy something, etc.: *The children subscribed 5p each to buy a present for Nick in hospital.* **subscribe to**, pay to get a newspaper, magazine, etc. at fixed times: *Mr. Murray subscribes to 'The Times'*.

subscription /səb'skrɪpʃn/ *n.* money that each person gives for something; money that you pay to get a newspaper, etc. at fixed times, or to belong to a club.

substance /'sʌbstəns/ *n.* sort of thing; material: *Stone is a hard substance*.

substitute /'sʌbstɪtjuːt/ *n.* person or thing that you put in the place of another: *The goalkeeper was ill so we found a substitute*.

subtract /səb'trækt/ *v.* take a number away from another number: *If you subtract 6 from 9, you will have 3.* **subtraction** /səb'trækʃn/ *n.: We do addition and subtraction in arithmetic.*

suburb /'sʌbɜːb/ *n.* one of the outside parts of a town or city: *Wimbledon is a suburb of London*.

subway /'sʌbweɪ/ *n.* path for people, which goes under a busy street.

succeed /sək'siːd/ *v.* **1** do what you were hoping and trying to do: *Did you succeed in booking the tickets?* **2** come after another person or thing and take his or its place: *Queen Elizabeth II succeeded her father, King George VI.*

success /sək'ses/ *n.* **1** (no *pl.*) doing what you were hoping and trying to do: *I wished Jill success with her studies.* **2** (*pl.* successes) someone who does something well: *Mary is a great success as a singer.* **3** (*pl.* successes) something that you have done well; something that pleases people: *The new sports centre is a big success.* **successful** *adj.: a successful actor.* **successfully** *adv.: Mr. Richards runs his business very successfully.*

succession /sək'seʃn/ *n.* **in succession**, that come one after the other: *We won three matches in succession.*

successor /sək'sesə(r)/ *n.* someone who comes after another person or thing and takes his or its place: *When the chairman leaves, who will his successor be?*

such /sʌtʃ/ *adj.* **1** of that sort: *I'd love a boat but such things are expensive.* **2** word that shows the cause of something: *It's such sweet tea that I can't drink it.* **such a,** words that you say when you tell how much, how big, etc.

something or someone is: *Don't be in such a hurry! He's such a nice man.* **such as this,** like this; of this sort. **such as that,** like that; of that sort: *I've never seen such a fruit as that before.* **such** *pron.*

suck /sʌk/ *v.* **1** pull liquid, etc. into your mouth through your lips: *A baby sucks milk from a bottle.* **2** hold something in the mouth and lick it: *She was sucking a sweet.*

sudden /'sʌdn/ *adj.* happening quickly; that comes when you do not expect it: *There was a sudden storm, and we all got wet.* **all of a sudden,** suddenly. **suddenly** *adv.: Suddenly the doorbell rang.*

suffer /'sʌfə(r)/ *v.* have pain, sadness, etc.: *He is suffering from toothache.*

sufficient /sə'fɪʃnt/ *adj.* as much as you need; as many as you need: *Is there sufficient time for a visit to the museum?*

suffix /'sʌfɪks/ *n.* (*pl.* suffixes) group of letters that you add to the end of one word to make another word: *We add the suffix -ly to make the adjective 'quick' into the adverb 'quickly'.*

suffocate /'sʌfəkeɪt/ *v.* **1** breathe with difficulty: *I'm suffocating in this hot room.* **2** stop someone from breathing; stop breathing and die: *The pillow suffocated the baby.* **suffocating** *adj.* **suffocation** /ˌsʌfə'keɪʃn/ *n.*

sugar /'ʃʊgə(r)/ *n.* (no *pl.*) sweet stuff that comes from some sorts of plant: *Do you have sugar in your tea?*

suggest /sə'dʒest/ *v.* say what you think someone should do, etc.: *Sal suggested that we should go for a swim.* **suggestion** /sə'dʒestʃn/ *n.: I don't know what to buy for her birthday—have you any suggestions?*

suicide /'sjuːɪsaɪd/ *n.* (no *pl.*) killing yourself. **commit suicide,** kill yourself: *He committed suicide by jumping out of a high window.*

suit[1] /suːt/ *n.* jacket and trousers, or jacket and skirt, that you wear together.

suit[2] *v.* **1** please you; be right for you; be what you want or need: *Will this car suit you or do you want a bigger one?* **2** look well on you: *The blue dress doesn't suit me.*

suitable /'suːtəbl/ *adj.* right for that person, happening, place, etc.: *Thick*

clothes are not suitable for hot weather.
suitably *adv.* in the right way: *Val was not suitably dressed for a walk in the country.*

suitcase /'su:tkeɪs/ *n.* thing that holds your clothes, etc., when you travel: *Have you packed your suitcase?*

suite /swi:t/ *n.* **1** set of furniture. **2** set of rooms in a hotel, etc.

sulk /sʌlk/ *v.* not speak because you are angry about something. **sulky** *adj.*: *a sulky face.* **sulkily** *adv.*

sullen /'sʌlən/ *adj.* unfriendly. **sullenly** *adv.*

sum /sʌm/ *n.* **1** piece of work in arithmetic: *Can you do simple sums in your head?* **2** answer that you have when you add two numbers: *18 is the sum of 12 and 6.* **3** amount of money: *£20,000 is a large sum.*

summer /'sʌmə(r)/ *n.* warm time of the year.

summit /'sʌmɪt/ *n.* top of a hill or mountain.

summon /'sʌmən/ *v.* call someone to you: *The director summoned his secretary.*

sun /sʌn/ *n.* **1 the sun**, the big, round thing in the sky, which gives light and heat: *The sun is shining.* **2** (no *pl.*) light and heat from the sun: *It's too hot in the sun—we'll sit in the shade.*

sunbathe /'sʌnbeɪð/ *v.* lie in the sun so that you become brown: *We sunbathed on the beach.*

sunburn /'sʌnbɜ:n/ *n.* (no *pl.*) brown or red colour of your skin when you have been in the hot sun. **sunburned** /'sʌnbɜ:nd/, **sunburnt** /'sʌnbɜ:nt/ *adj.*: *sunburnt arms.*

Sunday /'sʌndeɪ/ *n.* first day of the week: *On Sunday many people go to church.*

sung /sʌŋ/ *past part.* of *v.* sing.

sunglasses /'sʌngla:sɪz/ *n.* (*pl.*) dark glasses that you wear in strong light: *a pair of sunglasses.*

sunken /'sʌŋkən/ *adj.* that has gone under the water: *a sunken ship.*

sunlight /'sʌnlaɪt/ *n.* (no *pl.*) light from the sun. **sunlit** /'sʌnlɪt/ *adj.* full of sunlight: *a sunlit room.*

sunk /sʌŋk/ *past part.* of *v.* sink.

sunglasses

suitcase

suit¹

subway

sunny /'sʌnɪ/ *adj.* bright with light from the sun: *a sunny day.*

sunrise /'sʌnraɪz/ *n.* (no *pl.*) time when the sun comes up in the east; beginning of day: *The birds start to sing at sunrise.*

sunset /'sʌnset/ *n.* time when the sun goes down in the west; end of day.

sunshade /'sʌnʃeɪd/ *n.* sort of umbrella that keeps the sunlight off you.

sunshine /'sʌnʃaɪn/ *n.* (no *pl.*) bright light from the sun.

suntan /'sʌntæn/ *n.* brown colour of your skin when you have been in the hot sun. **suntanned** /'sʌntænd/ *adj.*

super /'su:pə(r)/ *adj.* wonderful; very big, great, etc.: *'That's a super new car!' said Robert.*

superb /su:'pɜ:b/ *adj.* wonderful; beautiful. **superbly** *adv.*

superintendent /,su:pərɪn'tendənt/ *n.* **1** manager; someone who controls what other people do. **2** senior police officer.

superior /su:'pɪərɪə(r)/ *adj.* better; cleverer, more important, etc. than another: *Fresh coffee is superior to instant coffee.*

superlative /su:'pɜ:lətɪv/ *adj.* form of adjectives and adverbs, showing the most of something: *'Best' is the superlative form of 'good' and 'worst' is the superlative form of 'bad'.*

supermarket /'su:pəma:kɪt/ *n.* big

food shop where you collect things in a basket and pay when you leave.

supersonic /ˌsuːpəˈsɒnɪk/ *adj.* faster than the speed of sound: *Concorde is a supersonic aeroplane.*

superstition /ˌsuːpəˈstɪʃn/ *n.* belief in magic; belief in good and bad luck because of signs that you see and hear: *It is a superstition to believe that breaking a mirror brings bad luck.* **superstitious** /ˌsuːpəˈstɪʃəs/ *adj.*: *a superstitious person.* **superstitiously** *adv.*

supervise /ˈsuːpəvaɪz/ *v.* watch to see that people are working correctly. **supervision** /ˌsuːpəˈvɪʒn/ *n.*: *There is strict supervision of exams.*

supper /ˈsʌpə(r)/ *n.* last meal of the day: *We eat our supper in the evening.*

supplies /səˈplaɪz/ *n.* (*pl.*) goods; things that people need: *A helicopter dropped supplies to farms cut off by the snow.*

supply¹ /səˈplaɪ/ *n.* (*pl.* supplies) amount of something. **a good supply**, plenty: *Mother always has a good supply of food in the house.*

supply² *v.* give or sell something that someone needs: *Butchers supply us with meat.*

support /səˈpɔːt/ *v.* **1** keep something or someone up; hold the weight of something: *That small chair isn't strong enough to support that heavy man.* **2** help someone by giving money, etc. **3** give food, clothes, and a home to someone: *Mr. Donovan has to support a large family.* **4** say that you think someone is best, right, etc.: *I supported Adam in the argument.* **support** *n.* supporting someone or something; thing that gives support: *We cheered to show support for our team.*

supporter /səˈpɔːtə(r)/ *n.* someone who helps, shows interest, gives money, etc.: *When our football team played in another town, all the supporters went to watch the game.*

suppose /səˈpəʊz/ *v.* **1** think that something is true when you are not totally sure: *It's late, so I suppose I must go home.* **2** think that something will probably happen.

supposed /səˈpəʊzd/ *past part.* of *v.* suppose. **be supposed to**, be expected to do something; must do something: *Are you supposed to do homework every day?* **not be supposed to**, not be allowed to do something: *We're not supposed to smoke in the bus.*

supposing /səˈpəʊzɪŋ/ *conj.* if: *Supposing it rains, will we still go to the market?*

supreme /suːˈpriːm/ *adj.* most important: *the Supreme Court.*

sure¹ /ʃʊə(r)/ *adj.* certain; knowing that something is true: *I am sure that the key is in the drawer because I put it there this morning.* **be sure to**, do not forget to do something: *Be sure to lock the door when you leave.* **make sure**, find out about something so that you are certain: *I think the party begins at six o'clock, but I'll phone to make sure.*

sure² *adv.* **sure enough**, as you thought: *I said it would rain, and sure enough it did.* **for sure**, certainly; definitely: *I don't know the number for sure—I'll look in the telephone book.*

surely /ˈʃʊəlɪ/ *adv.* **1** certainly; with no doubt: *He works so hard that he will surely pass.* **2** word that you say when you think something must be true: *Surely you know where your brother works?*

surf¹ /sɜːf/ *n.* (no *pl.*) white tops of big waves.

surf² *v.* stand up on a long piece of wood, etc. and ride on the big waves that come up on to a beach. **surfboard** *n.* piece of wood or plastic for surfing. **surfing** *n.* sport of riding on the tops of the waves.

surface /ˈsɜːfɪs/ *n.* **1** outside of something: *A tomato has a shiny, red surface.* **2** top of a liquid, a lake, the sea, etc.: *He dived below the surface.*

surgeon /ˈsɜːdʒən/ *n.* doctor who operates, and mends broken bones and parts inside you.

surgery /ˈsɜːdʒərɪ/ *n.* **1** (no *pl.*) cutting into the body to mend a part inside: *A bone in his foot is broken—he'll need surgery.* **2** (*pl.* surgeries) place where you go to see the doctor or dentist.

surname /ˈsɜːneɪm/ *n.* family name: *Sam Brown's surname is Brown.*

surprise¹ /səˈpraɪz/ *n.* **1** (no *pl.*) feeling that you have when an unexpected thing happens: *She stared in surprise when she* heard the news. **take someone by surprise**, do something that someone is not expecting: *Your phone call took me by surprise because I thought you were on holiday.* **to my surprise**, I was surprised that: *I thought he would be angry but, to my surprise, he smiled.* **2** (*pl.* surprises) an unexpected happening: *My sister arrived suddenly from Canada—what a surprise!* **give someone a surprise**, make someone feel surprise: *I went in quietly because I wanted to give her a surprise.*

surprise² *v.* do something that someone does not expect: *My good marks surprised my father.* **surprising** *adj.* that you do not expect: *surprising news.* **surprisingly** *adv.*

surrender /sə'rendə(r)/ *v.* stop fighting because you are not strong enough: *After six hours on the roof, the gunman surrendered to the police.* **surrender** *n.*

surround /sə'raʊnd/ *v.* be or go all round something: *Trees surrounded the lake.*

surroundings /sə'raʊndɪŋz/ *n.* (*pl.*) everything round a place, person, etc.: *Animals in a zoo are not living in their natural surroundings.*

survive /sə'vaɪv/ *v.* go on living through a difficult or dangerous time: *Camels can survive for many days with no water.* **survival** /sə'vaɪvl/ *n.*: *After eight days in an open boat with no food, his survival was a miracle.* **survivor** /sə'vaɪvə(r)/ *n.* someone who survives: *The government sent help to the survivors of the earthquake.*

suspect¹ /'sʌspekt/ *n.* someone whom you think has probably done wrong: *When the man was found dead, the police arrested two suspects.*

suspect² /sə'spekt/ *v.* think that something is true, but not be certain: *I suspect that she is ill, but I'm not sure.* **suspect someone of something**, think that someone has probably done something wrong: *I suspect that girl of taking my book.*

suspend /sə'spend/ *v.* hang something: *We suspended the lamp from the ceiling.*

suspense /sə'spens/ *n.* (no *pl.*) excitement or worry because you do not know what will happen: *They waited in suspense to hear the end of the story.* **keep someone in suspense**, make some-

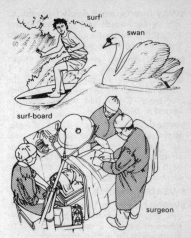

surf¹

swan

surf-board

surgeon

one wait to hear news, etc.: *Don't keep me in suspense—tell me what happened!*

suspicion /sə'spɪʃn/ *n.* idea that is not totally certain: *I have a suspicion that he is lying.* **suspicious** /sə'spɪʃəs/ *adj.* **1** not believing; not trusting: *I'm suspicious of his story because I know he sometimes tells lies.* **2** strange; making you think that something is wrong: *a suspicious noise.* **suspiciously** *adv.*: *The dog sniffed suspiciously at the stranger.*

swallow¹ /'swɒləʊ/ *n.* sort of small bird.

swallow² *v.* take something down the throat: *I can't swallow these tablets without a drink of water.* **swallow** *n.*

swam /swæm/ past tense of *v.* swim.

swamp¹ /swɒmp/ *n.* wet, soft ground. **swampy** *adj.*

swamp² *v.* fill or cover something with too much liquid: *A big wave swamped the boat and it began to sink.*

swan /swɒn/ *n.* big water-bird with a long neck.

swarm¹ /swɔːm/ *n.* **1** big group of flying insects: *a swarm of bees.* **2** big crowd of people.

swarm² *v.* fly or hurry in large numbers: *The children swarmed into the playground.* **swarm with**, be crowded with busy people, animals, etc.: *The streets are swarming with shoppers.*

sway /sweɪ/ v. move slowly from side to side or backwards and forwards; move something slowly to and fro: *The trees were swaying in the wind.*

swear /sweə(r)/ v. (*past part.* sworn /swɔːn/, *past tense* swore /swɔː(r)/) **1** make a strong promise; promise in the name of God: *He swears that he's telling the truth.* **2** say bad words. **swearword** n. bad word.

sweat /swet/ n. (no pl.) drops of water that come out of your skin when you are hot, afraid, etc. **sweat** v.: *He was sweating after the race.* **sweaty** adj. wet with sweat; smelling of sweat: *sweaty clothes.*

sweater /'swetə(r)/ n. jersey; pullover.

sweep[1] /swiːp/ n. **1** moving away dust, dirt, etc. with a brush or broom: *I gave the room a sweep.* **2** man whose job is to brush away the dirt in chimneys.

sweep[2] v. (*past part. & past tense* swept /swept/) **1** clean a floor, by moving away dust, dirt, etc. with a brush or broom: *She swept the floor.* **sweep up**, move away something that is on the floor, ground, etc. with a brush or broom: *In the autumn we sweep up the fallen leaves in the garden.* **2** push something along or away: *The floods have swept the bridge away.*

sweet[1] /swiːt/ adj. **1** with a taste of sugar: *Honey is sweet.* **2** with a good smell: *the sweet smell of roses.* **3** pleasant; nice: *What a sweet girl!* **sweetly** adv. **sweetness** n.

sweet[2] n. **1** small piece of sweet food: *Chocolates and toffees are sweets.* **2** pudding; dessert; sweet food that you eat at the end of a meal.

sweetheart /'swiːthɑːt/ n. boyfriend or girlfriend.

swell /swel/ v. (*past part.* swollen /'swəʊlən/, swelled /sweld/, *past tense* swelled) become bigger, thicker, fatter, etc.: *He blew into the balloon and it swelled bigger and bigger.* **swell up**, swell.

swelling /'swelɪŋ/ n. place on the body that has become bigger, fatter, etc.: *She has a swelling on her head where she hit it when she fell.*

swept /swept/ *past part. & past tense* of v. sweep.

swerve /swɜːv/ v. turn suddenly while you are driving or running: *The car swerved when the driver saw a child in the road.* **swerve** n.

swift /swɪft/ adj. quick; fast. **swiftly** adv.: *He ran swiftly up the stairs.*

swim /swɪm/ v. (*pres. part.* swimming, *past part.* swum /swʌm/, *past tense* swam /swæm/) move your body through the water: *Can you swim across the lake?* **swim** n.: *Let's go for a swim.*

swimming n.: *Swimming is my favourite sport.* **swimming-pool** n. special place or building for swimming. **swimmer** n. someone who is swimming. **swimsuit** /'swɪmsuːt/ n. piece of clothing that a woman or girl wears for swimming.

swindle /'swɪndl/ v. take money from someone by tricking him; cheat: *Don't buy a car from that garage—they will swindle you.* **swindle** n. **swindler** n. someone who swindles.

swing[1] /swɪŋ/ n. **1** (no pl.) moving backwards and forwards through the air. **2** (pl. swings) hanging seat for a child to move backwards and forwards through the air. **3** (no pl.) strong rhythm: *Jazz music has a lot of swing.* **go with a swing**, go well: *The party went with a swing and we all enjoyed it.* **in full swing**, happening; busy and going well: *The party was in full swing when we arrived.*

swing[2] v. (*past part. & past tense* swung /swʌŋ/) **1** hang and move from side to side or backwards and forwards through the air: *The monkey was swinging by its tail from the tree.* **2** turn in a circle; make something turn through the air: *The cowboy swung the lasso round and round.*

switch[1] /swɪtʃ/ n. small handle, knob, or button that turns electricity on and off: *a light switch.*

switch[2] v. **1** press a handle, knob, or button to turn electricity on or off. **switch on**, press a knob, etc. to start something that works by electricity. **switch off**, press a knob, etc. to stop electricity: *When the programme finished, we switched the radio off.* **2** change to something different: *He switched from a back seat to a front seat so that he could see more.*

switchboard /'swɪtʃbɔːd/ n. machine

with many small handles, for sending telephone calls to the right place, etc.

swollen /ˈswəʊlən/ *adj.* fatter, thicker, or fuller than usual: *a swollen ankle; a swollen river.*

swoop /swuːp/ *v.* come down quickly: *The bird swooped down on to the ground.* **swoop** *n.*

swop /swɒp/ *v.* (*pres. part.* swopping, *past part.* & *past tense* swopped /swɒpt/) give one thing and get another thing for it: *I swopped my knife for Kit's pen.*

sword /sɔːd/ *n.* very long, sharp knife for fighting.

swore /swɔː(r)/ *past tense* of *v.* swear.

sworn /swɔːn/ *past part.* of *v.* swear.

swot /swɒt/ *v.* (*pres. part.* swotting, *past part.* & *past tense* swotted /ˈswɒtɪd/) study hard: *Matthew is swotting for his exam.*

swum /swʌm/ *past part.* of *v.* swim.

swung /swʌŋ/ *past part.* & *past tense* of *v.* swing.

syllable /ˈsɪləbl/ *n.* part of a word that has one vowel sound: *The word 'big' has one syllable and the word 'Africa' has three syllables.*

symbol /ˈsɪmbl/ *n.* mark, sign, or picture that shows something: + *and* − *are symbols for plus and minus in arithmetic.*

sympathize /ˈsɪmpəθaɪz/ *v.* feel sorry for someone; share a feeling with someone; understand someone's feelings: *I sympathize with you—I have a naughty little brother like yours.* **sympathy** /ˈsɪmpəθɪ/ *n.: She wrote me a letter of sympathy when Dad died.* **sympathetic** /sɪmpəˈθetɪk/ *adj.: a sympathetic smile.* **sympathetically** *adv.: 'I'm so sorry you're ill', he said sympathetically.*

symptom /ˈsɪmptəm/ *n.* sign of an illness: *A sore throat is a symptom of a cold.*

synthetic /sɪnˈθetɪk/ *adj.* not natural; made by people: *Nylon is synthetic, but wool is natural.*

syrup /ˈsɪrəp/ *n.* (no *pl.*) thick, sweet liquid made with sugar and water or fruit juice.

system /ˈsɪstəm/ *n.* **1** group of things or parts that work together: *the railway*

system. **2** set of ideas; way of doing things: *a system of government.*

Tt

table /ˈteɪbl/ *n.* **1** piece of furniture that is a flat top on legs: *Dinner is ready—come to the table.* **lay the table**, put things on the table ready for a meal. **2** list: *a table of weights and measures.*

table-cloth /ˈteɪbl klɒθ/ *n.* piece of cloth that you put over a table when you have a meal.

table napkin /ˈteɪbl næpkɪn/ *n.* small piece of cloth that each person has at the table to keep his clothes clean, wipe his fingers on, etc.

tablespoon /ˈteɪblspuːn/ *n.* big spoon for putting food on to the plate of each person.

tablet /ˈtæblɪt/ *n.* **1** flat piece of something: *a tablet of soap.* **2** small, round, hard piece of medicine, which you swallow; pill: *aspirin tablets.*

table tennis /ˈteɪbl tenɪs/ *n.* (no *pl.*) game where you hit a small, white ball over a net on a big table; ping-pong.

tackle[1] /ˈtækl/ *n.* **1** (no *pl.*) special things that you need for a job or sport:

Did Ken take his fishing tackle with him to the river? **2** (*pl.* tackles) catching someone in a game and trying to take the ball from him.

tackle² *v.* **1** start to do a difficult, nasty job: *Please help me to tackle these sums.* **2** try to catch and hold someone: *The policeman tackled the thief.* **3** catch someone in a game and try to take the ball from him.

tact /tækt/ *n.* (no *pl.*) knowing how and when to say things so that you will not hurt people. **tactful** /'tæktfl/ *adj.* polite and careful with people's feelings: *Jack wrote me a tactful letter when I lost my job.* **tactfully** *adv.* **tactless** *adj.* rude and careless about people's feelings. **tactlessly** *adv.*

tag /tæg/ *n.* small piece of paper or metal that you fix on something to give information about it: *I looked at the price tag to see what the dress cost.*

tail /teɪl/ *n.* **1** part of an animal, bird, or fish that sticks out at the back and can move: *The dog wagged his tail when I came home.* **2** end or back part of something: *the tail of an aeroplane.*

tailor /'teɪlə(r)/ *n.* someone whose job is to make suits, coats, etc.

take /teɪk/ *v.* (*past part.* taken /'teɪkən/, *past tense* took /tʊk/) **1** get hold of something or someone; pick something up: *Please take my hand. The mother took the baby in her arms.* **2** carry something: *Shall I take that heavy basket home for you?* **3** remove something; make something disappear; steal something: *Who has taken my bicycle?* **4** lead or bring someone somewhere: *Geoff took me to the cinema.* **5** do or have something: *We took a walk in the park.* **6** eat or drink something: *Has James taken his medicine?* **7** travel in a vehicle: *I took a taxi.* **8** receive or accept something: *I'll take £6 for my old bicycle.* **9** buy something often: *Mr. Moore takes two daily newspapers.* **10** need something: *The journey will take two days. That dress will take four metres of cloth.* **take after**, look like someone: *Sean takes after his father.* **take something apart**, separate something into parts: *He took the engine apart to mend it.* **take something away, (a)** remove something: *I took the knife away from the baby.* **(b)** subtract a number from another number. **take something down**, write something on a piece of paper: *She took down my address.* **take someone** or **something for**, think that someone or something is: *I took him for a clever boy at first, but now I think he's rather stupid.* **take something for granted**, be so sure of something that you do not think about it: *I take it for granted that I'll always spend Christmas with my family.* **take someone in, (a)** let someone with no home stay in your house. **(b)** trick someone: *Don't believe him—he'll try to take you in.* **take something in**, make a piece of clothing smaller, etc.: *The dress was too big, so I took it in.* **take it that**, think or believe that: *When I did not hear from him, I took it that he was on holiday.* **take off**, leave the ground and start to fly: *The aeroplane took off an hour late.* **take someone off**, copy the way someone does things so that you make people laugh: *Everyone laughed when Mary took off the angry farmer.* **take something off**, remove a piece of clothing: *He came in and took off his coat.* **take something on**, accept a job; promise to do something: *Diana always takes on too much work.* **take something over**, look after a business, a machine, etc. when another person stops: *Alan took over the farm when his father died.* **take to something, (a)** start to do something often: *When did Emma take to smoking?* **(b)** go somewhere to escape from something: *He ran away from prison and took to the forest.* **take to someone**, begin to like someone: *Have the staff taken to the new manager?* **take up**, fill a space: *That big table takes up too much room.* **take a road, path, etc.**, go by a road, path, etc.: *If you take that road you'll reach the village.*

take-away /'teɪk əweɪ/ *n.* shop or restaurant that sells hot food that you buy and take out with you. **take-away** *adj.*: *a take-away meal.*

taken /'teɪkən/ *past part.* of *v.* take.

take-off /'teɪk ɒf/ *n.* moment when an aeroplane or rocket leaves the ground.

tale /teɪl/ *n.* story: *the tale of the hare and the tortoise.* **tell tales**, tell other people about the bad things that someone has done.

talent /'tælənt/ *n.* natural skill; something that you do naturally well: *Amanda has a talent for painting.*

talented /'tæləntɪd/ *adj.* very clever in a special way: *a talented footballer.*

talk¹ /tɔ:k/ *n.* **1** conversation between two or more people: *Dave and I had a long talk.* **2** speaking to a group of people: *Professor Wilson gave an interesting talk on birds.*

talk² *v.* say words; speak to someone: *She is talking to her boyfriend on the telephone.* **talk something over**, talk about something.

talkative /'tɔ:kətɪv/ *adj.* talking a lot.

tall /tɔ:l/ *adj.* **1** high; from top to bottom: *Ella is two metres tall.* **2** high; going up a long way: *Richard is a tall boy.*

tame /teɪm/ *adj.* not wild; that lives with people: *a tame fox.* **tame** *v.* make a wild animal tame: *He tames lions for the circus.*

tan¹ /tæn/ *n.* **1** (no *pl.*) yellow-brown colour. **2** (*pl.* tans) brown colour of your skin when you have been in the hot sun. **tan** *adj.* with a yellow-brown colour. **tanned** /tænd/ *adj.* brown from the sun: *a tanned face.*

tangerine /ˌtændʒə'ri:n/ *n.* fruit like a small, sweet orange, with a loose skin.

tangle /'tæŋgl/ *v.* mix or mess string, threads, hair, etc. so that it is difficult to undo: *The kitten played with my wool and tangled it.* **tangle** *n.* **tangled** /'tæŋgld/ *adj.*: *tangled hair.*

tank /tæŋk/ *n.* **1** container for holding oil or water: *the petrol-tank of a car.* **2** strong, heavy army vehicle with guns.

tanker /'tæŋkə(r)/ *n.* **1** ship with big tanks that carry oil. **2** lorry with a big tank that carries oil, etc.

tap¹ /tæp/ *n.* sort of handle that you turn to let water, gas, etc. come out of a pipe.

tap² *v.* (*pres. part.* tapping, *past part. & past tense* tapped /tæpt/) touch or hit something quickly and lightly: *He tapped the window and she looked up.* **tap** *n.*: *a tap on the window.*

tape /teɪp/ *n.* **1** ribbon; long, narrow strip of cloth. **2** long, narrow piece of sticky paper that you put on parcels, papers, etc. to fasten or mend them. **3** long strip of special stuff that records voices and music in a machine.

tail 2

tail 1

tape-recorder

tap¹

3 2

tape-measure

tape-measure /'teɪp meʒə(r)/ *n.* long, narrow band of cloth, plastic, or metal for measuring: *The tailor put a tape-measure round his waist to see how big it was.*

tape-recorder /'teɪp rɪkɔ:də(r)/ *n.* machine that can put sound on tapes and play it back later.

tar /tɑ:(r)/ *n.* (no *pl.*) black stuff that is thick and sticky when it is hot, and hard when it is cold: *We use tar for making roads.*

target /'tɑ:gɪt/ *n.* what you are trying to hit when you shoot a bullet or arrow.

tariff /'tærɪf/ *n.* list of prices for meals, hotel rooms, etc.

tarmac /'tɑ:mæk/ *n.* (no *pl.*) mixture of sand, small stones, and tar, which makes a smooth covering for roads, etc.

tart /tɑ:t/ *n.* piece of pastry with fruit or jam on it.

tartan /'tɑ:tən/ *n.* special pattern on cloth that comes from Scotland. **tartan** *adj.*: *tartan trousers.*

task /tɑ:sk/ *n.* job; piece of work: *Cooking is an enjoyable task.*

taste¹ /teɪst/ *n.* **1** (no *pl.*) feeling or recognizing food with the mouth: *When I have a cold, I lose my sense of taste.* **2** (*pl.* tastes) feeling that a certain food or drink gives in the mouth: *Sugar has a sweet taste and lemons have a sour taste.* **3** (*pl.* tastes) small amount of something to eat or drink: *I'll have a taste of the wine first, to see whether I like it.* **4** (no *pl.*) a little of anything that you do or have: *Did you like your first taste of riding?* **5** (*pl.* tastes) what you like: *She spends a lot of money on clothes because she has expensive tastes.*

taste[2] *v.* **1** feel or recognize a certain food or drink in your mouth: *I can taste onions in this dish.* **2** have a certain feeling when you put it in your mouth: *This tea tastes too sweet.* **3** eat or drink a little of something: *The cook tasted the stew to see if it had enough salt.*

tasty /'teɪstɪ/ *adj.* good to eat: *a tasty meal.*

tatters /'tætəz/ *n.* (*pl.*) rags. **in tatters**, full of holes; torn. **tattered** /'tætəd/ *adj.: a tattered coat.*

tattoo /tə'tu:/ *v.* make a picture or pattern on someone's skin, with a needle and dyes. **tattoo** *n.: The sailor had a tattoo of a ship on his arm.*

taught /tɔ:t/ *past part. & past tense* of *v.* teach.

tax /tæks/, **taxes** /'tæksɪz/ (*pl.*), **taxation** /tæk'seɪʃn/ (no *pl.*) *n.* money that the government takes from your pay or from the sale of some goods. **tax** *v.* make someone pay tax.

taxi /'tæksɪ/ *n.* car, with a driver, that you can hire for short journeys. **taxirank** *n.* place where taxis wait for customers.

tea /ti:/ *n.* **1** (no *pl.*) drink that you make with hot water and the dry leaves of a plant: *a pot of tea.* **2** (*pl.* teas) cup of tea. **3** (*pl.* teas) small afternoon meal with sandwiches, cakes, and cups of tea. **teapot** /'ti:pɒt/ *n.* pot for holding tea.

teach /ti:tʃ/ *v.* (*past part. & past tense* taught /tɔ:t/) **1** educate someone; tell or show someone how to do something: *My brother is teaching me to swim.* **2** have a job in a school: *Sue wants to teach when she grows up.* **teaching** *n.* the job of teaching in a school.

teacher /'ti:tʃə(r)/ *n.* someone who gives lessons.

team /ti:m/ *n.* **1** group of people who play sports together on one side: *A football match is between two teams of players.* **2** group of people or animals working together: *a team of oxen.*

tear[1] /tɪə(r)/ *n.* drop of water that comes from your eye when you are unhappy, etc. **burst into tears**, suddenly start crying. **be in tears**, be crying: *Why is Erica in tears?* **tearful** *adj.* crying; wet with tears: *Erica's tearful face.* **tearfully** *adv.*

tear[2] /teə(r)/ *n.* rough hole or split in cloth, paper, etc.: *Mother mended the tear in Andrew's trousers.*

tear[3] *v.* (*past part.* torn /tɔ:n/, *past tense* tore /tɔ:(r)/) **1** pull something apart; make a rough hole in something: *Carol tore her dress on a nail.* **tear something up**, pull something into small pieces. **2** take something roughly away from a person or place: *Tear a page out of your notebook.* **3** break; come apart: *Paper tears easily.* **4** run fast: *The children tore out of the classroom when the bell rang.*

tease /ti:z/ *v.* laugh at someone; make fun of someone in an unkind way: *The girls were always teasing her because she was so fat.* **teasingly** *adv.*

teaspoon /'ti:spu:n/ *n.* small spoon for putting sugar into tea, etc. and stirring it.

technical /'teknɪkl/ *adj.* of special, practical knowledge. **technical college** *n.* place where people go to study technical subjects. **technically** *adv.*

technician /tek'nɪʃn/ *n.* expert who works with machines, instruments, or tools.

technique /tek'ni:k/ *n.* way of doing something: *Dick Fosbury had a new technique for doing the high jump.*

teddy-bear /'tedɪ beə(r)/ *n.* sort of doll like a bear.

tedious /'ti:dɪəs/ *adj.* not interesting: *a tedious lecture.* **tediously** *adv.*

teenager /'ti:neɪdʒə(r)/ *n.* boy or girl between the ages of 13 and 19. **teenage** /'ti:neɪdʒ/ *adj.: a teenage girl.* **teens** /ti:nz/ *n.* the ages from 13 to 19: *boys and girls in their teens.*

teeth /ti:θ/ (*pl.*) of *n.* tooth. **grit your teeth**, be brave when there is trouble, pain, etc.

telegram /'telɪgræm/ *n.* message that you send quickly by electric wires or by radio.

telegraph /'telɪgrɑ:f/ *n.* (no *pl.*) way of

sending messages quickly by electric wires or by radio. **telegraph** v.

telephone /'telɪfəʊn/ n. **1** (no pl.) way of talking to someone in another place by using electric wires or by radio: *I spoke to him by telephone.* **2** (pl. telephones) instrument that you hold to talk to and listen to someone in another place. *answer the telephone*, pick up the telephone when it rings and speak to the person who is calling. *on the telephone*, talking to someone by telephone. **telephone call** n. speaking to someone on the telephone: *I had a telephone call from Pete in Leeds today.* **telephone box, telephone booth, telephone kiosk** n. small building with a public telephone. **telephone directory** n. book of people's names, addresses, and telephone numbers. **telephone** v. speak to someone on the telephone: *Oliver telephoned me to say that he had missed the train.*

telescope /'telɪskəʊp/ n. long instrument with special glass that makes distant things look bigger and nearer.

television /'telɪvɪʒn/ n. **1** (no pl.) way of sending pictures so that you can see what is happening in another place. **2** (pl. televisions) **television set**, special box with a screen that shows pictures of what is happening in another place.

tell /tel/ v. (past part. & past tense told /təʊld/) speak to someone about something; inform someone: *Has she told you her new address?* *can tell*, can know, guess, or understand something: *I can tell that she's unhappy because she's crying.* *tell someone off*, speak angrily to someone because he has done something wrong: *My boss told me off for my careless work.* *there's no telling*, no one knows: *There's no telling when the storm will end.* *you're telling me!* I know that already; I agree: *'It's hot today!' 'You're telling me!'*

telly /'telɪ/ abbrev. television.

temper /'tempə(r)/ n. how you feel. *fly into a temper*, become suddenly angry. *in a bad temper*, angry. *in a good temper*, happy. *keep your temper*, not become angry. *lose your temper*, become suddenly angry: *He lost his temper when Julia broke his new record.*

temperature /'temprətʃə(r)/ n. how hot

teddy-bear

telescope

telephone box

TELEPHONE

teapot

telephone 2

taxi

or cold something is: *On a very hot day, the temperature reaches 35°C.* *have or run a temperature, have or run a high temperature*, have a fever: *Jack was running a high temperature and his mother phoned the doctor.*

temple /'templ/ n. building where people pray and worship.

temporary /'temprərɪ/ adj. for a short time: *a temporary job.* **temporarily** adv.: *The road is temporarily closed while the workmen repair it.*

tempt /tempt/ v. **1** try to make someone do something wrong; give someone the idea of doing wrong: *The open door tempted him to go in and rob the house.* **2** make someone want it: *Those cream cakes tempt me!* **tempting** adj. that you want: *a tempting offer.* **temptation** /temp'teɪʃn/ n.

ten /ten/ n. number 10. **ten** adj.

tenant /'tenənt/ n. someone who pays money to live or work in another person's home, offices, etc.: *The tenants pay a monthly rent of £100 for their flat.*

tend /tend/ v. usually do something; be likely to do or be something: *Boys tend to be bigger than girls.* **tendency** /'tendənsɪ/ n.

tender /'tendə(r)/ adj. **1** that you can bite or chew easily: *tender meat.* **2** kind; gentle: *a tender mother.* **tenderly** adv. gently.

tennis /'tenɪs/ n. (no pl.) game for two or four players, with rackets and balls.
tennis-court n. piece of ground with lines on it where you play tennis.
tennis racket n. instrument for hitting a tennis ball.

tense[1] /tens/ adj. **1** tightly pulled: tense muscles. **2** excited because you are waiting for something to happen: The audience was tense as they waited for the acrobat to jump. **tensely** adv. **tension** /'tenʃn/ n.

tense[2] n. form of a verb that shows when something happens: 'I see' is present tense, 'I saw' is past tense, and 'I shall see' is future tense.

tent /tent/ n. house of cloth over poles, which you can put up or take down quickly.

tenth /tenθ/ n. 10th. **tenth** adj.: Bella's tenth birthday.

term /tɜːm/ n. **1** period of time: An American President's term of office is four years. **2** time when schools, universities, etc. are open: The summer term runs from April to July. **3** word; group of words; way of saying something. **4 terms** (pl.) conditions; things you promise and accept in a contract: What are the terms of the peace treaty? **on good** or **bad terms with**, friendly, or not friendly, with someone: We're on good terms with our neighbours.

terminal /'tɜːmɪnl/ n. **1** end of a railway line, bus route, etc. **2** place where the bus to the airport leaves and arrives.

terminus /'tɜːmɪnəs/ n. (pl. termini or terminuses) station at the end of a railway line; end of a bus or aeroplane route.

terrace /'terəs/ n. **1** flat strip of ground along the side of a hill. **2** flat strip of concrete, etc. above the ground outside a house: We sat on the terrace and looked at the sunset. **3** line of houses joined together. **terraced** /'terəst/ adj. joined in a line: Terraced houses are joined together.

terrible /'terəbl/ adj. **1** making you very afraid, very sad, or shocked: a terrible war. **2** very bad: They gave us terrible food at the hotel.

terribly /'terəblɪ/ adv. **1** in a terrible way: She was terribly injured in the crash. **2** very: I'm terribly sorry!

terrific /tə'rɪfɪk/ adj. **1** very great, loud, etc.: a terrific storm. **2** that pleases you very much; wonderful: That was a terrific party! **terrifically** adv.

terrify /'terɪfaɪ/ v. make someone very afraid: The thunder terrified the small children. **terrified** /'terɪfaɪd/ adj. very frightened.

territory /'terətrɪ/ n. (pl. territories) land; land that belongs to one government: Angola was once a Portuguese territory.

terror /'terə(r)/ n. **1** (no pl.) great fear: She screamed in terror. **2** (pl. terrors) a particular fear: a terror of the dark.

terrorist /'terərɪst/ n. someone who frightens, hurts, or kills others so that people will do what he wants. **terrorism** /'terərɪzəm/ n.

test /test/ v. **1** look at something carefully to find out how good it is; examine something: The doctor tested my eyes. **2** use something to find out if it works well: to test a new car. **3** ask someone questions to find out what he knows or can do: The teacher is testing our spelling tomorrow. **test** n.: a blood test; a maths test.

test-pilot /'test paɪlət/ n. someone who flies a new aeroplane to see whether it works.

test-tube /'test tjuːb/ n. long, narrow glass bottle for chemistry, etc.

textbook /'tekstbʊk/ n. book that teaches about something: a history textbook.

than /ðən/, /ðæn/, conj. word that you use when you compare things or people: Rob likes apples more than bananas.

thank /θæŋk/ v. tell someone that you are pleased with something he has done or given; show that you are grateful: I thanked Tim for his present. **thank you**, I thank you. **no thank you**, no, I don't want it; no, I don't want to do it. **thanks** n. **thanks for**, I thank you for something: Thanks for your help. **thanks to**, because of something: I stopped the car very quickly, thanks to the good brakes.

thankful /'θæŋkfl/ adj. very glad; grateful: I was thankful for a rest after the long walk. **thankfully** adv.

that[1] /ðət/, /ðæt/ adj. **1** the one there:

Who is that man? **2** word for something in the past: *At that time, there was no telephone in the village.*

that² *adv.* so: *The next village is ten kilometres away, and we can't walk that far in an hour.*

that³ *conj.* **1** word to show what: *Jo said that he would come.* **2** word to show result, what happens, etc.: *Katy was so happy that she cried.* **3** word to show purpose, why, etc. **so that**, in order that: *She packed the glass in straw so that it wouldn't break.*

that⁴ *pron.* **1** (*pl.* those) the one there: *This house isn't as big as that.* **2** (*pl.* those) word for something in the past: *Mother was in hospital all year—that was a terrible time.* **3** (*pl.* that) who; whom; which: *A lion is an animal that lives in Africa.*

thatch /θætʃ/ *n.* (no *pl.*) cover or roof of dried straw, reeds, etc. **thatch** *v.* put thatch over the roof of a house. **thatched** /θætʃt/ *adj.: a thatched cottage.*

thaw /θɔː/ *v.* warm something frozen so that it starts to melt; become warmer so that it melts: *The sun thawed the ice on the lake.* **thaw** *n.* weather that is warm enough to make snow and ice melt.

the¹ /ðə/, /ði:/ *def. art.* **1** word before the name of someone or something that you know of: *I had a present today. The present came from my girlfriend.* **2** word that you use before the names of rivers, oceans, mountains, some countries, etc.: *the Thames; the Atlantic; the United States.* **3** each; every: *a car that goes eight kilometres to the litre.*

the² *adv.* word that you use when you compare things: *The more he has, the more he wants.*

theatre /ˈθɪətə(r)/ *n.* building where you can see plays. **theatrical** /θɪˈætrɪkl/ *adj.: a theatrical company.*

theft /θeft/ *n.* stealing: *Have you told the police about the theft of your bicycle?*

their /ðeə(r)/ *adj.* of them: *They have brought their children.*

theirs /ðeəz/ *pron.* (no *pl.*) thing that belongs to them: *This car is mine and that car is theirs.*

them /ðəm/, /ðem/ *pron.* (*pl.*) word that you say when you speak about other

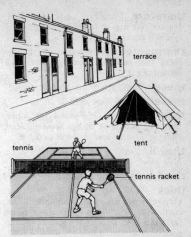

terrace

tent

tennis

tennis racket

people or things: *They are my flowers. Please give them to me.*

theme /θi:m/ *n.* subject; something to talk or write about, etc.: *What is the theme of the opera?*

themselves /ðəmˈselvz/, /ðemˈselvz/ *pron.* (*pl.*) **1** word that describes the people or things that you have just talked about: *They fell and hurt themselves.* **2** they and no other people: *They did it themselves.* **by themselves**, alone.

then /ðen/ *adv.* **1** at that time; at a time that you have just spoken of: *I was living at home then. I will be at college then.* **2** next; afterwards: *I went home for dinner and then went to the cinema.* **3** if that is so: *You feel ill? Then go home.*

theory /ˈθɪərɪ/ *n.* (*pl.* theories) idea that tries to explain something: *In old times people had a theory that the world was flat.*

there¹ /ðeə(r)/ *adv.* **1** in, at, or to that place: *Don't put the box here—put it there.* **here and there**, in different places. **2** word to show something: *There is a man at the door. In winter there are no leaves on the trees.* **3** word that you say with the verbs 'appear', 'seem', etc.: *There seems to be a lot of noise in the street.*

there² *exclam.* word to make people look or listen: *There comes the train! There's the bell for our class!*

therefore /'ðeəfɔ:(r)/ adv. for that reason: *Sue was on holiday and therefore couldn't come to our party.*

thermometer /θə'mɒmɪtə(r)/ n. instrument that tells you how hot or cold something is.

these[1] /ði:z/ (pl.) of adj. this.

these[2] (pl.) of pron. this.

they /ðeɪ/ pron. (pl.) word for more than one person or thing: *Bob and Jean came at 11 a.m. and they left at 6 p.m.*

they'll /'ðeɪəl/ = they will: *They'll be here soon.*

they're /'ðeɪə(r)/ = they are.

thick[1] /θɪk/ adj. **1** wide; how far through from one side to the other: *The castle walls are 80 cm thick.* **2** not thin; far from one side to the other: *You'll need a thick coat in that icy wind.* **3** with a lot of people or things close together: *a thick forest.* **4** that does not flow quickly: *thick oil.* **thickly** adv. **thickness** n.

thick[2] adv. close together: *Leaves lay thick on the ground.*

thief /θi:f/ n. (pl. thieves) someone who steals: *A thief has taken my car.*

thigh /θaɪ/ n. part of your leg above the knee.

thimble /'θɪmbl/ n. metal or plastic cap that you wear on the end of your finger when you are sewing.

thin /θɪn/ adj. (thinner, thinnest) **1** with little flesh; not fat: *thin, starving cattle.* **2** not thick; not far through: *thin cloth.* **3** like water: *thin stew.* **4** not close together: *the thin hair of an old man.* **thinly** adv.: *Sow the seed thinly.*

thing /θɪŋ/ n. **1** an object: *What is that thing in the sky?* **2** things (pl.) possessions; what you own: *Have you packed your things for the journey?* **3** happening; event: *A funny thing happened today.*

think /θɪŋk/ v. (past part. & past tense thought /θɔ:t/) **1** work with your mind: *Think before you answer the question.* **2** believe something: *I think it's going to rain.* **think about,** (a) have something or someone in your mind: *I often think about that day.* (b) consider whether to do something or not: *Paul is thinking about becoming a doctor.* **think badly of,** not like someone or something. **think**

better of, think about something and then not do it: *I was going to play tennis but I thought better of it when I heard the weather forecast.* **think highly of, think well of,** like someone or something very much. **think of,** (a) have something in your mind: *She cried when she thought of her dead cat.* (b) have an opinion about someone or something: *What do you think of that record?*

third /θɜ:d/ n. 3rd. **third** adj.: *March is the third month of the year.*

thirst /θɜ:st/ n. (no pl.) wanting to drink something: *The long walk gave him a thirst.*

thirsty /'θɜ:stɪ/ adj. **1** wanting something to drink: *Give me a glass of water because I'm thirsty.* **2** that makes you want to drink: *Digging is thirsty work.* **thirstily** adv.

thirteen /ˌθɜ:'ti:n/ n. number 13. **thirteen** adj. **thirteenth** /ˌθɜ:'ti:nθ/ adj. 13th.

thirty /'θɜ:tɪ/ n. (pl. thirties) number 30. **thirty** adj. **thirtieth** /'θɜ:tɪəθ/ adj. 30th.

this /ðɪs/ adj. **1** the one here: *I like this dress better than that.* **2** word for something in the present: *this morning; this week.* **this** pron.: *How much is this?*

thistle /'θɪsl/ n. plant with leaves that have sharp points.

thorn /θɔ:n/ n. sharp point that grows on the stem of a plant: *Roses have thorns on their stems.* **thorny** adj. with thorns: *a thorny plant.*

thorough /'θʌrə/ adj. **1** complete; well done: *Grace gave the room a thorough cleaning.* **2** careful to do a job well: *Jeremy is very thorough in his work.* **thoroughness** n.

thoroughly /'θʌrəlɪ/ adv. **1** done well and completely: *He cleaned the room thoroughly.* **2** totally: *He's thoroughly honest.*

those[1] /ðəʊz/ (pl.) of adj. that.

those[2] (pl.) of pron. that.

though[1] /ðəʊ/ adv. however: *He said he would come; he didn't though.*

though[2] conj. **1** although; in spite of the fact that: *Though she was in a hurry, she stopped to talk.* **2** even if; but: *I thought it was right though I wasn't sure.*

as though, in a way that makes you think something: *He frowned as though he didn't understand.*

thought¹ /θɔːt/ *n.* **1** (no *pl.*) thinking. **2** (*pl.* thoughts) idea: *Have you any thoughts about our next holiday?* **on second thoughts**, after thinking about something again.

thought² *past part.* & *past tense* of *v.* think.

thoughtful /'θɔːtfl/ *adj.* **1** thinking: *She had a thoughtful look on her face.* **2** kind; thinking and caring about other people: *It was thoughtful of Arthur to meet us at the station.* **thoughtfully** *adv.* **thoughtfulness** *n.*

thoughtless /'θɔːtlɪs/ *adj.* not thinking or caring about other people. **thoughtlessly** *adv.* **thoughtlessness** *n.*

thousand /'θaʊznd/ *n.* number 1,000. **thousand** *adj.* 1,000. **thousandth** /'θaʊzənθ/ *adj.* 1,000th.

thrash /θræʃ/ *v.* hit a person or animal very hard and often: *The cruel man was thrashing his horse.* **thrashing** *n.* beating.

thread¹ /θred/ *n.* long, thin piece of cotton, silk, wool, etc. for sewing or weaving.

thread² *v.* **1** put a piece of cotton, silk, wool, etc. through a needle. **2** put beads, etc. on a piece of cord.

threat /θret/ *n.* **1** promise to hurt someone if he does not do what you want. **carry out a threat**, do the harmful thing that you promised: *Do you think that the workers will carry out their threat to go on strike?* **2** sign of trouble, danger, etc.: *Dark clouds bring a threat of rain.*

threaten /'θretn/ *v.* **1** promise to hurt someone if he does not do what you want. **2** give a sign of something bad or dangerous: *The clouds threaten rain.* **threatening** *adj.* **threateningly** *adv.*: *to speak threateningly.*

three /θriː/ *n.* number 3. **three** *adj.*

threw /θruː/ *past tense* of *v.* throw.

thrill /θrɪl/ *v.* excite someone: *The news of Paul's prize thrilled his mother.* **thrill** *n.*: *The visit to the circus was a big thrill for the children.* **thrilled** /θrɪld/ *adj.* excited; very pleased, happy, etc. **thrilling** *adj.* exciting.

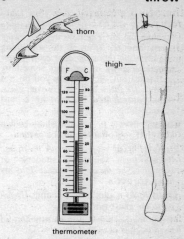

thorn

thigh —

thermometer

thriller /'θrɪlə(r)/ *n.* exciting story, play, or film.

throat /θrəʊt/ *n.* **1** front part of the neck. **2** tube that takes food from the mouth down into the body: *A bone stuck in the boy's throat and he couldn't swallow.*

throb /θrɒb/ *v.* (*pres. part.* throbbing, *past part.* & *past tense* throbbed /θrɒbd/) beat hard and fast: *His heart was throbbing with fear.* **throb** *n.*: *the throb of an engine.*

throttle /'θrɒtl/ *v.* hold someone's throat so tightly that you kill him.

through¹ /θruː/ *adv.* **1** from one end to the other; from one side to the other: *Drive round the town; don't drive through.* **2** from the start to the end; completely: *The book was too long—I couldn't read through.*

through² *prep.* **1** from one end to the other of; from one side to the other of: *We drove through the tunnel.* **2** from the start to the end of: *I must travel through the night.* **3** from; because of: *I heard about the meeting through Tom.*

throughout¹ /θruː'aʊt/ *adv.* in every part; all the time: *They painted the house throughout.*

throughout² *prep.* in every part of; from the start of to the end of: *We laughed throughout the film.*

throw /θrəʊ/ *v.* (*past part.* thrown

/θrəʊn/, *past tense* threw /θru:/) **1** move your arm quickly to send something through the air: *The boys were throwing stones into the river.* **2** do something quickly: *Don threw the door open.* **throw something away** or **out**, put something in the dustbin, etc. because you do not want it: *He threw away the broken glass.* **throw yourself into**, begin to work hard at something.

thrush /θrʌʃ/ *n.* (*pl.* thrushes) brown bird that you often see in the garden.

thrust /θrʌst/ *v.* (*past part.* & *past tense* thrust) push something suddenly or strongly: *She thrust the money into my hand.* **thrust** *n.*

thud /θʌd/ *n.* dull, heavy sound: *He fell on to the grass with a thud.*

thug /θʌg/ *n.* someone who attacks and harms other people.

thumb /θʌm/ *n.* short, thick finger on the inside of the hand: *He pressed the drawing pin into the board with his thumb.* **under someone's thumb**, always doing what another person wants: *That girl is under her mother's thumb.*

thump /θʌmp/ *v.* **1** hit something hard: *He thumped on the door.* **2** beat hard and fast: *His heart was thumping with fear.* **thump** *n.*

thunder /'θʌndə(r)/ *n.* (no *pl.*) **1** big noise in the sky when there is a storm. **2** big noise. **thunder** *v.*: *The lorries thundered down the street.*

thunderstorm /'θʌndəstɔːm/ *n.* storm with heavy rain, lightning, and thunder.

Thursday /'θɜːzdeɪ/ *n.* fifth day of the week: *Thursday comes before Friday.*

thus /ðʌs/ *adv.* **1** in this way: *Do it thus.* **2** for that reason; for this reason.

tick¹ /tɪk/ *n.* **1** sound that a clock or watch makes. **2** small mark (√): *The teacher puts a tick next to right answers and a cross next to wrong ones.*

tick² *v.* **1** make a sound like a clock or watch. **2** make a mark like this (√). **tick someone off**, speak angrily to someone because he has done something wrong: *My boss ticked me off for arriving late.*

ticket /'tɪkɪt/ *n.* small piece of card or paper that shows you have paid to travel on a train, bus, etc. or go to a cinema or theatre: *He bought a ticket at the railway station.* **ticket collector** *n.* someone whose job is to take tickets from people on trains, etc. **ticket office** *n.* place where you buy tickets.

tickle /'tɪkl/ *v.* **1** touch someone lightly so that he feels funny and laughs: *The mother tickled her baby's feet.* **2** have an itching feeling: *My nose tickles.* **tickle** *n.*

tide /taɪd/ *n.* rise and fall of the sea that happens twice a day.

tidy /'taɪdɪ/ *adj.* **1** with everything in the right place; neat: *a tidy room.* **2** liking to have things in good order: *a tidy boy.* **tidy** *v.* put things in their right places; make something clean and neat: *The waitress tidied the table.* **tidily** *adv.* **tidiness** *n.*

tie¹ /taɪ/ *n.* **1** long, narrow piece of cloth that a man wears round the neck of his shirt. **2** something that holds people together: *He doesn't want to live in London because of his family ties in Newcastle.* **3** equal marks, etc. in a game or competition: *The match ended in a tie, 2–2.*

tie² *v.* **1** make a knot or bow with two ends of string, rope, etc.: *Please tie a firm knot.* **tie someone up**, put a piece of rope round someone so that he cannot move: *The robbers tied up the shopkeeper.* **tie something up**, put a piece of string, rope, etc. round something to hold it firm: *I tied up the parcel.* **2** end a game or competition with the same marks, etc. for both sides: *The two boys tied in the examination—each got 88%.*

tiger /'taɪgə(r)/ *n.* big, wild animal with yellow fur and black stripes.

tight /taɪt/ *adj.* firm so that you cannot untie or undo it easily: *This knot is so tight I can't undo it.* **tightly** *adv.*

tighten /'taɪtn/ *v.* become tighter or firmer; make something tighter: *to tighten a screw.*

tightrope /'taɪtrəʊp/ *n.* piece of rope or wire above the ground, on which dancers and acrobats walk, etc.

tights /taɪts/ *n.* (*pl.*) stockings and pants all in one piece of clothing, for a woman or girl or dancer.

tile /taɪl/ *n.* thin piece of baked clay, etc. for making roofs, floors, etc.

till[1] /tɪl/ *conj.* up to the time when: *We'll wait till the rain stops.*

till[2] *n.* machine that holds money and adds up prices.

till[3] *prep.* **1** up to a certain time: *I'll be here till Monday.* **2** before: *I can't come till Tuesday.*

tilt /tɪlt/ *v.* lean to one side; move something so that it leans to one side: *If you tilt the table, the dishes will slide off on to the floor.* **tilt** *n.*

timber /'tɪmbə(r)/ *n.* **1** (no *pl.*) wood that is ready for building, making things, etc.: *We bought some timber to build a shed.* **2** (*pl.* timbers) long piece of heavy wood that holds up a roof, part of a ship, etc.

time[1] /taɪm/ *n.* **1** (no *pl.*) all the years, months, weeks, days, hours, and minutes: *Time passes quickly when you're busy.* **2** (no *pl.*) length of time; period: *We waited a long time.* **3** (no *pl.*) the hour of the day: *What time is it? It's six o'clock.* **4** (*pl.* times) a certain moment or occasion: *It's a long way—I'll go by bus next time.* **5** **times** (*pl.*) multiplied by: *Three times four is twelve.* **6** **times** (*pl.*) certain years in history: *There was a house in this field in Roman times.* **7** (*pl.* times) experience; something that you do, etc.: *We had a lovely time on holiday.* **8** how quickly something happens: *What was the winning runner's time?* **at a time**, together; on each occasion: *He carried six boxes at a time.* **at one time**, in the past: *At one time, Nigeria was a British colony.* **at the time**, then: *In 1969 the first men landed on the moon—I was twelve at the time.* **at times**, sometimes: *I like Bob but he's very annoying at times.* **for the time being**, now; for a short while: *She has a cold and is staying in bed for the time being.* **from time to time**, sometimes: *We get letters from our uncle from time to time.* **in a few days' time**, soon. **in time**, **(a)** not too late for something: *If you hurry, you'll be in time for the bus.* **(b)** at some time in the future; as time passes: *Swimming is difficult but you'll learn in time.* **in good time**, early: *We want to get to the station in good time, so that we can buy our tickets.* **in no time**, very quickly: *She was very thirsty and drank her milk in no time.* **it's about time, it's high time**, it is very necessary:

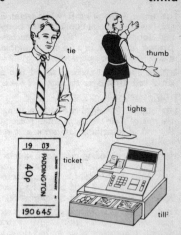

You're lazy—it's high time you started working hard. **have a good time**, enjoy yourself: *Have a good time at the party.* **just in time**, at the last moment: *I caught the child just in time before she fell into the river.* **kill time**, find something to do while waiting: *Let's kill time with a game of football until the train comes.* **on time**, at the right time; not early and not late: *The train was on time.* **spare time**, time free from work, when you can do other things: *Nick plays drums in his spare time.* **spend time**, use a certain time to do something: *He spent a lot of time mending the car.* **take your time**, not hurry; do something slowly: *Granny is tired, so she's taking her time to walk upstairs.* **tell the time**, read a clock or watch correctly. **time and time again**, often; again and again.

time[2] *v.* **1** plan something so that it will happen when you want it to: *Tom timed his journey so that he would be home before dark.* **2** measure how long something takes: *The teacher timed all the boys to see who could run the fastest.*

timetable /'taɪmteɪbl/ *n.* programme; plan or list of times when something will happen, be done, etc.: *The railway timetable shows the times when the trains arrive and depart.*

timid /'tɪmɪd/ *adj.* easily frightened; shy: *That timid boy won't talk to anyone.* **timidly** *adv.*

tin /tɪn/ *n.* **1** (no *pl.*) soft, white metal. **2** (*pl.* tins) can; metal container for keeping foods, etc.: *a tin of peaches.* **tinned** /tɪnd/ *adj.* in a tin or can so that it will stay fresh: *tinned milk.*

tinkle /'tɪŋkl/ *v.* make a sound like a small bell. **tinkle** *n.: the tinkle of bells.*

tiny /'taɪnɪ/ *adj.* very small.

tip¹ /tɪp/ *n.* **1** pointed end of something: *the tips of your fingers.* **2** small piece at the end of something: *an arrow with an iron tip.*

tip² *n.* **1** gift of money to a porter, waiter, etc. after he has done a job for you: *How much should we leave as a tip at the restaurant?* **2** little piece of advice: *He gave me some tips about gardening.*

tip³ *v.* (*pres. part.* tipping, *past part.* & *past tense* tipped /tɪpt/) give extra money to someone after he has done a job: *Shall I tip the porter?*

tip⁴ *v.* move something so that it leans to one side; lean to one side: *She tipped the tray and all the cups slid on to the floor.* **tip out**, turn something so that the things inside fall out: *Jock tipped the water out of his bucket.* **tip over**, turn something over; turn over: *The boat tipped over and we were all in the water.* **tip up**, move up at one side or at one end; make something move up at one side: *The tray tipped up and the plates slid off.*

tiptoe /'tɪptəʊ/ *v.* walk quietly on your toes. **tiptoe** *n.: He walked on tiptoe.*

tire /'taɪə(r)/ *v.* **1** make someone want to rest; become weary: *The long walk tired the children.* **2** want to stop doing something: *She never tires of talking about her children.* **be tired of**, have had enough of something: *I'm tired of this programme—let's switch it off.*

tired /'taɪəd/ *adj.* needing to rest: *The tired boy fell asleep at once.* **tired out**, totally tired.

tissue /'tɪʃuː/ *n.* paper handkerchief. **tissue paper**, thin paper for wrapping things.

title /'taɪtl/ *n.* **1** name of a book, film picture, etc. **2** word that we put in front of a person's name: *'Sir', 'Mr.', and 'Miss' are titles.*

to¹ /tuː/ *adv.* **to and fro**, backwards and forwards: *She swung to and fro on the swing.*

to² /tə/, /tʊ/, /tuː/ *prep.* **1** word that shows where someone or something is going, etc.: *We walk to town. Point to the blackboard.* **2** word that shows who is receiving something: *I gave the book to Mary.* **3** word that shows how many minutes before the hour: *It's ten minutes to six.* **4** as far as; until: *She read the book from the beginning to the end.* **5** word that shows where: *He tied the donkey to the tree.* **6** word that shows why: *He came to help me.* **7** word that shows a change: *The sky changed from blue to grey.* **8** word that shows the highest number, price, etc.: *Coats cost from £40 to £100.*

toad /təʊd/ *n.* animal like a frog, with a rough skin.

toast /təʊst/ *n.* (no *pl.*) piece or pieces of bread that you have grilled so that they are brown and crisp. **toaster** *n.* instrument for grilling bread. **toast** *v.*

toast *v.* hold up a glass of wine and wish someone happiness, etc.: *The wedding guests toasted the bride and bridegroom.* **toast** *n.:* to drink a toast.

tobacco /tə'bækəʊ/ *n.* (no *pl.*) dried leaves that you smoke in cigarettes, cigars, and pipes. **tobacconist** /tə'bækənɪst/ *n.* shopkeeper who sells tobacco.

toboggan /tə'bɒgən/ *n.* children's sledge for sliding down snowy slopes. **toboggan** *v.*

today /tə'deɪ/ *n.* (no *pl.*) **1** this day: *Today is my birthday.* **2** now; present time: *the young people of today.* **today** *adv.: I couldn't go yesterday but I am going today.*

toe /təʊ/ *n.* **1** one of the five parts like fingers at the end of the foot. **2** part of a sock, shoe, etc. that covers the end of the foot.

toffee /'tɒfɪ/ *n.* sort of sticky sweet.

together /tə'geðə(r)/ *adv.* **1** next to each other; close: *Hold the sticks together and see which is longer.* **2** with each other: *Grace and Catherine always walk to school together.* **3** at the same time: *All his troubles seemed to happen together.*

toilet /'tɔɪlɪt/ *n.* lavatory; W.C. **toilet paper** *n.* special paper that you use in the toilet.

token /'təʊkən/ *n.* sign or mark: *This present is a token of our friendship.*

told /təʊld/ *past part. & past tense* of *v.* tell. *I told you so!* I told you what would happen and now you see I am right.

tomato /tə'mɑːtəʊ/ *n.* (*pl.* tomatoes) soft, round, red fruit which we cook or eat raw.

tomb /tuːm/ *n.* grave. **tombstone** *n.* stone that you put on a grave, with the name of the dead person.

tomorrow /tə'mɒrəʊ/ *n.* (no *pl.*) the day after today: *It's Sunday today, so tomorrow is Monday.* **tomorrow** *adv.*: *We'll go tomorrow.*

ton /tʌn/ *n.* measure of weight = 1,016 kilograms. **tons of**, a lot of something; many: *He has tons of money.*

tone /təʊn/ *n.* sound of voice or music: *He spoke in an angry tone.*

tongs /tɒŋz/ *n.* (*pl.*) instrument for lifting and holding things: *a pair of coal tongs.*

tongue /tʌŋ/ *n.* **1** the part inside the mouth that moves when you talk, eat, lick, etc. **hold your tongue**, stop talking; not say anything: *She was angry but she held her tongue.* **2** language: *the English tongue.*

tonight /tə'naɪt/ *n.* (no *pl.*) this night: *Tonight will be fun.* **tonight** *adv.*: *I'm going to a party tonight.*

tonne /tʌn/ *n.* measure of weight.

too /tuː/ *adv.* **1** also; as well: *I want to go, too.* **2** more than you want; more than you can do, etc.: *That question is too hard—I can't answer it.*

took /tʊk/ *past tense* of *v.* take.

tool /tuːl/ *n.* instrument; thing for doing a job: *A hammer is a tool for knocking nails into wood.*

tooth /tuːθ/ *n.* (*pl.* teeth) **1** one of the hard, white things in the mouth, which bite and chew. **have a tooth out**, let someone pull your tooth out because it is bad, etc. **toothache** /'tuːθeɪk/ *n.* pain in a tooth. **toothbrush** /'tuːθbrʌʃ/ *n.* small brush for cleaning your teeth. **toothpaste** /'tuːθpeɪst/ *n.* special stuff for cleaning your teeth. **2** something like a tooth: *the teeth of a comb; the teeth of a saw.*

top¹ /tɒp/ *adj.* **1** highest: *the top shelf.* **2** best: *top marks.*

top² *n.* **1** highest part: *Clouds cover the*

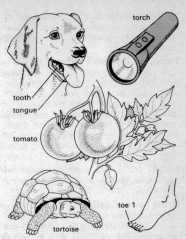

top of the mountain. **2** cover; lid: *Where's the top of the jam jar?* **at the top of your voice**, very loudly: *He shouted at the top of his voice.* **on top**, at or on the highest part: *The cake had sugar on top.* **on top of**, over or covering something: *We climbed on top of the wall.*

top³ *n.* child's toy that goes round and round very fast in the same place.

topic /'tɒpɪk/ *n.* something to talk or write about: *Football is his main topic of conversation.*

topple /'tɒpl/ *v.* fall over; make something fall over: *The pile of books toppled.*

torch /tɔːtʃ/ *n.* (*pl.* torches) small lamp, with batteries, that you carry to show the way in the dark.

tore /tɔː(r)/ *past tense* of *v.* tear.

torn /tɔːn/ *past part.* of *v.* tear.

tornado /tɔː'neɪdəʊ/ *n.* (*pl.* tornadoes) dangerous storm with very strong winds.

torpedo /tɔː'piːdəʊ/ *n.* (*pl.* torpedoes) sort of bomb that travels under the water to blow up a ship. **torpedo** *v.* hit and break up a ship with a torpedo.

torrent /'tɒrənt/ *n.* rush of water: *After the rain, the river became a torrent.* **torrential** /tə'renʃl/ *adj.*: *torrential rain.*

tortoise /'tɔːtəs/ *n.* animal with a hard shell on its back, which walks very slowly.

torture /'tɔːtʃə(r)/ v. hurt someone terribly; give someone great pain. **torture** n. **torturer** n. someone who tortures another person.

toss /tɒs/ v. **1** throw something quickly: *Jim tossed the ball to me.* **2** move roughly; make something move roughly: *The boat was tossing on the big waves.* *toss up, toss for it,* throw a coin into the air and let it fall to decide something. **toss** n. *win* or *lose the toss,* guess rightly or wrongly when a coin is thrown up: *Our captain won the toss, so our team batted first.*

total¹ /'təʊtl/ adj. complete; entire: *No one spoke, and there was total silence in the room.*

total² n. complete amount: *Add these figures together and find the total.* **total** v. (*pres. part.* totalling, *past part.* & *past tense* totalled /'təʊtld/) add up to an amount: *The cost of the trip totalled £30.*

totally /'təʊtəlɪ/ adv. completely: *A totally blind man can see nothing.*

touch¹ /tʌtʃ/ n. **1** (*pl.* touches) contact; when two things come together: *The horse became quiet at the touch of my hand.* **2** (no *pl.*) feeling in your hands, etc. that tells you about things: *A blind man reads by touch.* *be in,* or *get in touch with,* write to, telephone, or go to see someone: *I haven't been in touch with Mick since we left school five years ago.*

touch² v. **1** put a finger or another part of the body on or against something: *Don't touch the paint until it's dry.* **2** contact or meet something: *Your jeans are dirty at the bottom because they touch the ground.* **3** take food or drink: *The sick boy hasn't touched his lunch.* **4** make you feel sad or happy: *Her unhappy face touched me.*

touch-down /'tʌtʃ daʊn/ n. moment when an aeroplane or spacecraft comes down to the ground.

tough /tʌf/ adj. **1** strong in the body: *A mountain-climber must be tough.* **2** difficult; hard: *a tough job.* **3** that you cannot bite or chew easily: *tough meat.* **4** that you cannot break or tear easily: *A leather bag is tougher than a paper bag.*

tour /tʊə(r)/ n. **1** journey to see many places: *The Queen is making a tour of Canada.* **2** short visit to see a certain building: *a tour of the Tower of London.* **tour** v.: *Our American friends are touring Europe.*

tourist /'tʊərɪst/ n. someone on holiday who travels around to see places.

tournament /'tʊənəmənt/ n. sport competition: *a tennis tournament.*

tow /təʊ/ v. pull a boat, car, etc. with a rope or chain: *We tow a caravan behind our car.*

toward /tə'wɔːd/, **towards** /tə'wɔːdz/ prep. **1** to; in the direction of: *Walk towards me.* **2** at a time near: *Children become tired towards evening.* **3** to help; to help pay for: *He saves £2 every week towards his new bicycle.*

towel /'taʊəl/ n. cloth for drying something: *He dried his hands with a towel.*

tower /'taʊə(r)/ n. tall, narrow building; tall part of a building: *a church tower.* **tower** v. be very high: *The tree towers above our house.*

tower-block /'taʊə blɒk/ n. very high building.

town /taʊn/ n. place with houses, shops, offices, etc.: *Stratford-on-Avon is a small country town.*

town hall /,taʊn 'hɔːl/ n. building with offices and meeting rooms for the people who control the town.

toy /tɔɪ/ n. plaything for a child.

trace¹ /treɪs/ n. mark or sign that shows where someone or something has been: *They couldn't find any trace of the lost children.*

trace² v. **1** search for and find someone or something: *The police have traced the stolen car.* **2** put thin paper over a map, picture, etc. and draw over the lines to make a copy.

track¹ /træk/ n. **1** rough marks that people, animals, cars, etc. make when they go along: *I could see the bicycle tracks in the mud.* *on the track of,* following someone to catch him: *The police are on the track of the thief.* **2** rough, narrow road in the country. **3** rails where a train or tram runs: *The train stopped because there was a tree across the track.* **4** special road for races: *a running-track.*

track² v. follow an animal or criminal

by the marks he makes, etc.: *They tracked the bear through the forest.*

tracksuit /'træksu:t/ *n.* special warm clothes for a sportsman or sportswoman to wear before or after a race, etc.

tractor /'træktə(r)/ *n.* strong farm vehicle that pulls ploughs, heavy carts, etc.

trade[1] /treɪd/ *n.* **1** (no *pl.*) buying and selling: *foreign trade.* **2** (*pl.* trades) a business: *the clothes trade.* **3** (*pl.* trades) job: *Don is a plumber by trade.*

trade[2] *v.* buy and sell things: *Mr. Canon trades in furs.*

trader /'treɪdə(r)/, **tradesman** /'treɪdzmən/ (*pl.* tradesmen) *n.* someone whose job is buying and selling goods.

trade union /,treɪd 'ju:nɪən/ *n.* group of workers who have joined together to talk to their bosses about the way they work, the pay, etc.

tradition /trə'dɪʃn/ *n.* custom; what a group of people have always done: *In Britain it is a tradition to give children chocolate eggs at Easter.* **traditional** *adj.* **traditionally** *adv.*

traffic /'træfɪk/ *n.* (no *pl.*) all the vehicles and people that are moving in the roads and streets; aeroplanes that are flying in the sky. **traffic jam** *n.* when a road is so full of cars, etc. that none of them can move. **traffic lights** *n.* electric lights that change from green to yellow and red to control cars, etc.

tragedy /'trædʒədɪ/ *n.* (*pl.* tragedies) **1** sad or serious play for the theatre, cinema, etc.: *'Hamlet' is a tragedy.* **2** very sad thing that happens: *The child's death was a great tragedy.* **tragic** /'trædʒɪk/ *adj.* very sad. **tragically** *adv.*

trail[1] /treɪl/ *n.* **1** line of marks that people, animals, cars, etc. make when they go along: *a trail of blood from the wounded animal.* **2** rough, narrow road in the country.

trail[2] *v.* **1** pull something slowly behind; drag behind: *Her long dress was trailing along the ground.* **2** walk slowly: *The tired children trailed along behind their mother.* **3** follow a person or animal by the marks he makes.

trailer /'treɪlə(r)/ *n.* vehicle with no engine, which a car or lorry pulls.

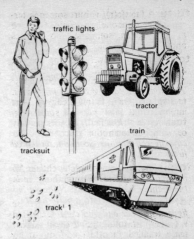

traffic lights

tractor

train

tracksuit

track[1] 1

train[1] /treɪn/ *n.* engine with railway coaches behind: *We travelled to Manchester by train.* **catch a train**, get on a train to travel somewhere: *We caught a train to Hull.* **change trains**, go from one train to another. **goods train**, train that only carries goods. **passenger train**, train for people.

train[2] *v.* **1** teach a person or animal to do something well: *He's training a horse for the race.* **2** study, learn, or prepare for something: *He is training to become a doctor.*

trainer /'treɪnə(r)/ *n.* someone who teaches people a sport; someone who teaches animals to do something.

training /'treɪnɪŋ/ *n.* (no *pl.*) teaching. **training college** *n.* college where you learn how to teach. **in training**, strong and ready for a sport: *You won't win the race if you're not in training!*

traitor /'treɪtə(r)/ *n.* someone who hurts his friend, his group, or his country, to help another person, group, or country: *The traitor told the enemy what our soldiers were planning.*

tram /træm/ *n.* electric bus that goes along rails in a street. **tramline** /'træmlaɪn/ *n.* rails where a tram runs.

tramp[1] /træmp/ *n.* **1** (no *pl.*) sound of heavy steps: *We heard the tramp of marching soldiers.* **2** (*pl.* tramps) long walk: *a tramp over the mountains.* **3** (*pl.* tramps) poor person with no home or work, who walks from one place to another.

tramp² v. **1** walk with heavy steps. **2** walk a long way: *They tramped all day.*

trample /'træmpl/ v. walk on something and push it down: *Don't trample on the flowers!*

transfer /træns'fɜː(r)/ v. (*pres. part.* transferring, *past part.* & *past tense* transferred /træns'fɜːd/) move something or someone to another place: *Pete's boss transferred him to Scotland.* **transfer** /'trænsfɜː(r)/ n.

transform /træns'fɔːm/ v. change the shape of someone or something; make something look different: *Nature transforms a caterpillar into a butterfly.*

transistor /træn'zɪstə(r)/ n. **1** small instrument in radios, etc. **2** small radio.

translate /trænz'leɪt/ v. give the meaning of words in another language: *Can you translate this German letter for me?*

translation /trænz'leɪʃn/ n. **1** (no *pl.*) putting a piece of writing into another language. **2** (*pl.* translations) piece of writing that has been translated.

transparent /træns'pærənt/ adj. that you can see through: *The glass in a window is transparent.*

transport¹ /'trænspɔːt/ n. (no *pl.*) **1** carrying people or things from one place to another: *We hired a van for transport.* **2** aeroplanes, cars, ships, etc.

transport² /træn'spɔːt/ v. carry people or goods from one place to another: *They transported the bricks in a lorry.*

trap¹ /træp/ n. **1** instrument for catching animals, etc.: *The farmer sets traps to catch the rats.* **2** plan to catch someone; trick to make someone do or say something.

trap² v. (*pres. part.* trapping, *past part.* & *past tense* trapped /træpt/) catch or trick a person or animal.

travel v. /'trævl/ v. (*pres. part.* travelling, *past part.* & *past tense* travelled /'trævld/) make a journey; visit other places. **travel agency** n. business that plans holidays and journeys for people.

traveller /'trævlə(r)/ n. **1** someone on a journey. **2** someone whose job is to go round selling things. **traveller's cheque** n. special cheque for taking your

money safely when you go to other countries.

trawler /'trɔːlə(r)/ n. fishing-boat.

tray /treɪ/ n. flat piece of wood, plastic, etc., with higher edges, for holding or carrying things: *She brought the cups in on a tray.*

treacherous /'tretʃərəs/ adj. **1** whom you cannot trust: *The treacherous servant told his master's enemies where they could find him.* **2** more dangerous than it seems: *Icy roads are treacherous.* **treacherously** adv.

tread /tred/ v. (*past part.* trodden /'trodn/, *past tense* trod /trod/) **1** walk on something: *Don't tread on my toes!* **2** press something down with your feet: *He trod his cigarette into the ground.* **tread** n. step.

treason /'triːzn/ n. (no *pl.*) hurting your own country to help another; telling the enemy secrets about your own country.

treasure /'treʒə(r)/ n. **1** store of gold, silver, jewels, money, or other valuable things: *The pirates hid the treasure in a cave.* **2** anything that is valuable to you: *The photo of her dead father is her greatest treasure.*

treasurer /'treʒərə(r)/ n. someone who looks after the money of a club or society.

treat¹ /triːt/ n. something unusual and special to please someone: *My aunt took me to the zoo as a treat.*

treat² v. **1** behave towards someone or something: *Mr. Brown beats his dog and treats it unkindly.* **treat something as**, think about something as: *He treated my plan as a joke.* **2** try to make a sick person better; try to cure an illness: *The doctors treated his fever with pills.*

treatment /'triːtmənt/ n. **1** way you behave towards someone or something: *I don't like his cruel treatment of those poor horses.* **2** way of curing an illness; doctor's care: *After the accident he had treatment in hospital.*

treaty /'triːtɪ/ n. (*pl.* treaties) written agreement between countries; contract: *a peace treaty.*

tree /triː/ n. big plant with one tall stem of wood: *Apples grow on a tree.*

trek /trek/ v. (*pres. part.* trekking, *past*

part. & past tense trekked /trekt/) go on a long journey. **trek** *n.*

tremble /'trembl/ *v.* **1** shake because you are afraid, cold, weak, etc.: *He was trembling with fear.* **2** shake: *The bridge trembled when the heavy lorry drove over it.* **tremble** *n.*

tremendous /trɪ'mendəs/ *adj.* **1** very big; very great: *That aeroplane flies at a tremendous speed.* **2** wonderful: *a tremendous singer.*

tremendously /trɪ'mendəslɪ/ *adv.* very.

trench /trentʃ/ *n.* (*pl.* trenches) long hole that you have dug in the ground.

trespass /'trespəs/ *v.* go on private land without the owner's permission: *There was a sign 'No Trespassing!' near the gate of the big house.* **trespass** *n.* **trespasser** *n.* someone who trespasses.

trial /'traɪəl/ *n.* **1** test; using something to see if it works well: *He gave the bicycle a trial before he bought it.* **2** examining someone in a law court to decide whether he has done a crime. **on trial, (a)** doing tests; for trying before you buy it: *I've got a new car on trial.* **(b)** in a law court because you are accused of a crime: *He was on trial for theft.*

triangle /'traɪæŋgl/ *n.* shape with three straight sides and three angles. **triangular** /traɪ'æŋgjʊlə(r)/ *adj.*

tribe /traɪb/ *n.* group of people with the same language, ancestors, and customs. **tribal** *adj.: tribal dances.*

tribute /'trɪbjuːt/ *n.* words, present, event, etc. to show respect for someone: *They built a statue in London as a tribute to the explorer Captain Scott.*

trick¹ /trɪk/ *n.* **1** something dishonest that you do to get what you want from someone: *He got the money from me by a trick.* **2** unkind game to make someone look silly: *The boys hid Jon's bike to play a trick on him.* **3** something clever that you do to entertain people or to make them laugh: *card tricks.*

trick² *v.* do something that is not honest to get what you want from someone: *He tricked the girl and she gave him all her money.* **trickery** *n.* telling lies; being dishonest.

trickle /'trɪkl/ *v.* flow slowly or in drops: *Tears trickled down her cheeks.* **trickle** *n.* thin line of running water.

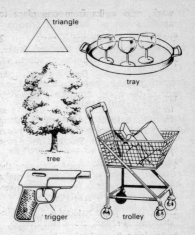

triangle

tray

tree

trigger

trolley

tricky /'trɪkɪ/ *adj.* difficult; hard to do: *a tricky job.*

tricycle /'traɪsɪkl/ *n.* cycle with three wheels.

tried /traɪd/ *past part. & past tense* of *v.* try.

trigger /'trɪgə(r)/ *n.* part of the gun that you pull with your finger to fire a bullet.

trim /trɪm/ *v.* (*pres. part.* trimming, *past part. & past tense* trimmed /trɪmd/) cut something to make it tidy: *The barber trimmed George's hair.* **trim** *n.*

trip¹ /trɪp/ *n.* journey: *We had a trip to the coast last Saturday.*

trip² *v.* (*pres. part.* tripping, *past part. & past tense* tripped /trɪpt/) catch your foot on something so that you fall or nearly fall: *He tripped over the step.* **trip someone up**, make someone fall: *Ken put out his foot and tripped me up.*

triumph /'traɪʌmf/ *n.* **1** (*pl.* triumphs) victory; winning. **2** (*no pl.*) joy of winning: *There were shouts of triumph when our football team won the cup.*

triumphant /traɪ'ʌmfənt/ *adj.* happy because you have done something well, won something, etc. **triumphantly** *adv.*

trod /trɒd/ *past tense* of *v.* tread.

trodden /'trɒdn/ *past part.* of *v.* tread.

trolley /'trɒlɪ/ *n.* **1** small table on wheels. **2** metal basket on wheels for carrying things in a supermarket.

troop /tru:p/ *n.* **1** group of people or animals: *troops of children.* **2 troops** (*pl.*) soldiers.

trophy /'trəʊfɪ/ *n.* (*pl.* trophies) prize for winning a competition in sport: *a tennis trophy.*

tropic /'trɒpɪk/ *n.* **the tropics**, the hot parts of the world. **tropical** /'trɒpɪkl/ *adj.* of or for hot countries.

trot /trɒt/ *v.* (*pres. part.* trotting, *past part. & past tense* trotted /'trɒtɪd/) run or ride slowly, with short steps: *The child trotted beside his mother.* **trot** *n.: to go for a trot.*

trouble[1] /'trʌbl/ *n.* **1** (no *pl.*) sadness and worry: *His life is full of trouble.* **2** (*pl.* troubles) problem; difficulty: *It's the car that's the trouble—it won't start.* **3** (no *pl.*) extra work; effort: *It won't be any trouble if you stay to dinner.* **save trouble, save the trouble of**, stop yourself from having problems or extra work: *Telephoning saves the trouble of writing.* **4** (*pl.* troubles) pain; illness: *stomach trouble.* **get into trouble**, make someone angry with you: *You'll get into trouble if you park your car here.* **get someone into trouble**, do something that brings problems to another person: *You'll get me into trouble if you tell Mum that I've lost my watch.* **go to trouble, take trouble**, do extra work; do something with extra care: *He went to a lot of trouble to help me.* **be in trouble**, have problems; have people angry with you because you have done wrong: *I'll be in trouble if I get home late.*

trouble[2] *v.* **1** worry someone; give someone pain or sadness: *His back is troubling him.* **2** give yourself extra work, etc.: *Please don't trouble to come with me—I can go by myself.* **troubled** /'trʌbld/ *adj.* sad and worried.

trough /trɒf/ *n.* long, open box that holds food or water for animals.

trousers /'traʊzəz/ *n.* (*pl.*) piece of clothing for the legs and lower part of the body: *a pair of trousers.*

trowel /'traʊəl/ *n.* small tool for digging, etc.: *Mrs. Mason dug up the plant with a trowel.*

truant /'tru:ənt/ *n.* child who stays away from school without permission. **play truant**, stay away from school.

truce /tru:s/ *n.* short time when two armies agree to stop fighting.

truck /trʌk/ *n.* **1** railway wagon for carrying heavy goods. **2** lorry; big vehicle that carries heavy loads.

trudge /trʌdʒ/ *v.* walk slowly, in a heavy, tired way: *The old man trudged up the hill.*

true /tru:/ *adj.* **1** correct; right: *Is it true that you have five brothers?* **come true**, really happen: *Her dream came true.* **2** faithful; real: *A true friend will always help you.*

truly /'tru:lɪ/ *adv.* really: *Are you truly happy in your work?*

trumpet /'trʌmpɪt/ *n.* sort of musical instrument that you blow.

trunk /trʌŋk/ *n.* **1** main stem of a tree, that grows up from the ground. **2** big strong box for carrying a lot of clothes, etc. when you travel. **3** long nose of an elephant.

trunk-call /'trʌŋk kɔ:l/ *n.* telephone call to a far place.

trunks /trʌŋks/ *n.* (*pl.*) short trousers for sport: *swimming trunks.*

trust[1] /trʌst/ *n.* (no *pl.*) faith; believing that someone or something is good, strong, right, honest, etc. **put your trust in**, believe in someone or something: *Children put their trust in their parents.*

trust[2] *v.* **1** feel sure that someone or something is good, right, honest, etc.: *I shall lend him money because I trust him.* **2** let someone have or do something, and not worry about him: *I trust Peter to go to the pool alone because he can swim well.* **3** hope: *I trust that you are well.* **trusting** *adj.* that shows trust. **trustingly** *adv.*

trustful /'trʌstfl/ *adj.* ready to believe other people. **trustfully** *adv.*

trustworthy /'trʌstwɜːðɪ/ *adj.* whom you can trust: *A trustworthy person does not lie or steal.*

truth /tru:θ/ *n.* (no *pl.*) being true; what is true: *He is lying and there is no truth in what he says.* **tell the truth**, say what is true: *Are you telling me the truth?*

truthful /'tru:θfl/ *adj.* **1** saying what is true: *a truthful person.* **2** true: *a truthful story.* **truthfully** *adv.*

try¹ /traɪ/ *n.* (*pl.* tries) **1** attempt: *Can I have a try on your bike?* **2** special score of three points in rugby.

try² *v.* **1** see if you can do something; attempt to do something: *I don't think I can mend this watch, but I'll try.* **try and do something**, try to do something: *Please try and come early.* **try for**, do your best to get or win something: *He's trying for a job in the Post Office.* **2** use something to see if it is good, nice, useful, etc.: *Try this new soap.* **try something on**, put on a piece of clothing to see whether it looks good, is big enough, etc.: *He tried the jacket on before he bought it.* **3** examine someone in a law court to decide whether he has done a crime: *They tried him for murder.*

T-shirt *n.* casual shirt with short sleeves and no collar.

tub /tʌb/ *n.* bowl or pot.

tube /tjuːb/ *n.* **1** long, thin pipe of metal, glass, or rubber. **2** container of soft metal, plastic, etc. with a hole and lid at one end: *a tube of toothpaste.* **3** underground railway: *the London tube.*

tuck /tʌk/ *v.* put or push something tidily into a small space: *He tucked his shirt inside his trousers.* **tuck someone in** or **up**, put the covers tightly over a person in bed.

Tuesday /'tjuːzdeɪ/ *n.* third day of the week.

tuft /tʌft/ *n.* group of hairs, feathers, etc. that are growing closely together: *a tuft of grass.*

tug¹ /tʌg/ *n.* **1** sudden hard pull: *He unkindly gave his sister's hair a tug.* **2** small, strong boat that pulls big ships.

tug² *v.* (*pres. part.* tugging, *past part.* & *past tense* tugged /tʌgd/) pull something hard: *The dog tugged at its lead.*

tuition /tjuː'ɪʃn/ *n.* (no *pl.*) teaching: *He needs extra tuition in English.*

tumble /'tʌmbl/ *v.* fall suddenly: *He tumbled off his bicycle.* **tumble down**, (*a*) fall down. (*b*) become a ruin: *The old house is tumbling down.* **tumble-down** *adj.* ruined: *a tumble-down castle.* **tumble** *n.* sudden fall.

tumbler /'tʌmblə(r)/ *n.* a glass for drinks.

tummy /'tʌmɪ/ *n.* (*pl.* tummies) stomach.

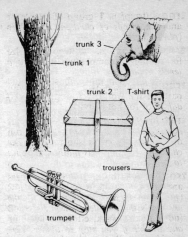

tune¹ /tjuːn/ *n.* group of notes that make a piece of music; melody: *He whistled a cheerful tune.*

tune² *v.* fix the strings of a musical instrument so that it makes the right sounds: *to tune a guitar.* **tune in**, turn a knob on the radio so that you can hear a broadcast: *I tuned in to Radio 4.*

tunnel /'tʌnl/ *n.* long hole through the ground for a road or railway. **tunnel** *v.* (*pres. part.* tunnelling, *past part.* & *past tense* tunnelled /'tʌnld/) make a tunnel: *The miners tunnelled through the mountain to find coal.*

turban /'tɜːbən/ *n.* piece of cloth that you wind round your head.

turkey /'tɜːkɪ/ *n.* big farm bird that we eat.

turn¹ /tɜːn/ *n.* **1** moving round: *a turn of the wheel.* **2** moving something round: *Give the knob a few turns.* **3** change of direction; bend; curve: *Drive on for a kilometre; then take a right turn.* **4** time for you to do something; opportunity: *Sam had a ride on the bike and then it was my turn.* **in turn**, (*a*) first one and then the other, then the first one again, etc.; alternately: *Sam and I rode the bike in turn.* (*b*) one after the other: *The teacher helped all the children in turn.* **take turns at, take it in turns to**, do something one after the other: *Sam and I took turns at riding the bike.* **5** action that may help someone. **do someone a good**

turn, help someone: *He did me a good turn when he found my lost key.* **6** piece of entertainment: *a star turn.*

turn² *v.* **1** move round and round: *Wheels turn.* **2** move something round: *Turn the handle to open the door.* **3** change direction; move something into a different position: *Turn right at the next corner. Turn the page of your book.* **4** make someone or something change: *The cold turned my nose red.* **5** become: *The weather has turned cold.* **turn against,** become unfriendly to someone: *Why has she turned against me?* **turn down,** say no to what someone wants to do, give you, etc.; refuse: *He turned down my invitation.* **turn in,** go to bed: *It's getting late, so I think I'll turn in.* **turn into,** change into; become: *In the winter, the water turns into ice.* **turn off,** stop something: *Turn off the tap.* **turn on,** start something: *Turn on the television.* **turn out,** **(a)** come outside to do something: *The whole town turned out to watch the procession.* **(b)** become: *It's turned out cold today.* **(c)** go: *How did your party turn out?* **turn out a light, etc.,** switch off a light, etc. **turn out a place,** take everything out of a place: *I'm turning out the cupboard to look for a lost key.* **turn someone out,** make someone leave a place: *He turned us out of his room because he wanted to study.* **turn over,** move, or move something, so that the other side is on top: *He was lying on his chest and then turned over to look up at the sky.* **turn to,** go to someone: *The child turned to its mother for help.* **turn up,** come; arrive: *Has Jake turned up yet?*

turnip /'tɜ:nɪp/ *n.* sort of vegetable.

turnstile /'tɜ:nstaɪl/ *n.* gate that turns to let one person go through at a time: *We went through the turnstile into the zoo.*

turntable /'tɜ:nteɪbl/ *n.* part of a record-player that holds the record.

tusk /tʌsk/ *n.* long, pointed tooth that grows beside the mouth of an elephant, etc.

tutor /'tju:tə(r)/ *n.* **1** private teacher for one child or one family. **2** teacher at a university.

T.V. /ˌti: 'vi:/ *abbrev.* television.

tweed /twi:d/ *n.* (no *pl.*) thick, woollen cloth for coats and suits. **tweed** *adj.: a tweed suit.*

tweezers /'twi:zəz/ *n.* (*pl.*) small instrument for holding very small things: *She pulled the splinter out of her finger with a pair of tweezers.*

twelve /twelv/ *n.* number 12. **twelve** *adj.: Ali is twelve years old today.* **twelfth** /twelfθ/ *adj.* 12th: *her twelfth birthday.*

twenty /'twentɪ/ *n.* (*pl.* twenties) number 20. **twenty** *adj.* **twentieth** /'twentɪəθ/ *adj.* 20th.

twice /twaɪs/ *adv.* two times: *Twice two is four.*

twig /twɪg/ *n.* small, thin stick on a bush or tree.

twilight /'twaɪlaɪt/ *n.* (no *pl.*) time between daylight and darkness; half light.

twin¹ /twɪn/ *adj.* **1** with a brother or sister of exactly the same age: *my twin brother.* **2** two of the same kind: *an aeroplane with twin engines.*

twin² *n.* one of two children who are born of the same mother at the same time.

twinkle /'twɪnkl/ *v.* shine brightly on and off; sparkle softly: *The stars twinkled.* **twinkle** *n.* **twinkling** *adj.*

twist /twɪst/ *v.* **1** turn something strongly: *He twisted the lid off the jar.* **2** turn in many directions; bend often: *The path twisted and turned through the forest.* **3** wind a number of threads, etc. together: *He twisted the sheets into a strong rope and escaped.* **twist** *n.* **twisted** /'twɪstɪd/ *adj.: twisted roots.*

twitter /'twɪtə(r)/ *n.* short, soft sounds that small birds make. **twitter** *v.*

two /tu:/ *n.* number 2. **two by two,** in pairs: *The children walked in two by two.* **two** *adj.*

type¹ /taɪp/ *n.* **1** (*pl.* types) sort; kind: *A bungalow is a type of house.* **2** (no *pl.*) letters that a machine makes on paper: *In this book, the headwords are in large type.*

type² *v.* make letters on paper, with a machine called a **typewriter** /'taɪpraɪtə(r)/: *His secretary typed the report.* **typist** /'taɪpɪst/ *n.* someone who types.

typical /'tɪpɪkl/ *adj.* that is a good example of its kind: *We had a typical English breakfast—bacon, eggs, toast, and tea.* **typically** *adv.*

typist /'taɪpɪst/ *n.* someone who uses a typewriter.

tyrant /'taɪrənt/ *n.* someone who rules in a cruel way: *Nero was a tyrant.* **tyrannical** /tɪ'rænɪkl/ *adj.*

tyre /'taɪə(r)/ *n.* rubber ring, full of air, that fits round the wheel of a motor-car, bicycle, etc. **flat tyre**, broken tyre with no air inside.

Uu

UFO /'ju:fəʊ/ *abbrev.* Unidentified Flying Object; a flying object, not an aeroplane, that people think they have seen in the sky.

ugly /'ʌglɪ/ *adj.* not beautiful; that does not please you when you look at it: *an ugly old woman.* **ugliness** *n.*

umbrella /ʌm'brelə/ *n.* special cover on a stick that you hold over you to keep off the rain, etc.: *When it started to rain she opened her umbrella.*

umpire /'ʌmpaɪə(r)/ *n.* someone who controls a sports match. **umpire** *v.*: *He is umpiring a tennis match this afternoon.*

unable /ʌn'eɪbl/ *adj.* not able to do something: *Jamie was unable to go to work today because he was sick.*

unaccustomed /ˌʌnə'kʌstəmd/ *adj.* **unaccustomed to**, not knowing something well; not used to something: *She was sick after the glass of wine because she is unaccustomed to drinking alcohol.*

unafraid /ˌʌnə'freɪd/ *adj.* not afraid.

unanimous /ju:'nænɪməs/ *adj.* with the agreement of every person: *a unanimous vote.* **unanimously** *adv.*: *The union decided unanimously to go on strike.*

unarmed /ʌn'ɑ:md/ *adj.* with no gun, etc.

unattractive /ˌʌnə'træktɪv/ *adj.* not pleasing to see, hear, etc.

unaware /ˌʌnə'weə(r)/ *adj.* not knowing something: *The birds were eating the crumbs, unaware that the cat was coming nearer.*

unawares /ˌʌnə'weəz/ *adv.* when you are not expecting it: *They attacked him unawares while he was reading.*

unbearable /ʌn'beərəbl/ *adj.* very unpleasant; that you do not like: *She left the room because the noise was unbearable.* **unbearably** *adv.*

unbelievable /ˌʌnbɪ'li:vəbl/ *adj.* difficult to believe; amazing: *What unbelievable luck!*

unbreakable /ʌn'breɪkəbl/ *adj.* that you cannot break; that will not break easily: *Our camping plates are unbreakable.*

uncertain /ʌn's3:tn/ *adj.* not sure; not definite: *My holiday plans are uncertain because I don't know how much money I shall have.*

unchanged /ʌn'tʃeɪndʒd/ *adj.* as it was before; not different: *The town was unchanged when Alan went back after ten years.*

uncle /'ʌŋkl/ *n.* brother of your father or mother; husband of your aunt.

uncomfortable /ʌn'kʌmftəbl/ *adj.* not comfortable; not pleasant: *tight, uncomfortable shoes.* **uncomfortably** *adv.*

uncommon /ʌn'kɒmən/ *adj.* that you do not often see, hear, etc.: *an uncommon name.*

unconscious /ʌn'kɒnʃəs/ *adj.* not knowing what is happening: *A cricket ball hit him on the head and he was unconscious for three days.* **unconsciously** *adv.* **unconsciousness** *n.*

uncontrolled /ˌʌnkən'trəʊld/ *adj.* not controlled: *The uncontrolled car rolled down the hill and crashed into a wall.*

uncooked /ˌʌn'kʊkt/ *adj.* raw; not cooked.

unco-operative /ˌʌnkəʊ'ɒprətɪv/ *adj.* not willing to work helpfully with other people: *It is difficult to dress an unco-operative child.*

uncover /ʌn'kʌvə(r)/ *1 v.* take away the cover, lid, cloth, etc. that is over something: *He lifted the stone and uncovered a worm.* **2** find out about something that was a secret: *The detective uncovered a plot to rob the bank.*

under[1] /'ʌndə(r)/ *adv.* in or to a lower place: *The canoe filled with water, then went under and sank.*

under[2] *prep.* **1** below; at or to a lower place: *The boat sailed under the bridge.* **2** less than something: *Children in primary schools are usually under 12 years.* **3** in the control of: *This team plays well under their new captain.*

underclothes /'ʌndəkləʊðz/ *n.* clothes that you wear next to your skin, under a shirt and trousers or under a dress.

undergo /ˌʌndə'gəʊ/ *v.* (*past part.* undergone /ˌʌndə'gɒn/, *past tense* underwent /ˌʌndə'went/) have something done or happen to you: *Laura has undergone an operation in hospital.*

undergraduate /ˌʌndə'grædʒʊət/ *n.* student at a university.

underground /'ʌndəgraʊnd/ *adj.* that is under the ground: *an underground tunnel.* **underground** *n.* underground railway: *We went by underground from Trafalgar Square to Paddington station.*

undergrowth /'ʌndəgrəʊθ/ *n.* (no *pl.*) bushes, etc. that grow below the tall trees in a wood.

underline /ˌʌndə'laɪn/ *v.* draw a line under a word, sentence, etc.

underneath /ˌʌndə'niːθ/ *adv.* below; in or to a lower place: *My hands are on top of the desk and my feet are underneath.* **underneath** *prep.*: *Maurice is wearing a red sweater underneath his jacket.*

understand /ˌʌndə'stænd/ *v.* (*past part.* & *past tense* understood /ˌʌndə'stʊd/) **1** know what something means, why something happens, why people do

things, etc.: *I don't understand this homework—can you explain it to me?* **2** know something because someone has told you about it: *I understand that the plane from Geneva will be late.*

understanding[1] /ˌʌndə'stændɪŋ/ *adj.* who listens to other people's problems and tries to understand them: *an understanding mother.*

understanding[2] *n.* (no *pl.*) knowing about something or someone; sympathy: *A teacher must have an understanding of children.*

understood /ˌʌndə'stʊd/ *past part.* & *past tense* of *v.* understand **make yourself understood**, make people understand you: *He spoke very bad English so it was difficult to make himself understood at the station.*

undertake /ˌʌndə'teɪk/ *v.* (*past part.* undertaken /ˌʌndə'teɪkən/, *past tense* undertook /ˌʌndə'tʊk/) agree to do something: *A local firm undertook the building.*

underwater /'ʌndəwɔː'tə(r)/ *adj.* that is below the top of the water: *underwater plants.*

underwear /'ʌndəweə(r)/ *n.* (no *pl.*) clothes that you wear next to your skin under a shirt and trousers or under a dress, etc.: *Vests and pants are underwear.*

underwent /ˌʌndə'went/ *past tense* of *v.* undergo.

undid /ʌn'dɪd/ *past tense* of *v.* undo.

undo /ʌn'duː/ *v.* (*past part.* undone /ʌn'dʌn/, *past tense* undid) **1** make a knot or bow loose: *Please undo this ribbon for me.* **2** take the string, rope, etc. off something: *Phil undid the parcel.* **3** open something that was tied or fixed: *I can't undo these buttons.*

undoubtedly /ʌn'daʊtɪdlɪ/ *adv.* certainly; with no doubt: *Carol is undoubtedly the best swimmer in the class.*

undress /ʌn'dres/ *v.* take off clothes: *She undressed her baby.*

uneasy /ʌn'iːzɪ/ *adj.* worried; feeling that something is wrong: *She felt uneasy when the children did not come home.* **uneasily** *adv.*

unemployed /ˌʌnɪm'plɔɪd/ *adj.* with no work: *unemployed men.*

unemployment /ˌʌnɪmˈplɔɪmənt/ *n.* (no *pl.*) when people have no work: *The factory closed and there was a lot of unemployment.*

uneven /ˌʌnˈiːvn/ *adj.* rough: *The car bumped up and down on the uneven road.*

unexpected /ˌʌnɪkˈspektɪd/ *adj.* that surprises you; that you do not expect: *an unexpected visitor.*

unfair /ˌʌnˈfeə(r)/ *adj.* not fair; not treating people in the right way: *an unfair decision.*

unfaithful /ˌʌnˈfeɪθfl/ *adj.* that you cannot trust.

unfamiliar /ˌʌnfəˈmɪlɪə(r)/ *adj.* strange; that you do not know: *a room full of unfamiliar faces.*

unfashionable /ˌʌnˈfæʃnəbl/ *adj.* not fashionable.

unfasten /ˌʌnˈfɑːsn/ *v.* **1** open something that was tied or fixed: *He unfastened his belt and took it off. He unfastened the door.* **2** take off something that was fixed to another thing: *Sue unfastened the brooch from her dress.*

unfavourable /ˌʌnˈfeɪvərəbl/ *adj.* not good; showing that you do not like something or someone: *an unfavourable school report.*

unfinished /ˌʌnˈfɪnɪʃt/ *adj.* not finished, not done, not eaten, etc.: *an unfinished meal.*

unfold /ˌʌnˈfəʊld/ *v.* open something out: *Mr. Wilkinson unfolded his newspaper and started to read.*

unfortunate /ˌʌnˈfɔːtʃʊnət/ *adj.* not lucky: *It's unfortunate that you were ill on the day of the pop festival.* **unfortunately** *adv.*

unfriendly /ˌʌnˈfrendlɪ/ *adj.* not kind, helpful, etc.; showing that you do not like another person: *an unfriendly letter.*

ungrateful /ˌʌnˈɡreɪtfl/ *adj.* not showing thanks when someone has helped you or given you a present: *I lifted the cat away from the dog and the ungrateful animal scratched me!*

unhappy /ˌʌnˈhæpɪ/ *adj.* sad: *The unhappy child was crying.* **unhappiness** *n.*

unhealthy /ˌʌnˈhelθɪ/ *adj.* not well; that can make you ill: *Mining is an unhealthy job.*

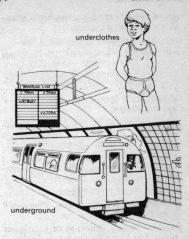

underclothes

underground

unhelpful /ˌʌnˈhelpfl/ *adj.* not giving help.

uniform /ˈjuːnɪfɔːm/ *n.* special clothes for a job, a school, a club etc.: *A policeman wears a uniform when he is working.*

unimportant /ˌʌnɪmˈpɔːtnt/ *adj.* **1** not powerful; not special. **2** that you need not do or have.

uninhabited /ˌʌnɪnˈhæbɪtɪd/ *adj.* where nobody lives: *an uninhabited island.*

uninteresting /ˌʌnˈɪntrəstɪŋ/ *adj.* dull; not interesting.

union /ˈjuːnɪən/ *n.* **1** (no *pl.*) coming together; putting things together: *Marriage is the union of a man and a woman.* **2** (*pl.* unions) group of workers, etc. who have joined together: *the National Union of Students.*

unique /juːˈniːk/ *adj.* being the only one of its sort: *a unique building.* **uniquely** *adv.*

unit /ˈjuːnɪt/ *n.* **1** one person; one thing; one group. **2** a measurement: *A metre is a unit of length and a kilogram is a unit of weight.*

unite /juːˈnaɪt/ *v.* join together to become one; put two things together to become one: *In 1603 James I united England and Scotland.* **united** /juːˈnaɪtɪd/ *adj.*: *the United States.*

universal /ˌjuːnɪˈvɜːsl/ *adj.* of all people; for all people. **universally** *adv.*

universe /'ju:nɪvɜ:s/ *n.* **the Universe,** this world and all space.

university /ˌju:nɪ'vɜ:sətɪ/ *n.* (*pl.* universities) place where people go to study more difficult subjects, when they have left school: *Keith studied medicine at Edinburgh University and is now a doctor.*

unjust /ˌʌn'dʒʌst/ *adj.* not fair; not treating people in the right way: *It's unjust to punish one naughty boy and not the other.*

unkind /ʌn'kaɪnd/ *adj.* not kind; cruel: *The unkind girl kicked the cat.*

unknown /ˌʌn'nəʊn/ *adj.* **1** that you do not know: *an unknown face.* **2** not famous: *an unknown painter.*

unless /ən'les/ *conj.* if not: *You won't catch the bus unless you run.*

unlike /ˌʌn'laɪk/ *prep.* not like; different from: *He is unlike his brother who is much fatter.*

unlikely /ʌn'laɪklɪ/ *adj.* that you do not expect will happen; not probable: *It is unlikely that we shall find a café there so bring sandwiches.*

unload /ʌn'ləʊd/ *v.* take things off a vehicle or ship: *The greengrocer unloaded the potatoes from the van.*

unlock /ˌʌn'lɒk/ *v.* open something with a key: *I've lost my key and can't unlock the front door.* **unlocked** /ˌʌn'lɒkt/ *adj.* not closed with a key.

unlucky /ʌn'lʌkɪ/ *adj.* **1** not having good things happen: *She's unlucky—she never wins a game.* **2** not bringing good things; bad: *Some people say it is unlucky to break a mirror.* **unluckily** *adv.*

unmarried /ˌʌn'mærɪd/ *adj.* not having a husband or wife.

unnatural /ʌn'nætʃrəl/ *adj.* not natural.

unnecessary /ʌn'nesəsrɪ/ *adj.* that you do not need; not important: *A coat is unnecessary on a hot day.*

unpack /ˌʌn'pæk/ *v.* take all the things out of a box, bag, etc.: *We arrived at the hotel and unpacked the luggage.*

unpaid /ˌʌn'peɪd/ *adj.* not paid.

unpleasant /ʌn'pleznt/ *adj.* not nice; that you do not enjoy: *the unpleasant smell of bad fish.* **unpleasantly** *adv.*

unpopular /ˌʌn'pɒpjʊlə(r)/ *adj.* not liked by many people.

unqualified /ˌʌn'kwɒlɪfaɪd/ *adj.* without the right knowledge and training: *He's unqualified—we can't give him this job.*

unreliable /ˌʌnrɪ'laɪəbl/ *adj.* that you cannot trust: *an unreliable car; an unreliable man.*

unsatisfactory /ˌʌnˌsætɪs'fæktərɪ/ *adj.* not good enough: *His work is unsatisfactory—I'm not pleased with it.*

unseen /ʌn'si:n/ *adj.* that you cannot see: *An unseen person makes the puppets dance.*

unselfish /ˌʌn'selfɪʃ/ *adj.* thinking about others, not about yourself.

unsteady /ˌʌn'stedɪ/ *adj.* that may fall: *Don't climb on that ladder—it's unsteady.* **unsteadily** *adv.*

unsuccessful /ˌʌnsək'sesfl/ *adj.* not doing what you were hoping and trying to do.

unsuitable /ˌʌn'su:təbl/ *adj.* not right for something or someone: *This murder film is unsuitable for children.*

unsympathetic /ˌʌnsɪmpə'θetɪk/ *adj.* not sympathetic; not understanding another person's feelings.

untidy /ʌn'taɪdɪ/ *adj.* **1** not neat; not in good order: *an untidy room.* **2** who does not keep things neat: *My untidy brother drops all his clothes on the floor.* **untidily** *adv.*

untie /ˌʌn'taɪ/ *v.* **1** make a knot or bow loose: *to untie a ribbon.* **2** take the string, rope, etc. off something or someone: *to untie a parcel.*

until[1] /ən'tɪl/ *conj.* up to the time when: *Wait here until I come back.*

until[2] *prep.* **1** up to a certain time: *She will stay until Saturday.* **2** before: *I can't come until tomorrow.*

untrue /ˌʌn'tru:/ *adj.* not correct: *an untrue story.*

untruthful /ˌʌn'tru:θfl/ *adj.* **1** telling lies: *Don't believe him—he's untruthful.* **2** not true: *an untruthful story.*

unusual /ʌn'ju:ʒl/ *adj.* strange; not happening often: *It is unusual to see a cat without a tail.* **unusually** *adv.*

unwanted /ˌʌn'wɒntɪd/ *adj.* not wanted: *The farmer drowned the unwanted kittens.*

unwelcome /ʌn'welkəm/ *adj.* not welcome; that you are not glad to receive, have, or see: *an unwelcome visitor.*

unwell /ˌʌnˈwel/ *adj.* ill; not well: *I went to bed because I was unwell.*

unwilling /ˌʌnˈwɪlɪŋ/ *adj.* that you do not do gladly: *I was unwilling to lend her my comb.* **unwillingly** *adv.*

unwrap /ˌʌnˈræp/ *v.* (*pres. part.* unwrapping, *past part. & past tense* unwrapped /ˌʌnˈræpt/) open something; take off the paper, cloth, etc. that is round something: *She unwrapped the parcel.*

up¹ /ʌp/ *adv.* **1** from a lower to a higher place: *Pull your socks up.* **2** from sitting or lying to standing: *She stood up in the bus and gave her seat to the old lady.* **3** out of bed: *When will you get up tomorrow?* **4** totally: *She ate the cake up and there was none for me.* **up to**, doing something: *What's that boy up to? **not up to much**, not very good: **What's up?** What's happening?: *I heard a shout—what's up?*

up² *prep.* **1** at, in, near, or towards a higher part: *We climbed up the mountain to the top.* **2** along: *We walked up the road.* **3** from the mouth of a river to its beginning: *They went up the Severn from Bristol to Gloucester.* **up and down**, one way and then the other way: *The dog ran up and down the stairs.* **up to**, (*a*) as far as; until: *Andrew has worked hard up to now.* (*b*) good enough for something: *This old car isn't up to a long journey.*

uphill /ˌʌpˈhɪl/ *adv.* up, towards the top of something: *to walk uphill.*

upon /əˈpɒn/ *prep.* on.

upper /ˈʌpə(r)/ *adj.* that is above another; top: *Gary has a moustache on his upper lip.*

upright /ˈʌpraɪt/ *adj.* that stands straight up: *The ladder was upright against the wall.*

uproar /ˈʌprɔː(r)/ *n.* loud noise from a lot of excited people: *There was uproar when our team scored the goal.*

uproot /ˌʌpˈruːt/ *v.* pull a plant from the ground with its roots: *The storm uprooted many trees.*

upset /ˌʌpˈset/ *v.* (*pres. part.* upsetting, *past part. & past tense* upset) **1** knock something so that it turns over and spills out: *She upset her tea over the table.* **2** make someone feel sick, etc.:

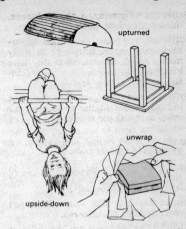

upturned

unwrap

upside-down

The rich food upset my stomach. **3** make someone feel sad: *The bad news upset Gail.* **4** spoil or stop something: *The bad weather will upset our plans for a picnic.* **upset** /ˈʌpset/ *n.: a stomach upset.*

upside-down /ˌʌpsaɪd ˈdaʊn/ *adv.* with the top part at the bottom: *The baby held the cup upside-down and all the milk poured out.*

upstairs /ˌʌpˈsteəz/ *adv.* to or on a higher floor of a building: *Our bedroom is upstairs.* **upstairs** *adj.: an upstairs room.*

up-to-date /ˌʌp tə ˈdeɪt/ *adj.* **1** fashionable; modern: *up-to-date furniture.* **2** with the newest information: *an up-to-date list of prices.*

upturned /ˈʌptɜːnd/ *adj.* with the top part at the bottom: *an upturned boat.*

upward /ˈʌpwəd/ *adj.* moving, going, etc. to a higher place: *an upward journey to the top of the mountain.* **upward, upwards** *adv.: If you look upwards you see the sky.*

urge¹ /ɜːdʒ/ *n.* strong wish: *I was afraid of the boy and I had an urge to run away from him.*

urge² *v.* try and make a person or animal do something: *He urged me to drive carefully on the icy roads.*

urgent /ˈɜːdʒənt/ *adj.* very important; that cannot wait: *There was an urgent telephone call and the doctor rushed to* *his car.* **urgently** *adv.: The ship called urgently for help.* **urgency** /ˈɜːdʒənsɪ/ *n.*

us /əs/, /ʌs/ *pron.* (*pl.*) word that you say when you speak about yourself and other people together: *We were pleased when he gave us a lift.*

use[1] /juːs/ *n.* **1** (no *pl.*) using: *A playground is for the use of children.* **go out of use,** finish; stop being used: *Shillings have now gone out of use.* **have the use of,** have the right to use something: *I have the use of his bicycle.* **make use of,** take something and do a job with it, etc.: *If you don't want that box I can make use of it.* **2** (*pl.* uses) function; what you can do with someone or something: *Water washes things; it also has many other uses.* **3** (no *pl.*) value. **of no use,** not good for anything: *These shoes are of no use—throw them away.*

use[2] /juːz/ *v.* do a job, etc. with something: *We use a pen for writing.* **use up,** use something until there is no more left: *We've used up all the sugar so we must buy some more.*

used[1] /juːzd/ *adj.* not new: *used clothes.*

used[2] /juːst/ *adj.* **be used to,** know something well because you have seen, heard, tasted, done it, etc. a lot: *I'm used to walking because I haven't got a car.*

used[3] /juːst/ *v.* **used to do something,** words that tell about something that often happened in the past: *My grandmother used to dance a lot when she was young.* **used to be,** words that tell about something that existed in the past: *There used to be a green field here—now there's a supermarket.*

useful /ˈjuːsfl/ *adj.* good for certain jobs; helpful: *A torch is useful at night when you are camping.* **usefully** *adv.* **usefulness** *n.*

useless /ˈjuːslɪs/ *adj.* **1** not good for anything: *A car is useless without petrol.* **2** not doing what you hoped: *a useless attempt.* **uselessly** *adv.* **uselessness** *n.*

usual /ˈjuːʒl/ *adj.* normal; happening often: *It's usual to have a holiday in the summer.* **as usual,** as always: *Tony arrived late, as usual!* **usually** *adv.* normally; mostly: *I usually go to church on Sunday.*

utensil /juːˈtensl/ *n.* instrument; thing

that you use in housework, etc.: *Pots and pans are kitchen utensils.*

utmost /ˈʌtməʊst/ *adj.* greatest: *a man of the utmost importance.* **utmost** *n.* **do your utmost,** try very hard: *Bill did his utmost to win the race.*

utter[1] /ˈʌtə(r)/ *adj.* total; complete: *The room was in utter darkness and I could not see anything.* **utterly** *adv.* totally; very.

utter[2] *v.* talk; make a sound with your mouth: *She uttered a cry of pain.*

Vv

v /viː/ *abbrev.* versus: *Liverpool v. Manchester United.*

vacant /ˈveɪkənt/ *adj.* **1** empty; with no one inside; with no one staying there: *a vacant house.* **2** with no one working in it: *a vacant job.*

vacancy /ˈveɪkənsɪ/ *n.* (*pl.* vacancies) **1** job that no one is doing; place for a new worker: *Mr. Seton's secretary is leaving so there is a vacancy.* **2** free room in a hotel: *Do you have any vacancies?*

vacation /vəˈkeɪʃn/ *n.* holiday from university.

vacuum /ˈvækjʊəm/ *n.* totally empty space; space with no air, etc.

vacuum-cleaner /ˈvækjʊəm kliːnə(r)/ *n.* machine that sucks in air and dirt with it: *We clean our carpets with a vacuum-cleaner.*

vacuum flask /ˈvækjʊəm flɑːsk/ *n.* special bottle that keeps hot liquids hot, or cold liquids cold.

vague /veɪg/ *adj.* not clear; not exact: *I couldn't find the house because he gave me such vague directions.* **vaguely** *adv.*

vain /veɪn/ *adj.* **1** thinking too well of your looks, etc.: *a vain man.* **2** useless: *They made a vain attempt to save him but he drowned.* **in vain,** with no success: *Shula knocked in vain—no one was at home.*

valley /ˈvælɪ/ *n.* low land, usually with a river, between hills or mountains: *the valley of the Nile.*

valuable /'væljʊəbl/ *adj.* **1** worth much money: *valuable jewels.* **2** useful or important: *Thanks for your help—it's been very valuable.* **valuable** *n.* something that is worth a lot: *She keeps her jewels, money, and other valuables in the bank.*

value[1] /'vælju:/ *n.* **1** (*pl.* values) how much money something is worth: *What is the value of this picture by Rubens?* **2** (no *pl.*) how useful or important something is to you: *Good books are of great value to students.*

value[2] *v.* think very highly of something that you have: *She values her freedom.*

van /væn/ *n.* **1** sort of big car or small, covered lorry for carrying goods: *The baker brings bread to our house in his delivery van.* **2** railway carriage for carrying goods.

vanilla /və'nɪlə/ *adj.* **vanilla ice-cream**, plain white ice-cream.

vanish /'vænɪʃ/ *v.* go away so that it cannot be seen; disappear: *The thief ran into the crowd and vanished.*

vanity /'vænəti/ *n.* (no *pl.*) thinking too well of your looks, etc.

variety /və'raɪəti/ *n.* **1** (no *pl.*) change; being different: *My job is boring— there's no variety.* **2** (no *pl.*) choice; number of different things: *There's a large variety of dishes on the menu.* **3** (*pl.* varieties) sort; kind: *This variety of apple is very sweet.*

various /'veərɪəs/ *adj.* different: *shoes of various sizes.*

varnish /'vɑːnɪʃ/ *n.* (*pl.* varnishes) clear paint with no colour, which you put on wood, pottery, etc. to make it hard and shiny. **nail-varnish** *n.* coloured varnish that women put on their fingernails. **varnish** *v.* put varnish on to something: *Ellen varnishes her nails red.*

vase /vɑːz/ *n.* pretty pot for holding flowers.

vast /vɑːst/ *adj.* very big: *Africa is a vast continent.* **vastly** *adj.*

vault[1] /vɔːlt/ *n.* room under the ground for keeping valuable or important things: *the vaults of a bank.*

vault[2] *v.* jump over or on to something, with hands or a pole: *Dan vaulted over the fence.* **vault** *n.*

veal /viːl/ *n.* (no *pl.*) meat from a calf.

veil

vacuum-cleaner   vase

valley

vegetable /'vedʒtəbl/ *n.* plant that we eat: *Potatoes, carrots, and beans are vegetables.*

vehicle /'vɪəkl/ *n.* any thing on wheels that transports people or goods: *Cars, buses, and lorries are all vehicles.*

veil /veɪl/ *n.* thin covering that a woman puts over her head or face: *The bride wore a veil at her wedding.*

velvet /'velvɪt/ *n.* (no *pl.*) sort of cloth that feels soft and thick on one side. **velvet** *adj.* made of velvet: *a velvet dress.* **velvety** *adj.* soft like velvet: *the puppy's velvety fur.*

vengeance /'vendʒəns/ *n.* (no *pl.*) revenge. **take vengeance on**, harm someone who has harmed you or your friends.

venture /'ventʃə(r)/ *v.* be brave or bold enough to do something; put yourself in danger: *Don't venture on the sea in that little boat.* **venture** *n.* risk: *Your journey to the Arctic is a brave venture.*

verandah /və'rændə/ *n.* covered place along the side of a building: *It was so hot that we sat on the verandah.*

verb /vɜːb/ *n.* word that tells what someone or something is, does, etc.; word marked '*v.*' in this dictionary: '*Go*', '*sing*', and '*swim*' are all verbs.

verdict /'vɜːdɪkt/ *n.* what a jury decides at the end of a case in a law court.

verse /vɜːs/ *n.* **1** (no *pl.*) poetry; piece of writing in lines that have a rhythm. **2**

(*pl.* verses) group of lines in a poem, hymn, etc.: *a poem of five verses.* **3** (*pl.* verses) group of lines in the Bible.

versus /'vɜːsəs/ *prep.* against; opposite; on the other side in a sport or fight: *Did you see the match yesterday—Manchester United versus Liverpool?*

vertical /'vɜːtɪkl/ *adj.* that stands straight up; upright: *a vertical line.*

very[1] /'verɪ/ *adj.* exact; same: *Ray! You are the very person I want!*

very[2] *adv.* word that makes the next word stronger: *London is a very big place.*

vest /vest/ *n.* piece of clothing that you wear next to the skin on the upper part of your body.

vet /vet/, **veterinary surgeon** /ˌvetrɪnrɪ 'sɜːdʒən/ *n.* doctor who looks after sick animals.

veto /'viːtəʊ/ *v.* say that something must not happen: *Grace's parents vetoed her plan to study in America.* **veto** *n.*

via /'vaɪə/ *prep.* through; by way of: *We drove from London to Exeter via Bristol.*

vicar /'vɪkə(r)/ *n.* priest in the Church of England. **vicarage** /'vɪkərɪdʒ/ *n.* vicar's house.

vice- /vaɪs/ *prefix* showing someone who is next to the leader: *The vice-captain leads the team when the captain is ill.*

vicious /'vɪʃəs/ *adj.* cruel; nasty: *The donkey gave him a vicious kick.* **viciously** *adv.*

victim /'vɪktɪm/ *n.* someone who suffers in an attack, murder, disaster, etc.: *The ambulance took the victims of the car accident to hospital.*

victor /'vɪktə(r)/ *n.* winner: *Who was the victor of the boxing-match?*

victorious /vɪk'tɔːrɪəs/ *adj.* successful; who have won: *We cheered the victorious football team.* **victoriously** *adv.*

victory /'vɪktərɪ/ *n.* (*pl.* victories) winning a game, fight, war, etc.

view /vjuː/ *n.* **1** (no *pl.*) seeing or being seen. **come into view**, come where you can see it: *They picked up their cases when the train came into view.* **in view**, where you can see it. **on view**, for you to see: *The Crown of England is on view at*

the Tower of London. **2** (*pl.* views) place that you look at; picture or photograph of a place: *a beautiful view.* **3** (*pl.* views) opinion; what you believe or think about something: *He holds strong views on race.* **in view of**, because of something: *I couldn't go to London in view of the train strike.*

viewer /'vjuːə(r)/ *n.* someone who is watching: *television viewers.*

vigorous /'vɪgərəs/ *adj.* **1** strong and active: *a vigorous man of 34.* **2** needing a strong body: *Running is vigorous exercise.* **vigorously** *adv.* **vigour** /'vɪgə(r)/ *n.*

vile /vaɪl/ *adj.* very bad; horrible: *The medicine tastes vile!*

villa /'vɪlə/ *n.* house.

village /'vɪlɪdʒ/ *n.* small town. **villager** *n.* someone who lives in a village.

villain /'vɪlən/ *n.* bad person; criminal.

vine /vaɪn/ *n.* plant where grapes grow.

vinegar /'vɪnɪgə(r)/ *n.* (no *pl.*) liquid with a sharp taste for cooking, etc.: *We mix oil and vinegar to put on salad.*

vineyard /'vɪnjəd/ *n.* piece of land where vines grow.

viola /vɪ'əʊlə/ *n.* musical instrument like a big violin.

violent /'vaɪələnt/ *adj.* strong and dangerous: *a violent wind.* **violently** *adv.* **violence** *n.*

violet /'vaɪələt/ *n.* **1** (*pl.* violets) small purple flower. **2** (no *pl.*) purple colour. **violet** *adj.*

violin /ˌvaɪə'lɪn/ *n.* musical instrument with strings. **violinist** /ˌvaɪə'lɪnɪst/ *n.* someone who plays a violin.

V.I.P. /ˌviː aɪ 'piː/ *abbrev.* very important person: *The prime minister is a V.I.P.*

visa /'viːzə/ *n.* special piece of paper or stamp in your passport to show that you can go into a country: *Foreigners must have visas when they visit the United States.*

visible /'vɪzəbl/ *adj.* that you can see: *Stars are only visible when the sky is dark.*

vision /'vɪʒn/ *n.* **1** (no *pl.*) sight; seeing: *He wears glasses because his vision is poor.* **2** (*pl.* visions) picture in your mind; dream: *Tom has visions of becoming a pop star when he grows up.*

visit /'vɪzɪt/ v. **1** go to see an interesting place; stay somewhere for a short time: *Have you ever visited Westminster Abbey?* **2** go to see a friend; stay with a friend for some time: *Let's visit Pippa this weekend.* **visit** n. *pay someone a visit*, go to see someone: *The doctor paid mother a visit when she was ill.*

visitor /'vɪzɪtə(r)/ n. someone who goes to see another person; someone who stays in a place: *Visitors are coming to lunch today.*

vital /'vaɪtl/ adj. very important; that you must do or have: *It's vital that the doctor comes quickly—her life is in danger.* **vitally** adv.

vivid /'vɪvɪd/ adj. **1** very bright: *vivid colours.* **2** clear: *I have a vivid memory of my first day at school.* **vividly** adv.

vocabulary /və'kæbjʊlərɪ/ n. (pl. vocabularies) **1** all the words in a language. **2** list of words in a lesson or book. **3** all the words that one person knows: *A young child has a small vocabulary.*

voice /vɔɪs/ n. (pl. voices) sound that you make when you speak or sing: *Alice has a very quiet voice.* *raise your voice*, speak loudly; shout.

volcano /vɒl'keɪnəʊ/ n. (pl. volcanoes) mountain with a hole in the top where fire, hot rock, ash, and gas come out: *Vesuvius is a volcano.* **volcanic** /vol'kænɪk/ adj.

volleyball /'vɒlɪbɔːl/ n. (no pl.) game where players try to hit a ball over a high net.

volume /'vɒljuːm/ n. **1** (no pl.) amount of space that something fills; amount of space in something: *What is the volume of that box?* **2** (no pl.) sound; loudness: *If you turn the volume down on your radio, it will be soft.* **3** (pl. volumes) a lot of something: *volumes of smoke.* **4** (pl. volumes) book.

voluntary /'vɒləntrɪ/ adj. **1** that you do willingly: *a voluntary confession.* **2** willing and unpaid: *Mrs. Thomas is a voluntary helper in a children's hospital.* **voluntarily** adv.

volunteer /ˌvɒlən'tɪə(r)/ v. offer to do a job that is unpleasant, difficult, or dangerous: *Two men volunteered to search for the missing climber.* **volunteer** n. someone who volunteers to do a job or to join the army.

vomit /'vɒmɪt/ v. be sick; bring back food from stomach through the mouth.

vote /vəʊt/ v. **1** put up your hand, etc. to show that you agree with a plan, etc.: *Did you vote yes or no?* **2** mark a piece of paper to choose your member of parliament, etc. in an election. **vote** n. *cast a vote*, choose someone in an election: *When did you cast your vote?* **voter** n. someone who votes.

vow /vaʊ/ n. serious promise. **vow** v.: *At his wedding, a man vows to look after his future wife.*

vowel /vaʊl/ n. one of the letters 'a', 'e', 'i', 'o', 'u'.

voyage /'vɔɪdʒ/ n. sea journey: *a voyage from London to New York.*

vulgar /'vʌlgə(r)/ adj. not polite; rough and rude. **vulgarly** adv.

Ww

wade /weɪd/ v. walk through water: *Can we wade across the river, or is it too deep?*

wag /wæg/ v. (pres. part. wagging, past part. & past tense wagged /wægd/) move to and fro; make something move from side to side or up and down: *The dog*

wagged his tail when he saw his master.
wag *n.*

wage /weɪdʒ/ *n.* money that you receive for work: *His wages are £70 a week.*

wagon, waggon /'wægən/ *n.* **1** cart on four wheels, which a horse or an ox pulls. **2** railway truck for goods.

wail /weɪl/ *v.* make a long, sad cry or noise: *The child wailed for his mother.*

waist /weɪst/ *n.* narrow part around the middle of the body: *Bob wears a belt around his waist.*

waistcoat /'weɪstkəʊt/ *n.* piece of clothing like a jacket with no sleeves.

wait /weɪt/ *v.* stay where you are until someone comes, something happens, etc.; not begin something for a while: *We waited at the bus-stop until the bus came.* **wait for**, wait until someone or something comes, etc.: *Please wait for me if I'm not ready.* **keep someone waiting**, be late or busy so that someone has to wait for you: *The doctor kept me waiting for half an hour.* **wait up**, not go to bed until someone comes home: *She always waits up for her husband when he's home late.* **wait** *n.*: *We had a long wait for the bus.* **lie in wait for**, hide somewhere to attack someone: *The cat lay in wait for the bird.*

waiter /'weɪtə(r)/ *n.* man who brings food to a table in a restaurant, etc.

waiting-room /'weɪtɪŋ rʊm/ *n.* room in a railway station, doctor's surgery, etc., where people can wait.

waitress /'weɪtrɪs/ *n.* (*pl.* waitresses) woman who brings food to a table in a restaurant, etc.

wake /weɪk/ *v.* (*past part.* woken /'wəʊkən/, *past tense* /wəʊk/) **1** stop sleeping: *I usually wake at six o'clock.* **2** make someone stop sleeping: *The noise woke me.* **wake up**, stop sleeping. **wake someone up**, make someone stop sleeping: *The alarm clock rings to wake us up.*

waken /'weɪkən/ *v.* make someone stop sleeping.

walk /wɔːk/ *v.* go on foot but not run: *She walked slowly upstairs to bed.* **walk** *n.* journey on foot: *The shop is a short walk from our house.* **go for a walk**, walk somewhere for pleasure: *It's a lovely afternoon—shall we go for a walk in the park?*

walkie-talkie /ˌwɔːkɪ 'tɔːkɪ/ *n.* small radio that a policeman, etc. carries so that he can send and receive messages.

wall /wɔːl/ *n.* **1** side of a building or room: *Clive hung a picture on the wall.* **2** something that you build with stones, bricks, wood, etc. round a garden, field, town, etc.: *There is a high wall around the prison.* **wall-paper** *n.* pretty paper that covers the walls of a room.

wallet /'wɒlɪt/ *n.* small case for paper money, etc., which you carry in your pocket or handbag.

walnut /'wɔːlnʌt/ *n.* sort of nut that you can eat.

waltz /wɔːls/ *n.* (*pl.* waltzes) **1** dance for a man and woman together. **2** music for this kind of dance. **waltz** *v.*

wander /'wɒndə(r)/ *v.* walk slowly with no special plan: *The boys wandered around the town with nothing to do.*

want[1] /wɒnt/ *n.* **1** (no *pl.*) not having something; not having enough: *The plants died from want of water.* **in want of**, needing something: *This broken fence is in want of repair.* **2** (*pl.* wants) what you wish for or need to live, be happy, etc.: *A mother looks after the wants of her baby.*

want[2] *v.* **1** desire or wish for something: *The horse wants an apple—I'll give it one.* **2** need something important or necessary that is not here: *This dirty floor wants a scrub.*

war /wɔː(r)/ *n.* fighting between countries: *the Korean War.* **at war**, fighting: *In 1775 England was at war with her American colonies.* **declare war**, start a war: *In 1812 Napoleon declared war on Russia.* **go to war**, start fighting. **wage war on**, fight another country. **civil war**, war between people in one country. **war-like** /'wɔːlaɪk/ *adj.* ready to fight; liking to fight.

ward /wɔːd/ *n.* room in a hospital or prison.

warden /'wɔːdən/ *n.* someone whose job is to control a hostel, public place, etc.

warder /'wɔːdə(r)/ *n.* man whose job is to guard people in prison. **wardress** /'wɔːdrɪs/ *n.* (*pl.* wardresses) female warder.

wardrobe /'wɔ:drəʊb/ n. cupboard where you hang your clothes.

ware /weə(r)/, **wares** (pl.) n. things that you see or buy: *We stopped at the stall to look at the wares.*

warehouse /'weəhaʊs/ n. building where you store goods, furniture, etc.

warm[1] /wɔ:m/ adj. **1** a little hot: *It's warm near the fire.* **2** that will make or keep you warm: *warm clothes.* **3** friendly; kind: *She has a warm heart.* **warmly** adv.: *Jill thanked me warmly.*

warm[2] v. become warm; make something warm: *Walter warmed his hands by the fire.* **warm up**, become warmer; make something hot or warmer: *Mum warmed up the stew for lunch.*

warm-hearted /ˌwɔ:m 'hɑːtɪd/ adj. kind.

warmth /wɔ:mθ/ n. (no pl.) **1** heat: *the warmth of a fire.* **2** friendliness; kindness.

warn /wɔ:n/ v. tell someone about danger or about a bad thing that will perhaps happen: *He warned me not to go near the horse because it kicks.* **warning** n.: *The radio gave a warning of bad weather.*

warrant /'wɒrənt/ n. piece of paper that gives you the right to do something: *The policeman had a warrant to arrest the man.*

warship /'wɔ:ʃɪp/ n. ship for fighting.

was /wɒz/ part of v. be, used with 'I', 'he', 'she', and 'it' in the past tense.

wash[1] /wɒʃ/ n. (no pl.) **1** cleaning with water: *Did you have a wash this morning?* **2** dirty clothes, towels, etc. that you must clean: *I've got a very large wash today.*

wash[2] v. **1** make something clean with water: *Wash those dirty hands, Pat!* **wash down**, clean something with water from a bucket, hose, etc.: *Frank washed down the car.* **wash up**, clean pots, plates, etc.: *We washed up after breakfast.* **2** move something with water: *The sea washed pieces of wood on to the beach.*

washing /'wɒʃɪŋ/ n. (no pl.) dirty clothes, etc. that you must clean; clothes, etc. that you are cleaning: *Pam hung the washing on the line to dry.*

washing-machine n. machine for

washing clothes. **washing-powder** n. soap powder for washing clothes, etc.

wasn't /'wɒznt/ = was not.

wasp /wɒsp/ n. flying insect that can sting people.

waste[1] /weɪst/ adj. that you do not want; not useful: *Throw the waste paper in the basket.* **wasteful** adj. throwing away something good. **wastefully** adv.

waste[2] n. (no pl.) **1** throwing away something good: *She never sings now— what a waste of a lovely voice.* **2** things that you throw away because they are not useful: *We put waste in the dustbin.* **a waste of time**, time that you spend in a useless way: *It's a waste of time to water the garden when it is raining.*

waste[3] v. throw away something good; not use something in a useful way: *You only need one piece of paper—don't waste any more.*

watch[1] /wɒtʃ/ n. (pl. watches) instrument that shows the time of day. You wear it on your wrist or carry it in your pocket.

watch[2] n. (no pl.) guard; looking to see that everything is in order, etc. **keep watch**, look out for danger: *The soldier kept watch at the gate.*

watch[3] v. **1** look at someone or something for some time; keep your eyes on someone or something: *The children watched the TV programme.* **2** guard something; look after something: *Will you watch my clothes while I go swimming?* **watch out for**, expect something; look and wait for a dangerous person or thing: *Watch out for ice on the road.* **watch over**, guard or look after someone or something: *She watched over her sick cat all night.*

watchman /'wɒtʃmən/ n. (pl. watchmen) man who guards a building.

water[1] /'wɔːtə(r)/ n. (no pl.) the liquid in rivers, lakes, seas, etc. **get into hot water**, get into trouble: *You'll get into hot water if you take apples from Mr. Scott's tree.*

water[2] v. **1** give water to something: *The gardener waters his plants in the summer.* **2** fill with tears: *Our eyes watered in the smoke.*

water-colour /'wɔːtə kʌlə(r)/, **water-colours** /'wɔːtə kʌləz/ (pl.) n. paints that you mix with water for painting pictures.

waterfall /'wɔːtəfɔːl/ n. place where a river falls from a high place to a lower place.

watering /'wɔːtərɪŋ/ adj. **watering can** n. can for pouring water on plants.

waterproof /'wɔːtəpruːf/ adj. that does not let water through: *A raincoat must be waterproof.*

wave[1] /weɪv/ n. **1** rough top of the water when the sea is not calm; rolling movement of the sea when it crashes on the beach: *A big wave swept the man off the boat.* **2** movement from side to side, up and down, etc.: *He gave a wave of the hand to say goodbye.* **3** gentle curve or bend: *Her hair has waves.* **4** movement like a wave that carries heat, light, sound, etc.: *radio waves.*

wave[2] v. **1** move gently to and fro: *The flag is waving in the wind.* **2** move something from one side to the other: *Ada waved her hand as the train left.* **3** make a sign to someone: *The policeman waved the driver to stop.*

wax /wæks/ n. (no pl.) soft stuff for making candles, etc. **wax** adj.

way /weɪ/ n. **1** (pl. ways) road, street, path, etc. **2** (pl. ways) route; how you go from one place to another: *Do you know your way home from here?* **3** (pl. ways) direction; where someone or something is going or looking: *Come*

this way. *Look that way.* **4** (no pl.) distance: *Glasgow is a long way from London.* **5** (pl. ways) manner; how you do something: *She smiled in a friendly way.* **way of life**, how you live: *A fireman has a dangerous way of life.* **by the way**, words that show you are going to tell a new thing that is not important but perhaps interesting. **feel your way**, use your hands to find where to go: *Sam felt his way to the door in the dark.* **find your way**, find where to go: *If you have a map you will be able to find your way to the hotel.* **force your way in**, break open a door, etc. to get into a place: *The burglar forced his way in.* **be in the way, get in the way**, block the road; stop someone's work, etc. because you are in the wrong place: *Don't get in the way while I'm trying to sweep the floor!* **give way, (a)** agree with someone after not agreeing: *After a long argument, Rob gave way.* **(b)** break: *The ladder gave way and Larry fell to the ground.* **(c)** let another person or thing go first: *Give way to cars that come from the left.* **go a long way, (a)** do well in the future: *That clever girl will go a long way.* **(b)** be enough; buy much: *His pay doesn't go a long way.* **a good way**, a long way: *It's a good way from here to the station, so you should get a taxi.* **lead** or **show the way to**, go in front of others so that they know where to go. **lose your way**, become lost: *Don't lose your way in the forest!* **make your way**, go: *Neil made his way to the station.* **on the way**, while you are going somewhere: *She fell down on the way to work.* **tell someone the way**, tell someone where to go: *Can you tell me the way to the station?* **the wrong way round**, back to front, inside out, etc.: *Your hat's on the wrong way round!*

wayside /'weɪsaɪd/ n. side of the road. **wayside** adj.: *a wayside café.*

w.c. /ˌdʌblju: 'siː/ n. toilet; lavatory.

we /wiː/ (pl.) of pron. I: *Joan and I are friends—we play together.*

weak /wiːk/ adj. **1** not strong in the body; not able to move heavy things: *a weak old man.* **2** that will break easily: *a weak chair.* **3** that you cannot see or hear clearly or taste easily: *weak tea.* **4** not able to make people do what you want: *a weak ruler.* **weakly** adv.

weakness /'wiːknɪs/ n. **1** (no pl.) not

being strong: *the weakness of old age.* **2**
(*pl.* weaknesses) fault: *Did Napoleon
have any weaknesses?*

wealth /welθ/ *n.* (no *pl.*) a lot of money,
land, etc.: *A rich man has great wealth.*
wealthy *adj.* rich.

weapon /'wepən/ *n.* instrument for
fighting: *Guns and swords are weapons.*

wear¹ /weə(r)/ *n.* (no *pl.*) **1** use; wearing: *I have jeans for everyday wear and
good trousers for special wear.* **2** clothes
in a shop: *That store sells men's wear.* **3**
using something and making it old: *My
bike gets a lot of wear.* **the worse for
wear**, not as good as it was because you
have used it a lot.

wear² *v.* (*past part.* worn /wɔːn/, *past
tense* wore /wɔː(r)/) **1** have clothes on
your body: *A policeman wears a uniform.* **2** show a feeling on your face: *She
was wearing a smile.* **3** use something so
much that it breaks, tears, becomes
weak, or becomes poor: *Tony has worn
his sock into holes.* **4** last for a long time:
Good leather will wear for years. **wear
off**, become less: *The excitement of
moving to a new town will soon wear off.*
wear out, **(a)** use something until it is
totally finished; become old and useless: *I
need some strong shoes that won't wear
out quickly.* **(b)** make someone very
tired: *That hard work will wear you out.*

weary /'wɪərɪ/ *adj.* tired: *I was weary
after a long day.* **wearily** *adv.* **wear-
iness** *n.*

weather /'weðə(r)/ *n.* (no *pl.*) how cold
or hot it is; how much sunshine, rain,
wind, etc. there is at a certain time: *I
wear a raincoat in wet weather.*

weave /wiːv/ *v.* (*past part.* woven
/'wəʊvn/, *past tense* wove /wəʊv/) **1**
make threads into cloth by crossing
them. **2** make a basket, etc. with straw,
cane, etc. **weaving** *n.* making cloth,
etc. **weaver** *n.* someone who weaves.

web /web/ *n.* fine net that a spider makes.

wed /wed/ *v.* (*pres. part.* wedding, *past
part.* wed, wedded /'wedɪd/, *past tense*
wedded) marry someone. **wedding** *n.*
marriage; ceremony when a man and a
woman marry.

Wednesday /'wenzdeɪ/ *n.* fourth day of
the week: *Wednesday comes after Tuesday and before Thursday.*

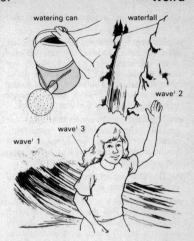

weed /wiːd/ *n.* wild plant that grows
where you do not want it: *a garden full
of weeds.* **weed** *v.* take weeds out of
the garden, etc.: *I spent all day weeding
the lawn.*

week /wiːk/ *n.* **1** any time of seven days:
The work will take a week. **2** seven days
from Sunday to Saturday: *this week;
next week.* **3** Monday to Friday;
Monday to Saturday: *The shops are
open in the week but not on Sundays.*
weekday *n.* any day except Sunday.

weekend /ˌwiːkˈend/ *n.* Saturday and
Sunday. **at the weekend**, on Saturday
and Sunday: *Are you going away at the
weekend?*

weekly /'wiːklɪ/ *adj.* done or happening
every week: *a weekly wage of £90.*
weekly *adv.*: *Mr. Davies pays me rent
weekly.*

weep /wiːp/ *v.* (*past part. & past tense*
wept /wept/) cry: *He wept when he heard
the sad news.*

weigh /weɪ/ *v.* **1** measure how heavy
something is: *The shopkeeper weighed
the tomatoes.* **2** show a certain number
of kilos, etc. on the scales: *The baby
weighs three kilos.*

weight /weɪt/ *n.* **1** how heavy something is: *The airline wants to know the
weight of your suitcase.* **2** piece of metal
that you put on scales.

weird /wɪəd/ *adj.* very strange; hard to

understand or explain: *What is that weird noise?*

welcome[1] /'welkəm/ *adj.* that you are glad to have, receive, or see: *A cool drink was welcome after the long, hot walk.* **be welcome to**, be allowed to do or have something: *You are welcome to use my pen if yours is broken.* **make someone welcome**, look after a visitor very well.

welcome[2] *v.* **1** show that you are pleased when someone or something comes: *Mr. Thomas welcomed us to his house.* **2** show that you like something: *He welcomed my plan.* **welcome** *n.*

well[1] /wel/ *adj.* in good health; not ill: *I hope your family is well.*

well[2] *adv.* **1** in a good or right way: *He sang well and won the first prize.* **2** hard; thoroughly: *Beat the eggs well.* **3** very much; a lot: *It's well past midnight.* **as well**, also: *Yvonne is learning French and English as well.* **as well as**, and also: *Scott has a flat in London as well as a house in Edinburgh.* **may as well**, there is no reason why you should not: *We've finished the work, so we may as well go home now.*

well[3] *exclam.* **1** word that you often say when you start speaking: *Well, I'm tired—I'll go to bed.* **2** word that shows surprise: *Well, you have grown!*

well[4] *n.* (no *pl.*) something good. **wish someone well**, wish someone good luck.

well[5] *n.* deep hole for getting water or oil from under the ground.

we'll /wi:l/ = we will; we shall.

wellington boots /ˌwelɪŋtən 'bu:ts/ *n.* (*pl.*) rubber boots that you wear in the rain, mud, etc.

well-known /'wel nəʊn/ *adj.* famous: *a well-known sportsman.*

well-off /ˌwel 'ɒf/ *adj.* rich.

went /went/ *past tense* of *v.* go.

wept /wept/ *past part. & past tense* of *v.* weep.

were /wɜ:(r)/ part of *v.* be, used with 'you', 'we', and 'they' in the past tense.

weren't /wɜ:nt/ = were not.

west /west/ *n.* (no *pl.*) one of the points of the compass: *The sun sets in the west.* **west** *adj.*: *a west wind.* **west** *adv.*: *Bristol is west of London.* **westerly** /'westəlɪ/ *adj.* from a place that is west: *a westerly wind.* **western** /'westən/ *adj.* of the west: *Glasgow is on the western side of Scotland.* **westwards** /'westwədz/ *adv.* towards the west.

wet /wet/ *adj.* (wetter, wettest) **1** covered with water; full of water or other liquid: *The ground is wet after rain.* **2** with rain: *a wet day.* **wet** *n.* **1** water. **2 the wet**, rain: *Come in out of the wet.* **wet** *v.* (*pres. part.* wetting, *past part. & past tense* wetted /'wetɪd/) make something wet: *The baby has wet the bed.* **wetting** *n.* becoming wet: *We had a wetting in the rain.*

whale /weɪl/ *n.* the biggest sea-animal.

wharf /wɔ:f/ *n.* (*pl.* wharves) place in a harbour where you tie a boat or ship so that you can take things on and off.

what[1] /wɒt/ *adj.* word that you say when you ask about a person or a thing: *What time is it? What colour is your car?*

what[2] *exclam.* word that shows any strong feeling: *What a hot day!*

what[3] *pron.* (no *pl.*) word that you say when you ask about something: *What is that bird? What happened?* **what about?**, words that you say when you suggest something: *I'm thirsty—what about a drink?* **what ... for?**, why? for what reason or job?: *What is this box for? It's for holding eggs.* **what ... like?**, words that you say when you want someone to describe something: *What is the hotel like? Very modern and comfortable.* **what's up?**, what is happening?; what is wrong?: *You look pale—what's up?*

whatever /wɒt'evə(r)/ *adj.* of any sort; however much. **whatever** *pron.*: *Do whatever you like.*

wheat /wi:t/ *n.* (no *pl.*) plant with grain that we make into flour.

wheel /wi:l/ *n.* thing like a circle that turns round and round: *A bicycle runs on two wheels. A car runs on four wheels.* **at the wheel**, driving a car: *Who was at the wheel when the accident happened?* **wheel** *v.* push or pull something on wheels: *Mary wheeled her bicycle up the hill.*

wheelbarrow /'wi:lbærəʊ/ *n.* small cart with one wheel at the front: *The gardener put dead leaves in the wheelbarrow.*

when¹ /wen/ *adv.* **1** at what time: *When did he come? He came at three.* **2** at which; on which: *Sunday is the day when I get up late.*

when² *conj.* at the time; during the time: *It was raining when we arrived.*

whenever /wen'evə(r)/ *adv.* **1** at any time: *Come again whenever you like.* **2** every time that: *The boys fight whenever they meet.*

where /weə(r)/ *adv.* **1** in what place: *I know where he lives—in Bath.* **2** word that you say when you ask what place: *Where are you going to? Where does he come from?* **3** in which; at which: *This is the room where I work.*

wherever /ˌweər'evə(r)/ *adv.* on, to, or at any place: *Sit wherever you like.*

whether /'weðə(r)/ *conj.* if: *I don't know whether I can come.*

which¹ /wɪtʃ/ *adj.* word that you say when you ask about a person or a thing; what: *Which boy is Jo—the tall one or the short one?*

which² *pron.* (no *pl.*) **1** what thing or things; what person or people: *Which is Jo—the tall boy or the short boy?* **2** that; and that: *They moved the fallen tree, which took a long time.*

whichever /wɪtʃ'evə(r)/ *adj.* any one: *Take whichever book you like.* **whichever** *pron.*: *Here are two books—take whichever you like.*

while¹ /waɪl/ *conj.* at a time during; for as long as; at the same time as: *Gillian watched television while she ate her supper.*

while² *n.* (no *pl.*) length of time: *I haven't seen him for a long while.* **once in a while**, sometimes; not often: *Theatre tickets are expensive so we only go to the theatre once in a while.* **worth your while**, good enough for the time, effort, etc. that you spend: *It isn't worth our while going swimming now, because the pool closes in half an hour.*

whilst /waɪlst/ *conj.* while: *She sang whilst she worked.*

whimper /'wɪmpə(r)/ *v.* make a soft cry of fear or pain: *The sick baby was whimpering in its cot.* **whimper** *n.*

whine /waɪn/ *v.* make a long cry or sound: *The dog was whining outside the door.* **whine** *n.*

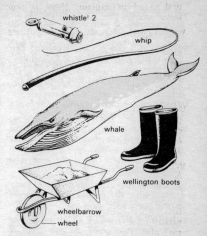

whistle¹ 2

whip

whale

wellington boots

wheelbarrow

wheel

whip /wɪp/ *n.* long piece of leather, cord, etc. on a handle, for hitting people or animals. **whip** *v.* (*pres part.* whipping, *past part.* & *past tense* whipped /wɪpt/) **1** hit a person or animal with a whip: *The rider whipped the horse to make it go faster.* **2** beat cream, etc. with a fork to make it stiff. **whipping** *n.*

whirl /wɜːl/ *v.* move quickly round and round; make something or someone move round fast: *The skaters whirled round the ice rink.* **whirl** *n.*

whisker /'wɪskə(r)/ *n.* **1** one of the hairs that grow on the sides of a man's face. **2** one of the long hairs that grow near the mouth of a cat, rat, etc.

whisky, whiskey /'wɪskɪ/ *n.* **1** (no *pl.*) sort of alcoholic drink. **2** (*pl.* whiskies) glass of whisky.

whisper /'wɪspə(r)/ *v.* speak very softly: *She whispered so that she would not wake the baby.* **whisper** *n.*: *They were talking in whispers.*

whistle¹ /'wɪsl/ *n.* **1** sound of air or steam when it goes through a small hole: *the whistle of a steam-engine; the whistle of a bird.* **2** small instrument that makes a sharp sound when you blow it: *The referee blew his whistle to end the match.*

whistle² *v.* blow through a small hole in an instrument, or through a small gap between your lips, to make a sound: *Dick whistled as he worked.*

white[1] /waɪt/ adj. **1** with the colour of snow or milk. **2** with a skin that is not black or brown: a white man.

white[2] n. **1** (no pl.) white colour: The bride was dressed in white. **2** (pl. whites) someone with a white skin. **3** (pl. whites) part of an egg that is round the yellow middle.

whizz /wɪz/ v. move very fast: The bullet whizzed by his head.

who /huː/ pron. (no pl.) **1** word that you say when you ask about a person; what person?: Who is that boy? I know who you are. **2** that: This is the man who wanted to meet you.

whoever /huːˈevə(r)/ pron. (no pl.) any person who; the person who: Whoever arrives early must wait.

whole[1] /həʊl/ adj. **1** all of; total: The whole class was quiet—no one spoke. **2** not broken; with no parts missing: He dropped the cup but luckily it's still whole.

whole[2] n. (no pl.) **1** something that is complete: Four quarters make a whole. **2** all of something: He spent the whole of the year in Egypt. **on the whole**, in general: Living in town is pleasant but, on the whole, I like the country better.

wholly /ˈhəʊli/ adv. completely; totally: I wholly agree with you.

whom /huːm/ pron. (no pl.) **1** word that you say when you ask about a person: To whom did you give the money? **2** that: She's the woman whom I met in Greece.

whose /huːz/ pron. (no pl.) of whom; of which: Whose house is this? Is that the boy whose sister I met last week?

why[1] /waɪ/ adv. for what reason: Why are you late?

why[2] exclam. word that shows surprise: Why, it's quite easy!

wicked /ˈwɪkɪd/ adj. very bad; evil: Murder is a wicked crime. **wickedly** adv. **wickedness** n.

wicket /ˈwɪkɪt/ n. three sticks behind a batsman in the game of cricket. **take a wicket**, defeat a batsman.

wide[1] /waɪd/ adj. **1** from side to side: The belt is 2 centimetres wide. **2** far from side to side; broad: a wide river. **3** fully opened: She started at me with wide eyes.

wide[2] adv. fully: She opened the door

wide. **wide apart**, a long way from each other: We planted the trees wide apart. **far and wide**, in many places: He travelled far and wide.

wide-awake /ˌwaɪd əˈweɪk/ adj. far from sleep.

widen /ˈwaɪdn/ v. become wider; make something wider: to widen a road.

widespread /ˈwaɪdspred/ adj. that you find in many places: There is widespread snow in Britain today.

widow /ˈwɪdəʊ/ n. woman whose husband is dead. **widower** n. man whose wife is dead.

width /wɪdθ/ n. how wide something is; measurement from side to side: The corridor has a width of two metres.

wife /waɪf/ n. (pl. wives) woman to whom a man is married.

wig /wɪg/ n. cap of hair that is not your own: The boy wore a wig when he played the part of a princess.

wild /waɪld/ adj. **1** that lives or grows in nature, not with people: wild flowers; wild animals. **2** fierce and dangerous: a wild bull. **3** angry and excited: He was wild with rage. **4** stormy: a wild night. **wildly** adv. in an excited, violent way: He laughed wildly.

will[1] /wɪl/ n. **1** (pl. wills) power of your mind that makes you choose, decide, and do things: He has a strong will, and nothing can stop him doing what he wants. **2** (no pl.) wish; plan: He was very ill but he got better because he had a will to live. **good will**, kind feelings: Christmas is a time of good will. **ill will**, unkind feelings. **of your own free will**, because you wish to: Nigel helped me of his own free will. **3** (pl. wills) piece of paper that says who will have your money, house, goods, etc. when you die: My aunt left me £2,000 in her will.

will[2] v. **1** word that forms the future with other verbs; word that shows something is going to happen: He will come tomorrow. **2** word that you say when you agree or promise to do something: I will help you if you need me: **3** word that you say when you ask a polite question: Will you pass the salt?

will[3] v. wish: Come when you will.

willing /ˈwɪlɪŋ/ adj. **1** ready and happy to do something: I'm willing to lend you *some money.* **2** that you do gladly: *willing help.* **willingly** *adv.: I'll willingly wait.* **willingness** *n.*

willow /'wɪləʊ/ *n.* sort of tree.

win /wɪn/ *v.* (*pres. part.* winning, *past part.* & *past tense* won /wʌn/) **1** do best in a game, competition, fight, etc.: *Doug came first and won the race.* **2** get or have something because you have worked well, tried hard, etc.: *Julie's courage won everyone's admiration.* **win someone over**, talk to someone and make him think the same way as you do. **win** *n.* doing best in a game, fight, etc.: *Our team has had five wins this year.* **winner** *n.* someone who wins. **winning** *adj.*

wind[1] /wɪnd/ *n.* air that moves: *The wind blew my hat over the wall.* **windy** *adj.* with a lot of wind: *a windy day.*

wind[2] /waɪnd/ *v.* (*past part.* & *past tense* wound /waʊnd/) **1** bend; curve; go round: *The road wound down the mountain.* **2** make something go round; twist string, etc. round and round to make a ball: *The nurse wound a bandage round my finger.* **3** turn a key or handle to make a machine go: *The clock will stop if you don't wind it.*

windmill /'wɪndmɪl/ *n.* building with sails that the wind blows round so that the machinery inside will grind flour, etc.

window /'wɪndəʊ/ *n.* opening, usually covered with glass, in a wall: *The room is cold—please shut the window.* **window-pane** /'wɪndəʊ peɪn/ *n.* piece of glass for a window. **window-sill** /'wɪndəʊ sɪl/ *n.* flat shelf at the bottom of a window.

windscreen /'wɪndskriːn/ *n.* big window at the front of a car, etc. **windscreen-wiper** *n.* thing that cleans rain, etc. off the windscreen while you are driving.

wine /waɪn/ *n.* alcoholic drink from grapes.

wing /wɪŋ/ *n.* part of a bird, insect, aeroplane, etc. that helps it to fly: *A bird has two wings.*

wink /wɪŋk/ *v.* shut and open one eye quickly to make a friendly or secret sign. **wink** *n.*

winner /'wɪnə(r)/ *n.* someone who does best in a game, fight, etc.

windmill / windscreen / wing / window

winning /'wɪnɪŋ/ *adj.* best in a race, game, etc.: *the winning team.*

winter /'wɪntə(r)/ *n.* cold time of the year. **winter** *adj.: winter sports.* **wintry** /'wɪntrɪ/ *adj.* cold: *wintry weather.*

wipe /waɪp/ *v.* rub something with a cloth to clean or dry it: *After you wash your hands, wipe them on a towel.* **wipe off**, take away something by rubbing: *He wiped the writing off the blackboard.* **wipe out**, (*a*) clean the inside of something: *to wipe out a cup.* (*b*) kill people; totally destroy a place, etc.: *The earthquake wiped out many villages.* **wipe up**, take up water, etc. with a cloth: *Wipe up that milk on the floor, please.* **wipe** *n.: Give your hands a wipe on this towel.*

wire /'waɪə(r)/ *n.* **1** thread of metal: *telephone wires.* **2** telegram: *He sent a wire to say that he was coming.*

wireless /'waɪəlɪs/ *n.* (*pl.* wirelesses) radio.

wise /waɪz/ *adj.* **1** knowing many things; knowing what is right and good: *a wise woman.* **2** good; sensible: *a wise idea.* **wisely** *adv.* **wisdom** /'wɪzdəm/ *n.*

wish[1] /wɪʃ/ *n.* **1** (no *pl.*) wanting: *I have no wish to go.* **2** (*pl.* wishes) what you want or desire: *I hope you get your wish.*

wish[2] *v.* **1** want or desire something: *Where do you wish to sit?* **2** want something impossible or unlikely: *I wish I could fly!* **3** hope that something will happen to someone: *I wish you a pleasant journey.* **wish for**, ask for; hope for: *He wished for a bicycle at Christmas.* **wish someone well**, hope that someone will have good luck.

wit /wɪt/ *n.* **1** (*pl.* wits) sense. **be at your wits' ends**, not know what to do or say. **2** (no *pl.*) saying things in a clever or funny way: *The audience laughed at the comedian's wit.* **witty** *adj.* said in a funny way; amusing: *a witty joke.* **wittily** *adv.*

witch /wɪtʃ/ *n.* (*pl.* witches) woman who uses magic to do bad things.

with /wɪð/ *prep.* **1** having; carrying: *a coat with two pockets; a man with a gun.* **2** word that shows what you are using: *He was writing with a pencil.* **3** word that shows things or people are together: *Harriet is playing with her friend.* **4** on the same side; agreeing: *Are you with us or against us?* **5** against: *The dog was fighting with the cat.* **6** because of: *The baby was crying with hunger.* **7** word that shows how something happens, how you do something, etc.: *He spoke with anger.* **8** in the same way as; at the same time as: *A tree's shadow moves with the sun.*

withdraw /wɪð'drɔː/ *v.* (*past part.* withdrawn /wɪð'drɔːn/, *past tense* withdrew /wɪð'druː/) **1** take something out or away: *I must withdraw some money from the bank.* **2** move back or away: *The enemy were withdrawing as our army moved forward.* **3** leave a team, club, etc.

wither /'wɪðə(r)/ *v.* dry up and die; make something dry up and die: *The grass withered in the hot sun.*

within /wɪð'ɪn/ *prep.* inside; before the end of; no further than, etc.: *There are 400 prisoners within the prison walls. I'll come within an hour.*

without /wɪð'aʊt/ *prep.* not having; not carrying: *You can't buy things without money!* **without doing**, and not do: *You can't make an omelette without breaking eggs.* **do without**, manage when someone or something is not there: *There's no sugar so we'll have to do without.*

witness[1] /'wɪtnɪs/ *n.* (*pl.* witnesses) **1** someone who sees something happen. **2** someone in a law court who tells about

what he saw: *The witness said he heard shots.* **witness-box** *n.* place in a law court where a witness stands.

witness[2] *v.* see something happening: *He witnessed a murder.*

witty /'wɪtɪ/ *adj.* funny; cleverly making you smile and laugh.

wives /waɪvz/ (*pl.*) of *n.* wife.

wobble /'wɒbl/ *v.* move unsteadily; make something move unsteadily: *The floor is rough so the table wobbles.* **wobbly** *adj.*

woe /wəʊ/ *n.* sadness; trouble.

woke /wəʊk/ *past tense* of *v.* wake.

woken /'wəʊkən/ *past part.* of *v.* wake.

wolf /wʊlf/ *n.* (*pl.* wolves) wild animal like a big dog, which hunts and kills other animals.

woman /'wʊmən/ *n.* (*pl.* women) grown-up female person: *men, women, and children.*

won /wʌn/ *past part. & past tense* of *v.* win.

wonder[1] /'wʌndə(r)/ *n.* **1** (no *pl.*) feeling that you have when you see, hear, or meet something strange, beautiful, etc.: *The children looked up in wonder at the big elephant.* **no wonder**, it is not surprising that: *No wonder you were late—you ate your breakfast so slowly.* **2** (*pl.* wonders) marvellous and surprising happening: *the wonders of modern medicine.*

wonder[2] *v.* **1** ask yourself; want to know: *I wonder who that boy is.* **2** feel surprised: *He was so ill, I wonder he didn't die.*

wonderful /'wʌndəfl/ *adj.* that pleases and surprises you very much: *What a wonderful present!* **wonderfully** *adv.*

won't /wəʊnt/ = will not.

wood /wʊd/ *n.* **1** (no *pl.*) stuff of a tree: *He chopped the wood for the fire.* **2** (*pl.* woods) big group of trees; small forest: *We had a picnic in the wood.* **wooden** /'wʊdən/ *adj.* made of wood: *a wooden box.*

woodland /'wʊdlənd/ *n.* land with many trees.

wool /wʊl/ *n.* **1** (no *pl.*) soft hair of sheep. **2** (*pl.* wools) thread, cloth, etc. made from sheep's hair. **woollen** /'wʊlən/, **woolly** *adj.* made of wool: *a woollen jersey.*

word /wɜːd/ n. **1** (pl. words) a sound that you make or write for a thing or an idea: *The baby's first word was 'mama'.* **have a word with**, speak to someone: *This bread is dry—I must have a word with the baker.* **will not hear a word against**, will not let you say anything bad about someone or something: *She thinks her son is wonderful—she will not hear a word against him.* **in other words**, saying the same thing in another way: *Joe doesn't like work—in other words, he's lazy!* **2** (no pl.) news; message: *Ben sent me word that he had arrived safely.* **3** (no pl.) promise: *He gave me his word that he would not smoke.* **be as good as your word, keep your word, be true to your word**, do what you promised. **break your word**, not do what you promised. **take someone at his word**, believe that someone will do what he promised.

wore /wɔː(r)/ past tense of v. wear.

work¹ /wɜːk/ n. **1** (no pl.) making or doing something: *Digging is hard work.* **get to work**, begin doing something: *'Let's get to work', said Gary and he picked up the spade.* **2** (no pl.) what you do to earn money; job: *A teacher's work is teaching.* **at work, (a)** at the place where you have a job: *I'm at work by 8 a.m.* **(b)** busy doing something: *Father's at work in his vegetable garden.* **out of work**, with no job that brings money: *Colin is out of work and he's looking for a job.* **3** (no pl.) what you are doing: *'We're going to eat now,' mother said, 'so please take your work off the table.'* **4** (no pl.) what you have made or done: *Mr. Baker paints pictures and sells his work to friends.* **5** (pl. works) book, painting, etc.: *the works of Shakespeare; works of art.* **6 works** (pl.) moving parts of a machine: *the works of a clock.* **7 works** (pl.) factory; place where people make things with machines: *the steel works; the gas works.*

work² v. **1** do or make something; be busy: *David worked hard and painted the whole house in a day.* **2** go correctly; function: *We can't watch the television because it's not working.* **3** control or operate something; make someone or something go: *Mother showed me how to work the sewing-machine.* **4** have a paid job: *Ken is working at the BBC.* **work out**, end well: *Did your plan work out?* **work something out, (a)** calculate an

wool 1

wool 2

woman

wolf

worm

amount, etc.: *He worked out the cost of the holiday.* **(b)** find the answer to: *I can't work out this sum.* **(c)** think of: *The scientists worked out a way of sending men to the moon.*

worker /ˈwɜːkə(r)/ n. someone who works: *a factory worker.*

workman /ˈwɜːkmən/ n. (pl. workmen) man who works with his hands, or with a machine.

workshop /ˈwɜːkʃɒp/ n. place where you make or repair things: *The carpenter was hammering in his workshop.*

world /wɜːld/ n. **1** the earth; all countries and people. **2** all the people who do the same kind of thing: *the world of sport.* **in the world**, at all: *Nothing in the world would make me pick up a spider.* **out of this world**, wonderful: *That meal was out of this world!* **think the world of**, like or admire someone a lot: *Mr. Peters thinks the world of you.* **world, world-wide** /ˌwɜːldˈwaɪd/ adj. that you find all over the world: *Football is a worldwide game.*

worm /wɜːm/ n. small animal, like a long thread, which lives in the ground or inside other animals.

worn /wɔːn/ past part. of v. wear. **worn out, (a)** old and totally finished because you have used it a lot: *I threw the shoes away because they were worn out.* **(b)** very tired: *She's worn out after a long, hard day.*

worry[1] /'wʌrɪ/ n. **1** (no pl.) feeling that something is wrong or will be wrong: *Her face showed signs of worry.* **2** (pl. worries) problem; something that makes you feel worried: *The leaking roof is a worry to Dad.*

worry[2] v. **1** feel that something is wrong or will be wrong: *I was worried when Barry didn't come back at the usual time.* **2** make someone feel that something is wrong: *Phil's bad health worries his parents.* **3** make someone rather angry: *Oh do stop worrying me with all these questions!* **worried** adj.: *You look worried—is something wrong?*

worse /wɜːs/ adj. **1** less good; more bad: *Killing is a worse crime than stealing.* **2** less good in health: *Vera is going to the doctor because she is worse than she was yesterday.* **worse** adv. more badly; **worse off**, poorer, more unhappy, etc. **worse** n. **none the worse for**, not hurt or damaged by something: *Luckily he was none the worse for his fall.*

worship /'wɜːʃɪp/ v. **1** believe in God or a god; pray to God or a god: *Christians worship in a church.* **2** think that someone is wonderful: *The girls worshipped the pop star.* **worship** n.

worst[1] /wɜːst/ adj. most bad: *The worst runner comes last in the race.* **worst** adv. **worst of all**, most badly: *Jim and Tim played badly, but I played worst of all!*

worst[2] n. (no pl.) most bad person or thing: *The worst of the weather comes in the winter.* **get the worst of it**, be beaten: *The smallest boy usually gets the worst of it in a fight.*

worth[1] /wɜːθ/ adj. **1** having a value of: *The house cost us £40,000 but it is not worth so much.* **2** good enough for; fine enough for: *Is this book worth reading?* **for all you are worth**, as much as you can: *He was running for all he was worth.*

worth[2] n. value: *a book of little worth.* **worth of**, words that show how much you can buy for an amount: *I bought £5 worth of petrol.* **worthless** adj. with no value.

worthwhile /wɜːθ'waɪl/ adj. good enough for the time, effort, etc. that you spend: *The hard work was worthwhile because I passed the exam.*

worthy /'wɜːðɪ/ adj. good enough; deserving something: *Danny is a good player and is worthy of a place in the team.*

would /wʊd/ **1** past tense of v. will: *He said he would come tomorrow.* **2** word to show what is probable: *It would be difficult to stop a car without any brakes.* **3** word that you say when you ask a polite question: *Would you like a cup of tea?* **4** word that you say after 'if' to show something possible but not likely: *If I were rich I would travel a lot.* **would rather**, would prefer to do something: *I would rather go tomorrow than today.*

wouldn't /'wʊdnt/ = would not.

wound[1] /waʊnd/ past part. & past tense of v. wind.

wound[2] /wuːnd/ v. hurt someone: *The bullet wounded him in the leg.* **wound** n.: *a knife wound.*

wove /wəʊv/ past tense of v. weave.

woven /'wəʊvn/ past part. of v. weave.

wrap /ræp/ v. (pres. part. wrapping, past part. & past tense wrapped /ræpt/) put paper or cloth round something or someone: *The nurse wrapped the baby in a shawl.*

wrapper /'ræpə(r)/, **wrapping** /'ræpɪŋ/ n. something for covering or packing: *She took the present out of its wrapping.*

wreath /riːθ/ n. ring of flowers or leaves: *They put wreaths on the grave.*

wreck /rek/ n. broken ship, car, building, etc. **wreck** v. totally break or destroy something: *The fire wrecked the hotel.*

wreckage /'rekɪdʒ/ n. (no pl.) broken remains of something: *the wreckage of a crashed aeroplane.*

wrench /renʃ/ v. **1** pull or twist something suddenly and strongly: *He wrenched the bag from my hand.* **2** hurt something by twisting: *Tony fell and wrenched his ankle.* **wrench** n.

wrestle /'resl/ v. **1** fight with someone; fight for sport. **2** try hard to do something: *He was wrestling with his sums.* **wrestler** n. someone who wrestles as a sport. **wrestling** n. fighting for sport.

wretched /'retʃɪd/ adj. **1** unhappy; ill;

feel wretched with this cold. **2** poor; bad; making you feel unhappy: *wretched houses.*

wriggle /'rɪgl/ *v.* turn and twist quickly: *Worms wriggle.*

wring /rɪŋ/ *v.* (*past part. & past tense* wrung /rʌŋ/) twist something with your hands to make water come out: *She wrung the clothes and put them on the line.*

wrinkle /'rɪŋkl/ *n.* line in your skin or in cloth, etc.: *The old woman's face is covered with wrinkles.* **wrinkled** /'rɪŋkld/ *adj.:* *her wrinkled face.*

wrist /rɪst/ *n.* place where the arm joins the hand.

wristwatch /'rɪstwɒtʃ/ *n.* (*pl.* wristwatches) watch that you wear on your wrist.

write /raɪt/ *v.* (*past part.* written /'rɪtn/, *past tense* wrote /rəʊt/) **1** make words with a pen, pencil, etc. on paper, etc.: *She wrote her name on the list.* **2** send a letter: *My boyfriend writes to me every week.* **3** make a story, book, newspaper article, etc.: *Wordsworth wrote poetry.* **write something down**, make a note of something: *She wrote down my telephone number in her diary.* **writer** *n.* someone who writes books, stories, etc.: *Charles Dickens was a well-known writer.*

writing /'raɪtɪŋ/ *n.* **1** (no *pl.*) how you form words with a pen, etc.: *His small writing is very hard to read.* **2** (no *pl.*) putting words on paper: *Writing is slower than telephoning.* **in writing**, on paper. **3 writings** (*pl.*) books: *the writings of Jane Austen.* **writing pad** *n.* book of paper for writing letters.

written /'rɪtn/ *past part.* of *v.* write.

wrong[1] /rɒŋ/ *adj.* **1** bad; that the law does not allow: *Crime is wrong.* **2** not correct: *It is wrong to say that* $2 + 2 = 5$. **3** not the best: *We're late because we took the wrong road.*

wrong[2] *adv.* not correctly: *You spelt my name wrong.* **go wrong,** (*a*) go on a path or road that you do not want. (*b*) not happen as you hope or wish: *All our plans went wrong.* (*c*) not work normally: *Something has gone wrong with the engine.*

wrong[3] *n.* (no *pl.*) what is bad, not right, etc.: *He did wrong to steal.*

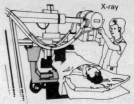

X-ray

xylophone   wrestle

wreck

wrongly /'rɒŋlɪ/ *adv.* not correctly: *The letter didn't arrive because it was wrongly addressed.*

wrote /rəʊt/ *past tense* of *v.* write.

wrung /rʌŋ/ *past part. & past tense* of *v.* wring.

Xx

Xmas /'krɪsməs/ *n. abbrev.* Christmas.

X-ray /'eks reɪ/ *n.* **1** (no *pl.*) instrument with rays that shows parts inside the body and takes photographs of them. **2** (*pl.* X-rays) picture of things inside the body: *The doctor took some X-rays of Simon's broken arm.*

xylophone /'zaɪləfəʊn/ *n.* musical instrument that you hit with small, wooden hammers.

Yy

yacht /jɒt/ *n.* **1** light sailing-boat. **2** very big motor-boat for a rich person who wants to cruise or race: *the Royal Yacht 'Britannia'.*

yard[1] /jɑːd/ *n.* measure of length = 90 centimetres.

yard[2] *n.* piece of hard ground with a fence or wall around it, near a building: *We play games in the school yard.*

yawn /jɔːn/ *v.* open your mouth wide because you are sleepy, etc.: *He yawned because the lesson was boring.* **yawn** *n.*

year /jɜː(r)/ *n.* **1** time of 365 days from 1 January to 31 December: *I was born in the year 1969.* **year in year out**, all the time; every year: *Old Mr. Parkinson has worked here year in year out since he was a boy.* **2** any time of 365 days: *He is 12 years old and he has been going to school for six years.* **all the year round**, through all the year: *He lives in a caravan all the year round.*

yearly /jɜːlɪ/ *adj.* done or happening once a year: *Christmas is a yearly festival.* **yearly** *adv.*: *The sports club members pay the fee yearly.*

yearn /jɜːn/ *v.* want something very much: *David yearned to see his parents again.*

yeast /jiːst/ *n.* stuff that makes bread rise.

yell /jel/ *v.* shout: *The crowd yelled when he scored a goal.* **yell** *n.*: *a yell of fear.*

yellow /'jeləʊ/ *adj.* with the colour of the sun: *Daffodils are yellow.* **yellow** *n.*

yelp /jelp/ *v.* make a short, sharp cry: *The dog yelped when the boy kicked it.* **yelp** *n.*

yes /jes/ *n.* (*pl.* yesses) word that you say when you agree: *Have you the key? Yes, here it is.*

yesterday /'jestədeɪ/ *n.* (no *pl.*) the day before today: *Today is Monday and yesterday was Sunday.* **yesterday** *adv.*: *We went swimming yesterday.*

yet[1] /jet/ *adv.* **1** up to now: *I haven't finished the book yet.* **2** up to then: *He told me that his brother had not yet arrived.* **as yet**, up to now: *As yet, I haven't decided what I'll do when I leave school.*

yet[2] *conj.* but; however: *He worked hard, yet he failed.*

yield /jiːld/ *v.* **1** give fruit, crops, etc.: *The tree has yielded a lot of apples this year.* **2** stop fighting because you are not strong enough; give in: *At first mother said no but in the end she yielded and let us go to the film.* **yield** *n.* amount of fruit, crops, etc.

yoghurt, yoghourt /'jɒgət/ *n.* (no *pl.*) sort of milk food.

yolk /jəʊk/ *n.* round, yellow part in an egg.

you /juː/ *pron.* (*pl.* you) **1** the person or people I am speaking to: *Come here and then I can see you.* **2** one; any person: *You buy stamps at a post office.*

you'd /juːd/ **1** = you had: *You'd better not be late!* **2** = you would: *It's a marvellous film—I'm sure you'd enjoy it.*

you'll /juːl/ = you will: *You'll come, won't you?*

young[1] /jʌŋ/ *adj.* not old; in the early part of life: *A child of one year old is too young to go to school.*

young[2] *n.* (*pl.*) **1 the young**, children. **2** baby birds and animals: *Birds build nests for their young.*

youngster /'jʌŋstə(r)/ *n.* child.

your /jɔː(r)/ *adj.* belonging to you; of you: *Show me your hands.*

you're /jɔː(r)/ = you are: *You're sure, are you?*

yours /jɔːz/ *pron.* (*pl.* yours) thing that belongs to you: *That pencil is yours.* **Yours . . .**, words that you write at the end of a letter: *Yours sincerely; Yours faithfully.*

yourself /jɔː'self/ *pron.* (*pl.* yourselves) **1** word that describes you, when I have just talked about you: *Did you hurt yourself when you fell over?* **2** you and no other person: *Did you make that dress yourself?* **by yourself**, alone: *Do you live by yourself?*

youth /juːθ/ *n.* **1** (no *pl.*) the time when you are young. **in my youth**, when I was young. **2** (*pl.* youths) boy or young man. **3** (*pl.*) young men and women: *the youth of our country.* **youth** *adj.*: *youth clubs.* **youth hostel** *n.* cheap place where young travellers, or people on holiday, can stay at night.

Zz

zebra /ˈziːbrə/ *n.* big, wild animal like a horse, with stripes. **zebra crossing** *n.* wide path of white stripes where people can walk safely over the road because cars must stop.

zero /ˈzɪərəʊ/ *n.* **1** the number 0; nought. **2** point between + and − on a thermometer, etc.

zig-zag /ˈzɪg zæg/ *n.* line or path that turns sharply left and then sharply right. **zig-zag** *adj.: a zig-zag line.*

zinc /zɪŋk/ *n.* (no *pl.*) sort of metal.

zip /zɪp/, **zipper** /ˈzɪpə(r)/, **zip-fastener** /ˌzɪpˈfɑːsnə(r)/ *n.* long fastener in clothes, bags, etc. You pull a small thing from one end to the other and this locks two sides together. **zip** *v.* (*pres. part.* zipping, *past part.* & *past tense* zipped /zɪpt/) open or close something with a zip: *She zipped the bag shut.* **zip up**, close something with a zip: *He zipped up his trousers.*

zone /zəʊn/ *n.* certain area: *the border zone.*

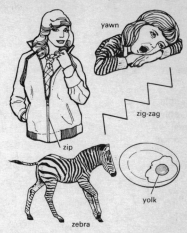

zoo /zuː/ *n.* place where you can see many sorts of animals; zoological gardens.

zoology /zəʊˈɒlədʒɪ/ *n.* (no *pl.*) study of animals. **zoological** /zəʊəˈlɒdʒɪkl/ *adj.* **zoologist** /zəʊˈɒlədʒɪst/ *n.* someone who studies animals.

zoom /zuːm/ *v.* move fast: *The cars zoomed up the motorway.*

Key to pronouncing common suffixes

suffix	phonetic spelling	example word	phonetic spelling of example word
-able	/-əbl/	fashionable	/ˈfæʃnəbl/
-ably	/-əblɪ/	comfortably	/ˈkʌmftəblɪ/
-al	/-l/ /-əl/	magical	/ˈmædʒɪkl/
-ance	/-əns/	assistance	/əˈsɪstəns/
-ate	/-ət/	affectionate	/əˈfekʃənət/
-er	/-ə(r)/	farmer	/ˈfɑːmə(r)/
-ery	/-ərɪ/	trickery	/ˈtrɪkərɪ/
-ily	/-ɪlɪ/	sulkily	/ˈsʌlkɪlɪ/
-ing	/-ɪŋ/	astonishing	/əˈstɒnɪʃɪŋ/
-ly	/-lɪ/	accurately	/ˈækjərətlɪ/
-ment	/-mənt/	arrangement	/əˈreɪndʒmənt/
-ness	/-nɪs/	kindness	/ˈkaɪndnɪs/
-or	/-ə(r)/	conjuror	/ˈkʌndʒərə(r)/
-ous	/-əs/	poisonous	/ˈpɔɪznəs/
-y	/-ɪ/	dusty	/ˈdʌstɪ/